# 汉英分类插图词典

## A CLASSIFIED AND ILLUSTRATED
## CHINESE-ENGLISH DICTIONARY

# 本词典主要编写人员
## Chief Compilers

| | | | | |
|---|---|---|---|---|
| 吴 楚 | 王多恩 | 翁显良 | 蔡文显 | 张鸾铃 |
| 张华诚 | 梁洪浩 | 吴继辉 | 黎 导 | 曾宪才 |
| 林成荣 | 许国烈 | 钟鸣砧 | 陈兆忠 | 刘初昆 |
| 周佐伦 | | 徐学娴 | 白健纯 | |

## 总 编 General Editors

王多恩　　翁显良　　梁洪浩　　曾宪才

# 汉英分类插图词典

## A CLASSIFIED AND ILLUSTRATED
## CHINESE-ENGLISH DICTIONARY

广州外国语学院《汉英分类插图词典》编写组编

By the Compiling Group of
**A Classified and Illustrated Chinese-English Dictionary**
**Guangzhou Institute of Foreign Languages**

生活·读书·新知三联书店香港分店
**Joint Publishing Company**
**(Hongkong Branch)**

责任编辑 Responsible Editor

曾 戈

插 图 Illustrator

若 峪

汉 英 分 类 插 图 词 典

广州外国语学院《汉英分类插图词典》编写组编

\*

生活·读书·新知三联书店香港分店出版发行

香港域多利皇后街九号

广东新华印刷厂印刷

广州市光明中路270号

1931年7月第1版　1931年7月第1次印刷

定价 HK$ 35.00

ISBN 962·04·0098·4

本词典由广东人民出版社在广州同时出版

This dictionary is simultaneously published in
Guangzhou by Guangdong People's Publishing House


Published and distributed by
Joint Publishing Co. (Hongkong Branch)
9 Queen Victoria St., Hongkong
© Joint Publishing Co. (Hongkong Branch), 1981
All rights reserved
First published in July, 1981
Printed by Xinhua Printing House of Guangdong
270 Guangming Road, Guangzhou

# 目 录

# Contents

# 出 版 说 明

　　《汉英分类插图词典》是由广州外国语学院特设编写组编写的一部以事物名称为主、从汉语查英语的词典。同类型的词典，坊间也有一些，但大都是从外语词典翻译过来，有关中国事物的词条当然很少，甚至没有。这本《汉英分类插图词典》因为是由中国学者编写的，不但具备一般分类词典的优点，而且补充了不少中国事物的词条。

　　本词典共收常用词条85,000条。词典按内容分为大众科技；文教卫生，财贸、服务；工业、交通、通讯及农业五个部分；各部分均收有具参考用途的附录。为利便使用者理解词条的含意，一些词条配有简明插图。

　　本词典不但内容较新，词条较多，而且在准确性、知识性和实用性上均达到一定的水平。对以汉语或英语为母语的人士学习对方语言文字、翻译工作者和从事中国贸易的人士都有参考价值。

　　本词典除由广东人民出版社在广州出版外，同时由本店出版香港版，发行港澳和海外地区。

　　读者在使用本词典过程中，如发现任何缺点、错误和疑问之处，欢迎赐函本店编辑部，以便转达编写单位。

三联书店香港分店编辑部

一九八一年三月

# FOREWORD

*A Classified and Illustrated Chinese-English Dictionary* is a bilingual dictionary compiled by the special compiling group of the Guangzhou Institute of Foreign Languages. It is a specialized dictionary dealing with the names of things in the main. Though other dictionaries of the kind can also be found, special requirements of the public are still not met as most of these dictionaries are mere translations of dictionaries in foreign languages and, therefore, are lacking in entries of things Chinese. Compiled by Chinese scholars, *A Classified and Illustrated Chinese-English Dictionary* has not only all the merits of a classified dictionary but is also enriched with the inclusion of numerous entries of terminology particular to Chinese usage.

Containing 35,000 entries of common terms, the Dictionary is divided according to the nature of things into five parts under the headings of: Popular Science and Technology; Culture, Education and Health; Finance, Commerce and Service Industries; Industry, Transport and Communications; and Agriculture. Attached to each of the five parts are appendices of great reference values. To give the users a clearer idea, some of the entries are precisely illustrated.

Not only is the Dictionary comparatively new in content and rich in entries, it is highly commendable for its accuracy and academic and practical values. It is, therefore, an important reference work for translators, China traders, and all those who are learning Chinese and English.

The Dictionary is published in Guangzhou by the Guangdong People's Publishing House as well as in Hongkong by the Joint Publishing Company (Hongkong Branch) for the purpose of distributing the Dictionary in Hongkong, Macau and overseas areas.

We sincerely hope that users of the Dictionary will gratefully point out what they find to be shortcomings and mistakes of the Dictionary so that we can have their friendly comments conveyed to the compilation committee.

Editorial Board,
Joint Publishing Co.(HK Branch)
March, 1981

# 凡　例

1. 本词典是按内容分类、从汉语查英语的,利用每部分正文前面的详细目录检索词目。各部分内容分若干大类,每类分若干项,每项又分若干目。

2. 词目的排列顺序,或按照事物的科学分类,或按照生产(业务)程序,视各项目的具体内容而定。

3. 凡是有插图的词目均用数码标明。

4. 词目形式包括单词、词组和句子。

　　名词一般用单数形式,必要时才用复数形式;冠词一般省略;

　　表现行动一般用动名词,偶尔也用动词的其他形式;

　　凡属布告性质的词句,一律加引号,以示区别。

5. 一物多名,选最常用的,有时也列俗名,加上括号;

　　一物二名,一英一美,一并列举,必要时注明(Br.)、(Am.)或(U.S.)。

6. 括号内的词语,或表示可省略,或表示可换用,或表示学名,或作说明、注释等。

7. 单词拼写采用英国通行形式。

8. 连字号可用可不用时,一律不用。

# HOW TO USE THIS DICTIONARY

1. This dictionary being classified according to the nature of its content and indexed in Chinese, the user will have to look up the appropriate entry in the index preceding the text of each part. The contents of the parts of the book are grouped under a number of main headings, further subdivided into several items and subitems.

2. The order in which the entries are arranged may fall in line with scientific classification or with the operational process, depending on the specific nature of the case.

3. Illustrated entries are marked with numerals.

4. Entries appear in the form of individual words, phrases, or sentences.

   Nouns are generally given in the singular but, if required, the plural form is used instead.

   The article is usually omitted.

   As a rule, the gerund is used to express an action, the use of the other forms of a verb being an occasional deviation.

   For purposes of distinction, expressions partaking of the tone of a public notice are given in quotation marks without exception.

5. When an object is known under several names, the

one most commonly used is chosen. Sometimes, a popular name is also given with brackets attached. When two different words, one British English and the other American English, are used for the same thing, they are given side by side with labels to indicate their origin where necessary.

6. A word or term thrown in brackets may mean an omissible part, or an alternative, or a scientific name. It may also serve as an explanation, an annotation, etc.

7. Conventional spelling forms used in Great Britain are followed in this book.

8. A hyphen, if not essential, is always dispensed with.

# 第一部分

# 大 众 科 技

## Part I

## Popular Science and Technology

# 第一部分

# 大众科技

## Part I

## Popular Science and Technology

# 目 录

# Contents

# 学科名称 Fields of Study

分类学 taxonomy, systematics
拓扑学 topology
统计力学 statistical mechanics
结构力学 structural mechanics
流体力学 hydrodynamics
磁流〔体〕力学 magnetohydrodynamics
高能物理学 high energy physics
分子电子学 molecular electronics, molectronics
微电子学 microelectronics
放射化学 radiation chemistry
海洋化学 oceanographic chemistry
空气热动力学 aerothermodynamics
航海天文学 nautical astronomy
射电天文学 radio astronomy
恒星天文学 stellar astronomy
行星学 planetology
火星学 areology
火〔星表〕面学 areography
月面学 selenography
宇宙学 cosmology
天体演化学 cosmogony
宇宙化学 cosmochemistry
天体地质学 astrogeology

天体物理学 astrophysics
天体力学 celestial mechanics
高层大气物理学 aeronomy
天文地球物理学 astrogeophysics
天体照相学 astrophotography
天体测量学 astrometry
宇宙航行动力学 astrodynamics
陨星学 meteoritics
光谱学 spectroscopy
天体光谱学 astrospectroscopy
分光光度学 spectrophotometry
干涉量度学 interferometry
地质学 geology
地质力学 geomechanics
地质年代学 geochronology
构造地质学 tectonics
地球化学 geochemistry
地球物理学 geophysics
地壳构造物理学 tectonophysics
地层学 stratigraphy
岩石学 petrology
火山学 volcanology
地貌学 geomorphology
大地测量学 geodesy
地理学 geography
自然地理学 physical geography
气候学 climatology
冰川学 glaciology
水文学 hydrology

物候学　phenology
水文地理学　hydrography
水文地质学　hydrogeology
地图学　cartography
摄影测量学　photogrammetry
生物学　biology
植物学　botany
动物学　zoology
微生物学　microbiology
外层空间生物学　exobiology
细菌学　bacteriology
血清学　serology
免疫学　immunology
生物化学　biochemistry
生物物理学　biophysics
生物群落学　biocoenology
天体生物学　astrobiology
胚胎学　embryology
细胞学　cytology
组织学　histology
遗传学　genetics
生物统计学　biometrics, biometry, biostatistics
古生物学　paleontology
古植物学　paleobotany
古动物学　paleozoology
新生物学　neontology
孢粉学　palynology
生态学　ecology
生物生态学　bioecology
古生态学　paleoecology
灵长类学　study of Primates
人类学　anthropology
人类形态学　human morphology
人体测量学　anthropometry
人类社会学　anthroposociology
人类地理分布学　anthropography

古人类学　paleoanthropology
人种学　ethnology
人种起源学　ethnogeny
淡水生物学　fresh water biology
海洋生物学　marine biology
生物气候学　bioclimatology
生物气象学　biometeorology
植物形态学　plant morphology
植物解剖学　phytotomy
植物分类学　phytotaxonomy, systematic botany
植物胚胎学　plant embryology
植物病理学　phytopathology
植物生理学　plant physiology
植物区系学　florology
植物地理学　plant geography, phytogeography
植物生态学　plant ecology, phytoecology
植物群落学　phytocoenology
植物寄生物学　phytoparasitology
植物化石学　phytopaleontology
藻类学　algology, phycology
真菌学　mycology
地衣学　lichenology
苔藓〔植物〕学　bryology, muscology
蕨类〔植物〕学　pteridology
动物分类学(动物系统学)　zootaxy
动物胚胎学　zooembryology
生理学　physiology
动物生理学　zoonomy, animal physiology
生物生态学　bioecology

| | |
|---|---|
| 动物生态学 zooecology | 脊椎动物学 vertebrate zoology |
| 动物地理学 zoogeography | |
| 动物病理学 zoopathology | 鱼类学 ichthyology |
| 动物心理学 zoopsychology | 鱼族学 ichthyography |
| 动物〔比较〕解剖学 zootomy | 爬虫学(爬行类学) herpetology |
| 寄生虫学 parasitology | 鸟类学 ornithology |
| 人体寄生虫学 human parasitology | 哺乳动物学 mammalogy |
| | 优生学 eugenics |
| 家畜寄生虫病学 veterinary parasitology | 植虫学 zoophytology |
| | 两栖类学 amphibiology |
| 无脊椎动物学 invertebrate zoology | 宇宙医学 space medicine |
| | 环境工程学 environmental engineering |
| 原生动物学 protozoology | |
| 蚁学 myrmecology | 人居学 ekistics |
| 蠕虫学 helminthology | 系统工程学 systems engineering |
| 贝类学 conchology | |
| 昆虫学 entomology | |

# 数 学 Mathematics

## 算 术 Arithmetic

| | |
|---|---|
| 数 number | 基数 cardinal number |
| 自然数 natural number | 序数 ordinal number |
| 奇数 odd number | 倍数 multiple |
| 偶数 even number | 公倍数 common multiple |
| 合数 composite number | 最小公倍数 least common multiple (LCM) |
| 倒数 reciprocal | |
| 名数 denominate number | 约数 divisor |
| 复名数 compound number | 因数 factor |
| 素数(质数) prime number | 公约数 common divisor |
| 互素(互质) relatively prime | 公因数 common factor |

最大公约数　greatest common divisor (GCD)

分数　fraction

分子　numerator

分母　denominator

约分　reduction of a fraction

既约分数　reduced fraction

不可约分数　irreducible fraction

真分数　proper fraction

假分数　improper fraction

普通分数　common fraction, vulgar fraction

带分数　mixed fraction

繁分数　complex fraction

通分　reduction of fractions to a common denominator

公分母　common denominator

连分数　continued fraction

收敛连分数　convergent continued fraction

循环连分数　recurring continued fraction

有尽连分数　terminating continued fraction

小数　decimal

有尽小数　finite decimal, terminating decimal

无尽小数　infinite decimal

循环小数　recurring decimal, repeating decimal

比　ratio

比例　proportion

百分比(百分率)　percentage (percent)

正比例　direct proportion

反比例　inverse proportion

正比　direct ratio

反比　inverse ratio

复比　compound ratio

连比　continued ratio

比例中项　mean terms of proportion

黄金分割　golden section

四则运算　four fundamental operations

加法　addition

减法　subtraction

乘法　multiplication

除法　division

被加数　summand

加数　addend

被减数　minuend

减数　subtrahend

被乘数　multiplicand

乘数　multiplier

被除数　dividend

除数　divisor

和　sum

差　difference

积　product

商　quotient

乘数表(九九表)　multiplication table, nine-times table

交换律　commutative law

结合律　associative law

分配律　distributive law

整除　exact division, exactly divisible

辗转相除法　division algorithm

十进制　decimal system

舍入法　rounding-off method

舍入数　rounded number, rounding number

四舍五入　rounding off

速算法　short-cut method of counting

捷乘法　abridged multiplica-

tion
捷除法　short division,
　abridged division
珠算　operation on the abacus

优选法　optimum seeking
　method
运筹学　operations research

## 初等代数　Elementary Algebra

正数　positive number
负数　negative number
整数　integer
有理数　rational number
无理数　irrational number
实数　real number
代数数　algebraic number
超越数　transcendental number
绝对值　absolute value
近似值　approximate value
代数和　algebraic sum
对数　logarithm
底数　base
对数的首数与尾数　characteristic and mantissa of logarithms
常用对数(布里格斯对数)　common logarithm (Briggs' logarithm)
自然对数(讷皮尔对数)　natural logarithm (Napierian logarithm)
余对数　cologarithm
幂　power
分指数幂　fractional exponent
负指数幂　negative exponent
乘方　involution
阶乘　factorial
复数　complex number
复数的模　modulus of a complex number

幅角　argument (amplitude)
共轭复数　conjugate complex numbers
共轭虚数　conjugate imaginary numbers
虚数　imaginary number
纯虚数　pure imaginary number
棣莫佛定理　De Moivre's theorem
棣莫佛公式　De Moivre's formula
指数　exponent, index
平方　square
立方　cube
开方　evolution, extraction of a root
开平方　extraction of a square root
开立方　extraction of a cube root
根号　radical sign
平方根　square root
立方根　cube root
不尽根　surd root
代数式　algebraic expression
多项式　polynomial
多项式的次数　degree of polynomial
单项式　monomial
二项式　binomial
三项式　trinomial

有理式 rational expression

有理分式 rational fraction

无理式 irrational expression

齐次多项式 homogeneous polynomial

不可约多项式 irreducible polynomial

部分分式 partial fraction

等式 equality

不等式 inequality

恒等式 identity

最高公因式 highest common factor (HCF)

因式分解 factoring, factorization

根式 radical

共轭根式 conjugate radicals

行列式 determinant

对称多项式 symmetrical polynomial

方程 equation

方程的根 root of an equation

一次方程 first-order equation, equation of first-order

二次方程 quadratic equation

双二次方程(四次方程) biquadratic equation (quartic equation)

高次方程 equation of higher degree

线性方程(一次方程) linear equation (simple equation)

联立方程(方程组) simultaneous equations

联立线性方程(联立一次方程) simultaneous linear equations

联立二次方程 simultaneous quadratic equations

有理方程 rational equation

有理整方程 integral rational equation

无理方程 irrational equation

分式方程 fractional equation

齐次方程 homogeneous equation

代数方程 algebraic equation

超越方程 transcendental equation

不定方程 indefinite equation

代数基本定理(高斯定理) fundamental theorem of algebra (Gauss' theorem)

综合除法 synthetic division

判别式 discriminant

剩余定理(余数定理) remainder theorem

因子定理 factor theorem

二项式定理 binomial theorem

二项展开式 binomial expansion

二次公式 quadratic formula

中国剩余定理(孙子剩余定理) Chinese remainder theorem

算术平均(等差中项) arithmetic mean, average (av)

几何平均(等比中项) geometric mean

数学归纳法 mathematical induction

同余 congruence

组合 combination

排列 permutation

置换 substitution

# 三角学　Trigonometry

平面三角学　plane trigonometry

球面三角学　spherical trigonometry

三角函数　trigonometric function

正弦　sine

余弦　cosine

正切　tangent

余切　cotangent

正割　secant

余割　cosecant

正矢　versed sine (versine)

余矢　coversed sine(coversine)

互反函数　reciprocal function

插值法(内推法)　interpolation

正角　positive angle

负角　negative angle

反三角函数　inverse trigonometric function

函数的周期性　periodicity of functions

反正弦　arc sine (inverse sine)

反余弦　arc cosine (inverse cosine)

反正切　arc tangent (inverse tangent)

反余切　arc cotangent (in-

verse cotangent)

主值　principal value

三角方程　trigonometric equation

单位根　roots of unity

欧拉公式　Euler's formula

正弦定理　law of sines

余弦定理　law of cosines

正切定理　law of tangents

倍角　double angle

半角　half angle

角度　degree of an angle

弧度　radian

象限　quadrant

球面三角形　spherical triangle

正弦—余弦定理　sine-cosine law

球面直角三角形　spherical right triangle

讷皮尔定律　Napier's rules

斜角球面三角形　oblique spherical triangle

球面度　spherical degree

圆的极点　pole of a circle

极三角形　polar triangle

原始三角形　primitive triangle

象限球面三角形　quadrantal triangle

# 几何学　Geometry

平面几何学　plane geometry

立体几何学　solid geometry

解析几何学　analytic geometry

几何学基础　foundations of

geometry

几何元素　geometrical element

几何作图　geometric construction

几何图形　geometric figure

点　point

线　line

面　surface

平面　plane

曲面　curved surface

立体　solid

直线　straight line

线段　line segment

射线(半线)　ray (half line)

折线　broken line

两线相交　intersection of two lines

相交线　intersecting lines

交点　intersection point, point of intersection

端点　end point

边　side

底边　base

角的始边　initial side of an angle

角的终边　terminate side of an angle

平行　parallel

垂直(正交)　perpendicularity

平行线　parallel lines

垂线　perpendicular, vertical

平行公理　axiom of parallels

面积　area

体积(容积)　volume

距(离)　distance

勾股定理　Pythagoras' theorem, Pythagorean theorem

中心对称　central symmetry

对称轴　axis of symmetry

角度制　degree measure (of an angle)

弧度制　circular measure (of

an angle)

角　angle

平角　straight angle

直角　right angle

周角　round angle

锐角　acute angle

钝角　obtuse angle

余角　complementary angle

补角　supplementary angle

邻角　adjacent angles

对顶角　vertical angles, vertically opposite angles

错角　alternate angles

外错角　alternate exterior angles

内错角　alternate interior angles

同傍外角　exterior angles on the same side

同傍内角　interior angles on the same side

同位角　corresponding angles

角等分线　angular bisector

三等分角　trisection of an angle

三角形　triangle

锐角三角形　acute (-angled) triangle

直角三角形　right (-angled) triangle

钝角三角形　obtuse (-angled) triangle

等腰三角形　isosceles triangle

等边三角形(正三角形)　equilateral triangle

不等边三角形　scalene triangle

中垂线　perpendicular bisector

中线　median line, median

顶垂线(高线)　altitude

垂心　orthocentre

形心(重心)　centroid, centre of figure

垂足　foot of a perpendicular

内心　incentre

外心　circumcentre

旁心　excentre

三角形旁切圆　escribed circle of a triangle

多边形　polygon

凸多边形　convex polygon

凹多边形　concave polygon

四边形　quadrilateral

平行四边形　parallelogram

梯形　trapezoid

等腰梯形　isosceles trapezoid

长方形(矩形)　rectangle

正方形　square

菱形　rhombus

正多边形　regular polygon

五边形　pentagon

多边形的角　angles of a polygon

内角　interior angle

外角　exterior angle

对角线　diagonal

相似形　similar figures

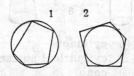

圆内接多边形①　inpolygon (inscribed polygon)

圆外切多边形②　circumscribed polygon

外接圆　circumcircle (circumscribed circle)

内切圆　incircle (inscribed circle)

圆　circle

圆心　centre of a circle

圆周　circumference

半径　radius

直径　diameter

半圆　semicircle

弦　chord

弧　arc (of a circle)

圆心角　central angle

圆周角　angle of circumference

圆周率　π(pi) (the ratio of the circumference of a circle to its diameter)

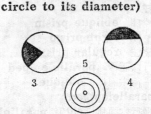

扇形③　sector

弓形④　segment of a circle

同心圆⑤　concentric circles

曲线　curve

割线　secant

切线　tangent line

公切线　common tangent

切点　point of tangency

抛物线　parabola

椭圆　ellipse

椭率　ellipticity

双曲线　hyperbola

正弦曲线　sine curve

余弦曲线　cosine curve

正切曲线　tangent curve
余切曲线　cotangent curve
二面角　dihedral angle
三面角　trihedral angle
四面角　tetrahedral angle
平面角　plane angle
多面角　polyhedral angle
面角　face angle
多面体　polyhedron
凸多面体　convex polyhedron
凹多面体　concave polyhedron
四面体　tetrahedron
五面体　pentahedron
六面体　hexahedron
八面体　octahedron
十二面体　dodecahedron
二十面体　icosahedron
棱柱　prism
斜棱柱　oblique prism
直棱柱　right prism
正棱柱　regular prism
平行六面体　parallelepiped
斜平行六面体　oblique
　parallelepiped
直平行六面体　right parallele-
　piped
长方体　cuboid
正方体(立方体)　cube

棱锥①　pyramid
棱〔锥〕台②　truncated
　pyramid
棱　edge
侧棱　lateral edge

侧面　lateral face
截面　cross section
正多面体　regular polyhedron
正四面体　regular tatrahedron

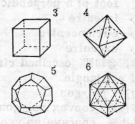

正六面体③　regular hexahe-
dron
正八面体④　regular octahe-
dron
正十二面体⑤　regular dode-
cahedron
正二十面体⑥　regular icosa-
hedron
旋转体　solid of rotation
母线　generatix, generator
旋转轴　axis of rotation
旋转面　surface of revolution

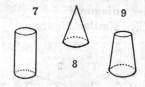

圆柱⑦　cylinder
圆柱面　cylindrical surface
圆锥⑧　cone
圆锥面　circular conical
surface
圆〔锥〕台⑨　truncated cone
球　sphere
球体　spheroid

| | |
|---|---|
| 球心　centre of a sphere | 球带　spherical zone |
| 球面　spherical surface, surface of a sphere | 球面角　spherical angle |
| 大圆　great circle | 立体角　solid angle |
| 小圆　small circle | 向量　vector |
| 球冠　spherical crown | 张量　tensor |

## 解析几何(平面)　Analytic Geometry in the Plane

| | |
|---|---|
| 笛卡儿直坐标　rectangular Cartesian coordinate | 范式(法线式)　normal form |
| 正射影　orthogonal projection | 直线系　system of straight lines |
| 倾角(直线的)　inclination of a line | 完全四线形(完全四边形)　complete quadrilateral |
| 斜率(直线的)　slope of a line | 直线的参数方程　parametric equation of straight line |
| 分点　point of division | 方向角　direction angle |
| 内分　internal division | 方向余弦　direction cosine |
| 外分　external division | 点圆(半径为零的圆)　point-circle (a circle whose radius is zero) |
| 分割比　ration of division | |
| 中点　middle point | |
| 闭合线　closing line | |
| 轨迹　locus | 圆系　system of circles |
| 方程式的轨迹　locus of an equation | 正交圆　orthogonal circles |
| | 极限点　limiting point |
| 比较原则　principle of comparison | 坐标　coordinate |
| | 极坐标　polar coordinates |
| 方程式的讨论　discussion of an equation | 向量径　radius vector |
| | 向量角(极角)　vectorial angle |
| 闭曲线　closed curve | 极轴　polar axis |
| 对称曲线　symmetrical curve | 双纽线　lemniscate |
| 双曲挠线(三次双曲线)　cubical hyperbola | 坐标的变换　transformation of coordinates |
| 代数曲线　algebraic curve | 变换方程式　equation of transformation |
| 截距　intercept | |
| 超越曲线　transcendental curve | 轨迹方程式　equation of a locus |
| 波状曲线　wave curve | 心脏线　cardioid |
| 方程的图　graph of equation | 轴的平移　translation of axes |

轴的平移方程式 equations for translating the axes

轴的旋转 rotation of axes

轴旋转方程式 equations for rotating the axes

圆锥曲线 conic section

焦点 focus

准线 directrix

离心率(偏心率) eccentricity

主轴 principal axis

极点(顶点) vertex

中心二次曲线(有心二次曲线) central conic

长轴 major axis

短轴 minor axis

横截轴 transverse axis

共轭轴 conjugate axis

等轴双曲线(直角双曲线) equilateral hyperbola

共轭双曲线 conjugate hyperbolas

渐近线 asymptote

退化的 degenerate

二次曲线系 system of conics

共焦的 confocal

辅助圆 auxiliary circle

切距 length of tangent

法距 length of normal

次切距 subtangent

次法距 subnormal

相切条件 condition for tangency

渐近方向 asymptotic direction

共轭直径 conjugate diameters

参数方程式 parametric equation

箕舌线 witch of Agnesi

蚌线 conchoid, conchoidal

curve

旋轮线(摆线) cycloid

圆内旋轮线(内摆线) hypocycloid

四尖圆内旋轮线(四尖内摆线) hypocycloid of four cusps

长辐旋轮线 prolate cycloid

短辐旋轮线 curtate cycloid

圆的渐伸线 involute of a circle

圆外旋轮线(外摆线) epicycloid

同位曲线 corresponding curves

准圆 director circle

不变式 invariant

绝对不变式 absolute invariant

欧几里得变换 Euclidean transformation

位移 displacement

不变点 fixed point, invariant point

对称变换 symmetry transformation

〔同〕位〔相〕似变换 homothetic transformation

〔同〕位〔相〕似图形 homothetic figures

相似变换 similitude transformation

反演 inversion

蔓叶线 cissoid

环索线 strophoid

三等分角线 trisectrix

极点 pole

极线 polar

配极 polar reciprocation

对射 correlation

## 数学分析　Mathematical Analysis

常量(常数)　constant
变量(变数)　variable
区间　interval
序列(数列)　sequence (number sequence)
有限序列(有限数列)　finite sequence
无限序列(无限数列)　infinite sequence (unending succession of numbers)
递增序列(递增数列)　increasing sequence
递减序列(递减数列)　decreasing sequence
有界序列(有界数列)　bounded sequence
无界序列(无界数列)　unbounded sequence
极限　limit
无穷大　infinity
无穷小　infinitesimal
集　set
元素　element
函数　function
自变量　independent variable

定义域　field of definitions
函数的图　graph of function
极大和极小　maximum and minimum
极大极小判据　maxi-min criterion
反函数　inverse function
线性函数(一次函数)　linear function
二次函数　quadratic function
指数函数　exponential function
对数函数　logarithmic function
周期函数　periodic function
微积分〔学〕　calculus
原函数　primitive function
级数　progression, series
算术级数(等差级数)　arithmetic(al) progression (AP), arithmetic(al) series
公差　common difference
几何级数(等比级数)　geometric(al) progression (GP), geometric(al) series
公比　common ratio
计算尺　slide rule

## 微分学　Differential Calculus

有界量　bounded quantity
无界量　unbounded quantity
邻域　neighbourhood
邻域半径　radius of neighbourhood
邻域中心　centre of neigh-

bourhood
允许值　permissible value
闭区间　closed interval
开区间　open interval
显函数　explicit function
隐函数　implicit function

初等超越函数　elementary transcendental function

自变数　argument

增量　increment

连续函数　continuous function

不连续函数(间断函数)　discontinuous function

导数〔微商〕　derivative

导出函数　derivative function, derived function

线性函数变化率　rate of change of linear function

函数在点X上的导数　derivative of the given function at the point X

求已知函数的微分　differentiating a given function

微分法　differentiation

极限位置　limiting position

曲线的法线　normal to a curve

曲线的斜率　slope of a curve

微分公式　formula of differentiation

幂函数　power function

合成函数　composite function

模数　modulus

单调函数　monotonic function, monotone function

递增函数　increasing function

递减函数(下降函数)　decreasing function

严格单调函数　strictly monotonic function

一阶导数　first derivative, derivative of the first order

二阶导数　second derivative, derivative of the second order

高阶导数　derivatives of higher order

逐次微分　successive differentiation

极值　extreme, extremum

极值点　extreme point, extremum point

平稳点　stationary point

凹向下的　concave downward

凹向上的　concave upward

拐点(反凹点，变曲点)　point of inflection

中值定理(平均值定理)　theorem of mean

近似计算　approximate calculation

## 积分学　Integral Calculus

逆运算　inverse operation

反导数(反微商)　antiderivative

积分　integral

不定积分　indefinite integral

积分符号　sign of integration

被积函数　integrand

任意常数　arbitrary constant

展开法　expansion method

置换积分法(换元积分法)　integration by substitution

三角函数置换法　trigonometric substitution

定积分　definite integral

定积分下限　lower limit of

the definite integral
定积分上限 upper limit of the definite integral
积分之和 integral sum
子区间 subinterval
牛顿—莱布尼兹公式 Newton-Leibniz formula
瓦雷斯公式 Wallis formula
梯形公式 trapezoid formula
辛卜生公式 Simpson formula

分部积分法 integration by parts
递化积分法 integration by successive reduction
部分分数积分法 integration by partial fraction
微分方程的积分 integral of differential equation
积分微分方程 integrodifferential equation

## 计算数学 Computational Mathematics

运算器 arithmetic-logic unit
存贮器 storage unit
输入输出部件 input-output unit
控制器 control unit
程序编制 program composition
数据 data
二进制 binary system
二进制运算 binary operation
逻辑代数(开关代数) logic algebra (switching algebra)
八进制 octal system
二—十进制转换 binary-to-decimal conversion
二—八进制 binary octal system
十—二进制转换 decimal-to-binary conversion
完点 fixed point
浮点 floating point
完点运算 fixed point operation
浮点运算 floating point operation
原码形式 true form

补码 (true) complement
补码形式 complement form
n进制补码 complement on n
n进制反码 complement on n-1
编码 coding
循环码 cyclic code
奇偶校验 even-odd check
算术运算 arithmetic operation
逻辑运算 logical operation
逻辑加法("或"运算) logical addition (OR-operation)
逻辑乘法("与"运算) logical multiplication (AND-operation)
反相("非"运算) inversion (NOT-operation)
逻辑函数 logical function
"或非" NOR
"与非" NOT-AND, NAND
代入规则 rule of substitution
反演 reversing
对偶 pairing
最小项 lowest term
逻辑网络 logical network

溢出检验　overflow check
循环移位　cyclic shift
误差　error
绝对误差　absolute error
相对误差　relative error
舍入误差　rounding error
舍入误差累加器　round-off accumulator
乘法电路　multiplying circuit
除法电路　dividing circuit
乘法同余法　multiplicative congruential method
加同余法　additive congruential method

寄存器　register
计数器　counter
计数寄存器　counter register
译码器　decipherer, decoder
译码网络　decoding network
五—二码　quibinary code
商—差算法　quotient-difference algorithm
乘数—商数寄存器　quotient-multiplier register
脉冲编码器　pulse encoder
脉冲分配器　pulse distributor
时序电路　sequential circuit

# 物理学　Physics

## 总 类　General

经典物理学　classical physics
统计物理学　statistical physics
统计力学　statistical mechanics
量子统计　quantum statistics
费米—狄拉克统计　Fermi-Dirac statistics
玻色—爱因斯坦统计　Bose-Einstein statistics
物质　matter

运动　motion
静止　rest
时间和空间　time and space
空间　space
时空连续统　space-time continuum
实物　real object
场　field
能量守恒　conservation of energy

能的转变 transformation of energy

能量守恒定律 law of conservation of energy

质量守恒定律 law of conservation of mass

质量能量守恒 conservation of mass and energy

质能方程式 mass-energy equation

能量不守恒 non-conservation of energy

宇称不守恒 non-conservation of parity

数学物理 mathematical physics

固态物理学 solid-state physics

超高压 supervoltage

原子说 atomic theory

宏观的 macroscopic

物理量 physical quantity

标量 scalar

矢量 vector

量纲 dimension

单位制 system of units

绝对单位制 absolute units

厘米克秒制 centimetre-gram-second system (cgs system)

米公斤秒制 metre-kilogram-second system (mks system)

米吨秒制 metre-ton-second system

测量误差 measuring error

视差 parallax

测量精度 measuring accuracy

公制 metric system

厘米 centimetre (cm)

米 metre (m)

公里 kilometre (km)

平方厘米 square centimetre (sq cm)

平方米 square metre (sq m)

平方公里 square kilometre (sq km)

公亩 are (a)

公顷 hectare (h)

立方厘米 cubic centimetre

立方米 cubic metre

升 litre

克 gram (g)

公斤 kilogram (kg)

公吨 metric ton, tonne

英美制 British and US system

英寸 inch (in)

英尺 foot (ft)

码 yard (yd)

英里 mile (mi)

海里 nautical mile

节 knot

链 cable's length

平方英寸 square inch (sq in)

平方英尺 square foot (sq ft)

平方码 square yard (sq yd)

平方英里 square mile (sq mi)

英亩 acre

立方英寸 cubic inch

立方英尺 cubic foot

立方码 cubic yard

品脱 pint (pt)

夸特 quart (qt)

加仑 gallon (gal)

蒲式耳 bushel (bu)

盎司 ounce (oz)

磅 pound (lb)

# 力 学 Mechanics

理论力学 theoretical mechanics

运动学 kinematics

动力学 dynamics

静力学 statics

质点 material particle, particle

物体 body

刚体 rigid body

参照构架(参照系) frame of reference, reference frame

坐标系 coordinate system

直线运动 rectilinear motion

曲线运动 curvilinear motion

圆周运动 circular motion

机械运动 mechanical movement

平动(平移) translation

移动 shift

转动 rotation

位移 displacement

角位移 angular displacement

速度 velocity

线速度 linear velocity

瞬时速度(即时速度) instantaneous velocity

平均速度 average velocity

速率 speed

角速度 angular velocity

加速度 acceleration

线加速度 linear acceleration

角加速度 angular acceleration

匀速运动 uniform motion

匀加速运动 uniformly accelerated motion

减速度 deceleration

匀减速运动 uniformly decelerated motion

变速运动 variable motion

匀变速运动 uniformly varying motion

切向加速度 tangential acceleration

法向加速度 normal acceleration

切向力 tangential force

法向力 normal force

向心力 centripetal force

离心力 centrifugal force

相对运动 relative motion

绝对运动 absolute motion

相对速度 relative velocity

绝对速度 absolute velocity

绝对时空 absolute space-time (absolute time)

三维空间 three-dimensional space

四维空间 four-dimensional space

力 force

大小 magnitude

方向 direction

作用点 point of application

力的合成 composition of forces

合力 resultant force, resultant

分力 component of force, component

力的平衡 equilibrium of forces

达因　dyne (dyn)

牛顿　newton (N)

力矩　moment of force

力偶　couple

力臂　arm of force

万有引力定律　law of universal gravitation

万有引力　gravitation

重力　gravity

重力加速度　acceleration of gravity

自由落体运动　ideal unimpeded falling motion of a body

引力场(重力场)　gravitational field

重量　weight

重心　centre of gravity

质心　centre of mass

碰撞　collision

摩擦　friction

摩擦力　friction force

滑动摩擦　sliding friction

静摩擦　static friction

动摩擦　dynamical friction

滚动摩擦　rolling friction

稳定平衡　stable equilibrium

不稳定平衡　unstable equilibrium

随意平衡　indifferent equilibrium

稳度　stability

牛顿运动定律　Newton's laws of motion

牛顿第一定律(惯性定律)　Newton's first law (law of inertia)

牛顿第二定律　Newton's second law

牛顿第三定律(作用与反作用定律)　Newton's third law (law of action and reaction)

惯性(惯量)　inertia

质量　mass

转动惯量　moment of inertia

转矩　torque

扭力　torque force

能〔量〕　energy

机械能　mechanical energy

动能　kinetic energy

势能(位能)　potential energy

功　work

功率　power

尔格　erg

动量　momentum, quantity of motion

动量守恒定律　law of conservation of momentum

平行四边形法则　principle of parallelogram

张力　tension

压力(压强)　pressure

巴(压强单位)　bar

大气压　atmospheric pressure

回转稳定器　gyrostabilizer

回转罗盘　gyrocompass

回转仪(陀螺仪)①　gyroscope

密度　density

比重　specific gravity

流体力学　fluid mechanics

流体静力学　hydrostatics

流体动力学　**hydrodynamics**
伯努利定理　**Bernoulli's theo-
　rem**
涡流　**vortex flow**
稳定流(稳流)　**steady flow**
紊流(湍流)　**turbulent flow,
　turbulence**
层流(片流)　**laminar flow**
射流　**efflux**
射流技术　**fluidics**
阿基米德原理　**Archimedes'
　principle**
浮力　**buoyancy**
帕斯卡定律　**Pascal's law**
液压机(水压机)　**hydraulic
　press**
虹吸现象　**siphonage**
流率　**flow rate, rate of flow**
空吸作用　**suction**
机械效率　**mechanical effi-
　ciency**
滑轮①　**pulley**
轮轴　**wheel and axle**
斜面②　**inclined plane**
螺旋　**screw**

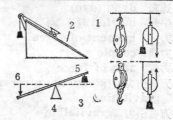

杠杆③　**lever**
杠杆原理　**lever principle**
支点④　**fulcrum (point of
　support)**
重点⑤　**weight, load**
力点⑥　**force, effort**
形变　**deformation**
弹性　**elasticity**
塑性(范性)　**plasticity**
展性　**malleability**
延性　**ductility**
应力(胁强)　**stress**
应变(胁变)　**strain**
胡克定律　**Hooke's law**
弹簧秤　**spring balance**
弹性极限　**elastic limit**
硬度　**hardness**

## 分子物理学　Molecular Physics

热运动　**thermal motion**
布朗运动　**Brownian move-
　ment**
分子运动　**molecular motion**
起伏(涨落)　**fluctuation**
扩散　**diffusion**
固体　**solid**
液体　**liquid**
分子力　**molecular force**
内聚力　**cohesion (cohesive
　force)**
附着力　**adhesion (adhesive
　force)**
表面张力　**surface tension**
毛细现象　**capillarity**
毛细管　**capillary tube**
毛细下降　**capillary depres-
　sion**
毛细上升　**capillary rise**
弯月面　**meniscus**
渗透　**osmosis**
渗透压强　**osmotic pressure**
半透膜　**semipermeable mem-
　brane**

聚集态　state of aggregation
物态　state
固态　solid state
气态　gaseous state
液态　liquid state
熔化　melting
熔解　fusion
熔点　melting point
熔解热　heat of fusion
凝固　solidification
凝固点　freezing point
冰点　ice point
液化　liquefaction
凝结　coagulation
汽化　vaporization
蒸发　evaporation
沸腾　boiling (ebullition)
沸点　boiling point
升华　sublimation
汽化热　heat of vaporization
蒸气　vapour
蒸汽(水蒸气)　steam
饱和汽　saturated vapour
饱和蒸汽　saturated steam
未饱和汽　unsaturated vapour
未饱和蒸汽　unsaturated steam
饱和汽压　saturated vapour pressure
过饱和汽　supersaturated vapour
临界状态　critical state
临界点　critical point
临界温度　critical temperature
临界压强　critical pressure
临界体积　critical volume
临界常数　critical constant
相平衡　phase equilibrium

相变　phase change
湿度　humidity
绝对湿度　absolute humidity
相对湿度　relative humidity
气体　gas
气体分子运动论　kinetic theory of gases
理想气体(完全气体)　ideal gas (perfect gas)
永久气体　permanent gas
实际气体(非理想气体)　real gas (imperfect gas)
阿伏伽德罗定律　Avogadro's law
玻意耳—马略特定律　law of Boyle-Mariotte
盖—吕萨克定律　Gay-Lussac's law
查理定律　Charles' law
气体常数　gas constant
阿伏伽德罗常数(阿伏伽德罗数)　Avogadro constant (Avogadro number)
物态方程(状态方程)　equation of state
标准状况　standard conditions
托　torr
标准大气压　standard atmospheric pressure
气压计　barometer
水银气压计　mercury barometer
无液气压计(膜盒气压计)　aneroid barometer
真空　vacuum
真空泵(抽气机)　vacuum pump
流体　fluid
雷诺耳数　Reynolds' number

## 热 学 Heat

热 heat
热质说 caloric theory of heat
热能 thermal energy
热力学 thermodynamics
准静态过程 quasi-static process
热动平衡 thermodynamic equilibrium
动态平衡 dynamical equilibrium
热平衡 thermal equilibrium
等温过程 isothermal process (constant temperature process)
等温变化 isothermal trans-process
等压过程 constant pressure process
等容过程 constant volume process
绝热过程 adiabatic process
循环 cycle
热效率 thermal efficiency
热力学第一定律 first law of thermodynamics
热力学第二定律 second law of thermodynamics
永恒运动 perpetual motion
内能 internal energy
温度 temperature
温标 thermometric scale
摄氏温标 Celsius' thermometric scale
华氏温标 Fahrenheit's thermometric scale
绝对温标(开氏温标) absolute

(temperature) scale (Kelvin scale)
温度计 thermometer
摄氏温度计 Celsius thermometer
华氏温度计 Fahrenheit thermometer
气体温度计 gas thermometer
高温计 pyrometer
辐射高温计 radiation pyrometer
光测高温计 optical pyrometer
电阻温度计 resistance thermometer
恒温器 thermostat
低温物理学 low temperature physics
量热学 calorimetry
热量 quantity of heat
量热器(卡计) calorimeter
热功当量 mechanical equivalent of heat
焦耳 joule (J)
卡〔路里〕 calorie
大卡 major calorie
热容量 thermal capacity
比热 specific heat
原子热 atomic heat
分子热 molecular heat
热绝缘 thermal insulation
热传递 heat transfer
传导 conduction
对流 convection
辐射 radiation
红热 red heat

白热　white heat
膨胀　expansion
收缩　contraction
热膨胀　thermal expansion
线性膨胀　linear expansion
膨胀系数　coefficient of
　expansion

线胀系数　coefficient of
　linear expansion
体胀系数　volume expansion
　coefficient
压缩系数　coefficient of com-
　pressibility, compressibil-
　ity

## 振动和波　Vibration and Wave

振动　vibration, vibratory
　motion
谐运动(谐振动, 简谐运动)
　harmonic motion (harmonic
　vibration, simple harmonic
　motion (SHM))
周期　period
频率　frequency
赫兹　hertz (Hz)
振幅　amplitude
固有振动　natural vibration
固有频率　natural frequency
阻尼谐动　damped harmonic
　motion
阻尼振动(阻尼振荡)　damped
　oscillation
受迫振动　forced vibration
共振　resonance
相角　phase angle
波(波动)　wave (wave motion)
波阵面　wave front
平面波　plane wave
表面波　surface wave
球面波　spherical wave

重力波　gravity wave
纵波　longitudinal wave
横波　transverse wave
纵振动　longitudinal vibration
横振动　transverse vibration
弹性波　elastic wave
冲击波　shock wave
波峰　crest
波谷　trough
波速　wave velocity
行波　travelling wave
驻波　standing wave
波长　wavelength
反射　reflection
折射　refraction
干涉　interference
衍射　diffraction
衍射栅　diffraction grating
偏振　polarization
单摆(数学摆)　simple pendu-
　lum (mathematical pen-
　dulum)
复摆(物理摆)　compound pen-
　dulum (physical pendulum)

# 声 学 Acoustics

几何声学 geometrical acoustics, ray acoustics
物理声学 physical acoustics
分子声学 molecular acoustics
水声学 underwater acoustics, hydroacoustics
电声学 electroacoustics
超声学 ultrasonics
大气声学 atmospheric acoustics
音乐声学 musical acoustics
建筑声学 architectural acoustics
噪声控制 noise control
声 sound
声源 sound source
声音的传播 propagation of sound
次声 infra-audible sound, infrasonic sound
响度 loudness
音量(声量) volume
声强 sound intensity
回声 echo
拍 beat
拍频 beat frequency
声共鸣 acoustic resonance
音品(音色) timbre, tone quality
谐音 harmonics
基音 fundamental tone
泛音 overtone
乐音 musical sound
噪声 noise
声波 sound wave

声速 speed of sound, sonic velocity, velocity of sound
音调 pitch

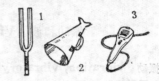

音叉① tuning fork
共鸣器 acoustical resonator
传声筒② megaphone
传声器③ microphone
探声器 sound probe
声纳(水声测位仪) sonar (sound navigation and ranging)
留声机 gramophone, phonograph
录音(录声) sound recording
超声物理学 ultrasonic physics
超声波 ultrasonic wave
超声波发生器 ultrasonic generator
超声振荡器 ultra-sonator
超声波发射器 ultrasound transmitting transducer
超声波洗涤 ultrasonic cleaning
超声波探伤器 ultrasonic reflectoscope, ultrasonic flaw detector
超声钻孔 ultrasonic drilling
超声显微镜 ultrasonic microscope

超声波接收器 ultrasonic re-
  ceiver
超声透镜 ultrasonic lens
超声鱼群探测器 ultrasonic
fish-detector, ultrasonic
fish-finder
超声凝聚 ultrasonic coagula-
tion

## 光 学 Optics

光 light
光度学 photometry
光源 light source
可见光 visible light
光线 light ray
光波 light wave
光的波动说 wave theory of
  light
惠更斯原理 Hugens' principle
光的电磁说 electromagnetic
  theory of light
光的微粒说 corpuscular
  theory of light
光子说 photon theory
光的直线传播 rectilinear
  propagation of light
光速 velocity of light, speed
  of light
光束 light beam
埃 angstrom (A)
色 colour
单色光 monochromatic light
多色光 heterochromatic light
光程 optical path, optical
  length
镜 mirror
平面镜 plane mirror
球面镜 spherical mirror
凸镜 convex mirror
凹镜 concave mirror
透镜 lens

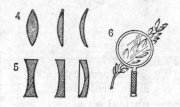

凸透镜(会聚透镜)④ convex
  lens (converging lens)
凹透镜(发散透镜)⑤ concave
  lens (diverging lens)
放大镜⑥ magnifier, magni-
  fying glass
望远镜 telescope
天文望远镜 astronomical tele-
  scope
折射望远镜 refracting tele-
  scope
反射望远镜 reflecting tele-
  scope
伽利略望远镜 Galilean tele-
  scope
棱镜双目望远镜 prismatic bi-
  nocular telescope
双目望远镜(观剧镜) binocu-
  lar telescope, binoculars
  (opera glasses)
放大率 magnifying power,
  magnification
物镜 object lens, objective

目镜　eyepiece, eyeglass

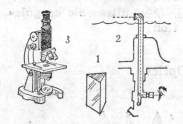

棱镜①　prism
潜望镜②　periscope
显微镜③　microscope
幻灯　slide projector
光轴　optical axis

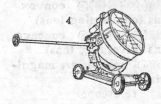

探照灯④　searchlight
视角　visual angle
本影　umbra
半影　penumbra
反射定律　law of reflection
折射定律　law of refraction
折射率　refractive index,
　index of refraction
光密媒质　optically denser
　medium
光疏媒质　optically thinner
　medium
入射线　incident ray
入射点　point of incidence
入射角　angle of incidence

反射角　angle of reflection
折射角　angle of refraction
漫反射　diffuse reflection
全反射　total reflection
临界角　critical angle
偏向角　angle of deviation
焦距　focal length, focal
　distance
焦点　focus (focal point)
主焦点　principal focus
实焦点　real focus
虚焦点　virtual focus
焦平面　focal plane
聚焦　focusing
焦度　focal power
屈光度　diopter, dioptre
可变焦距透镜　zoom lens
象　image
实象　real image
虚象　virtual image
倒象　inverted image
光心　optical centre
天然光　natural light
散射　scattering
色散　dispersion
红　red
橙　orange
黄　yellow
绿　green
蓝　blue
靛　indigo
紫　violet
紫外线　ultraviolet ray
红外线　infrared ray
红外跟踪　infrared tracking
红外线摄影　infrared photo-
　graphy
红外通信　infrared communi-
　cation

远红外通信　far-IR communication
红外步枪瞄准镜　sniperscope
黑体　blackbody
黑体辐射　blackbody radiation
发光　luminescence
荧光　fluorescence
磷光　phosphorescence
吸收　absorption
光度计　photometer
发光强度　luminous intensity
光通量　luminous flux
照度　illuminance, illumination
发光率　luminance
亮度　brightness
烛光　candle power
流明　lumen (lm)
勒克司(米烛光)　lux (metre-candle)
熙提(亮度单位)　stilb
摄谱仪　spectrograph

分光镜　spectroscope
光谱学　spectroscopy
光谱　spectrum
太阳光谱　solar spectrum
原子光谱　atomic spectrum
带光谱　band spectrum
连续光谱　continuous spectrum
发射光谱　emission spectrum
吸收光谱　absorption spectrum
明线光谱　bright line spectrum
暗线光谱　dark line spectrum
夫琅和费谱线　Fraunhofer's lines
光谱分析　spectrum analysis
荧光灯　fluorescent lamp
日光灯　daylight lamp
白炽灯　incandescent lamp
激光光普　laser spectrum
激光通讯　laser communication

## 电磁学　Electromagnetics

电〔学〕　electricity
电动力学　electrodynamics
麦克斯韦方程组　Maxwell (field) equations
电荷　electric charge
正电荷(阳电荷)　positive charge
负电荷(阴电荷)　negative charge
电量　electric quantity
自由电子　free electron
自由电荷　free charge
库仑定律　Coulomb's law
摩擦起电　frictional electricity

电场　electric field
磁场　magnetic field
电磁场　electromagnetic field
电场强度　electric field strength
电子论　electron theory
电力线　line of electric force
磁力线　magnetic line of force
电通量　electric flux
磁通量　magnetic flux
导体　conductor
电介质　dielectric
绝缘体　insulator
电势(电位)　electric potential

零电势(零电位) zero potential

电势差(电位差) electric potential difference

电压 voltage

路端电压(端电压) terminal voltage

电动势 electromotive force (E.M.F.), electromotance

静电感应 electrostatic induction

感生电荷 induced charge

电流 electric current

电流密度 electric current density

直流电 direct current (DC)

交流电 alternating current (AC)

变压器 transformer

电流强度 current intensity, current strength

电容 capacitance, electric capacity

电导 electric conductance

电路 electric circuit

串联 series

并联 parallel, multiple

电阻 resistance, electrical resistance

电源 power supply

内电阻 internal resistance

电阻率 resistivity

欧姆定律 Ohm's law

安培定律 Ampere's law

焦耳—楞次定律 Joule-Lenz's law

楞次定律 Lenz's law

充电 charging

左手定则 left-hand rule

右手定则 right-hand rule

逆电动势 counter electromotive force (counter E.M.F.)

磁学 magnetics

磁性 magnetism

磁现象 magnetic phenomenon

磁体(磁铁) magnet

磁铁矿(磁石) magnetite (lodestone)

天然磁铁 natural magnet

人造磁铁 artificial magnet

永久磁铁 permanent magnet

条形磁铁① bar magnet

蹄形磁铁② horseshoe magnet

磁针③ magnetic needle

磁极 magnetic pole

〔指〕北极 north pole

〔指〕南极 south pole

地球磁场 geomagnetic field

地磁 geomagnetism, terrestrial magnetism

磁偏角 magnetic declination

磁倾角 magnetic dip, magnetic inclination

磁场强度 magnetic intensity

磁力 magnetic force

洛伦磁力 Lorentz force

磁感应 magnetic induction

电磁感应 electromagnetic induction

感生电动势(应电动势) induced electromotive force (induced E.M.F.)

电感 inductance
自感现象 self inductance
感生电流(应电流) induced current
磁化 magnetization
去磁 demagnetization

4

电磁铁④ electromagnet
电谐振(电共振) electric resonance
电磁振荡 electromagnetic oscillation
电磁波 electromagnetic wave
电弧 electric arc
放电 discharging
尖端放电 point discharge
螺线管 solenoid
电池 battery
伏打电池 Voltaic cell
干电池 dry battery, dry cell
蓄电池 storage battery
电极 electrode

5

6

阴极 cathode (negative electrode)
阳极 anode (positive electrode)
光电管⑤ photocell, photoelectric cell
电子学 electronics
微波 microwave
整流器 rectifier

8
9
7

阴极射线管 cathode ray tube
同步 synchronism
电子计算机 electronic computer
电子显微镜⑥ electron microscope
验电器⑦ electroscope
安培计⑧ ammeter, amperemeter
静电计⑨ electrometer

瓦特计(功率表)　**wattmeter**
瓦时计(电度表)　**watthour me-ter**
安伏欧计(万用电表)　**avometer**
电量计(库仑计)　**voltameter (coulometer)**
电流计　**galvanometer**
伏特计(电压表)　**voltmeter**
伏安计　**voltampere meter**
伏安时计　**volt-ampere-hour meter**

电阻箱①　**resistance box**
电阻器　**resistor**
变阻器　**rheostat**
电容器　**capacitor**
检波(探测)　**detection**
调制　**modulation**

调幅　**amplitude modulation (AM)**
调频　**frequency modulation (FM)**
调相　**phase modulation (PM)**
放大　**amplification**
安培　**ampere (A)**
伏特　**volt (V)**
瓦特　**watt (W)**
库仑　**coulomb (C)**
欧姆　**ohm ($\Omega$)**
奥〔斯试〕(磁场强度单位)　**oersted (Oe)**
高斯(磁感应单位)　**gauss (G)**
法拉(电容单位)　**farad (F)**
微法〔拉〕　**microfarad ($\mu$F)**
韦伯(磁通量单位)　**weber (Wb)**
麦〔克斯韦〕(磁通量单位)　**maxwell (Mx)**
亨〔利〕(电感单位)　**henry (H)**
静电系单位　**electrostatic units (esu)**

## 半导体　Semiconductor

锗　**germanium**
硅　**silicon**
纯半导体(本征半导体)　**intrinsic semiconductor**
杂质半导体　**impurity semicon-ductor**
半导体中掺杂质　**doping the semiconductor**
施主　**donor**
施主杂质　**donor impurity**
受主　**acceptor**
受主中心　**acceptor centre**
掺杂补偿　**doping compensa-tion**

空穴传导　**hole conduction**
储孔效应　**hole storage effect**
扩散电容　**diffusion capaci-tance, diffusion capacity**
冲穿效应　**punch-through effect**
箍断效应　**pinch-off effect**
霍耳效应　**Hall effect**
霍耳迁移率　**Hall mobility**
复合作用　**recombination action**
n型半导体　**n-type semicon-ductor**
p型半导体　**p-type semicon-**

ductor

p—n结　p-n junction

半导体整流器　semiconductor rectifier

点接触整流器　point-contact rectifier

阻挡层　blocking layer

p—n—p 结构　p-n-p structure

n—p—n 结构　n-p-n structure

单晶　single crystal

复晶　compound crystal

晶体生长　crystal growth

籽晶　seed crystal

引上法单晶　Chochralski single crystal

单晶拉制炉　crystal pulling furnace

区域平均法　zone levelling method

区熔提纯法　floating zone refining method

温差电效应(塞贝克效应) thermoelectric effect (Seebeck effect)

晶体管　transistor

单极晶体管　unipolar transistor

二极晶体管　diode transistor

三极晶体管　triode transistor

四极晶体管　tetrode transistor

场效应晶体管　field effect transistor

结型场效应晶体管　junction field effect transistor

p—n—i—p 晶体管　p-n-i-p transistor

漂移晶体管　drift transistor

晶体检波器　crystal detector

源　source

栅　grid

漏　drain

沟道　channel

发射极　emitter

发射区　emitter region

基极　base

基区　base region

集电极　collector

集电区　collector region

隧道效应　tunnel effect

隧道二极管　tunnel diode

多数载流子　majority carrier

少数载流子　minority carrier

半波整流器　half-wave rectifier, single-way rectifier

锗整流器　germanium rectifier

可控硅整流器　silicon-controlled rectifier

硒整流器　selenium rectifier

半导体化合物　semiconducting compound

金属间半导体　intermetallic semiconductor

超金属　supermetal

半导体光电池　semiconductor photocell

光生伏打效应　photovoltaic effect

光生伏打电池　photovoltaic cell

太阳能电池　solar battery

光敏电阻　photoresistance

光电导管　photoconductive tube

阻挡层光电池　blocking layer photocell

固体电路　solid-state circuit

集成电路 integrated circuit
大规模集成电路 large scale integrated circuit
温差发电器 thermal converter, thermoelectric generator

温差致冷器 thermoelectric cooler
热敏电阻 thermistor, thermal resistor
微电子学 microelectronics

## 原子物理学 Atomic Physics

原子核物理学 nuclear physics
波粒二象性 wave-particle duality
德布罗意波 de Broglie wave
物质波 matter wave
薛定谔方程 Schrödinger equation
宇称 parity
宇称守恒定律 law of parity conservation
相对论 relativity theory, theory of relativity
质能关系式 equation of mass-energy relation
相对性原理 relativity principle
以太 ether
光速不变原理 the axiom that the velocity of light is absolute
量子论 quantum theory
量子 quantum
玻尔学说 Bohr theory
量子数 quantum number
量子力学 quantum mechanics
场论 field theory
经典场论 classical field theory
量子场论 quantum field theory

统一场论 unified field theory
玻尔轨道 Bohr orbit
卢瑟福实验 Rutherford experiment
能级 energy level
能级图 energy level diagram
跃迁 transition
自旋 spin (spinning)
基态 ground state
激发态 exited state
电离 ionization
电离电势(电离电位) ionization potential
电离能 ionization energy
阴极射线 cathode ray
阳极射线 anode ray
阳射线 positive ray
X射线(伦琴射线) X-ray (Röntgen ray)
光电效应 photoelectric effect
超导性 superconductivity
超导体 superconductor
电子云 electron(ic) cloud
等离子体(物质第四态) plasma (fourth state of matter)
同位素分离 isotope separation
基本粒子 fundamental particle
微观粒子 microscopic particle

电子 electron
正电子 positron (positive electron)

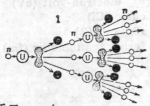

质子 proton
中子 neutron
核子 nucleon
中微子 neutrino
介子 meson, mesotron
超子 hyperon
光子(光量子) photon (light quantum)
反粒子 antiparticle
反物质 antimatter
宇宙射线 cosmic ray
原子核 atomic nucleus
核力 nuclear force
裂变 fission
核反应 nuclear reaction
链式反应① chain reaction
氘核 deuteron, deuton
原子能(核能) atomic energy (nuclear energy)
原子能发电站 atomic power plant
原子核反应堆 nuclear reactor
反应堆 reactor
核燃料 nuclear fuel
减速剂 moderator
靶 target
热核反应 thermonuclear reaction
聚变 fusion

放射性 radioactivity
人工放射性 artificial radioactivity
天然放射性 natural radioactivity
核辐射 nuclear radiation
嬗变 transmutation
衰变 decay
α 蜕变 alpha disintegration
γ 辐射 gamma radiation
β 蜕变 beta disintegration
蜕变 disintegration
α 粒子 alpha particle
β 粒子 beta particle
α 射线(甲种射线) alpha ray (α-ray)
β 射线(乙种射线) beta ray (β-ray)
γ 射线(丙种射线) gamma ray (γ-ray)
放射性尘埃 radioactive ash
放射性微粒回降 radioactive fallout
放射性雨 radioactive rain
放射性沾染 radioactive contamination
半衰期 half-life, half-value period
X射线管(伦琴射线管)② X-ray tube (Röntgen ray tube)
云室(威尔逊云室) cloud chamber (Wilson cloud chamber)

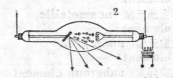

加速器　accelerator
计数管　counter tube
盖革—弥勒计数管　Geiger-Müller tube
盖革—弥勒计数器　G-M (Geiger-Müller) counter
电离室　ionization chamber
普朗克常数(普朗克恒量)　Planck constant
原子质量单位　atomic mass unit
电子伏特　electron-volt (eV)
居里　curie (Ci)
伦琴　röntgen (R)
费米　fermi, femtometer (fm)

# 化　学　Chemistry

## 化学元素　Chemical Elements

同位素　isotope
放射性同位素　radioisotope
同位素量　isotopic weight
质量数　mass number
原子序数　atomic number
同素异形体　allotrope, allotropic form
同质多晶(同质异象)　polymorphism
金属元素　metallic element
半金属元素　semimetallic element
非金属元素　nonmetallic element
主族元素　main group element
副族元素　subgroup element
过渡元素　transition element, transition metal
元素符号　symbol of element
化学符号　chemical symbol
铂族元素(贵金属元素)　platinum family element (precious metallic element)
稀有元素　rare element
稀土元素(稀土金属)　rare-earth element (rare-earth metal)
镧系元素　lanthanide series
放射性元素　radioactive element, radioelement
超铀元素(铀后元素)　transuranium element, transuranic element
超钚元素　transplutonium element
锕系元素　actinide series

## 物理化学　Physical Chemistry

理论化学　theoretical chemistry

热化学　thermochemistry

电化学　electrochemistry

胶体化学　colloidal chemistry

表面化学　surface chemistry

放射化学　radiochemistry

辐射化学　radiation chemistry

〔元素〕周期律　periodic law

〔元素〕周期表　periodic table

化合价(原子价)　valency, valence

原子团　atomic group

基　radical

物理性质　physical property

化学性质　chemical property

克分子体积　molecular volume

阿伏伽德罗常数　Avogadro number, Avogadro constant

组成　composition

混合物　mixture

化合物　compound

分子结构　molecular structure

化学键　bond

共价键　covalent bond

离子键(电价键)　ionic bond (electrovalent bond)

极性键　polar bond

非极性键　non-polar bond

氢键　hydrogen bond

金属键　metallic bond

共价化合物　covalent compound

物理变化　physical change

化学变化　chemical change

化学反应　chemical reaction

化学作用　chemical action

氧化　oxidation

还原　reduction

氧化剂　oxidizing agent, oxidizer

还原剂　reducing agent

自燃　spontaneous ignition

燃烧　combustion

火焰　flame

氧化焰　oxidizing flame

还原焰　reducing flame

着火点(燃点)　ignition temperature, ignition point

气体常数　gas constant

分解　decomposition

化合　chemical combination

复分解　metathesis

潮解　deliquescence

风化　efflorescence

挥发　volatilization

升华　sublimation

可逆反应　reversible reaction

不可逆反应　irreversible reaction

理想气体　ideal gas

标准情况(标准状况)　normal conditions

理想溶液　ideal solution

浓度　concentration

当量浓度　normality

当量溶液　normal solution

克分子浓度　molarity, molar concentration

重量克分子浓度 weight-molarity, weight molar concentration

百分浓度 percentage concentration

重量百分浓度 concentration expressed in percentage by weight

体积百分浓度 concentration expressed in percentage by volume

〔体积〕克分子分数 molar fraction

饱和溶液 saturated solution

过饱和溶液 supersaturated solution

母液 mother liquor, mother solution

稀释 dilution

蒸馏 distillation

固溶体 solid solution, sosoloid

阿伏伽德罗定律 Avogadro's law

法拉第定律 Faraday's law

原子说(原子论) atomic theory

分子说(分子论) molecular theory

燃素说 phlogiston theory

结晶 crystallization

晶体 crystal

晶形(结晶单形) crystal form

光合作用 photosynthesis

溶解热 heat of solution

燃烧热 heat of combustion

汽化热 heat of vaporization

熔化热 heat of fusion

生成热 heat of formation

热效应 heating effect

反应热 heat of reaction, reaction heat

吸热反应 endothermic reaction

放热反应 exothermic reaction, exothermal reaction

离解 dissociation

化学平衡 chemical equilibrium

反应速度 reaction velocity

催化作用 catalytic action

催化反应 catalytic reaction

助催化剂(促进剂) promoter

链式反应 chain reaction

放射性 radioactivity

蜕变 disintegration

原子的蜕变 atomic disintegration

原子嬗变 atomic transmutation

价电子 valence electron

电离 electrolytic dissociation

电离度 degree of electrolytic dissociation

离子化合物 ionic compound

电极 electrode

电解 electrolysis

电解氧化 electrolytic oxidation

电解还原 electrolytic reduction

电子云 electron cloud

胶体(胶质) colloid

胶体溶液(溶胶) colloidal solution

吸附 adsorption

化学吸附(活化吸附) chemical adsorption

物理吸附 physical adsorption

扩散 diffusion

凝结 coagulation

丁铎尔现象 Tyndall phenomenon

胶体颗粒(胶粒) colloidal particle

悬胶体(悬浊液，悬浮体) suspension colloid(suspensoid)

布朗运动 Brownian movement, Brownian motion

质能守恒定律 law of conservation of mass and energy

气体反应定律 law of gas reaction

## 无机化学 Inorganic Chemistry

无机化合物 inorganic compound

氧化物 oxide

酸性氧化物 acid oxide, acidic oxide

碱性氧化物 basic oxide

过氧化物 peroxide

超氧化物 superoxide, hyperoxide

酸酐 acid anhydride

氢氧化物 hydroxide

碱 base

碱性反应 alkali reaction, alkaline reaction

强碱 strong base

弱碱 weak base

酸 acid

无机酸(矿酸) inorganic acid (mineral acid)

强酸 strong acid

弱酸 weak acid

酸根 acid radical

含氧酸 oxy-acid, oxygen acid

氢酸(无氧酸) hydro-acid, hydrogen acid

酸性反应 acid reaction

中性反应 neutral reaction

两性〔化合〕物 amphoteric compound

两性氧化物 amphoteric oxide

两性氢氧化物 amphoteric hydroxide

氢离子浓度 hydrogen ion concentration

氢离子指数 hydrogen ion exponent

pH值 pH value

盐 salt

碱式盐 basic salt

酸式盐 acid salt

正盐 normal salt

复盐 double salt

硬水 hard water

软水 soft water

重水(氧化氘) heavy water (deuterium oxide)

水合物(水化物) hydrate

结晶水 water of crystallization

水解 hydrolysis

金属 metal

非金属 nonmetal

碱金属 alkali metal

碱土金属 alkaline-earth metal

重金属 heavy metal

轻金属 light metal

贵金属 noble metal

合金 alloy

催化剂 catalyst

接触剂 contact agent

单质 simple substance

原子 atom

分子 molecule

当量 equivalent

原子量 atomic weight

分子量 molecular weight

克分子 mol(e), gram molecule

克原子 gram atom

克当量 gram equivalent

化学式 chemical formula

分子式 molecular formula

化学反应式(化学方程式) chemical equation

反应物 reactant

生成物 product

离子 ion

阳离子(正离子) cation(positive ion)

阴离子(负离子) anion(negative ion)

电解质 electrolyte

强电解质 strong electrolyte

弱电解质 weak electrolyte

非电解质 non-electrolyte

离子反应 ionic reaction

离子方程式 ionic equation

溶剂(溶媒) solvent

溶质 solute

溶液(溶体) solution

溶解度 solubility

氘(重氢) deuterium (heavy hydrogen)

氚 tritium

氢化物 hydride

氯化钠(食盐) sodium chloride (common salt)

次氯酸盐 hypochlorite

硝酸盐 nitrate

硝酸钠(智利硝石) sodium nitrate(Chile saltpetre)

亚硝酸盐 nitrite

磷酸钠 sodium phosphate

硅酸钠(水玻璃) sodium silicate(water glass)

过氧化钠 sodium peroxide

氢氧化钠(烧碱, 苛性钠) sodium hydroxide (caustic soda)

硫酸钠 sodium sulfate

碳酸钠(纯碱, 苏打) sodium carbonate (washing soda)

碱灰(苏打灰) soda ash

氨碱法(苏尔维法) ammonia soda process (Solvay process)

碳酸氢钠(小苏打, 焙烧苏打) sodium bicarbonate (baking soda)

溴化钠 sodium bromide

硫化钠 sodium sulfide

氯化钾 potassium chloride

氯酸钾 potassium chlorate

溴化钾 potassium bromide

碘化钾 potassium iodide

硝酸钾 potassium nitrate

硝石(火硝) nitre

碳酸钾(钾碱, 珠灰) potassium carbonate (potash)

氢氧化钾(苛性钾) potassium hydroxide (caustic potash)

过硫酸钾 potassium persulfate

高锰酸钾(灰锰养) potassium permanganate

硫酸钾 potassium sulfate

黄铜矿 chalcopyrite, copper pyrites

硫酸铜(胆矾，蓝矾) copper sulfate, cupric sulfate

氧化铜 copper oxide

氯化铜 copper chloride

氧化银 silver oxide

溴化银 silver bromide

氯化银 silver chloride

碘化银 silver iodide

硝酸银 silver nitrate

氯化镁 magnesium chloride

碳酸镁 magnesium carbonate

硫酸镁(泻盐) magnesium sulfate (Epsom salt)

氧化镁(苦土) magnesium oxide

氯化钙 calcium chloride

磷酸钙 calcium phosphate

过磷酸钙 calcium superphosphate

碳化钙(电石) calcium carbide

碳酸钙 calcium carbonate

石灰(生石灰) lime (quicklime)

氧化钙 calcium oxide

氢氧化钙(熟石灰) calcium hydroxide (slaked lime)

石灰水 limewater

石灰乳 milk of lime

硫酸钙 calcium sulfate

石膏(生石膏) gypsum (plaster stone)

烧石膏(熟石膏) calcined gypsum (plaster of Paris)

硫酸钡 barium sulfate

重晶石 barite, baryte(s), heavy spar

氧化钡(重土) barium oxide

硫化钡 barium sulfide

氯化钡 barium chloride

硫化锌 zinc sulfide

硫酸锌(皓矾) zinc sulfate

氯化锌 zinc chloride

汞(水银) mercury

硼酸 boric acid

氧化铝 aluminium oxide

矾土 bauxite

氢氧化铝 aluminium hydroxide

硫酸铝 aluminium sulfate

明矾 alum

金刚石(金刚钻，钻石) diamond

石墨 graphite

炭黑 carbon black

活性炭 activated carbon, active carbon

碳化物 carbide

二氧化碳(碳酸气) carbon dioxide (carbonic acid gas)

碳酸 carbonic acid

碳酸盐 carbonate

一氧化碳 carbon monoxide

二硫化碳 carbon disulfide

碳化硅(金刚砂) silicon carbide (carborundum)

二氧化硅(硅石) silicon dioxide (silica)

石英 quartz

水晶 rock crystal

硅酸 silicic acid

硅酸盐 silicate

石棉 asbestos

硅酸铝 aluminium silicate

一氧化铅(密陀僧，黄丹) lead monoxide

四氧化三铅(铅丹，红铅) trilead tetroxide (minium, red lead)

碱式碳酸铅(铅白) basic lead

carbonate (white lead)

氯化铅　lead chloride

氮化物　nitride

氧化氮　nitrogen oxide

一氧化二氮(笑气)　nitrous oxide (laughing gas)

硝酸　nitric acid

发烟硝酸　fuming nitric acid

亚硝酸　nitrous acid

王水　aqua regia

合成氨　synthetic ammonia

氨水　ammonia water, aqua ammonia

氢氧化铵　ammonium hydroxide

铵盐　ammonium salt

氯化铵(硇砂)　ammonium chloride (sal ammoniac)

硫〔酸〕铵　ammonium sulfate

硝酸铵　ammonium nitrate

碳酸铵　ammonium carbonate

碳酸氢铵(酸式碳酸铵)　ammonium bicarbonate (ammonium acid carbonate)

白磷(黄磷)　white phosphorus (yellow phosphorus)

五氧化二磷(磷酸酐)　phosphorus pentoxide (phosphoric anhydride)

磷酸　phosphoric acid

磷酸盐　phosphate

臭氧　ozone

过氧化氢(双氧水)　hydrogen peroxide

黄铁矿(硫铁矿)　pyrite

硫化氢　hydrogen sulfide

氢硫酸　hydrosulfuric acid

硫化物　sulfide

三氧化硫(硫酸酐)　sulfur trioxide (sulfuric anhydride)

二氧化硫　sulfur dioxide

硫酸　sulfuric acid

发烟硫酸　fuming sulfuric acid

亚硫酸　sulfurous acid

硫酸盐　sulfate

亚硫酸盐　sulfite

二氧化硒　selenium dioxide

钨酸　tungstic acid

卤素(卤族元素)　halogen

卤化物　halide, halogenide

氟化氢　hydrogen fluoride

氢氟酸　hydrofluoric acid

氟化物　fluoride

氟化钙(萤石)　calcium fluoride (fluorite, fluorspar)

氯化氢　hydrogen chloride

盐酸(氢氯酸)　hydrochloric acid

氯酸　chloric acid

氯酸盐　chlorate

高氯酸　perchloric acid

高氯酸盐　perchlorate

氯化物　chloride

溴化物　bromide

溴化氢　hydrogen bromide

碘化氢　hydrogen iodide

碘化物　iodide

二氧化锰　manganese dioxide

惰性气体(稀有气体)　inert gas, noble gas (rare gas)

氧化铁　iron oxide

硫酸亚铁　ferrous sulfate

# 有机化学　Organic Chemistry

高分子化学　high polymer
chemistry, macromolecular

chemistry

立体化学　stereochemistry, spatial chemistry

有机合成　organic synthesis

同分异构　isomerism

互变异构　tautomerism

立体异构　stereoisomerism

光学异构(旋光异构)　optical isomerism

几何异构(顺反异构)　geometric isomerism

同系列　homologous series

同系物　homologue, homolog

结构式　structural formula

衍生物　derivative

游离基(自由基)　free radical

官能团(功能团)　functional group

烃基　hydrocarbon, hydro-carbon group

烷基(有时指烃基)　alkyl, alkyl group

甲基　methyl, methyl group

乙烯基　vinyl, vinyl group

苯基　phenyl, phenyl group

苄基(苯甲基)　benzyl, benzyl group

氢氧基(氢氧根,羟基)　hydroxy, hydroxyl group

氢硫基(巯基)　sulfhydryl, mercapto group

羰基　carbonyl, carbonyl group

羧基　carboxyl, carboxyl group

磺基　sulfonic group

硝基　nitro⁻, nitro group

氨基　amino⁻, amino group

氰基　cyano⁻, cyano group

偶氮基　azo⁻, azo group

自动氧化　auto-oxidation

氢化　hydrogenation

水合(水化)　hydration

烷基化　alkylation

卤化　halogenation

氯化　chlorination

磺化　sulfonation

氯磺化　chloro-sulfonation

芳构化　aromatization

异构化　isomerization

硝化　nitration

氨化　ammoniation

脱水　dehydration

脱氢　dehydrogenation

偶合　coupling

聚合　polymerization

单体　monomer

聚合物　polymer

缩合　condensation

缩聚〔反应〕　condensation polymerization

银镜反应　silver mirror reaction

分子重排　molecular rearrangement

置换反应(取代反应)　substitution reaction

加成反应　addition reaction

有机〔化合〕物　organic compound

高分子化合物　high molecular compound, macromolecular compound

有机金属化合物(金属有机化合物)　organometallic compound

有机硅〔化合物〕　organosilicon (compound)

硅烷　silane

| 油脂 | fat |
|---|---|
| 蛋白质 | protein |
| 碳水化合物(糖) | carbohydrate |
| 还原糖 | reducing sugar |
| 纤维素 | cellulose |
| 淀粉 | starch |
| 生物碱 | alkaloid |
| 饱和化合物 | saturated compound |
| 不饱和化合物 | unsaturated compound |
| 脂肪族化合物 | aliphatic compound |
| 碳环化合物 | carbocyclic compound |
| 芳族化合物 | aromatic compound |
| 脂环族化合物 | alicyclic compound |
| 杂环化合物 | heterocyclic compound |
| 烃(碳氢化合物) | hydrocarbon |
| 饱和烃 | saturated hydrocarbon |
| 烷烃(石蜡烃) | methane series (paraffin series) |
| 不饱和烃 | unsaturated hydrocarbon |
| 烯烃 | ethylene series |
| 炔烃 | acetylene series |
| 环烃 | cyclic hydrocarbon, ring hydrocarbon |
| 脂环烃 | alicyclic hydrocarbon |
| 芳族烃(芳香烃) | aromatic hydrocarbon |
| 蜡 | wax |
| 醇〔类〕 | alcohol |
| 酚〔类〕 | phenol |
| 醚〔类〕 | ether |

| 醛〔类〕 | aldehyde |
|---|---|
| 酮〔类〕 | ketone |
| 醌〔类〕 | quinone |
| 羧酸〔类〕 | carboxylic acid |
| 有机酸 | organic acid |
| 脂肪酸 | fatty acid |
| 氨基酸(胺酸) | amino acid |
| 磺酸 | sulfonic acid |
| 酯〔类〕 | ester |
| 腈〔类〕 | nitrile |
| 胩〔类〕 | carbylamine |
| 肼〔类〕 | hydrazine |
| 腙〔类〕 | hydrazone |
| 肟〔类〕 | oxime |
| 脎〔类〕 | osazone |
| 胍〔类〕 | guanidine |
| 胂〔类〕 | arsine |
| 砜〔类〕 | sulfone |
| 胺〔类〕 | amine |
| 重氮盐 | diazonium salt |
| 重氮化合物 | diazo compound |
| 偶氮化合物 | azo compound |
| 甲烷 | methane |
| 乙烷 | ethane |
| 丙烷 | propane |
| 丁烷 | butane |
| 戊烷 | pentane |
| 己烷 | hexane |
| 庚烷 | heptane |
| 辛烷 | octane |
| 乙烯 | ethylene |
| 乙炔 | acetylene |
| 苯 | benzene |
| 萘 | naphthalene |
| 乙醇(酒精) | ethyl alcohol |
| 葡萄糖(右旋糖) | glucose (dextrose) |
| 麦芽糖 | maltose |
| 乙酸(醋酸) | acetic acid |

尿素(脲，碳酰胺) urea (carbamide)

芥子气(双氯乙基硫，二氯乙硫醚) mustard gas, yperite (dichloroethyl sulfide)

糖精 saccharin

## 分析化学 Analytical Chemistry

化学分析 chemical analysis

无机分析 inorganic analysis

有机分析 organic analysis

定性分析 qualitative analysis

定量分析 quantitative analysis

重量分析 gravimetric analysis

容量分析 volumetric analysis

微量分析 microanalysis

半微量分析 semimicroanalysis

超微量分析 supermicroanalysis

元素分析 elemental analysis

碳氢氮元素分析仪 CHN analyzer

气体分析 gas analysis

吹管分析 blowpipe analysis

光谱分析 spectrum analysis

原子吸收光谱法 atomic absorption spectrometry (AAS)

原子发射光谱法 atomic emission spectrometry (AES)

极谱分析 polarography

色谱分析 chromatography

滴定法 titration, titrimetric method

酸碱滴定法 acid-base titration

氧化还原滴定法 oxidation-reduction titration

(滴定)突跃 break

差示扫描量热法 differential scanning calorimetry (DSC)

焰色反应 flame reaction

火焰光度计检测器 flame photometric detector (FPD)

标准溶液(规定溶液) standard solution

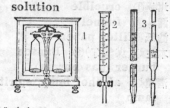

准确度 accuracy

灵敏度 sensitivity

试剂 reagent

分析纯试剂 analytical reagent (AR)

指示剂 indicator

试纸 test paper

石蕊试纸 litmus paper

姜黄试纸 turmeric paper

酚酞 phenolphthalein

化学天平 chemical balance

分析天平① analytical balance

砝码 weight

滴定管② burette, buret

吸量管(移液管)③ pipette, pipet

量瓶(容量瓶)④ measuring flask (volumetric flask)

量筒⑤ measuring cylinder

蒸发皿⑥ evaporating dish

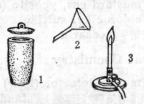

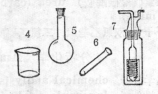

钳埚① crucible
漏斗② funnel
滤纸 filter paper
本生灯(煤气灯)③ Bunsen burner (gas burner)
酒精灯 alcohol lamp, spirit lamp
钾碱球管 potash bulb
烧杯④ beaker
烧瓶⑤ flask
试管⑥ test tube
洗气瓶⑦ gas washing bottle
干燥器⑧ desiccator, exsiccator
基普发生器⑨ Kipp generator
化学纯 chemically pure (CP)
化学电离 chemical ionization (CI)

离子交换剂 ion exchanger
极谱仪 polarograph
比浊计 turbidimeter
比色计 colorimeter
酸度计 acidimeter
折射计 refractometer
沉淀 precipitation
共沉淀 coprecipitation
中和作用 neutralization

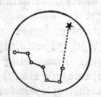

# 天文学 Astronomy

## 天文观测和描述 Astronomical Observation and Description

天文台 observatory

射电天文学 radio astronomy

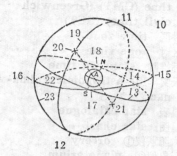

天球⑩　celestial sphere
天轴　celestial axis
天极　celestial pole
北天极⑪　north celestial pole
南天极⑫　south celestial pole
天〔球〕赤道⑬　celestial equator
黄道⑭　ecliptic
夏至点⑮　summer solstice
冬至点⑯　winter solstice
春分点⑰　vernal equinox
秋分点⑱　autumnal equinox
（地面A点的）天球子午圈⑲
　celestial meridian (for point
　A on Earth's surface)
（A点的）天顶⑳　zenith (for A)
（A点的）天底㉑　nadir (for A)
交点㉒　node
二至圈㉓　solstitial colure
天球坐标　celestial coordi-
nates
赤道坐标系　equatorial system
　of coordinates
赤经　right ascension
赤纬　declination
黄道坐标系　ecliptic system
　of coordinates
黄极　ecliptic pole
黄经　ecliptic longitude

黄纬　ecliptic latitude
黄道带　zodiac
黄道十二宫㉔　12 signs of the
　zodiac
天体　celestial body
恒星自行　proper motion of
　stars
视差　parallax
视差位移　parallactic dis-
　placement
秒差距　parsec (pc)
视位〔置〕　apparent position
视〔运〕动　apparent motion
大气折射(蒙气差)　astronomi-
　cal refraction
周日运动　diurnal motion
周日〔平行〕圈　diurnal circle
中天　meridian transit
星等　magnitude
绝对星等　absolute magnitude
光度　luminosity
视星等　apparent magnitude
视亮度　apparent brightness
赫罗图　Hertzsprung-Russell
　diagram (HRD)
光谱型　spectral type

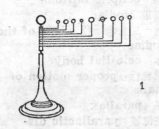

1

质光关系　mass-luminosity relation
主星序　main sequence
主序星　main sequence star
天文单位　astronomical unit (AU)
光年　light year
时间计量　time measurement
恒星日　sidereal day
恒星时　sidereal time (ST)
真太阳日　true solar day
太阳时　solar time
平(太阳)时　mean solar time
历书时　ephemeris time (ET)
格林威(尼)治平时(格林威(尼)治民用时)　Greenwich mean time (GMT) (Greenwich civil time) (GCT)
时区　time zone
区时　zone time
标准时　standard time
天文年历　astronomical almanac
星表　star catalogue
星图　star chart
太阳系仪①　orrery
天象仪②　planetarium

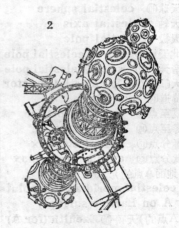

2

# 天文仪器　Astronomical Instruments

圭表③　gnomon
日规(日晷)④　sundial
漏壶⑤　water clock, clepsydra
沙漏⑥　hourglass
浑仪⑦　armillary sphere
天球仪⑧　celestial globe
象限仪⑨　quadrant
望远镜　telescope
折射望远镜　refractor
物镜　objective, object glass
目镜　eyepiece
十字丝　cross hair, spider line
光阑　diaphragm
入射光瞳　entrance pupil
出射光瞳　exit pupil
放大率　magnifying power
测微器　micrometer
反射望远镜　reflector, mirror telescope

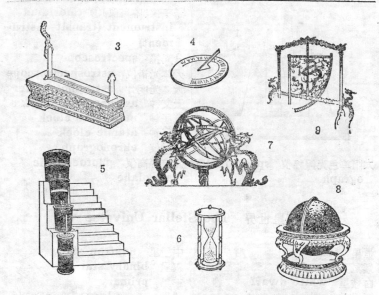

牛顿〔式〕反射望远镜 **Newtonian reflector**

平面镜 **flat mirror**

抛物面镜 **parabolic mirror**

卡塞格林〔式〕反射望远镜 **Cassegrain reflector**

照相望远镜 **photographic telescope**

导星镜 **guiding telescope**

寻星镜 **finder**

寻彗镜 **comet seeker**

施密特〔式〕照相望远镜 **Schmidt photographic telescope**

改正镜片 **correcting plate**

曲焦面 **curved focal surface**

球面镜 **spherical mirror**

赤道〔式〕装置 **equatorial mounting**

望远镜筒 **telescope tube**

赤纬轴 **declination axis**

极轴 **polar axis**

转仪装置 **driving mechanism**

转仪钟 **driving clock**

光电倍增管 **photomultiplier**

光电象管 **photoelectric image tube**

折轴望远镜 **coude telescope**

浮动天顶仪 **floating zenith telescope (FZT)**

射电望远镜 **radio telescope**

赤道仪 **equatorial**

经纬仪 **theodolite**

日冕仪 **coronagraph**

天文摄影机 **astrophotocamera**

双筒天体照相仪 **double astrograph**

摄谱仪 **spectrograph**

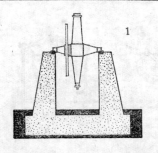

太阳单色光照相仪　spectroheli-
ograph

子午仪(中星仪)① meridian
instrument (transit instrument)
分光镜　spectroscope
天体光谱仪　astrospectroscope
天体光度计　astrophotometer
天文钟　astronomical clock
分子钟　molecular clock
原子钟　atomic clock
记时仪　chronograph
光电等高仪　photoelectric
astrolabe

## 恒星世界　The Stellar Universe

恒星　star
矮星　dwarf
白矮星　white dwarf
亚巨星　subgiant
巨星　giant
红巨星　red giant
超巨星　supergiant
红超巨星　red supergiant
变星　variable star
食变星(食双星)　eclipsing
variable (eclipsing binary)
脉动变星　pulsation variable
造父变星　Cepheid
光变周期　light period
周光关系　period-luminosity
relation
天琴RR型变星　RR Lyrae vari-
able
爆发变星　explosive variable
新星　nova
超新星　supernova
脉冲星　pulsar (pulsating
radio source)

中子星　neutron star
双星　binary star
主星　primary
伴星　secondary, companion
分光双星　spectroscopic binary
聚星　multiple star
巴纳德星　Barnard star
柯伊伯星　Kuiper star
佛耳夫—拉叶星(W型星)
Wolf-Rayet star (W star)
哈罗—赫比格天体　Haro-Herbig
object
星团　star cluster
疏散星团　open star cluster
昴星团　Pleiades
毕星团　Hyades
球状星团　globular star clus-
ter
星协　association
O星协　O-association
T星协　T-association
岛宇宙　island universe
星系　galaxy

旋涡星系　spiral galaxy
银河　Milky Way
银河系　Milky Way Galaxy
银〔河系中〕心　galactic centre
银盘　galactic disc
银核　galactic nucleus
银晕　galactic halo
星族　stellar population
银道坐标②　galactic coordinates
银道③　galactic equator
北银极④　north galactic pole
南银极⑤　south galactic pole
银心方向⑥　direction of galactic centre
银经⑦　galactic longitude

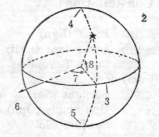

银纬⑧　galactic latitude
棒旋星系　barred spiral galaxy
椭圆星系　elliptical galaxy
不规则星系　irregular galaxy
双重星系　binary galaxy
三重星系　triple galaxy
射电星系　radio galaxy
类星射电源　quasar (quasi-stellar radio source, QSS)
类星星系　quasi-stellar galaxy (QSG)
星系团　cluster of galaxies
超星系　supergalaxy
总星系　metagalaxy
宇宙〔射〕线　cosmic rays
宇宙起源　origin of the Universe
天体演化　cosmogony
宇宙模型　cosmological model
膨胀〔宇宙〕模型　expanding model
大爆炸宇宙论　Big Bang theory
稳恒态宇宙论　Steady State theory
振动宇宙论　Oscillation theory

## 星 云　Nebula

银河星云　galactic nebula
弥漫星云　diffuse nebula
亮星云　luminous nebula, bright nebula
尘埃星云　dust nebula
反射星云　reflection nebula
气体星云　gaseous nebula
发射星云　emission nebula
猎户座大星云　great nebula in Orion

麒麟座玫瑰星云　Rosette nebula in Monoceros
金牛座蟹状星云　Crab nebula in Taurus
天鹅座网状星云　Network nebula in Cygnus
天鹅座北美洲星云　North America nebula in Cygnus
天鹅座鹈鹕星云　Pelican nebula in Cygnus

暗星云　dark nebula

猎户座马头星云　Horse-Head nebula in Orion

"煤袋"〔暗星云〕　Coalsack

变光星云　variable nebula

行星状星云　planetary nebula

宝瓶座耳轮星云　Helical nebula in Aquarius

狐狸座哑铃星云　Dumbbell nebula in Vulpecula

天琴座环状星云　Ring nebula in Lyra

河外星云　extragalactic nebula, anagalactic nebula

椭圆星云　elliptical nebula

旋涡星云　spiral nebula

纺锥状星云　spindle nebula

不规则星云　irregular nebula

仙女座星云　Andromeda nebula

三角座旋涡星云　Triangulum Spiral

大麦〔哲伦〕云　Large Magellanic Cloud (LMC)

小麦〔哲伦〕云　Small Magellanic Cloud (SMC)

北冕座河外星云团　cluster of extragalactic nebulae in Corona Borealis

## 星座名称　Names of Constellations

北天星座①　northern constellations

小熊座②　Ursa Minor (UMi)

天龙座③　Draco (Dra)

仙王座④　Cepheus (Cep)

仙后座⑤　Cassiopeia (Cas)

鹿豹座⑥　Camelopardalis (Cam)

大熊座⑦　Ursa Major (UMa)

猎犬座⑧　Canes Venatici (CVn)

牧夫座⑨　Boötes (Boö)

北冕座⑩　Corona Borealis (CrB)

武仙座⑪　Hercules (Her)

天琴座⑫　Lyra (Lyr)

天鹅座⑬　Cygnus (Cyg)

蝎虎座⑭　Lacerta (Lac)

仙女座⑮　Andromeda (And)

英仙座⑯　Perseus (Per)

御夫座⑰　Auriga (Aur)

天猫座⑱　Lynx (Lyn)

小狮座⑲　Leo Minor (LMi)

后发座⑳　Coma Berenices (Com)

巨蛇座㉑　Serpens (Ser)

蛇夫座㉒　Ophiuchus (Oph)

盾牌座㉓　Scutum (Sct)

天鹰座㉔　Aquila (Aql)

天箭座㉕　Sagitta (Sge)

狐狸座㉖　Vulpecula (Vul)

海豚座㉗　Delphinus (Del)

小马座㉘　Equuleus (Equ)

飞马座㉙　Pegasus (Peg)

三角座㉚　Triangulum (Tri)

黄道星座　zodiacal constellations

白羊座㉛　Aries (Ari)

金牛座㉜　Taurus (Tau)

双子座㉝　Gemini (Gem)

巨蟹座㉞　Cancer (Cnc)

狮子座㉟　Leo (Leo)

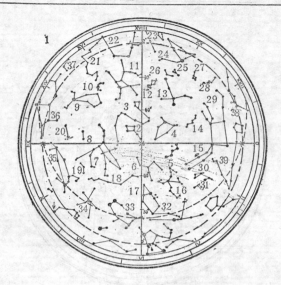

| 室女座㊱ | **Virgo (Vir)** | **(CrΛ)** | |
| --- | --- | --- | --- |
| 天秤座㊲ | **Libra (lib)** | 显微镜座⑯ | **Microscopium** |
| 宝瓶座㊳ | **Aquarois (Aqr)** | **(Mic)** | |
| 双鱼座㊴ | **Pisces (Psc)** | 天坛座⑰ | **Ara (Ara)** |
| | | 望远镜座⑱ | **Telescopium (Tel)** |
| 南天星座① | **southern constel-** | 印第安座⑲ | **Indus (Ind)** |
| **lations** | | 天鹤座⑳ | **Grus (Gru)** |
| 天蝎座② | **Scorpius (Sco)** | 凤凰座㉑ | **Phoenix (Phe)** |
| 人马座③ | **Sagittarius (Sgr)** | 时钟座㉒ | **Horologium (Hor)** |
| 摩羯座④ | **Capricornus (Cap)** | 绘架座㉓ | **Pictor (Pic)** |
| 鲸鱼座⑤ | **Cetus (Cet)** | 船帆座㉔ | **Vela (Vel)** |
| 波江座⑥ | **Eridanus (Eri)** | 南十字座㉕ | **Crux (Cru)** |
| 猎户座⑦ | **Orion (Ori)** | 圆规座㉖ | **Circinus (Cir)** |
| 麒麟座⑧ | **Monoceros (Mon)** | 南三角座㉗ | **Triangulum** |
| 小犬座⑨ | **Canis Minor (CMi)** | **Australe (TrA)** | |
| 长蛇座⑩ | **Hydra (Hya)** | 孔雀座㉘ | **Pavo (Pav)** |
| 六分仪座⑪ | **Sextans (Sex)** | 南鱼座㉙ | **Piscis Austrinus** |
| 巨爵座⑫ | **Crater (Crt)** | **(PsA)** | |
| 乌鸦座⑬ | **Corvus (Crv)** | 玉夫座㉚ | **Sculptor (Scl)** |
| 豺狼座⑭ | **Lupus (Lup)** | 天炉座㉛ | **Fornax (For)** |
| 南冕座⑮ | **Corona Australis** | 雕具座㉜ | **Caelum (Cae)** |

1

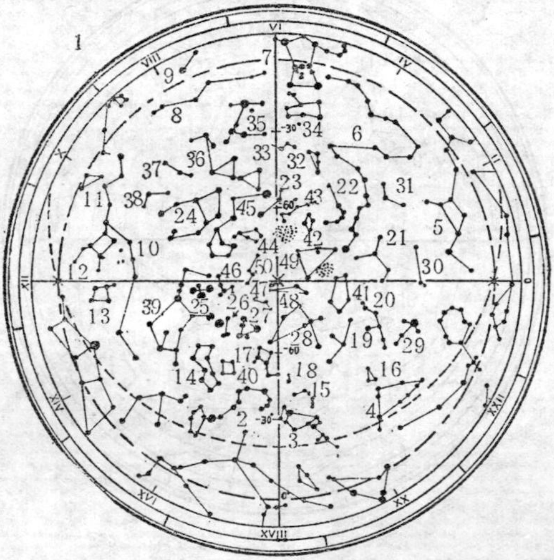

天鸽座㉝ **Columba (Col)**
天兔座㉞ **Lepus (Lep)**
大犬座㉟ **Canis Major (CMa)**
船尾座㊱ **Puppis (Pup)**
罗盘座㊲ **Pyxis (Pyx)**
唧筒座㊳ **Antlia (Ant)**
半人马座㊴ **Centaurus (Cen)**
矩尺座㊵ **Norma (Nor)**
杜鹃座㊶ **Tucana (Tuc)**
网罟座㊷ **Reticulum (Ret)**
剑鱼座㊸ **Dorado (Dor)**
飞鱼座㊹ **Volans (Vol)**
船底座㊺ **Carina (Car)**
苍蝇座㊻ **Musca (Mus)**
天燕座㊼ **Apus (Aps)**
南极座㊽ **Octans (Oct)**
水蛇座㊾ **Hydrus (Hyi)**
蝘蜓座㊿ **Chamaeleon (Cha)**

## 重要星名 Names of Important Stars

北极星(勾陈一, 小熊座α)(51) **Polaris (α Ursae Minoris), polestar**
北斗七星(52) **Big Dipper**
天枢(北斗一, 大熊座α) **Dubhe (α Ursae Majoris)**
天璇(北斗二, 大熊座β) **Merak (β Ursae Majoris)**
天玑(北斗三, 大熊座γ) **Phecda (γ Ursae Majoris)**

（β Tauri）

毕宿五（金牛座α）　**Aldebaran**
（α Tauri）

昴宿六（金牛座η）　**Alcyone**
（η Tauri）

大火（心宿二，天蝎座α）
**Antares**（α Scorpii）

北河二（双子座α）　**Castor**
（α Geminorum）

北河三（双子座β）　**Pollux**
（β Geminorum）

北落师门（南鱼座α）　**Fomal-**
**haut**（α Piscis Austrini）

角宿一（室女座α）　**Spica**
（α Virginis）

牵牛星（河鼓二，天鹰座α）
**Altair**（α Aquilae）

织女星（织女一，天琴座α）
**Vega**（α Lyrae）

南河三（小犬座α）　**Procyon**
（α Canis Minoris）

水委一（波江座α）　**Achernar**
（α Eridani）

轩辕十四（狮子座α）　**Regulus**
（α Leonis）

五帝座一（狮子座β）　**Denebola**
（β Leonis）

参宿四（猎户座α）　**Betelgeuse**
（α Orionis）

参宿五（猎户座γ）　**Bellatrix**
（γ Orionis）

参宿七（猎户座β）　**Rigel**（β
Orionis）

室宿一（飞马座α）　**Markab**
（α Pegasi）

室宿二（飞马座β）　**Scheat**（β
Pegasi）

壁宿一（飞马座 γ）　**Algenib**
（γ Pegasi）

天权（北斗四，大熊座δ）
**Megrez**（δ Ursae Majoris）

玉衡（北斗五，大熊座ε）
**Alioth**（ε Ursae Majoris）

开阳（北斗六，大熊座ζ）
**Mizar**（ζ Ursae Majoris）

辅（大熊座ζ₂）　**Alcor**（ζ₂ Ursae
Majoris）

摇光（北斗七，大熊座η）
**Alkaid, Benetnasch**（η Ursae
Majoris）

右枢（紫微右垣一，天龙座α）
**Thuban**（α Draconis）

大角（牧夫座α）　**Arcturus**
（α Boötis）

天船三（英仙座α）　**Mirfac**
（α Persei）

大陵五（英仙座β）　**Algol**
（β Persei）

天狼星（大犬座α）　**Sirius**
（α Canis Majoris）, **Dog**
**Star**

老人星（船底座α）　**Canopus**
（α Carinae）

天津四（天鹅座α）　**Deneb**
（α Cygni）

五车二（御夫座α）　**Capella**
（α Aurigae）

五车五（金牛座β）　**Elnath**

星宿一(长蛇座 α)　Alphard
　(α Hydrae)
娄宿三(白羊座 α)　Hamal
　(α Arietis)
天囷一(鲸鱼座 α)　Menkar
　(α Ceti)
蒭藁增二(鲸鱼座O)　Mira

(o Ceti)
奎宿九(仙女座 β)　Mirach
　(β Andromedae)
侯(蛇夫座 α)　Rasalhague
　(α Ophiuchi)
王良四(仙后座 α)　Schedar
　(α Cassiopeiae)

## 太阳系　The Solar System

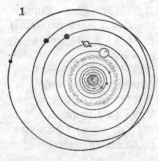

太阳系① the solar system
太阳　sun
光球　photosphere
太阳圆面　disc of the sun
(圆面)边缘　limb
临边昏暗　limb darkening
太阳黑子(日斑)　sunspot
前导黑子　leading sunspot

后随黑子　following sunspot
黑子周　sunspot cycle
光斑　facula
(日面)米粒　granule
色球(层)　chromosphere
日珥　solar prominence
日冕　solar corona
太阳单色光观测②　spectrohe-
　liographic investigation
棱镜③　prism
透镜④　lens
狭缝⑤　slit
光谱⑥　spectrum
太阳单色光照片　spectrohelio-
　gram
谱斑　plage
太阳辐射　solar radiation
射电宁静太阳　radio quiet sun
电离层暴　ionospheric storm

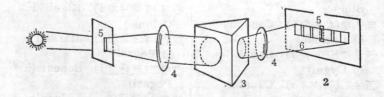

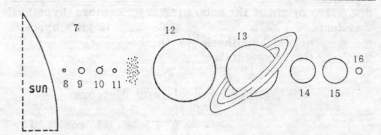

| | |
|---|---|
| 耀斑　solar flare | 阿波罗小行星　Apollo |
| 磁暴　magnetic storm | 赫米斯小行星　Hermes |
| 太阳风　solar wind | 伊卡鲁斯小行星　Icarus |
| 黄道光　zodiacal light | 小行星带　asteroidal belt |
| 行星　planet | (小行星带外的)外行星　outer planets |
| 九大行星⑦　9 principal planets | (小行星带内的)内行星　inner planets |
| 水星⑧　Mercury | (地球轨道外的)外行星　superior planets |
| 金星⑨　Venus | (地球轨道内的)内行星　inferior planets |
| 地球⑩　Earth | |
| 火星⑪　Mars | 类木行星　Jovian planets |
| 木星⑫　Jupiter | 类地行星　terrestrial planet |
| 土星⑬　Saturn | 卫星　satellite |
| 土星光环　Saturn's rings | 火卫　Martian satellites |
| 天王星⑭　Uranus | 木卫　Jovian satellites |
| 海王星⑮　Neptune | 土卫　Saturnian satellites |
| 冥王星⑯　Pluto | 天〔王〕卫　Uranian satellites |
| 冥外行星　trans-Plutonian planet | 海〔王〕卫　Neptunian satellites |
| 小行星　asteroid, planetoid, minor planet | 开普勒行星运动三定律　Kepler's three laws of planetary motion |
| 谷神星　Ceres | 托勒密体系(地心体系)　Ptolemaic system (geocentric system) |
| 智神星　Pallas | |
| 婚神星　Juno | |
| 灶神星　Vesta | |
| 义神星　Astraea | 哥白尼体系(日心体系)　Copernican system (heliocentric system) |
| 爱神星　Eros | |
| 阿基里斯小行星　Achilles | |
| 阿多尼斯小行星　Adonis | |

太阳系起源 origin of the solar system

星云假说 nebula hypothesis

潮汐假说 tidal hypothesis

俘获假说 capture hypothesis

霍伊尔假说 Hoyle's hypothesis

## 彗星和流星 Comets and Meteors

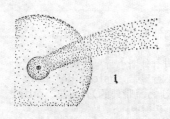

彗星① comet

彗头 head of comet

彗核 nucleus of comet

彗发 coma

氢云 hydrogen cloud

彗尾 tail of comet

直彗尾 straight tail

曲彗尾 curved tail

多重彗尾 multiple tail

反常彗尾 anomalous tail

恩克彗〔星〕 Encke's comet

哈雷彗〔星〕 Halley's comet

彗星群 comet group

木族彗〔星〕 comet of Jupiter family

土族彗〔星〕 comet of Saturn family

天〔王〕族彗〔星〕 comet of Uranus family

海〔王〕族彗〔星〕 comet of Neptune family

交食彗 eclipse comet

母彗星 parent comet

彗生流星雨 cometary stream

流星 meteor, shooting star

火流星 fireball

仙女流星群 Andromedids

宝瓶流星群 Aquarids

仙后流星群 Cassiopeids

天龙流星群 Draconids

双子流星群 Geminids

天琴流星群 Lyrids

狮子流星群 Leonids

天秤流星群 Librids

麒麟流星群 Monocerids

猎户流星群 Orionids

英仙流星群(八月流星群) Perseids (August meteors)

金牛流星群 Taurids

小熊流星群 Ursids

流星雨 meteor shower

流星雨辐射点 meteor shower radiant

流星尘 meteoric dust

流星轨迹 meteor trajectory

流星余迹 meteor trail

陨星 meteorite

陨星雨 meteorite shower

陨星坑 meteorite crater

## 地月系统　The Earth-Moon System

质量中心　centre of mass
地球自转　rotation of the Earth
地〔球自转〕轴　rotation axis of the Earth
地球公转　revolution of the Earth
轨道　orbit
轨道面　orbital plane
近日点　perihelion
远日点　aphelion
地平圈　horizon
地球进动　precession of the Earth
地球章动　nutation of the Earth
月球　moon
白道　moon's orbit, lunar orbit
近地点　perigee
远地点　apogee

黄白交角　inclination of the lunar orbit
交点　node
交点线　line of nodes
偏心率(离心率)　eccentricity
月球天平动　lunar libration, libration of the moon
月相②　phases of the moon
朔(新月)③　new moon
蛾眉月④　crescent
上弦⑤　first quarter
凸月⑥　gibbous moon
望(满月)⑦　full moon
下弦⑧　last quarter
盈月　waxing moon
亏月　waning moon
地月交互作用　Earth-moon interaction
潮汐　tides
太阴潮　lunar tide
太阳潮　solar tide
涨潮　flood tide
落潮　ebb tide
大潮　spring tide
小潮　neap tide
大气潮　atmospheric tide
陆潮　earth tide
长潮力　tide raising force
潮汐力　tidal force
潮汐摩擦　tidal friction
月震　moonquake
月面　lunar surface
(月面)环形山　lunar crater
(月面)圆谷　lunar circus
(月面)沟纹　rill (rille)

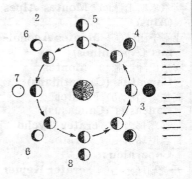

| | |
|---|---|
| 月面图① **lunar map** | 汽海⑪ **Mare Vaporum (Sea of Vapours)** |
| 风暴洋② **Oceanus Procellarum (Ocean of Storms** | 冷海⑫ **Mare Frigoris (Sea of Cold)** |
| 湿海③ **Mare Humorum (Sea of Moisture)** | 阿尔泰山脉⑬ **Montes Altai (Altai Mountains)** |
| 云海④ **Mare Nubium (Sea of Clouds)** | 阿尔卑斯山脉⑭ **Montes Alpes (Alps)** |
| 雨海⑤ **Mare Imbrium (Sea of Rains)** | 亚平宁山脉⑮ **Montes Apenninus (Apennines)** |
| 酒海⑥ **Mare Nectaris (Sea of Nectar)** | 喀尔巴阡山脉⑯ **Montes Carpatus (Carpathians)** |
| 静海⑦ **Mare Tranquillitatis (Sea of Tranquillity)** | 高加索山脉⑰ **Montes Caucasus (Caucasus)** |
| 澄海⑧ **Mare Serenitatis (Sea of Serenty)** | 第谷环形山⑱ **crater Tycho** |
| 丰富海⑨ **Mare Foecunditatis (Sea of Fertility)** | 哥白尼环形山⑲ **crater Copernicus** |
| 危海⑩ **Mare Crisium (Sea of Crises)** | 开普勒环形山⑳ **crater Kepler** |
| | 柏拉图环形山㉑ **crater Plato** |

## 交食和掩星　Eclipses and Occultations

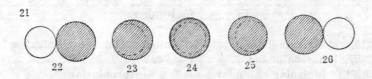

交食　eclipse

食年　eclipse year

沙罗周期　saros

食限　eclipse limit

交食预测　prediction of eclipses

偏食始(初亏)　beginning of partial eclipse (first contact)

食甚　middle of eclipse, maximum phase

偏食终(复圆)　end of partial eclipse (last contact)

日全食五个阶段㉑　five phases of a total solar eclipse

初亏㉒　first contact

食既(全食始)㉓　second contact (beginning of totality)

食甚㉔　totality, middle of eclipse

生光(全食终)㉕　third contact (end of totality)

复圆㉖　fourth contact, last contact

日食㉗　solar eclipse, eclipse of the sun

本影㉘　umbra

半影㉙　penumbra

全食㉚　total eclipse

偏食㉛　partial eclipse

环食㉜　annular eclipse

日全食　total solar eclipse

日偏食　partial solar eclipse

全食带　belt of totality

月食　lunar eclipse, eclipse of the moon

月全食　total lunar eclipse

月偏食　partial lunar eclipse

半影月食　penumbral lunar eclipse, lunar appulse

卫星食　satellite eclipse

食分　magnitude of eclipse, degree of obscuration

掩食时间　duration of eclipse

全食时间　duration of totality

掩星　occultation

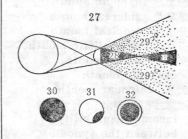

掩始　immersion
复现　emersion
水星凌日　**transit of Mercury**

金星凌日　**transit of Venus**
初切　**ingress**
终切　**egress**

## 历　法　Calendar

阳历　**solar calendar**
阴历　**lunar calendar**
阴阳历　**lunisolar calendar**
太初历(三统历)(公元前104年采用)　**Taichu calendar (Santong calendar) (adopted in 104 B. C.)**
祖冲之创制的大明历　**Daming calendar constructed by Zu Chongzhi**
郭守敬的授时历　**Shoushi calendar by Guo Shoujing**
儒略历　**Julian calendar**
格〔雷果〕里历(1582年开始颁行)　**Gregorian calendar (introduced in 1582)**
恒星年　**sidereal year**
回归年(太阳年)　**tropical year (solar year)**
历年　**calendar year**
平年　**common year**
闰年　**leap year**
月　**month**
朔望月　**synodic month**
恒星月　**sidereal month**
分至月　**tropical month**
近点月　**anomalistic month**
交点月　**nodal month, draconic month**
历月　**calendar month**
朔望月和回归年的不可通约性　**incommensurability between the synodic month and the tropical year**
置闰　**intercalation**
闰月　**intercalary month**
闰日　**intercalary day**
太阴周(默冬章)　**lunar cycle (Metonic cycle)**
十九年七闰月　**7 intercalary months in 19 years**
十二次　**12 intervals on the ecliptic**
二十四节气　**24 solar terms**
季　**season**
春　**spring**
夏　**summer**
秋　**autumn**
冬　**winter**
春分　**vernal equinox**
秋分　**autumnal equinox**
岁差　**precession of the equinoxes**
夏至　**summer solstice**
冬至　**winter solstice**
二十八宿　**28 lunar mansions**
甲子周期(干支周期)　**sexagenary cycle**
天干　**'celestial stems'**
地支　**'terrestrial branches'**
星期(周)　**week**
日　**day**
平太阳日(民用日)　**mean solar day (civil day)**

# 气象学　Meteorology

## 大　气　The Atmosphere

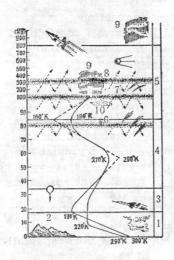

对流层①　troposphere
对流层顶②　tropopause
平流层③　stratosphere
中间层④　mesosphere
热成层⑤　thermosphere
D层⑥　D-layer
E层⑦　E-layer

F层⑧　F-layer
极光⑨　aurora
夜光云⑩　noctilucent clouds
臭氧层　ozonosphere
光化层　chemosphere
电离层　ionosphere
外逸层　exosphere
磁性层　magnetosphere
摩擦层　frictional layer
自由大气　free atmosphere
空气密度　air density
气压　atmospheric pressure
标准大气压　standard atmos-
　phere pressure
毫巴　millibar (mb)
气温　air temperature
度　degree
摄氏温〔度〕标(百分温标)　Cel-
　sius' temperature scale
　(centigrade temperature
　scale) (C)
华氏温〔度〕标　Fahrenheit
　temperature scale (F)
绝对温〔度〕标　absolute
　temperature scale (K)
绝对湿度　absolute humidity

| 相对湿度　relative humidity | 暖气团　warm air mass |
| --- | --- |
| 饱和空气　saturated air | 锋　front |
| 饱和水汽压　saturation vapour pressure | 锋面　frontal surface |
| | 锋线　frontal line |
| 露点　dew point | 冷锋　cold front |
| 气团　air mass | 暖锋　warm front |
| 冷气团　cold air mass | 静止锋　stationary front |

# 风　Wind

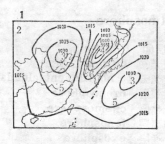

大气环流　atmospheric circulation

海平面气压　sea level pressure

气压图①　pressure chart

等压线②　isobar

高气压③　high pressure

低气压④　low pressure

高压脊⑤　pressure ridge

低压槽⑥　pressure trough

高压等值线　pleiobar

低压等值线　meiobar

槽线　trough line

气压梯度　pressure gradient

气压梯度力　pressure (-gradient) force

地球自转偏向力　deflection force of Earth rotation

热量平衡　heat balance

平流　advection

平流变化　advective change

辐合　convergence

辐散　divergence

对流　convection

热对流　thermal convection

动力对流　dynamical convection

气块　air parcel

浮力　buoyancy

重力　gravity

绝热过程　adiabatic process

绝热变化　adiabatic change

干绝热直减率　dry adiabatic lapse rate

湿绝热直减率　wet adiabatic lapse rate

温度直减率　lapse rate of temperature

大气垂直稳定度　vertical stability of the atmosphere

涡旋运动　vortex motion

切变　shear

小〔型〕环流　minor circulation

陆风　land breeze

海风　sea breeze

谷风　valley breeze

山风　mountain breeze

焚风　foehn wind

融雪风　snow eater
气旋　cyclone
反气旋　anticyclone
热带气旋　tropical cyclone
热带扰动　tropical disturb-
　ance
热带低压　tropical depression
中等热带风暴　moderate
　tropical storm
强热带风暴　severe tropical
　storm
飓风　hurricane
台风　typhoon
台风眼　typhoon eye
飑　squall
水龙卷(海龙卷)　waterspout
陆龙卷　landspout, tornado

(twister)
尘卷　dust devil, dust whirl
尘暴　dust storm
沙暴　sandstorm
风带　wind belt
东风带　easterly belt
西风带　westerly belt
东风槽　easterly trough
西风槽　westerly trough
东风波　easterly wave
西风波　westerly wave
赤道无风带　doldrums, equa-
　torial calms
副热带无风带　horse latitudes
信风　trade winds
反信风　antitrades
季风　monsoon

# 云　雾　Cloud and Fog

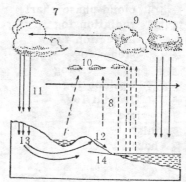

水分循环⑦　hydrological
　cycle
蒸发⑧　evaporation
水汽　water vapour
海洋气团⑨　maritime air
　mass
大陆气团⑩　continental air

mass
凝结　condensation
降水⑪　precipitation
河流和片流⑫　streams and
　sheet flow
渗透⑬　infiltration
潜水面(地下水面)⑭　water
　table
绝热冷却　adiabatic cooling
辐射冷却　radiation cooling
尘粒　dust particle
凝结核　condensation nucleus
凝华　sublimation
凝华核　sublimation nucleus
悬浮于空中的微细水滴　fine
　particles of water suspend-
　ed in the air
云滴　cloud droplet
雾滴　fog drop

国际云图　International Cloud Atlas
云属　cloud genera
高云　high clouds
卷云①　cirrus (Ci)
卷层云②　cirrostratus (Cs)
卷积云③　cirrocumulus (Cc)
中云　middle clouds
高层云④　altostratus (As)
高积云⑤　altocumulus (Ac)
低云　lower clouds
层积云⑥　stratocumulus (Sc)
层云⑦　stratus (St)

雨层云⑧　nimbostratus (Ns)
直展云　heap clouds, (Am.) clouds with vertical development
积云⑨　cumulus (Cu)
积雨云⑩　cumulonimbus (Cb)
旗状云　banner cloud
盔云　crest cloud
云底　cloud base
云顶　cloud top
云幂　ceiling
云带　cloud band
云堤　cloud bank
云的调控　cloud modification
消云　cloud dissipation
云的催化　cloud seeding
云催化剂　cloud-seeding agent
卫星云图　satellite cloud picture
云相图　cloud-phase chart
辐射雾　radiation fog
平流雾　advection fog
蒸汽雾　steam fog
海〔面蒸汽〕雾　sea fog
上坡雾　upslope fog
锋面雾　frontal fog
雾凇　rime
霭　mist
霾　haze

## 雨雪雷电　Rain, Snow, Thunder, Lightning

雨　rain
梅雨　plum rain
台风雨　typhoon rain
毛毛雨　drizzle
晴空雨　serein

阵雨　shower
雷阵雨　thunder shower
连续雨(绵雨)　continuous rain
暴雨　cloudburst

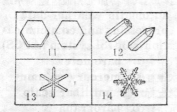

冻雨　freezing rain
雨淞　glaze
雪　snow
雪花　snow-flake
雪晶　snow crystal
片状晶⑪　plate crystal
柱状晶⑫　columnar crystal
星状晶⑬　stellar crystal
枝状晶⑭　dendritic crystal
雪花环　snow garland
雪阵　snow flurry
高吹雪　blowing snow
低吹雪　drifting snow
大风雪　driving snow
雪暴　snowstorm
米雪　snow grains
霰(软雹)　snow pellets,
　graupel (soft hail)
冰雹　hail
冰雹胚胎　hail embryo

雹块　hailstone
雹暴　hailstorm
防雹　hail suppression
消雹　hail mitigation
霜　frost
白霜　hoarfrost, white forst
黑霜(霜冻)　black frost
永冻　permafrost
冰晶　ice crystal
冰核带电　electrification of
　ice nucleus
闪电　lightning
枝状闪电　streak lightning
片状闪电　sheet lightning
球状闪电　ball lightning
雷　thunder
霹雳　thunderclap
雷暴　thunderstorm
虹　rainbow
虹彩　iridescence
晕　halo
日晕　solar halo
月晕　lunar halo
彩光〔环〕　glory
华盖　aureole
峨眉宝光　Brocken spectre,
　Brocken bow
海市蜃楼　mirage
上现蜃景　upper mirage
下现蜃景　lower mirage

## 气象观测　Meteorological Observation

探测　sounding
气球火箭探测　rockoon sound-
ing
气象火箭　meteorological
rocket
火箭探空仪　rocketsonde

气象卫星　meteorological
satellite
同步气象卫星　synchronous
meteorological satellite
(SMS)
卫星探测　satellite sounding

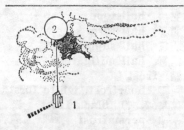

无线电探空仪① radiosonde

探空仪气球② radiosonde balloon

气象区 meteorological region

气象台站网 meteorological network

气象台 meteorological observatory

气象站 meteorological station

气象哨 meteorological post

气象雷达 meteorological radar

多普勒雷达 Doppler radar

激光雷达 lidar (light detecting and ranging)

多色激光雷达 polychromatic lidar

声雷达 sodar (sound detecting and ranging)

天气监视雷达 weather surveillance radar (WSR)

测云雷达 cloud detection radar

云的回波 cloud echo

测云镜 mirror nephoscope, cloud mirror

彩色自旋扫描摄云照相机 multicolour spin scan cloud camera (MSSCC)

天气雷达资料处理分析器 weather radar data processor and analyzer (WERAN)

自动天气资料加工和通信控制系统 automatic weather-data processing and communication control system (APCS)

气压表④ barometer

水银柱⑤ mercury column

毫巴标尺⑥ millibar scale

气压计⑦ barograph

记录筒⑧ recording drum

空盒⑨ aneroid boxes

记录杆⑩ recording lever

温度表⑪ thermometer

温度计⑫ thermograph

测量元件⑬ measuring element

湿度表⑭ hygrometer

毛发⑮ hair

标尺⑯ scale

干湿球湿度表⑰ wet and dry bulb hygrometer

风杯风速表⑱ cup anemometer

旋转风杯⑲ revolving cups

风向标⑳ wind vane

雨量器㉑ rain gauge

漏斗㉒ funnel

收集器㉓ collector

量杯㉔ graduated glass cylinder

百叶箱㉕ instrument shelter, thermometer screen, thermoscreen

直接日射强度表㉖ pyrheliometer

量雪器 snow gauge

〔量〕雪尺 snow stake, snow scale

气象资料 meteorological data

气象要素 meteorological element

气象图 meteorological map

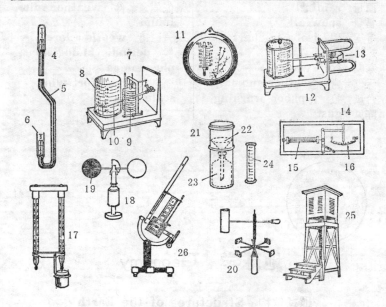

## 天气预报 Weather Forecasting

天气型 **weather type**

天气分析 **weather analysis**

数值天气预报 **numerical weather prediction (NWP)**

单站预报 **single station forecast**

中期预报 **medium-range forecast (MRF)**

长期预报 **long-range forecast (LRF)**

(预报)时效 **valid time**

订正预报 **forecast amendment**

预报准确率 **forecast accuracy**

预报检验 **forecast verification**

预报员 **forecaster**

天气图 **weather map**

填图 **plotting**

填图符号 **plotting symbols**

风向 **wind direction**

风速 **wind speed, wind velocity**

云量 **cloud cover, cloudage, cloudiness**

云高 **cloud height**

无云 **clear, cloudless**

晴 **fine**

少云 **somewhat cloudy**

多云 **cloudy**

阴 **overcast**

鱼鳞天 **mackerel sky**

能见度 **visibility**

| | |
|---|---|
| 雨量　rainfall | 最低气象条件　weather minimum |
| 雪量　snowfall | 天气谚语　weather lore |
| 等压面图　isobaric chart | 物候　periodic biological phenomena |
| 热浪　heat wave | 蒲福风级　Beaufort wind scale |
| 寒潮　cold wave | |
| 天气异常　weather anomaly | |
| 台风警报　typhoon warning | |
| 阵风　gust | |

# 地球学　Geonomy

## 地球结构　Structure of the Earth

地球的主要分层① main layers of the Earth
地壳② Earth crust
上地幔③ upper mantle
过渡带④ transition zone
下地幔⑤ lower mantle
地核⑥ Earth core
外核⑦ outer core
内核⑧ inner core

海洋⑨ ocean
大陆阶地⑩ continental terrace
大陆地壳⑪ continental crust
硅铝带⑫ sial
海洋地壳⑬ oceanic crust
硅镁带⑭ sima
莫霍〔洛维奇契〕不连续面（莫霍面）⑮ Mohorovičić discontinuity (Moho)
地幔⑯ mantle

岩石层　lithosphere
软流层　asthenosphere
地壳运动　crustal movement
收缩说　contraction theory
大陆漂移说　continental drift theory
大陆块　continental block
联合古陆⑰　Pangaea
劳亚古陆⑱　Laurasia
冈瓦纳古陆⑲　Gondwana
当代各大陆的位置⑳　contemporary position of the continents
板块大地构造　plate tectonics
板块　plate
板块运动　plate movement
海底扩张　sea floor spreading
(软流层中的)对流　convection currents (in the asthenosphere)
地壳均衡　isostasy
均衡补偿　isostatic compensation
地壳翘曲　crustal warping
褶皱　folding
断裂　faulting
地壳变形㉑　deformation of the Earth crust
单斜褶皱㉒　monocline
对称向斜㉓　symmetrical syncline
对称背斜㉔　symmetrical anticline
倾斜背斜㉕　inclined anticline

伏褶皱㉖　recumbent fold
逆掩褶皱㉗　overthrust fold
正常断层㉘　normal fault
逆断层㉙　reverse fault
横推断层㉚　transcurrent fault
斜滑正常断层㉛　oblique-slip normal fault
旋转断层㉜　rotation fault
地垒㉝　horst
地堑㉞　graben
盐丘㉟　salt dome
盐栓㊱　salt plug
水平断层　horizontal fault
转换断层　transform fault
造陆　continent making, epeirogeny
上升　uplift
下沉　subsidence
造山　mountain building, orogeny
造山带　orogenic belt
地槽　geosyncline

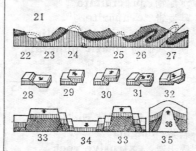

## 地球化学循环 Geochemical Cycle

大循环　major cycle
小循环　minor cycle
元素的丰度　abundance of elements
元素在岩石带中的迁移　migration of elements in the lithosphere
花岗岩化〔作用〕　granitization
深熔作用　anatexis
再生作用　palingenesis
花岗岩精　granitic ichor
混合作用　migmatization
混合岩　migmatite
交代〔作用〕　metasomatosis
内成作用　endogenic process
深成作用　deep-seated process
外成作用　exogenic process
地表作用　surficial process
化学风化　chemical weathering
沉积物的分类　classification of sediments
水解产物　hydrolyzate
氧化物　oxidate
沉淀物　precipitate
蒸发岩　evaporite
生物沉积物　biogenic sediment
镁铁质矿物　mafic minerals

长英矿物　felsic minerals
粘土矿物　clay minerals
成岩作用　diagenesis
地球化学异常　geochemical anomaly
异常集中　abnormal concentration
分散　dispersion
分散模式　dispersion pattern
成矿区　metallogenetic province
分散晕　dispersion halo
渗漏晕　leakage halo
元素的释放和再分布　release and redistribution of elements
胶体溶液　colloidal solution
胶体悬浮　colloidal suspension
侧向迁移　lateral migration
分散扇　dispersion fan
分散流　dispersion train
比色分析　colorimetric analysis
色谱分析　chromatographic analysis
极谱分析　polarographic analysis

## 岩 石 Rock

火成岩　igneous rock
岩浆　magma
喷出岩　extrusive rock

侵入岩　intrusive rock
岩基　batholith
岩株　stock

| | |
|---|---|
| 岩颈 neck, plug | 片麻岩 gneiss |
| 粒状岩 granular rock | 大理岩(大理石) marble |
| 细粒岩 fine-grained rock | 石英岩 quartzite |
| 粒度 grain size | 酸性岩 acid rock |
| 花岗岩 granite | 中性岩 intermediate rock |
| 玄武岩 basalt | 基性岩 basic rock |
| 斑状〔结构〕 porphyritic | 生物岩 biolith |
| 斑晶 phenocryst | 响岩 phonolite, clinkstone |
| 基质 matrix | 侵蚀 erosion |
| 黑曜岩 obsidian | 风化 weathering |
| 浮岩 pumice | 页状剥落 exfoliation |
| 火成碎屑岩 pyroclastic rock | 溶蚀 solution |
| 凝灰岩 tuff | 刻蚀 corrasion |
| 火山角砾岩 volcanic breccia | 磨蚀 abrasion |
| 隐晶结构 aphanitic texture | 冰蚀 glaciation |
| 流纹岩 rhyolite | 风棱石 ventifact, glyptolith, rillstone |
| 沉积岩(水成岩) sedimentary rock | 巨砾 boulder |
| 成层岩 stratified rock | 中砾 cobble |
| 砾岩 conglomerate rock | 小砾 pebble |
| 砂岩 sandstone | 粗砾 shingle |
| 石英 quartz | 砂砾 gravel |
| 方解石 calcite | 岩溶 karst |
| 粘土 clay | 洞穴 cave, grotto |
| 粉砂岩 siltstone | 桂林岩洞 Kweilin's karst grottoes |
| 页岩 shale | 地下洞穴 cavern |
| 石灰岩 limestone | 落水洞 sinkhole, sink |
| 白云岩 dolomite | 石笋 stalagmite |
| 变质岩 metamorphic rock | 钟乳石 stalactite |
| 板岩 slate | 石枝 helictite |
| 千枚岩 phyllite | |
| 片岩 schist | |

## 地质调查 Geologic Survey

| | |
|---|---|
| 矿物资源 mineral resources | 勘探 prospecting |
| 分布 distribution | 矿床 ore deposit, mineral deposit |
| 储〔藏〕量 reserve | |

矿脉 vein, lode, ledge
矿脉结构 vein texture
脉尖 apex of vein
露头 outcrop
地球物理勘探 geophysical prospecting
重力法 gravitational method
重力仪 gravimeter
扭秤 torsion baldnce, torsion gravimeter
磁法 magnetic method
磁力仪 magnetometer
电法 electrical method
电位测量 measurement of electric potential
电位计 potentiometer
电阻率法 resistivity method
地震法 seismic method
反射法 reflection method
折射法 refraction method
地下岩系 subsurface rock formation
构造 structure
层理 bedding
节理 jointing
劈理 cleavage
矿层 ore bed
矿体 ore body

砂矿 placer
钻孔 borehole, drillhole
电测井 electrical logging
初探浅井 trial pit
表生矿床 superficial deposit
厚度 thickness
基岩 bedrock
采样 sampling
采样单位 sampling horizon
槽探取样 pit sampling
取样器 sampler
岩样 rock sample
(岩石)薄片 slice (of rock)
偏振光显微镜 polarizing microscope
电子显微镜 electron microscope
放射性元素 radioactive element
子原素 daughter element
放射性衰变率 radioactive decay rate
半衰期 half-life (period)
放射性碳(碳14) radiocarbon (C14)
放射性碳测定年代 radiocarbon dating
地质图 geological map

# 地 貌 Land Form

地块 land mass
地盾 shield
地台 platform
大陆 continent
亚洲 Asia
非洲 Africa
欧洲 Europe

美洲 America
大洋洲 Oceania
次大陆 Subcontinent
大陆边缘 continental margin
大陆坡 continental slope
大陆架 continental shelf
褶皱山 fold mountain

| | |
|---|---|
| 断块山　fault-block mountain | 高原　plateau |
| 山系　mountain system | 黄土高原　loess plateau |
| 山链　mountain chain | 准平原　peneplain |
| 山脉　mountain range | 平原　plain |
| (美洲)雁列山脉　cordillera | 剥蚀平原　plain of denudation |
| 山岭　mountain ridge | 冲积平原　alluvial plain |
| 山梁　flat-topped ridge | 海岸平原　coastal plain |
| 刃岭　arête | 湖成平原　lacustrine plain |
| 山口　pass | 泛滥平原　flood plain |
| 山脊垭口　saddle | 黄土平原　loess plain |
| 山肩　shoulder | 洼地　depression |
| 高山口　col | 地峡　isthmus |
| 峰　peak | 半岛　peninsula |
| 山嘴　mountain spur | 岬角　cape, promontory |
| 平顶山　table mountain | 海岸　coast |
| 山麓　foot of the mountain, | 海岸线　coastline |
| 　piedmont | 海滩　beach |
| 丘陵　hill | 海湾　gulf, bay |
| 小丘　hillock | 开展海湾　bight |
| 圆丘　knoll | 小湾　cove |
| 土岗　earth hummock | 峡湾　fiord |
| 山麓丘陵　foothills | 海峡　strait |
| 山麓冲积平原　mountain apron | 岛　island |
| 高山平地　alb | 陆边岛　continental island |
| 盆地　basin | 洋中岛　oceanic island |
| 山间盆地　intermontane basin | 列岛　island chain, islands |
| 锅状盆地　ca(u)ldron basin | 岛弧　island arc |
| 阶地　terrace, bench | 群岛　islands, isles, archipel- |
| 谷　valley | 　ago |
| 宽谷　dale | 礁　reef |
| 峡谷　gorge | 暗礁　sunken reef, submerged |
| 大峡谷　grand canyon | 　reef |
| 幽谷　dingle | 裙礁　fringing reef |
| 悬崖　cliff | 珊瑚礁　coral reef |
| 断层崖　fault scarp | 堤礁　barrier reef |
| 断线崖　fault-line scarp | 环礁　atoll |
| 巉崖　crag | |

## 江河湖沼 Streams, Lakes, Swamps

水系 river system
江河 river
幼年河 young river
壮年河 mature river
老年河 old river
小河 rivulet, (Am.) creek
溪 brook
细流 rill
分水岭 watershed
分水界 water parting
集水面积 catchment area
流域 drainage basin
河源 river source
源头 headwater
河道 river course, river channel
河岸 riverbank
河边陡岸 riverside bluff
河床 riverbed
干流 trunk stream
支流 tributary, affluent
汇流点 confluence, junction
侧流 effluent
网状水道 braided channel
上游 upper reaches
中游 middle reaches
下游 lower reaches
急流 rapids
石滩 rocky shallows
河口 river mouth
河口湾 estuary
冲积扇 alluvial fan
三角洲 delta
沙洲 sandbar
沙嘴 spit

浅滩 shoal
河川径流 stream flow
流量 discharge
河流坡降 stream gradient
水位 water level
(河流)改道 diversion
(河流)袭夺 piracy, beheading
断头河 beheaded river
断尾河 betrunked river
运河 canal
冲刷 scour
沉积 deposit
淤积 siltation
河泥 river silt
塘泥 pond silt
瀑布 waterfall
小瀑布 cascade
(瀑布)跌水潭 plunge basin, plunge pool
牛轭湖 oxbow lake
潟湖 lagoon
内陆湖 inland lake, interior lake
堰塞湖 dammed lake, barrier lake
火〔山〕口湖 crater lake
苦湖 bitter lake
盐湖 salt lake
低盐湖 brackish lake
沼泽 swamp, marsh
红树林沼泽 mangrove swamp
高沼 moor
泥炭沼泽 peat bog
颤沼 quaking bog

| | |
|---|---|
| 潮沼 tidal marsh | 地下水 groundwater |
| 盐沼 salt marsh | 泉 spring |
| 盐碱滩 alkali flat | 喷泉 fountain |
| 淤泥滩 mud flat | 矿泉 spa |
| 蓄水层 aquifer | 温泉 hot spring |
| 受水区 intake area | 自流泉 artesian spring |

## 冰 川 Glaciers

| | |
|---|---|
| 高山冰川 mountain glacier, alpine glacier | 冰塔 sérac |
| 谷冰川 valley glacier | 冰川瓯穴 moulin, glacier mill |
| 山麓冰川 piedmont glacier | 冰瀑 ice cascade |
| 高原冰川 plateau glacier | 冰桌 glacier table |
| 大陆冰川 continental glacier | 雪面波纹 sastrugi |
| 小冰川 glacieret | (冰川)动态 regime |
| 极地冰川 polar glacier | 堆积 accumulation |
| 温带冰川 temperate glacier | 消融 ablation |
| 雪线 snow line | 融水 meltwater |
| 雪原 snow field | (冰)崩解 calving |
| 粒雪 firn, névé | 冰水沉积 outwash |
| 冰原 ice field | 冰水沉积平原 outwash plain, outwash apron |
| 冰盖 ice sheet | 冰山 iceberg |
| 冰帽 icecap | 浮冰 ice floe |
| 冰碛 moraine, glacial drift | 积冰 pack ice |
| 侧碛 lateral moraine | 盘冰 ice pan |
| 中碛 medial moraine | 饼冰 pancake ice |
| 终碛 terminal moraine | 碎冰 brash ice |
| 冰隙 crevasse | 雪崩 avalanche |
| 冰斗 cirque, cwm, corrie | |

## 植 被 Vegetation

| | |
|---|---|
| 植被型 vegetation type | 混合林 mixed forest |
| 北部林 boreal forest | 阔叶林 broadleaf forest |
| 泰加林(西伯利亚针叶林) taiga | 温带雨林 temperate rain forest |
| 针叶林 conifer forest | |

热带雨林　**tropical rain forest**

原始林　**virgin forest, primeval forest**

季雨林　**monsoon forest**

亚热带林　**subtropical forest**

热带旱生林　**thorn forest**

热带丛林　**jungle**

高山矮曲林　**elfinwood**

红树林　**mangrove**

灌木　**shrub**

密灌丛　**scrub**

冻原　**tundra**

草原　**grassland**

干草原　**steppe**

(北美)高草原　**prairie**

(南美)大草原　**pampas**

热带稀树草原　**savanna**

热带稀树草原林地　**savanna woodland**

热带无树大草原　**llano**

草甸　**meadow**

灌丛地　**bushland**

石楠荒原　**heath**

沙漠　**desert**

戈壁　**gobi**

沙丘　**sand dune**

流沙　**shifting sand**

石〔质沙〕漠　**stone desert**

盐漠　**salt desert**

绿洲　**oasis**

# 气　候　Climate

大气候　**macroclimate**

中气候　**mesoclimate**

小气候　**microclimate**

赤道　**equator**

北回归线　**Tropic of Cancer**

南回归线　**Tropic of Capricorn**

北极圈　**Arctic Circle**

南极圈　**Antarctic Circle**

热带　**torrid zone**

温带　**temperate zone**

寒带　**frigid zone**

热带气候　**tropical climate**

温带气候　**temperate climate**

副极带气候　**subarctic climate**

极地气候　**polar climate**

干燥气候　**arid climate, dry climate**

湿润气候　**humid climate**

潮湿气候　**wet climate**

大陆〔性〕气候　**continental climate**

海洋〔性〕气候　**maritime climate**

岛屿〔性〕气候　**insular climate**

高山气候　**alpine climate**

山岳气候　**mountain climate**

高原气候　**plateau climate**

森林气候　**forest climate**

草原气候　**steppe climate**

季风气候　**monsoon climate**

地中海气候　**Mediterranean climate**

沙漠气候　**desert climate**

气候循环　**climatic cycles**

气候变化　**climatic change**

气候异常　**climatic anomaly**

第四纪冰期　**Quaternary Ice Age**

冰期　**glacial period**

间冰期　**interglacial period**

冰后期　postglacial period
洪积期　pluvial period
小冰期　Little Ice Age
气候要素　climatic elements
气候因子　climatic factors
温度变化　temperature variation
温度日较差　diurnal temperature range

平均年温差　mean annual temperature range
等温线　isotherm
平均年降水量　mean annual rainfall
气候图　climate map, climatic map
气候图表　climograph, climagraph, climatograph

## 地图制作　Map Making

地图　map
裱装地图　mounted map
地图册　atlas
普通地图　general map
国际百万分之一地图　international map
半球图　hemisphere map
平面图　planimetric map
地形图　topographic map, relief map
政区图　political map
经济地图　economic map
交通图　communications map
土地利用图　land-use map
地籍图　cadastral map
分片着色地图　colour-patch map
分层着色地图　layer-tinted map
略图　outline map, sketch map
详图　detailed map
(大地图内的)插图　inset
(地图)编绘　compilation
草绘　drafting
清绘　delineation

刻图　scribing
绘等高线　contouring
等高线　contour line
等高距　contour interval
晕滃　hachure
晕渲　shading
着色　colouring
(地图)比例尺　scale
直线比例尺①　linear scale
地图坐标系　map coordinates system
坐标格网　grid
经度　longitude
纬度　latitude
经线　meridian
纬线　parallel
地图符号　map symbols
图例　map legend
注记　lettering
图幅　sheet
图廓注记　border information, marginal information

1

图廓　map border, map margin

地图投影　map projection

圆锥投影① conic projection

多圆锥投影　polyconic projection

圆柱投影② cylindrical projection

墨卡托投影　Mercator projection

球心投影　gnomonic projection

球面投影　stereographic projection

正射投影　orthographic projection

椭圆投影　oval projection

航摄像片　aerial photo

航空摄影制图　aerial photomapping

精密立体测图仪　stereoplanigraph

视距仪　tacheometer

光电测距仪　geodimeter

雷达测距仪　tellurometer

面积仪　planimeter

体视比较仪　stereocomparator

地图数据库　cartographic data bank

计算机图形处理　computergraphics

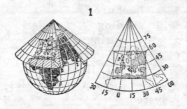

正形投影　conformal projection, orthomorphic projection

方位投影(天顶投影)③ azimuthal projection (zenithal projection)

等距投影　equidistant projection

等积投影　equal-area projection

等距方位投影　azimuthal equidistant projection

全球投影　globular projection

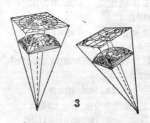

# 地震学 Seismology

## 地震成因 Generation of Earthquakes

地震 earthquake

地震构成线 seismotectonic lines

活动带 mobile belt

地震带 earthquake zone, seismic zone

环太平洋带 circumpacific belt

喜马拉雅——地中海带 Himalayas—Mediterranean belt

火山 volcano

火山带 volcanic belt

活火山 active volcano

休眠火山 dormant volcano

死火山 extinct volcano

复合火山横断面④ cross-section through composite volcano

岩浆房⑤ magma chamber

火山筒⑥ pipe

火山锥⑦ cone

火山口⑧ crater

熔岩灰⑨ lava ash

熔岩流⑩ lava flow

岩墙(岩脉)⑪ dike, dyke

岩床⑫ sill

岩盖⑬ laccolith, laccolite

盾形火山⑭ shield volcano

复合火山⑮ composite volcano

火山渣锥⑯ cinder core

溶岩滴丘⑰ hornito

破火山口⑱ caldera

喷发 eruption

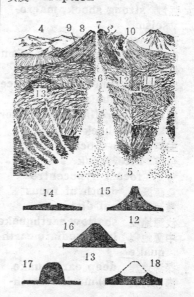

| | |
|---|---|
| 喷溢口 vent of eruption | 构造地震 tectonic earthquake |
| 喷硫期 solfatara stage | 挤压力 compressional force |
| 喷气期 fumarole stage | 张力 tensional force |
| 碳酸喷气孔 mofettelava | 切向力 tangential force |
| 熔岩 lava | 应力 stress |
| 块状熔岩 block lava | 断层 fault |
| 绳状熔岩 corded lava, pahoehoe | 滑动 slip |
| | 位移 displacement |
| 火山弹 volcanic bomb | 深成地震 plutonic earthquake |
| 火山砾 lapilli | 爆裂地震 explosion earthquake |
| 火山云 volcanic cloud | |
| 火山灰 volcanic ash | 火山地震 volcanic earthquake |
| 地震区 earthquake region, seismic region | 间歇泉 geyser |
| | 泥火山 mud volcano |
| 震群 earthquake swarm | |

## 地震观察和预报 Earthquake Observation and Prediction

| | |
|---|---|
| 地震台站 seismic station | quake |
| 强震 strong shock, macroseism | 海啸 tsunami, seismic sea wave |
| 弱震 weak shock | 湖震 seiche |
| 微震 slight shock, microseism | 裂缝 fissure |
| 地颤 earth tremor | 山崩 landslide |
| 发震时刻 time of occurrence of earthquake | 泥石流 debris flow |
| | 地下喷水 ground water discharge |
| 初期微震 preliminary tremor | |
| 前震 foreshock | 震中 epicentre |
| 主震 main shock | 震中距 epicentral distance |
| 余震 aftershock | 震中区 epicentral area |
| 震源 focus, hypocentre | 地震波 earthquake waves |
| 震源深度 depth of focus | 体波 body waves |
| 震源距 focal distance | 纵波(P波) longitudinal wave, primary wave (P wave) |
| 浅源地震 shallow earthquake | |
| 中源地震 intermediate earthquake | 横波(S波) transverse wave, secondary wave (S wave) |
| 深源地震 deep earthquake | 面波 surface waves |
| 海(底)震 submarine earthquake | 勒夫波(Q波) Love wave |

(Q wave)

瑞雷波(R 波)　Rayleigh wave (R wave)

弹性波　elastic wave

冲击波　shock wave

走时　travel time

时距曲线　travel time curve

(地震)烈度　intensity

烈度表　intensity scale

麦氏烈度表　Mercalli Scale of Felt Intensity

震级　magnitude

里氏震级表　Richter magnitude scale

六级地震　Force Six earthquake

地震仪　seismograph

张衡于公元132年发明的世界上第一台地震仪　the first seismograph in the world invented by Zhang Heng in the year 132

地震(波曲线)图　seismogram

测震表　seismometer

地震检波器　seismic detector

地震放大器　seismic amplifier

扭地震计　torsion seismometer

加速度地震检波器　accelerometer-type seismometer

地震波显示仪　seismoscope

等震线　isoseismal line

等震线图　isoseismal map

地震征兆　premonitory symptoms of earthquake

地球磁场变化　fluctuations in the geomagnetic field

磁场强度　magnetic field intensity

磁倾角　magnetic inclination

磁偏角　magnetic declination

地下水位变化　changes in the water table

地下水中氡气含量的变化　changes in radon content of groundwater

海平面变化　sea level fluctuations

地震波传播速度的变化　variations in the speed of propagation of seismic waves

重力异常　gravity anomaly

地温异常　ground temperature anomaly

地面倾斜　inclination of the ground

反常的天气　abnormal weather

动物的异常反应　strange reactions of animals

地震警报　earthquake alarm

地震破坏　earthquake damage

抗震建筑　earthquake-proof construction, earthquake-resistant structure

# 海洋学　Oceanography

## 海洋　Ocean

太平洋　Pacific Ocean
大西洋　Atlantic Ocean
印度洋　Indian Ocean
北冰洋　Arctic Ocean
南冰洋　Antarctic Ocean
海　sea
滨线　shoreline
高潮线　high watermark
低潮线　low watermark
潮间带　intertidal zone
滨海带　littoral zone
亚滨海带　sublittoral zone
浅海带　neritic zone
半深海带　bathyal zone
远洋带　pelagic zone
光亮带　euphotic zone
深海底带　abyssal zone
远洋生物　pelagic organism
游泳生物　nekton, swimming organism
浮游生物　plankton, floating organism
浮游动物　zooplankton

浮游植物　phytoplankton
海底生物　benthos
生物发光　bioluminescence
海洋沉积　marine sediment, marine deposit
沉积速率　rate of sedimentation
深海软泥　deep-sea ooze, abyssal ooze
抱球虫软泥　globigerina ooze
有孔虫软泥　foraminiferal ooze
翼足虫软泥　pteropod ooze
放射虫软泥　radiolarian ooze
硅藻软泥　diatom ooze
海水的自然性质　physical properties of sea water
盐度　salinity
氯含量　chlorinity
赤潮　red tide
马尾藻海　Sargasso Sea
海洋同温层　oceanic stratosphere, cold-water sphere

## 海洋水流  Ocean Currents

海洋环流　oceanic circulation
风海流　wind current
密度流　density current
倾斜流　slope current
补偿流　compensation current
暖流　warm current
北赤道海流①　north equatorial current
南赤道海流②　south equatorial current
赤道逆流③　equatorial counter current
北太平洋海流④　North Pacific current
阿拉斯加海流⑤　Alaska current

东澳大利亚海流⑥　East Australian current
日本海流(黑潮)⑦　Japan current (Kuroshio)
厄加勒斯海流⑧　Agulhas current
莫桑比克海流⑨　Mozambique current
马达加斯加海流⑩　Madagascar current
北大西洋海流⑪　North Atlantic current
(墨西哥)湾流⑫　Gulf Stream
西格陵兰海流⑬　West Greenland current
挪威海流⑭　Norwegian current

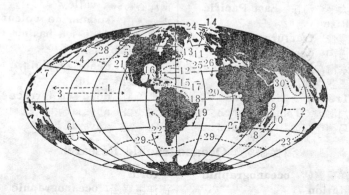

安的列斯海流⑮　**Antilles current**

佛罗里达海流⑯　**Florida current**

加勒比海流⑰　**Caribbean current**

圭亚那海流⑱　**Guiana current**
巴西海流⑲　**Brazil current**
几内亚海流⑳　**Guinea current**
埃尔——宁诺海流　**El Niñ5**
寒流　**cold current**
加利福尼亚海流㉑　**California current**
秘鲁海流㉒　**Peru current**

西澳大利亚海流㉓　**West Australian current**

东格陵兰海流㉔　**East Greenland current**

拉布拉多海流㉕　**Labrador current**

加那利海流㉖　**Canaries current**

本格拉海流㉗　**Benguela current**

亲潮㉘　**Oyashio**
漂流　**drift**
西风漂流㉙　**west wind drift**
季风漂流㉚　**monsoon drift**

## 海底地形　Submarine Topography

洋底　**ocean floor**
洋盆　**ocean basin**
海脊　**midocean ridge**
大西洋中央海脊　**Mid-Atlantic Ridge**
洋底地堑　**midocean rift**
洋底峡谷　**midocean canyon**
海丘　**oceanic rise**
东太平洋海丘　**East Pacific Rise**
破裂带　**fracture zone**
深海沟　**deep-sea trench**
日本海沟　**Japan Trench**
马里亚纳海沟　**Marianas Trench**
汤加海沟　**Tonga Trench**
克马德克海沟　**Kermadec**

Trench
秘鲁海沟　**Peru Trench**
智利海沟　**Chile Trench**
海台　**oceanic bank**
海渊　**ocean deep**
海床　**seabed**
海山　**seamount**
平顶海山　**guyot**
海底谷　**sea valley**
海底火山　**submarine volcano**
深海盆地　**deep-sea basin, abyssal basin**
深海平原　**deep-sea plain, abyssal plain**
深海阶地　**deep-sea terrace**
深海缺口　**abyssal gap**
深海丘陵　**abyssal hill**

## 海洋研究　Oceanographic Research

海洋观测站　**oceanographic station**
水文站　**hydrographic station**
海洋作业台　**offshore plat-**

form
海洋考察船　**oceanographic vessel, research ship**
潜水艇支援船　**support vessel**

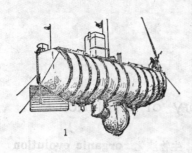

1

for submersible

小型潜水艇　small submersible

深海潜水器① bathyscaph(e)
球形深海潜水器　bathysphere
潜水钟　diving bell
碟形潜水器　diving saucer
深海探测器　seaprobe
测深仪　bathymeter
回声测深仪　echo sounder
海洋地质研究　marine geolo-gical research
洋底剖面　profile of the ocean floor
海水测温仪　bathythermome-ter (BT)
南森采水器　Nansen bottle
水样　water sample
(海底)采泥器　bottom sampler
浮游生物采集网　plankton net
盐度计　salinometer
流速计　current meter
海流板　drogue
遥控水下电视摄影机　remote-controlled underwater television camera
遥控水下操作器　remote-con-trol underwater manipula-tor (RUM)
海洋磁力仪　marine magneto-meter
海洋重力仪　sea gravimeter
锰结核　manganese nodules

# 进化论 Theory of Evolution

物种学 speciology
达尔文主义 Darwinism
新达尔文主义 Neo-Darwinism
拉马克主义 Lamarckism
新拉马克主义 Neo-Lamarck-ism
用进废退说 theory of use and disuse
创造进化论 creative evolution
异变说 emergent evolution
有生源说(生生说，生源说) biogenesis
无生源说 abiogenesis
无生源新说 neo-abiogenesis
自然发生说 autogenesis, spontaneous generation
后成说 epigenesis
自然更生 spontaneous regeneration
个体发育(个体发生) ontogeny, ontogenesis
系统发育(系统发生) phylogeny, phylogenesis
渐进发育 gradual development
重演〔性〕发生 palingenesis
后生变态 c(a)enogenesis
重演性变态 palingenetic metamorphosis

生物演化 organic evolution
生物发生律 biogenetic law
重演 recapitulation
重演律 law of recapitulation
进化 evolution
人类的起源与进化 origin and evolution of mankind
进化的机械基础 mechanical basis of evolution
退化 devolution, degeneration
变态 metamorphosis
渐进变态 gradual metamorphosis
变异 variation
变型 aberration
适应 adaptation
彷徨变异 fluctuation
物种变异 mutation of species
自然选择(自然淘汰) natural selection
人工选择 artificial selection
定向选择 consecutive selection
无意识选择 unconscious selection
性选择 sexual selection
系统选种 line selection
生存竞争 struggle for existence

种内竞争　intraspecific competition
种间竞争　interspecific competition
分异　segregation
分离规律　law of segregation
系统树　genealogical tree, family tree
进化树　evolution tree
同源　isogeny
物种　species
细胞演发　cell development
物种形成　speciation, formation of species
亚种　subspecies
亚变种　subvariety
变种(突变)　mutation
品种　variety
系　line
纯系　pure line, inbred line
纯种　purebred
宗　race

生物宗　biological race
杂种　hybrid
栽培　cultivation
栽培〔变种〕　cultivation variety
趋异〔作用〕　divergence
趋同〔作用〕　convergence
极端趋同原理　principle of extreme convergence
种内进化　intraspecific evolution
跳跃演化　saltatory evolution
更代　substitution
更生　regeneration
演变　transmutation
植物群进化　floral evolution
微进化　microevolution
倒位杂种　inversion hybrid
营养杂种　vegetative hybrid
嫁接杂种　graft hybrid
居间杂种　intermediate hybrid
直向演化　orthogenesis

# 细胞学　Cytology

细胞生理学　cytophysiology
细胞生物学　cytobiology
细胞化学　cytochemistry

细胞形态学　cytomorphology
细胞结构(细胞性)　cellularity

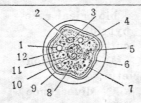

细胞 cell
液泡① water vacuole, vacuole
中心粒② centriole
中心球③ centrosphere
后成质④ metaplasm
高尔基体⑤ Golgi body (dictyosome)
细胞壁⑥ cell wall
原生质膜⑦ protoplasm membrane
腺粒体⑧ mitochondrion, chondriosome
真细胞核⑨ plasmosome
核液⑩ karyolymph, nuclear sap
染色质⑪ chromatin
染色质核仁⑫ chromatin nucleolus, karyosome
细胞板 cell plate
细胞体 cell body
细胞液 cell sap
细胞肛 cytopyge
细胞膜 cell membrane
细胞口 cytostome
细胞质 cytoplasm
胞质丝 cytoplasmic filament
核仁 nucleolus
细胞核穿壁运动 intercellular migration of nucleus
核配合 karyogamy
核外染色粒 chromidium
有色体 chromoplast, chro-

moplastid
叶绿体 chloroplast, chlorophyll body
微粒体 microsome
无性生殖单体 parthenogonidium
载色体(色素细胞) chromatophore
赤道板 equatorial plate

染色体⑬ chromosome
〔正常男性人体〕淋巴细胞染色体 chromosome from a lymphocyte (of a normal human male)
异染色体 heterochromosome
常染色体 autosome, euchromosome
性染色体 sex chromosome
染色性 chromaticity
丝间质 paramitome
滋养质 deutoplasm
非染色质 achromatin
染色质粒 chromatin granule
染色质网 chromatin network
细胞分化 cell differentiation
细胞分裂 cell division
胞质分裂 cytokinesis
无丝分裂 amitosis, amitotic division
有丝分裂 mitosis
减数分裂 meiosis
异型分裂 heterolypic division, allotypic division
核分裂 nuclear division,

karyokinesis

单价〔染色〕体 monovalent chromosome

双价〔染色〕体 bivalent chromosome

多价〔染色〕体 multivalent chromosome

细胞发生 cytogenesis

细胞变态 cytomorphosis

细胞并合 cell fusion

细胞反应 cell effect

细胞混合 cytomixis

细胞集合 cell aggregation

细胞增殖 cell multiplication

细胞张力 cell turgidity

细胞感应性 irritability of cell

胞质运动 cytoplasmic movement

细胞内运动 intracellular movement

胞间消化 intercellular digestion

细胞外消化 extracellular digestion

母细胞 mother cell

子细胞 daughter cell

生殖细胞 generative cell, reproductive cell

生殖母细胞(性母细胞) auxocyte

性细胞 sex cell

无核细胞 akaryote

单核细胞 uninuclear cell

营养细胞 vegetative cell

滋养细胞 nutrient cell

蜜腺细胞 nectarous cell

# 遗传学 Genetics

遗传学说 theory of heredity

遗传生态学 genecology

细胞遗传学 cytogenetics

群体遗传学 colony genetics

米丘林学说 Michurinism

孟德尔主义 Mendelism

变性 denaturation

代谢型 metabolic type

生存条件 condition for existence

发育条件 condition for development

生活规律 law of life

发育规律 developmental mechanism, law of development

生活力 vigour, vitality, viability

遗传器官 organ for inheritance

遗传物质 substance of heredity

遗传影响 genetic implication

遗传变异性 variability of

heredity

遗传基本规律 fundamental laws of heredity

遗传的保守性 conservatism of heredity

融合遗传(混合遗传) blending heredity

定向育种(定向培育) directive breeding

引种 introduction

嵌合体 chimera

杂交 hybridization

有性杂交 sexual hybridization

无性杂交 asexual hybridization

营养杂交 vegetative hybridization

混精杂交 heterosperminous hybridization, hybridization by means of mixed sperms

嫁接杂交 graft hybridization

相反杂交(反交) reciprocal crossing

媒介法(居间法) intermediary method

嫁接 grafting

胚芽嫁接 embryo-grafting

属间胚芽嫁接 intergeneric embryo-grafting

远距离杂交(远缘杂交) distant hybridization

〔品〕种间杂交 intervarietal crossing

属间杂交 intergeneric hybridization

远缘杂种不育性 infertility of distant hybrid

单倍体育种 monadic breeding

异花授粉 cross-pollination

异花受粉 cross-fertilization

人工授粉 artificial pollination

异体受精 allogamy, cross-fertilization

人工受精 artificial insemination, artificial fertilization

远亲交配 outbreeding

近亲交配 inbreeding

异型有性世代交替 heterogeny, heterogenesis

传粉 pollination

传粉媒介 fertilizer, pollinator

遗传性载体 genetic carrier

自由授粉 free pollination

自体能育性 self-fertility

自体不育性 self-sterility

去雄 emasculation

去势 castration

人工引变 artificial induction of hereditary changes

人工变性 experimental sex reversal

诱变剂(诱变因素) mutagenic agent

性特征 sexual characteristics

遗传性状 hereditary character

数量性状 quantitative character

获得性状 acquired character

获得性状遗传 inheritance of acquired character

机体再生说(泛生说) pangenesis

亲本(母本) parent

亲株 parental plant

子株 daughter plant

子代₁ first filial generation (F₁)

子代₂ second filial generation (F₂)

杂交 crossbrceding, hybridization

杂交结合力 crossability

杂交物种 hybrid species, crossbreeding species

后代 progeny, descendent, descendant, offspring

杂种后代 offspring of hybrid, descendent of hybrid

显性性状 dominant character, dominant

隐性性状 recessive character, recessive

基因型(遗传型) genotype

表〔现〕型 phenotype

生活型 life form

反交杂种 reciprocal hybrid

居间杂种 intermediate hybrid

单杂交种(单性杂种) unisexual hybrid

双杂交种(两性杂种) bisexual hybrid

回交(逆代杂交) backcross

分离 segregation

有性分离 sexual segregation

无性分离 asexual segregation

两性融合 amphimixis

杂种优势 heterosis

遗传因子 genetic factor

遗传性载体 genetic carrier

复制 replication

遗传信息 genetic information

遗传密码 genetic code

遗传组合 genetic composition, genetic combination, genetic constitution

遗传变量(遗传方差) genetic variance

遗传相关 genetic correlation

遗传性阻碍 genetic block

遗传工程 genetic engineering (GE)

遗传获得量(遗传进展) genetic gain, genetic advance

配子生殖 gametic reproduction

单亲生殖 monogony, monogenetic reproduction

有性生殖 sexual reproduction

人工单性生殖(人为孤雌生殖) artificial parthenogenesis

分裂生殖 schizogamy, schizogenesis

授精 insemination

繁殖 propagation

营养繁育 vegetative multiplication

自体繁殖 self-reproduction

无性繁殖 vegetative propagation

无性生殖 asexual reproduction, vegetative reproduction

单性生殖 parthenogenesis, parthenogeny

有性生殖 sexual reproduction

单性〔生殖〕世代 parthenogenetic generation

(有性生殖与无性生殖)世代交替

metagenesis

自体受精　self-fertilization

体外受精　external fertilization

体内受精　internal fertilization

闭花受精　cleistogamy

因子　factor

基因　gene

显性基因　dominant gene

隐性基因　recessive gene

等位基因　allele, allel, allelomorph

基因学说　theory of genes

配子　gamete

雌配子　female gamete

雄配子　male gamete

数量遗传　quantitative heredity, quantitative inheritance

性〔别〕决定　sex determination

雌雄同体　hermaphrodite

细胞质遗传　cytoplasm heredity

返祖遗传(隔代遗传)　atavism

母体遗传　parental heredity

突变　mutation

基因突变　gene mutation

突变型(突变体)　mutant

突变子　muton

突变学说　theory of mutation

变异　variation

定向变异　directed variation

芽条变异　bud variation

倒位　inversion

受孕　impregnation

性状稳定　stabilization of characteristics

异体性别　heterogametic sex

取向　orientation

自体能育性　self-fertility

自体不育性　self-sterility

雄性不育性　male sterility

基因重新组合　recombination of genes

电离辐射引起的突变　mutation induced by ionizing radiation

遗传的基本规律　fundamental laws of heredity

分离规律　law of segregation

自由组合规律　law of independent assortment

连锁和交换规律　law of linkage and exchange

# 遗传工程　Genetic Engineering (GE)

遗传工程设计　genetic engineering project

分子生物学　molecular biology

微生物学 microbiology

遗传工程实验 genetic engineering experiment

遗传结构 genetic structure

遗传胶质 genetic glue

遗传指令 genetic command

遗传杂种 genetic hybrid

遗传特性 hereditary trait

遗传移植技术 genetic transplantation technique

遗传畸形(遗传异常) genetic abnormality, genetic freak

遗传适应性 genetic adaptation

遗传进展 genetic advance, genetic gain

遗传选型交配 genetic assortative mating

遗传性阻碍 genetic block

遗传密码 genetic code

遗传组分 genetic component

遗传缺陷 genetic defect

遗传死亡 genetic death

遗传异质性 genetic heterogeneity

遗传参数 genetic parameter

重复力 repeatability

遗传力 heritability

遗传相关 genetic correlation

从性遗传 sex-influenced inheritance

限性遗传 sex-limited inheritance

伴性遗传 sex-linked inheritance

核 nucleus

染色体 chromosome

减数分裂 meiosis

有丝分裂 mitosis

核酸 nucleic acid

核糖核酸 RNA (ribonucleic acid)

脱氧核糖核酸 DNA (deoxyribonucleic acid)

嘌呤 purine

嘧啶 pyrimidine

胸腺嘧啶 thymine

分子模型 molecular model

双螺旋 double helix

双螺旋DNA duplex DNA

双链DNA twin-stranded DNA

单链DNA single-stranded DNA

染色体DNA chromosomal DNA

环状DNA circular DNA, cyclic DNA

DNA病毒 DNA virus

RNA病毒 RNA virus

质粒 plasmid

质粒嵌合体 plasmid chimera

重组 recombination

重组技术 recombinant technique

重组子(交换子) recon

生命的主要分子 master molecule of life

创造新的生命形式 creating new forms of life

遗传工程育出的细菌 bug developed by genetic engineering

人造细菌 artificial bacteria

对抗菌素有免疫力的人造细菌 artificial bacteria immune to antibiotics

"安德洛墨达种"细菌 "Andromeda strain" bacteria

人工突变 man-made mutation

繁育杂交动物 breeding hybrid animals

培育杂交植物 cultivating hybrid plants

基因 gene

结构基因 structural gene

控制基因 control gene

调节基因 regulator gene

操纵基因 operator gene

阻遏物(阻遏蛋白) repressor

诱导物 inducer

操纵子 operon

表〔现〕型 phenotype

异体基因 foreign gene

基因的复制品 replica of genes

制造移植基因的复制品 making duplicates of a transplanted gene

抑制基因 inhibitory gene

基因库 gene bank, gene pool

基因基础 gene basis

基因流动 gene-flow

基因位点 gene locus

基因突变 gene mutation

基因激素 genohormone

胞质基因(类基因) genoid

基因组合 gene combination

基因移植 gene transplantation, implantation of genes

基因重组 gene recombination

生长激素释放的抑制因子 somatostatin

新品系 new strain

杂交 cross-breeding, hybridization

分子杂交 molecular hybridization

DNA—RNA杂交物 DNA—RNA hybrid

杂交分子 hybrid molecule

物种屏障 species barrier

酶 enzyme

限制性内切酶 restriction enzyme

修饰酶 modification enzyme

细菌酶 bacterial enzyme

核酸内切酶 endonucleases

核酸外切酶 exonucleases

纤维素酶 cellulase

酶解剖刀 enzymatic scalpel

大肠杆菌 Escherichia coli, E. coli

大肠杆菌的变种 mutated strain of E. coli

K—12大肠杆菌 E. coli K—12

病原体 pathogen, disease organism, disease carrying bacteria

肾上腺素 adrenalin(e), adrenine

激素 hormone

胰岛素 insulin

胰〔腺〕 pancreas

制造固氮细菌 creation of nitrogen-fixing bacteria

退化碳氢化合物 degrading hydrocarbons

无害细菌基因 harmless bacterial gene

极安全的实验室 ultra-secure laboratory

完全密封的环境 totally sealed environment

防污染系统 decontamination system

密封的培育箱 sealed cabinet

抑制程序 containment proce-

dure
保护措施 safeguard
致病力强的病菌 virulent bug
突变种 mutant variety
突变型(突变体) mutant

保护膜 protective membrane
(中间)缺失 deletion
特制的细菌 tailor-made
  microbe
变形细菌 transmuted bug

# 微生物学　Microbiology

细菌学 bacteriology
病毒学 virology, inframicro-
  biology
血清学 serology
免疫学 immunology
微生物 microorganism,
  microbe
病毒 virus
天花病毒 variola virus
过滤性病毒 filterable virus
粘病毒 mucous virus
虫媒病毒 entomophilous
  virus
腺病毒 glandular virus
噬菌体 fungivorous body
细菌 bacterium (pl. bac-

teria)
球菌状① coccus forms
杆菌状② bacillus forms
螺旋菌状③ spirillum forms
真菌 fungus (pl. fungi)
菌根 mycorrhiza
菌丝 hypha
菌〔丝〕体 mycelium
杆菌 bacillus (pl. bacilli)
球菌 coccus (pl. cocci)
敏感菌 sensitized bacterium
敏感菌苗 sensitized vaccine
磷细菌 phosphorous bacterium
好气细菌 aerobic bacterium
厌气细菌 anaerobic bacterium
厌气性微生物 anaerobic
  microorganism
好气性微生物 aerobic micro-
  organism
分解纤维细菌 cellulolytic
  bacterium
链球菌 streptococcus
葡萄球菌 staphylococcus

大肠杆菌　colibacillus, Escherichia coli (E.coli)

痢疾杆菌　shigella, dysentery bacterium, bacteria of the Shigella genus

嗜血杆菌　haemophilus

自生固氮菌　azotobacter

根瘤菌　rhizobium, root-nodule bacterium

毛霉　mucor

氨细菌　ammonium bacterium

螺菌　spirillum

硫〔黄〕细菌　sulphur bacterium

原生质体　protoplast

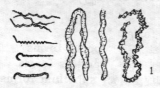

螺旋体①　spirochaete, spirochaetale

镰刀菌　fusarium

霉菌(丝状菌)　mould, mold

酵母菌　saccharomycete

酵母菌的芽生情况②　blastogenesis of saccharomycetes

菌珠　strain

曲霉　aspergillus

抗生菌(拮抗菌)　antagonistic microorganism

包涵体　inclusion body

芽胞　gemma

抗菌素　antibiotic

毒素　toxin

疫苗(菌苗)　vaccine

疫源(疫病中心)　epidemic focus

生物制品　biotic preparation

免疫　immunity

自然免疫性　natural immunity

抗原　antigen

抗原分析　antigenic analysis

抗原性　antigenicity

抗体　antibody

抗毒素　antitoxin, toxolysin

抗霉素　antimycin

腐生　saprophytism

兼腐生　facultative saprophytism

产腐菌　saprogenic bacterium

腐生菌　saprophytic bacterium

自养微生物　autotrophic microorganism

异养微生物　heterotrophic microorganism

氮素循环　nitrogen cycle

细菌光合作用　bacterial photosynthesis

化能合成作用　chemosynthesis

自溶作用　autolysis

溶菌作用　bacteriolysis

溶菌素　bacteriolysin

抑菌作用(制菌作用)　bacteriostatic activity, antimicrobial action

抑菌　bacteriostasis

杀菌作用　sterilization

噬菌作用　fungivorous action

传染(感染)　infection

侵扰　infestation

接触传染 contagion, contagious infection
发酵 fermentation
菌种保藏 type culture collection
微生物培养法 culture of microorganism
接种 vaccination
冷冻干燥(冷藏干燥) freeze-drying lyophilization
消毒 sterilization, disinfection
防腐 antisepsis
培养基 culture medium
发酵培养基 fermentation medium
发酵管 fermentation tube
杜汉氏发酵管③ Durham's fermentation tube
斯密司氏发酵管④ Smith's fermentation tube
培养皿 Petri dish, petri dish
生长曲线 curve of growth

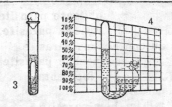

碳源 origin of carbon
氮源 origin of nitrogen
生长因子 growth factor
敏感性 sensibility
耐受性 tolerance
耐药性(抗药性) resistance to drugs
补体 complement
抗毒血清 antitoxic serum
发酵饲料 fermented fodder
菌类饲料 fungus fodder
曲酶 inulase, inulinase
玉米浆 maize jelly
原胶原 procollagen
抗原性 antigenicity
抗原分析 antigenic analysis

# 寄生虫学 Parasitology

寄生物形态学 morphology of parasites
人体寄生虫学 parasitology of humans
寄生现象 parasitism
共生现象 commensalism

互惠共生现象 mutualism
转主寄生现象 heteroecism
寄生物 parasite
外寄生物 ectoparasite
兼性寄生物 facultative parasite

专性寄生物　obligate parasite
固有寄生物　autistic parasite, autochthonous parasite
定主寄生物　specific parasite
不定主寄生物　incidental parasite
半寄生物　hemiparasite
相互寄生物　reciprocal parasite
依生生物　mutualist
共生生物　commensal
寄生〔蠕〕虫　parasitic worm, helminth
人体寄生虫　parasite of humans
多宿主寄生虫　pleophagous parasitic worm
体内寄生虫　endoparasite
寄生变形虫　parasitic amoeba
寄生纤毛虫　parasitic ciliate
寄生细菌　parasitic bacterium
腐生物(死物寄生菌)　saprophyte
(寄生于动物的)真菌　epiphyte
细胞内寄生菌　intracellular parasite
病原　pathogen, pathogene
寄生生活方式　parasitic mode of life
宿主(寄主)　host
终宿主　final host
暂时寄主　temporary host
定局宿主　definitive host
中间宿主　intermediate host
营养体(滋养体)　vegetative organ, nutrient body
利杜体　Leishman-Donovan body, LD body
毛蚴　caterpillar larva

稚虫　naiad
尾蚴　cercaria
囊蚴　bladder larva, encysted cercaria
原尾蚴　procercoid
囊尾蚴　cysticercous cercaria
幼虫　larva
丝虫(血丝虫)　filaria
肝胚　fluke
线虫　nematode
钩虫　hookworm

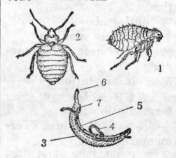

蚤①　flea
虱②　louse
血吸虫　schistosoma, blood fluke
雄血吸虫③　male schistosoma
雌血吸虫④　female schistosoma
腹沟⑤　ventral groove
口⑥　mouth
腹吸盘⑦　ventral sucker
传染媒介　intermediate vector
病媒昆虫(媒介昆虫)　insect vector
传病媒介　vector
漂浮法　floating method, floatation

沉淀法 precipitating method,
  precipitation
寄生虫的生活周期 life cycle
  of parasites
纤毛胚 ciliated embryo
幼虫期 larval stage
吸盘 sucking disc
产卵器 ovipositor
白血球 leucocyte
抗体 antibody
遗传变异 heritable variation
寄生虫毒力(寄生虫毒性) para-

site virulence
寄主免疫 host immunity
寄主专一性 host specificity
寄生物寄生生态系统 parasito-
  cenose
综合防治措施 comprehensive
  preventive health measures
相互作用 interplay, inter-
  action, mutual action
宿主病毒相互作用 host-virus
  interaction
相关性 correlation

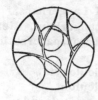

# 组织学 Histology

上皮组织 epithelial tissue,
  epithelium
间皮 mesothelium
内皮 endothelium
分泌上皮 secretory
  epithelium
毛囊 hair follicle
汗腺 sweat gland
皮下组织 subcutaneous tissue
结缔〔组〕织 connective tissue
纤维〔组〕织 fibrous tissue
间质组织 interstitial tissue
淋巴组织 lymphoid tissue
胶原纤维 collagen fibre
弹性组织 elastic tissue
网状纤维 reticular fibre
软骨膜 cartilage membrane
骨化 ossification

哈弗氏系统 Haversian system
血液 blood
血浆 blood plasma
血清(浆液) blood serum,
  serum
血清白蛋白 serum albumin
血清球蛋白 serum globulin
血细胞 haemocyte, haemato-
  cyte
血球 blood corpuscle,
  corpuscle
红〔血〕细胞(红血球) red blood
  cell, red blood corpuscle
  (RBC)
白血细胞(白血球) white blood
  cell, white blood corpuscle
  (WBC)
血小板 blood platelet, throm-

bocyte
淋巴 lymph
肌肉组织 muscle tissue
肌原纤维 muscular fibril, muscle fibril, myofibril
心内膜 endocardium
心外膜 epicardium
神经 nerve
神经原 neuron
神经组织 nerve tissue
神经鞘(神经膜) neurilemma
神经细胞 nerve cell
神经末梢 nerve ending
神经节 ganglion
神经纤维网 neuropil
味蕾 taste bud
角膜 cornea
巩膜 sclera
视网膜 retina
结膜 conjunctiva
虹膜 iris
釉质 enamel
齿质 dentine
腺 gland
无管腺 ductless gland

内分泌腺 endocrine gland
唾液腺(涎腺) salivary gland
甲状腺 thyroid gland
泪腺 lacrimal gland
淋巴结(淋巴腺) lymph gland
乳腺 mammary gland
胃腺 gastric gland
浆膜层 serosa
粘膜 mucous membrane, mucosa
肺泡 alveolus
肾小管 uriniferous tubule
黄体 corpus luteum
胰岛 islet of Langerhans, island of Langerhans, islet of the pancreas, pancreatic island
网状细胞 reticulocyte
网状组织 reticulum
网状内皮组织 reticuloendothelium
基质 stroma
共生体 symbiont
组织再生 tissue regeneration
组织培养 tissue culture

# 胚胎学 Embryology

动物胚胎学 zooembryology
实验胚胎学 experimental embryology
比较胚胎学 comparative embryology

化学胚胎学 chemical embryology
生殖细胞(性细胞) generative cell, reproductive cell, sex cell

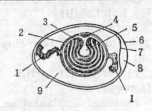

卵　egg, ovum
鸡蛋　hen's egg
卵〔黄系〕带①　chalaza
卵黄膜②　yolk membrane
黄养料卵黄③　yellow food yolk
胚泡④　germinal vesicle
白卵黄⑤　white yolk
壳⑥　shell
壳膜⑦　shell membrane
气腔⑧　air chamber
白蛋白(白朊)⑨　albumin, white of the egg
精子　sperm, spermatozoon
卵子发生　oogenesis, ovogenesis, ovigenesis
精子发生　spermatogenesis
精子形成　spermiogenesis
排卵　ovulation
受精　fertilization
体内受精　internal fertilization
体外受精　external fertilization
受精卵　fertilized egg
有性生殖　sexual reproduction
同配生殖　homogamy
异配生殖　heterogamy
单性生殖(孤雌生殖)　parthenogenesis, parthenogeny
无性生殖　asexual reproduction
卵胎生　ovo-viviparity

胎生　viviparity
胎盘　placenta
胎盘循环　placental circulation
(哺乳动物的)胎儿　foetus, fetus
动物〔性〕极　animal pole
植物极　plant pole
〔受精〕卵〔分〕裂　cleavage
胚胎　embryo
胚胎发生　embryogeny
囊胚　blastula
囊胚形成　blastulation
胚基　blastema
囊胚基质　blastostroma
原肠胚　gastrula
胚层(胚盘)　blastoderm
胚根　radicle
胚乳　endosperm
胚乳细胞　endosperm cell
胚外体壁　extra-embryonic somatopleure
胚外体腔　exocoelom, extra-embryonic coelom
胚胎发育　embryonic development
胚细胞　blastocyte
胚膜　embryonic membrane
羊膜　amnion, amniotic membrane
羊膜腔　amniotic cavity
羊水　amniotic fluid, amnion fluid
羊膜细胞　amniotic cell
绒毛膜　chorion
尿〔囊〕膜　allantois
卵泡　follicle
卵囊　nidamental capsule
卵黄囊　vitellus capsule

脐带 umbilical cord
胞衣(胞囊) chorion
植入(着床) implantation
分化 differentiation
原基 primordium, anlage
神经胚 nerve embryo
神经板 nerve plate
神经管 nerve duct
神经嵴 nerve ridge
鳃裂 cleft
孵育 incubation
孵化 hatching

孵化性 hatchability
变态 metamorphosis
变态发育 interrupted development
人工受精 artificial fertilization
外植 external implantation
卵子移植 transplantation of ovum
受精卵移植 transplantation of fertilized egg

# 植物学 Botany

植物分类学 Phytotaxonomy
常绿植物 evergreen plant
常绿草本植物 evergreen herbage
常绿小灌木 evergreen undershrub
蕨类植物 fern, pteridophyte, pteridophyta
蕨类一年生植物 pteridotherophyte
有花植物 flowering plant
显花植物 phanerogamia, phanerogam
隐花植物 cryptogamia, cryptogam
隐芽植物 cryptophyte
单子叶植物 monocotyledon, monocotyledonous plant
双子叶植物 dicotyledon,

dicotyledonous plant
食虫植物 insectivorous plant
食菌植物 fungivorous plant
自养植物 autophyte
树上附生植物 epiphyte arboricosa
半附生植物 hemiepiphyte
寄生植物 parasite plant
寄主植物 host plant
内长植物 endogenous plant, endophyte
外长植物 exogenous plant
土著植物(乡土植物) indigenous plant
外来植物 exotic plant, introduced plant
阳性植物 light-demanding plant
阴性植物 shade-demanding

plant

木本植物　ligneous plant

草本植物　herbaceous plant

高草本植物　altoherbosa

短生植物　ephemeral plant

春季短生植物　vernal ephemeral plant

针叶植物　conifer

阔叶植物　broadleaved plant

高山植物　alpine plant, acrophyte

草原植物　psilophyte

森林植物　forestry growth

砂土植物　silicicole

先锋植物　pioneer

优势植物　dominant plant

广域分布植物　curychoric plant

气生植物　aerial plant

陆生植物　terrestrial

水生植物　aquatic plant, hydrophyte

沼生植物　helophyte

两栖植物　amphiphyte, amphibious plant

沉水植物　submerged plant

水底植物　benthophyte, phytobenthon, benthon

多年生植物　perennial, perpetual

一年生植物　annual

水生一年生植物　hydrotherophyte

维管植物　vascular plant

水生维管束植物　aquatic vascular plant

动物形植物　zoophyte

酸性土指示植物　oxylophyte

单细胞植物　unicellular plant

种子植物　seed plant

中温植物　mesotherm

无叶植物　aphyllous glant

阴地植物　shade plant, sciophyte

兽媒植物　zoophilous plant

虫媒植物　entomophilous plant

近亲植物　close relative plant

伴人植物　synanthropic plant

古老植物　relic plant

裸子植物　gymnosperm

鳞茎植物　bulb plant

肉茎植物　stem succulent

喜雨植物(适雨植物，好雨植物)　ombrophile, ombrophilous plant

喜湿植物(好湿植物，适湿植物)　hygrophilous plant

喜温植物(适温植物，好温植物)　thermophilous plant

旱生植物　xerophilous plant

喜蚁植物(适蚁植物，好蚁植物)　ant plant, myrmecophilous plant, myrmecophyte

喜砂植物(适砂植物，好砂植物)　psammophilous plant

喜硷植物(适硷植物，好硷植物)　alkaline plant, basephilous plant

喜盐植物(适盐植物，好盐植物)　halophilous plant

喜氮植物(适氮植物，好氮植物)　nitrophilous plant

喜钙植物(适钙植物，好钙植物)　calciphilous plant

嫌雨植物(避雨植物)　ombrophobe, ombropholous plant

嫌风植物(避风植物)　anemo-

110

phobe

嫌钙植物(避钙植物) calciphobous plant, calcifuge, calciphobe

嫌寒植物(避寒植物) frigofuge

嫌硷植物(避硷植物) basifuge

嫌酸植物(避酸植物) oxyphobe

嫌雪植物(避雪植物) chionophobous plant

嫌盐植物(避盐植物) halophobe

栽培植物 cultivated plant

木材植物 xylplant

纤维植物 fibrous plant

油料植物 oil-pressing plant, oil plant

染料植物 dye plant

芳香植物 scent plant

蜜腺植物 nectarous plant

# 植物生理学　Plant Physiology

叶绿素 chlorophyll

叶绿体 chloroplast

光合作用 photosynthesis

碳水化合物的新陈代谢 carbohydrate metabolism

渗透作用 osmosis

渗透压 osmotic pressure

外渗 exosmosis

膨压(涨压) turgor pressure

根〔部〕压〔力〕 root pressure

吸水力 water-absorbing power

吸胀作用 imbibition

蒸腾作用 transpiration

气孔 stoma

呼吸作用 respiration

气孔运动 stomatal movement, stomatic movement

吐水 guttation

光周期 photoperiod

临界光周期 critical photoperiod

叶黄素 xanthophyll

花青素 anthocyanidin, cyanidin

黄化现象 aetiolation, etiolation, blanching, yellowing

白化现象 albinism

固氮作用 nitrogen fixation

半纤维素 semicellulose

木〔质〕素 lignin

营养生长 vegetative growth

生殖生长 reproductive growth

植物激素 phytohormone, plant hormone

光敏色素 phytochrome

脱落现象 abscission

脱果现象 abscission of fruit

春化(春化作用，春化处理) vernalization

人工催熟 artificial ripening

向性运动 tropic movement

向光性 phototropism

向日性　heliotropism
向热性　thermotropism
向地性　geotropism
感性运动　nastic movement

感夜性　nyctinasty
感应性　irritability
感药性　chemonasty

## 植物解剖学　Phytotomy

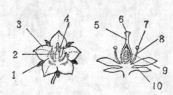

花　flower
萼片① sepal
雌蕊② pistil
花瓣③ petal
雄蕊④ stamen
花柱⑤ style
柱头⑥ stigma
花药⑦ anther
花丝⑧ filament
子房⑨ ovary
胚珠⑩ ovule
叶型　leaf types
长叶片⑪ linear leaf
披针形叶⑫ lanceolate leaf
渐尖叶⑬ acuminate leaf
急尖叶⑭ acute leaf
匙形叶⑮ spatulate leaf

圆头叶(钝叶)⑯ obtuse leaf
卵圆形叶⑰ ovate leaf
齿状叶⑱ serrate leaf
箭头形叶⑲ sagittate leaf
双生叶⑳ binate leaf
抱茎叶㉑ amplexicaul leaf
十字形对生叶㉒ decussate leaf
掌状叶㉓ digitate leaf
复叶㉔ compound leaf
叶各部分　leaf parts
完全叶　complete leaf
无托叶的叶　exstipulate leaf
无柄叶　sessile leaf
草叶　leaf of grass
松树针状叶　needlelike leaves of pine
草片(叶片)　blade
叶柄　petiole
托叶　stipule
鞘　sheath
叶舌(舌状叶)　ligule
矮枝　dwarf branch

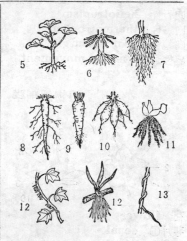

叶脉序　leaf venation
平衡脉① parallel vein
羽状脉② pinnate vein
掌状脉③ palmate vein
二叉脉④ dichotomous vein
叶脉　vein
中〔肋〕脉 midrib vein
根的种类 kinds of roots
不定根⑤ adventitious roots
支撑根和其它不定根⑥ prop
and other adventitious
roots
纤维不定根⑦ fibrous adven-
titious roots
主根(直根，初生根)⑧ taproot
(primary root)
肉质主根⑨ fleshy taproot
肉质簇生不定根⑩ fleshy fas-
cicled adventitious root
水生不定根⑪ aquatic adven-
titious roots
气生不定根⑫ aerial adventi-
tious roots

寄生根(吸根)⑬ parasitic
roots (haustorial roots)
果　fruit
瓣⑭ valve
隔膜(中隔)⑮ septum
囊果皮⑯ pericarp
胚胎⑰ embryo
胚乳⑱ endosperm
籽⑲ seed
空间⑳ space
外皮㉑ periderm
翼瓣㉒ wing

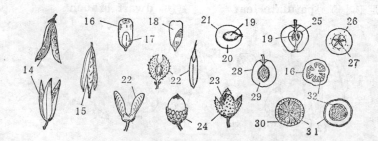

坚果〔仁〕㉓ nut
花被㉔ involucre
内果皮㉕ endocarp
花管㉖ floral tube
核仁㉗ core

外果皮㉘ exocarp
中果皮㉙ mesocarp
油腺㉚ oil gland
果皮㉛ rind, peel
胎座㉜ placenta

# 动物学 Zoology

动物生理学 zoophysiology, animal physiology
电生理学 electrophysiology
机体 organism
机制 mechanism
神经反射性机制 nervous reflex mechanism
肌肉无力 myasthenia
肌肉疲劳 muscular fatigue
肌萎缩 muscular atrophy
肌觉 muscular sensation
肌体吸收 absorption by tissue
刺激作用 stimulation
条件刺激 conditioned stimulus
暂时刺激 temporary stimulus
反应 response
抑制 inhibition
兴奋与抑制 excitation and inhibition

兴奋性 excitability
刺激阈 stimulus threshold
潜伏期 incubation, period of incubation
神经冲动 nervous impulse
神经统御 nervous control
神经性诱发 neural induction
生物电流 bioelectric current
生物电势 bioelectric potential
(神经的)膜电位 membrane potential (of nerve)
网状结构 reticular formation, reticular structure
神经中枢 nerve centre
突触 synapse
介质(递质) medium
锥体神经原 pyramidal neuron
反射 reflex
条件反射 conditioned reflex

非条件反射(无条件反射) **unconditioned reflex**

腹壁反射 **abdominal reflex**

二头肌反射 **biceps reflex**

三头肌反射 **triceps reflex**

角膜反射 **corneal reflex**

瞳孔反射 **pupilary reflex**

翻正反射 **righting reflex**

腱反射 **tendon reflex**

跖反射 **plantar reflex**

姿势反射 **postural reflex**

不随意反射动作 **involuntary reflex action**

分析器 **analyzer**

本能 **instinct**

睡眠 **sleep**

催眠 **hypnosis**

冬眠 **hibernation**

信号系统 **signal system**

第一信号系统 **first signal system**

第二信号系统 **second signal system**

感觉 **sensation**

色觉 **sense of colour**

五种官能 **the five senses**

触觉 **sense of touch**

视觉 **sense of sight**

听觉 **sense of hearing**

味觉 **sense of taste**

嗅觉 **sense of smell**

直觉(第六官能) **cenesthesia (the sixth sense)**

内脏感觉(第七官能) **visceral sense (the seventh sense)**

错觉 **illusion**

错视 **optical illusion**

体液 **body fluid**

血型 **blood groups, blood types**

给血者的红血细胞 **red blood cells of donor**

受血者的血清 **serum of acceptor**

有凝集反应 **having agglutination reaction**

无凝集反应 **having no agglutination reaction**

血液循环 **blood circulation**

体循环(大循环) **systemic circulation**

肺循环(小循环) **pulmonary circulation**

血压 **blood pressure**

心音 **cardiac sound**

心〔搏频〕率 **heart rate, heart beat frequency**

心输出量 **cardiac output**

脉搏 **pulse**

呼吸作用 **respiration**

内呼吸 **internal respiration**

外呼吸 **external respiration**

肺活量 **vital capacity**

缺氧 **anoxia, oxygen deficit**

消化 **digestion**

绒毛运动 **ciliary movement**

新陈代谢(代谢) **metabolism**

基础代谢 **basal metabolism**

呼吸商 **respiratory quotient**

体温 **body temperature**

排泄 **excretion**

分泌 **secretion**

内分泌 **endocrine**

性周期(动情周期) **estrous cycle**

月经 **menstruation**

性征 **sex character**

再生 **regeneration**

| | |
|---|---|
| 吞噬作用 phagocytosis | 吸血动物 bloodsucker |
| 代偿现象 compensation phenomenon | 游行动物 nekton |
| 动物分类学 animal taxonomy | 食鱼动物 piscivorous animal |
| 门 phylum | 单食性动物 monophagous animal |
| 亚门 subphylum | 多食性动物(杂食性动物) omnivore, omnivorous animal, polyphagous animal |
| 纲 class | |
| 目 order | 单配偶动物 monogamous animal |
| 科 family | |
| 属 genus | 多配偶动物 polygamous animal |
| 种 species | |
| 无脊椎动物 invertebrate | 多足动物 myriapod |
| 原生动物 protozoa | 四足动物 quadruped |
| 原口动物 protostomia | 有蹄动物 ungulate |
| 腔肠动物 coelenterate | 外寄生动物 ectoparasite |
| 海绵动物 sponge | 寄生动物 parasitic animal, zooparasite |
| 蠕形动物 verme | |
| 节肢动物 arthropod | 反刍动物 ruminant |
| 软体动物 mollusc | 温血动物(定温动物) warm-blooded animal (homoiothermic animal) |
| 棘皮动物 echinoderm | |
| 脊索动物 chordate | |
| 脊椎动物 vertebrate (craniate) | 冷血动物(变温动物) coldblooded animal (poikilothermic animal) |
| 鱼 fish | |
| 两栖动物 amphibian | 甲壳动物 crustacean |
| 爬行动物 reptile | 常见动物 common animal |
| 鸟 bird | 稀有动物 rare animal |
| 哺乳动物 mammal | 野生动物 wild animal |
| 啮齿动物 rodent | 热带动物 tropical animal |
| 食虫动物 insectivore, insectivorous animal | 亚热带动物 subtropical animal |
| 食肉动物 carnivore, carnivorous animal, zoophagous animal | 温带动物 animal of the temperate zone |
| | 寒带动物 animal of the frigid zone |
| 食腐动物 scavenger, saprophagous animal | 大洋动物 pelagic fauna, oceanic fauna |
| 食草动物 herbivore, herbivorous animal, phytophagous animal, vegetarian | 蜘蛛类动物 arachnid |

多细胞动物　multicellular animal
单细胞动物　unicellular animal, single-cell animal
共生动物　commensal

# 动物界　Animal Kingdom

原生动物亚界　Subkingdom Protozoa
原生动物门　Phylum Protozoa
原生质　protoplasm
细胞质　cytoplasm
细胞器　organelle
鞭毛纲　Class Mastigophora (Flagellata)
全植型营养(自养型营养)　holophytic nutrition
全动型营养(异养型营养)　holozoic nutrition
肉足纲　Class Sarcodina (Rhizopoda)
伪足　pseudopodia

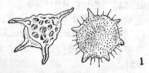

放射虫①　radiolarian
有孔虫②　foraminifera
变形虫③　amoeba
变形虫目　Order Amoabida
孢子纲　Class Sporozoa
配子形成　gamete formation
复分裂　multiple fission

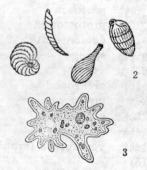

合子　zygote
营养体　trophozoite
裂殖子　schizozoite
孢子被　sporocyst
孢子虫　sporozoite
单食性动物　monophagous animal
多食性动物(杂食性动物)　omnivore, omnivorous animal, polyphagous animal
纤毛纲　Class Ciliophora
表膜　outer pellicle
纤丝　fibril
外质　ectoplasm
大核　macronucleus
小核　micronucleus

多孔动物门(海绵动物门)
  **Phylum Porifera (Spongia)**

海绵 **sponge**

多细胞动物 **multicellular animal**

固着(座生)的幼体 **sessile larva**

海绵排水孔 **osculum**

针状体 **spicule**

海绵硬蛋白 **spongin**

后生动物亚界 **Subkingdom Metazoa**

无脊椎动物 **invertebrate**

腔肠动物门 **Phylum coelenterata**

外胚层 **ectoderm**

内胚层 **endoderm**

中胶层 **mesogloea**

辐射对称 **radial symmetry**

浮浪幼体(腔肠动物幼体) **planula**

刺细胞腔肠动物亚门 **Subphylum Cnidaria**

刺细胞 **cnidoblast**

水螅纲 **Class Hydrozoa**

钵水母纲 **Class Scyphozoa**

珊瑚虫纲 **Class Actinozoa (Anthozoa)**

螅形 **polypoid form**

水母形 **medusoid form**

二态〔形〕性 **dimorphism**

水螅④ **hydra**

4

刺丝囊 **nematocyst**

5

海蜇⑤ **jellyfish**

生殖腺 **gonad**

芽体 **bud**

钵口幼体 **scyphistoma**

碟状幼体 **ephyra larva**

眼点 **ocellus**

腔肠 **enteron**

隔膜 **mesentery**

6

海葵⑥ **(sea) anemone**

共生动物 **commensal**

珊瑚 **coral**

隔膜 **septum**

珊瑚环礁 **coral atoll**

栉水母亚门 **Subphylum Ctenophora**

侧腕水母 **sea goosebury**

触手 **tentacle**

粘细胞 **colloblast**

生物光 **bioluminescence**

扁形动物门 **Phylum Platyhelminthes**

扁虫 **flatworm**

两侧对称 **bilateral symmetry**

背腹扁平 **being flattened dorso-ventrally**

酶 enzyme
中胚层 mesoderm
盲囊 caecum
排泄系 excretory system
神经系 nervous system
生殖系 reproductive system
涡虫纲 Class Turbellaria
吸虫纲 Class Trematoda, fluke
有尾幼虫 cercaria
绦虫纲 class cestoda
绦虫 tapeworm
节裂(横裂) strobilization, strobilation
节裂体(横裂体) strobila
节片 proglottis, proglottid
(绦虫)头节 scolex
纽虫门 Phylum Nemertea (Nemertinea)
线形动物门 Phylum Nematoda

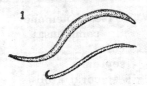

蛔虫① roundworm
化感器 amphid
植物寄生线虫 plant nematode
可外翻喙 eversible proboscis
刺体动物门 Phylum Nematomorpha
棘头虫门 Phylum Acanthocephala
轮虫门 Phylum Rotifera
轮虫② rotifer
轮器 wheel-organ

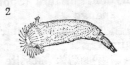

腹毛门 Phylum Gastrotricha
动吻虫门 Phylum Kinorhynchia (Echinoderida)
鳃曳虫门 Phylum Priapulida
内肛动物门 Phylum Endoprocta (Entoprocta)
环节动物门 Phylum Annelida
多毛纲 Class Polychaeta
沙蚕 Nereis
寡毛纲 Class Oligochaeta
蚯蚓 earthworm
水蛭纲 Class Hirudinea
原环虫纲 Class Archiannelida
螠虫纲 Class Echiuroidea
星虫纲 Class Sipunculoidea
分节现象 metameric segmentation, metamerism
头向集中 cephalization
角质层 cuticle
几丁质 chitin
背神经节 dorsal ganglia
腹神经节 ventral ganglia
腹神经索 ventral nerve cord
开型循环系 closed blood system
原肾 nephridia
肾孔 nephridiopore
体腔 coelom
腔 lumen

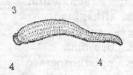

水蛭③ leech
吸盘④ sucker
前吸盘 anterior sucker
后吸盘 posterior sucker
口前叶 preoral lobe
两性体 hermaphrodite
雌雄异体 dioecism
卵袋 cocoon
寄生 parasitism
外寄生 ectoparasitism
食腐动物 scavenger
捕食动物 predator
疣足 parapodia
打地洞 burrowing
触毛 cirri
节肢动物门 Phylum Arthropoda
附肢 appendage
颚 jaw
硬外骨骼 hard exoskeleton
抓爪 grasping claw

书肺⑥ book lung
有爪纲 Class Onychophora
大颚 mandible, mandibula
多足纲 Class Myriapoda
毒腺 poison gland
双节 diplo-segment
蜈蚣亚纲 Subclass Chilopoda
马陆亚纲 Subclass Diplopoda
结合纲 Class Symphyla
昆虫纲 Class Insecta
    (Hexapoda)
头 head
胸 thorax
腹 abdomen

蝎子⑤ scorpion
尾倒刺 tail barb
呼吸结构 respiratory
    structure
鳃片 gill
气管 trachea

触角⑦ antenna
复眼 compound eye
气门 spiracle

若虫⑧ nymph

成虫　imago (pl. imagines or imagos)

脱皮　molt

龄期　stadium, instar

不完全变态　incomplete metamorphosis

蛴螬　grub

静止期　resting stage

蛹　pupa

完全变态　complete metamorphosis

独居的　solitary

聚生的　gregarious

集群组合社会　society

成群迁徙的　swarming and migratory

螫针　sting

隐藏色　cryptic colouration

保护性拟态　protective mimicry

保护性形肖　protective resemblance

无翅亚纲(无变态亚纲)　Subclass Apterygota (Ametabola)

有翅亚纲(变态亚纲)　Subclass Pterygota (Metabola)

传病媒介昆虫　vector

虱　louse (pl. lice)

蚤　flea

蝇　fly

蚜虫　aphid

产卵力　fecundity

蚊①　mosquito

蜘蛛②　spider

纺绩器　arachnidium

丝腺　silk gland

吐丝器　spinneret

前体　prosoma

后体　opisthosoma

捕握螯　prehensile pincers

须肢　pedipalp (pl. pedipalpi)

毒液　venom

螯肢　chelicera

蝗虫③　locust

甲壳纲　Class Crustacea

鳃足亚纲　Subclass Branchiopoda

躯干　trunk

小颚　maxilla

颚足　maxilliped

蔓足　cirri

胸肢　thoracic appendage

螯　chela

藤壶　barnacle

等足类　isopod

十足类　decapod

软体动物门　Phylum Mollusca

石鳖纲　Class Amphineura

腹足纲　Class Gastropoda

掘足纲　Class Scaphopoda

双壳纲(瓣鳃纲)　Class Lamellibranchiata (Bivalvia)

头足纲　Class Cephalopoda

大脑神经节　cerebral ganglia

内脏囊　visceral sac

软体套膜　mantle

介壳　shell

排泄管 excretory duct

血管肺 vascular lung

齿舌 radula

闭壳肌 adductor muscle

滤食性动物 filter feeder

水管 siphon

丝足 byssus

(介壳的)真珠层 nacreous layer

真皮 dermis

载色体 chromatophore

墨囊 ink sac

发光器 light organ, luminous organ

蹼 web

外肛动物门 Phylum Ectoprocta

腕足动物门 Phylum Brachiopoda

毛颚动物门 Phylum Chaetognatha

帚虫门 Phylum Phoronidea (Phoronida)

棘皮动物门 Phylum Echinodermata

海星纲 Class Asteroidea

阳遂足纲(蛇尾纲) Class Ophiuroidea

海胆纲 Class Echinoidea

海参纲 Class Holothuroidea

有柄亚门 Subphylum Pelmatozoa

小骨片 ossicle

萼体 stalk

萼体冠 calyx

育幼袋(育囊) brood pouch

五趼节对称 pentaonerous symmetry

管足 tube foot

前月面 lunch

羽枝 pinnule

脊索动物门 Phylum Chordata

半索动物亚门 Subphylum Hemichorda

须腕动物亚门 Subphylum pogonophora

尾索类(被囊类)亚门 Subphylum Urochorda (Tunicata)

头索动物亚门(无头亚门) Subphylum Cephalochordata (Acrania)

脊索 notochord

脊髓 spinal cord

脊柱 vertebral column

脑 brain

颅骨 skull, cranium

鳍 fin

肢 limb

吻 proboscis

脊椎动物亚门(有头亚门) Subphylum Vertebrata (Craniata)

无颌总纲 Superclass Agnatha (Marsipobranchii)

圆口纲 Class Cyclostoma

软骨骼 cartilaginous skeleton

鼻囊 nasal sac

有颌总纲 Superclass Gnathostomata

鱼类 Pisces

软骨鱼纲 Class Elasmobranchii (Chondrichthyes)

游行动物 nekton

胸鳍 pectoral fin

腹鳍 pelvic fin

背鳍 dorsal fin

臀鳍 anal fin

鳞 scale

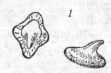

盾鳞① placoid scale
食鱼动物 piscivorous animal
心房 atrium
动脉圆锥 conus arteriosus
腹侧主动脉 ventral aorta
鳃动脉 gill artery
变温动物 cold-blooded
　　animal, poikilotherm
肠 intestinum
螺旋瓣 spiral valve
有黄卵 yolky egg
(某些鲨和虹的)硬壳卵 mer-
　　maid's purse
卵胎生 ovoviviparity
卵子发生 ovogenesis, oogene-
　　sis
鳍脚 clasper
硬骨鱼纲 Class Osteichthyes
鳃盖骨 operculum
气鳔 air bladder
游泳鳔 swim bladder
瓣胸鳍 lobed pectoral fin
吻鼻 snout
韦伯氏器 Weberian appara-
　　tus
发光器 photophore
放电器 electric(al) organ
食草动物 herbivore
食肉动物 carnivore
伪眼 mock eye
两栖纲 Class Amphibia
五趾型肢 pentadactyl limb
蝌蚪 tadpole
卵囊 egg capsule

幼征滞留 neolony
无尾总目 Superorder
　　Salientia (Anura)

蛙② frog
蟾蜍③ toad
口腔 buccal cavity
子宫 uterus
副性征(次级性征) secondary
　　sexual characteristics
爬行纲 Class Reptilia
多次换齿 polyphyodonty
龟鳖类 chelonians, (Am.)
　　turtles
鳖 turtle
龟 tortoise

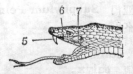

蜥蜴④ lizard
蚺蛇属大蟒 python

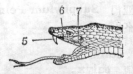

毒蛇 viper
毒蛇的毒牙⑤ fang
毒管⑥ venom duct, poison
　　duct

毒腺⑦ venom gland, poison gland

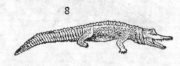

鳄鱼⑧ crocodile
鸟纲 Class Aves
羽 feather

羽根(翮)⑨ quill
外气囊 extra air sac
胸骨 sternum
锁骨 clavicle, clavicula
胸部飞行肌 pectoral flight muscle
脊棱 keel
肋骨 rib
翼 wing
角质喙 horny beak
恒温动物 warm-blooded animal, idiothermous animal
食虫鸟 insectivorous bird
嘴 bill
卵白 albumen
一窝(蛋) clutch
雏鸟 fledgeling
平胸类鸟(不能飞的鸟) ratitae, (primitive flightless bird)

驼鸟⑩ ostrich
食肉鸟 bird of prey

爪⑪ claw
鹰爪 talons
蹼足⑫ webbed foot
哺乳动物纲 Class Mammalia
毛 hair
毛皮 fur
汗腺 sweat gland
皮脂腺 sebaceous gland
乳腺 mammary gland
乳头 nipple, teat
肺 lung
膈 diaphragm
双循环 double circulation
左动脉弓 left systemic arch
异形齿 heterodont teeth
两次生齿的 diphyodont
双后头髁 double occipital condyle
骨化中心 centre of ossification
外耳壳 external ear, finna
脑半球 cerebral hemisphere
胎生 viviparity

胎生动物　viviparous animal
子宫　womb
有袋哺乳动物　mausupial,
　　pouched mammal

袋鼠① 　kangaroo
林栖的　arboreal
夜出的　nocturnal
蝙蝠　bat
感音器　sonar
翅膜　patagium

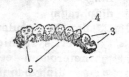

獠牙②　tusk
门齿③　incisor
犬齿④　canine tooth
臼齿⑤　molar
前臼齿　premolar
啮齿动物　rodent

穿山甲(鲮鲤)⑥　pangolin
有蹄动物　ungulate

角⑦　horn

茸角⑧　antler
角蛋白　keratin
指甲(趾甲、嚓甲)　nail
四足动物　quadrupedal
　　animal, quadruped
双足走路习惯　bipedal habit
灵长类　primates
鬼狒　drill

| | |
|---|---|
| 山魈⑨ mandrill | 大猩猩 gorilla |
| 狒狒 baboon | 单配偶动物 monogamous animal |
| 类人猿 anthropoid ape, man-like ape | 多配偶动物 polygamous animal |
| 长臂猿 gibbon | |

# 生态学 Ecology

| | |
|---|---|
| 森林生态学 forest ecology | 陆地生态学 terrestrial ecology |
| 动态生态学 dynamic ecology | |
| 群落生态学 synecology | 港湾生态学 estuarine ecology |
| 昆虫生态学 insect ecology | |
| 鸟类生态学 bird ecology | 溪流生态学 stream ecology |
| 海洋生态学 marine ecology | 草地生态学 grassland ecology |
| 淡水生态学 fresh water ecology | 个体生态学 autecology |
| | 古生态学 palaecology |

## 人类生态学 Human Ecology

| | |
|---|---|
| 人类社会 human community | 社会形态学 social morphology |
| 社会 society | |
| 社会组织形式 pattern of social organization | 政治制度 political institution |
| | 政体 polity, system of government |
| 社会制度 social system | |
| 原始社会 primitive society | 政府 government |
| 阶级社会 class society | 权力所在地 locus of authority |
| 奴隶制度 slavery | 政权 state power |
| 封建制度 feudalism | 国家 state, country |
| 资本主义制度 capitalist system | 阶层 stratum |
| | 阶级 class |
| 社会主义制度 socialist system | 资产阶级 bourgeoisie |
| 共产主义制度 communist system | 小资产阶级 petty bourgeoisie |
| | 无产阶级 proletariat |

工人阶级　working class
农民　peasantry
地主阶级　landlord class
阶级斗争　class struggle
生产斗争　struggle for production
科学试验　scientific experiment
人在自然的地位　man's place in nature
改造自然　transformation of nature, transforming nature
适应方式　mode of adaptation
人种论　ethnography
部落　tribe
少数民族　minority nationality
民族　nation
家庭　family
家属关系结构　kinship structure
住宅区　settlement unit
人口聚集　aggregation of population
人口生态学　population ecology
出生率　natality, birth rate
死亡率　mortality, death rate
人口增长　population growth
人口增长决定因素　determinant of population growth
农业人口　agricultural population
工业人口　industrial population
人口规模　population size
人口密度　density of population

tion
人口稀少　underpopulation
人口过剩　overpopulation
计划生育　family planning
节制生育　birth control
人口突增　population explosion
人口可容量　population potential
最适宜的人口　optimal population
人口循环　population cycle
人口平衡　population equilibrium
人口调查　census
人口普查　taking a census
人口统计学　demography
人类地理分布学　anthropography
生活方式　way of life
农村生活方式　rural mode of existence, rural style of life
城市生活方式　urban mode of existence
当代大城市社会　contemporary metropolitan community
城市社会学　urban sociology
经济活动　economic activity
社会分工　social division of labour
生产　production
生产劳动　productive labour
生产力　productivity
生产方式　mode of production
生产关系　relations of production
生产资料　means of production
生产资料所有制　ownership of

the means of production

生活资料 means of livelihood, means of subsistence

生活必需品 subsistence needs, necessities of life

文明 civilization
创造 creation
发现 discovery
发明 invention
开发(发展) development
技术革新 technical innovation
工业化 industrialization
现代化 modernization
革命化 revolutionization
城市化 urbanization
污染 pollution
环境公害 environmental hazard

环境污染 environmental pollution

环境 environment

自然环境 natural environment

人类同环境的斗争 man's struggle with his environment

保护自然环境 preservation of the natural environment

植物覆盖率 rate of plant coverage, rate of vegetation

水土保持 conservation of soil and water

造林 forestation

重新造林 reforestation, reafforestation

自然保护区 nature reserve

## 动物生态学 Animal Ecology (Zooecology)

共生 symbiosis
共栖 messmatism
蛰伏(休眠) dormancy
休眠期 resting period
冬眠(冬蛰) hibernation, winter sleep
冬眠场所(越冬巢) hibernaculum
夏眠 aestivation, estivation
夏眠场所 estivaculum
季节调整 seasonal adjustment
空中调整 aerial adjustment
水中调整 aquatic adjustment
陆上调整 terrestrial adjustment
空中呼吸 respiration in air
水中呼吸 respiration in water
特化适应性 specialized adaptation

专化特性 specialized feature
生态平衡 ecological balance
种间关系 interspecies relation
生物量 biomass
食物链(营养链) vegetative chain
植食性 herbivorous character
肉食性(捕食性) carnivorous character (predacity)
多食性(泛食性,杂食性) polyphagia
腐食性 saprophagous character
单食性(寡食性) monophagous character
动物区系 fauna

动物群落　zoocoenosis, zoo-
biocoenose, zoocoenosium

大生物群落　macrofauna,
macrobiocoenosium

顶极　apical pole

周期变形　periodical meta-
morphosis

种群生长型　growth form of
population

复苏现象　resurgence

风土驯化　acclimation

生态气候　ecological climate

生态价(生态值)　ecological
value

动物性极　animal pole

动物地理学　zoogeography

动物地理区　zoogeographical
region

生境　habitat

小生境　microhabitat

生态小生境　ecological niche

生境变坏(生境退化)　habitat
deterioration

地理宗(地理亚种)　geographic
race

生态宗　ecological race

本地种(地方种)　aboriginal
species

固有种　autochthonous species

迁入种　ecdemic species

迁移(迁徙,洄游)　migration

广温性生物　eurythermal
organism

广温动物　eurythermal
(animal)

广盐性生物　euryhalin(e)
organism

广生性动物(广适性动物)　eury-
topic animal

广分布种　eurytopic species

永久留兽　permanent
resident

永久群落　permanent
community

大洋动物　pelagic fauna

海底动物区系　bottom fauna

留鸟　resident bird

漂鸟　wandering bird

候鸟　migratory bird, bird of
passage

冬候鸟　winter resident

旅鸟　travelling bird

迷鸟　stray bird

移栖　migration

洄游鱼　migratory fish

迁徙区　zone of migration

大陆漂移说　theory of conti-
nental drift

南陆区(南极区)　Antarctic
realm

新陆区　New Continental
realm

北寒带　Frigid zone

澳大利西亚区(澳大利亚区)
Australasian region
(Australian region)

热带区(埃塞俄比亚区)　tropical
realm (Ethiopian realm)

新热带区　New Tropical
realm, neotropical region

东洋区(东方区)　Oriental
realm, oriental region

新北区　neoarctic realm,
nearctic region

古北区　palaeoarctic realm,
palaearctic region

区系简化　faunal simplifica-
tion

物质和生物环境 **physical and biotic environments**

生理要求 **physiological requirement**

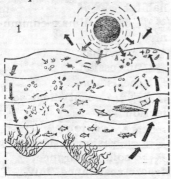

海洋食物循环① **marine food cycle**

太阳能 **solar energy**

浮游植物 **phytoplankton**

光 **light**

热 **heat**

浮游动物 **zooplankton**

浮游动物以浮游植物为食物 **zooplankton feeds on phytoplankton**

鲸鱼和鱼类以浮游动物和浮游植物为食物 **Whales and fish feed on zooplankton and phytoplankton**

深海无光地区 **abysmal region (lightless)**

营养盐 **nutrient salt**

营养化学物 **nutrient chemical**

演替原理 **principle of succession**

自然地理演替 **physiographic succession**

生物演替 **biotic succession**

光底(发端)期 **bare bottom (pioneer) stage**

沉水植被 **submerged vegetation**

浮现植被 **emerging vegetation**

山毛榉和枫树林(演替顶极)期 **beech and maple forest (climax) stage**

趋同现象 **convergence**

趋同现象原理 **principle of convergence**

## 植物生态学 Plant Ecology (Phytoecology)

生态环境 **ecological condition, ecotope**

生态幅度 **ecologic(al) range**

生态分布 **ecological distribution**

生活型 **life form**

植被型 **vegetation form**

生态型 **ecotype**

生态种 **eco-species**

生态系统 **ecosystem**

植被 **vegetation, vegetation cover**

草本植被 **herbosa**

沼泽植被 **swamp vegetation**

荒漠植被 **desert vegetation, eremo-vegetation**

自然植被 **natural vegetation**

地面植被(地被) **ground layer, ground vegetation**

木本植被 **lignosa**

针叶林 **forest of conifer species**

落叶林 **deciduous forest**

温带落叶林 **temperate decidu-**

ous forest
泰加林(泰加群落) taiga
阔叶林 broad-leaved forest
常绿阔叶林(照叶林) evergreen broad-leaved forest
常绿季雨林 evergreen seasonal forest
苔原 tundra
赤道雨林 equatorial rain forest
雨绿林 hiemisilvae
丛林 jungle
季雨林 seasonal rain forest, monsoon forest
防风林 windbreak forest
多层林 polylayer forest
红树林 mangrove
草原 grassland
热带草原 tropical grassland
草甸 meadow
草地 grassland
热带雨林 tropical rain forest
植物群落 phytocommunity, phytocoenosium, botanical colony
小植物群落 plantlet community
残留种 deleted species
世界种 world species
特有种(特产种) endemic species
偶见种 rare species
亚优生种 sub-dominant species
优势种 dominant species
休眠 dormancy, quiescence
样方 quadrat
植被〔类型〕图 vegetation chart

生态系统 ecosystem
生态系列 ecological spectrum
演替系列 succession spectrum
演替环境 successional habitat
演替顶极群落 climax community
演替顶极 climax
演替 succession
定居 ecesis
生态变种选择 ecotypical selection
群落交错区 ecotone
耐磨性 abrasion resistance
耐寒性 cold endurance, freeze resistance, low-temperature resistance
耐病性 disease tolerance
耐荫性 shade tolerance
耐旱性 drought hardiness
耐雨性 rain fastness
向食性 sitotropism
向湿性 hygrotropism
趋湿性 hygrotaxis
向水性 hydrotropism
向地性 geotropism
向光性 phototropism
向气性(向氧性) aerotropism
向日性 heliotropism
向性 tropism
抗滑性 skid resistance
抗风性 wind resistance
野生性 wildness
生境因素 site factor
生境型 site type
森林生境 site
集群 colony
植物类群 phyto-group
植物群丛复合体 association

complex
演替植物群丛 associes
复合群丛 multiple association
植物群丛 plant association

群丛 association
稀疏群系 open formation
群系 formation
植物区系 flora

# 生物化学 Biochemistry

有机生物化学 organic bio-
  chemistry
有机矿物 organic mineral
有机磷化物 organic phospho-
  rous compound
碳水化合物 carbohydrate
多糖 polysaccharide, polysac-
  charose
葡萄糖 glucose
右旋糖 dextrose
果糖 fructose
核糖 ribose
糖甙(配糖体) glucoside
蔗糖 cane sugar
麦芽糖 maltose, malt sugar
乳糖 lactose
乳糖酶 lactase, milk sugar
糊粉 aleurone
糊精 dextrin, starch gum
糊精酶 dextrinase
果胶 pectin
淀粉 starch
淀粉胶 amylan
淀粉酶 amylase
纤维素 cellulose
纤维蛋白(纤维朊) fibrin

纤维蛋白原(纤维朊原) fibrino-
  gen
丝〔心〕蛋白(丝纤朊) fibroin
糖元(动物淀粉) glycogen, ani-
  mal starch
氨基糖 aminosugar
葡聚糖 dextran
脂肪(真脂) fat
脂肪粒 fat granule
脂肪蛋白 lipoprotein
醛 aldehyde
醛固酮(醛甾酮) aldosterone
脂肪族化合物 aliphatic com-
  pound, fatty compound
脂肪酸 fatty acid
棕榈酸(软脂酸) palmitic acid
硬脂酸(油脂酸) stearic acid
葡萄糖酸 gluconic acid
叶酸 folic acid
乳酸 lactic acid
草酸 oxalic acid
磷脂 phosphatide
谷氨酸 glutamic acid
氨基酸 amino acid
胆酸 bile acid
甾族化合物(类固醇) steroid

甾醇(固醇) sterol

麦角甾醇(麦角固醇) ergosterol

谷甾醇 sitosterol

胆甾醇(胆固醇) cholesterol

肌醇 inositol

精氨酸 arginine

丙氨酸 alanine

多肽 polypeptide

杆菌肽 bacitracin

蛋白质 protein

白蛋白 albumin

糖蛋白 glycoprotein, glucoprotein

脂蛋白 lipoprotein

核蛋白 nucleoprotein (NP)

球蛋白 globulin

蛋白酶 proteinase

胆红素 bilirubin

胆绿素 biliverdin

血红素 heme

肌球蛋白 myosin

肌动蛋白 actin

卵白蛋白 egg albumin (EA)

精朊 protamin

乳蛋白 lacto-protein

乳白朊 lactalbumin

血浆蛋白 plasma proteins

胨 peptone

胶体(胶质) colloid

等电点 isoelectric point

电泳 electrophoresis

氢键 hydrogen bond

变性作用 denaturalization

核酸 nucleic acid

核糖核酸 ribonucleic acid (RNA)

正常核糖核酸 normal ribonucleic acid

脱氧核糖核酸 de(s)oxyribonucleic acid (DNA)

核糖〔核蛋白〕体 ribosome

核苷酸 nucleotide

多核苷酸 polynucleotide

核苷 nucleoside

嘌呤 purine

嘧啶(间二氮苯) pyrimidine

嘧啶化合物 pyrimidine compound

脒 amidine

醚 ether

酶 enzyme

生物氧化 biological oxidation

细胞色素 cytochrome

转氨酶 transaminase

酚酶 phenolase

激活作用 activation

抑制作用 inhibition, inhibitory action

解脂作用 hydrolysis of fat, lipolysis

新陈代谢 metabolism

同化代谢 assimilation

组成代谢 anabolism

分解代谢 catabolism

生物合成 biosynthesis

生物测定(生物检定) bioassay

解毒作用 antidotal action

尿素 urea, carbamide

尿酸 uric acid

糖化作用 saccharification

抗代谢物 antimetabolite

维生素 vitamin

激素 hormone

甲状腺素 thyroxine

胰岛素 insulin

肾上腺素 adrenalin, epinephrin

雄性激素 androgen, male

hormone
雌性激素 estrogen, female hormone
前列腺素 prostaglandin
抗体 antibody
抗体生成 antibody formation

蛋白质密码学 protein crypto-graphy
促性腺激素 gonadotrop(h)in
催产素(放乳激素) oxytocin (let-down hormone)

# 生物物理学 Biophysics

放射生物学(辐射生物学) radio-biology, radiation biology
分子生物学 molecular biology
生物力学 biomechanics
生物动力学 biodynamics
致死量(致死剂量) lethal dosage, lethal dose
半致死量(半数致死剂量) half lethal dose (HLD), median lethal dose, lethal dose50 (LD50)
最小致死量(最小致死剂量) min-imal lethal dose, minimum lethal dose (MLD)
示踪元素 tracer element
示踪原子 tracer atom
同位素标记法 isotope labell-ing method
渗入作用 infiltration
渗透分析(渗析) dialysis
冷冻真空干燥(冻干) vacuum freeze-drying
离子运转 ion revolution
生物电流 bioelectric current

生物电势 bioelectric poten-tial, biopotential
生物发光现象 biological lu-minescence
生物高分子 biological high polymer
荧光计 fluorometer, fluori-meter
高空恐怖 aerophobia
动作电流 action current
致死基因 lethal gene
致死突变 lethal mutation
光适应 light adaptation
暗视野显微镜 dark-field mi-croscope
光生物学 photobiology
生物声学 bioacoustics
生物电 bioelectricity
生物电子学 bioelectronics
生物电源 biogalvanic source
生物宇宙航行学 biocosmonaut-ics
生物工程学 bioengineering
助听器 acouophone, hearing

| | |
|---|---|
| aid | effect |
| 人造器官 artificial organ | 磁生物学 magnetobiology |
| 人造耳 artificial ear, bionic ear | 动物磁性 zoomagnetism |
| 人造眼 visilog | 生物发光 bioluminescence |
| 人造心脏 artificial heart | 生物钟 biological clock |
| 人造动脉 artificial artery | 生物运动摄影术 biography |
| 人造肺 artificial lung | 失重 weightlessness |
| 人造肾 artificial kidney | 语音打字机 voice actuated typewriter |
| 人造臂(假臂) artificial arm | 语音合成器 voder |
| 人造腿(假腿) artificial leg | 自动语音合成仪(音码器) vocoder |
| 人造牙(假牙) artificial tooth | 语音控制器 voice controller |
| 人造喉 artificial larynx | 静脉波图 venogram |
| 人造细胞 artificial cell | 脉搏描记图 arteriograph |
| 人工呼吸器 biomotor, spirophore | 心电场 cardioelectric field, cardiac electric field |
| 仿生学 bionics | 心音图 cardiophonogram |
| 仿生自动机 bio-robot | 心脏起搏器 cardiac pacemaker |
| 生物环境调节技术 biotronics | 心动图 cardiogram |
| 生物宇航试验 biological space probe | 心电图 electrocardiogram (ECG) |
| 载生物卫星 biosatellite | 心电学 elecyrocardiology |
| 生物磁效应 biomagnetic | |

# 考古学 Archaeology

## 古动物 Ancient Animals

| | |
|---|---|
| 恐龙 dinosaur | 马门溪龙 Mamenchisaurus |

| 梁龙① | diplodocus | 剑齿虎⑦ | sabre-toothed tiger |
|---|---|---|---|
| 雷龙 | brontosaur(us) | 乳齿象 | mastodon |
| 霸王龙 | tyrannosaur(us) | 始祖象 | moerithere |
| 禄丰龙② | Lufengosaurus | 剑齿象 | stegodon |
| 青岛龙③ | Qingdaosaurus | 猛犸⑧ | mammoth |
| 剑龙 | stegosaur | 始祖马⑨ | hyracothere |
| 甲龙 | ankylosaur | 三趾马 | hipparion |
| 蛇颈龙④ | plesiosaurus | 爪蹄兽 | chalicothere |
| 鱼龙 | ichthyosaur | 雷兽 | brontothere |
| 翼指龙 | pterodactyl | 板齿犀 | elasmothere |
| 准噶尔翼龙⑤ | Dsungaripterus | 披毛犀⑩ | woolly rhinoceros |
| 始祖鸟⑥ | archaeopteryx | 大角鹿⑪ | megaloceros |
| 古鸟 | archaeornis | 洞穴鬣狗 | cave hyena |
| 洞熊 | cave bear | 化石 | fossil |
| 洞狮 | cave lion | | |

## 人类进化　Evolution of Man

森林古猿　**Dryopithecus**
西瓦古猿　**Sivapithecus**
拉玛古猿　**Ramapithecus**
(非洲)南方古猿　**Australopith-**
　**ecus**
傍人　**Paranthropus**
迩人　**Plesianthropus**
东非人　**Zinjanthropus**
巨猿　**Gigantopithecus**
中国猿人　**Sinanthropus**
元谋人　**Yuanmou man**

1　　2

蓝田人①　**Lantian man**
北京人②　**Beijing man**
直立猿人(爪哇人)　**Pithecan-**
　**thropus erectus (Java man)**
非洲猿人　**Africanthropus**
弗洛里斯巴德人　**Florisbad**
　**man**

罗得西亚人　**Rhodesian man**
海德堡人　**Heidelberg man**
原始人　**primitive man**
古人　**Paleoanthropus**
尼安德特人　**Neanderthal man**
马坝人　**Maba man**
长阳人　**Changyang man**
丁村人　**Dingcun man**
梭罗人　**Solo man**
博斯科普人　**Boskop man**
新人　**Neoanthropus**
瓦贾克人　**Wadjak man**
奥瑞纳人　**Aurignacian man**
克罗马努人　**Cro-Magnon man**
河套人　**Hetao man**
山顶洞人　**Shandingdong man**
柳江人　**Liujiang man**
资阳人　**Ziyang man**
麒麟山人　**Qilinshan man**
格里马尔迪人　**Grimaldi man**
桑地亚人　**Sandia man**
福尔索姆人　**Folsom man**
人种　**race**
蒙古人种　**Mongoloid**
尼格罗人种　**Negroid**
欧罗巴人种(高加索人种)　**Euro-**
　**poid (Caucasoid)**

## 文化遗存　Cultural Remains

石器时代　**Stone Age**
石器　**stone tool, stone**
　**implement**
砾石石器　**pebble tool**
石核石器　**core tool**

石片石器　**flake tool**
尖状器　**point**
砍砸器　**blade**
刮削器　**scraper**
雕刻器　**graver**

钻孔器　borer, perforator
手斧　hand ax(e)

石锛③　stone adz(e)
磨光燧石镞　polished flint arrowhead
细石器④　microlith
角器　horn tool
(鹿角制成的)指挥棒　baton de commandement
骨器　bone tool
鱼叉⑤　harpoon
投矛器　spear thrower
曙石器　eolith
旧石器　paleolith
新石器　neolith
曙石器时代　Eolithic Age
旧石器时代　Paleolithic Age
中石器时代　Mesolithic Age
新石器时代　Neolithic Age
新石器时代早期文化　early Neolithic culture
新石器时代中期文化　mid-Neolithic culture
新石器时代晚期文化　late Neolithic culture
仰韶文化　Yangshao culture
马家窑文化　Majiayao culture
大汶口文化　Dawenkou culture
青莲岗文化　Qingliangang culture

屈家岭文化　Qujialing culture
齐家文化　Qijia culture
龙山文化　Longshan culture
良渚文化　Liangzhu culture
细石器文化　microlithic culture
典型遗址　type station, type site
发掘　excavation
遗骸　skeletal remains
器物　artifact
半地穴式房屋　pit house
(巴基斯坦)索安文化　Soan culture
(缅甸)安雅特文化　Anyathian culture
(越南)和平文化　Hoa Binh culture
(越南)北山文化　Bac Son culture
(巴勒斯坦)那图夫文化　Natufian culture
(欧洲)阿布维尔文化(舍利义化)　Abbevillian culture (Chellean culture)
(欧洲)阿修尔文化　Acheulean culture
(欧洲)穆斯特文化　Mousterian culture
(欧洲)奥瑞纳文化　Aurignacian culture
(欧洲)梭鲁特文化　Solutrean culture
(欧洲)马格德林文化　Magdalenian culture
(欧洲)阿齐尔文化　Azilian culture
(欧洲)塔登诺阿文化　Tardenoisian culture

138

(美洲)桑地亚文化　Sandia culture
(美洲)福尔索姆文化　Folsom culture
大石文化　megalithic culture
大石　megalith
独石　monolith, menhir

大石棚(支石墓)①　dolmen
图腾　totem
洞画　cave painting
岩画　rock picture
石刻书画　petroglyph, petrograph

金石并用时代　Aeneolithic Age
青铜器时代　Bronze Age
殷墟　Waste of Yin
卜骨　oracle bone
龟甲　tortoise shell
卜辞　oracular inscription
(印度河流域)哈拉帕文化　Harappa culture
摩亨约—达罗　Mohenjo-daro
(欧洲)米诺斯文化　Minoan culture
(欧洲)迈锡尼文化　Mycenaean culture
(两河流域)乌鲁克文化　Uruk culture
(越南)东山文化　Dong Son culture
木乃伊　mummy
罗塞达碑　Rosetta stone
铁器时代　Iron Age

# 空间技术　Space Technology

## 航　天　Space Flight

宇宙空间　space
近地空间　terrestrial space
外层空间　outer space
地月间空间　cislunar space
行星际空间　interplanetary space
行星〔轨道〕外空间　extra-planetary space
恒星际空间　interstellar space
星系际空间(银河际空间)　inter-

galactic space

空间探测 space exploration

空间探测器 space probe

装备测量仪表的空间探测器 instrumented space probe

航天器 spacecraft, space vehicle

载人航天 manned space flight (navigation)

航天员(宇航员) astronaut, (USSR) cosmonaut

航天服 spacesuit

引力范围 gravisphere

地球重力场 gravitational field of the Earth

轨道速度(环绕速度) orbital velocity (circular velocity)

分离速度 separation velocity

逃逸速度 escape velocity

宇宙火箭 cosmic rocket

(火箭)点火试车 test firing

发射 launching

离地直升 lift-off

发射场 launch(ing) site

发射台 launch(ing) pad

发射塔 launch(ing) tower

发射井 silo

加速阶段 boost period

动力飞行阶段 powered period

惯性飞行阶段 coasting period

初始加速度 initial acceleration

最大加速度 peak acceleration

飞出大气层 exit from the atmosphere

(由发射轨道进入飞行轨道的)转向 doglegging

航天轨道② space-flight trajectory

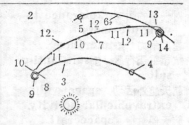

出发行星的轨道③ path of departure planet

出发行星的最终位置④ final position of departure planet

目的行星的初始位置⑤ initial position of target planet

目的行星的轨道⑥ path of target planet

行星际过渡轨道⑦ interplanetary transfer trajectory

上升到驻留轨道⑧ ascending and attaining parking orbit

驻留轨道上惯性飞行⑨ coasting in parking orbit

进入行星际过渡轨道⑩ going into interplanetary transfer trajectory

行星际过渡轨道上惯性飞行⑪ coasting in interplanetary transfer trajectory

临时校正轨道的飞行动作⑫ occasional trajectory correction manoeuvres

到达新的驻留轨道⑬ attaining new parking orbit

下降着陆⑭ descending and landing

失重 weightlessness, zero gravity

对失重的耐力　tolerance to weightlessness

超重耐力　g-tolerance

抗超重飞行服　g-suit, anti-g suit

航天舱外活动　space walk, extravehicular activity

航天器对接　spacecraft docking

会合对接　rendezvous docking

再入(重返)　reentry

利用升力再入　lifting reentry

再入热防护系统　reentry thermal protection system

减速度　deceleration

硬着陆　hard landing

软着陆　soft landing

溅落　splashdown

回收　recovery

回收系统　recovery system

航天器上的计算机　on-board computer

空间飞行器试验发射中心　spaceport

空间站①　space station

空间渡船　space shuttle

1

天空实验室　skylab

地面站　ground station

跟踪站　tracking station

光跟踪　optical tracking

光传感器　optical sensor

电子跟踪　electronic tracking

跟踪〔问答〕信标　tracking beacon

米尼跟踪系统(干涉仪跟踪系统,飞行器载无线电跟踪装置)　minitrack

干涉仪　interferometer

空间探测跟踪系统　space detection and tracking system (SPADATS)

## 宇宙飞船　Spaceship

航天封舱　space capsule

适配舱　adapter module

服务舱　service module

指挥舱　command module

登月舱　lunar module

蜂窝夹层板　honeycomb sandwich panel

高温材料　high-temperature material

超合金　superalloy

耐火合金　refractory alloy

微粒辐射　corpuscular radiation

宇宙辐射　cosmic radiation

辐射防护屏　radiation shield

烧蚀　ablation

抗热层　heat shield

热沉(吸热器)　heat sink

蒸发冷却　transpiration cooling

热耗散  heat dissipation
运载火箭  carrier rocket, launch vehicle
多级火箭  multistage rocket
助推  boost
助推火箭  booster rocket

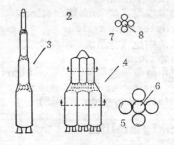

助推器系统②  booster system
串联式系统③  tandem system
簇式系统④  clustered system
第一级⑤  first stage
第二级⑥  second stage
第三级⑦  third stage
第四级⑧  fourth stage
级间结构  interstage structure
主级火箭  sustainer rocket
减速火箭(制动火箭)  retrorocket (braking rocket)
微调火箭  vernier rocket
速度调整  velocity adjustment
(推进剂箱中的)气垫  ullage
气垫增压火箭  ullage rocket
过氧化氢火箭  hydrogen peroxide rocket
姿态控制  attitude control
火箭推进  rocket propulsion
火箭推进剂  rocket propellant
单组元推进剂  monopropellant
双组元推进剂  bipropellant
液体推进剂  liquid propellant

固体推进剂  solid propellant
燃料  fuel
氧化剂  oxidizer
添加剂  additive
推力  thrust
火箭发动机  rocket engine, rocket motor

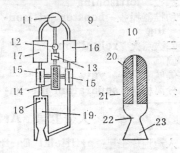

液体〔推进剂〕火箭发动机⑨  liquid-propellant rocket engine
固体〔推进剂〕火箭发动机⑩  solid-propellant rocket engine
低压容器⑪  low pressure vessel
过氧化氢箱⑫  hydrogen peroxide tank
气体发生器⑬  gas generator
燃气涡轮(燃气透平)⑭  gas turbine
推进剂泵⑮  propellant pump
燃料箱⑯  fuel tank
氧化剂箱⑰  oxidizer tank
喷嘴⑱  injector
推力室⑲  thrust chamber
推进剂⑳  propellant
外壳㉑  case
喉道㉒  throat
喷管㉓  nozzle

万向〔悬挂式〕发动机　gimbaled engine, gimbal-mounted engine

有效载荷　payload

发动机关闭　shutdown

熄火时〔飞行〕速度　burnout velocity, all-burnt velocity

抛投　jettisoning

助推器抛投　booster jettisoning

二次点火　reignition

偏航　yaw

偏航阻尼器　yaw damper

分离机构　separation mecha-nism, kickoff mechanism

分离速度　separation velocity

制导系统　guidance system

全惯性制导系统　all-inertial guidance system

滚动俯仰程序机构　roll and pith programmer

故障探测系统　malfunction detection system

紧急中止飞行系统　abort system

空中故障传感和处理系统　abort sensing and implemen-tation system (ASIS)

## 人造卫星　Artificial Satellite

人造地球卫星　artificial Earth satellite

主星〔体〕　primary (body)

科学〔研究〕卫星　scientific research satellite

应用技术卫星　applications technology satellite

大地测量卫星　geodesic satel-lite

有源卫星　active satellite

无源卫星　passive satellite

上升弹道　ascent trajectory

送入轨道　injecting into orbit

极轨道　polar orbit

赤道轨道　equatorial orbit

同步轨道　synchronous orbit, geostationary orbit

转移到同步轨道　transferring into synchronous orbit

初始近地点　initial perigee

初始远地点　initial apogee

最大远地点　peak apogee

远地点〔起动〕发动机　apogee motor

〔卫星〕最后定位　final posi-tioning

轨道平面　orbital plane

轨道倾角　orbit inclination

轨道参数　orbital parameters

轨道周期　orbital period

大气阻力　atmospheric drag

轨道衰减　orbital decay

卫星寿命　satellite lifetime

仪器组件　instrument package

子系统技术　subsystem technology

恒星传感器　star sensor

红外线水平传感器　infrared horizon sensor

太阳传感器　sun sensor

太阳电池　solar cell

太阳电池板　solar panel

火花室　spark chamber

旋转〔控制〕喷管　spin nozzle

旋转稳定　spin stabilization

冷气稳定系统　cold gas sta-

bilization system
消〔自〕转 despinning
全向天线系统 omnidirectional antenna system
遥测天线 telemetry antenna
遥测资料 telemetry data
双道辐射计 bi-channel radiometer
扫描微波辐射计 scanning microwave radiometer
反符合计数器 anticoincidence counter
γ射线望远镜 gamma-ray telescope
阻抗探测器 impedance probe

测量电子密度 measuring electron density
紫外线分光仪 ultraviolet spectrometer
测度太阳辐射强度 measuring the intensity of solar radiation
测量太阳中子发射 measuring solar neutron emission
测量太阳γ发射 measuring solar gamma emission
测量电离层参数 measuring ionospheric parameters
地球资源勘测 Earth resources survey

# 环境科学 Environmental Science

## 环境问题 Environmental Problems

无计划的发展 random development
邻近市镇的合并 merging of neighbouring towns
集合城市 conurbation
中心城市的扩展 expansion of central city
超级城市 supercity
一系列的集合城市 series of conurbations

城市密布的地区 region densely scattered with cities
特大都市群 megalopolis
都市化程度 degree of urbanization
自然规模(占地面积) physical size (area covered)
城市改造 reforming of cities
重建市区 urban renewal
扩展郊区 suburban sprawl

人口规模　population size
人口密度　population density
布局　layout
市区　urban area
市中心　town centre
行政中心　administrative centre
工业区　industrial area
商业区　commercial area
住宅区　residential area
贫民窟　slum
木屋区　shantytown
环境损害　environmental damage
矿物燃料　fossil fuels
二氧化碳的释放　release of carbon dioxide
二氧化碳在大气中的积聚　accumulation of carbon dioxide in the atmosphere
逆温　temperature inversion
逆温层　inversion layer
温室效应　greenhouse effect
红外线放射的障碍　barrier to infrared radiation
上层大气的温度上升　temperature rise in the upper atmosphere
不完全燃烧　incomplete combustion
未燃烧的碳氢化合物　unburned hydrocarbons
微粒物质　particulate matter
气溶胶　aerosol
有毒的烟雾　toxic smog
过乙酰硝酸酯　peroxyacetyl nitrate (PAN)
污水污染　sewage pollution

未经处理的污水　untreated sewage
养分过多　eutrophication, excessive fertilization
有害的藻类大量滋长　rank growth of harmful algae
工厂化的农场经营　factory farming
农药的滥用　indiscriminate use of pesticides
空中喷洒　aerial spraying
农药污染　pesticide pollution
废热　waste heat
热污染　thermal pollution
(对鱼类)氧气供应的减少　reduction of oxygen supply (to fish)
油污染　oil pollution
噪音污染　noise pollution
核发电厂的废物　waste from nuclear power station
放射性公害　radioactive hazard
生命层(生物圈)　biosphere
自然环境　natural cycle
再循环　recycling
食物链　food chain
降解　degradation
生物可以降解的物质　biodegradable substance
生物不能降解的物质　nonbiodegradable substance
野生动物绝种　extinction of wild animals
(居民)逃离市区　escape from urban areas
遁逃城市的形成　creation of escape cities

## 环境保护  Environmental Protection

环境保护论者  environmentalist

环境控制  environmental control

环境卫生  environmental health, environmental hygiene

城市规划  city planning

以人为尺度的规划  planning on the human scale

环境美化  landscaping

花园城市  garden city

房屋密布区  built-up area

绿化区  green area

街坊  neighbourhood

街坊活动中心  neighbourhood centre

人车分道  separation of pedestrians from automobiles

禁止行车的林荫小道  pedestrian mall

减少拥塞  decongestion

徙置计划  rehousing program-(me)

住宅新村  housing estate, housing development

市郊  city outskirts

城市近郊住宅区  suburbs

城市远郊住宅区  exurbs

市郊商店区  shopping centre

城乡边缘地带  rural-urban fringe

城乡结合  integration of town and country

聚居型式  settlement pattern

集结村落  nucleated rural settlement

分散村落  dispersed rural settlment

空旷地区  open space

重新造林  reforestation

废物处理  waste disposal

空气污染控制  air pollution control

黑烟的减少  dark smoke reduction

闭循环式焚化炉  closed cycle incinerator

空气检验  air monitoring

水污染控制  water pollution control

污水处理区  sewage disposal area

污水处理工厂  sewage plant

(下水道)出口地点的选定  siting of outfall

离子交换法  ion exchange method

逆渗透  reverse osmosis

电渗析  electrodialysis

水质检验  water quality monitoring

噪音控制  noise control

隔声  sound insulation

减震  vibration damping

消音器  silencer

农业废物还田  return of farm wastes to the land

# 小型化 Miniaturization

## 小型化设计 Miniaturization Design

减轻重量 reducing the weight

减小体积 reducing the volume

减少组件数目 reducing the number of components

减少动力消耗量 reducing power consumption

减少焊接 reducing the number of soldered connections

提高设备的可靠性 increasing the reliability of equipment

组件设计 component design

模拟板(试验板) breadboard

模拟设计 breadboard design

微型化 microminiaturization

微程序 microprogram

微程序设计 microprogramming

微型逻辑 micrologic

微矩阵 micromatrix

## 微型电路 Microcircuit

印刷电路 printed circuit

印刷线路板 printed wiring board

绝缘基体 insulating base

掩模 mask

蚀刻(腐蚀) etching

光刻 photoetching

光致抗蚀剂(感光胶) photoresist

腐蚀剂 etchant

导电图形 conductive pattern

薄膜 thin film

薄膜微型电路 thin-film microcircuit

基片(衬底) substrate

蒸涂 evaporation

溅射 sputtering

淀积 deposition

厚膜电路 thick-film circuit

厚膜混合集成电路 thick-film hybrid integrated circuit

陶瓷基片 ceramic substrate

丝网印刷 screen printing

烧结 firing

| | |
|---|---|
| 喷涂　spraying | module |
| 火焰喷涂　flame spraying | 铸模树脂　casting resin |
| 微型元件　microelement | 分立元件　discrete element |
| 微电子元件　microelectronic element | 内接元件　intraconnection element |
| 叠层　stacking | 外接元件　outward element |
| 互连　interconnection | 显微操作设备　micromanipu- lator |
| 埋入　potting | |
| 热固化合物　thermosetting compound | 封装　packaging |
| | 密封　encapsulation |
| 埋入的微型元件　potted micro- element | 封装电路　rescap, packaged circuit |
| 微型组件　micromodule | 多层布线　multilayer wiring |
| 堆叠式微型组件　tinkertoy | |

# 摄　影　Photography

## 摄影器材　Photographic Apparatus

| | |
|---|---|
| 照相机　camera | lens (converging lens) |
| 折合式照相机　folding camera | 负透镜(发散透镜)　negative lens (diverging lens) |
| 皮腔　(collapsible) bellows | |
| 双镜头反光式照相机　twin-lens reflex camera (TLR) | 消色差透镜　achromatic lens |
| | 复消色差透镜　apochromatic lens |
| 单镜头反光式照相机　single-lens reflex camera (SLR) | |
| | 消球差透镜　aspheric(al) lens |
| 全景照相机　panoramic camera | 分光透镜　beam-splitting lens |
| | 大孔径透镜　high-aperture lens |
| 立体照相机　stereocamera | 标准镜头　normal lens |
| 即印照相机　instant camera | 正光镜头(去象散透镜)　anastig- mat |
| 镜头(透镜)　lens | |
| 正透镜(会聚透镜)　positive | 双正光镜头　double anastigmat |

对称式镜头 symmetrical lens

非对称式镜头 asymmetric lens

三合镜头 triplet

可变焦距镜头 zoom lens

远摄镜头 telephoto lens

广角镜头 wide-angle lens

附加镜头 supplementary lens

延伸筒 extension tube

遮光罩 lens hood

滤色镜 colour filter

玻璃滤色镜 glass filter

明胶滤色镜 gelatin filter

天空滤色镜 sky filter

偏振镜 polarizing filter

滤色镜因数 filter factor

双射光组 catadioptric system

视界 coverage, covering power

光阑 diaphragm

可变光阑 iris diaphragm

焦距 focal length

超焦距 hyperfocal distance

相对口径 relative aperture

焦距比 focal ratio

光圈数 f-number

光圈数刻度 f/stop

分散光圈(模糊圈) circle of confusion (blur circle)

调焦 focusing

调焦屏 focusing screen

物距 object distance

测距器 rangefinder

截影式测距器 split-image rangefinder

双象式测距器(叠影式测距器)

double-image rangefinder

连动测距器 coupled rangefinder

取景器 viewfinder

万能取景器 universal finder

五角棱镜取景器 pentaprism finder

焦深 depth of focus

景深 depth of field

景深表 depth-of-focus scale

快门 shutter

镜中快门 between-the-lens shutter

焦面快门 focal plane shutter

电子快门 electronic shutter

快门速度 shutter speed

快门速度表 shutter speed scale

空气减震器 air damper

管件 plumbing

光电二极管 photo-diode

光发射二极管 light emitting diode (LED)

示波器接合器 oscilloscope adapter

半导体开关元件 thyristor

测光表 exposure meter

自拍器 self-timer

电子闪光器 electronic flash

反光罩 reflector

直射闪光 direct flash

反射闪光 bounce flash

附件 accessory

附件插座(蹄插) accessory shoe

通电蹄插 hot shoe

三脚架 tripod

## 拍摄和洗印　Shooting and Processing

影象　image
象距　image distance
象角　image angle
象圈　image circle
象场　image field
象场弯曲　curvature of field
象畸变　image distortion
象差　aberration
彗形象差　coma
带象差　zonal aberration
球面象差　spherical aberration
色差　chromatic aberration
焦距的色别　chromatic difference of focal length
色视差　chromatic parallax
环形效应　doughnut effect
渐晕效应　vignetting
幻象　ghost
象衬比技术　image contrast technique
感光片　sensitive plate and film
硬片　plate
软片　film
单页软片　sheet film
散页软片包　film pack
卷片　roll film, (Am.) cartridge
色盲片(无色片)　colour-blind film
分色片　ortho (chromatic) film
全色片　panchromatic film
特快全色片　ultraspeed pan
红外线片　infrared film

负片　negative film
正片　positive film
透明片　transparency
感光速度　film speed
(感光片)增速　hypersensitizing, hypersensitization
反差　contrast
反差系数极限(伽马极限)　gamma infinity
分析力　resolving power
宽容度(伸缩性)　latitude
银粒〔度〕　grain
曝光　exposure
自动曝光　automatic exposure
对数曝光　logarithm exposure
曝光不足　underexposure
曝光过度　overexposure
直射光　direct light
散漫光　diffuse light
顺光　frontlighting
侧光　sidelighting
逆光　backlighting
暗室　darkroom
潜影(潜象)　latent image
显影　developing
显影液　developer
促进剂　accelerator
保护剂　preservative
抑制剂　restrainer
停显液　stop bath
坚膜液　hardener
定影　fixing
定影液　fixing bath, fixer, fix
大苏打定影液(海波)　hypo
清晰度　definition
影调　tone

淡色调　high key
深色调　low key
明暗层次　gradation
明暗变化　chiaroscuro
灰度等级　grey scale
灰雾　fog
印相　printing
印相器　printer
相纸　printing paper
光面纸　glossy paper

半光面纸　semi-gloss paper
无光面纸　mat(te) paper
细绒面纸　semi-mat(te) paper
绸纹面纸　silk-finish paper
布纹面纸　textured paper
修版　print finishing
相片样张　proof
即印相片　instant print
放大　enlarging
放大机　enlarger

## 彩色摄影　Colour Photography

感色性　colour sensitivity
色调　hue
饱和度　saturation
亮度　brightness
原色　primary colour
红　red
绿　green
蓝　blue
补色　complementary colour
青　cyan
品红　magenta
黄　yellow
间色(二次色)　secondary col-
　our, binary colour
复色(三次色)　tertiary colour
色值　colour value
暖色　warm colour
冷色　cold colour
色温　colour temperature
色温计　colour temperature
　meter
加色法　additive process
减色法　subtractive process
分色负片　separation negative
彩色负片　colour negative
彩色反转片　colour reversal

film
彩色正片　colour positive
彩色透明正片　positive colour
　transparency
多层彩色片　multilayer colour
　film
防光晕层　antihalation back-
　ing
片基　film support, film base
底层　substratum
感红层　red-sensitive layer
感绿层　green-sensitive layer
黄滤光层　yellow filter layer
感蓝层　blue-sensitive layer
黄色影象　yellow image
品红色影象　magenta image
青色影象　cyan image
柔和滤光器　diffuse filter
紫外线滤光器　ultraviolet fil-
　ter
红外线滤光器　infrared filter
补偿滤色镜　compensating
　filter
彩色构图　colour composition
彩色和谐　colour harmony
彩色反差　colour contrast

彩色表现　colour rendition
强烈的彩色　strong colours
柔和的彩色　pastel shades
彩色平衡　colour balance
偏色　colour cast
掩色　masking
彩色改正　colour correction

二次曝光　reversal exposure
彩色显影液　colour developer
耦合剂　coupler
彩色相纸　colour paper
即取彩色照片　take-away
　colour print

## 全息摄影　Holography

气体激光全息摄影　gas laser
　holography
巨脉冲全息摄影　giant-pulse
　laser holography
光源　light source
点〔光〕源　point source
激光①　laser
平面波②　plane wave
物体③　objects
反射波④　reflected wave
摄影底片⑤　photographic
　plate
激光照射　laser illumination
全息图⑥　hologram
观察者⑦　viewer
再现象⑧　reconstructed
　image
相干性　coherence
空间相干性　space coherence
相干光　coherent light

参考镜(基准镜)　reference
　mirror
镜面反射　reflection from
　mirror
参考光束(基准光束)　reference
　beam
物体反射　reflection from
　object
球面波　spherical wave
驻波　standing wave
波列　wave train
波阵面　wavefront
干涉　interference
相长干涉　constructive inter-
　ference
相消干涉　destructive inter-
　ference
干涉图样　interference
pattern
波扰动　wave disturbance

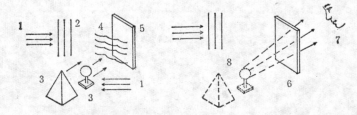

波扰动幅度　amplitude of wave disturbance

相位分布　phase distribution

光栅　raster

衍射　diffraction

缝隙衍射　diffraction by slit

波带片　wavestrip

光图象　optical image

实象　real image

虚象　virtual image

幻视象　pseudoscopic image

三维象　three-dimensional image

光全息图　optical hologram

聚焦象全息图　focused image hologram

多色全息图　multicolour hologram

非光全息图　nonoptical hologram

声全息图　acoustic hologram

微波全息图　microwave hologram

信息含量　information content

全息图再现　reconstruction of hologram

# 附 录 Appendices

## （一）袖珍数字电子计算机
## (I) Pocket-sized Digital Computer

电源开关① power switch
交流电转接器接头② AC adaptor connecting terminal
显示器③ display
键盘 keyboard
数字键④ numeral keys
十进制定点键⑤ decimal point key
四则运算键⑥ four arithmetic calculation keys
加法键 addition key
减法键 subtraction key
乘法键 multiplication key
除法键 division key
等于键(结果键) equals key
变号键⑦ change sign key
输入存储键⑧ memory-in key
取存储键⑨ recall memory key
存储累加键⑩ memory plus key
清洗键⑪ clear key
清洗输入键⑫ cleary entry key
函数键⑬ function keys
第二函数标志键⑭ second

fundtion designation key
平方根与平方键 squareroot and square key
乘方与立方根键 yˣ and cube root key
60进制与10进制换算键⑮ degree/minute/second⟷ decimal degrees conversion key
三角函数与反三角函数键 trigonometric and inverse trigonometric key
阶乘键⑯ factorial key
指数键⑰ enter exponent key
圆周率与倒数键 Pi and reciprocal key
自然对数与反对数键 natural logarithm and anti-logarithm key
常用对数与反对数键 common logarithm and anti-logarithm key
交换键⑱ exchange key
度/弧度/梯度选择器⑲ degree/radian/grad selector

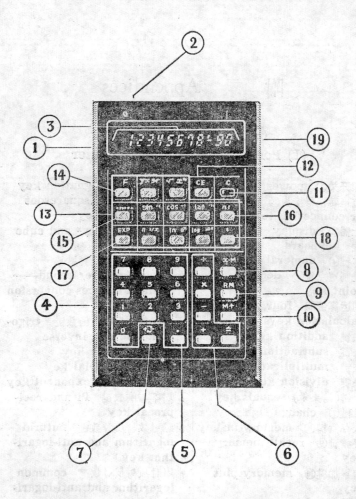

# (二)化学元素 (II) Chemical Elements

氢 hydrogen (H)
氦 helium (He)
锂 lithium (Li)
铍 beryllium (Be)
硼 boron (B)
碳 carbon (C)
氮 nitrogen (N)
氧 oxygen(O)
氟 fluorine (F)
氖 neon (Ne)
钠 sodium (Na)
镁 magnesium (Mg)
铝 aluminium (Al)
硅 silicon (Si)
磷 phosphorus (P)
硫 sulphur (S)
氯 chlorine (Cl)
氩 argon (Ar)
钾 potassium (K)
钙 calcium (Ca)
钪 scandium (Sc)
钛 titanium (Ti)
钒 vanadium (V)
铬 chromium (Cr)
锰 manganese (Mn)
铁 iron (Fe)
钴 cobalt (Co)
镍 nickel (Ni)
铜 copper (Cu)
锌 zinc (Zn)
镓 gallium (Ga)
锗 germanium (Ge)
砷 arsenic (As)
硒 selenium (Se)
溴 bromine (Br)

氪 krypton (Kr)
铷 rubidium (Rb)
锶 strontium (Sr)
钇 yttrium (Y)
锆 zirconium (Zr)
铌 niobium (Nb)
钼 molybdenum (Mo)
锝 technetium (Tc)
钌 ruthenium (Ru)
铑 rhodium (Rh)
钯 palladium (Pd)
银 silver (Ag)
镉 cadmium (Cd)
铟 indium (In)
锡 tin (Sn)
锑 antimony (Sb)
碲 tellurium (Te)
碘 iodine (I)
氙 xenon (Xe)
铯 caesium (Cs)
钡 barium (Ba)
镧 lanthanum (La)
铈 cerium (Ce)
镨 praseodymium (Pr)
钕 neodymium (Nd)
钷 promethium (Pm)
钐 samarium (Sm)
铕 europium (Eu)
钆 gadolinium (Gd)
铽 terbium (Tb)
镝 dysprosium (Dy)
钬 holmium (Ho)
铒 erbium (Er)
铥 thulium (Tm)
镱 ytterbium (Yb)

| | | | |
|---|---|---|---|
| 镥 | lutecium (Lu) | 铅 | lead (Pb) |
| 铪 | hafnium (Hf) | 铋 | bismuth (Bi) |
| 钽 | tantalum (Ta) | 钋 | polonium (Po) |
| 钨 | tungsten (W) | 砹 | astatine (At) |
| 铼 | rhenium (Re) | 氡 | radon (Rn) |
| 锇 | osmium (Os) | 钫 | francium (Fr) |
| 铱 | iridium (Ir) | 镭 | radium (Ra) |
| 铂 | platinum (Pt) | 锕 | actinium (Ac) |
| 金 | gold (Au) | 钍 | thorium (Th) |
| 汞 | mercury (Hg) | 镤 | protactinium (Pa) |
| 铊 | thallium (Tl) | 铀 | uranium (U) |

## 超铀元素  Transuranic Elements

| | | | |
|---|---|---|---|
| 镎 | neptunium (Np) | 锎 | californium (Cf) |
| 钚 | plutonium (Pu) | 锿 | einsteinium (Es) |
| 镅 | americium (Am) | 镄 | fermium (Fm) |
| 锔 | curium (Cm) | 钔 | mendelevium (Md) |
| 锫 | berkelium (Bk) | 锘 | nobelium (No) |

---

注：此表以原子序数为序。

# （三）度 量 衡 表

## （Ⅲ）Tables of Measures and Weights

### 1. 公制 The Metric System

| 类　别 Classification | 汉语名称 Chinese Name | 英　语　名　称 English Name | 缩写或符号 Abbreviation or Symbol | 对主单位的比 Ratio to the Primary Unit | 折合市制 Approximate Chinese Equivalent |
|---|---|---|---|---|---|
| 长　　　度 **Length** | 毫微米 | millimicron | mμ | 1/1,000,000,000 | |
| | 微米 | micron | μ | 1/1,000,000 | |
| | 忽米 | centimillimetre | cmm. | 1/100,000 | |
| | 丝米 | decimillimetre | dmm. | 1/10,000 | |
| | 毫米 | millimetre | mm. | 1/1,000 | |
| | 厘米 | centimetre | cm. | 1/100 | |
| | 分米 | decimetre | dm. | 1/10 | |
| | 米 | metre | m. | Primary Unit 主单位 | =3市尺 |
| | 十米 | decametre | dam. | 10 | |
| | 百米 | hectometre | hm. | 100 | |
| | 公里 | kilometre | km. | 1,000 | =2市里 |

| | 中文 | English | 缩写 | Primary Unit 主单位 | |
|---|---|---|---|---|---|
| **Area**<br>面积及地积 | 平方米 | square metre | sq.m. | Primary Unit 主单位 | =9平方市尺 |
| | 公亩 | are | a. | 100 | =0.15市亩 |
| | 公顷 | hectare | ha. | 10,000 | =15市亩 |
| | 平方公里 | square kilometre | sq.km. | 1,000,000 | =4平方市里 |
| **Weight and Mass**<br>重量和质量 | 毫克 | milligram(me) | mg. | 1/1,000,000 | |
| | 厘克 | centigram(me) | cg. | 1/100,000 | |
| | 分克 | decigram(me) | dg. | 1/10,000 | |
| | 克 | gram(me) | g. | 1/1,000 | |
| | 十克 | decagram(me) | dag. | 1/100 | |
| | 百克 | hectogram(me) | hg. | 1/10 | |
| | 公斤 | kilogram(me) | kg. | Primary Unit 主单位 | =2市斤 |
| | 公担 | quintal | q. | 100 | =200市斤 |
| | 公吨 | metric ton | MT(或t.) | 1,000 | =2,000市斤 |
| **Capacity**<br>容量 | 微升 | microlitre | μl. | 1/1,000,000 | |
| | 毫升 | millilitre | ml. | 1/1,000 | |
| | 厘升 | centilitre | cl. | 1/100 | |
| | 分升 | decilitre | dl. | 1/10 | |
| | 升 | litre | l. | Primary Unit 主单位 | =1市升 |
| | 十升 | decalitre | dal. | 10 | |
| | 百升 | hectolitre | hl. | 100 | |
| | 千升 | kilolitre | kl. | 1,000 | |

## 2. 英美制 The British and U.S. System

| 类别 Classification | 汉译 Chinese Translation | 名称 Name | 缩写 Abbreviation | 等值 Equivalent | 折合公制 Metric value |
|---|---|---|---|---|---|
| 长度 Length | 哩 | mile | mi. | 880fm. | =1.609公里 |
| | 噚 | fathom | fm. | 2yd. | =1.829米 |
| | 码 | yard | yd. | 3ft. | =0.914米 |
| | 呎 | foot | ft. | 12in. | =30.48厘米 |
| | 吋 | inch | in. | | =2.54厘米 |
| 海程长度 Nautical Measure | 海里,浬 | nautical mile | | 10cables' length | 英=1.853公里 国际海程制 =1.852公里 |
| | 链 | cable's length | | | 英=185.3米 国际海程制 =185.2米 |
| 面积及地积 Area | 平方哩 | square mile | sq. mi. | 640a. | =2.59平方公里 |
| | 英亩 | acre | a. | 4,840sq. yd. | =4,047平方米 |
| | 平方码 | square yard | sq. yd. | 9sq. ft. | =0.836平方米 |
| | 平方呎 | square foot | sq. ft. | 144sq. in. | =929平方厘米 |
| | 平方吋 | square inch | sq. in. | | =6.451平方厘米 |

## 重 量　Weight

| 类别 | 中文 | English | 略语 | 折合 | 公制 |
|---|---|---|---|---|---|
| **常衡 Avoirdupois** | 吨 | ton | tn.(英t.) | | |
| | 长吨 | long ton | | 20cwt.<br>2,240lb. | =1.016公吨 |
| | 短吨 | short ton | | 2,000lb. | =0.907公吨 |
| | 英担 | hundredweight | cwt. | 英112lb.<br>美100lb. | =50.802公斤<br>=45.359公斤 |
| | 磅 | pound | lb. | 16oz. | =0.454公斤 |
| | 盎司，啢 | ounce | oz. | 16dr. | =28.35克 |
| | 打兰，英钱 | dram | dr. | | =1.771克 |
| **金衡 Troy** | 磅 | pound | lb. t. | 12oz. t. | =0.373公斤 |
| | 盎司，啢 | ounce | oz. t. | 20dwt. | =31.103克 |
| | 英钱，喱 | pennyweight | dwt. | 24gr. | =1.555克 |
| | 谷，喱 | grain | gr. | | =64.8毫克 |
| **药衡 Apothecaries'** | 磅 | pound | lb. ap. | 12oz. ap. | =0.373公斤 |
| | 盎司，啢 | ounce | oz. ap. | 8dr. ap. | =31.103克 |
| | 打兰，英钱 | dram | dr. ap. | 3scr. ap. | =3.887克 |
| | 吩 | scruple | scr. ap. | 20gr. | =1.295克 |
| | 谷，喱 | grain | gr. | | =64.8毫克 |

| 容量 Capacity | | | | | |
|---|---|---|---|---|---|
| 干量 Dry Measure | 蒲式耳 | bushel | bu. | 4pks. | 英=36.368升<br>美=35.238升 |
| | 配克 | peck | pk. | 8qts. | 英=9.092升<br>美=8.809升 |
| | 加仑 | gallon(英)* | gal. | 4qts. | =4.546升 |
| | 夸脱 | quart | qt. | 2pts. | 英=1.136升<br>美=1.101升 |
| | 品脱 | pint | pt. | | 英=0.568升<br>美=0.55升 |
| 液量 Liquid Measure | 加仑 | gallon | gal. | 4qts. | 英=4.546升<br>美=3.785升 |
| | 夸脱 | quart | qt. | 2pts. | 英=1.136升<br>美=0.946升 |
| | 品脱 | pint | pt. | 4gi. | 英=0.568升<br>美=0.473升 |
| | 及耳 | gill | gi. | | 英=0.142升<br>美=0.118升 |

* gallon 作干量单位仅用于英制。

# 第 二 部 分

# 文 教 卫 生

## Part II

## Culture, Education and Health

# 目　录

# Contents

# 文 化 Culture

## 文艺革命 Revolution in Literature and Art

文艺应成为整个革命机器的一个组成部分 Literature and art should fit into the whole revolutionary machine as a component part

批判地继承 inheriting in a critical way

批判地吸收文学艺术遗产 critically assimilating the legacies of literature and art

古为今用, 洋为中用 Make the past serve the present and foreign things serve China.

百花齐放, 推陈出新 Let a hundred flowers blossom, weed through the old to bring forth the new.

政治和艺术的统一 unity of politics and art

内容和形式的统一 unity of content and form

革命的政治内容和尽可能完美的艺术形式的统一 unity of revolutionary political content and the highest possible perfection of artistic form

革命现实主义和革命浪漫主义相结合 combining (integrating) revolutionary realism with revolutionary romanticism

歌颂工农兵英雄 eulogizing worker, peasant and soldier heroes

暴露反面人物的丑恶形象 laying bare the ugly features of a negative character

反映现实生活 reflecting real life

反映现代生活 reflecting present-day life

干预生活 intervening (interfering) in life

强烈的生活气息 strong smack of everyday life

丰富的表现能力 rich expressive power

浓厚的中国民族特色 rich Chinese national colour

用民族风格表现新的思想内容
**presenting new ideological** | **content with a national flavour**

## 文艺工作者　Literature and Art Workers

文化界　cultural circles

文艺界　literary and artistic circles

文坛　literary world (circle), literary forum

文艺队伍　ranks of writers and artists

中国文学艺术界联合会　All-China Federation of Literary and Art Circles

中国作家协会　Association of Chinese Writers

中国美术家协会　Association of Chinese Artists

中国音乐家协会　Association of Chinese Musicians

中国戏剧家协会　Association of Chinese Dramatists

中国电影家协会　Association of Chinese Movie Workers

中国舞蹈家协会　Association of Chinese Dancers

中国曲艺家协会　Association of Chinese Musical Artists

中国摄影家协会　Society of Chinese Photographers

文工团　art ensemble, art troupe, cultural troupe

业余文工团　amateur art ensemble, amateur cultural troupe

业余作家　amateur writer

诗人　poet

散文家　prose writer, proser

小说家　novelist

剧作家　dramatist, playwright

导演　director

男演员　actor

女演员　actress

音乐家　musician

歌唱家　singer, vocalist

作曲家　composer

美术家　artist

画家　painter

漫画家　cartoonist, caricaturist

布景画家　scene-painter

雕塑家　sculptor

雕刻师　carver

电影剧本作者　scenario writer, (film) scenarist

业余文艺宣传队　amateur art propaganda team

业余演出队　amateur performance troupe

文艺轻骑兵　light cavalry of art and literature

乌兰牧骑　mobile cultural troupe in Inner Mongolia, *Ulanmuqi*

文艺工作　literary and artistic work

文艺工作者　literary and art workers, workers in the literary and artistic fields, writers and artists

文人　literary man, man of letters

艺人　artist, professional player (singer, performer)
民间艺人　folk artist
文学家　writer, man of letters
艺术家　artist
美学家　aestheticist
文艺批评家　literary critic

作家　writer
专业作家　professional writer
摄影师　cameraman
舞蹈家　dancer
杂技演员　acrobat
魔术师　conjuror, juggler
驯兽师　tamer, animal trainer

# 文　学　Literature

韵文(诗)　verse
诗歌　poetry
一首诗　poem
史诗　epic
叙事诗　narrative poetry
抒情诗　lyric, lyrical poetry
讽刺诗　satirical poetry
剧诗　dramatic poetry
哲理诗　philosophic poetry
说教诗　didactic poetry
田园诗　pastoral, pastoral poetry
歌　song
民歌(民谣)　folk song, ballad
颂歌(颂诗)　ode
挽歌　elegy
十四行诗　sonnet
无韵诗(素体诗)　blank verse
新诗　modern verse
旧体诗　classical verse, verse in classical forms
散文诗　prose poem, poetry in prose
自由诗　free verse
律诗　"standard" form of poetry, with strictly regulated tones and rhythm, usually consisting of eight line with five or seven words each—*lüshi*

绝句　poem with four lines to a stanza, each line consisting of five or seven words—*jueju*
词(长短句)　a special poetic form using sentence patterns based on song melodies (as word to music)—*ci*
赋　a special form of rhapsodic poem, chiefly in parallel constructions, often written for celebration of event, a descriptive poetic prose—*fu*
歌行　a poem that can be set to music and sung
乐府　folk rhyme, ancient songs for court entertainment
对联　couplet, couplet written on scrolls
打油诗　doggerel, a light poem, satiric poetry
散文　prose
抒情散文　lyric prose
叙事文　narrative prose
说明文　expository prose
描写文　descriptive prose
论说文　argumentative prose

政论文　political prose
讽刺文　satire
小品文(随笔)　essay
杂文　satirical essay
特写　sketch, feature
故事　story, tale
神话　myth, mythology, fairy tale
传说　legend
寓言　fable, allegory
童话　fairy tale
传记　biography
自传　autobiography
回忆录　reminiscences, memoirs
游记　travels, travel sketch
书评　book review
书信　letter, correspondence
通讯　news despatch, newsletter
新闻报道　newspaper report, news coverage
社论　editorial

评论　commentary, comment
报告文学　reportage
儿童文学(儿童读物)　children's literature
文学评论　literary criticism
小说　fiction, novel
短篇小说　short story
中篇小说　novelette
长篇小说　novel
历史小说　historical novel
社会风俗小说　novel of manners
冒险小说　novel of adventures, adventure story
侦探小说　detective story
讽刺小说　satirica
科学幻想小说　science fiction
连载小说　serial story
民间文学(民俗文学)　folk literature
民间故事　folk tale
动物故事　animal story

## 文学创作　Literary Creation

文学作品　literary works, works of literature, creative writings
创作源泉　fountain-head of literary and artistic creation, source of creative writing
创作思想　ideas guiding creation in literature and art
逻辑思维　thinking in terms of logic
形象思维　thinking in terms of images
背景　background

题材　subject matter
主题　theme
内容　content
形式(样式，体裁)　form
构思　conceiving, conception
情节　plot (of a story or play), story
细节　details
序幕(序诗)　prologue
序曲(前奏曲)　prelude
插曲　interlude
高潮　climax
尾声　epilogue
结尾　end

三部曲  trilogy

人物  character, figure, personage

人物描写(人物刻画)  characterization, character delineation (portrayal)

主要人物(主角)  main (chief) character, leading role

次要人物(配角)  minor character

正面人物  positive character, hero

反面人物  negative character, villain

主人公  hero, leading role

女主人公  heroine

典型  type, model

典型性  typicality

典型形象(典型性格)  typical image, typical character, model personalities

典型环境  typical enviroment

表现手法(表现技巧)  technique of expression

叙述  to narrate, narration

倒叙(闪回)  flashback

描绘  to depict, to portray, to describe

对话  dialogue

风格(文体)  style

夸张  to exaggerate, to magnify, exaggeration, hyperbole

衬托  to make…stand out in high relief, to serve for contrast

## 文艺批评  Literary and Art Criticism

作品评价  appraisal or evaluation of literary works

批评标准  criterion of criticism

真实性  truthfulness, authenticity

思想性  ideological content (level)

艺术性  artistic quality(level), artistry

真善美  the true, the good, and the beautiful

革命现实主义  revolutionary realism

艺术成就  artistic merit

写光明  writing about the bright

写黑暗  writing about the dark

歌颂光明  eulogizing(praising) what is bright

暴露黑暗  exposing the dark

文化遗产  cultural heritage

文学遗产  literary heritage, legacy of literature

厚今薄古  paying more attention to the present than to the past

艺术流派  genre, school

艺术鉴赏  virtuosity

艺术借鉴  referenceinart

作品欣赏  appreciation of literary works

批判现实主义  critical realism

## 戏 剧　Drama

话剧　(stage) play, modern drama

独幕剧　one-act play

多幕剧　many-act play, full-length drama

三幕五场(剧)　(a play) in three acts and five scenes

喜剧　comedy

悲喜剧　tragi-comedy

悲剧　tragedy

历史剧　historical play

现代剧　modern play

滑稽戏(闹剧)　farce

情节剧　melodrama

活报剧　skit

歌剧　opera

小歌剧　operetta

音乐剧　musical

舞剧　dance drama

小型歌舞讽刺剧　musical review, revue

现代舞剧　modern dance drama

哑剧　pantomine

木偶戏　puppet show

皮影戏　shadow show

雕塑剧　tableau vivant

京剧　Beijing opera

折子戏　selected scenes

地方戏　local opera

昆曲　Kunqu opera

徽剧　Anhui opera

沪剧　Shanghai opera

越剧　Shaoxing opera

粤剧　Guangdong opera

潮剧　Chaozhou opera

评剧　Northeast opera, *pingju* opera

湘剧　Hunan opera, *xiangju* opera

湖南花鼓戏　(Hunan) *huagu* opera

淮剧　*huaiju* opera

汉剧　Wuhan opera, *hanju* opera

黄梅戏　*huangmei* opera

赣剧　Jiangxi opera, *ganju* opera

桂剧　*guiju* opera

僮剧　Guangxi opera, *zhuangju* opera

川剧　Sichuan opera,

豫剧　Henan opera

藏剧　Xizang opera, *zangju* opera

晋剧　Shanxi opera, *jinju* opera

秦腔　Shǎnxi opera, *qinqiang* opera

剧团　troupe

业余剧团　amateur theatrical troupe, amateur dramatic group

业余演出队　amateur performance troupe

巡回演出队　mobile performance troupe

实验剧团　experimental theatre

儿童剧团　children's dramatic troupe

木偶剧团　troupe of puppet show

话剧团　modern drama troupe

京剧团　Beijing opera troupe

中国京剧团　China Beijing Opera Troupe

舞剧团　dance drama troupe

# 编 剧 Play Writing

(话剧)剧本 **play**

(戏曲，歌剧)剧本，脚本 **libretto**

(电影，电视)剧本 **script**

上演本 **stage version**

传统剧目 **traditional theatrical pieces**

序幕 **prologue**

第一(第二、第三…)幕 **act 1 (2, 3…), first (second, third…) act**

尾声 **epilogue**

主题 **theme**

情节 **plot**

背景 **background, setting**

戏剧冲突 **dramatic conflict**

剧情发展 **development of action**

高潮 **climax**

(剧情)转折起伏 **peripeteia**

(剧情)突降 **anticlimax**

结局(收场) **dénoument**

(情节)插曲 **episode**

间奏曲 **intermezzo**

人物 **character**

形象 **image**

角色 **part, role**

剧名角色 **title role**

主要人物(主角) **leading character (role)**

男主人公 **hero**

女主人公 **heroine**

次要人物(配角) **minor charac-ter**

正面人物 **positive character (role), hero**

反面人物 **negative character (role), villain**

台词 **(one's) lines**

对话 **dialogue**

独白 **monologue**

旁白 **aside**

合编 **collaborating, collaboration**

同…合写一个剧本 **collaborating on a play with sb.**

改编(移植) **adapting, adaptation**

由小说改编的剧本 **a play adapted from a novel**

改编为京剧 **being adapted for Beijing opera**

剧本创作思想 **ideas guiding creation of a play**

主题明确 **(with) a clear-cut theme**

结构谨严 **(with) a tightly-knit structure (plot)**

人物突出 **(with) characters that stand out**

感人肺腑 **deeply moving, touching**

振奋人心 **soul-stirring**

紧凑 **close-knit**

精练(洗练) **refined**

## 剧 院 Theatre

剧院(剧场) theatre

露天剧场 open-air theatre, amphitheatre

歌剧院 opera house

舞剧院 ballet theatre, theatre of dance drama

实验剧场 experimental theatre

人民艺术剧院 people's art theatre

儿童剧院 children's theatre

木偶剧场 puppet show theatre, marionette theatre

礼堂 auditorium

售票处 booking-office, ticket office

订票 booking seats (tickets)

排队买票 queueing up for tickets

入口 entrance

正厅入口 entrance to the auditorium

出口 exit

太平门 emergency exit

门厅 vestibule

衣帽间 cloakroom, check room

休息室 lobby, foyer

正厅前座 stalls

正厅后座 pit

包厢 box

楼厅(二楼)前座 dress circle

楼厅(二楼)后座 upper circle

三层楼座 balcony

顶层楼座 gallery

座位 seat

排 row

座号 number of the seat

单号 odd numbers

双号 even numbers

(座位中的)走道 aisle

小吃部 refreshments room

乐池 orchestra pit

乐队席 orchestra stalls, orchestra seat

看戏用小望远镜 opera glasses

舞台 stage

后台 back stage

旋转舞台 revolving stage

竞技场式舞台 arena-type stage

舞台前部(幕和乐队席之间) proscenium

舞台两侧 wings

幕 curtain

后幕 back curtain

布景 scenery, setting

吊景 drop scenery

道具 properties, props

化装 make-up

化装室 dressing room

服装(戏装) costume

灯光 lighting

舞台照明 stage illumination

顶灯 top light

脚灯 foot light

聚光灯 spotlight

提词厢 prompter's box

舞台设计 stage design

舞台装置 stage set(ting), décor

舞台美术 décor, scenic ornamental painting

舞台效果　stage effect
音响效果　sound effect
灯光效果　light effect

舞台经验　stage experience
舞台艺术(技巧)　stagecraft

## 戏剧演出　Performance

演出(上演)　putting on a play, producing a play, performing a play
首次演出　first performance, première
告别演出　farewell performance
巡回演出　tour
观摩演出(汇演)　festival
搬上舞台　presenting on the stage, staging a play
重新搬上舞台　restaging
排演　rehearsing, rehearsal
彩排　dress rehearsal
扮演(某一角色)　playing (acting, performing) the role of …
初次登台　one's first appearance in …, début
演员表　cast
海报　theatre posters on program, show bill
节目单　program
剧情简介　synopsis
保留节目　repertoire
预备节目　possible encore
日场　day show, matinée
早场　morning show
夜场　evening show
观众　audience, spectators
客满(满座)　house full, full house
幕启(开幕)　The curtain rises

(goes up).
幕落(闭幕)　The curtain falls (drops).
(幕间)休息　interval, intermission
灯光暗下来.　The lights are going down.
精彩表演　superb performance
喝彩(鼓掌)　applauding, applause
再来一次!　Encore!
加唱(奏)一曲　giving an encore
谢幕　taking (answering, responding to) curtain calls
向…献花　presenting a bouquet (a basket of flowers) to …
京剧　Beijing opera
京剧唱腔　rhyme scheme of Beijing opera
主要唱段　main arias
板眼　musical beat
道白　dialoguing, recitative
真嗓子　natural voice
假嗓子　falsetto
做功　acting
台步　stage walk
亮相　making (striking) a stage pose
面部表情　facial expression
脸谱　theatrical mask, make-up

上装 facial make-up

武打 stylized combat, acrobatics

各色武艺 various skills in boxing, fighting with sword, spear, etc.

翻筋斗 turning a somersault, turning somersaults

传统角色 traditional role

生 *sheng*, role of male actor

旦 *dan*, role of female actress

净 *jing*, actor with a paint- ed face

丑 *chou*, role of a clown

京剧的独特风格 special characteristics of Beijing opera

象征性的 symbolic

程式化的 stylized

艺术夸张 artistic exaggeration

传统京剧 traditional Beijing opera

现代京剧 modern Beijing opera

## 戏剧工作人员　Theatrical Workers

编剧(剧作家) playwright

专业剧作家 professional playwright

业余剧作家 amateur playwright

演出者 producer

导演 director, stage director

男演员 actor

女演员 actress

男(女)主要演员 chief actor (actress)

艺术指导 art director

乐队指挥 conductor

乐队人员 orchestra

合唱队人员 theatre chorus

合唱队指挥 chorus master

歌唱家 singer

男歌唱家 male vocalist

女歌唱家 female vocalist

舞台监督 stage manager

舞台工作人员 stage hand

布景设计人 setting designer

布景画家 scene-painter

布景员 scene-man

化装师 make-up man

道具管理员 property man

提词人 prompter

报幕员 announcer, master (mastress) of ceremonies

验(检)票员 ticket-taker

男(女)引座员 usher (usherette)

服务员 attendant

## 影　片　Film

电影 film, cinema, movie, motion (moving) picture

宽银幕电影 wide-screen film, wide-screen

全景电影 panorama film, panorama

全景宽银幕电影 cinepanoramic

立体电影 three-dimensional (3-D) film

宽银幕立体电影 cinerama

深景电影 vista-vision

无声影片 silent film
有声影片 sound film
黑白片 black-and-white film, non-colour film
彩色片 colour film, technicolour film
天然色彩片 natural colour film
配音片(翻译片) dubbed film
故事片 feature film, story film
新闻短片(新闻简报) newsreel
纪录片 documentary film
大型(彩色)纪录片 full length documentary (colour) film
舞台纪录片(戏曲片) opera film, film adapted from an opera
艺术纪录片 artistic documentary
舞剧片 ballet film
歌舞片(音乐片) musical film
由剧本(小说)改编的影片 film adapted from a play (novel)
电视电影 telecinema
电视纪录片 televised documentary
科教片 scientific and educational film

科普片 popular science film
体育片 sports film, athletic film
医学片 medical film
动画片 cartoon, animated cartoon
木偶片 puppet (marionette) film
美术片 cartoon and puppet film
儿童片 film for children
童话片 fairy film, film adapted from a fairy tale
军事片(战争片) military film, war film
侦探片 detective film
惊险片 adventure film
(教学用)电影胶片 film-strip
幻灯片 lantern slide, film-strip
短片 short
预告片 trailer
电影业 the cinema, filmdom
电影摄影学 cinematography
电影文献 film document
电影编年史 film chronicle
电影艺术 cinematographic art
电影音乐 cinema music
电影美学 cinema aesthetics

## 电影制片厂 Film Studio

新闻纪录电影制片厂 newsreel and documentary film studio
中央新闻纪录电影制片厂 Central Newsreel and Documentary Film Studio
艺术(故事)电影制片厂 feature (story) film studio

美术电影制片厂 animation film studio
科学教育电影制片厂 scientific and educational film studio
摄影车间 cinematographing department
录音车间 film recording

department

对口型录音室 lip-synchroniza-
tion studio

配音室 dubbing studio

洗印车间 film laboratory

特技车间 stunt photography
department, trick photo-
graphy department

美工车间 art designing de-
partment

造型车间 make-up department

剪辑车间 film-editing de-
partment

放映车间 film projection
department

电影资料馆 cinematheque

电影图书馆(档案馆) film li-
brary, film archives

外景拍摄场 location, outdoor

filming ground, studio
grounds

半圆形透视背景 cyclorama

拷贝 copy

标准拷贝 standard copy

一盘(一本) reel

(未经剪辑的)工作样片 work
print, rush

复制 duplication

电影事业管理局 cinema ad-
ministration bureau

电影生产 film production,
cinema production

制片费用 net cost, cost price

影片发行 film renting (let-
ting out, hiring), film distribution

电影发行公司 film distribu-
tion corporation

## 电影摄制 Filming

电影剧本(脚本) script, scena-
rio

编写电影剧本 scenarizing

拍成电影(搬上银幕) screen-
ing, filming (a stage play,
a novel, etc.)

电影技术 film technique,
cinematographic technique

电影摄影 cinematography

摄影艺术 photography, art
of photography

拍摄电影 shooting a film

拍摄计划 shooting plan

拍摄程序 shooting procedure

外景摄影 location (exterior,
outdoor) shooting

内景摄影 floor work, indoor
shooting

摄影室 studio

摄影棚 pavilion, sound stage

电影摄影机 cine-camera,
motion picture camera,
film camera

隔音摄影机 sound-proof film
camera

磁性录音摄影机 magnetic-
sound camera

新闻摄影机 newsreel camera

声画摄影机 picture-sound
camera

慢(快)速摄影机 slow-(rapid-,
quick-)motion camera

特技摄影机 stunt film cam-
era

立体声摄影机 stereophonic
camera

连续摄影机 chrono-photographic camera

摄影枪 photographic fusil

(摄影机)三脚架 tripod

摄影机升降架 camera crane, studio crane, dolly crane

旋转摄影器 photographic revolver

X光摄影 cinematographic X-ray, X-ray photography

移动摄影 travelling photography

显微电影摄影 micro-photography

特技摄影 stunt photography, trick photography

镜头 shot, photographic shot

试镜头 trial photography

镜头剪辑(蒙太奇) montage

特写镜头 close-up

近景 bust

中景 medium shot

远景 long shot

全景 full scene

透镜旋转台 turret

可变焦距透镜 zoom lens

宽银幕变形镜头 wide-screen adjustable (anamorphous, cylindrical, distorting) lens

洗印 film processing

洗片机 film-developing machine

印片 printing, film printing

印片机 film-printing machine

接触式声画片印片机 contact picture-sound-printing machine

黑白洗印机 b/w (black/white) film processor

彩色转片洗印机 colour reversal film processor

彩色印刷片 colour printing film

染印法 dyeing transfer process

基色 primary colours

电影胶片 cinematographic film

电影胶片打孔机 film punching machine

正片 positive

底片 negative

水洗(冲洗) washing

暗室 darkroom, photographic laboratory

暗室灯 darkroom lamp

曝光 exposition, exposure

感光乳剂 emulsion

显影 development

录音 sound recording

配音 dubbing, synchronization

对口型录音 lip-synchronization

摄制后配音 post-synchronization

音乐配音录音 music recording

录音机 recorder, recording machine

配音机 dubbing machine

光学声带录音机 optical sound recording machine

摄影室录音箱 studio sound box (booth)

回声室 echo studio

录音车 recording van (truck)

录音放大器　recording ampli-
　　fier
音响效果　sound effect
音画结合　audio-visual coun-
　　terpoint
声音编辑机　Moviola(moviela),
　　sound editor
华语配音　synchronization in
　　Chinese
剪接　editing, cutting
接片(衔接)　collage
集成照片(集成照片制作法)
　　photo-montage
蒙太奇节奏　montage rhythm
平行式蒙太奇　parallel mon-
　　tage
电影剪辑机　motion picture
　　editing machine
看画机　viewing machine
声画剪辑机　picture and sound
　　editor (editing machine)
接片机　splicer, splicing ma-
　　chine
热接片机　hot splicer
磁带片接片机　splicer for
　　magnetic film
布景　scenery, setting
场景(场面)　scene, tableau
布景装置　décor
内景(室内景物)　scenes shot
　　indoors
外景(室外景物)　outdoor shots
构图设计(图样)　design

场面背景　scenic background
成套布置　complex
影片结构　film composition
画面结构　tableau composition
静态构图　static composition
动态构图　dynamic composi-
　　tion
灯光　lighting
灯光效果　light effect
照明　illumination
照明器械　illuminating appa-
　　ratus
照明装置　illuminator
照明强度　illumination inten-
　　sity
能见度(明显度)　visibility
弧光灯　Klieg light, arc lamp
　　(light)
聚光灯　spotlight
聚光器　condenser
水银灯　mercury vapour lamp
水银弧光灯　mercury arc lamp
回旋灯　praxinoscope
感光度　sensitivity
感光计　sensitometer
散光器　diffuser
反射器(反光镜)　reflector
服装　costume, costuming
化装　make-up
舞台装置　stage machinery
道具　properties, props
大小道具　accessories
道具间(室)　property room

## 电影院　Cinema

电影院　cinema, picture house
小汽车电影院　built-in cinema
售票处　cinema box office
电影票　cinema ticket

电影观众　film-goers, cinema-
　　goers
电影舞台　cinema stage
舞台前部　proscenium

银幕 screen, silver screen
银幕前幕布 screen curtain
字幕 caption, subtitle
观众大厅 auditorium
太平门 emergency exit
电影放映室 film projector room
电影放映机 projector
左手放映机 left-hand projector
右手放映机 right-hand projector
16毫米轻便放映机 16 mm. portable projector
逐格放映机 graded projector
幻灯片放映机 slide projector
放映机镜头(透镜) projector lens
倒片机 film winder
影片盒 film magazine
(放映机)上下胶片盒 top and bottom film box
胶片卷轴 film spool
胶片卷 film roll
流动(巡回)放映队 mobile cinema team
放映电影 releasing (showing)
a film
预映(试映) preview
电影在…放映 The film is on at…
今晚电影跑片 The film is shown in (by)relay tonight.
轮回上映(电影放映网) circuits
发行(租片) letting out, renting
上映比率 quota
上映影片目录 film repertoire
一场电影 séance, sitting
日场 day show
早场 morning show
夜场 evening show
海报 show bill
广告 advertisement
解说词 commentary
说明书(故事梗概) synopsis
观众人次 frequentation
轰动一时的片子 sensatinal film
影迷 film-(cinema-) fan
电影展览 film exhibition
电影节 film festival
国际电影节 international film festival

## 电影工作人员 Cinematic Workers

电影工作者 film worker, cinema worker
电影编剧(电影剧本作者) scenarist, scenario writer
导演 director
副导演 assistant director
助理导演 assistant
剪辑导演 montage director
录音导演 sound recording director
对话导演 dialogue director
配音导演 dubbing director
音乐指挥 conductor
全体演员 cast
男(女)演员 movie actor (actress)
男(女)主角 hero (heroine)
电影明星 film star
主演 starring in, playing the lead, acting the leading role (part)
译制(配音)演员 dubber

| | |
|---|---|
| 对口型录音者 lip-synchronist | 混合配音员 dubbing mixers |
| 无声配角 super-numerary | 动画片画家 cartoonist |
| 制片厂经理 studio manager | 化装师 make-up artist, make-up man |
| 制片主任 executive producer | |
| 制片人 producer | 剪辑员 film-cutter, film-editor |
| 制片顾问 consultant, adviser | |
| 科学顾问 science consultant (adviser) | 布景员 scene-man |
| | 布景画家 scene-painter |
| 摄影主任 chief camera-man, director of photography | 服装员 costumer |
| | 道具管理员 property man |
| 摄影师 camera-man, camera operator | 解说员 commentator |
| | 放映员 projectionist |
| 摄影助理 assistant operator | 检票员 ticket-taker |
| 录音技师 sound recordist, sound engineer | 男(女)引座员 usher (usherette) |

# 音 乐 Music

| | |
|---|---|
| 民族音乐 national music | 二重奏(二重唱) duet |
| 古典音乐 classic music | 三重奏(三重唱) trio |
| 民间音乐 folk music | 四重奏(四重唱) quartet |
| 广东音乐 Guangdong music | 五重奏(五重唱) quintet |
| 戏剧音乐 theatrical music | 弦乐四重奏 string quartet |
| 舞蹈音乐(舞曲) dance music | 乐谱 musical notation, score sheets, music book |
| 标题音乐 program (me) music | |
| 无标题音乐 absolute music | 五线谱 staff |
| 轻音乐 light music | 简谱 numbered musical notation |
| 室内乐 chamber music | |
| 管弦乐 orchestral music | 总谱 score |
| 交响乐 symphony | 大谱表 great stave |
| 爵士音乐 jazz | 谱号 clef |
| 流行音乐(歌曲) pop | 高音谱号 treble clef, G clef |
| 摇摆音乐 rock music | 低音谱号 bass clef, F clef |
| 怨曲(美国黑人民歌) the blues | 乐谱夹 music case |
| 声乐 vocal music | 乐谱架 music stand |
| 器乐 instrumental music | 指挥棒 baton |
| 独奏(独唱) solo | 音名 musical alphabet |
| 独奏(独唱)会 recital | 音符 note |
| 音乐会(演奏会) concert | 休止符 rest |
| 合奏(重奏) ensemble | 符点 dot |

装饰音 grace note, grace, ornament

二全音符 breve

全音符 semi-breve

二分音符 half note, mimin

四分音符 quarter note, crotchet

八分音符 eight note, quaver

十六分音符 sixteenth note, semi-quaver

三十二分音符 thirty-second note, demi-semi-quaver

三连音符 triplet

切分音 syncopation

小节 bar, measure

反复 repeat

拍 beat

拍号 time signature

拍子 time

二拍子 duple time

三拍子 triple time

四拍子 quadruple time

调 key

调号 key signature

转调 modulation

移调 transposition

升号 sharp

降号 flat

大调(长调) major

小调(短调) minor

乐句 phrase

乐段 period

乐章 movement

终曲(最后乐章) finale

主题(主旋律) theme, main theme

变奏 variation

反复 repetition

结尾 coda

小结尾 codetta

曲调(旋律) tune, melody

节奏 rhythm

和谐(和声) harmony

和弦 chord

音(音调) tone

音律 tone-system

音长 tonal length

音质 tone quality

音高 tonal height, pitch

音量 volume

音程 interval

八度 octave

音色 timbre, tone colour

音域 compass, range

音阶 scale

速度 tempo

调音 tuning

弱 p (piano)

强 f (forte)

稍弱 mp (mezzo piano)

稍强 mf (mezzo forte)

最弱 pp (pianissimo)

最强 ff (fortissimo)

渐弱 dim. (diminuendo)

渐强 cresc. (crescendo)

作曲 composing, composition

作曲法 composition

…作曲 music by…

…作词 words by…

为曲调配词 setting words (to a tune)

为诗词谱曲 setting (a poem) to music

(由管弦乐)改写的钢琴曲 an arrangement (of orchestral music) for the piano

配乐法 orchestration

## 音乐团体　Music Organization

乐团(乐队)　orchestra, music ensemble (troupe)

歌舞团　song and dance ensemble

管弦乐队　orchestra

管乐队(吹奏乐队)　band

弦乐队　string orchestra

铜管乐队　brass band

军乐队　military band

交响乐团(队)　symphony orchestra

合唱团(队)　chorus troupe, choir

民族乐团　national music ensemble (orchestra)

民族歌舞团　nationalities song and dance ensemble

歌剧院　opera house

中央乐团　Central Philharmonic Society

中央乐团合唱团　Central Philharmonic Chorus

中央乐团管弦乐队　Central

Philharmonic Symphony Orchestra

音乐学院　conservatory

音乐学校　music school

音乐家　musician

音乐大师　virtuoso

专业音乐家　professional musician

业余音乐家　amateur musician

歌唱家　singer, vocalist

作曲家　composer

乐队指挥　conductor, musical director

独奏(独唱)者　sololist

伴奏者　accompanist

某人钢琴伴奏　with…at the piano

钢琴演奏者　pianist

小提琴手　violinist

手风琴演奏者　accordionist, accordion player

乐队队员　bandsman

## 歌曲与乐曲　Song and Music

国歌　national anthem

《国际歌》　The Internationale

民间歌曲　folk songs

进行曲　march

舞曲　dance music

组曲　suite

芭蕾舞组曲　ballet suite

回旋曲　rondo

协奏曲　concerto

奏鸣曲　sonata

小奏鸣曲　sonatina

狂想曲　rhapsody

幻想曲　fantasia

夜曲　nocturne, nocturn

小夜曲　serenade, serenata

浪漫曲　romance

序曲　overture

前奏曲　prelude

间奏曲　intermezzo

终曲　finale

| | |
|---|---|
| 练习曲 **étude** | 即兴曲 **impromptu** |
| 圆舞曲(华尔兹) **waltz, valse** | 诙谐曲 **humoresque** |
| 摇篮曲(催眠曲) **lullaby** | 音诗 **tone poem** |

## 声 乐 Vocal Music

| | |
|---|---|
| 独唱 **solo** | 二重唱 **duet** |
| 合唱 **chorus, ensemble** | 三重唱 **trio** |
| 大合唱 **cantata** | 四重唱 **quartet** |
| 男声合唱 **male chorus** | 五重唱 **quintet** |
| 女声合唱 **female chorus** | 伴唱(伴奏) **accompaniment** |
| 混声合唱 **mixed chorus** | 钢琴伴奏 **with piano accompaniment** |
| 齐唱 **unison, singing in unison** | |
| 轮唱 **round** | 歌 **song** |
| 对唱 **antiphonal responses** | 歌词 **verse, words** |
| 独唱会 **recital** | 歌谱 **music, music composition** |
| 咏叹调 **aria** | |
| 朗诵调 **recitative** | 副歌(选句) **refrain** |

## 乐 器 Musical Instruments

弦乐器 **stringed instruments**
弓弦乐器 **bowed stringed instruments**
小提琴 **violin**
中提琴 **viola**
大提琴① **cello, violoncello**
低音提琴 **double-bass, contrabass**
拨弦乐器 **plucked instruments**
竖琴② **harp**
曼陀林③ **mandolin**
吉他(六弦琴)④ **guitar**
夏威夷吉他 **Hawiian guitar**
班卓琴 **banjo**
三角琴 **balalaika**

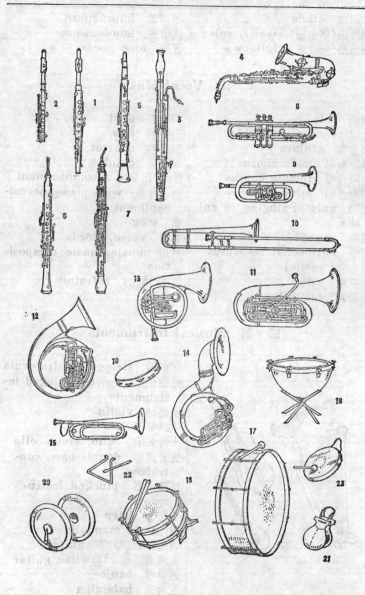

管乐器(吹奏乐器)　wind instruments, winds

木管乐器　wood-wind instruments, wood-winds

铜管乐器　brass-wind instruments, brass-winds, brasses

口琴　mouth-organ, harmonica

长笛① flute

短笛② piccolo

巴松管(大管)③ bassoon

萨克斯管④ saxophone

单簧管⑤ clarinet

双簧管⑥ oboe

中音双簧管　alto oboe

英国号(双簧管的一种)⑦ English horn

小号⑧ trumpet

短号⑨ cornet

中音号　alto horn, althorn

长号(拉管)⑩ trombone

高音长号　tenor trombone

大号(低音号)⑪ tuba, bass tuba

黑里康大号⑫ helicon

法国号(圆号)⑬ French horn, horn

军乐大号⑭ sousaphone

军号⑮ bugle

打击乐器　percussion instruments

定音鼓⑯ kettel-drums, timpani

大鼓⑰ bass drum

小鼓⑱ side drum, snare drum

铃鼓(手鼓)⑲ tambourine, timbrel

钹⑳ cymbals

响板㉑ castanets

三角铁㉒ triangle

锣㉓ gong

木琴㉔ xylophone

组钟　chimes

键盘乐器　keyboard instruments

钢琴㉕ piano

大钢琴(三角钢琴)㉖ grand piano, concert piano

小钢琴(竖式钢琴)　upright piano

管风琴　pipe organ, organ

簧风琴㉗ reed organ, harmonium

手风琴　accordion

钢片琴　celesta

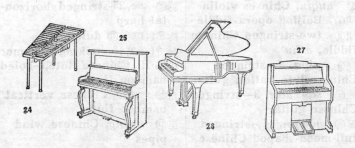

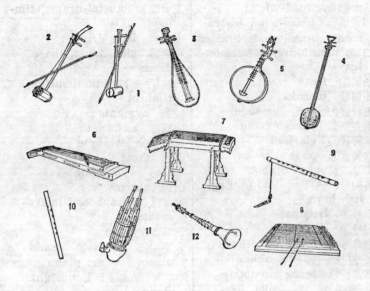

中国乐器　**Chinese musical instruments**

胡琴　*huqin,* Chinses violin

京胡①　**Beijing opera fiddle**

二胡②　**two-stringed Chinese fiddle,** *erhu*

琵琶③　*pipa,* **4—stringed Chinese lute, ballon guitar**

三弦④　*sanxuan,* **3—stringed Chinese guitar**

月琴⑤　*yueqin,* **4—stringed full-moon-shaped Chinese mandolin**

筝⑥　*zheng,* **13—14 stringed Chinese harp**

瑟⑦　*se,* **25-stringed horizontal harp**

扬琴(洋琴)⑧　**dulcimer**

琴竹(琴签)　**striking hammer**

笛⑨　*di,* **Chinese flute, 8-holed bamboo flute**

箫⑩　*xiao,* **Chinese vertical bamboo flute**

笙⑪　*sheng,* **Chinese wind pipes**

唢呐⑫　*suona,* **Chinese clarinet**

号角　horn
螺号　conch, shell trumpet
鼓　drum
大鼓　big drum
小鼓　small drum
腰鼓　waist drum
板鼓　time-beater
搭板　wooden clapper,
　　musical clapping board
木鱼　wooden fish
钟　bell
铃铛　hand bell
磬　single sonorus stone,
　　struck by a hammer
编磬　stone-chime, composed
　　of 16 stones
锣　gong
钹　cymbals
乐器部件　instrumental parts
弓　bow

弓杆　stick
弓弦　hair
弓根　nut
弦　string
聚弦板　tail piece
琴头　head
琴颈　neck
琴马　bridge
琴拨(拨子)　plectrum, pluck
腮垫　chin-rest
指板　finger-board
键盘　keyboard
踏板　pedal
号嘴　mouthpiece
喇叭口　bell
哨子(簧片)　reed
音叉　tuning fork
弱音器　mute, sordino
松香　rosin

## 曲 艺 Musical Arts

曲艺　*quyi*, musical arts,
　　balladry, ballad-singing
　　and story-telling
表演唱　song with action, an
　　item combining singing,
　　dancing and acting
清唱　(Chinese opera) singing
　　selections without stage
　　makeup
对口词　theatrical (rhymed)
　　dialogues
评弹　*pingtan*, balladry, story-
　　telling accompanied by a
　　Chinese lute
说书(评书)　monoloque story-
　　telling with accompani-

ment and gestures
大鼓书　monoloque story-tell-
　　ing in rhythmic language,
　　accompanied by a hand
　　drum
鼓词　drum ballad
弹词　fiddle ballad
京音大鼓　monoloque story-
　　telling in Beijing dialect
山东大鼓　monoloque story-
　　telling in Shandong dialect
梆子腔(秦腔)　music or opera
　　in Shanxi marked by use
　　of *bangzi*
坠子　a form of folk enter-
　　tainment, song and narra-

tive recitation, with drum accompaniment

昆腔 music and opera of Kunshan

昆曲 a form of opera developed at Kunshan

吹腔(弋腔) a type of local opera with flute accompaniment

西皮 *xipi*

二簧 *erhuang*

吹打 playing flutes, horns or trumpets and beating drums

吹弹 music for occasions (with horns and string)

莲花落 *lianhualuo* (a popular song or melody)

单口相声 monoloque comic talk

对口相声 witty dialogue, cross talk

快板 *kuaiban*, clapper verses accompanied by bamboo castanets, song to quick patter

双簧(唱双簧) an act of entertainment, with one person making mouth gestures and another hidden behind making the voice

口技 ventriloquism, ventriloquy, vocal imitation

口技表演者 ventriloquist

曲艺团(队) recitation and ballad-singing troupe

评弹团 balladry (*pingtan*) troupe

## 舞 蹈 Dance

舞曲(舞歌) dance song

舞剧 dance drama

歌舞 song and dance

舞蹈家 dancer

独舞(单人舞) solo dance

双人舞 pas de deux

民间舞(土风舞) folk dance

秧歌舞① yangko dance

芭蕾舞② ballet

芭蕾舞演员 ballet-dancer

女芭蕾舞演员 ballerina

舞蹈设计者 choreographer

爵士舞 jazz

探戈舞 tango

摇摆舞 rock-and-roll

的士高舞 disco

草裙舞 hula-hula

脱衣舞 strip tease

查尔斯顿舞 Charleston

康康舞 can can

康茄舞 conga

方块阿哥哥舞 square ago-go

勃罗斯舞 blues

扭摆舞(扭腰舞) twist

曼波舞 mambo

恰恰舞 cha-cha

吉特巴舞 jitterbug

方块舞 square dance

森巴舞 samba

狐步舞 fox trot

轮摆舞 rumba

华尔兹舞 waltz

茶舞　tea dance

交际舞③　social dancing

伴舞　acting as dance partner

舞伴　dancing partner

舞男　gigolo

舞女　dancing hostess

舞会　dancing party, ball

化装舞会　fancy dress ball

舞场(舞厅)　dance hall

舞池　dancing floor, space for dancing in night club

舞术　art of dancing

舞步　dance step

传统舞蹈　traditional dance

舞龙　dragon dance

舞狮　lion dance

凤舞　phoenix dance

鹤舞　stork dance

苗彝跳月　Miao and Yi custom of communal dance, followed by selection of girls and boys for mates

新疆舞④　Xinjiang dance

蒙古舞⑤　Mongolian dance

西藏舞⑥　Tibetan dance

朝鲜舞⑦　Korean dance

舞蹈动作　dance movements

舞蹈造型　dance poses

舞蹈语言　dance vocabulary

表现手法(技巧)　technique of expression

(舞蹈的)基调　dominant notes (of the dances)

技巧和手法　technique and method

鲜明对比　sharp contrast

层次清晰　distinctive nuance

精湛的艺术表演　superb artistry

完美的表演技巧　perfect playing skill

## 杂 技 Acrobatics

魔术(变戏法) conjuring, juggling

古彩戏法 traditional (Chinese) magic circus

节目 items

索上空翻① somersault on the tight rope

走钢丝 wire-rope walking, wire-rope dancing

飞叉 flying trident

飞刀 flying knife

耍碗 twirling bowls

顶碗 pagoda of bowls

转碟子 plate-spinning

踢碗转盘 bowl-topping and plate-spinning

耍坛子② jar-balancing (vat juggling)

钻圈(钻环)③ jumping through hoops (rings)

套索 lasso trick

水流星④ juggling with meteorlike bulbs, spinning bowls of water

木砖顶 balancing on wood bricks

晃板⑤ balancing on a plank

晃梯 balancing on a free-stand ladder

踩高跷 stilt walk, walk on stilts

倒立 hand-stand

单手倒立 one-handed hand-stand

椅上(桌上)倒立 hand-stand on a chair (table)

叠椅倒立⑥ balancing on a pyramid of chairs

爬杆 climbing the pole

杠杆⑦ long-pole tricks, acrobatics on a bamboo pole

翻筋斗 turning somersaults

前空翻 forward somersault in the air

后空翻 about-turn in the midair

劈叉 split

力气表演 feats of strength

叠罗汉 pyramid, make a human pyramid

技巧 acrobatic gymnastics

狮子舞⑧ lion dance (two men masquerading as a lion)

车技 trick-cycling

独轮脚踏车 unicycle

高台定车⑨ bicycle stabilizing feat on a raised platform

伞上走车⑩ cycling on an umbrella

高秋千(空中飞人) trapeze

抛掷表演 throwing act

平衡表演 balancing act

杂技团 acrobatic troupe, circus

马戏团 circus

流动(旅行)马戏团 travelling circus, touring circus

杂技表演 acrobatic performance

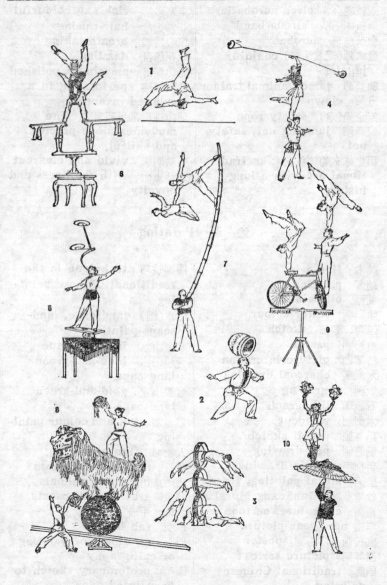

杂技晚会　soiree acrobatics
杂技团乐队　circus band
杂技演员　acrobat
魔术师(变戏法者) conjuror juggler
驯兽师　tamer, animal trainer
丑角　clown
安全绳(索)　safety rope
安全网　jumping net, safety net
历史悠久的传统艺术　a traditional art with a long history

丰富多彩　rich and colourful
非常惊险　hair-raising
惊心动魄　breath-taking
眼花缭乱　dazzling
无比精练　amazingly polished
表演从容　performing in a relaxed manner
动作准确, 灵巧自如　The movements are precise and skilful.
生动明快　vivid and clearcut
别开生面　with freshness and novelty

## 绘 画 Painting

美术　fine arts
绘画　painting
油画　oil painting
水彩画　water colour
速写, 素描　sketch
粉彩画　pastel
腊笔画　picture in crayon
木炭画　charcoal drawing
版画　engraving
石版画　lithograph
木刻画　woodcut
铅笔画　pencil sketch
钢笔画　pen drawing
手指画　finger drawing
壁画　mural painting, fresco
敦煌壁画　Dunhuang Murals
漫画　caricature, cartoon
年画　new year picture
宣传画, 广告画　poster
连环画　picture series
国画　traditional Chinese painting

国画技巧　technique in the traditional Chinese painting
山水(画)　landscape, landscape-painting
水墨山水　ink landscape
青绿山水　blue-and-green landscape
金碧山水　gold-and-green landscape
彩墨画　ink and colour painting
人物画　figure painting
花卉　flowers and plants
翎毛　birds and animals
草虫　grasses and insects
卷轴, 手卷　scroll
扇面　fan leaf
册页　an album of painting or calligraphy
画稿　preliminary sketch to be painted over

题跋　annotations or remarks on a painting

题诗　poem inscribed on a painting

篆刻　carving in seal script

篆章　seal

静物画　still life

肖像画, 画像　portrait

自画像　self-portrait

全身像　full-length portrait

半身像　half-length portrait

花鸟画　flower-bird works

古典画　classical painting

工笔画　painting very carefully and precisely executed, painting done with fine delicate strokes

写意画　free sketch

现代绘画　modern painting

原作　original

临摹(本)　copy, reproduction

写生　painting from life

复制品　reproduction, replica

真品　genuine article

赝品　imitation article, fake article

图案花纹　pattern, design

花形图案　a design (pattern) of flowers

云纹　cloud pattern

直纹　perpendicular pattern

花纹繁缛　variegated in pattern

画廊, 美术馆　gallery

画笔　painting-brush, brush

宣纸　good paper for painting (or calligraphy) from Xuancheng County in Anhui

墨　ink, ink stick

砚　stone ink-slab

图章, 图记　seal, stamp

画板　drawing board

油画画布　canvas

调色板　palette

调色刀　palette knife

写生簿, 速写本　sketch-block, sketch-book

构思　drawing up a mental outline, conceiving

构图　making a sketch of a painting

主题　theme

笔锋, 笔法　stroke

形象　image

风格　style

流派　school

绘画技巧(手法)　painting technique

完美的技巧(手法)　perfection of execution

画面结构　composition of a picture

透视画法　perspective

大胆的构思　boldness of conception

主题的处理　treatment of the theme

粗犷, 雄浑的线条　(in) bold and rough lines

浓淡映衬, 明暗对比　chiaroscuro

光与影的运用, 光暗对比　play of light and shadow

绘(一张)画　drawing (painting) a picture

绘油画　painting in oils

绘水彩画　painting in watercolours

绘国画　painting in the traditional Chinese style

绘画作品　**paintings, works of painting, pictures**

杰作　**masterpiece**

画家　**painter**

绘画大师　**master painter**

古典画家　**classical painter**

现代画派　**modern schools**

抽象派　**abstractionism**

立体派　**cubism**

表现派　**expressionism**

印象派　**impressionism**

点彩派　**pointillism**

超现实主义派　**super-realism**

野兽派　**fauvism**

将来派　**futurism**

旋涡派　**vorticism**

达达派　**Dadaism**

## 雕　塑　Sculpture

雕塑, 雕刻　**sculpture, carving**

雕刻品　**carved works, carvings**

浮雕　**relief**

半浮雕　**bas-relief, low relief**

园雕　**circular carving**

冰雕　**ice carving**

石雕　**stone carving, stone sculpture**

石刻品　**stone composition, stone carvings**

青田石雕　**Qingtian stone (soapstone) carving**

松石刻花片　**carved turquoise plaque**

（天安门广场）汉白玉华表　**marble (cloud) pillar (Tian An Men Square)**

人民英雄纪念碑　**Monument to The People's Heroes**

汉白玉浮雕　**marble bas-relief**

（故宫博物院）云龙石雕　**carved stone "Dragon Pavement" (Palace Museum)**

（颐和园）石舫　**Marble Boat (Summer Palace)**

"万寿山昆明湖"汉白玉碑　**Marble Monument — Longevity Hill-Kunming Lake**

云岗石窟　**Yungang Caves (Datong, Shanxi)**

龙门石窟　**Longmen Caves (Luoyang, Henan)**

石雕佛像　**stone statue of Buddha**

佛龛　**niche for Buddha**

碑刻　**carved stone inscription**

莲花宝盖　**lotus canopy**

云纹　**cloud patterns**

卷草纹　**floral scrolls**

几何纹　**geometric designs**

宝相花　**designs of composite flowers**

木雕　**wood carving**

木刻　**woodcut**

版刻, 雕版　**engraving**

浮雕木刻　**wooden carvings in relief**

木雕像　**wood figurine**

木雕佛像　**wood carvings of Buddha**

黄杨木雕　**boxwood carving(s)**

檀香木雕　**sandal-wood carving(s), red sandal-wood carving(s)**

竹雕 bamboo carving

竹片线雕 bamboo veneer with fine "thread carving"

竹板平雕 bamboo board with shallow carving

竹片诗雕 bamboo veneer with Chinese calligraphy in poetic verse

骨雕 bone sculpture, bone carving

贝雕 shell carving

橄核雕 olive kernel carving

象牙雕刻 ivory carving

(4—30层)象牙同心花球 (4—30 layers) concentric ivory balls one enclosing another

象牙通花扇 ivory fan (open-work)

象牙画舫 gayly decorated pleasure boat of ivory

象牙龙舟 ivory dragon boat

玉雕 jade carving

玉雕器 jade carved objects

玉雕锁链花瓶 jade vase decorated with chains of inter connecting links

翡翠西瓜 jadeite (green jade) watermelon with vines

玉佛 jade Buddha

白玉观音 white-jade statue of Guanyin (the Goddess of Mercy)

玉带 jade belt

玉如意 jade *ruyi* ("as-you-wish")

塑像,铸像 statue

人像 image, moulded figure, figurine

石像 stone statue

铜像 bronze statue

石膏像 plaster statue, plaster figure

大理石像 marble statue

(石、铜、石膏)半身像 (stone, bronze, plaster) bust

与真人大小相等的泥像 lifesize clay figure

泥塑 clay figure modelling

泥像,泥人 clay statuette, clay figurine

蜡像 waxwork

陶瓷像 pottery figure porcelain figure

瓷雕 porcelain carving

美术陶瓷 artistic ceramics

(卧佛寺)卧佛塑像 clay statue (figure) of the Sleeping Buddha (Temple of the Sleeping Buddha)

(碧云寺)罗汉塑像 clay statues (figures) of the Arhats (Temple of the Azure Clouds)

(北海公园)九龙壁 Nine-Dragon Wall (Bei Hai Park)

(故宫博物院)铜仙鹤香炉 bronze cranes used as incense burners (Palace Museum)

青铜鼍龙 bronze legendary animal with the head of a dragon and body of a turtle

铜牛 bronze ox

雕刻师 carver

雕刻家 sculptor

雕塑(雕刻)技巧 carving technique, technique of sculpture

## 书　法　Calligraphy

汉字　**Chinese character or script**

书法　**calligraphy**

象形字　**pictographic character**

篆书①　**seal script (style)**

大篆　**big-seal style**

小篆　**small-seal style**

隶书②　**script in square style, official style, clerical writing**

八分书　**style of script, balanced right and left, of Han Dynasty**

楷书③　**regular (proper) style, formal script**

行书　**running script, half way between formal script (楷书) and cursive script (草书)**

草书④　**cursive script (style)**

半行半草　**midway between running and cursive script**

大字　**big Chinese character**

小字　**small chinese character**

碑帖　**rubbings from ancient tablets**

习字帖　**models for learning calligraphy, models of calligraphy**

对联  couplets
卷轴  scroll
条幅  vertical scroll
横轴,横披  horizontal scroll
匾额  horizontal tablet over door or on wall, inscribed hall name
招牌  shop sign, sign-board
题字,题词  autograph, writing inscription or a few words, dedicatory script
题跋,附记  postscript, remarks on scrolls of calligraphy or painting
题诗  poem inscribed on a scroll, picture, etc.
题签  book title written on book cover
题额  inscription on top of tablet
题匾  inscription fronting a shop or hall
题壁  writing lines or a poem on wall
题款  (on a scroll) name of writer and the person it is dedicated to, signature on scroll or inscription
上款  inscription (to person) in a scroll
下款  signature in a scroll
题署,署名  sign (signature) on scroll, tablet, etc.
篆刻  carving in seal script
图章,图记  seal, stamp
笔法,笔触  stroke (in Chinese calligraphy)
点  point, dot
横  horizontal bar (stroke)
竖  vertical bar (stroke)
撇  slanting stroke towards the left
捺  slanting downward stroke towards the right
提  slanting upward stroke towards the right
勾  stroke with a hook
折  stroke with a bend or twist
书法家  calligrapher

## 工艺美术  Arts and Crafts

手工艺  crafts
手工艺,技艺  craftsmanship
手工艺工人  craftsman, artisan
艺术工匠  artist craftsman
雕刻工  sculptor, carver
制模工  moulder
陶工  potter
陶瓷工  ceramist
玉雕工  jade carver, jade grinder
绣工  embroiderer
编织工  weaver
编结工,针织工  knitter
地毯编织工  carpet weaver
油漆工,画工  painter
缝工,裁缝  tailor
玩具制作者  toyman
雕刻品  carved works, carvings
木器  wood ware
木雕小像  wood figurine
木花制品  wood chip products
竹器  bamboo articles (objects)

竹丝玩具 toy made of bamboo filament

竹编织品 bamboo-splint woven articles

椰壳雕 coconut-shell carving

桃核雕 peach-stone(nut) carving

橄榄核雕 olive-stone(nut) carving

彩塑 colour modelling

面人 dough figurine

漆器 lacquer ware

雕漆 carved lacquer ware

脱胎漆 bodiless lacquer

镶嵌漆器 inlaid lacquer ware

金(银)漆镶嵌 gold-(silver-) inlaid lacquer ware

福建镶嵌银丝大花瓶 Fujian lacquer vase with filigree marquetry

雕漆葫芦瓶 gourd-shaped carved lacquer vase

堆漆 embossed lacquer

金器 gold objects (articles)

银器 silverware

花丝, 金银丝 filigree

烧瓷(搪瓷)制品 enamelware

料器 glassware

景泰蓝 cloisonne

彩蛋 painted egg

彩蚌 painted shell

绢画 silk painting

竹帘画 bamboo screen (scroll) painting

内画 inside-bottle painting

树皮画 tree bark picture

贝雕画 shell picture, shell mosaics

麦秆画 wheat straw (wheat stalk) patchwork

羽毛画 feather patchwork

漆画 lacquer painting

玻璃画 glass painting

铁画 iron openwork, iron (wall) picture

火烙画 burnt picture, poker work

高粱秆画 picture made of sorghum stalk

螺钿镶嵌画 mother-of-pearl inlay work

软木画 cork patchwork

牛角画 ox horn mosaics

水粉画 qouache

皮毛画 fur patchwork

描金 gold drawing

拓片 rubbing from tablet

剪纸 paper-cut

风筝 kite

刺绣 embroidery

雕绣 cutwork embroidery

万缕丝绣 venetian embroidery

十字绣 cross-stitch embroidery

平绣 plain embroidery

双面绣 double sided (reversible) embroidery

色贴布绣 coloured applique work

麻布对丝彩绣 linen article with spoke-work and colour embroidery

绒线绣 woollen needle-point embroidery

绒线绣制品 woollen needle-point tapestry

发绣 hair embroidery

丝绣　silk embroidery
刺绣画片　silk embroidered picture
织锦　brocade
风景织锦　silk-woven landscape
抽纱　drawn work
花边　lace, trimming
挑花　hand-stitching work
补花　patchwork
手工钩针制品　hand crochet articles
线结袋　cotton crochet bag
绒制玩具　chenille toys
绒鸟兽　velvet birds and animals
绢花　silk flower
绢人　silk figurine
塑料花　plastic flower
蜡果　wax fruit
刻蜡　art candle
通草纸花　rice-paper flower
纸拉花　paper garlands
翻花　magic flower
宫灯　palace lantern
纱灯　gauze lantern
壁灯　wall lantern
走马灯　revolving scenic lamp
花彩　festoon
仿古玩　imitation antiquities
皮影　shadow figures
草织品　straw articles (products)
草织盛具　grass basketry
藤织品　cane (rattan) products
棕编制品　palm woven ware
棕榈纤维玩具　palm-fibre toy

柳条制品　wicker work, willow twig products
蒲制品　rush products
玉米皮制品　maize-leaf articles
草地席　floor mat
地毯　carpet, rug
壁毯, 挂毯　tapestry
烟具　smoking set
茶具　tea set
咖啡具　coffee set
酒具　cocktail set
餐具　dinner set
屏风　(parlour) screen
八扇屏风　floor screen (8-leaf big screen)
插屏　table screen
挂屏　hanging panel, wall panel
立体挂屏　relief panel
果盘　fruit tray
花插　flower receptacle
笔筒　brush barrel
书签　bookmark, marker
镇纸　paper-weight
盘垫　traycloth
茶碗垫　doily
手提包　handbag
宫扇　mandarin fan
绢扇　silk fan
羽毛扇　feather fan
葵扇　palm fan
折扇　folding fan
檀香扇　sandal wood (folding) fan
图案设计　pattern design
艺术风格　artistic style
浮雕细工　fretwork
透雕细工　openwork

| | |
|---|---|
| 隆起花纹 raised flower pattern | 制胎 body-making, base-making |
| 镶嵌细工 marquetry | 上漆 varnishing, coating of lacquer |
| 镀金 gold-plated, gilded | |
| 馏金 gold-coated | 上色 colouration |
| 贴金 gold-overlaid | 上釉 glazing |
| 开料 rough shape cutting | 点蓝 enamel-filling |
| 磨制 grinding | 烧焊 soldering |
| 磨光 polishing | 组装 assembling |

## 出土文物 Unearthed Relics

| | |
|---|---|
| 文物 relics, cultural relics | 宝库 treasure trove |
| 出土文物 unearthed relics, unearthed cultural objects | 窖藏 buried objects, underground storage |
| 历史文物 historical relics | 圆形窖穴 round storage pit |
| 文物保护 protection of historical relics | 墓地 graveyard, tomb |
| | 墓穴 grave, tomb chamber |
| 文物发掘 excavation of historical relics | 墓门 door of tomb |
| | 墓道 paved front leading to grave |
| 文化遗址 historical culture sites | |
| | 墓碑 tombstone |
| 遗迹 remains, vestiges | 墓表 memorial tablet at grave |
| 罕见文物 rare relics | |
| 保存完整 in a good state of preservation, being fairly well preserved | 墓碣 memorial tablet |
| | 墓志铭 biographical sketch engraved on memorial tablet, epitaph |
| 完整无损 intact | |
| 制作精巧 done with exquisite technique | 外城墙 barbican wall |
| | 门楼 gate tower |
| 整理复原 being restored (as they were original) | 明楼 soul-tower |
| | 石柱 corbel |
| 光亮如新 show their original lustre | 石棺床 coffin platform |
| | 椁室 coffin chamber |
| 高超工艺水平 high artistic and technical level | 棺, 内棺 coffin |
| 陵墓 emperor's mausoleum | 椁外棺 outer coffin |
| 古墓 ancient tomb | 棺葬 coffin burial |
| | 瓮葬 urn burial |
| 陪陵, 陪葬 satellite tombs | 瓮棺 funerary urn |

单人葬　single burial
双人葬　double burial
合葬　joint burial urn
奴隶殉葬墓　tomb with immolated slaves
殉葬奴隶　immolated slaves
木俑　wooden figurine
泥俑　earthen figurine
陶俑　pottery figurine
上釉陶俑　glazed pottery figurine
武士俑　figurine of warrior
木雕仪仗俑　wooden entourage figurines
乐、舞、杂技陶俑群　pottery figurines of musicians, dancers and acrobats
车马具　chariots and harness
殉葬品　sacrificial object
随葬品　funeral object
明器　specially made funerary object
石器　stone vessel, stone objects
青铜器　bronze, bronze ware
铁器　iron ware
金银器　gold and silver ware
玉器　jade objects (articles)
陶器　pottery, potter vessel, earthenware
瓷器　porcelain
竹器　bamboo utensil
木器　wooden utensil
漆器　lacquer ware
丝织品　silk fabrics
麻织品　hemp fabrics
甲骨　oracle bone
甲骨文　inscription on oracle bones

砍砸器　chopper
刮削器　scrapper
石斧　stone axe
石臼　stone mortar
石磨盘　stone saddle-quern
瓢　gourd ladle
勺　ladle
耳杯　eared cup
案　tray
俎　*zu* (oblong bench or table for carving meat)
彩陶　painted pottery
赤陶　terracotta
陶熏炉　pottery incense burner
炭盆,火盆　brazier
彩绘陶盘　colour painted pottery dish with short stem
彩绘陶盉　colour painted pottery pot (seasonings mixer)
彩绘陶钟　colour painted pottery vessel for wine
红陶鼎　red pottery tripod
黑陶缕孔盘　black pottery platter engraved with holes
玉环　jade ring
玉镯　jade bracelet
珮　pendant
玺　imperial seal
如意　*ruyi* ("as-you-wish")
朝珠　court beads
充耳　ear stuff
玉圭　jade tablet (bar) for ritual services
玉带　jade belt
铜器　copperware
朱雀灯　bronze "scarlet bird" lamp
铜漏　copper clepsydra

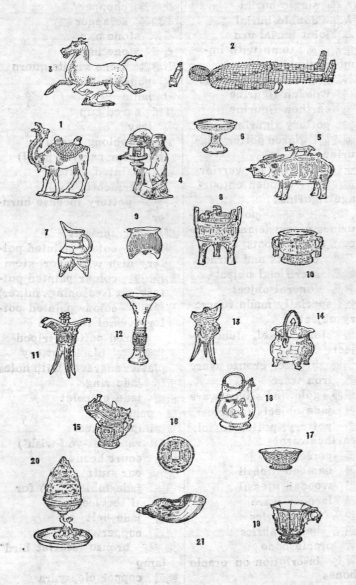

釉瓷① glazed porcelain

金缕玉衣② jade clothes, jade burial suit sewn with fine gold wire

青铜奔马③ bronze galloping horse

长信宫灯④ gilded bronze figurine with a lamp

瓶 vase, bottle

壶 ewer, kettle

瓮, 罐 jar

钵 bowl

盆 pot, tub

尊⑤ jar, wine vessel

盅, 碗 cup

盏 small cup

盒 casket

豆⑥ stemmed bowl

鬶⑦ *gui*, water pitcher

鼎⑧ tripod, cauldron

鬲⑨ *li*, cooking tripod with hollow legs

簋⑩ *gui*, food container

爵⑪ *jue*, wine vessel

觚⑫ *gu*, wine vessel, beaker

角⑬ vessel for heating wine

卣⑭ *you*, jar with swing handle for containing wine

觥⑮ *gong*, wine vessel

盂 basin

魁 ladle

五铢钱 *wuzhu* coin

开元通宝⑯ Kai Yuan Tong Bao coin

刀钱 knife money

楚国郢爰金币 gold coins (of the State of Chu)

马蹄形碎金 pieces of horseshoe-shaped coin

金箔 gold foil

刻花金碗⑰ gold bowl with flower patterns

银壶⑱ gilded silver wine pot

环柄八棱杯⑲ octagonal cup with ringed handle

桃形盘 peach-shaped dish

六曲盘 six-lobed bowl

提梁壶 pot with loop handle

盝顶银盒 silver casket with bas-relief

错金博山炉⑳ Boshan incense burner inlaid with gold decorations

景泰蓝 cloisonne

珐琅器 enamel vessels (wares)

玛瑙 onyx, agate

琥珀 amber

珊瑚 coral

朱砂 cinnabar

宝石 gem

红宝石 ruby

绿宝石 emerald

蓝宝石 aquamarine

翡翠 (chrysolite) jadeite, green jade

水晶 crystal

兵器 weapons

戈 halberd

矛 spear

戟 *ji*, halberd

斧 hatchet, battle-axe

钺 *yue*, axe

戚 *qi*, axe

刀 sword

长矛 lance, spear

狼牙棒 toothed club

弓　bow

弩　cross-bow

箭,矢　arrow

镞,箭头　barbed head of an arrow, arrowhead

剑　sword, double-edged sword

剑鞘,刀鞘　sheath

皮甲　leather armour

甲胄　mail-armour and helmet

盔甲　helmet and armour

战车　chariot

御具,车具　chariot accessories, pieces of harness

乐器　musical instruments

彩绘扁磬　musical stones with coloured engravings

竽　*yu*, pipes

排管　reed pipes

木瑟　wooden *se*, zither

十二竹音律管　12 pitch-pipes made of bamboo

木板漆画　wooden screen with lacquer painting

彩绘帛画　colour painting on silk

幡　funeral banner

香囊　incense bag

奁盒　dressing case

竹简　inscribed bamboo-slips

字画卷轴　scrolls of calligra-phy and painting

经卷　buddhist text, buddhist scripture, sūtra

抄本　manuscript

佚书　lost book

(印刷)木板　(printing) wood-block

铺绒　silk embroidered in satin stitch

(暗花杯纹罗地)锁绣　chain-stitch embroidery (on loz-enge-patterned damask)

(绛地)五色彩绣　embroidery in five colours (on red background)

羽毛贴花绢　silk with rhombic design pasted with down

素纱禅衣　garment of plain silk gauze

丝锦缎　silk damask

彩条纹锦　polychrome silk

(花鸟纹饰)锦缎　silk damask (with flower and bird pattern)

(云头)锦鞋　silk damask shoes (with cloud pattern toe)

乌纱帽　hat made with black gauze

朝服　court dress

龙袍　dragon robe

王冠　diadem, crown

# 教 育 Education

## 教育制度 Educational System

我们的教育方针，应该使受教育者在德育、智育、体育几方面都得到发展，成为有社会主义觉悟的有文化的劳动者。 Our educational policy must enable everyone who receives an education to develop morally, intellectually and physically and become a worker with both socialist consciousness and culture.

提高整个中华民族的科学文化水平 Raise the scientific and cultural level of the entire Chinese nation.

教育事业 educational undertaking

教育设施 educational institution

教育机构 educational establishment

教育制度 educational system

学制 school system

学分制 credit system

三级制 three-tier system

单轨制 one-track system

双轨制 dual-track system

阶梯制 ladder system

学龄前教育 preschool education

幼儿园教育 kindergarten education

初等教育 elementary education, primary education

中等教育 secondary education

普及教育 universal eduction

普及中等教育 making secondary education universal

高等教育 higher education

义务教育 compulsory education, free education

成人教育 adult education

进修教育 further education, continuing education

思想政治教育 ideological and political education

科学技术教育 scientific and technical education

职业教育 vocational education

广泛的职业教育 career education

男女同校教育 co-education

因材施教的教育 progressive education

世俗教育 lay education

教会教育 ecclesiastical education

回归教育 recurrent education

补偿教育 compensatory education

## 学 校 Schools

托儿所 nursery (school)

幼儿园 kindergarten

小学 elementary school, primary school, (Am.) grade school

中学 secondary school, middle school, (Am.) high school

初级中学 junior middle school, junior high school

高级中学 senior middle school, senior high school

十年一贯制学校 compound school of ten-year system

中等专业学校 specialized middle school

全日制正规学校 full-time regular school

二部制学校 two-shift school

半工半读学校 part-work and part-study school

附属学校 affiliated school

附中(小) attached middle (primary) school

实验学校 experimental school

民办学校 school run by the local people

重点学校 key school

业余学校 spare-time school

夜校 evening school

扫盲班 literacy class

速成班 accelerated course

补习班 supplementary class

进修学校(补习学校) continuation school

师范学校 normal school

幼儿师范学校 school for kindergarten teachers

职业学校 vocational school

函授学校 correspondence school

巡回学校 mobile school

水上流动学校 waterborne school

帐篷学校 tent school

少年业余体育学校 youth amateur athletic school, youth sparetime sports school

聋哑学校 school for deaf-mutes

盲人学校 school for the blind

寄宿学校 boarding school

〔美〕公立中学 public school

〔英〕公学 public school

文法中学 grammar school

技术中学 technical school

综合中学 comprehensive school

教区学校 parochial school

寺院学校 monastic school

慈善学校 charity school

主日学校 Sunday school

教会学校 missionary school

实行种族隔离的学校 segregated school

教育园 educational park

## 高等院校  Institutions of Higher Learning

综合性大学 comprehensive university

文科大学 university of liberal arts

理工科大学 university of science and engineering

科学技术大学 university of science and technology

师范学院(大学) teachers' college, normal university

工学院 engineering institute

综合性工艺学院 polytechnical institute

农学院 agricultural college

林学院 forestry college

医学院 medical college

药学院 college of pharmaceutical science

中医学院 institute of traditional Chinese medicine

教育学院 college of education

政法学院 institute of political science and law

外国语学院 institute of foreign languages

外贸学院 institute of foreign trade

海运学院 institute of marine transport

邮电学院 posts and telecommunications institute

海洋学院 oceanology college

体育学院 physical cultural institute

民族学院 institute for nationalities

工艺美术学院 institute of arts and crafts

美术学院 academy of fine arts

音乐学院 academy of music, conservatory of music

戏剧学院 drama institute

电影学院 cinema college

舞蹈学校 dancing school

军事学院 military academy

军医大学 army medical college

广播电视大学 radio and television courses

开放大学 open university

终身大学 lifetime university

初级学院 junior college

社区学院 community college

工人大学 workers' college

共产主义劳动大学 communist labour university

## 学校人员  School Members

小学校长 schoolmaster

中学校长 principal

大学校长 president, chancellor

教务长 dean

院长 college head, dean

系主任 department head

注册主管员 registrar

财务主管员 bursar

教学人员 teaching staff, faculty

教师 teacher

特级教师 teacher of a special grade

大学教员 college teacher

助教 assistant

讲师 lecturer, instructor

高级讲师 reader, senior-lecturer

副教授 associate professor

教授 professor

名誉教授 honorary professor

荣誉退休教授 emeritus professor, professor emeritus

交换教授 exchange professor

客座教授 visiting professor

外籍教师 foreign teacher

班主任 head teacher, class adviser

政治辅导员 assistant for political and ideological work

全体学生 student body

小学生 school child, pupil

小先生 pupil teacher

中学生 middle school student, secondary school student

大学生 college student

大学肄业生 undergraduate

一年级学生 first-year student, freshman

二年级学生 second-year student, sophomore

三年级学生 third-year student, junior

四年级学生 fourth-year student, senior

毕业生 graduate

退学生 dropout

离校生 school-leaver

研究生 postgraduate, research student, fellow

兼教学的研究生 teaching fellow

"尖子"学生 top student

走读生 day student, commuting student

住校生 boarder

旁听生 associate student, auditor

转学生 transfer student

教学实习生 student teacher

同学 schoolmate

同班同学 classmate

班长 monitor

男校友 alumnus, (pl.) alumni

女校友 alumna, (pl.) alumnae

男女校友 alumni

专家 specialist

学者 scholar

顾问 advisor

教育工作者 educational worker, educator

教育学家 education(al)ist

## 学位学衔 Academic Degrees and Titles

学士学位 bachelorship, bachelor's degree

学士 bachelor

文学士 Bachelor of Arts, Bachelor of letters, Litt. B.

理学士 Bachelor of Science

| | |
|---|---|
| 硕士学位 mastership, master's degree | 文学博士 Doctor of Literature, Litt. D. |
| 硕士 master | 理学博士 Doctor of Science |
| 博士学位 doctorate, doctor's degree | 医学博士 Doctor of Medicine |
| 博士 Doctor, Dr., D. | 名誉学士 honorary degree |
| 哲学博士 Doctor of Philosophy, Ph. D. | 授予学位 conferring of degrees |
| | 学位文凭 diploma |

## 课程设置和专业 Curricula and Disciplines

| | |
|---|---|
| 基础课 basic course | 图书馆学 Library Science |
| 基础理论课 course on basic theory | 档案管理学 Science of Archive administration |
| 普通课 general knowledge course | 天文学 Astronomy |
| 专业课 specialized course | 气象学 Meteorology |
| 政治课 political course | 地理学 Geography |
| 体育课 physical education | 地质学 Geology |
| 必修课 required course, compulsory course | 岩石学 Petrology |
| 选修课 optional course, selective course | 矿物学 Mineralogy |
| 速成课程 crash course | 考古学 Archaeology |
| 在职训练 in-service training | 人类学 Anthropology |
| 中国语言文学 Chinese Language and Literature | 理论数学 Pure Mathematics |
| 外国语言 Foreign Languages | 应用数学 Applied Mathematics |
| 东方语言 Oriental Languages | 力学 Mechanics |
| 西方语言 Occidental Languages | 物理学 Physics |
| 历史学 History | 地球物理学 Geophysics |
| 哲学 Philosophy | 天体物理学 Astrophysics |
| 政治经济学 Political Economy | 高能物理学 High Energy Physics |
| 教育学 Pedagogy | 激光物理学 Laser Physics |
| 心理学 Psychology | 激光光谱学 Laser Spectroscopy |
| 法律学 Law | 电真空物理学 Electro-vacuum Physics |
| 国际关系 International Relations | 电光学 Electrooptics |
| | 非线性光学 Non-linear Optics |
| | 核子科学 Nuclear Science |

电子学　Electronics
计算机科学　Computer science
空间科学　Space Science
化学　Chemistry
无机化学　Inorganic Chemistry
有机化学　Organic Chemistry
物理化学　Physicochemistry
电化学　Electrochemistry
放射化学　Radiochemistry
稀有元素化学　Rare Elements Chemistry
生物学　Biology
生物化学　Biochemistry
生理学　Physiology
植物学　Botany
动物学　Zoology
昆虫学　Entomology
细菌学　Bacteriology
遗传学　Genetics
遗传工程　Genetic Engineering
农学　Agriculture
农业机械　Agricultural Machinery
园艺学　Horticulture
冶金学　Metallurgy
采矿工程　Mining Engineering
机械工程　Mechanical Engineering
电机工程　Electrical Engineering
无线电工程　Radio Engineering
化学工程　Chemical Engineering
石油化工　Petrochemical Engineering
高分子合成　High Polymer Synthesis
直接合成工艺　Technology of Direct Synthesis
土木工程　Civil Engineering
水利工程　Hydraulic Engineering
建筑工程　Architectural Engineering
造船工程　Naval Architecture, Shipbuilding
航空工程　Aeronautical Engineering
微电子技术　Microelectronics
遥感技术　Remote Sensing Techniques
环境科学　Environmental Science
教育工学　Educational Technology

## 学校制度，管理与设备　Scholastic Institutions, Administration and Installations

教学原则　teaching principles
教学计划　teaching plan
教学大纲　teaching program, syllabus
招生制度　enrol(l)ment system
考试制度　examination system
入学考试　entrance examination
入学资格　admission qualifications

入学者 enrollee

择优取录 admitting the best, selecting the best, matriculating the best of the examinees

全面衡量 all-round appraisal

放榜 announcement of examination results

注册入学 matriculation

按程度分班组 streaming, grouping according to ability

学习智能测验 Scholastic Aptitude Test, SAT

智力测验 intelligence test

智(力)商(数) intelligence quotient, I. Q.

学年 school year, scholastic year

学期,半学年 semester, term

学期,四分之一学年 quarter

校历 school calendar

秋季学期 autumn term

春季学期 spring term

暑假 summer vacation (holi days)

寒假 winter vacation (holidays)

升留级制度 system of promoting or holding back students

升级 being promoted to a higher grade

留级 staying in the same grade

跳级一年 jumping a year, skipping a year

班主任制 system of putting a teacher in charge of each class

导师制 tutorial system

教学活动 teaching activities

学文 learning book knowledge, learning science and culture

对口实习 doing practice geared to the needs of the job

教学实习 doing practice teaching

野外实习 conducting fieldwork

军训 military training

课外活动 extracurricular activities

校外活动 after-school activities

文娱活动 recreation, recreational activities

作息制度 work-and-rest system

课程表 schedule, timetable

一节课 period

课间休息 break, interval

毕业考试 graduation exam(-ination)

毕业论文 graduation thesis, graduate's dissertation

毕业设计 diploma-winning design

毕业答辩会 graduation oral exam(ination)

毕业证书 graduation certificate, diploma

学分 credit

学院 college, school

系 department, faculty

专业 speciality

教研组 teaching research

group

研究院 postgraduate research institute, graduate school

大学附设部分 university extension

学校建筑 school architecture

学校建筑物 campus building

校舍 school building

校园,学校场地 campus

教学楼 classroom building

办公楼 school office

礼堂 auditorium

宿舍 dormitory, hall of residence

运动场 playground

体育馆 gym, gymnasium

图书馆 library

科学馆 science building

实验室 laboratory

## 教　学　Teaching and Learning

教材 teaching materials

油印活页教材 mimeographed sheets of teaching materials

课本 textbook

教法 teaching method

注入式 cramming method, method of spoon feeding

启发式 method of elicitation

讨论式 method of discussion

因材施教法 individualized method of instruction

由浅入深 from the shallower to the deeper

由易到难 from the easier to the more advanced

深入浅出 explaining profound theories in simple language

基础知识 basic knowledge

基础理论 basic theory

基本训练 basic training

基本功 basics, basic skill

系统性 systematization

连贯性 consistency

课堂教学 classroom teaching

上课 attending class

上数学课 taking classes in math.

讲课 giving a lecture, delivering a lecture

发给学生的讲课提纲 handout

听课 attending a lecture

记笔记 taking notes

对笔记 comparing notes

做练习 doing exercises

做功课 doing schoolwork

课外作业 homework

课外辅导 instructions after class

个别辅导 individual coaching

精读 intensive reading, perusal

泛读 extensive reading

规定的阅读 prescribed reading

复习 reviewing

写作 writing

写概要 precising

讨论 discussion

辩论 debate

讨论会 seminar

分析 analysis, analyzing

综合 synthesis, synthesizing

假设 hypothesis, hypothesizing

验证 verification, verifying

归纳 induction, inducing

演绎 deduction, deducing

推断 inference, inferring

抽象 abstraction, abstracting

概括 generalization, generalizing

现场教学 on-the-spot teaching

实物教学 object teaching

示范教学 teaching by demonstration

电化教学 teaching with electric audio-visual aids

实地调查考察 field work

实地旅行参观 field trip

实验 experiment, experimenting

观察 observation, observing

循序渐进的教学 programmed instruction

利用附题解的课本进行的自学 programmed learning

自学课本 programmed teaching book

计算机辅助的学习 computer-assisted (aided) learning

线性教学程序设计 linear programming

分枝式教学程序设计 branching programming

理论联系实际 integrating theory with practice

使学习生动活泼 livening up the studies

培养独立分析问题和解决问题的能力 cultivating the ability to analyze and solve problems independently

培养科学研究能力 cultivating (raising) the ability to do scientific research

实现教育手段现代化 modernizing the means of education

提高业务能力 raising vocational proficiency

提高教学水平 raising the level of teaching

提高教学质量 improving the quality of teaching

检查学习情况 checking up (on) studies

考核 check-up

考查 test, quiz

笔试 written test, written examination

口试 oral test, oral examination

掌握程度考试 achievement test

熟练程度考试 proficiency test

补考 make-up examination

学期终考试 end-of-term examination

离校考试 school-leaving examination

开卷考试 open-book exam

评分标准 standards of grading

百分制 one hundred point (s) scale

五分制 five point(s) scale

分数 marks

及格分数 pass mark

好分数 **good mark**
不好的分数 **bad mark**
满分 **full marks**
考试及格 **passing an exam**

考试不及格 **failing in an exam(ination), flunking in an exam(ination)**

## 教 室 Classroom

讲台 **platform**
讲桌 **teacher's desk**
黑板 **blackboard**
滑动黑板 **sliding blackboard**
墙板 **wallboard**
黑板擦 **blackboard eraser**
黑板抹布 **blackboard cloth**
海绵擦 **sponge**
粉笔 **chalk**
教鞭 **pointer**
阶梯式教室 **lecture theatre**
阶梯式示范室 **demonstration theatre**
地图 **map**
教学用图 **picture for teaching**

图表 **diagram, chart, graph**
实物 **object**
陈列柜 **display case, showcase**
模型 **model**
标本 **specimen**
剥制的袋鼠 **stuffed kangaroo**
剥制的猫头鹰 **stuffed owl**
地球仪 **(terrestrial) globe**
墙报 **wall newspaper**
学生园地 **Students' Corner**
外语园地 **foreign languages corner**
废纸篓 **waste (-paper) basket**
课桌 **school desk**

## 视听教具 Audio-Visual Aids

识字卡片 **flash card**
法兰绒板示教图 **flannelgraph**
毡板 **feltboard**
剪切品 **cut-out, cut-out object**
塑性粘着物 **plastic adhesive**
塑性图片 **plastigraph**
活动挂图 **mobile**
立体教具 **three-dimensional aid**
粘胶模型 **plasticine model**
沙盘 **sand tray**
缩型立体布景 **diorama**
幻灯机 **slide projector**
幻灯片 **slide, transparency**

不透明投影 **opaque projection**
透明静止投影 **transparent projection**
投影放大器 **episcope**
显微映画器 **micro-projector**
投影幻灯机, 投射器 **overhead projector**
电影放映 **cineprojection**
电影放映机 **film projector, cineprojector**
电影胶片 **filmstrip**
无声影片 **silent film**
有声影片 **sound film, cine-sound film**
光泽面 **shiny side**

无光泽面　dull side

帧幅　frame

声带　sound track

链轮齿孔　sprocket hole

拼接处　splice

银幕　screen

单速留声机　one-speed gramo-phone

电唱机　record player

三速晶体管唱机　three-speed transistorised player

转盘　turntable

唱片　record

慢转密纹唱片　long-play disc (record)

磁带录音机　tape recorder, magcorder

教学机　teaching machine

教育电视节目　educational television program(me)

创作电视节目　originating a television program(me)

播送电视节目　transmitting a television program(me)

播送区域　transmission area

闭路电视　closed circuit tele-vision, C.C.T.V.

(电视)接收机　receiver

电视荧光屏　television screen

磁带录像　video (tape) re-cording

录像磁带　videotape

磁带录像机　video (tape) re-corder

盒式录像机　video cassette re-corder

电视唱片, 录像片　video disc

电视黑板　tele-board

电传课文　teletext

计算机终端机　computer termi-nal

## 语言实验室　Language Lab

视听中心　audio-visual centre

听力语言实验室　audio-passive L L

听练语言实验室　audio-active L L

听练比较语言实验室　audio-ac-tive comparative L L

视听语言实验室　audio-visual L L

听力座　listening booth

视听座　visual-listening booth

二(音)轨磁带录音机　twotrack tape recorder

四(音)轨磁带录音机　fourtrack

tape recorder

盒式磁带录音机　cassette tape recorder

磁带　magnetic tape

供带盘　feed reel

卷带盘　take-up reel

抹音磁头　erase head

录音磁头　record head

放音磁头　playback head

话筒　microphone

耳机　earphone

耳机话筒组　headset

洗掉磁带上的录音　erasing the existing recording on tape

录新材料　recording new material

倒带　rewinding the tape

听教师的录音　listening to the teacher's recording (the master recording)

录自己的模仿　recording one's own imitation

录自己的回答　recording one's own response

播放录音　playing back the recording

监听学生的讲读　monitoring a student's performance, listening in to a student's performance

找出差错　diagnosing faults

提供正确讲法　offering correction

提出意见, 进行指点　offering advice

中央控制台　control console

呼叫录音室按键　REC ROOM CALL Button

录音室指示灯　FROM REC ROOM Lamp

转录按键　TO TAPE Button

解除按键　RESET Button

对讲录音开关　INTERCOM REC Switch

监听录音开关　REC MONITOR Switch

录音室话筒音量控制　REC ROOM MIC Volume Control

实验室喇叭音量控制　LAB SP Volume Control

节目选择器　Program(me) Selector

耳机插座　Earphone Jack

## 物理仪器　Physical Apparatuses

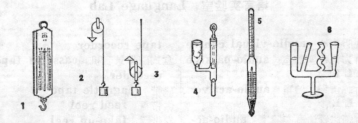

弹簧测力计①　spring dynomometer

起重滑车　hoisting tackle

滑车组　block and tackle

固定滑车②　fixed pulley

滑动滑车③　movable pulley

回转仪　gyroscope

液压器④　hydraulic press

液体比重计⑤　hydrometer

连通器⑥　communicating vessel

毛细管装置⑦　device for demonstrating capillarity

毛细管⑧　capillary tube

教育 221

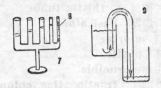

虹吸管⑨ siphon, syphon
音叉 tuning fork
共振摆 resonance pendulum
检声器 sound detector
弧光灯 arc lamp
凸透镜 convex lens
凹透镜 concave lens
会聚透镜(凸透镜) converging lens
棱镜 prism
棱镜座 prism table
分光计⑩ spectrometer
分度圈 graduated circle
望远镜 telescope

准直管 collimator
显微镜 microscope
莱顿瓶 Leyden jar
导电棒 conducting rod
放电叉 discharge tongs
静电发生器⑪ electrostatic generator
锡箔条 strip of tin foil

伏打电池 Voltaic cell
本生电池 Bunsen cell
碳棒 carbon stick
锌筒 zinc cylinder
验电器 electroscope
实验变压器 experimental transformer
原线圈 primary coil
副线圈 secondary coil
蹄形磁体 horseshoe magnet
衔铁 keeper, armature
磁针 magnetic needle

## 化学仪器 Chemical Apparatuses

酒精灯 alcohol lamp
本生灯 bunsen burner
烧杯 beaker
烧瓶 flask, boiling flask
量筒 graduate, measuring cylinder

U形管 U-tube
试管 test tube
试管架 test-tube stand
搅棒 stirrer
气体洗涤瓶 wash-bottle for gases

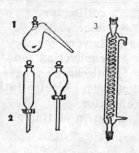

曲颈瓶① **retort**
分液漏斗② **separatory funnel**
旋管冷却器③ **coiled conden-**
**ser**
吸气瓶 **aspirator bottle**

气体发生器 **gas generator**
长梗漏斗 **thistle tube**
干燥器 **desicator**
臼 **mortar**
杆 **pestle**
坩埚 **crucible**
分馏柱 **fractionating column**
吸滤器 **suction filter**
滤网 **silter sieve**
分析天平 **analytical balance**
滴定管 **burette**
液体吸气计 **absorptionmeter**
水银温度计 **mercurial ther-**
**mometer**
酒精温度计 **alcohol thermo-**
**meter**

# 图书馆　Library

图书馆学 **library science**
目录室 **catalogue room**
总目录 **repertory catalogue,**
**cumulative catalogue**
新书目录 **accession cata-**
**logue, accession list**
新书预告 **announcement of**
**forthcoming books**
馆际图书编目 **interlibrary**
**cataloguing**
分科排列的目录 **catalogue**
**raisonne**
按字母顺序分类目录 **alphabet-**
**ic-classed catalogue**
卡片目录 **card catalogue**
卡片目录柜 **card catalogue**
**cabinet**
书名卡 **title card**
主题卡 **subject card**
作者卡 **author card**

分类卡 **classified card**
指引卡 **guide card**
互见卡 **cross reference card**
缩微卡 **microcard**
期限卡 **date card**
穿孔卡 **punched card**
期刊登记卡 **periodical record**
**card**
图书流通室 **delivery room,**
**circulation room**
借书台 **delivery desk,lending**
**counter**
开放时间 **hours of loan ser-**
**vice**
借书证 **library card, borrow-**
**er's card, reader's card**
索书单 **book slip**
索书号 **call number**
借者登记 **borrower's register**
借阅天数 **days of loan service**

催还通知　overdue notice
还书　discharging, returning
续借　renewal, redating
预约　reserving
注销　cancelling
(图书馆)借出　to lend
(读者)借回　to borrow
已借出去的书　books out in circulation
"不外借"　"Not for circulation"
"本馆存"　"Library has"
孤本　the only copy extant
保存本　reserved copy
两星期到期　being due in two weeks
过期七天　being seven days overdue
暂停借书权　suspending the right of borrowing books
阅览室　reading room
指定图书阅览室　reserved books department
读报室　newspaper (reading) room
期刊阅览室　periodical (reading) room
报纸夹　newspaper rod
杂志夹　magazine binder
杂志架　periodical rack
挂图架　scroll picture rack
卷轴架　scroll rack
报刊缩印版　microscopic edition
缩微印刷品　microprint
缩微胶片带　microstrip, microfilm strip
缩微影片　microfilm
显微阅读机　microfilm reader

缩微影片摄影机　microfilm camera
复印机　duplicating machine
影印机　photostat
编目部　cataloguing department
编目员　cataloguer
图书编目　cataloguing
改编目录　recataloguing
图书分类　classifying
图书分类员　classifier
图书整理上架　preparing books for the shelves, processing
交换藏书　exchanging collections
书库　stack room, stacks
书橱　bookcase
架叠书橱　bookstack
双面书架　double-sided bookshelf
滑动书架　roller shelf, sliding shelf
旋转书架　revolving bookcase
公开书架　open shelf
参考书书架　reference shelf
不出借书书架　reserve shelf
辞书架(台)　dictionary stand
图书馆自动化　library automation, computer-based library operation
情报检索　information retrieval
使用计算机检索　using a computer for retrieval
借出图书如有遗失或损坏, 应按章赔偿　Loss or damage of library books should be paid for according the regulations.

# 新闻出版 Press and Publishing

## 报刊 The Press

报纸　newspaper
日报　daily paper, daily
晨报　morning paper
下午报　afternoon paper
晚报　evening paper
星期日报　Sunday newspaper
号外　extra
特刊, 专刊　special edition, special issue
增刊　supplement
增页　extra page
插页　insert
机关报　organ
喉舌　mouthpiece
(政府, 大学)公报　gazette
小报　tabloid
期刊　periodical
不定期刊物　non-periodical
周报, 周刊　weekly
双周刊　biweekly, fortnightly
三周刊　triweekly
月刊　monthly
双月刊　bimonthly
季刊　quarterly

年刊, 年鉴　annual, year book
杂志　magazine
画报　pictorial
黄色报刊　yellow press, scandal sheet
新闻采访　news-gathering
新闻报道　news report, news story, news coverage
新闻公报　press communique
新闻通报　press handout
新闻简报　bulletin
新闻照片　news picture
新闻信札　news letter
新闻分析　news analysis
新闻杂志　newsmagazine
新闻人物　news maker
国内新闻　home news
国际新闻　international news, world news
国外新闻　foreign news
头条新闻　top news, top-line news
本地新闻　local news
独家新闻　exclusive news

内幕新闻 inside story, inside dope
花边新闻 box news
抢先发表的独家新闻 scoop
(付印时加的)最新消息 stop press
小道新闻 grapevine news
丑闻 scandal
珍闻,趣闻 titbit, tidbit
传闻 hearsay
消息来源 source of news
权威方面 authoritative source
消息灵通人士 well-informed sources
提供消息的人 informant
新闻发布会 (news) briefing
新闻发布官员 briefing officer
新闻电讯 dispatch
短讯 flash
新闻稿 news release, press release
标题 headline, head
通栏标题 banner headline
栏外标题 running headline
副标题 subtitle
栏顶标题 tophead
小标题 subhead, subheading
导语 lead
社论 editorial, leading article

评论 commentary, comment, review
专论,专题文章 monograph
署名文章 signed article
特写 feature story
访问记 interview
编者按语 editor's note
作者姓名(的一)行 byline
笔名 pseudonym
读者园地 readers' corner
副刊 supplement
连载 serial
连载小说 serial story
人物简介 profile
小品文 feuilleton
漫画 cartoon
连环漫画 comic strip
版面 format
报头 head of a paper
报眼 ear
专栏 special column
栏吋 column inch
书评专栏 book review column
体育部分 sports section
科技版 science and technology page
宣传工具 mass media, mass communications
民意测验 public opinion poll
报业辛迪加,特稿供应社 syndicate

## 报 社 Newspaper Office

编辑部 editorial department, copy desk
出版部 publishing department, production department

营业部 business department
发行部 circulation department
订阅部 subscription department

广告部　advertising department

参考图书馆　reference library

资料室　morgue

发行人　publisher

总编辑　editor-in-chief

主编,编辑主任　managing editor

副主编　associate managing editor, deputy managing editor

编辑　editor, copy reader

改写员　rewriteman

电讯编辑　cable editor, telegraph editor

新闻编辑　news editor

图片编辑　picture editor

版面编辑　make-up editor

社论撰写人　editorialist

高级编辑　senior editor

特约编辑　contributing editor

投稿人　contributor

特约撰稿人　staff writer

本市新闻编辑　city editor

〔英〕商业金融栏编辑　City editor

责任编辑　responsible editor

助理编辑　sub-editor

评论员　commentator

新闻分析员　news analyst

专栏作家　columnist

特写作家　feature writer

自由(采访)撰稿人　free lance, free-lancer

新闻工作者　journalist

新闻记者　newspaperman

女新闻记者　newspaperwoman

记者,采员　reporter

战地记者　war correspondent

常驻记者　resident correspondent

驻国外记者　foreign correspondent

特派记者　staff correspondent

巡回记者　roving reporter

摄影记者　press photographer, cameraman

政治漫画作者　political cartoonist

记者招待会　press conference, news conference

(议会中)记者席　press gallery

(运动会等)记者席　press box

## 通讯社　News Agencies

新华社(新华通讯社)　Xinhua (Xinhua News Agency)

中国新闻社　China News Service

路透社(路透通讯社)　Reuter(s) (Reuter's News Agency)

美联社(美国联合通讯社)　AP (Associated Press)

合众国际社　UPI, United Press International

美国新闻处　USIS, United States Information Service

国际交流署　International Communications Agency

法新社(法国新闻社)　AFP (L' Agence France-Presse)

共同社　KYODO (Kyodo News Agency)

时事社(时事通讯社)　JIJI(Jiji News Agency)

德新社(德意志新闻社)　**DPA**
　**(Deutsche Presse Agentur)**
安莎社(安莎通讯社)　**ANSA**
　**(Ansa News Agency)**
塔斯社(苏联电讯社)　**TASS**
　**(Telegraph Agency of the**
　**Soviet Union)**
苏联新闻社　**Novosti Agency,**
　**Novosti Press Agency**
罗马尼亚通讯社　**AGERPRES**
南通社　**TANJUG**

安塔拉通讯社　**ANTARA**
中东社(中东通讯社)　**MENA**
　**(Middle East News Agen-**
　**cy)**
拉美社　**Prensa Latina**
不结盟国家通讯社联盟　**Non**
　**Aligned Nations News**
　**Agency**
普尔新闻交换网　**News Agency**
　**Pool of Non-Aligned and**
　**Developing Countries**

## 出　版　Publishing

出版社　**publishing house,**
　**publisher**
出版物　**publication**
教科书　**textbook**
读本　**reader**
参考书,工具书　**reference book**
手册　**handbook, manual**
小册子　**booklet, pamphlet**
选集　**selected works, selec-**
　**tion**
全集　**complete works**
(诗文等)选集　**anthology**
公文,文件　**document, papers**
文摘　**digest, abstracts**
文献集,档案　**archives**
科学文献　**scientific literature**
科普读物　**popular science**
　**readings**
论文　**thesis**
专题报告　**memoir**
会议录　**proceedings**
议事录　**transactions**
地图　**map**
地图册　**atlas**

画册　**album of paintings,**
　**book of plates**
版画　**engraving**
纪念刊　**memorial volume**
纪念册　**souvenir album**
图画书　**picture book**
书目提要　**bibliography**
索引书　**index volume**
畅销书　**best seller**
百科全书　**encyclop(a)edia**
大百科全书　**macrop(a)edia**
小百科全书　**microp(a)edia**
版本　**edition**
初版　**first edition**
再版　**second edition, repub-**
　**lication**
第三版　**third edition**
第一次印刷　**first impression**
原版(书)　**original edition**
修订版　**revised edition**
增订版　**enlarged edition**
重版书　**reprint**
平装本　**paperback edition**
普及本　**popular edition**

廉价本　cheap edition, low-price edition
图书馆版　library edition
精装本　hardback edition
高级精装本　deluxe edition
袖珍本　pocket edition
缩印本　compact edition
影印本　photographic reprint edition
直接影印本　photostat (copy)
缩微本　microcopy
珍本　rare book, scarce book
孤本　the only extant copy
节本　abridged edition
题署本　autographed copy, signed copy

毛边书　rough edge edition
硬纸面　stiff paper binding
布面　cloth binding
皮面　leather binding
塑料面　plastic cover
护封　jacket
色边　coloured edge
金边　gilt edge
对开本　folio
四开本　quarto
八开本　octavo
十六开本　sixteen-mo, 16-mo
三十二开本　thirty-two-mo, 32-mo
六十四开本　sixty-four-mo, 64-mo

## 广播，电视　Broadcast and Television

广播节目　broadcast(ing) program(me)
新闻广播　newscast
国内新闻广播　home news broadcast
国际新闻广播　world news broadcast
实况广播　live broadcast
实况广播报道　running commentary
实况广播员　commentator
录音报道　transcribed report, tape-recorded report
联播　network broadcast, chain broadcast
转播　relay broadcast, re-broadcast
有线转播　rediffusion on wire
定向广播　directional broadcast

有线广播　wire broadcasting
立体声广播　stereophonic broadcast
呼号　call signal
报时信号　time signal
广播电台　broadcasting station, broadcaster
转播电台　relay station
录音室　recording room
录音员　sound engineer
磁带录音机　(magnetic) tape recorder
盒式磁带录音机　cassette tape recorder
立体声录音机　stereo recorder
多声道录音机　multichannel recorder
循环磁带录音机　endless tape recorder
混音桌　mixing desk

监听扬声器 monitoring (check) loudspeaker

播音室 studio

播音员 announcer, broadcaster

悬挂式话筒 suspended microphone

桌上用话筒 desk microphone

广播稿 script, broadcast message

广播剧 radio play

广播讨论会 panel discussion

有声资料 sound archives

电视广播 telecast(ing), television broadcasting

黑白电视 monochrome television, black-and-white television

彩色电视 colour television

电视节目 television program

电视与无线电同时联播(节目) simulcast

电视演播室 television studio

电视广播员 telecaster

电视记者招待会 televised news conference

实况电视转播 live television coverage, live telecast

电视转播 television relay

电视广播剧 teleplay

电视电影 telecine

电视观众 televiewers

电视台 television (broadcast) station

电视塔 television tower

电视转播卫星 television transmission satellite

电视网 television network

电视机 television receiver, TV set

电视信道 television channel

频道 band of frequencies

荧光屏 fluorescent screen

电视摄像员 camera operator

电视摄像机 television camera

电视录像 television recording

电视唱片 video disc

录像机 video (tape) recorder

盒式录像机 video-cassette recorder

录像磁带 videotape

# 体 育 Physical Culture

## 体育运动 Physical Culture and Sports

发展体育运动,增强人民体质 **Promote physical culture and sports and build up the people's health.**

友谊第一,比赛第二 **Friendship first, competition second.**

切磋技艺,交流经验 **studying techniques and exchanging experiences**

体育锻炼 **physical training**

群众性体育锻炼 **mass sports activities**

"国家体育锻炼标准"证书 **"National Physical Fitness Training Programme" Certificate**

"国家体育锻炼标准"证章 **"National Physical Fitness Training Programme" Badge**

训练量 **volume of exercise**

运动量 **amount of exercise**

准备活动 **warming-up (exercises)**

整理活动 **cooling-down (exercises), warming-down (exercises)**

球类运动 **ball games**

乒乓球 **table tennis**

羽毛球 **badminton**

网球 **tennis**

排球 **volleyball**

篮球 **basketball**

足球 **football, association football, soccer**

棒球 **baseball**

垒球 **softball**

手球 **handball**

曲棍球① **hockey**

冰球② **ice hockey**

水球③ **water polo**

马球④ **polo**

板球⑤ **cricket**

橄榄球⑥ **Rugby football, rugger**

高尔夫球⑦ **golf**

台球(弹子球)⑧ **billiards**

槌球⑨ **croquet**

滚球戏(九柱戏)⑩ **skittles, ninepins, bowls**

康乐球⑪ **caroms**

回力球⑫ **pelota, jai alai**

田径运动 **track and field**

体操 **physical exercises, gymnestics**

| | |
|---|---|
| 跑步 **running** | 摩托车运动 **motor-cycling** |
| 爬山 **mountain climbing** | 登山运动 **mountaineering** |
| 爬绳 **rope climbing** | 滑冰 **skating** |
| 爬杆 **pole climbing** | 滑雪 **skiing** |
| 跳绳 **rope skipping** | 射箭 **archery** |
| 跳橡皮筋 **rubber-band skipping** | 射击 **shooting** |
| 拔河 **tug-of-war** | 现代五项运动 **modern pentathlon** |
| 荡秋千 **playing on the swing** | 赛马 **horse race** |
| 高秋千 **high swing** | 赛牦牛 **yak race** |
| 跳板 **springboard jumping** | 拳击 **boxing** |
| 跳跷跷板 **see-saw jumping** | 击剑 **fencing** |
| 游泳 **swimming** | 摔跤 **wrestling** |
| 跳水 **diving** | 武术 *wushu* |
| 划艇运动 **canoeing** | 国际象棋 **chess** |
| 划船运动 **rowing, boating** | 象棋 **Chinese chess** |
| 龙舟竞渡 **dragon boat race** | 围棋 *weiqi*, **go** |
| 摩托艇运动 **motor-boating** | 相扑〔日〕 **sumo** |
| 帆船运动 **yachting** | 柔术，柔道〔日〕 **judo** |
| 自行车运动 **cycling** | 徒手自卫武术〔日〕 **karate** |

## 运动会 Sports Meet

| | |
|---|---|
| 全国运动会 **National Games** | 列队退场 **march-off** |
| 亚洲运动会 **Asian Games** | 授奖仪式 **prize-awarding ceremony** |
| 奥林匹克运动会 **Olympic Games, Olumpiad** | 比赛 **competition, contest** |
| 组织委员会 **organizing committee** | 友谊赛 **friendly match** |
| 技术委员会 **technical committee** | 邀请赛 **invitational tournament** |
| 仲裁委员会 **appeal committee** | 主队 **home team** |
| 比赛地点 **venue** | 客队 **visiting team, guest team** |
| 东道国 **host country** | 国际比赛 **international tournament** |
| 竞技场(比赛场地) **arena** | 锦标赛 **championships** |
| 开幕式 **opening ceremony** | 表演赛 **exhibition match** |
| 闭幕式 **closing ceremony** | 选拔赛 **selective trials** |
| 列队入场 **march-in** | |

| | | | |
|---|---|---|---|
| 对抗赛 | duel meet | 冠军 | champion, title |
| 淘汰赛 | elimination series | 亚军 | runner-up |
| 循环赛 | round-robin series | 名列第一 | taking the first place |
| 小组循环赛 | group round robin | | |
| 第一轮 | first round | 名列第三 | getting the third place |
| 及格赛 | qualifying heats, qualifying trials | | |
| | | 金质奖章获得者 | gold medallist, gold medal winner |
| 预赛 | preliminaries | | |
| 复赛 | quarter-finals | 银质奖章 | silver medal |
| 半决赛 | semi-finals | 铜质奖章 | bronze medal |
| 决赛 | finals | 奖品 | prize, trophy |
| 安慰赛 | consolation event | 纪念品 | souvenir |
| 三(五)局两(三)胜 | best of three (five) games | 纪念章 | souvenir badge |
| | | 奖状 | certificate of award |
| 甲队对乙队 | A team versus B team.(A team plays B team.) | 奖杯 | cup |
| | | 比分 | score |
| 正式项目 | title event | 累积比分 | running score, aggregate score |
| 团体项目 | team event | | |
| 个人项目 | individual event | 报分 | calling the score |
| 保持纪录 | holding a record, keeping a record | 以…分获胜 | winning by… points |
| | | 以…分败局 | losing by… points |
| 打破纪录 | breaking a record | 以…分领先 | leading by… points |
| 平纪录 | equalizing a record | | |
| 创造纪录 | setting a record, creating a record | 击败 | defeating…, outplaying…, beating… |
| | | 败给 | losing (the match) to… |
| 创造好成绩 | chalking up good results | 打成平局 | playing even |
| | | 扳成平局 | equalizing the score |
| 少年纪录 | junior record | 现在几比几? | What's the score? |
| 国家纪录 | national record | 零比零 | love all |
| 世界纪录 | world record | 三比零 | three to zero |
| 世界纪录保持者 | world record holder | 五比三,甲队领先. | Five to three in A team's favour. |
| 名次 | placing, ranking | | |
| 名次排列表 | ranking list | | |

## 体育人员　Sports Staff

| | | | |
|---|---|---|---|
| 运动员 | athlete, sportsman | 优秀运动员 | top-notch player, ace player |
| 老练运动员 | veteran player | | |

| | |
|---|---|
| 老练运动员　veteran player | 种子队　seeded team |
| 全能运动员　all-round sports-man | 队员　team member |
| 有希望的运动员　up-and-com-ing player | 同队队员　teammate |
| | 预备队员　reserve, substitute |
| 一级运动员　first-class sports-man | 对手　opponent |
| | 领队　team leader |
| 二级运动员　second-class sportsman | 队长　captain |
| | 场上队长　field captain |
| 三级运动员　third-class sportsman | 不参加比赛的队长　non-playing captain |
| 运动健将　master of sports | 随队人员　team follower |
| 新手　beginner | 教练　coach |
| 选手　selected player, se-lected contestant | 教练员　trainer |
| | 受训练人　trainee |
| 种子选手　seeded player | 运动爱好者　sports fan, sports enthusiast |
| 职业运动员　professional | |
| 半职业运动员　semi-profes-sional | 啦啦队　cheering section |
| | 体育工作者　sports worker, physical culture worker |
| 业余运动员　amateur | |
| 参加半决赛运动员　semi-final-ist | 裁判员　referee, umpire, judge |
| 参加决赛运动员　finalist | 主裁判员　chief referee |
| 运动队　team | 司线员　linesman |
| 男队　men's team | 终点裁判员　judge at the finish line |
| 女队　women's team | |
| 青年队　youth team | 发令员　starter |
| 少年队　junior team | 记分员　scorekeeper |
| 国家队　national team | 计时员　timekeeper |
| 选手队　selection team | 宣告员　announcer |
| | 甲队由…上场　A team fields… |

## 体育场　Stadium (Sports Field)

| | |
|---|---|
| 训练场地　training ground | 露天看台　bleachers |
| 比赛区　playing area | 坐位数量　seating capacity |
| (篮、排、网、羽毛)球场　court | 裁判台　referee's platform, referee's stand |
| (足、手、棒)球场　field | |
| 看台　stand | 裁判椅　referee's chair |

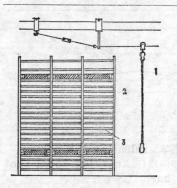

受奖台 victory rostrum, podium
公告牌 bulletin board
成绩公布牌 results board
记分牌 score board, score indicator
电子计时器 electronic timer
光电计时记分器 photoelectric timing and scoring device
哨子 whistle
号令枪 starter's pistol
秒表 chronograph, stopwatch
体育馆 gym, gymnasium
照明设备 lighting installation
电力控制可移看台 electrically controlled movable stand

翻椅 tip-up seat
体操设备 gymnastic equipment
体操器械 gymnastic apparatus
技巧弹跳器械 rebound tumbling apparatus
保护带 safety belt
保护滑车① safety pulley
肋木② wall bars, rung
肋木条③ rung
杠梯 balancing ladder
伏虎,滚轮④ gyro wheel, Rhön wheel
轻器械 hand apparatus
瓶状棒⑤ Indian club
哑铃 dumb-bell
握力器⑥ spring-grip dumb-bell
拉力器⑦ chest expander, chest developer

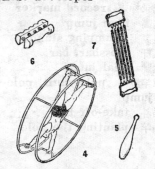

# 田 径 Track and Field

田径运动 track and field sports, athletics
田径运动员 track and field athlete, athlete
田赛项目 field events
径赛项目 track events
田径场 playing field
十项运动 decathlon

| 五项运动 | pentathlon |
|---|---|
| 跳远 | long jump, broad jump |

五项运动　pentathlon
跳远　long jump, broad jump
跳远运动员　long jumper
三级跳远①　hop, step and jump, triple jump
单脚跳(三级跳远第一跳)②　hop
跨步跳(三级跳远第二跳)③　step
跳跃(三级跳远第三跳)④　jump
起跳板⑤　take-off board
沙坑　jumping pit, sand pit
空翻跳远　somersault long jump
纪录标志　record marker
跳高　high jump
跳高架　jumping stand
横杆　crossbar, bar
试跳　trial jump
撑竿跳高　pole-vault, pole-jump
插斗　take-off box
插竿　planting the pole

撒竿　releasing the pole
碰倒横杆　knocking down the bar
剪式跳高　scissors jump
俯卧式跳高　belly roll jump
跳过…米　jumping over…metres, clearing…metres
推铅球⑥　shot put, putting the weight
铅球运动员　shot putter
铅球投掷圈　putting circle
掷铁饼　discus throw, throwing the discus
投掷圈　throwing circle
掷标枪⑦　javelin throw, throwing the javelin
掷链球⑧　hammer throw, throwing the hammer
安全护笼⑨　safety cage
试掷　trial throw
投掷…米　throwing…metres

## 赛 跑 Race, Running

全天候跑道 all-weather track

塑胶跑道 synthetic surface track

分道 lane

里道, 里圈 inside lane, inner lane

外道, 外圈 outside lane, outer lane

第一圈 first lap

最后一圈 last lap

计圈器 lap-counting apparatus

电动计时器 electric time-keeping device

起跑线⑩ starting line

起跑器⑪ starting block

发令枪 starting pistol

起跑信号 starting signal, pistol shot

抢跑⑫ jumping the gun

起跑犯规 false start

终点线 finishing line

终点带 finishing tape

冲刺 spurt, sprint

撞线⑬ breasting the tape

短跑 sprint, dash

短跑运动员 sprinter

100米赛跑 100-metre sprint

200米赛跑 200-metre dash

中距离赛跑 middle-distance race

长距离赛跑 long-distance race

马拉松赛跑 Marathon (race)

环城赛跑 round-the-city race

越野赛跑 cross-country race

障碍赛跑 obstacle race, steeplechase

跨栏赛跑 hurdle race, hurdles

110米高栏 110-metre high hurdles

200米低栏 200-metre low hurdles

400米中栏 400-metre intermediate hurdles

接力赛跑⑭ relay race, relay

接力棒⑮ relay baton

接力区 change-over area

接力区标志 change-over mark

传接棒 baton exchange

第一棒运动员 first runner

最后一棒运动员　anchor man

竞走　heel-to-toe walking, walking race, competitive walking

"各就各位！"　"On your marks!"

"预备！"　"Set!" "Get set!"

"跑！"　"Go!"

在赛跑中领先　having the lead in a race

遥遥领先　holding a safe lead

恢复领先地位　regaining the lead

## 体　操　Gymnastics (Exercises)

体操运动员　gymnast

体操表演　gymnastic display, gymnastic exhibition

柔软体操　callisthenics

双人体操　couples exercise, companion exercises

团体操　group callisthenics, group exercises

广播操　broadcast callisthenics, setting-up exercises done to broadcast music

工间操　physical exercises during break

课间操　between-classes exercises

马背体操①　horseback gymnastics

医疗体操　therapeutic gymnastics, curative gymnastics

哑铃操　dumb-bell exercises

藤圈操　hoop exercises, exercises with rattan hoops

垫上运动　mat exercises

自由体操　free exercises, floor exercises

技巧运动　acrobatic gymnastics

规定动作　compulsory exercise, prescribed exercise

自选动作　optional exercise, voluntary exercise

艺术体操　artistic gymnastics

音乐伴奏　music accompaniment

完成预定动作情况　execution

难度　difficulty

高难度　superior difficulty

协调　harmony

准确　accuracy

流畅　fluency

优美　gracefulness, elegance

独创性　originality

评分　making evaluation

满分　full score

加分　bonus point

1

## 体操与技巧动作　Exercises and Tumbling

开始姿势　starting position

足尖站立　standing on tiptoe

两臂前平举　arms forwards

两臂侧举　arms sideways

两臂上举　arms upwards

两臂屈伸　arms bending and stretching

右腿向前举　right leg forwards

左腿向后举　left leg backwards

体前屈②　trunk bending forwards

体后仰③　trunk bending backwards

两手叉腰, 体右屈④　trunk bending to the right, hands on hips

体旋转⑤　trunk circling

弓箭步⑥　forward lunge

侧弓箭步⑦　lateral lunge, sideways lunge

桥⑧　back bend, bridge

肩倒立⑨　shoulder stand

头手倒立⑩　headstand

手倒立⑪　handstand

侧手翻⑫　cartwheel, lateral wheel

后手翻⑬　flip-flop, flip-flap

劈叉⑭　split

纵劈叉　sidesplit

俯撑　front support

俯卧推起　push-up

直角支撑　"L" support

| | |
|---|---|
| 分腿 straddle | 平衡 scale, balance |
| 跪 kneeling | 转体 turn, twist, pirouette |
| 卧 lying down | 鱼跃 dive |
| 仰卧 lying flat on back | 滚翻 roll |
| 蹲 squat, crouch | 软翻 reversal |
| 助跑 approach prun | 直体空翻 stretched smersault |
| 跳跑 spring run | 团身空翻 tucked somersault |
| 快滑步 chasse step | 技巧一系列动作 routine |

## 器械体操 Exercises on Apparatus

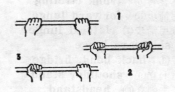

| | |
|---|---|
| 体操器械 gymnastic apparatus | 反握② reverse grip, underhand grip |
| 上(体操器械) mounting | 正反握③ combined grip |
| 下(体操器械) dismounting | 引体向上 chin-up |
| 单杠 horizontal bar | 屈伸上 upstart |
| 单杠握法 grasps on the horizontal bar | 挂臂屈伸上 upstart from upperarm |
| 正握① ordinary grip, over grip | 摆动 swing |
| | 悬垂 hang, suspense |
| | 翻上 swing up |
| | 向前大回环④ giant circle forward |
| | 骑撑⑤ straddle support |
| | 脱手 releasing the grip |
| | 再握杠 regrasping the bar |
| | 后空翻离杠 backward somersault from the bar |

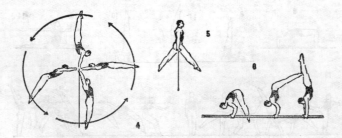

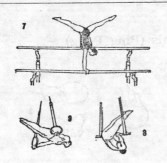

双杠　parallel bars
支撑动作　movement of support
用力动作　movement of strength
平衡动作　movement of balance
杠下动作　movement below the bars
双臂屈伸　dip
屈臂撑行进　bent arms support walk
摆动手倒立　handstand with swing
慢起手倒立⑥　handstand with press
高低杠　uneven parallel bars, high-low bars
高杠　top bar
低杠　lower bar
倒十字支撑⑦　cross handstand
平衡木　balance beam
保持平衡　keeping the balance

燕式平衡　front horizontal scale
吊杠⑧　trapeze
翻上向前　upward circle forward
吊环　rings, hand rings
静止吊环　stationary rings
摆动吊环　swinging rings
倒悬垂　inverted hang
水平支撑⑨　horizontal support
鞍马⑩　pommelled horse
纵跳马　long horse
横跳马　side horse
鞍部　saddle
摆越　half leg circle
交叉⑪　scissors
全旋　circle
移位　travel
俯腾越⑫　front vault, face vault
背腾越⑬　rear vault, back vault
侧腾越⑭　side vault
分腿腾越　vaulting over with straddled legs
屈腿腾越⑮　vaulting over with legs together and bent
跳跃器　vaulting back
跳桌　vaulting table
跳箱　vaulting box
弹跳板　springboard

## 乒乓球  Table Tennis (Ping Pong)

乒乓球  table tennis ball, ping pong ball
球拍  bat, paddle, racket
橡胶拍  rubber bat
海绵拍  sponge bat
颗粒胶  pimpled rubber
正贴海绵拍  sandwich with pimpled rubber turned outwards
反贴海绵拍  sandwich with pimpled rubber turned inwards
拍身  blade
拍柄  handle
球拍套  racket case
球台  table
台面  playing surface
右半区  right half court
左半区  left half court
台角  corner of table
台边  edge of table
端线  end line
边线  side line
中线  centre line
网  net
白边  white-top
网柱  pole, support
球网支架  clamp
网眼  mesh
直拍握法①  pen-hold grip
横拍握法②  hand-shake grip, tennis grip
执拍手  racket hand
不执拍手  free hand
左手执拍者  left-hand player

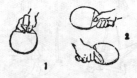

攻击型选手  attacking player, aggressive
防守型选手  defensive player
合法发球  good service
发球员  server
抛球  throwing the ball, projecting
发平击球  flat service
发弹击式急球  flip service
下蹲式发球  squat(ting) service
变化并加转的发球  varied and heavily spun service
巧妙的发球  tricky service
重发球  service let
擦网球  net ball
发球得分  serving a winner, ace service
发球抢攻  attacking after service, hitting the service-return
发球失误  missed service
发球违例  service fault
发球未触及本区台面  volleyed service
接发球  returning the service
合法还击  good return
接发球得分  killing the service

接发球抢攻　**counter-hitting the service**

回球失误　**making a faulty return**

抽球　**drive**

扣杀　**smash**

推球　**push**

挡球　**block**

推挡③　**half volley with push**

弧圈球　**loop**

削球　**cut, slice**

搓球④　**chop**

上旋　**topspin**

下旋　**underspin, backspin**

侧旋　**sidespin**

长球　**long shot**

短球　**short shot, drop shot**

高球　**lob, high ball**

扫球　**flat hit**

正手远抽⑤　**forehand long drive**

反手击球⑥　**backhand stroke**

直线球　**straight shot, side-line shot**

斜线球　**diagonal shot, cross shot**

擦边球　**edge ball, touch**

滚网球　**net-cord ball**

追身球　**close-to-the-body-shot**

超身球　**passing shot**

木板球　**wood shot**

定位球　**placement shot**

对抽　**exchanging drives**

对搓　**chopping the chops**

拉球　**lifting the ball**

加转　**giving spin to the ball**

长抽短吊　**combining long drives with drop shots**

左右开弓　**attacking on both sides, smashing from both wings**

近台快攻　**fast attack over the table**

远台削球⑦　**off-table chop**

近台防守　**close-table defence**

放高球防守　**balloon defence**

滑板　**feint play**

空档　**opening, open side**

打球出界　**overdriving, over-hitting a shot**

打球落网　**netting the ball**

步法　**footwork**

站位　**positioning**

救险球　**saving a seemingly impossible ball, retrieving an impossible shot**

局末平分　**deuce**

"准备!"　**"Ready!"**

"比赛开始!"　**"Play ball!"**

"发球犯规!"　**"Fault!"**

"手扶球台!"　**"Hand on table!"**

"台内阻挡!"　**"Over table!"**

"拦击!"　**"Volleyed!"**

"错区!"　**"Wrong court!"**

"错接球！" "Wrong player!"
"触网！" "Touched net!"
"两跳！" "Double bounce!"
"连击！" "Double hit!"
"出界！" "Out!" "Off!"

"得分！" "Point!"
"失分！" "No!"
轮换发球法 expedite system
(轮换发球法)还击12次 making 12 returns

# 羽毛球 Badminton

羽毛球 shuttlecock
塑料羽毛球 plastic shuttle
(球)底托 cork base
羽毛顶点 feather tip
羽毛圈 crown of feathers
球拍 racket
球场 court
前场 forecourt
后场 backcourt
中区 midcourt
左场区 backhand court
右场区 forehand court
端线 base line
端线外空地 back room
正手握拍法 forehand grip
反手握拍法 backhand grip
发远球 long service
发短球 short service
发平(线)球 level service, flat service
发球方 serving side
接球方 receiving side
掌握发球权一方 In side, "in" side
不掌握发球权一方 OUT side, "out" side
发球权 right to serve
失误 miss
失发球权 loss of service
有发球权 hand-in

无发球权 hand-out
失去发球权一方 retired side
重发球 let
正拍扣球① forehand smash
反拍扣球② backhand smash
头顶扣球 overhead smash
高远球 high clear
大力扣杀 hard smash
吊网前球 drop-shot
平抽球③ drive

网前推托 **pushing a shot just across the net**

扣吊结合 **combining smashes with drop shots**

近网挑球 **lift**

网前轻挑短球④ **hairpin shot**

一方保持发球权时间 **inning(s)**

回合, 往返拍击 **rally**

打赢一回合 **winning a rally**

获得一分 **scoring a point**

再赛 **setting**

选择"再赛"权 **choice of "setting"**

击球犯规 **foul hit**

连击 **double hit**

木球 **wooden shot**

持球 **holding, carrying**

触网 **touching the net**

"零比零, 开始比赛!" **"Love all, play!"**

"发球错区!" **"Wrong court!"**

"换发球!" **"Service Over!"**

(双打)"第二发球员发球!" **"second server!"**

"再赛x分!" **"Set x points!"**

# 网　球　Tennis

草地网球 **lawn tennis**

网球 **tennis ball**

网球拍 **tennis racket, tennis racquet**

拍柄 **racket handle**

(球拍)线 **gut, string**

(球拍)竖线 **main string**

(球拍)横线 **cross string**

球拍夹 **racket press**

扣紧螺丝 **tightening screw**

挡眼罩 **eyeshade**

网球场 **tennis court**

草地球场 **grass court, tennis lawn**

硬地球场 **hard court**

端线 **base line**

双打边线 **side line for doubles**

单打边线 **side line for singles**

单打边线与双打边线之间的狭长地带 **alley**

发球线 **service line**

发球区 **service box, service court**

中线 **centre (service) line**

中点标志 **centre mark**

网柱 **net post**

网中心固定装置 **net strip**

网中心高度调节器 **net adjuster**

网中心布带 **centre band**

发球⑤ **service**

发削球⑥ **slice service**

发球员 **server**

接球员 **receiver, striker-out**

正拍握拍法 **forehand groundstroke**

| | |
|---|---|
| 反拍握拍法　backhand groundstroke | 大抡拍　long swing |
| 发球失误　faulty service | 截球　intercepting |
| 发球触网　net | 失误　miss |
| 触线球　line ball | 换位　change of positions |
| 脚步犯规　foot fault | 换边　change of sides |
| 发球得分　service ace | 主裁判　call umpire |
| 截击空中球　volley | 副裁判　net umpire |
| 低截球　low volley | 发球裁判　foot fault judge |
| 击反弹球①　playing a half volley | 司线员　linesman |
| 高压球②　smash | 记分员　marker |
| 高球扣杀　overhead smash | 局　game |
| 正手拦球③　forehand volley | 盘　set |
| 反手扣杀　backhand volley | 场　match |
| 正手抽球　forehand drive | 一局中得一分　fifteen |
| 反手抽球④　backhand drive | 一平　fifteen all |
| 跃起扣杀　jump smash | 一局中得两分　thirty |
| 吊高球　lob | 二平　thirty all |
| 滚球　spin | 一局中得三分　forty |
| 切球　cut | 三平　forty all, deuce |
| | 一局中的决胜分　game point, game ball |

## 排　球　Volleyball

| | |
|---|---|
| 排球场　volleyball court | 网顶帆布带　canvas band |
| 网柱　net post | 标志杆　vertical rod |

标志带　vertical side marker

排球　volleyball

球胆　bladder

皮壳　leather case

橡皮壳　rubber case

发球区　service area, service box

后区　back zone

攻击区, 前区　attack zone

"死角"　"dead area"

网前位置　net position

前排队员　frontline player, net player

后排队员　backline player, backcourt player

后排右(1号位队员)　right back (player No.1)

前排右(2号位队员)　right forward (player No.2)

前排中(3号位队员)　centre forward (player No.3)

前排左(4号位队员)　left forward (player No.4)

后排左(5号位队员)　left back (player No.5)

后排中(6号位队员)　centre back (player No.6)

拦网队员　blocker

攻击手, 扣手　attacker, spiker

主攻手　ace spiker

发球权　right of service

抛起(发球动作)　toss-up

发保险球　safe service

上手发球　overhand service

下手发球　underhand service

过头发球　overhead service

大力发球　drive service

发下坠球　drop service

发高球　lobbing service

勾手发球　hook service

勾手大力发球⑤　cannon-ball service

助跑发球　running service

发飘球⑥　floating service

发球得分　scrve point, service ace

换发球　change of service

失去发球权　loss of service

一传　first pass

一传手　first passer

单手下手垫球　one-hand under toss

二传　set, set up

二传手　setter

上手传球　overhand pass, face pass

跑动传球　running pass

跳起传球　jump pass, jump toss

传近网球　close set

传远网球　deep set

背传⑦　back pass, backward set

传拉开球　wide set

倒地传球　fall down pass

一次扣杀　direct spike

二次扣杀　one-pass attack, two-count spike

快扣　quick spike

大力扣杀　powerful smash

大抡臂扣球　windmill attack

打拦网手扣杀　smash on the block

超手扣球　spike over the block

甩腕扣球　snap down with the wrist

躲拦网手扣球　spike past the block

快攻球　wide-cat spring attack

斜线扣球　crosscourt smash, cross spike

直线球　straight ball

斜线球路　cross course

直线球路　straight course

封网,拦网　block

单人拦网　one-man block

双人拦网　two-man block

拦网成功　shut out

拦网得分　block point

击入空当得分　scoring a placement

用手掌击球　batting the ball

吊球　dropping the ball

救球　retrieving a ball

鱼跃救球⑧　making a diving save

将网上球救起　recovering a ball from net

捞球　scooping up a ball

推球　pushing a ball, shoving a ball

铲球　digging up a ball

手腕动作　wrist work

步法　footwork

跨步　stride

垫步　skip

滑步　slide

侧步　sidestep

晃跳　trick jump

犯规　foul

持球　holding, catching

连击　double hit

四次击球　four-hit

越过中线　off-side

过网　over net

触网　touching the net

## 篮　球　Basketball

篮球场　basketball court

篮板　backboard, bank

篮圈　ring, hoop, basket

篮柱　basket post

篮网　cord net

边线　side-line

底线 end-line
三秒区 3-second zone, foul lane
罚球区 free-throw area
罚球线 free-throw line
中线 division line
中圈 centre circle
篮球运动员 basketballer, basketball player
(上场)篮球队 quintet, five
中锋 centre
前锋 forward
后卫 guard
跳球队员 jumper
跳球 jump ball
中圈跳球 tip-off
投篮 shooting
空心球 clean shot, open shot
原地投篮 set shot
单手投篮 one-hand shot
双手头上原地投篮① two-hand overhead set shot
勾手投篮② hook shot
急停投篮 stop shot
跳起投篮 jump shot
急停跳投 stop-jump shot
行进间单手投篮③ running one-hand shot
运球投篮 drive shot
近距离投篮 close-in shot
不受干扰的近投 crisp shot
转身投篮 pivot shot
面向球篮投篮 facing shot
背向球篮转身投篮 back-up shot
高弧度投篮 high arch shot
"扣篮" over-the-rim shot
擦板入篮 bank shot
轻拨入篮 flipping the ball into the basket
补篮,托球入篮 rebound shot, tip-in shot
切入篮 lay-up shot
跨步上篮 stride lay-up
投中 shooting the ball in, making a basket
投篮不中 missing the basket
投中得分 making a goal
判投中有效 allowing a goal
判投中无效 cancelling a goal
抢篮板球 backboard recovery
长传球 long pass
短传球 short pass

单手肩上传球④ **baseball pass**

单手低手向前传球⑤ **bowling pass**

低传球 **low pass**

高吊传球 **lob pass**

弧形传球 **loop pass**

侧传 **side pass**

侧臂传球 **sidearm pass**

横传球 **cross pass, lateral pass**

反弹传球 **bounce pass**

传滚地球 **floor pass, rolling pass**

勾手传球⑥ **hook pass**

跳起传球 **jump pass**

手递手传球 **hand-off**

背后传球⑦ **back-flip pass, around-the-back**

两手交叉传球 **cross-hand pass**

双手胸前传球 **two-hand snap pass**

双手低手传球⑧ **two-hand under-hand pass**

回传球 **return pass**

假传球 **fake pass**

假装投篮的传球 **fake-shot pass**

双手把传来的球迅速传出 **shove pass**

拨球传递 **shovel pass**

花样传球 **fancy pass**

三人传球 **three-man inter-passing**

"之"字形传球 **zigzag passing**

突破 **breakthrough**

切入 **cutting in**

补防 **filling-in**

封死传球路线 **cutting off the passing lane**

运球 **dribbling**

接球 **catching the ball**

截球 **intercepting the ball**

夺球 **stealing the ball**

重新掌握球 **recovering the ball**

快攻 **fast break, quick attack**

交叉进攻 **alternating attack**

区域联防 **five-man defence, zone defence**

人盯人 **man-for-man defence**

混合防守 **combination defence**

密集防守 **bunched defence**

跟进的打法 **trailer play**

中锋策应 **centre-pivot play**

拖延时间的战术 **delaying tactics**

违例 **violation**

带球走 **walking**

两次运球 **double (dribble)**

技术犯规 **technical foul**

侵人犯规 **personal foul**

推人犯规 **pushing**

打人犯规 **striking**

打手犯规 **hacking**

拉人犯规 **grabbing**

撞人犯规 **charging**

阻挡犯规 **blocking**

双方犯规 **double foul**

暂停 **time-out**

罚球 **free throw**

罚球得分 **converting a free throw**

放弃罚球 **forfeiting a penalty**

被罚出场 **foul out**

# 足 球 Football, Soccer

足球场　football field
球门　goal
(球门)横木　cross bar
球门线　goal line
球门网　goal net
球门区　goal area
罚球区　penalty area
罚球点　penalty spot
角球区　corner area
角旗　corner flag
边线　touch line
端线　end line
中线　halfway line
中圈　centre circle, kick-off circle
足球队　football team, the eleven
足球队员　footballer, football player
传统阵容　traditional line-up
守门员　goal keeper, goalie
右后卫　right full back
左后卫　left full back
右前卫　right half (back)
左前卫　left half (back)
中卫　centre half (back)
右边锋　outside right (forward), right wing
左边锋　outside left (forward), left wing

右内锋　inside right (forward)
左内锋　inside left (forward)
中锋　centre forward
现代阵容　modern line-up
后卫　defenders, (full) backs
中场队员　midfield link men
前锋　strikers, forwards
足球鞋　football boot, studded boot
足球袜　football sock
护胫　shinguard, shinpad
护膝　kneeguard, kneepad
开球　kick-off
定位球　place kick
球门球　goal kick
角球　corner ball, corner kick
直接任意球　direct free kick
间接任意球　indirect free kick
人墙①　wall of players
组"墙"　lining up a wall, setting a wall
掷界外球　throw-in
脚背正面踢球　kicking with the instep
倒勾踢球②　overhead kick
顶球③　heading
射门④　shooting
跑动踢球　running kick

传球　passing the ball, pass
地面传球　pass along the ground
空中传球　volley pass, overhead pass
交叉传球　scissors pass
三角传球　triangular pass
高吊传球　lobbed pass
接传球　picking up a pass
停球　stopping the ball
脚底停反弹球　trapping a rebound with the sole
运球　dribbling
带球越过对手　dribbling past an opponent
截球　intercepting
胸部停球　intercepting with the chest
突破　break-through
跳起顶球　heading with a jump
顶球入门　heading in
争球　rushing for the ball
盯人　marking an opponent

射门机会　scoring chance
攻进一球　scoring a goal, netting a goal
劲射　snap shot, hard shot
弧线射门　curved shot
凌空射门　volley shot
高吊射门　high shot
反弹球射门　drop kick
拦阻对手　screening an opponent
假动作　trick movement, feinting
危险动作　dangerous play
混战　mêlée, scramble
越位　off-side
手触球犯规　hand ball
罚点球　ll-metre penalty kick
(守门员)将球击出　punching the ball clear
用拳击球　fisting the ball
接住球　catching the ball
鱼跃救球　making a diving save
救险球　retrieving an impossible shot

## 手　球　Handball

手球场　handball field
球门区　goal area
球门区线　goal-area line
7米线　seven-metre line
7米球　seven-metre throw
任意球线　free-throw line
开球　throw-off
持球①　holding the ball
打持球　striking the ball out of an opponent's hands
单手低手传球　one-hand underhand pass

双手胸前传球②　two-hand chest pass
背后传球③　pass behind the body
手腕传球　snap pass
反手传球　reverse pass
反弹传球　bounce pass
掷球技术　throwing technique
掷界外球　throw-in
掷球门球　throw-out
掷角球　corner throw
掷球越过防守人墙　throwing

over the wall
原地射门　standing shot
单手肩上射门　one-hand shoulder shot
跳起射门④　jump shot
鱼跃射门⑤　diving jump shot
转身射门　turnaround shot, pivot shot

身体假动作⑥　body feint
罚球　penalty shot
四步违例　walking violation
侵区犯规　line violation
持球超过三秒　overtime
守门员　goalkeeper
场上队员　field player
监门员　goal judge

## 棒球，垒球　Baseball and Softball

分指手套　glove
连指手套　mitt
护面　mask
护胸　chest protector
护胫　shinguard
棒球场　baseball field, baseball park
内场　infield, diamond
外场　outfield
本垒　home base
本垒板　home plate
一垒　first base
二垒　second base

三垒　third base
垒包　base bag
投手板　pitcher's plate, pitcher's rubber
投手区　pitcher's box
接手区　catcher's box
左手击球员区　left-handed batter's box
右手击球员区　right-handed batter's box
界内场地　fair territory, fair ground
界外场地　foul territory

场外指导员区 coach's box
防守队 fielding team
投手① pitcher
接手② catcher
内场手 infielder
一垒手 first baseman
二垒手 second baseman
三垒手 third baseman
游击手 shortstop
右外场手 right outfielder
中外场手 centre outfielder
左外场手 left outfielder
投球 delivering
平直球 liner
内曲线球 incurve
外曲线球 out-curve
下坠球 drop
快球 fast ball
慢球 slow ball
(投手)暴投 wild pitch
不合法投球 illegal delivery,
 illegal pitch
接球 catching
接球失误 muff
接手漏接球 passed ball

投手犯规 balk
传球 pass
肩上传球 overhand throw
体侧传球 sidearm throw
低手传球 underhand throw
封杀 force-out
触杀 touch out, tag out
夹杀 run-down
被杀出局 put-out
传杀,双杀 double play, doub-
 le kill
击球队,攻方 batting team,
 side at bat
棒球③ baseball
击球员④ batter, batsman
棒球棒⑤ baseball bat
长挥击球法 long swing
短挥击球法 short swing
触击球 bunting
界内球 fair ball
界外球 foul ball
腾空球 fly ball
地滚球 ground ball, grounder
擦棒球 foul tip
跑垒 base running
击跑员 batter-runner
跑垒员 base-runner
滑垒 sliding
向前扑垒 bead-first
偷垒 stealing
安全进垒 safe
安全打 safe hit
一垒安全打 one-base hit,
 single
二垒安全打 two-base hit,
 two-bagger
三垒安全打 three-base hit,
 three-bagger
本垒打 home run

四环球安全上一垒　**base on balls**
三击不中, 击球员出局　**striking out**
牺牲打　**sacrifice hit**
得一分　**scoring a run**
局　**inning**
决胜局　**extra-inning**
场　**game**
司球裁判员　**plate umpire**
司垒裁判员　**base umpire**

"好球!", "一击!"　**"Strike!"**
"坏球!", "一球!"　**"Ball!"**
"击球员进场!"　**"Batter up!"**
"击球员出局!"　**"Batter out!"**
"击跑员出局!"　**"Batter-runner out!"**
"跑垒员出局!"　**"Base-runner out!"**
"暂停!"　**"Time!"**
"比赛结束!"　**"Game set!"**

## 游　泳　Swimming

游泳池　**swimming pool**
室外游泳池　**outdoor pool, open air pool**
室内游泳池　**indoor pool, swimming bath**
有看台的游泳池　**swimming stadium**
游泳馆　**natatorium**
浅水池　**shallow pool, non-swimmers' pool**
深水池　**deep pool, swimmers' pool**
洗脚池　**foot bath**
淋浴室　**shower room**

更衣室　**dressing room, changing room**
更衣室单间　**cubicle**
设有衣柜的更衣室　**locker room**
池壁休息台　**rest ledge**
扶手　**handrail**
游泳姿式　**swimming strokes**
自由泳⑥　**freestyle**
蝶泳⑦　**butterfly stroke**
仰泳⑧　**back stroke**
侧泳　**side stroke**
蛙泳⑨　**frog style**
海豚泳⑩　**dolphin stroke**
爬泳　**crawl stroke**

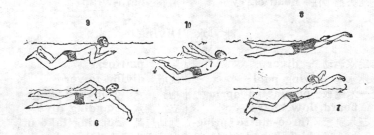

特拉金式泳法 trudgen stroke
俯泳 breast stroke
狗爬式 dog paddle
潜泳 underwater swimming
个人混合泳 individual medley
放松游 swimming easy
用力游 swimming hard
划水 stroke
打水, 踢水 kick
踩水 treading water
跳入水中 plunging into water
出发跳水 starting plunge
出发姿势 starting position
触池壁 touching the side
转身 turning
蹬壁 push-off
换气, 呼吸 breathing
呼气 breathing out, exhaling
吸气 breathing in, inhaling
侧面呼吸 side breathing
爆发式呼吸 explosive breathing
两侧呼吸 bilateral breathing
喘气 gasping
救生 life saving
救生员 life guard, life saver
救生用具 life preserver
橡皮浮圈 rubber float
托头拖带法 head carry

resuscitation
扣颈拖带法 neck carry
托下颏的拖带法 chin carry
胸前拖带法 cross-chest carry
痉挛, 抽筋 cramp
人工呼吸 artificial respiration
嘴对嘴人工呼吸 mouth-to-mouth
游泳比赛 swimming race
出发台 starting block, starting platform
发令员 starter
出发跳水 starting dive
比赛泳道 racing lane
泳道线 lane rope
计时员 time keeper
触壁检查员 touch umpire
转弯检查员 turn umpire
电子计时触板 electronic timing pad
电子裁判计时设备 electronic judging and timing equipment
游泳衣 swimming suit, bathing suit
男泳裤 swimming-trunks, bathing slips
游泳帽 swimming cap
浴衣 bath-wrap

## 跳 水 Diving

跳水运动员 diver
跳水池 diving pool
一米跳板 one-metre springboard, low board
三米跳板 three-metre springboard, high board

跳台 platform
跳塔 diving tower
抱膝跳水 crouched jump
立定跳水 standing dive
跑动起跳 running take off
在跳板上弹跳 bouncing on

the springboard

直体 straight
屈体 pike
抱膝 tuch
向前跳水 forward dive, front dive
向后跳水 backward dive, back dive
低难度跳台跳水 plain high diving
高难度跳台跳水 variety high diving
燕式跳水 swallow dive, swan dive

向前直体跳水① forward header dive
向后屈体跳水② back-jack-knife dive
面对池反身跳水③ reverse dive
面对板向内跳水④ inward dive
向后翻腾两周 double backward somersaults
跑动转体跳水⑤ running twist dive
旋转式跳水⑥ screw dive

## 举 重 Weight Lifting

举重运动员 weight lifter, lifter
称量体重 weighing-in
减体重 reducing bodyweight

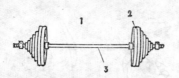

体重级别　weight category
次最轻量级　flyweight
最轻量级　bantamweight
次轻量级　featherweight
轻量级　lightweight
中量级　middleweight
轻重量级　light-heavyweight
次重量级　middle-heavyweight
重量级　heavyweight
超重量级　super-heavyweight
杠铃①　barbell
杠铃片②　disc, dick
横杠③　bar
标准举重台　regulation platform
摸粉　chalking up one's hands

走向杠铃　approaching the bar
推举④　press
提铃至胸　lifting the barbell to the chest
推铃到头顶上　pushing the barbell overhead
挺举⑤　clean and jerk
上挺(两脚可移动)　jerk
抓举　snatch
下蹲式抓举⑥　squat snatch
箭步式抓举⑦　split snatch
三项共举起…　lifting…in three goes
两项总成绩　two-lift total
握法　method of grip
窄握　narrow grip
宽握　broad grip
普通握　thumbs around grip
锁握　hook grip
空握　thumbless grip
辅助动作　assistance movement
坐推　seated press
卧推　bench press

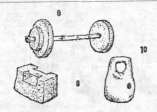

硬举　dead lift
石锁⑧　stone lock
石担⑨　stone barbell
壶铃⑩　kettle bell

## 登山运动　Mountaineering

登山运动员　mountaineer, alpinist, climber
登山队　mountaineering party, climbing party
突击组　assault party
支援组　support party
营救组　rescue party
大本营　base camp
旅途营地　approach camp
高山营地　alpine base
向山脚行军　approach march
适应性训练　acclimatization training
登上顶峰　ascending a peak, scaling a peak, conquering a peak
山谷　valley
顶峰　peak
山隘　pass
山肩　shoulder
鞍形山脊　saddle
山壁　face
山麓碎石　scree
冰隙　crevasse
陡峭山脊　arête
狭窄岩缝　chimney
高原　plateau

山口　col
冰川　glacier
冰碛　moraine
冰川侧碛　lateral moraine
冰川终碛　terminal moraine
攀岩作业　rock climbing
攀岩技术　rock technique
结绳技术　rope technique
"活绳"　live rope
抓结　prusik knot
单"8"字结　figure-of-eight knot
布林结⑪　bowline knot
叉开腿攀登法⑫　straddling technique
用背和脚作支点的登攀法⑬　backand-foot technique

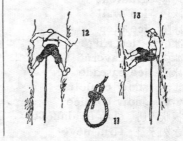

保护绳套　belay sling, belay loop

攀登狭窄岩缝　chimney climbing

用背和膝盖作支点的攀登法　backand-knee technique

踩人攀登法　courte échelle

绕绳下降　roping down, abseiling

主绳绕单腿下降①　thigh rappel

主绳绕双腿下降②　double thigh rappel

自由下降, 坐式下降③　free rappel

冰雪作业　snow and ice climbing

冰坡　ice slope

坡度　gradient

冰崖　ice wall

冰阶　ice step

冰山脊　ice ridge

冰穴　ice cavern

冰瀑　ice cascade

雪沟　snow couloir

雪檐　snow cornice

板状雪崩　slab avalanche

永久冰雪　firn, névé

永久积雪线　firn line

攀登冰坡　negotiating an ice slope, climbing an ice slope

过冰川　crossing a glacier

跳过冰裂缝　jumping a crevasse

沿着缝隙走　skirting a fissure

临时赶搭绳梯　rigging up a rope ladder

登山装备　mountaineering equipment

带齿钉登山靴　nailed climbing boot

尖钉, 冰爪　crampon

鸭绒衣　down jacket

防风衣　anorak

防护眼镜　snow goggles, snow glasses

探测棒④　alpenstock

冰镐⑤　ice axe

镐尖⑥　pick

镐刃⑦　blade

岩锥⑧　rock piton, rock peg

冰锥⑨　ice piton, ice peg

锥锤⑩　piton hammer

铁锁⑪　snaplinkm karabiner

# 滑 冰 Skating

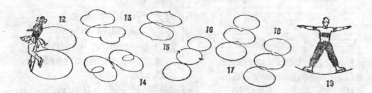

滑冰场　skating rink
人工冰场　artificial ice rink
滑冰运动员, 滑冰者　skater
速度滑冰　speed skating
速滑跑道　speed skating track
滑行腿　skating leg
浮腿　free leg
蹬冰　stroke
利用体重蹬冰　taking off by weight, pushing off by weight
收腿　drawing back the leg
上体前倾　leaning forward from the waist
保持平衡　keeping balance
直道滑跑　straight skating
进入弯道　entering a curve
弯道滑跑　curve skating
花样滑冰　figure skating
单人花样滑冰　single skating
双人花样滑冰　pair skating
规定图形　compulsory figure, school figure
滑一个"3"字　doing a figure of three
"8"字形⑫　curve eight, figure of eight
(弧线上的)双"3"字⑬　double three

结环形⑭　loop
括弧形⑮　bracket
同轴上三个圆形⑯　serpentine
内勾手形⑰　rocker
外勾手形⑱　counter
横一字⑲　spread eagle
自由滑　free skating
冰上舞蹈　ice dancing
单人旋转⑳　solo spin
环绕㉑　spiral
托举　lift
跳跃　jump
滑脚㉒　employed foot
浮脚㉓　unemployed foot
冰球运动　ice hockey
冰球运动员　ice hockey player, puckster
冰球门　cage, goal

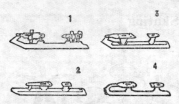

界墙,板墙　boards, fence
冰球杆　ice hockey stick
冰球杆柄　stick handle
冰球杆刃　stick blade

冰球　puck
冰刀　skate
双刃刀①　hollow-ground blade
内刃　inside edge
外刃　outside edge
跑刀②　racing skate
冰球鞋冰刀③　ice hockey skate
花样滑冰刀④　figure skate
轱辘鞋　roller skate

## 滑雪 Skiing

上坡⑤　climbing, ascending
梯形上坡⑥　side step ascent
倒"八"字形上坡⑦　herringbone ascent
上山吊椅　ski-lift, chair-lift
下坡滑行　downhill running
快速降下　downhill racing
斜线滑下　downhill traversing
滑行步　skating step
犁式制动⑧　snowplough

障碍滑雪　slalom
障碍跳跃　obstacle jump
撑杖跳过障碍　field jump
斜线跳跃⑨　oblique jump
跳跃转弯　jump turn
踢腿转弯⑩　kick turn
弓步式转弯⑪　telemark turn
半犁式转弯⑫　stem turn
跳台飞跃　ski-jumping
飞跃跳台　run-down tower

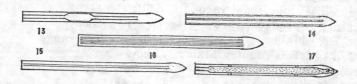

助滑坡　run-down, in-run
飞跃起跳台　take-off platform
滑雪装备　ski outfit, skiing outfit
旅行雪板⑬　touring ski
降下用雪板⑭　down-hill ski
比赛雪板⑮　racing ski
飞跃用雪板⑯　jumping ski
上坡防滑皮⑰　climbing skin
雪板固定装置⑱　ski-binding
前夹⑲　fore-tightener, fore-clamp
脚趾搭扣带⑳　toe-strap

铁耳㉑　toe-iron
脚板㉒　foot plate
螺旋弹簧㉓　spiral spring
滑雪靴　ski boot
滑雪衣　parka, anorak
滑雪杖㉔　ski pole, ski stick
雪杖轮盘㉕　stick disc

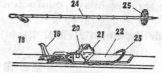

## 国防体育　National Defence Sports

航空运动　aviation sports
航空模型　model airplane
飞行　flying
滑翔机　glider
滑翔　gliding
降落伞　parachute
跳伞　parachuting, parachute jumping
跳伞塔　parachuting tower
集体定点跳伞　group precision landing
水上运动　marine sports
航海模型　model ship
划船　rowing

划船比赛　boat race, regatta
全体船员　crew
舵手　coxswain
桨手　oarsman
帆船比赛　yacht race
张帆　stretching a sail
卷帆减速　taking in a sail
顺风航行　sailing before the wind
几乎顶风航行　sailing aginst the wind
左舷受风航行　sailing on the port tack
右舷受风航行　sailing on the

starboard tack

摩托艇比赛 motorboat race

快艇比赛 speedboat race

徒步旅行 hiking

越野步行 cross-country hike

行军 march, marching

徒涉 fording

野营训练 marching and camping exercises

赛马 horse race

骑术 horsemanship

摩托车运动 motorcycling

掷手榴弹 hand grenade throwing

劈刺训练 bayonet drill

负重障碍赛跑 obstacle race carrying heavy equipment

"三防"演习 "three anti" drills, antiair raid, atomic and chemical warfare drills

射箭(术) archery

射箭场 archery range

弓 bow

弓弦 bow string

箭 arrow

箭杆 arrow shaft

箭筒 arrow-case, quiver

拉弓 drawing the bow

射箭 shooting the arrow

旗语,手旗通讯 semaphore signalling

手旗 semaphore flag

无线电作业 radio operation

无线电收发报 transmitting and receiving radio messages

## 射 击 Shooting

射击技术 marksmanship

射手 marksman, shooter

射击场 shooting range, shooting gallery

射击台 shooting platform

射击眼镜 shooting spectacles

靶 target

人像靶 silhouette target

移动靶 moving target

靶心 bull's-eye

靶环 scoring ring, ring

小口径步枪 small-bore rifle

标准步枪 standard rifle

自选步枪 free rifle

军用步枪 service rifle

手枪 pistol

汽手枪 air pistol

立射 shooting from standing position

跪射 shooting from kneeling position

卧射 shooting from prone position

瞄准 taking aim

瞄准练习 aiming exercise

中靶,命中 hitting

脱靶 missing

弹着环数 shot value

标准步枪300米三种姿势比赛 standard rifle 300 m. three positions

小口径步枪50米三种姿势比赛 small-bore rifle 50 m. three positions

手枪速射25米赛　rapid-fire pistol 25 m.

跑兽靶50米赛　running game target 50 m.

跑猪　running boar

跑鹿　running deer

飞靶射击　trap-shooting

多向飞靶射击　skeet (shooting)

泥鸽,碟靶　clay pigeon

泥碟　clay disc

飞碟靶场　clay-pigeon range

双向飞碟靶场　skeet field

"清场完毕!"　"All clear!"

"装子弹!"　"Load!"

"退子弹!"　"Unload!"

"射击!"　"Fire!"

"命中!"　"Dead!", "Killed!"

"脱靶!"　"Lost!"

"全体停止射击!"　"Lay down all guns!"

"关保险!"　"Safety catch!"

# 武　术　Wushu

武术　wushu, traditional Chinese fighting arts

拳术①　quanshu, traditional Chinese boxing

太极拳②　tai ji quan, traditional Chinese tai ji boxing

简化太极拳　simplified tai ji quan

五禽戏  Five-Animal Exercises

起势  beginning form

收势  closing form

绵绵不断的动作  flowing movement

舒松肌肉关节  limbering up muscles and joints

短兵器  short weapon

长兵器  long weapon

软兵器  soft weapon

双兵器  double weapon

匕首  dagger

单刀  curlas(s)

刀  sabre

刀术③  sabreplay

大刀  broadsword

剑  sword

剑术④  swordplay

枪  spear

枪术⑤  spearplay

棍  cudgel

棍术⑥  cudgelplay

三节棍⑦  three-section cudgel

叉  fork

三叉⑧  trident

戟  halbert, halberd

绳镖  rope-dart

流星锤  meteor hammer

九节鞭  nine-section whip

双钩  double hook

双剑  double rapier

盾牌  shield

藤牌  rattan shield

套路  set pattern, routine

规定套路  required routine

手型  hand form

手法  hand position

拳法  fist position

腿法  foot position

步法  stepping position

拳打  fisting, hitting with the fist

脚踢  kicking

踢脚  kicking with toes leading

蹬脚  kicking with heel leading

推掌  pushing the palm

扭身  twisting

直戳  straight lunging

斜刺  diagonal stabbing

侧击  side striking

徒手练习  bare-handed practice

对练  paired practice

对打  encounter, duel

器械练习  armed practice

单刀对枪  single sword against spear

空手对棍  empty hands against cudgel

# 医疗卫生 Medical Treatment and Public Health

## 保健工作 Health Protection

公费医疗 free medical service

劳保医疗 labour-protection medical care

自费医疗 self-paid medical care

半费医疗 semi-paid medical care

减费医疗 discount medical care

免费医疗 free medical care

保健费 health subsidies

就近医疗原则 principle of attending for treatment at the nearest place

送医上门 bringing medical care to the patient's home

田间医疗站 medical station in the fields

巡回医疗队 mobile medical team

工人医生 worker-doctor

保健人员的培训 training of health workers

内科医生和外科医生的培养 training of physicians and surgeons

保健机构 health institution

保健网 health protection network

保健站 health station

保健所 health centre

健康咨询站 health consultation centre

医疗网 medical and health network

成功率 rate of success

发病率 disease incidence

死亡率 mortality rate

人口自然增长率 rate of natural increase of population

人口增长率 rate of population growth

人口增长 population growth, human increment

全国人口增长统计数字 national statistics on population increase

进行人口普查　taking a census of the population

使(……病)的死亡率降低到百分之……　keeping the mortality rate (from…) down to… percent

定期体格检查　regular physical examination, regular health examination

体格检查　physical check-up

卫生检查　sanitary inspection, hygiene examination

身体状况　physical condition

职业病的预防和治疗　prevention and cure of occupational diseases

疗养院　sanatorium

疗养　recuperation

疗养期　period of recuperation

恢复健康　recuperating one's health

增加体重　gaining (putting on) weight

过有规律的生活　leading a regular life

规定的饮食　diet

富有营养的食物　nourishing food, nourishment

降低医疗费用　lowering medical fees

减少常见病的死亡率　reducing the mortality rate of common diseases

医务人员的精心照顾　meticulous care of medical workers

挨家逐户为患者治疗　giving medical treatment to the patients' homes

合作医疗制度　System of Co-operative Medical Care

赤脚医生　barefoot doctor

集训　training course

防病灭病的方法　ways to prevent and wipe out disease

公社卫生院　commune hospital

大队卫生所　bridge clinic

改进农村医疗卫生状况　improving public health and medical conditions in the rural areas

业余卫生员　spare-time health worker

挂号费　registration fee

出诊费　fee for making home calls

注射费　fee for giving injections

助产费　fee for delivering babies

预防流行病　preventing endemic diseases

除害防病　eliminating pests and preventing diseases

预防与治疗相结合　combining treatment with prevention

保健措施　hygienic measures

预防措施　preventive health measures

预防注射　protective inoculation

菌苗　vaccine

对某人接种病菌　inoculating virus on (or into) somebody

对某人注射……预防针　inocula-

ting somebody against…
防疫注射 immunization inoculation
种痘, 接种 vaccination
家庭访问 home visit

卫生习惯 sanitary habit
卫生知识 sanitary knowledge
车间保健员 workshop medical attendant

## 妇幼保健 Maternal and Child Hygiene

妇幼保健站 health centre for women and children, child and maternity clinic
儿童诊疗所 children's polyclinic
儿童疗养院 children's sanatorium
从新生婴儿到14岁的儿童 from new-born infants to children up to 14 years old
托儿所 nursery
日托托儿所 day-nursery
幼儿园 kindergarten
托婴所 crèche
哺乳室 feeding (nursing) room for mothers
托儿站 child-care centre
婴儿 infant
儿童 child
接种牛痘 giving vaccines, vaccinating, vaccination against smallpox
卡介苗预防接种 BCG(Bacillus-Calmette-Guèrin) inoculation, BCG vaccination
控制若干常见病的发生或蔓延 controlling the outbreak or spread of some common diseases
麻疹 measles
小儿麻痹症 infantile paralysis, polio (myelitis)

麻疹疫苗 attenuated living measles vaccine
小儿麻痹疫苗 attenuated living poliomyelitis vaccine
早产儿 premature infant
早产儿保育器, 暖箱 incubator
母亲喂养 breast feeding
产前检查 pre-natal check-up (diagnosis)
产后检查 post-natal check-up (diagnosis)
无生育, 不孕 sterility
新式接生法 modern delivery method
接生 delivering a baby, maternity services, obstetric services
接生站 child birth station, maternity centre
生产, 分娩 giving birth to a baby, delivery
产科病案 delivery case, obstetric case
无痛分娩 painless childbirth, psychopro-phylactic painless parturition
产房 maternity ward, labour room
待产妇 mother-to-be
胎位正常 baby in correct position
婴儿保健 health care for

infant
婴儿死亡率 **infant mortality rate**
死胎 **stillbirth**

死产的 **stillborn**
出生率 **birth rate**
试管婴儿 **tube baby**

## 爱国卫生运动 Patriotic Health and Sanitation Campaign

增强人民体质 **building up the people's health**
治疗不如预防 **Prevention is better than cure.**
环境卫生 **environmental sanitation**
个人卫生 **personal hygiene**
卫生习惯 **hygienic habit**
不卫生习惯 **unhealthy habit**
卫生面貌 **health conditions**
预防注射,接种 **inoculation**
通过空气或水的传染 **infection**
通过接触的传染 **contagion**
传染源 **contagion source**
传染媒介 **contagion intermediary**
传染途径 **route of contagion**
控制疾病流行 **controlling the spread of diseases**
人人动手防病治病 **Everybody lends a hand in preventing and curing diseases.**
盖厕所 **building latrines**
公共厕所 **public toilet, public lavatory**
粪车 **night-soil cart**
露天粪坑 **open manure pit**
马桶 **commode, night-com-**

mode
挖卫生井 **digging hygienic well**
粪便管理 **control of manure**
人粪 **human excrement or faeces, night-soil**
填平坑洼 **filling up holes and hollows**
清除垃圾 **cleaning waste matter**
疏通沟渠 **opening up ditches and gutters**
除尘 **dust cleaning**
治理环境污染 **combating enviromental pollutions**
口罩 **mouth mask**
痰盂 **spittoon**
防疫站 **anti-epidemic station**
卫生检查 **health inspection**
臭水塘 **stagnant pond**
消除病源 **getting rid of the source of infection**
带菌者 **bacteria carrier**
消毒站 **sterilization station**
垃圾箱 **garbage pan, rubbish-bin**
废纸篓 **waste(paper)basket**
垃圾 **refuse, garbage**

垃圾堆 refuse dump, rubbish heap

垃圾车 garbage wagon

垃圾处理 garbage disposal

捕蝇拍 fly-swatter, flapper

灭蛆 exterminating maggots

白蛉子 midges

臭虫 bedbug

蚤 flea

虱 louse(pl. lice)

下水道 sewer

雨后积水 water collection after rain

疏通积水 draining away the collected water

污水处理 sewage treatment

污水唧站 drainage pump station

绿化城市 beautifying the city by planting trees

清洁队 clean-up squad

堵鼠洞 plugging (up) rat holes

堵树洞 plugging (up) tree holes

蚊蝇孳生地 breeding grounds for flies and mosquitoes

翻坛倒罐 turning jugs and jars upside down

消灭蝇 exterminating house-flies

蝇卵 housefly eggs

消灭子孓 exterminating larvae of mosquitoes

防疫队 anti-epidemic unit

细菌武器 bacteriological weapon

细菌传染病毒媒介 germ(infection) carriers

街道清洁员 street cleaner

街道清洁队 street cleaning team

城市环境卫生 the city's environmental hygiene

把垃圾堆去指定地点 dumping the garbage at appointed spots

用泥封垃圾堆加以发酵 sealing the dumps with clay to ensure fermentation

堆肥 compost

改善环境卫生 improving environmental sanitation

管理粪水和净化饮水 disposing of the night-soil and purifying the drinking water

## 计划生育 Family Planning

计划生育 birth control, family planning, planned parenthood

避孕法 contraception

药物避孕 medical contraception

器具避孕 instrumental contraception

输卵管结扎 tubal ligation

放子宫托 fixing a pessary

放子宫帽 fixing a contraceptive diaphagm (uterine cap)

放避孕环 fixing the intra-uterine contraception ring

输精管结扎 ligation of spermatic duct
阴茎套 condom
口服避孕药 oral contraceptive
避孕胶冻 contraceptive jelly

育龄妇女 women at child-bearing-age
每对夫妇只生一个小孩。 Each couple has only one child.

## 人体器官 Organs of Human Body

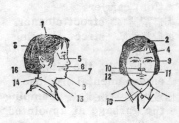

头 head

头顶① vertex, top (crown) of the head
头发② hair of the head
后头部③ back of the head
脸 face
额④ forehead, frontal eminence, frontal bump, superciliary arch, bulge of the forehead
太阳穴⑤ temple
颊⑥ cheek
酒窝 dimple in the cheek, dimple at the corner of the mouth
口⑦ mouth
下巴窝 dimple in the chin
颏⑧ chin
眼⑨ eye
鼻⑩ nose

鼻唇沟⑪ line (furrow) from the nose to the corner of the mouth
人中(上唇中沟)⑫ philtrum (the groove at the median line of the upper lip)
颈⑬ neck
项(部)⑭ nape (scruff) of the neck
喉(咙)⑮ throat, gullet
颌, 颚⑯ jaw
颚骨 jaw bone
脑 brain
大脑 cerebrum
小脑 cerebellum
脑桥 pons
延髓 medulla oblongata
眼 eye
眉⑰ eyebrow, brows
上眼睑⑱ upper lid
下眼睑⑲ lower lid
睫毛⑳ eye lash
虹膜㉑ iris

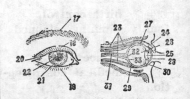

瞳孔㉒ **pupil**
眼肌㉓ **eye muscles, eye strings**
眼球㉔ **eye ball**
晶状体㉕ **(crystalline) lens**
玻璃液㉖ **vitreous humour**
玻璃体㉗ **vitreous body**
角膜㉘ **cornea**
视网膜㉙ **retina**
巩膜㉚ **sclera**
视神经㉛ **optic nerve**
盲点㉜ **blind spot**
中央凹㉝ **central fovea**

## 耳 ear

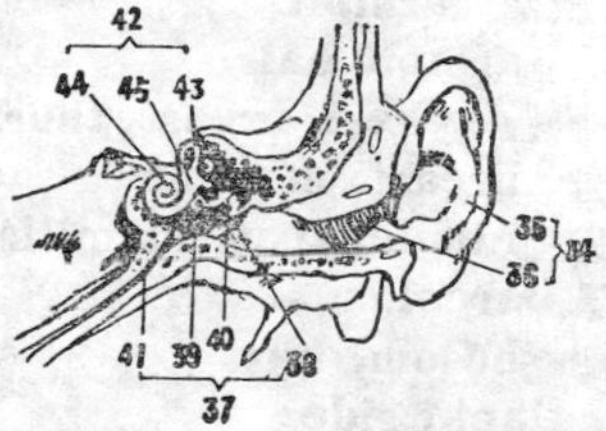


外耳㉞ **external ear**
耳廓㉟ **auricle**
耳垂 **lobe of the ear (lobule)**
外耳道㊱ **external auditory meatus (cannal)**
中耳㊲ **middle ear**
鼓膜㊳ **tympanic membrance**
鼓室㊴ **ear drum, tympanic cavity, (tympanum)**
听小骨㊵ **ossicles**
锤骨 **hammer, malleus**
砧骨 **anvil, incus**
镫骨 **stirrup, stapes**
耳咽管(咽鼓管)㊶ **Eustachian tube. Eustachian cannal. auditory tube**
内耳㊷ **inner ear, internal ear**
半规管㊸ **labyrinth**
耳蜗㊹ **cochlea**
前庭㊺ **vestibule**
听神经 **auditory nerve**

## 鼻 nose

鼻梁㊻ **bridge of nose**
鼻孔㊼ **nostril**
鼻中隔 **nasal septum**
鼻腔㊽ **nasal cavity**
鼻骨㊾ **nasal bone**
鼻旁窦㊿ **paranasal sinus**
鼻甲(51) **nasal concha, turbinal**
鼻后孔(52) **choana**
鼻翼 **wings of nosc**
鼻道(53) **nasal passage**
鼻毛 **vibrissae**

## 口腔和咽 cavity of the mouth and pharynx

上唇(54) **upper lip**
下唇(55) **lower lip**
牙龈(56) **gum**
牙(57) **tooth**
硬腭(58) **hard palate**
软腭(59) **soft palate, velum**

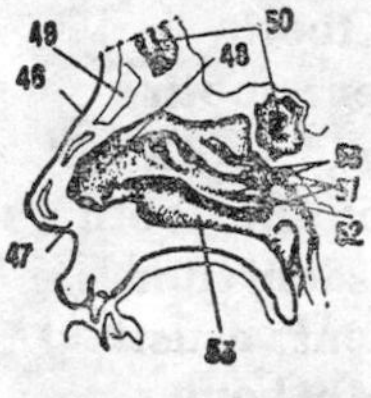

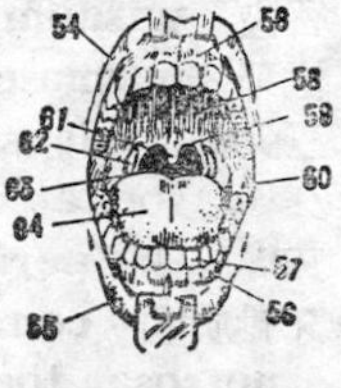

口角⑥ corner of the mouth, angle of the lips

悬雍垂(小舌)⑥ urula

(腭)扁桃体⑥ (palative) tonsil

咽(峡)⑥ pharynx, pharyngeal cavity

舌⑥ tongue

喉 throat, larynx

会厌 epiglottis

声带 vocal chords, cords

声门 glottis

牙 tooth

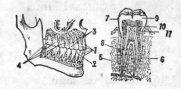

切齿, 门齿① incisor, front tooth

尖牙, 犬牙② canine tooth, eyetooth

双尖牙, 前磨牙, 前臼齿③ premolar tooth

磨牙, 臼齿(后牙)④ molars, back tooth, double tooth

乳牙(暂齿) milk tooth, temporary tooth

智齿 wisdom tooth

恒牙 permanent tooth

三尖牙 tricuspid tooth

牙槽 socket of the tooth

牙周膜⑤ perisdon tium

牙骨质⑥ cement, crusta petrosa, tooth bone

牙冠⑦ crown

牙根⑧ root, fang

牙釉质⑨ enamel, encaustum

牙质⑩ dentine

牙髓⑪ pulp, dental pulp

血管和神经 blood vessels and nerve fibres

人体 human body

肩 shoulder

肩甲骨 shoulder blade

腰 loins, waist

骶骨部 loins

腰背部 small of the back

腋, 腋窝 armpit

腋毛 armpit hair

胸, 胸腔 chest, breast, thorax

乳房 breast, mamma

乳头 nipple, teat, mamilla

乳晕 areola

胸部 bosom, bust

胁 flank, side

臀部 hip, haunch

脐 naval, belly button

腹部 belly, abdomen

上腹 upper abdomen

下腹 lower abdomen

腹股沟 groin

屁股 buttocks, bottom, backside, posterior

臀皱 posterior ruga bend of the upper thigh

上臂 upper part of the arm, upper arm

下臂, 肱 forearm

肘 elbow

臂弯 bend (crook) of the arm

腕 wrist

拳　fist

大腿　thigh

膝, 膝盖　knee

腘, 腘窝　hollow of the knee, back of the knee

小腿胫　shank, lower part of the leg

腓肠肌, 小腿肚　calf

腿　leg

手　hand

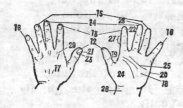

拇指⑫　thumb

食指⑬　fore finger, index finger

中指⑭　middle finger, second finger, long finger

无名指, 环指⑮　ring finger

小指⑯　little finger

手背⑰　back of the hand

手掌⑱　palm of the hand, thenar

挠(骨)侧⑲　radial side of the hand

尺(骨)侧⑳　ulnar side of the hand

指甲㉑　finger nail

指纹㉒　fingerprint

甲晕㉓　moon

拇指腕掌(鱼际)㉔　ball of the thumb, thenar eminence, thenar prominence

掌纹㉕　lines of the palm

腕㉖　wrist, carpus

腕关节　carpal joint

指骨㉗　phalanx, finger cushion

指尖㉘　finger tip

指关节骨㉙　knuckle

脚　foot

拇趾㉚　big (great) toe

二趾㉛　second toe

三趾㉜　third toe

四趾㉝　fourth toe

小趾㉞　little toe

趾甲㉟　toe nail

拇趾球㊱　ball of the foot

踝　ankle, malleolus

外踝㊲　external malleolus

内踝㊳　internal malleolus

脚面(跗)㊴　instep, arch

脚底㊵　sole of the foot

脚跟㊶　heel

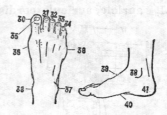

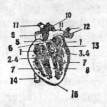

## 心脏　heart

心房① atrium
三尖瓣② tricuspid valve
二尖瓣③ mitral valve (bi-
　cuspid valve)
瓣尖④ cuspid
主动脉瓣⑤ aortic valve
半月瓣 semilunar valve
肺动脉瓣⑥ pulmonary valve
心室⑦ ventricle
室中隔⑧ ventricular septum,
　septum muscular ventri-
　culorum cordis
上腔静脉⑨ superior vena
　cava
主动脉⑩ aorta
肺动脉⑪ pulmonary artery
肺静脉⑫ pulomonary vein
冠状动脉⑬ coronary artery
下腔静脉⑭ inferior vena
　cava
心耳 auricle, auricula cordis

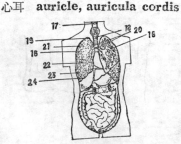

右心耳 auricula dextra
左心耳 auricula sinistra
心包 pericardium
心肌 myocardium
心尖⑮ apex of the heart

肺⑯ lung

喉⑰ throat, larynx
气管⑱ wind pipe, trachea
肺尖⑲ apex of the lung
左支气管⑳ left brochi
右支气管⑳ right brochi
肺叶 lobe of the lung
上肺叶㉑ upper lobe
中肺叶㉒ middle lobe
下肺叶㉓ lower lobe
肺底㉔ base of the lung
肺门 hilus of the lung
肺泡 lung alveolus (pl. al-
　veoli)
肺泡孔 lung alveolar pores
胸膜 pleura
纵膈 mediastinum

## 消化系统　digestive system

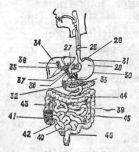

食管㉕ gullet
贲门㉖ orifice of the stom-
　ach

| | |
|---|---|
| 幽门㉗　pylorus | 尿道㉒　urethra |
| 胃㉘　stomach | 精囊㊾　seminal vesicle |
| 胃小弯㉙　lesser curvature | 前列腺㊴　prostate, prostate gland |
| 胃大弯㉚　greater curvature | |
| 胃底㉛　fundus of stomach | 输精管㊵　spermatic duct |
| 十二指肠㉜　duodenum | 睾丸㊶　testis, testicle |
| 胰㉝　pancreas | 附睾㊷　epididymis |
| 肝㉞　liver | 阴囊　scrotum, purse |
| 肝镰状韧带　lateral ligament of the liver | 阴茎㊸　penis |
| | 包皮㊹　foreskin, prepuce |
| 肝(右、左)叶　(right, left) lobe of the liver | 龟头㊿　glans penis |
| | 海绵体㉛　corpus cavernosum and spongiosum |
| 肝管㉟　hepatic duct | |
| 胆囊㊱　gall bladder | 子宫㉢　uterus, womb, matrix |
| 胆总管㊲　common bile duct | 子宫体腔㉣　uterine cavity |
| 胆囊管　cystic duct | 输卵管㉤　Fallopian tube |
| 门静脉㊳　portal vein | 卵巢㉥　ovary |
| 空肠㊴　jejunum | 输卵管伞㉦　fimbria |
| 回肠㊵　ileum | 子宫颈㉧　cervix |
| 大肠　large intestine | 子宫颈口㉨　os uteri |
| 盲肠㊶　caecum | |
| 阑尾㊷　(vermiform) appendix | |
| 升结肠㊸　ascending colon | |
| 横结肠㊹　transverse colon | |
| 降结肠㊺　descending colon | |
| 直肠㊻　rectum | |
| 肛门　anus | |
| 括约肌　sphincter | |

泌尿生殖系统　urogenital system

| |
|---|
| 肾脏㊼　kidney |
| 肾盂㊽　renal pelves |
| 肾盏㊾　calyx |
| 肾上腺　adrenal gland |
| 肾小球　glonerule |
| 输尿管㊿　ureter |
| 膀胱㊿　bladder |

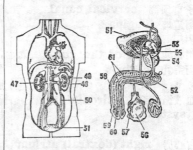

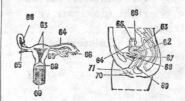

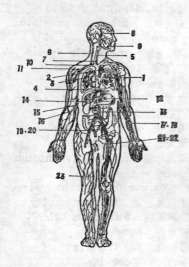

子宫颈管　cervical canal
阴道⑥⑨　vagina
阴门　vulva
阴唇⑦⓪　lips of the vulva
阴蒂⑦①　clitoris

**血液循环系统　circulatory system**

右心房　right (dextral) atrium
左心房　left (sinister) atrium
右心室　right (dextral) ventricle
左心室　left (sinister) ventricle
肺动脉①　pulmonary artery

肺静脉　pulmonary vein
毛细血管　blood capillary
主动脉　aorta
主动脉弓②　aortic arch
上腔静脉③　superior vena cava
下腔静脉④　inferior vena cava
颈动脉⑤　carotid artery
颈外静脉⑥　external jugular vein
颈内静脉⑦　internal jugular vein
颞动脉⑧　temporal artery
颞静脉　temporal vein
面动脉⑨　frontal (facial) artery
面静脉　frontal (facial) vein
头静脉　cephalic vein
锁骨下动脉⑩　subclavian artery
锁骨下静脉⑪　subclavian vein
腹腔动脉⑫　abdominal artery
腹主动脉⑬　abdominal aorta
门静脉⑭　portal vein
贵要静脉⑮　basilic vein
肘正中静脉⑯　median cubital vein
桡动脉⑰　radial artery
桡静脉⑱　radial vein
髂内动脉⑲　internal iliac artery
髂内静脉⑳　internal iliac vein
股动脉㉑　femoral artery
股静脉㉒　femoral vein
大隐静脉㉓　great saphenous vein

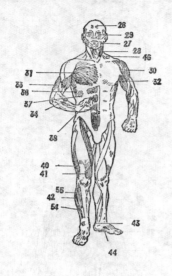 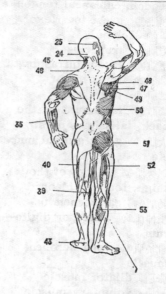

肌肉组织　muscular system (musculature)

肌　muscle
枕肌㉔　occipital muscle
面肌　facial muscle
颞肌㉕　temporal muscle
颈肌　cervical muscle
额肌㉖　frontal muscle
咬肌㉗　great masticatory muscle (masseter)
胸锁乳突肌㉘　stermocleidom-astoid, amuent muscle
眼轮匝肌㉙　orbicularies oculi
三角肌㉚　deltoid (muscle)
胸肌　the pectoral muscle
胸大肌㉛　greater pectoral muscle, pectoris major
肱二头肌㉜　biceps, brachial biceps

肱三头肌㉝　triceps (brachial triceps)
肱桡肌㉞　trachio radialis
桡侧腕屈肌㉟　flexor carpi radialis
鱼际肌　thenar muscle
前锯肌㊱　serratus anterior
腹肌　abdominal muscle
腹外斜肌㊲　the oblique abdominal muscle, oblianus abdominis
腹直肌㊳　straight abdominal muscle, transversus abdominis
缝匠肌㊴　sartoruis
股外肌㊵　vastus lateralis
股内肌㊶　vastus medialis
胫骨前肌㊷　anterior tibial muscle
跟腱㊸　heel string, Achilles,

tendon, calcaneal tendon

趾屈肌㊹ **great-toe flexor**

夹肌㊺ **splenuis**

斜方肌㊻ **trapezius**

罔下肌㊼ **fascia infraspinata**

小圆肌㊽ **teres minor**

大圆肌㊾ **teres major**

背阔肌㊿ **latissimus of the back, latissimus dorsi**

臀大肌(51) **great gluteal muscle**

股二头肌(52) **biceps of the thigh, femoral biceps**

腓肠肌(53) **gastrocnemius**

趾长伸肌(54) **extensor digitorum**

腓骨长肌(55) **long peroneal muscle**

扩张肌 **dilator muscle**

随意肌 **voluntary muscle**

不随意肌 **involuntary muscle**

平滑肌 **non-striated muscle, smooth muscle**

横纹肌 **striated muscle**

合作肌 **synergistic muscle**

骨骼 **skeleton, osseous framework**

颅① **skull, cranium**

额骨② **frontal bone**

鼻骨③ **nasal bone**

顶骨④ **parietal bone**

枕骨⑤ **occipital bone**

颞骨⑥ **temporal bone**

上颌骨⑦ **upper jaw bone, maxilla**

下颌骨⑧ **lower jaw bone, mandible**

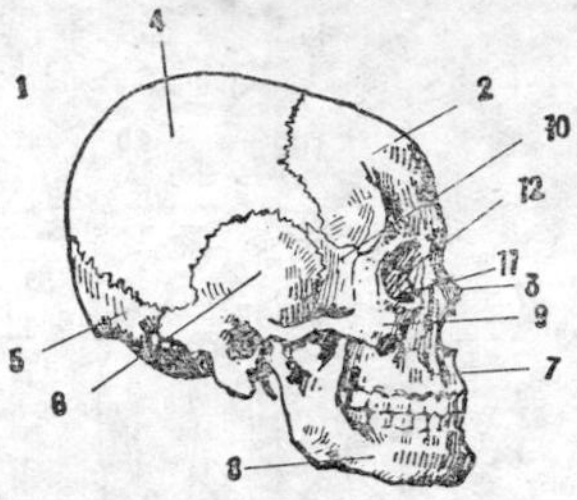

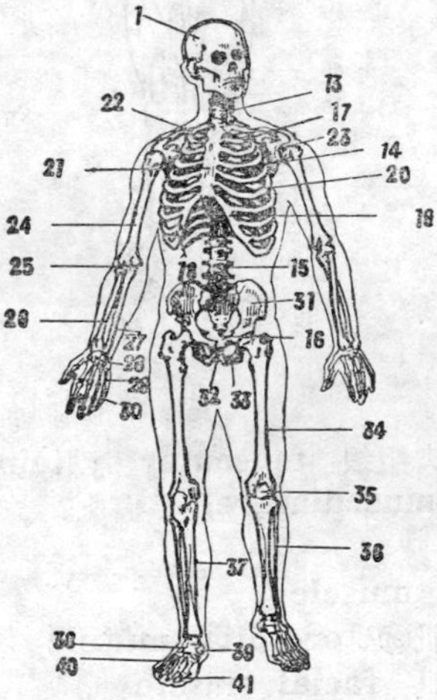

颧骨⑨ **cheek bone, zygomatic bone**

蝶骨⑩ **sphenoid bone**

筛骨⑪ **ethmoid bone, ethmoid**

泪骨⑫ **lacrimal (lachrimal) bone**

脊柱 **vertebral column, spine, back-bone**

颈椎⑬ **cervical vertebra(e)**

胸椎⑭ **thoracic (dorsal) vertebra(e)**

腰椎⑮ **lumbar vertebra(e)**

尾骨⑯　coccyx, coccygeal vertebrae, tail bone

真肋⑰　true (sternal) ribs

假肋⑱　false ribs

浮肋　floating ribs

肋软骨⑲　cartilage eibs

肋骨⑳　ribs

胸骨㉑　breast bone, sternum

锁骨㉒　collarbone, clavicle

肩胛骨㉓　shoulder blade, scapula

上肢骨　arm bone

肱骨㉔　bone of the upper arm, humerus

肘关节㉕　elbow-joint

桡骨㉖　radius

尺骨㉗　ulna

腕骨㉘　carpal bones, wrist bones

掌骨㉙　metacarpal bones, metacarpus

指骨㉚　phalanx

骨盆　pelvis

髂骨㉛　ilium

耻骨㉜　pubic bone

耻骨联合　pubic symphysis

坐骨㉝　ischium

下肢骨　leg bone

股骨㉞　thigh bone, femur

膝盖骨㉟　kneecap, patella

腓骨㊱　splint bone, calf bone, fibula

胫骨㊲　shin bone

跗骨㊳　tarsal bone

跟骨㊴　heel bone, calcaneum

蹠骨㊵　metatarsal bone, metatarsus

趾骨㊶　phalanges, toe bone

神经系统　nervous system

神经　nerve

中枢神经系统　central nervous system

周围神经系统　peripheral nervous system

大脑㊷　cerebrum

小脑㊸　cerebellum

脊髓㊹　spinal marrow (spinal cord)

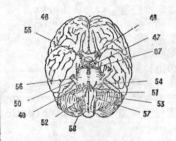

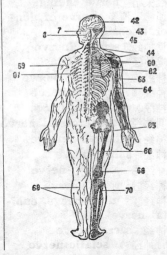

延髓㊺ **medulla**
脑神经㊻ **cranial nerve**
动眼神经㊼ **oculomotor nerve**
视神经㊽ **optic nerve**
面神经㊾ **facial nerve**
听神经 **auditory (acoustic) nerve**
嗅神经 **olfactory nerve**
三叉神经㊿ **trigeminal nerve**
舌咽神经(51) **glossopharygeal nerve**
舌下神经(52) **hypoglossal nerve**
迷走神经(53) **vagus nerve**
展神经(54) **abducent nerve**
脑垂体(55) **hypophysis cerebri**
脑桥(56) **pons**
传出神经 **efferent nerve**
传入神经 **afferent nerve**
交感神经 **sympathetic nerve**
副交感神经 **parasympathetic nerve**
神经末梢 **nerve endings**
普通感觉神经 **nerve of general sensibility**
感觉神经 **sensory nerve**
味觉神经 **nerve of taste**
副神经(57) **accessory nerve**
颈神经(58) **cervical nerve**
臂神经(59) **brachial nerve**
肋间神经(60) **intercostal nerve**
胸神经(61) **thoracic nerve**
脊神经 **spinal nerve**
腋神经(62) **axillary nerve**
桡神经(63) **radial nerve**
尺神经(64) **ulnar nerve, cubital nerve**
骶神经 **sacral nerve**
坐骨神经(65) **sciatic nerve**
股神经(66) **femoral nerve**
滑车神经(67) **trochlear nerve**
胫神经(68) **tibial nerve**
腓肠神经(69) **sural nerve**
腓神经(70) **peroneal nerve**
内脏神经 **splanchnic nerve**
营养神经 **trophic nerve**
神经干 **nerve trunk**
神经细胞 **nerve cell**
神经根 **nerve root**
淋巴 **lymph**
淋巴结 **lymph node**
淋巴腺 **lymphatic gland**
淋巴管 **lymph-vessel, lymphatic vessel**
淋巴组织 **lymphoid tissue**
淋巴球, 淋巴细胞 **lymphocyte**
腺 **gland**
内分泌腺 **endocrine gland**
泪腺 **lacriminal gland**
乳腺 **mamanary gland**
腮腺 **parotid gland**
涎腺 **salivary gland**
皮脂腺 **sebaceous gland**
汗腺 **sweat gland**
血管 **blood vessel**
脉管 **pulse artery**
毛细管 **capillary**
血液 **blood**
血浆 **plasma**
血球 **blood corpuscle**
白血球 **white blood cell, leucocyte**
红血球 **red blood cell, erythrocyte**
血小板 **blood platelets, thrombocyte**
血红蛋白 **haemoglobin**

## 看 病 Consulting a Doctor

看医生 visiting (seeing, consulting) a doctor

请医生 sending for a doctor, having a doctor in, calling a doctor

挂号 registering

预约(某时)诊病 having a doctor's appointment at …, making an appointment

候诊室 waiting room

候诊 waiting for one's turn to see the doctor

病史 medical history, case history

病历 record of disease

填写病历 filling in the record of disease

诊脉 feeling one's pulse

探热 taking one's temperature, having one's temperature taken

量血压 checking (taking) one's blood pressure

听心肺 listening to one's heart and lung

验血 having one's blood tested

检验屎尿 having one's stool and urine tested

照X光 being X-rayed

观察 observation

住院(治疗) being hospitalized (for treatment)

入院 being admitted into hospital

门诊病人 out-patient

诊断为…… diagnosing the case as…

压诊, 检查肝胃 checking one's liver, stomach by pressing

处方, 药方 prescription, formula

开处方 making out a prescription

送进医院 sending to hospital

要住院 ought to be hospitalized

(开)病情证明 (making out) a medical (sickness) certificate

(开)病假证明 (making out) a sick leave certificate

急诊 urgent medical aid, emergency treatment

交处方 taking a prescription to a chemist's

配药 filling a prescription

患……病 suffering from…

做手术 performing an operation

接受手术 undergoing an operation

卧床(三天) keeping to one's bed (for three days)

(医生)规定(病人)饮食 putting (a patient) on a diet

(病人)进清淡饮食(流质饮食, 半流质饮食) going on a light (liquid, semi-liquid) diet

哪里不舒服? what's the trouble?

# 症 状　Symtom

早期症状　early symtoms

前驱症状　premonitary symtoms, prodrome

自觉症状　subjective symtoms

主要症状　cardinal symtoms

全身症状　constitutional symtoms

临床症状　clinical symtoms

脸部表情　facial expression

迟钝　dullness

苍白　pallor, paleness

面色不好　being off colour

营养不良　poor nutritional state

发热(40度C)　having a fever, running a fever, running a temperature (of 40 degrees C)

体温上升　temperature rising

体温下降　temperature dropping(falling)

高热　high temperature, high fever

低热　low fever, low grade fever

退热　the fever being kept down

热正常　normal temperature

寒战　shivering, shivering with cold

发冷　feeling chilly

感到不舒服　feeling very bad, not feeling well

全身不适　general malaise

生病　falling ill, being ill, being taken ill

生……病　being ill with…, suffering from…

水肿　edema

浮肿　dropsy

全身水肿　anasarca

发肿,肿胀　swelling

(脚……)水肿　having swollen (legs…), (legs) swelling up

消肿　keeping the swelling down

眼睑虚肿　puffiness of eyelids

感到虚弱无力　feeling weak

焦躁不安　feeling restless and anxious

疲乏不堪　feeling exhausted, being tired out

过度疲劳　excessive fatigue

没有精神　feeling listless

(胸、肚、背、腰、耳……)痛　having a pain(in the chest, abdomen, back, side, ear…)

全身疼痛　general aching, aching all over

钝痛　dull aching

剧痛　severe pain, sharp pain

撕裂般痛　tearing pain

闪痛　lightning pain

锥痛　boring pain

触痛,压痛　tenderness

咬痛　gnawing pain

游走性痛　wandering pain

心前区痛　precardial pain

痛放射至……　radiation of pain to…

头痛　headache

偏头痛　migraine, hemicrania

牙痛　toothache

胃痛　stomachache

呼吸困难　respiratory difficulty, having difficulty in breathing

气促　shortness of breath, dyspn(o)ea

充血　congestion, hyperemia, engorgement

出血　hemorrhage, bleeding

皮下出血　subcutaneous hemorrhage

内出血　internal hemorrhage (bleeding)

外出血　external hemorrhage (bleeding)

伤口出血　the wound bleeding

大出血　bleeding profusely

咯血　spitting of blood, hematemesis

皮下出血　subcutaneous ecchymoma

郁血　stagnation of blood, stasis of blood

呕血　vomiting of blood, hematemesis

呕吐　vomiting

恶心　nausea, feeling nausea

食欲不振　losing appetite, poor appetite

无力　asthenopia

流涎　salivation

反胃　regurgitation of food

消化不良　indigestion

不想吃油腻食物　losing appetite for fatty food

嘴发苦　having a bad taste in the mouth

口臭　fetid oris

腹泻　having loose bowels, diarrhea

上腹痛　pain in upper abdomen

绞痛　colic, colicky pain

腹绞痛　angina abdominis

腹鸣　borborygmus

便秘　constipation, being constipated

里急后重　tenesmus

大便不正常　irregular bowel movement

大便失禁　incontinence of feces

小便失禁　incontinence of urine

小便……次　having…motions

突然想大便　being taken short

有舌苔　coated(furred) tongue

舌苔很厚　tongue heavily coated

干呕　retching

呃逆　hiccup, hiccough

胃酸多　gastric hyperacidity

胃酸少　gastric hyporacidity

黄疸　jaundice

肝肿大　enlargement of liver, hepatomegaly

脾肿大　enlargement of spleen, splenomegaly

胀感　feeling swelling

腹胀　abdominal distension, meteorism

放屁　breaking wind, passing flatus, farting

腹水　ascites, ascitic fluid

咳嗽　cough

干咳　dry cough, hacking cough

阵咳 paroxysmal cough, a fit of coughing
咳痰 coughing up phlegm
反射性咳 reflex cough
剧咳 having a bad cough
喷嚏 sneezing
流鼻涕 having a running nose
鼻子不通 having a stuffed-up nose, nose clogged up
痰 sputum
浓痰 purulent sputum
鼻涕 snivel, mucus in(from) the nose
口水, 唾液 saliva, spittle
流泪 (eyes) running with tears, having watery eyes
喉疼 sore throat
声嘶 being hoarse
发绀 cyanosis
紫癜 purpura
瘀点, 瘀斑 petechia, ecchymosis(pl. ecchymoses)
痉挛 spasm, cramp
惊厥 convulsions
震颤 tremor
萎缩 atrophy
(局部肌肉)抽搐 tic
发炎 inflamation
兴奋 excitation
膝反射 knee jerk, knee reflex, patellar
眼球突出 exophthalmos, exophthalmus
瞳孔扩张 dilated pupil
瞳孔缩小 contracted pupil
出汗 sweating, perspiring
盗汗 night sweat
冷汗 cold sweat, being in a cold sweat
气喘 asthma, being short of breath
喘鸣 stridor
脉速 rapid pulse
迟脉 retarded pulse
脉弱 weak pulse
心悸 palpitation
血压 blood pressure
收缩压 systolic pressure
舒张压 diastolic pressure
血压120/80 The blood pressure 120 over 80.
干罗音 dry rale
湿罗音 moist rale
心搏 heart beat
心动过速 tachycardia
心动徐缓 bradycardia
心音 cardiac sound
心脏杂音 heart murmur
心律不齐 arrhythmia
心绞痛 angina pectoris
呼吸急促 tachypnea
呼吸徐缓 bradypnea
嗜眠 somnolence
昏睡 in a coma
昏迷 coma, to faint, fainting
休克 shock
发晕 feeling faint
昏倒 swooning, fainting, passing out
耳鸣 having a ringing sound in the ear
眩晕 dizziness, vertigo, gliddiness, feeling dizzy
失眠 insomnia, sleeplessness, not being able to sleep
神志昏迷, 谵妄 delirium
神经不正常 nervous disorder

幻觉　hallucination
幻视　photism
幻听　phonism
淋巴结肿大　enlargement of the lymph nodes
甲状腺肿　goiter
语音震颤　vocal fremitus
失去知觉　loss of sense
语言障碍　lalopathy
语言不清　alalia
失语　aphasia
发痒　itch
全身发痒　itching all over
尿闭　ischuria
尿频　sychnuria, pollakiuria
排尿困难　difficulty in urination
血尿　hematuria, blood urine
乳糜尿　chylous urine
便血　occult blood in the feces
黑便　passing tarry stools
遗尿　enuresis, urorrhea
早泄　prospermia
遗精　emission
月经不调　irregular menstruation, menoxnia
月经过多　menorrhea,

menorrhagia
痛经　dysmenorrhea
经闭　amenorrhea
消瘦　losing weight
肥胖症　obesity
外伤　trauma
溃疡　ulcer
流脓　running with pus
化脓　suppurating
脓　pus
感染　infection
水疱　blister
疹　rash
(全身)出疹　breaking out with rashes (all over)
脱水　dehydration
虚脱　collapse
脱发　dropping of hair
蚁走感　formication
辗转不安　jactitation
视觉模糊　dimness of vision
肿块　mass
腹内肿块　abdominal mass
血块　clot, blood clot
失认识能　agnosia
失听觉　auditory agnosia
失视觉　optical agnosia
失运动能　akinesia

# 疾　病　Disease

急性病　acute disease
慢性病　chronic disease
传染病　communicable (infectious) disease
接触传染病　contagious disease
小病　ailment
地方病　endemic disease
流行病　epidemic disease

大流行病　pandemic disease
间发病　intercurrent disease
器质性疾病　parenchymal disease
官能性疾病　functional disease
职业病　occupational disease
原发性病　primary disease
继发病　secondary disease
热带病　tropical disease

先天病　congenital disease
后天病　acquired disease
常见病　common disease, commonly encountered disease
多发病　disease of frequent occurence, reocurrent disease
并发病　complication

传染病　infectious diseases

伤风(感冒)　coryza, cold
流行性感冒　influenza, flu
麻疹　measles
风疹　rubella
水痘　chicken-pox
天花　small pox
猩红热　scarlet fever
白喉　diphtheria
百日咳　whooping cough, pertusis
流行性腮腺炎　mumps, epidemic parotitis
流行性脑膜炎　epidemic cerebrospinal meningitis
伤寒　typhoid, typhoid fever
副伤寒　paratyphoid
细菌性痢疾　bacterial dysentery
阿米巴痢疾　amoeba dysentery
传染性肝炎　infective hepatitis
霍乱　cholera
脊髓灰质炎(小儿麻痹症)　polio, poliomyelitis (infantile paralysis)
蛔虫病　ascariasis
蛲虫病　enterobiasis, ringworm disease

姜片虫病　fasciolopsiasis
绦虫病　cestodiasis, taeniasis, tape worm disease
包虫病　echinococcosis, hyddtid disease
锥虫病　trypanosomiasis
华支睾吸虫病　clonorchiasis
肺吸虫病　paragonimiasis
疟疾　malaria
丝虫病　filariasis
黑热病　black fever, kala-azar
回归热　relapsing fever
流行性出血热　epidemic hemorrhagic fever
鼠疫　plague, pest
流行性乙型脑炎　epidemic encephalitis B
斑疹伤寒　typhus (fever)
恙虫病　tsutsugamushi disease
黄热病　yellow fever
钩虫病　ancylostomiasis, hookworm disease, ankylostomiasis
血吸虫病　schistosomiasis, snail fever
钩端螺旋体病　leptospirosis
炭疽　anthrax
狂犬病　rabies
结核病　tuberculosis
喉结核　laryngeal tuberculosis
肺结核　pulmonary tuberculosis (TB)
急性粟粒性结核　acute miliary TB
干酪性肺炎　caseous pneamonia
结核性脑膜炎　meningitis tuberculosis

结核性胸膜炎　tuberculous pleuritis

活动性结核　active tuberculosis

开放性结核　open TB

肠结核　tuberculosis of intestine

结核性腹膜炎　tuberculous peritonitis

肾结核　renal tuberculosis

骨结核　tuberculosis of bones

关节结核　tuberculosis of joints

皮肤结核　dermal tuberculosis

淋巴结结核　tuberculosis of lymph nodes

颈淋巴结核　tuberculosis of the cervical lymph nodes

呼吸系统疾病　diseases of respiratory system

上呼吸道感染　upper respiratory tract infection

支气管炎　bronchitis

急性支气管炎　acute bronchitis

慢性支气管炎　chronic bronchitis

支气管扩张症　bronchiectasis

支气管哮喘　bronchial asthma

老年气管炎　bronchitis suffered by the old people

肺炎　pneumonia

大叶性肺炎　lobar pneumonia

小叶性肺炎　lobular pneumonia

原发性非典型性肺炎　primary atypical pneumonia

肺脓肿　suppuration of the lung

肺气肿　emphysema

胸膜炎　pleuritis, pleurisy

化脓性胸膜炎　suppurative pleurisy

脓胸　empyema

气胸　pneumothorax

心血管疾病　cardiovascular diseases

心脏病　heart trouble

风湿性心脏病　rheumatic heart disease

慢性风湿性心脏病　chronic rheumatic heart disease

肺原性心脏病　cor pulmonale

冠状动脉粥样硬化性心脏病　coronary atheroselerotic heart disease

心绞痛　angina pectoris

心肌梗塞　myocardial infarction

高血压病　hypertension

动脉粥样硬化　atherosclerosis

心包炎　pericarditis

低血压病　hypotension

心内膜炎　endocarditis

肺动脉栓塞　pulmonary embolism

梅毒性心管病　syphilitic cardiovascular disease

先天性心血管病　congenitial cardiovascular disease

先天性心脏病　congenital heart disease

心间隔缺损　auricular septal defects

心室间隔缺损　ventricular

septal defects

主动脉狭窄　aortostenosis, aortarctia

心肌炎　myocarditis

心律不齐　irregular pulse, cardiac arrhythmias

窦性心律不齐　sinus arrhythmia

窦性心动过缓　sinus bradycardia

窦性心动过速　sinus tachycardia

窦房结暂停　sinus arrest

异位搏动　ectopic beat

脱漏搏动　dropped beat

过早搏动　premature beat

期前收缩　premature contraction

心房扑动　auricular flutter

纤维性颤动　fibrillation

心房纤维性颤动　auricular fibrillation, atrial fibrillation

心室纤维性颤动　ventricular fibrillation

心脏传导阻滞　disturbances in conduction

房室传导阻滞　atrioventricular block

束支传导阻滞　bundle branch block

心血管神经官能症　neurocirculatory asthenia, cardiac neurosis

心肌衰弱　myocardia

心力衰竭　cardiac failure, heart failure

脑溢血　cerebral apoplexy, cerebral hemorrhage

克山病　Kenshan disease

偏瘫(半身不遂)　hemiplegia

消化系统疾病　diseases of the digestive system

食管炎　esophagitis

食道炎　esophagitis, inflammation of the esophagus

食道扩张　esophagectasic

胃炎　gastritis

急性胃炎　acute gastritis

慢性胃炎　chronic gastritis

肠胃炎　enterogastritis

急性胃肠炎　acute gastroenteritis

胃溃疡　gastric ulcer

十二指肠溃疡　duodenal ulcer

肠炎　enteritis

十二指肠炎　duodenitis

结肠炎　colitis

胃肠神经官能症　gastro-intestinal neurosis

胃下垂　gastroptosis, ptosis of the stomach

胃扩张　dilatation of stomach

肝炎　hepatitis

病毒性肝炎　viral hepatitis

中毒性肝炎　toxic hepatitis

无黄疸型肝炎　anicteric hepatitis

急性突发型肝炎　acute fulminating hepatitis

肝硬变　cirrhosis of the liver

肝昏迷　hepatic coma

肝脓肿　liver abscess

肝肿大　enlargement of the liver, hepatomegaly

胆石症　gall (bladder) stone,

cholelithiasis

胆囊炎 cholecystitis

胰腺炎 pancreatitis

急性胰腺炎 acute pancreatitis

慢性胰腺炎 chronic pancreatitis

腹膜炎 peritonitis

小肠炎 inflammation of the small intestine

大肠炎 inflammation of the large intestine

肠套叠 intussusception

脾肿大 splenomegoly, splenomegalia

黄疸病 jaundice

肠溃疡 enterelcosis

肠胃炎 enterogastritis

习惯性便秘 habitual constipation

便秘 constipation

肠结肠炎 enterocolitis

肠痉挛 enterospasm

腹泻 diarrhea


泌尿生殖系统疾病 diseases of urigenital system


肾病 disease of the kidney

肾炎 nephritis

肾小球性肾炎 glomerulonephritis

慢性肾小球性肾炎 chronic glomerular nephritis

急性肾小管性肾病 acute tubular necrosis

肾盂炎 pyelitis

肾盂肾炎 nephropyelitis

尿毒症 uremia

肾盂积水 hydronephrosis

肾结石 kidney stone

肾硬变 nephrosclerosis

尿道炎 urethritis

遗尿症 nocturnal enuresis

尿道出血 urethrorrhagia, hemorrhage of the urethra

膀胱结石 bladder stone

尿闭 suppression of urine, anuria

尿潴留 retention of urine

血尿 bloody urine, urina cruenta

乳糜尿 urina chyli

乳状尿 urina galactodes

排尿困难 difficult urination

排尿痛感 painful urination

尿频 frequent urination

肾结核 tuberculosis of the kidneys

前列腺肥大 hypertrophy of the prostate

输精管精囊炎 vasovesicalitis


造血系统疾病 diseases of hematopoietic system


贫血 anemia

恶性贫血 septicaemia, anemia, pernicious anemia

白血球增多 leukocytosis, leucocytosis

红血球增多症 polycythaemia, polycythemia

白血病 leukaemia

血友病 hemophilia

败血病 septicaemia, septicemia

血小板溶解 thrombocytolysis

血小板减少性紫癜 thrombocytopenic purpura

过敏性紫癜　anaphylactic purpura

粒性白细胞缺乏症　agranulocytosis

粒性白细胞减少症　granulocytopenia

神经系统疾病和精神病　diseases of the nervous system and psychoses

三叉神经痛　trigeminal neuralgia

坐骨神经痛　sciatica

面神经瘫痪　facial paralysis

神经炎　neuritis

多发性神经炎　polyneuritis

中风　apoplexy, apoplectic fit

癫痫　epilepsy

癔病(歇斯底里)　hysteria

神经痛　neuralgia

舞蹈病　chorea

精神分裂症　schizophrenia, schizophrenosis

神经官能症　neurosis

脑震荡　cerebral concussion

神经衰弱　neurasthenia

偏头痛　migraine

脑膜炎　meningitis

脑炎　encephalitis

脑血管意外　cerebral vascular accident

脑溢血　cerebral hemorrhage

脑血栓形成　cerebral thrombosis

脑栓塞　cerebral embolism

蛛网膜下腔出血　subarachmoid hemorrhage

脑肿瘤　brain tumour

脑脓肿　abscess

记忆减退　hypomnesia

遗忘症　amnesia

妄想　dillusion

痴呆　dementia

职业病及物理、化学及其他因素引起的疾病　occupational diseases and diseases due to physical, chemical and other agents

中暑　heat stroke, hyperpyrexia

热虚脱　heat exhaustion

日射病　sun stroke

热痉挛　heat cramps

矽肺　silicosis

肺尘埃沉着病　pneumoconiosis chalicotica

一氧化碳中毒　carbon monoxide poisoning

铅中毒　lead poisoning

砷中毒　arsenial poisoning

煤气中毒　gas poisoning

罐头食物中毒　can poisoning, tin sickness

药物中毒　drug poisoning

食物中毒　food poisoning

酸中毒　acid poisoning, acidism

碱中毒　alkali poisoning, lye poisoning

工业中毒　industrial poisoning

汞中毒　mercurial poisoning

银中毒　silver poisoning

苯中毒　benzol poisoning

杀虫剂中毒 insecticide poisoning

金属中毒 metallic poisoning

蜈蚣咬中毒 myriapedes, myriapedes poisoning

蛇咬中毒 snake venom poisoning

蝎咬中毒 scorpion bite poisoning

血中毒 blood poisoning

漆中毒 varnish poisoning, rhus poisoning

战争毒气中毒 war gas poisoning

急性中毒 acute poisoning

慢性中毒 chronic poisoning

酒精中毒 alcoholism

溺水 drowned, drowning

电击 electric shock

晕车 car sickness

晕船 seasickness

晕机 airsickness

运动病 motion sickness

放射病 irradiation sickness

登山病 mountain sickness

减压病 decompression illness

冻伤 frostbite

冻疮 chilblain

内分泌系统疾病 disease of ductless glands, disease of endocrine glands

新陈代谢疾病 disease of metabolism

甲状腺机能亢进 hyperthyroidism

甲状腺机能减退 hypothyroidism

甲状腺机能不全 thyropenia

克汀病(呆小病) cretinism

粘液性水肿 myxedema

甲状腺肿 goiter

甲状腺毒症 thyrotoxicosis

糖尿病 diabetes, diabetes mellitus

肥胖病 obesity

肾上腺皮质机能亢进 hyperfunction of adrenal cortex

肾上腺皮质机能减退 adrenal cortical insufficiency

电解质平衡紊乱 disturbance of electrolytes balance

运动系统疾病 diseases of locomotor system

风湿性关节炎 arthritis rheumatica, rheumarthritis

类风湿性关节炎 rheumatoid arthritis

骨关节病 osteoarthritis

纤维组织炎 fibrositis

营养缺乏病 deficiency diseases

蛋白质缺乏 protein deficiency

营养不良 malnutrition

维生素缺乏病 vitamin deficiency, hypovitarninosis

维生素A缺乏病 vitamin A deficiency

脚气病 beriberi

核黄素缺乏病 riboflavin deficiency, ariboflavinosis

糙皮病 pellagra

儿科疾病　paediatric disease

新生儿硬化症　sclerema neonatorum
佝偻病　rickets
婴儿湿疹　eczema infantum
急惊风　convulsion
惊厥　eclampsia
软骨病　cartilage

妇产科疾病　obstetric and gynecologic disease

痛经　dysmenorrhea
月经不调　abnormal menstruation
月经过多　menorrhagia
月经过少　hypomenorrhea
月经紊乱　menstrual disturbance
月经频繁　polymenorrhea
经闭　amenorrhea, amenia
绝经　menopause
子宫出血(血崩)　metrorrhagia, meno-metrorrhagia
子宫脱垂　metroptosis
子宫后屈　retrocession of uterus
子宫后移　retroflexion of uterus
子宫后倾　retroversion of uterus
子宫内翻　inversio uteri, inversion of uterus
子宫前倾　anteversio uteri
功能性子宫出血　functional memorrhagia
子宫炎　metritis
子宫内膜异位症　endometriosis, adenomyosis
子宫内膜炎　endometritis
子宫收缩功能紊乱　uterine dysfunction
子宫肌炎　myometritis
子宫周围结缔组织炎　parametritis
子宫穿孔　perforation of uterus
子宫破裂　rupture of uterus
子宫颈炎　cervicitis
子宫颈肥大　cervicical hypertrophy
子宫颈息肉　cervical polyp
双子宫　double uterus
子宫颈糜烂　cervical erosion
子痫　eclampsia
外阴白斑症　leukoplakia vulvae
外阴瘙痒　pruitus vulvae
外阴炎　vulvitis
阴道炎　vaginitis
滴虫性阴道炎　trichomonas vaginitis
白带　leukorrhea, whites
阴道出血　vaginal hemorrhage
附件炎　adnexitis
输卵管炎　inflamation of oviduct, salpingitis
输卵管卵巢炎　salpingoovaritis
卵巢囊肿　ovarian cyst
乳腺炎　mastitis
盆腔炎　pelvic infection
慢性盆腔炎　chronic pelvic inflamation
处女膜闭锁　imperforate hymen
不孕　infertility, sterility
怀孕, 妊娠　pregnancy, gesta-

tion

| | |
|---|---|
| 宫外孕 | ectopia pregnancy |
| 妊娠水肿 | edema of pregnancy |
| 妊娠呕吐 | vomiting of pregnancy |
| 妊娠高血压 | hypertension of pregnancy |
| 妊娠中毒症 | toximia of pregnancy |
| 轻度妊娠中毒 | mild toximia |
| 流产 | abortion |
| 晚期流产 | miscarriage |
| 习惯性流产 | habitual abortion |
| 先兆流产 | threatened abortion |
| 人工流产 | artificial abortion |
| 不完全流产 | incomplete abortion |
| 完全流产 | complete abortion |
| 先露部分 | presenting part |
| 头先露 | cephalic presentation |
| 头顶先露 | vertex presentation |
| 足先露 | footling presentation |
| 肩先露 | shoulder presentation |
| 枕骨先露 | occipicat presentation |
| 混合臀先露 | mixed breech presentation |
| 单臀先露 | frank breech presentation |
| 臀先露 | breech presentation |
| 面先露 | face presentation |
| 产后出血 | post-partum homorrhage |
| 早产 | premature birth, premature labour |
| 早产儿 | premature |
| 剖腹产术 | cesarotomy |
| 产褥感染 | puerperal infection |
| 产褥热病 | puerperal fever |
| 羊水 | amniotic fluid |
| 羊水过少 | oligohydramnios |
| 羊水过多 | polyhydramnios |
| 会阴破裂 | perineal tear |
| 良性葡萄胎 | Hydatidiform Mole |
| 恶性葡萄胎 | chorioadenoma destruens |
| 初产妇 | primipara |
| 经产妇 | multipara |
| 初孕妇 | primigravida |
| 经孕妇 | multigravida |
| 初乳 | colostrum |
| 更年期 | climacterium |
| 输卵管妊娠 | tubal gestation |
| 卵巢妊娠 | ovarian pregnancy (gestation) |
| 刮宫 | dilation & curettage (D. & C.) |
| 胎儿畸形 | fetal anomalies |
| 胎头吸引术 | vaccum extraction of fetal head |
| 胎足倒转术 | cephalic version |
| 胎盘 | placenta |
| 胎盘早期剥离 | abruptio placenta |
| 胎盘滞留 | retention of placenta |
| 胎膜早破 | premature rupture of membranes |
| 剖腹子宫切除 | abdominal hysterectomy |
| 子宫切除 | hysterectomy |
| 原发性卵巢癌 | primary ovarian carcinoma |
| 脐带 | umbilical cord |
| 脐带先露 | cord presentation |
| 胎产式 | lie |

直产式 longitudinal lie

横产式 transverse lie

胎位 position of the fetus

胎位不正 fetus in wrong position

斜产式 obligue lie

绒毛膜上皮癌 chorio epithelioma, choriocarcinoma

新生儿呼吸暂停 apnea neonatorum

新生儿窒息 asphyxia neonatorum

输卵管通气术 tubal insufflation

输卵管切除 salpingectomy

分娩, 生产 labour, accouchment, giving birth, delivery

顺产 normal labour

难产 difficult labour

剖腹产(术) Caesarean section (operation)

引产 induced labour

接生 delivery

过期分娩 postponed labour

滞产 prolonged labour

产伤 birth injury

产后痛 after-pains

死产 still birth

迫产 forced labour

死胎不下 missed labour

干产 dry labour

外科疾病 surgical disease

疖 furuncle

痈 carbuncle

脓肿 abscess

血肿 hematoma

蜂窝织炎 cellulitis, phlegmon

丹毒 erysipelas

类丹毒 erysipeloid

淋巴管炎 lymphangitis

淋巴结炎 lymphadenitis

静脉炎 phlebitis

血栓性静脉炎 thrombophlebitis

感染 infection

破伤风 tetanus

气性坏疽 gas gangrene

急性乳房炎 acute mastitis

烧伤 burns

冻伤 frost-bite

冻疮 chilblain

蛇咬中毒 ophiotoxaemia, ophidismus, snake venom poisoning

蛇咬伤 snake bite

昆虫咬伤 insect bite

下肢静脉曲张 varicose vein of the leg

慢性溃疡 indolent ulcer, chronic ulcer, callous ulcer

痔 hemorrhoids, piles

肛门裂 fissure in ano

外痔 external piles

内痔 internal piles

肛门瘘 anal fistula

脱肛 prolapse of anus

直肠息肉 polip of rectum

脑震荡 coneussion of brain, cerebral concussion

挫伤 contusion

扭伤, 捩伤 sprain

外伤, 创伤 being injured, being wounded, injury, wound, trauma

咬伤 bite

脱位 dislocation, subluxation

劳损 strain
畸形 deformity
脓泡 pustule
脓 pus
水疱 blister
褥疮 bedsore
化脓 suppuration
溃疡 ulcer
溃疡形成 ulceration
发炎 inflammation
发肿 swelling
充血 congestion, hyperemia
肌萎缩 muscular atrophy
坏死 necrosis
腰痛 lumbago, lumbodynia, lower back pain
胃穿孔 gastric perforation
胃扩张 dilotation of stomach
疝 hernia
外科急腹症 surgical acute abdomen
急性阑尾炎 acute appendicitis
小儿麻痹后遗症 sequel of polio
后遗症 sequela
(急性)肠梗阻 (acute) intestinal obstruction
弓形腿(膝内翻) bowleg
骨折 fracture
开放性骨折 open fracture
闭合性骨折 closed fracture
粉碎性骨折 comminuted fracture
不完全骨折 incomplete fracture
完全骨折 complete fracture
嵌入骨折 impacted fracture
出血 bleeding, hemorrhage

外科感染 surgical infection
脓性感染 purulent infection
动脉出血 arterial hemorrhage
静脉出血 venous hemorrhage
微血管出血 capillary hemorrhage
晕厥 syncope
虚脱 collapse
休克 shock
开放性伤口 open injury
伤口 wound(s)
化脓性伤口 suppurative wound
闭合性伤口 closed injury
血中毒, 脓毒病 blood poisoning, sepsis
血管梗塞 infarct
血栓形成 thrombosis
栓塞 embolism
动脉瘤 aneurysm
静脉曲张病 varicosis
血栓性血管炎 thromboagiitis
良性肿瘤 benign tumours
恶性肿瘤 malignant tumours
血管瘤 angioma(s)
肌瘤 myoma
神经纤维瘤 neurinoma
神经胶质瘤 glioma
(鼻……)受伤 injury(ies) (to nose…)
(颈……部)伤 wounds (of the neck…)
(颅……部)骨折 fractures (of the skull…)
(鼻……部)出血 hemorrhage (from the nose…)
(耳, 咽……部)异物 foreign body (in the ear, in the pharynx…)

中耳炎　inflammation of the middle ear

瘘　fistula

唇裂(兔唇)　harelip

坏疽性口炎　noma, water cancer

下颚脱位　dislocation of the lower jaw

甲状腺肿　goiter

狭窄　stenosis, stricture

喉狭窄　laryngeal stenosis

幽门狭窄　tricuspid stenosis

食管狭窄　stenosis of the Esophagus

气胸　pneumothorax

脓胸(化脓性胸膜炎)　purulent pleurisy

先天性心脏缺损　congenital cardiac defects

后天性心脏缺损　acquired cardiac defects

腹膜炎　peritonitis

腹水　ascites

胃溃疡　gastric ulcer

十二指肠溃疡　duodenal ulcer

胃穿孔　gastric perforation

阑尾穿孔　appendicular perforation

肠穿孔　intestinal perforation

肠套叠　intussusception

直肠不通　atresic of the rectum

肝破裂　rupture of the liver

胆囊炎　inflammation of the gallbladder

胆管病　cholepathy

胆石病　cholelithiasis, biliary calaulus, gallstone

胆蛔虫病　biliary ascariasis

急性胰腺炎　acute pancreatitis

膀胱结石　calculus vascularis, cystolith, vesical calculus

肾结石　calculus renalis, nephrolithus, kidneystone

前列腺肥大　hypertrophy of the prostate

水囊肿　hydrocele

腰椎间盘突出　protrusion of lumbar intervertabal

骨髓炎　osteomyelitis

化脓性骨髓炎　purulent osteomyelitis

腱鞘炎　tendovaginitis, tendo-vaginitis, vaginal synovitis

化脓性腱鞘炎　purulent tendovaginitis

(化脓性)汗腺炎　(purulent) hidradenitis

甲沟炎　paronychia

**皮肤病　skin disease**

皮肤病　dermatosis

带状疱疹　herpes zoster

单纯疱疹　herpes simplex

疣　wart

脓疱疮　impetigo

疖　furunculus

毛囊炎　folliculitis

丹毒　erysipelas

结核皮肤病　tuberculosis cutis

狼疮　lupus

癣　tinea, ringworm

雅司病　yaws

头癣　tinea capitis

体癣　tinea corporis

手癣　tinea manuum

足癣　tinea pedis, tinea of the foot

念珠菌病　candidiasis

疥疮　scabies

冻疮　perniosis, chilblains

痱子　miliana rubra

擦烂红斑　erythema intertrigo

尿布红斑　napkin erythema

皮炎　dermatitis

湿疹　eczema

红斑性湿疹　eczema erythem-
atosum

丘疹性湿疹　eczema papulosum

水泡性湿疹　eczema vesiculo-
sum

脓泡性湿疹　eczema pustulo-
sum

湿润性湿疹(糜烂性湿疹)
eczema madidans

结痂性湿疹　eczema crustosum

鳞屑性湿疹　eczema squamo-
sum

婴儿湿疹　eczema infantum

药物性皮炎　dermatitis
medicamentosa

荨麻疹(风疹)　urtica, urticana,
nettle rash

职业性皮肤病　occupational
dermatoses

工业职业性皮肤病　industrial
occupational dermatoses

农业职业性皮肤病　agricultural
occupational dermatoses

水稻田皮炎　dermatitis of the
rice field

红斑性狼疮　lupus erythema-
tosis

硬皮病　sclerodorma

紫癜　purpura

瘙痒　pruritus

神经性皮炎　neurodermatitis

牛皮癣(银屑病)　psoriasis

扁平苔癣　lichen planus

玫瑰糠疹　pityriasis rose

天疱疮　pemphigus

维生素缺乏病　hypovitaminosis

核黄素缺乏病　ariboflarinosis

白癜病(白斑病)　vitiligo, leu-
coderma

雀斑　ephelides

皮脂溢出症　seborrhea

皮脂溢性皮炎　dermatitis
seborrheica

痤疮　acne

酒渣鼻　rosacea

臭汗症　bromidrosis

斑秃　alopecia areata

早秃　alopecia prematura

滤泡炎　folliculitis

鸡眼　corn, callosity

性病　venereal disease, V. D.

淋病　gonorrhea

麻风　leprosy

梅毒　syphilis

先天性梅毒　congenital
syphilis

眼科疾病　Ophthalmic disease

慢性泪囊炎　chronic dacryocys-
titis

急性泪囊炎　acute dacryocys-
titis

睑缘炎(红眼边)　blepharitis

睑下垂　blepharoptosis

睑痉挛　blepharospasm

睑外翻　ectropion

睑内翻　entropion, blephare-
losis

睑板腺炎　meibomianitis,

blepharoadenitis
眼干燥　xerophthalmia
眼球突出　exophthalmos
倒睫　trichiasis
眼浓溢　blennophthalmia
急性结膜炎(火眼)　acute conjunctivitis
慢性结膜炎　chronic conjunctivitis
沙眼　trochoma
泡性结膜炎　phlyctaenulosa conjunctivitis
结膜干燥　xeroma
泪腺炎　dacryoadenitis
角膜炎　keratitis
角膜软化症(夜盲症)　keratomalacia(nyotalopia, night blindness)
角膜溃疡　keratohelcosis
间质性角膜炎　kerotitis interstitialis
角膜结膜炎　keratoconjunctivitis
白内障　cataract
青光眼　glaucoma
虹膜睫状体炎　iridocyclitis
脉络膜炎　choroiditis
脉络膜视网膜炎　choroidoretinitis
视网膜炎　retinitis
乳头视网膜炎　papillorentinitis
视神经炎　neuropapillitis, ophthalmoneuritis, optic neuritis
视神经萎缩　optic atrophy
眼眶炎　orbititis
眼色素层炎　uveitis
眼炎　ophthalmia, ophthalmitis

感光眼炎　photophthalmia
远视　hypermetropia, hyperopia, far-sight
近视　myopia, myopy, nearsight
老视　old sight, presbyopia
色盲　colour blindness
散光　astigmatism, astigmia
斜眼　squint, strabismus
雪盲　snow blindness
昼盲　day blindness
色觉模糊　dimness of vision
眼花　vertigo
麦粒肿　hordeolum
霰粒肿　chalazion

耳鼻喉科疾病　ENT disease

急性鼻炎　acute rhinitis
慢性鼻炎　chronic rhinitis
鼻堵塞　obstruction of nose
鼻疖　furuncle of nose
鼻中隔弯曲　deviation of nasal septum
鼻中隔穿孔　perforation of nasal septum
萎缩性鼻炎　atrophic rhinitis
肥厚性鼻炎　hypertrophic rhinitis
鼻出血(鼻衄)　epistaxis
鼻部结核　tuberculosis of nose
鼻窦炎　sinusitis
化脓鼻窦炎　suppurative sinusitis
变态反应性鼻炎(过敏性鼻炎)　allergic rhinitis
鼻息肉　nasal polyp
腺样体增生肥大　hyperplasia and hypertrophy of adenoid

急性扁桃体炎　acute tonsillitis

扁桃体周围脓肿　peritonsillar abscess

慢性扁桃体炎　chronic tonsillitis

急性咽炎　acute pharyngitis

慢性咽炎　chronic pharyngitis

咽后脓肿　retropharyngeal abscess

软腭瘫痪　paralysis of soft palate

咽感觉紊乱　sensory disturbances of pharynx

咽良性肿瘤　benign tumour of pharynx

咽恶性肿瘤　malignant tumours of pharynx

咽痛　pharyngalgia

咽峡炎　angina, sore throat

急性喉炎　acute laryngitis

喉脓肿　laryngeal abscess

慢性喉炎　chronic laryngitis

肥厚性喉炎　hypertrophic laryngitis

萎缩性喉炎　atrophic laryngitis

喉结核　tuberculosis of larynx

喉肌麻痹　paralysis of laryngeal muscles

喉异物　foreign body of larynx

喉良性肿瘤　benign tumours of larynx

喉恶性肿瘤　malignant tumours of larynx

喉阻塞　laryngeal obstruction

坏疽性喉炎　gangrinous laryngitis

外耳道疖　furuncle of the external auditory canal

外耳道异物　foreign body in the external auditory canal

耳鸣　tinnitus (aurium)

耵聍栓塞　cerumen impaction

外耳湿疹　eczema of the external ear

弥漫性外耳道炎　diffused otitis externa

急性卡他性中耳炎　acute catarrhal otitis media

慢性卡他性中耳炎　chronic catarrhal otitis media

粘连性中耳炎　adhesire otitis media

急性化脓性中耳炎　acute supperative otitis media

急性乳突炎　acute mastoiditis

慢性化脓性中耳炎　chronic suppurative otitis media

慢性乳突炎　chronic mastoiditis

结核性中耳炎　tuberculosis otitis media

耳原性面神经麻痹　otogenic facial paralysis

硬脑膜外脓肿　extradural abscess

横窦血栓　lateral sinus thrombosis

耳原性脑膜炎　otogenic meningitis

耳原性脑脓肿　otogenic brain abscess

迷路炎　labyrinthitis

神经性耳聋　nerve deafness

耳硬化症　otosclerosis

美尼亚氏病　Meniere disease

聋症　deafness

中耳癌  cancer of middle ear

噪声性耳聋  deafness due to
　noise trauma

耳痛  otalgia

耳炎  otitis

耳溢  otorrhea


**肿瘤疾病  tumours**

良性肿瘤  benign tumour

恶性肿瘤  cancer, malignant
　tumour, carcinoma

乳头状瘤  papilloma

乳头状癌  papillocarcinoma

皮脂腺囊肿(粉瘤)  sebaceous
　cyst

纤维瘤  fibroid tumour,
　fibroma

脂瘤, 脂肪瘤  lipoma

血管瘤  hemangioma

肉瘤  sarcoma

鼻咽癌  cancer of nasopha-
　rynx, nasopharyngeal car-
　cinoma

淋巴肉瘤  sarcoma lymphati-
　cum, lymphosarcoma

腺瘤  adenoma, glandular
　tumour

血管瘤  angioma, vascular
　tumour

肌瘤  myama, muscular
　tumour

子宫肌瘤  myoma of uterus

神经瘤  neurinoma, nerve
　tumour

神经胶质瘤  glioma, brain
　tumour

囊肿  cyst

囊瘤  cystoma

上皮瘤, 上皮癌  epithelioma

软骨瘤  chondroma,
　cartilaginous tumour

脑癌  cancer of the brain

肺癌  cancer of the lungs,
　pulmonary cancer

皮肤癌  cancer of the skin

骨癌  cancer of the bone

子宫癌  uterine cancer, can-
　cer of the uterus

子宫内膜癌  endometrial
　carcinoma

子宫体癌  carcinoma of
　corpus uteri

子宫颈癌  carcinoma of
　cervix uteri

直肠癌  cancer of the rectum

食道癌  cancer of the
　oesophagus

淋巴腺癌  cancer of the
　lymph glands

胃癌  cancer of the stomach

乳癌  cancer of the breast,
　breast cancer

前列腺癌  cancer of the
　prostate gland

肝癌  cancer of the liver

肠癌  cancer of intestines

睾丸癌  cancer of the testis

原发性癌  primary cancer

转移  mestastasis, metaptosis

扩散  spreading, development

溃疡形成  ulcerating,
　ulceration


**口腔疾病  diseases in the
　oral cavity**

龋齿  dental caries, caries

dentis

牙髓炎 pulpitis

牙痛 toothache

自发性疼痛 spontaneous pains

牙周炎 periodontitis

(牙周炎)急性发作 (periodontitis) in the acute stage

牙松 looseness of the tooth

化脓性牙周炎 purulent periodontitis

牙龈红肿 redness and swelling of the gum

牙接触性疼痛 pains upon contact with the tooth

病牙 affected tooth

发热感 pyrexia

冠周炎 pericoronitis

拔牙后出血 hemorrhage following tooth extraction

牙槽炎 alveolitis

口炎 stomatitis

龈口炎 gingivostomatitis

口角炎 angular stomatitis

滤泡性口炎 stomatitis follicularis

雪口症(鹅口疮) stomatitis mycotica, stomatitis mycetogenetica, thrush

龈炎 gingivitis

龈瘤 epulis

脓肿 abscess

牙槽脓肿 alveolar abscess

龈脓肿 parulis

牙槽骨髓炎 alveolar osteomyelitis

颌骨髓炎 osteomyelitis of the jaw

颌骨骨折 jaw fracture

上颌骨折 maxillary fracture

下颌骨折 mandibular fracture

兔唇 cleft lip

# 化 验 Laboratory Test

化验室 laboratory

化验员 laboratory technician

化验单 laboratory test report

验大便 stool test, having one's stool tested

验小便 urine test

验痰 sputum test

验血 blood test

血样 specimens of one's blood

抽血 drawing blood

血常规分析(试验) routine analysis of blood

作……试验 putting one throughtest

血型 blood group

O型 group O

肝(肾)功能试验 test for liver (kidney) function

抗"O" antistreptococcolysin O

血沉 erythrocytic sedimentation rate (ESR)

血脂 blood lipoids

胆固醇 choleterol

血清 serum

三酸甘油脂 triglyceride

麝香浊度试验 thymol turbidity test (TTT)

硫酸锌浊度试验 Zinc Sulphate

turbidity test

脑磷脂胆固醇絮状试验 cephalincholesterol flocculation test (CCFT)

谷丙转氨酶 glutamicpyruvic transaminase (GPT)

血清谷氨酸草酰乙酸转氨酶测定 serum glutamic oxaloacetic transaminase (SGOT)

黄胆指数 Icterus Index

红血球计数 red blood cells count (RBC)

白血球计数 white blood cells count (WBC)

(白细胞)分类计数 differential count (DC)

红细胞平均血红蛋白浓度 mean corpuscular hemoglobin concentration (MCH)

平均红细胞容积 mean corpuscular volume (NCV)

压紧血细胞容积 packed cell volume (PCV)

基础代谢率 basal metabolic rate (BMR)

半乳糖(果糖)耐量试验 glatactose (frutose) tolerance test

菊粉(脲)廓清试验 inulin (urea) clearance test

肌酐(木糖)廓清试验 creatinine (xylose) clearance test

胰岛素葡萄糖水耐量试验 insulinglutose-water tolerance test

乳酸脱氢酶测定 lactic acid dehydrogenase determination

癌胚抗原 carcinoembryonic antigen

α—胎儿蛋白 α-fetoprotein (AFP)

阳性反应 positive reaction

阴性反应 negative reaction

## 医疗方法 Therapy

临床观察 clinical observation

病例 case

试脉 feeling one's pulse

量体温 taking one's temperature

量血压 taking (checking) one's blood pressure

收缩压 systolic pressure

舒张压 diastolic pressure

听诊 auscultation

叩诊 percussion

触诊 palpation

问诊 inquiry

望诊 inspection

检查眼(耳、鼻) examining the eyes (ears, nose)

全身检查 general checking-up

常规检查 routine examination

复查 follow-up examination

会诊 consultation

出诊 visit, paying a call

急诊 emergency case, emergency treatment

诊断 diagnosis, diagnosing

确诊 identifying one's disease, making a definitive diagnosis of…

预后　prognosis

康复　recovery

复发　relapse

病灶　focus (pl. foci)

肛门指诊　rectal touch

阴道指诊　vaginal touch

X 线检查　X-ray examination, being X-rayed

X 线照片　X-ray film, roentgenogram

X 线照相　X-ray film taking, radiography

透视检查　examination by fluoroscopy

胸部透视　having one's chest X-rayed

钡餐检查　barium meal examination

化验结果　laboratory report

心电图检查　ECG (electrocardiogram) examination

二杯试验　two-glass test

三杯试验　three-glass test

皮肤试验(过敏检查)　skin test

肾盂造影术　pyelography

静脉肾盂造影术　intravenous pyelography

逆行肾盂造影术　retrograde pyelography

X 线缩影照片　miniature radiograph

脑电图检查　EEG (electroencephalogram) examination

穿刺术检查　examination by centesis (by puncture)

病理切片　pathological section

基础代谢　basal metabolism

基础代谢率　basal metabolic rate (B. M. R.)

显微镜检查　microscopic examination

肉眼检查　macroscopic examination

活组织检查　biopsy

内窥镜检查　endoscopy

青蛙试验　toad test

治疗　treatment, giving treatment

临床治疗　clinical treatment

开药方　writing out a prescription

开药　prescribing for an illness, prescribing a medicine

配药　filling a prescription

抓药　having a prescription made up (filled)

打针　injecting, giving an injection

放松肌肉　relaxing one's muscle

打(……C.C.青霉素)针　an injection of (…c.c. of penicillin)

接受打针　receiving (having) an injection

对……过敏　being allergic to…

过敏反应　allergic reaction

青霉素反应　having a penicillin reaction

没有副作用　being free from side effects

盐水注射　saline infusion

预防注射　inoculating, protective inoculation

皮下注射　hypodermic

(subcutaneous) injection

肌肉注射 intramuscular injection

静脉注射 intravenous injection

静脉滴注 infusion by intravenous drip

关节内注射 intra-articular injection

激发注射 booster injection

血管注射 intravascular injection

输液 fluid infusion

输血 blood transfusion

过敏试验 test for hypersensitivity

服药 taking medicine

内服(药) for oral administration

外用(药) for external use

剂量 dose

剂量大小 the size of a dose

空腹服 to be taken on an empty stomach

饭后(饱食后)服 to be taken on a full stomach, after food, p.c. (post cibum)

每四小时服一次 to be taken at four-hour intervals, q.h. (quartis horis), four hourly

临睡前服 to be taken at bedtime

必要时服 to be taken when necessary, p.r.n. (pro re nate), whenever necessary

一天服三次 taking medicine 3 times a day, t.i.d. (ter in die)

一日四次 q.i.d. (quater in die); four times a day

每次服一茶匙 taking a spoonful (of medicine) each time

饭后服 taking medicine after meals

服药前摇晃药瓶 shaking the bottle well before use

睡前(服) hor. decub. (hora decubitus), at bedtime

每晚(服) o.n. (omni nocte), every night

每晨(服) o.m. (omni mane), every morning

遵医嘱服用 to be taken according to the instructions of the doctor

献血 blood donation

献血者 blood donor

血库 bank of blood

验血型 test of blood group

血型 blood group

O型 Group O

A型 Group A

B型 Group B

血清 serum

血浆 plasm

热敷 hot compress

冷敷 cold compress

敷贴 application

导尿 urethral catheterization

洗胃 gastric lavage

灌肠 enema

止血 hemostasis

滴注法 instillation

脊椎抽液 spinal tap

抽腹水 tapping the abdomen

包扎 dressing

包扎创伤 dressing a wound

上绷带 bandaging

换药 changing the dressings

消毒 disinfecting, sterilizing

切口，切开 incision

切开引流 incision and drainage

排脓 clearing out the pus, letting out the pus

抽脓 extraction of pus

封闭疗法 block therapy

缝合 suture, surgical stitching

缝合创口 suturing (sewing up) the wound

缝合切口 sewing up the incision

拆线 taking out (removing) the stitches

人工呼吸 artificial respiration

脱臼复位 replacing dislocated joints

按摩 massage

固定 fixation

夹板与绷带 splint and bandage

石膏绷带 plaster bandage

骨折复位 reduction of the fracture

结扎 ligation

扩张术 dilation

施行手术 performing an operation

大手术 major operation

小手术 minor operation

给病人做手术 operating on a patient

接受手术 undergoing an operation

麻醉 an(a)esthesia

全身麻醉 general an(a)esthesia

局部麻醉 local an(a)esthesia

人工冬眠 artificial hibernation

混合麻醉 mixed an(a)esthesia

低温麻醉 hypothermic an(a)esthesia

脊髓麻醉 spinal an(a)esthesia

药物麻醉 drug an(a)esthesia

针刺麻醉 acupuncture an(a)esthesia

中药麻醉 herbal an(a)esthesia

冷冻麻醉 refrigeration an(a)esthesia

切除术 resection, removal, excision

局部切除 local excision

扁桃体切除 tonsillectomy

胃切除 gastrectomy

肺切除 pneumonectomy

甲状腺切除 thyroidectomy

乳房切除 mastectomy

阑尾切除 appendectomy

脾切除 splenectomy

食管部分切除 esophagectomy

子宫颈切除 cervicectomy

子宫切除 hysterectomy, uterectomy

子宫肌瘤切除 hysteromyomectomy

全子宫切除 panhysterectomy

血栓切除 thrombectomy

附睾切除 epidiclymectomy

直肠切除 proctectomy

肾切除 nephrectomy

肾石切除 nephrolithotomy

前列腺切除 prostatectomy

迷走神经切除 vagotomy

叶切除术(切除肝、脑、肺等的一叶)

lobectomy
膀胱石切除　lithotomy
胆石切除　cholelithotomy
胆囊切除　cholecystectomy
淋巴结切除　lymphadenectomy
痔切除　hemorrhoidectomy
肝叶切除　hepalobectomy
肝切开　hepatomy
输尿管石切除　ureterolithotomy
输卵管切除　salpingectomy
脓肿切开　incision of abscess
颅骨切开　craniotomy
开颅术　craniotomy
静脉切开　venesection
耻骨切开　pubiotomy
舌系带切开　frenotomy
会阴切开　perineotomy
气管切开　tracheotomy
尿道切开　urethrotomy
瘤切除　removing a tumour
胸廓切开　thoracotomy
疝修补术　hernia repair, herniorrhaphy
体外循环　extracorporeal circulation
剖腹探查　abdominal laparotomy, exploratory laparotomy
剖腹术　laparotomy
剖腹产术　Caesarian section, Caesarian operation
引产术　induction of labour
产钳分娩　forceps delivery
无痛分娩　painless childbirth
刮子宫　uterine curettage
人工流产　artificial abortion
绝育　sterilization
截肢　amputation

断肢再植　reattaching a severed limb, replantation of a severed limb
断指再植　reattaching a severed finger, replantation of a severed finger
再植, 再接　reattaching, rejoining, replantation
坏死　gangrene
连接动脉静脉　connecting (joining) arteries and veins
冲洗　douche, irrigation
止血法　hemostasis
固定　fixation
植皮　skin-grafting
灸术　moxibustion
揉捏　kneading
心脏按摩　cardiac massage
人工气胸　artificial pneumothorax
正骨　bone-setting
关节固定术　arthrodesis
卧床休息　bed rest
骨胳牵引　skeletal traction
复位术　reduction
俯卧位　prone position
仰卧位　supine position
日光浴　sun bath
水浴　water bath
酒精浴　alcohol bath
热气浴　hot-air bath
手术疗法　operative treatment
非手术疗法　non-operative treatment
综合疗法　complex treatment, composite treatment
辅佐疗法　adjuvant treatment
保守疗法　conservative

treatment

姑息疗法 palliative treatment

根治法 radical treatment, radical cure

特效疗法 specific treatment

物理疗法 physiotherapy

电疗 electrotherapy, electrical treatment

水疗 hydrotherapy, hydropathic treatment

泥疗 mud-bath treatment

日光疗法 sun-rays treatment

日光灯疗法 sun-lamp treatment

紫外线疗法 ultraviolet ray treatment

热疗法 heat treatment

放射线疗法 radiotherapy

超短波疗法 ultra-short-wave treatment

超声波疗法 ultrasonic treatment

(生理)睡眠疗法 (physiological) sleep therapy

饮食疗法 dietotherapy

体育疗法 physical exercise therapy

牵引 traction

推拿, 按摩 massage

针刺疗法 acupuncture therapy

气功疗法 breathing technique therapy

新针疗法 new acupuncture therapy

组织疗法 tissue therapy

埋线疗法 thread burial

中西医综合治疗 treatment with combined therapy of traditional Chinese and Western medicine

化学疗法 chemotherapy

矿泉疗法 crenotherapy

家庭治疗 domestic treatment, home treatment

药物疗法 drug treatment

卧床治疗 treatment in the bed

气候疗法 climatic treatment, climatotherapy

机械疗法 mechanical treatment, mechanotreatment, mechanotherapy

蜡疗法 paraffin therapy

内科治疗 medical treatment

外科治疗 surgical treatment

矫形 orthopedic treatment

休息疗法 rest treatment

常规疗法 routine treatment

温热疗法 thermotherapy

预防处理 preventive treatment

卫生处理 hygenic treatment

精神疗法 mental therapeutics

氧气治疗 oxygen treatment

发汗治疗 treatment by sweating

饮食 diet

易消化的饮食 light diet

特定的饮食 special diet

最低维持饮食 subsistance diet

低热量饮食 low calory diet

低脂肪饮食 low fat diet

低蛋白饮食 low protein diet

素食 vegetable diet

流质饮食 liquid diet, liquid

**food**

半流质饮食　**semi-liquid diet**

食谱　**diet-table, dietary**

断奶　**weaning**

眼保健操　**ocular gymnastics**

斜视手术　**strabotomy**

腭成形术　**uraoplasty, palatoplasty**

医治烧伤　**healing of burns**

三(四)度烧伤　**third (fourth) degree burns**

焦痂　**eschar**

皮瓣　**skin flap**

真皮　**corium**

表皮　**epidemis**

移植　**transplanting**

控制细菌感染　**control of bacterial infection**

排出结石　**discharging stones, passing stones**

镶牙　**fixing a false tooth, having a denture made, dental prosthesis**

补牙　**filling a hollow tooth, filling the cavity of a tooth**

拔牙　**having a tooth pulled out (extracted)**

钻孔　**drilling**

做牙罩　**crowning a tooth**

# 药　物　Medicine

药物　**drug, medicine**

丸药　**pill**

片药　**tablet**

胶囊丸　**capsule**

药粉　**powder**

药水　**liquid medicine**

药膏(软膏)　**ointment, salve, unguentum**

漱口剂　**gargle, mouth-wash**

混合剂　**mixture**

搽剂　**liniment**

乳剂　**emulsion**

糖浆　**syrup**

针剂　**injection**

吸入剂　**inhalation**

硬膏,膏药　**plaster**

糊剂　**paste**

洗剂　**lotion**

栓剂　**suppository**

消毒剂　**disinfectant**

滴鼻剂　**nasal drops**

滴眼剂　**eye drops**

洗眼剂　**eye lotion**

成药　**patent medicine**

煎药　**decoction, decoctum**

预防药　**preventive medicine**

止痛药　**pain-killer, analgesics**

退热药　**antipyretics**

阿斯匹林　**aspirin**

复方阿斯匹林　**APC**

氨基比林　**amidopyrine**

安替比林　**antipyrine**

匹拉米洞　**pyramidon**

安乃近　**analgin**

索密痛,去痛片　**somidon**

头痛片　**headache tablets**

吗啡　**morphine**

度冷丁　**dolantin**

镇静药　**sedatives**

溴化钠　**sodium bromide**

溴化钾　**potassium bromide**

溴化铵 ammonium bromide
安眠药 sleeping pill
眠尔通 miltoum
冬眠灵 wintermin, chlorpromazine
利眠宁 librium
非那根 phenargan
鲁米那 luminal
巴比妥 barbital
消毒防腐剂 disinfectants and preservatives
酒精(乙醇) alcohol (ethanol)
乙醚 ether
碘 iodine
碘酊 tincture of iodine
红汞 mercurochrome
龙胆紫 gentian violet, methyl violet
高锰酸钾,灰锰氧 kalii permanganas
来苏 lysol
福马林 formalin
蒸馏水 distilled water
盐水 normal saline solution
祛痰药 expectorant
镇咳药 antitussive
咳嗽合剂 cough mixture
复方甘草合剂 brown mixture
咳必清 toclase
利尿药 diuretics
醋唑磺胺 diamox
尿素 urea
利尿素 diuretin
麻醉药 narcotics, anesthetics
普鲁卡因 procaine
盐酸普鲁卡因 procainum hydrochoricum, novocain
盐酸邦妥卡因(的卡因) pontocaini hydrochoridum

(dicaine)
泻药 eccoprotica, cathartic
蓖麻油 castor oil
止血药 hemostatic
止血散 styptic powder
止泻药 antidiarrheal
解毒药 antidote
止痒药 antipuritic
止汗药 antiperspirant
发汗药 diaphoretic
收敛药 astringent
杀菌药 germicide
抗风湿药 antirheumatic
血管舒张药 vasodilator
血管收缩药 vasoconstrictor
抗肿瘤药 antineoplastic
抗癌药 anticarcinogen
抗结核药 antituberculotic
抗血吸虫药 antichistosomal
抗凝剂 anticoagulant
杀菌剂 bactericide
制菌剂 bacteriostatic
消炎药 anti-inflammatory, antiphlogistic
通经药 emmenagogue
催吐药 emetic
特效药 specific medicine
堕胎药 aborticide
刺激剂 irritant
兴奋剂 stimulants
健胃药 stomachic tonic
强心药 cardiac tonic
中风药 apoplectic
子宫收缩药 uterine tonic
催生药 oxytocic
催乳药 galactostasis
解痉药 antipasmodic
镇痫药 antiepileptic
补药 tonic

抗菌素　antibiotics

青霉素　penicillin

长效西林(苄星青霉素)　tardo-
　cillin

土霉素　terramycin

四环素　tetracycline

合霉素　syntomycin

链霉素　streptomycin

氯霉素　chloromycetin,
　chloramphenicol

庆大霉素　gentamicin

灰黄霉素　griseofulvin

红霉素　erythromycin

春雷霉素　kasugamycin

卡那霉素　kanamycin

新霉素　neomycin

磺胺类药　sulfa drugs

磺胺嘧啶　sulfadiacine (S.D.)

磺胺噻唑　sulfadiazole (S.T.)

磺胺脒　sulfaguanidine (S.G.)

长效磺胺　SMP

磺胺增效剂　trimethoprim
　(TMP)

磺胺增效片A　bactrim

颠茄　belladonna

阿托品　atropine

菠萝蛋白酶　bromelain

乳酶生,表飞鸣　biofermin

胃蛋白酶　pepsin

胰酶　pancreatin

胰蛋白酶　trypsin

辅酶A　coenzym A

胃舒平　gastropin

食母生(酵母)　yeast

痢特灵,呋喃唑酮　furazolidone

黄连素　berberine

胰岛素　insulin

利血平　reserpine

降压灵　verticil

地巴唑　dibazal

肝太乐　glucurolastone

肌甙　inosine

谷氨酸　glutamic acid

洋地黄　digitalis

洋地黄毒甙　digitoxin

狄高辛　digoxin

西地兰　cedilanid

氨茶碱　aminophylline

麻黄碱　ephedrine

喘息定　isoprenaline

肾上腺素　adrenaline

色甘酸二钠　disodium cromo-
　glycate

黄体酮　progesterone

睾丸素　testosterone

奎宁　quinine

息疟定　pyrimethamine

雷米封(异烟肼)　rimifon

对氨水杨酸钠　PAS

利福平　rifampin (RFP)

胎盘球蛋白　globulin placenta

丙种球蛋白　r-globulin

三磷酸腺甙　A.T.P.

甲状腺片　thyroid tab

他巴唑　tapazol

碘化钾　Pot. lodide

促皮质素　ACTH

激素　hormones

可的松　cortisone

强的松　prednicone

药特灵(安痢生)　yatren

驱蛔灵　piperazine

山道年　santonin

维生素丸　vitamin pill

维生素A　vitamin A

维生素$B_2$　vitamin $B_2$

复合维生素B　vitamin B Co.

维生素C　vitamin C

鱼肝油(维生素甲、丁)　cod liver oil (vit. A+D)

维丁胶性钙注射液　Inj. calciferol and calcium colloid

维生素B$_6$　vitamin B$_6$

维生素B$_{12}$　vitamin B$_{12}$

葡萄糖　glucose

蜂王精　royal jelly

肝浸膏　liver extract

轻泻药　laxative

酚酞　phenolphthalein

苯海拉明　benadryl

扑尔敏　chlorphenamine

安其敏　buclizine

甘油　glycerin

石膏　plaster

煅石膏　plaster of paris

石灰水　lime water

松节油　turpentine oil

清凉油　cooling oil

咖啡因　caffeine

乳酸钙　calcium lactate

葡萄糖酸钙　calcium gluconate

鱼石脂　ichthyol

肤轻松　fluocinolone acetonide

消炎灵,炎痛静　benzydamine

消炎痛　antifan

晕海宁　dimenhydrinate

薄荷　peppermint

青霉素眼药水　penicillin eye drops

鼻眼净　naphazoline

四环素眼膏　tetracycline eye ointment

滴滴涕　DDT

敌百虫　dipterex

樟脑　camphor

淀粉　starch

滑石粉　tarcum powder

漂白粉　bleaching powder

六六六　benzene hexachloride, hexachlorocyclohexane

卡介苗　BCG vaccine

口服脊髓灰质炎疫苗　OPV (oral poliomyelitis vaccine)

牛痘苗　borine vaccine

伤寒副伤寒甲乙三联菌苗　TAB vaccine

(药物)适应症说明　indications

失效期　expiration date

吸收　resorption

剂量　dosage

首次量　initial dose

过量　over dose

中毒量　toxic dose

有效量　effective dose

副作用　side effect

## 医疗器械设备　Medical Apparatuses and Instruments

检床　examination couch

诊床　diagnostic couch

叩诊器　percussion hammer

听诊器　stethoscope, phonendoscope

压舌板　tongue spatula, tongue depressor

体温表　thermometer

血压计　blood pressure gauge, sphygmomanometer

额镜　head mirror
鼻镜,鼻窥器　rhinoscope, nasal speculum
喉镜　laryngoscope, laryngeal mirror
耳镜,耳窥器　ear speculum, ear mirror
橡皮手套　rubber glove
夹板　splint
镊子　pincette
刮刀　scaler
注射器　syringe
皮下注射器　hypodormic syringe
注射器针头　syringe needle
脱脂棉(卷)　absorbent cotton (roll)
橡皮膏(卷)　adhesive plaster (roll)
纱布(卷)　gauze (roll)
脱脂纱布　absorbent gauze
酒精灯　alcohol burner, spirit burner
消毒器　sterilizer
探子,探针　probe, sound
外科钳　surgical forceps
手术刀　scalpel
绷带　bandage
暖水袋　hot water bag
冰袋　ice-bag
剪刀　scissors
宽嘴瓶　wide mouth bottle
滴注器械　instruments for instillation
滴瓶　drop bottle
支架　stand
长颈瓶　flask
止血器　hemostat
滴管　dropper

音叉　tuning-fork
视力计　optometer
视力表　visual testing chart
便盆　bed pan
尿壶　urinal
脓盆　pus-basin
冲洗器　irrigator
安瓿　ampoule
试管　test tube
钳,镊　forceps, tweecers, nippers
量筒　cylinder
敷料　dressing
敷料钳　dressing forceps
刺血针　lancet
软膏刀　spatula
石膏绷带　plaster bandage
纱布绷带　gauze bandage
丁字带　T bandage
口罩　mask, mouth mask
纱布垫　pad
棉花签　cotton swab
纱布拭子　gauze swab
橡皮导尿管　rubber catheter
灌肠器　enemator
(尚未使用的)缝线　suture
(伤口上的)缝线　stitch
肠线　catgut suture
扩张器　dilator
牵开器　retractor
氧气吸入器　oxygen inhalator
计算仪表　gauge, metre
氧气箱　oxygen tank, oxygen cylinder
橡皮管　rubber tube
出诊医药箱　medical box
配药瓶　dispensing bottle
湿敷巾　wet compress
液吸管　glass dropper, pipet

| | |
|---|---|
| 急救箱 | first-aid case |
| 废物箱 | refuse bin |
| 废物桶 | pail for used dressings |
| 药瓶 | medicine bottle |
| 药包 | medicine package |
| 药柜 | medicine cupboard, medicine cabinet |
| 身高测量器 | height measuring gauge |
| 体重秤 | scales, weighing-machine standard |
| (器械、药物……)手推车 | (instrument, medicine…)trolley |
| 插管,套管 | cannula |
| 小夹 | clip |
| 外科小夹 | surgical clip |
| 肾形盆 | kidney-shaped bowl, kidney dish |
| 急救车 | ambulance |
| 病案卡 | card index of patients |
| X线机 | X-ray machine, X-ray apparatus |
| X线片 | X-ray film |
| 荧光屏 | fluorescent screen |
| 人工心肺机 | heart-lung machine |
| 心电图机 | electro-cardiograph |
| 脑电图机 | electro-encephalograph |
| 超声波诊断仪 | supersonic diagnostic set |
| 同位素扫描仪 | isotope scanner |
| 血细胞计数器 | hemacytometer |
| 血红蛋白计 | hemoglobinometer |
| 离心机 | centrifuge |
| 示踪器 | tracer |
| 示波器 | oscillograph |
| 止血带 | tourniguet |
| 引流管 | drain |
| 显微镜 | microscope |
| 肺活量计 | spirometer |
| 超短波治疗机 | instrument for ultra-short wave treatment |
| 电子显微镜 | electro-microscope |
| 玻片 | slide |
| 紫外线灯 | ultra-violet ray lamp |
| 红外线灯 | infra-red lamp |
| 血球计数机 | blood counter |
| 担架 | litter, stretcher |
| 床车 | wheeled litter |
| 电针治疗机 | electric apparatus for acupuncture treatment |
| 短波电疗机 | short wave diathermy machine |
| 体外循环装置 | extra-corporeal circulation apparatus |
| 牵引器 | tractor |
| 胃镜 | gastroscope |
| 直肠镜 | rectoscope, proctoscope |
| 子宫镜 | uteroscope |
| 膀胱镜 | cystoscope |
| 食管镜 | esophagoscope |
| 检眼镜 | ophthalmoscope |
| 气管镜 | thoracoscope |
| 早产儿保温箱 | incubator |
| 牙科综合治疗机 | dental unit |
| 植皮刀 | dermatome |
| 手术室 | operating theatre, operating room |
| 手术台 | operating table |

万能手术台  universal operation table, all-round operation table
手术灯  operating lamp
无影灯  shadowless lamp
手术胶手套  rubber operating glove
白大衣  overall
手术衣  operating coat
病人推床  wheeled stretcher
轮椅  wheel chair
洗手盆  wash-basin
用肘推动的水龙头  elbow operated tap
滤水器  water-distilling apparatus, water distiller
外科镊  surgical forceps
输血器  blood transfusion apparatus
电热烧灼器  electric cautery set
可调靠椅  chair with adjustable back
温度描记  temperature graph
温度描记表  temperature chart
外科止血器  tourniquet
人造血管  artificial blood vessel
麻醉机  anaesthesia machine
丝血管  silk blood vessel
外科缝针  surgical suture needle
羊肠缝线  catgut suture
皮背心  leather jacket
海绵垫(床)  sponge, bath bed
石膏床  plaster of paris bed

(P.P. bed)
高压蒸气灭菌器  autoclave sterilizer
煮沸灭菌器  boiling sterilizer
分娩椅  obstetric chair
产钳  obstetrical forceps, midwifery forceps
分娩台  obstetric table
婴儿恒温室  constant heat cabinet for infants
石英水银灯  quartz mercury lamp
水银蒸气灯  mercury vapor lamp
助听器  hearing aid
漏斗  funnel
电冰箱  electrical ice box
放大镜  magnifier
量杯  graduated cylinder
坩埚  crucible
研钵  mortar
研棒  pestle
牙科治疗坐椅  dental chair
牙托  denture
上牙托  upper denture
固定桥  fixed bridge
(牙)冠  crown
人造冠  artificial crown
牙瓷  dental porcelain
瓷牙  porcelain tooth
充填料  filling
口镜  mouth mirror
口内照灯  mouth lamp
牙刮器  tooth scaler
拔牙钳  extraction forceps
牙挺  elevator
牙根挺  tooth-root elevator

## 医疗机构和人员　Medical Institutions and Workers

医务工作者　medical worker

医院院长　director of the hospital

科主任, 处主任, 部主任　head of a department

医务部(处)主任　head of the department of medical administration

门诊部主任　head of the out-patient department

住院部主任　head of the in-patient department

护理部主任　head of the nursing department

内科主任　head of the medical department

外科主任　head of the surgical department

药房主任　head of pharmacy

医生, 大夫　doctor, physician

中医医生　doctor of traditional Chinese medicine

西医医生　doctor of Western medicine

专科医生　specialist

主任医生　chief physician

主治医生　physician (surgeon) in charge, attending doctor

内科医生　physician, internist

住院医生　resident physician

外科医生　surgeon

妇科医生　gynecologist

产科医生　obstetrician

儿科医生　paediatrician, pediatrist

耳鼻喉科医生　ENT (ear-nose-throat) doctor

泌尿科医生　urologist

眼科医生　oculist, eye-doctor

牙科医生　dentist, dental surgeon

皮肤科医生　dermatologist

耳科学家　otologist, aurist

鼻科学家　rhinologist

喉科学家　laryngologist

结核病医生　doctor for tuberculosis

传染病医生　doctor for infectious diseases

肿瘤科医生　oncologist

心脏外科医生　cardiac surgeon

心脏血管专家　cardiovascular specialist

神经病科医生(专家)　neuropathist, nerve specialist

整形外科医生　plastic surgeon

矫形外科医生, 骨科医生　orthopedic surgeon, orthopedist

营养医生　dietician, dietitian

脑科专家　brain specialist

药物学家　pharmacologist

放射科医师　radiologist

针刺医生　acupuncture doctor

值班医生　doctor on duty

实习医生　intern

放射科技师　radiographer

麻醉师　anaesthetist

药剂师　pharmacist, druggist

X光医师(技师)　roentgenologist (X-ray technician)

化验员　laboratory technician
技术员　technician
护士　nurse
护士长　head nurse
实习护士　student nurse
病房护士　ward nurse
日班护士　day nurse
夜班护士　night nurse
手术室护士　operating theatre nurse
手术助理护士　scrub nurse
值班护士　nurse on duty
赤脚医生　barefoot doctor
医士　feldsher
助产士　midwife
挂号员　registrar
医院各部门　departments of the hospital
医院　hospital
医院管理部门　administration office of the hospital
门诊部　out-patient department (OPD)
住院部　in-patient department
挂号处　registration office
入院处　admission office, admitting office
候诊室　waiting room
急诊室　emergency room
观察室　room for further observation, observation ward
隔离室　isolation room
诊室　consulting (consultation) room
治疗室　room for medical treatment
手术室　operation room (theatre), operating room

化验室　laboratory
药房　dispensary, pharmacy
病房　ward
内科　department of internal medicine, medical department
外科　surgical department, department of surgery
普通外科　general surgery
创伤外科　fraumatology department
心脏外科　department of cardiac surgery
脑外科　department of cerebral surgery
整形科　department of plastic surgery
矫形外科　orthopedic surgery department
小儿科　paediatrics department
妇产科　obstetrics and gynecology department
耳鼻喉科　ENT (ear-nose-throat) department
口腔科　stomatological clinic, department of oral surgery
眼科　ophthalmology department
泌尿科　urology department
皮肤科　dermatalogy department, skin department
中医科　department of traditional Chinese medicine
骨科　orthopedics department, department of osteologia
推拿科　manipulation clinic
按摩科　massage clinic

生化室　bio-chemical test room

细菌检验室　bacteriological laboratory

X光室　X-ray room

理疗室　department of physiotherapy

电疗室　electrotherapy room

消毒室　sterilizing room, disinfection room

心电图室　electrocardiographic room

储藏室　store room

洗涤室　laundry room

配膳室　dietician's room

供应室　supply room

停尸室, 太平间　mortuary, morgue

尸体解剖室　autopsy room

血库　blood bank

病史室　case history room

医药组织机构　medical institutions and organizations

卫生部　Ministry of Public Health

中国医学科学院　Chinese Academy of Medical Sciences

中华医学会　China Medical Association

中国红十字会　China Red Cross Society

中医研究院　academy of traditional Chinese medicine

儿科研究所　institute of paediatrics

寄生虫病研究所　institute of parasitic diseases

寄生虫病防治研究所　research institute of anti-parasitic diseases

皮肤性病研究所　institute of dermatology and venereology

劳动卫生、环境卫生、营养卫生研究所　research institute of industrial health, environmental health and nutrition

肿瘤研究所　institute of oneology

放射医学研究所　institute of radiology

心血管疾病研究所　institute of cardio-vascular diseases

输血血液研究所　institute of transfusion and hematology

药物研究所　institute of pharmacology

实验医学研究所　institute of experimental medicine

病毒研究所　institute of viruses

结核病研究所　tuberculosis research institute

眼科研究所　ophthamological research institute

生物制品研究所　institute of biological products

生理研究所　institute of physiology

耳鼻咽喉科研究所　research institute of ear, nose and throat

实验生物研究所　institute of experimental biology

卫生研究所　institute of health

针灸研究所　research institute

of acupuncture and
moxibustion

中药研究所 institute of
Chinese materia medica

医学生物学研究所 institute of
biological medicine

综合医院 general hospital

妇产医院 maternity hospital

儿童医院 children's hospital

牙科医院 dental hospital

传染病医院 infectious hospital

结核医院 tuberculosis
hospital

肿瘤医院 tumour hospital

整形外科医院 plastic surgery
hospital

陆军医院 army medical
hospital

中医医院 hospital of Chinese
medicine

野战医院 field hospital

后方医院 base hospital

隔离医院 isolation hospital

口腔医院 stomatology hospital

附属医院 affiliated (attached) hospital

教学医院 teaching hospital

精神病院 mental disease
hospital, insane asylum

麻风医院 leprosy hospital,
leprosarium

红十字会医院 Red Cross hospital

## 中 医 Traditional Chinese Medicine

中医学 traditional Chinese
medical science

《黄帝内经》 Huang Di Nei
Jing (The Yellow Emperor's Classic of Internal
Medicine)

《黄帝外经》 Huang Di Wai
Jing (The Yellow Emperor's Classic of External
Medicine)

《伤寒论》 Shang Han Lun
(Treatise on Fevers)

整体观念 concept of the
whole

辨证施治 determination of
treatment based on the
differentiation of symptoms
and signs, determination
of treatment according to

different conditions

审因施治 ascertaining the
causes of a disease and
giving treatment

五行学说 the theory of five
elements

金 metal

木 wood

水 water

火 fire

土 earth

八纲辨证 differentiation and
classification of symptoms
and signs based on eight
principal notions

阴 *ying*

阳 *yang*

表 external

里 internal

冷　cold

热　hot

虚　*xu* (being insufficient, weakness)

实　*shi* (being excessive, superfluity)

五脏　five solid viscera

心　heart

肝　liver

脾　spleen

肺　lung

肾　kidney

六腑　six hollow viscera

胆　gallbladder

胃　stomach

小肠　small intestine

大肠　large intestine

膀胱　bladder

三焦　"sanjiao" (three portions of the body cavities housing the internal organs and antimating their functions)

诊断(学)　diagnostics

四诊　four methods of diagnosis

望　observation of the patient's complexion, expression, movements, tongue, etc.

闻　auscultation and smelling

问　interrogation

切　pulse feeling and palpation

经络　*jing* and *lo* (channels and collaterals)

穴位　acupuncture points

内伤七情: 喜、怒、忧、思、悲、恐、惊　internal causes: joy, anger, worry, thought, grief, surprise and fear

外感六淫: 风、寒、暑、湿、燥、火　external causes: wind, cold, dryness, humidity, fire and heat

病因辨证　differentiation and classification of diseases according to different etiological factors

卫气营血辨证　differentiation and classification of the feverrish diseases according to the four processes of the diseases: 卫 (protection), 气 (energy), 营 (nourishment), 血 (blood)

切脉　feeling the pulse

触诊　tapping or pressing or stroking various parts of the patient's body

脉象　types of pulse, pulse conditions

舌苔　fur on the tongue

表证　symptoms indicating that the exterior of the human body has been attacked by exogenous harmful factors

里证　symptoms indicating that the internal organs have been affected

寒证　symptoms, caused by the cold factors, indicating chronic functional decline of internal organs

热证　symptoms, caused by febrile factors, indicating infectious diseases or morbid increase of metabolism

虚证 symptoms showing the deficiency of vital energy of the patient to ward off diseases

治疗学 therapeutics

正治 treatment by normal process

反治 treatment by reverse process

标、本、缓、急 the branch, the root, the chronic, the acute

理气 reestahlishing of vital energy

活血 invigorating of blood circulation

去瘀 elimination of blood stasis

八法 eight therapeutic methods

汗法 diaphoresis—sweating the patient

吐法 emetic measures—making the patient vomit

下法 purgation—making the patient evacuate what is harmful or superfluous

清法 antipyretic measures and sedation—bringing fever down and getting rid of the febrile factors

温法 warming and stimulation—making the patient's internal organs active

和法 counteraction and harmonization—counteracting the disease by adjusting the functional relation of the internal organs

消法 resolution—dispersing inflammatory or other lesions

补法 invigoration—giving the patient tonics

捏积 squeezing stasis

按摩 massage

推拿 manipulation

气功疗法 traditional Chinese breathing exercises, breathing technique therapy

枯痔疗法 withering therapy for hemorrhoids, mummification of hemorrhoids

刮痧 treatment of acute gastroenteritis by scraping the patient's neck, chest or back with a coin or something of the like moistened with water or vegetable oil

揪痧 treatment of sunstroke or angina by repeatedly pinching the patient's neck or the bend of the arm until signs of blood congestion appear

捏脊 chiropractic massage along the spinal column to cure the digestive troubles of children

中药 traditional Chinese medicine

草药 medicinal herbs

单方 single drug prescription

验方 proved recipe

秘方 secret prescription of

excellent curative effect

偏方 folk prescription, traditional popular prescription

成方 set prescription

丸剂 pill, bolus

丹剂 pill and powder made of melted or sublimated minerals

散剂 powder medicine

膏药 plaster

药膏 medical ointment

汤剂 herb soup, medical broth, decoction

药酒 medical liquor, tincture, medicated wine

饮片 medical herb in pieces

露剂 distillate of medicinal herbs

药材 medicinal material

四气:寒、热、温、凉 four properties (of medicinal herbs): cold, hot, warm and cool

五味:酸、苦、甘、辛、咸 five tastes (of medicinal herbs): sour, bitter, sweet, hot and salty

常用中药 Chinese materia medica in frequent use

发汗解表药 diaphoretics for the treatment of colds and influenza

清热解毒药 antipyretics for the treatment of fever, carbuncles and inflammation

活血药 medicines for the treatment of stasis and for the improvement of blood circulation

止血药 haemostatics

止咳平喘药 medicines for the treatment of cough and asthma

渗湿利尿药 diuretics for the treatment of dropsy, humidness and jaundice

治痢止泻药 medicines for the treatment of dysentery and diarrhea

泻下通便药 cathartics

健胃消化药 digestives and stomachics

跌打损伤药 medicines for the treatment of fracture and injury

治蛇虫咬伤药 medicines for the treatment of bites and stings

治烧伤药 medicines for the treatment of burns

镇惊安神药 sedatives for the treatment of insomnia, tachycardia, amnesia, vertigo and hyperkinesia

滋补气血药 tonic medicines for the treatment of anaemia, asthenia and the deterioration of the functions of the organs

理气止痛药 anodynes serving to assuage pain caused by functional disorder of various organs

祛风湿药 medicines for the treatment of rheumatism and arthritis

桔红, 桔皮 tangerine peel

桔络 dried tangerine fibres

姜 ginger

桔梗 root of ballon flower

金银花 flower of Japanese honey-suckle

菊花 mother chrysanthemum

芦根 reed thizome

麻黄 Chinese ephedra

麻仁 hemp seed

麦芽 malt

人参 ginseng

西洋参 root of American ginseng

鹿茸 young pilous antler

菟丝子 dodder seeds

桑椹 mulberry

枇杷叶 loquat leaf

枇杷膏 loquat leaf extract

乌梅 dark Japanese apricot

蒲公英 dandelion

甘草 licorice root

远志 root of Chinese slenderleaved polygala

柏子仁 seeds of Chinese arborviate

莱菔子 radish seeds

当归 *danggui*, angelica root

党参 *dangshen*, root of hairy asiabell

黄芪 root of membranous milk vetch

黄连 rhizome of Chinese goldthread, coptis

龙胆草 Japanese gentian root

牛黄 bezoar of ox

麝香 musk

赤芍 root of herbaceus peony (with bark)

白芍 root of herbaceus peony (without bark)

桃仁 peach kernel

仙鹤草 hairvein agrimony

白芨 tuber of bamboo-leaved orchid

白果 gingko, ginkgo

荷叶 lotus leaf

莲蓬 lotus seed-pod

藕节 node of lotus root

艾叶 moxa leaf, Chinese mugwort leaf

贝母 fritillary bulb

杏仁 apricot seed

百合 lily bulb

车前草 plantain herb

茵陈 stem (leaf) of capillary sagebrush

滑石 talc

山楂 fruit of Chinese hawthron

山慈姑 bulb of edible tulip

鸡内金 membrane of chicken gizzard

神曲 medicated leaven cake

薄荷 dried peppermint herb

陈皮 dried orange peel

沉香 heartwood of agalloch

大黄 rhubarb

丹皮 root bark of tree peony

地榆 garden burnet root

杜仲 bark of eucommia

阿胶 asses' glue

蜂蜜 honey

佛柑 fruit of finger citron

茯苓 tuckahoe

枸杞子 fruit of Chinese

wolfberry

地骨皮 root bark of Chinese wolfberry

桂皮 cassia bark

桂枝 cassia twig

何首乌 tuber of fleece-flower

厚朴 bark of official magnolia

檞寄生 stem of mistletoe

槐花 flower of Chinese scholartree

槐角 pod of Chinese scholartree

槟榔 areca-nut, betel-nut

朱砂 cinnabar

紫河车 dry human placenta

蜈蚣 centipede

蚯蚓 earth-worm

哈士蟆 dried oviduct fat of forest frog

蝉蜕 cicada ecdysis

穿山甲 pangolin scales

明矾 alum

安息香 benzoin

豆蔻 cardamon

半夏 pinellia

山道年 santonin

藏红花 saffron

车前草 plantain

连翘 forsythia

蜂王浆 royal jelly

人参精 panax ginseng extraction

参茸药酒 ginseng antler medical liquor

参茸卫生丸 ginseng antler pills

虎骨酒 tiger bone liquor

鹿茸 pilose antler

羚羊角 antelope's horn

犀角 rhinoceros horn

# 针 灸 Acupuncture and Moxibustion

针刺法 acupuncture

新针疗法 new acupuncture therapy, new method of acupuncture

电针(疗法) galvanic acupuncture, acupuncture with electric stimulation, electro-puncturing therapy

梅花针(疗法) "plum-blossom" shaped needling therapy

手针(疗法) hand-puncturing therapy

耳针(疗法) auricular needling, ear puncturing, needling of the pinna (exter-nal ear)

指针(疗法) finger puncturing (acupuncture) therapy

面针(疗法) face puncturing (acupuncture) therapy

头针(疗法) scalp acupuncture therapy

足针(疗法) foot puncturing therapy

穴位 acupuncture point

扎针,进针 inserting the needle, pushing the needle in

深扎 deep insertion, deep puncture

浅扎 shallow insertion

运针 handling the needle

行针 manipulating the needle

捻针 rotating (twirling) the needle

留针 retention of the needle in the body

不留针 non-retention of the needle

快针 swift insertion

透穴 penetration puncture

强刺激 strong stimulation

酸 (sense of) soreness, feeling sore

麻 (sense of) numbness, feeling numb

胀 (sense of) distension, swelling, feeling distensible

沉 (sense of) heaviness, feeling heavy

热感 sense of hotness

冷感 sense of coldness

触电感 electric stick sensation

蚁走感 creeping sensation

弱刺激 weak stimulation

针刺镇痛 using acupuncture to stop pain

针刺麻醉 acupuncture anaesthesia

哑门穴 "yamen" point

打开"禁区" opening up a "forbidden zone"

恢复听力和说话能力 restoring the hearing and speech

恢复视力 regaining vision

人中穴 "Renzhong" point

产生麻醉效能 producing the analgesic effect

在针刺麻醉下施行手术 performing an operation under acupuncture anaesthesia

手术时完全清醒 perfectly conscious during operation

(对)痛觉迟钝或消失 being dull or insensible to pain

穴位注射疗法(水针疗法) point-injection therapy

穴位埋线疗法 surgical suture imbedding therapy, catgut embedding therapy

挂线疗法 method for treating the anal fistula by tying its end with rubber band or silk thread, "thread-drawing method"

艾灸术 moxibustion

艾柱 moxa stick

在适当穴位烧艾卷 cauterizing the proper points with moxa rolls

拔火罐疗法 cupping

拔火罐 cup

挑治疗法 prick (pick) therapy

# 第三部分

# 财贸、服务

## Part III

## Finance, Commerce and Service Industry

# 目　录

330

# Contents

332

# 财政金融　Finance

## 一　般　General

财政部　Ministry of Finance, (Brit.) the Exchequer

财政　finance

财政金融政策　financial and monetary policy

赤字财政政策　compensatory fiscal policy

国家财政　national finance

赤字财政　deficit financing, compensatory finance

财政体制　financial system

财政纪律　financial regulations

财政检查　financial scrutiny

财政状况　financial condition

财政金融情况　financial and monetary situation

财政困难　financial stress

财政危机　financial crisis

财政灾难　financial disaster

开源节流　opening up new sources of revenue and cutting back on expenditures

群众理财　financial management by the masses

掌握财权　exercising the power of the purse (finance)

建立严格的财政信贷监督制度　instituting rigid supervision and control over financial credits

财政与贸易　finance and trade (commerce)

财贸战线　financial and commercial front

财贸政策　financial and trade policy

财贸工作　financial and trade work

精打细算　Be shrewd in money matters.

每一分钱都很重要。Every penny counts.

力求节省，用较少的钱办较多的事　striving to practise economy and do more things with less money

积少自然成多。Take care of the pence and the pounds will do themselves.

努力提高管理水平　striving to

improve the level of management

使用最先进的技术和方法　employing the most advanced technology and methods

把世界上一切好的东西尽量吸收过来　assimilating as far as possible everything good elsewhere in the world

反对补漏洞的方法。Oppose the stop-gap measures.

削减支出　cut-back in expenditure

大规模削减政府开支　sweeping reductions in government expenditure

人民的购买力　people's purchasing power

控制购买力　curb on spendings

控制社会机团购买力　curb on purchasing power of public institutions and social groups

资金的合理分配　rational allocation of funds

反对大手大脚花钱的作风。Oppose the free-spending attitude.

贪污和浪费是极大的犯罪。Corruption and waste are very great crimes.

## 预　算　Budget

预算　budget

预算政策　budgetary policy

决算　actual budget

(年度)国家预算　(annual) national budget

临时预算　interim budget, extraordinary budget

追加预算　supplementary budget

军事预算　military budget

国防预算　defence budget

战时预算　wartime budget

修正的预算　revised budget

外汇预算　foreign exchange budget

实行的预算　working budget

收支平衡的预算　balanced budget, budget in balance

赤字预算　red-letter budget

黑字预算　black-letter budget

预算编制人　budgeteer (budgeter)

预算控制　budget control

预算控制报告　budget control statement

预算法　budget law

概算　budget estimate

预算提案　budget proposal

预算收入　budgetary revenue

预算开支　budgetary expenditure

预算盈余　budget surplus

预算赤字　budget deficit

增加预算　increasing a budget

削减预算　cutting down a budget

预算内资金　budgetary fund

预算外资金　extra-budgetary fund

为下一年度编制预算　budgeting

for the coming year

回顾过去一年的财经情况和政府开支 review of the past year's economic conditions and government expenditure

制订来年的计划和预告 working out plans and forecasts for the coming year

编制预算 making a budget, preparing a budget

财政年度, 会计年度 (Brit.) financial year, (U.S.) fiscal year

制订预算时留有余地 budgeting for a surplus

提出预算 introducing a budget, opening a budget

表决预算 voting (on) a budget

批准(通过)预算 ratifying a budget, passing a budget

国家预算中的项目 item in the national budget

决算表 financial statement

国库 state treasury

国库剩余 surplus in the state treasury

## 收入与支出 Revenue and Expenditure

财政收入 revenue

国库收入 public revenue

国家收入 national revenue

总收入 total revenue

收入来源 source of revenue

开辟财源 opening up sources of revenue

工业(包括建筑业)提供的收入 revenue from industry (including construction)

农业提供的收入 revenue from agriculture

运输及其他公用事业提供的收入 revenue from transportation and other public utilities

贸易、商业提供的收入 revenue from trade and commerce

服务行业提供的收入 revenue from service industries

企业和事业提供的收入 revenue from enterprises and undertakings

国家投资提供的利润 profit from state investment

外汇收入 earnings from foreign exchange

非贸易外汇收入 non-trade revenue from foreign exchange

外债提供的息金 interest from loans to foreign countries

债务本息提供的收入 revenue from principal and interest on loans

国内税收 inland revenue

关税收入 customs revenue

收入不足 deficit in revenue

弥补赤字 making up the deficit

财政支出 expenditure

总支出 total expenditure

政府行政管理开支 government administrative expenditure

国防支出 expenditure on

national defence

军事开支 military expenditure, military spending

海外军事开支 overseas military expenditure

行政管理费用 administrative costs

其他行政支出 expenditure on other civil services

国库拨出的款项 appropriation from the state treasury

拨款 allocation of funds, appropriation of funds

信贷资金拨款 appropriation of credit funds

中央给地方的拨款 grant-in-aid from the central to the local government

工资 allocation to wages

基本建设费用 capital expenditure

国家投资拨款 appropriation for state investment

基本设备投资 investment in capital goods

(工、农业等)再投资 re-investment(in industry, agriculture, etc.)

设备添置和更新拨款 appropriation for buying new equipments and renovating existing ones

预算拨款的各项基金 funds appropriated from the budget

(设备)修缮基金 repair and maintenance funds for equipments

文教事业基金 culture and education fund

教育事业的追加预算 additional budget allocation for (to) education

研究基金 research fund

奖学金基金 scholarship fund

助学金基金 student aid fund

医药卫生基金 health care fund

社会福利基金 social welfare fund

退职金基金 retirement fund

救济基金 relief fund

公益金 public welfare fund

职工福利基金 welfare funds for staff and workers

统一基金 consolidated fund

国债息金的支付 interest payment on national debt

公债息金的支付 interest payment on bonds

分期偿债基金 sinking fund, amortization fund

公积金 accumulation fund

对外援助支出 aid to foreign countries

军援 military aid

经济援助 economic aid

偿还内、外债款的支出 repayment of domestic and foreign loans

其他(杂项)开支 other (miscellaneous) expenditure

财政收支平衡 revenue and expenditure in balance

国家收支 national balance sheet

赤字开支 deficit spending

以收入抵销支出 offsetting expenditure with revenue

## 税 收 Taxation

税收　taxation
双重税　double taxation
税收政策　tax policy
税务法令　tax law
税务法庭　tax court
税款　tax dues
税种　category of taxes
税目　tax item
征税单　tax bill
报税单　tax return
税款核计　tax audit
免税地　tax haven
印花税票　revenue stamp,
　duty stamp
补交拖欠的税款　back pay-
　ment
减退税款　tax rebate
特种免税　tax remission
免税　tax exemption
无须课税　tax-free
减税　tax reduction
税　tax
国税　state tax, national tax
财政税　revenue tax
直接税　direct tax
间接税　indirect tax
累进税　progressive tax
累减税　regressive tax
所得税　income tax
公司所得税　corporation tax,
　(U.S.) corporate income tax
个人所得税　individual
　income tax
累进所得税　graduated income
　tax, progressive income tax
工商业所得税　tax on industry

and commerce returns
利润税　profits tax
工商统一税　consolidated
　industry and commerce tax
商品税　commodity tax
特许经营税　franchise tax
营业税　sales tax, business
　tax
娱乐税　entertainment tax
国内消费税　excise duty,
　excise tax
消费税　consumption tax
盐的消费税　consumption tax
　on salt
奢侈品税　luxuries tax
农业税　agricultural tax
自行车税　bicycle tax
交通税　road traffic tax
公路通行税　road toll
酒税　wine tax
烟草税　tobacco tax
人头税　per capita tax, poll-
　tax
社会保险税　social security
　tax
继承遗产税　(U. S.) inheritance
　tax, (Brit.) death duty
立遗嘱人死后的动产税　probate
　duty
不动产税　real estate tax
房地产税　housing and land
　tax
增值税　value added tax
印花税　stamp duty
同比例税　proportional tax
附加税　surtax

追加税 additional tax
苛捐杂税 onerous taxation
税率 tax rate
税务局 (inland) revenue bureau
税务所 tax collecting station
税务员 excise-man, excise officer, tax collector
估税员 tax assessor
税务调查员 tax investigator

纳税人 taxpayer
拖欠税款者 delinquent taxpayer
滞纳金 negligence penalty
对……课税 levying tax on…, making a levy on…
撤销一项税收 repealing a tax
偷税(逃税) tax dodging, tax evasion
偷税人 tax dodger

## 股票与证券 Stocks and Bonds

证券 security
有价证券 marketable security (negotiable instrument)
长期证券 long-term security
短期证券 short-term security
最可靠的(金边)证券 gilt-edged (security)
优先证券 senior security
可取回本金的证券 redeemable security
不能取回本金的证券 unredeemable security, irredeemable security
债券 (Brit.) stock, (U.S.) bond
股票 (Brit.) share, (U.S.) stock
普通股票 (Brit.) ordinary share, (U.S.) common stock
高级普通股票 blue chip, quality common stock
优先股票 (Brit.) preference share, (U.S.) preferred stock
工业(实业)股票 industrial stock

公用事业股票 utility stock
银行股票 bank stock
按票面值出售的股票 par
无票面值的股票 no-par
长期以来利润稳步上升企业的股票 growth stock
成交活跃的股票 active stock
(在股票市场上起领导作用的)大公司股票 leader
(英国公司发行的有别于股票的)债券 (Brit.) debenture
(美国政府以公共资产或信贷为抵押所发行的)公债券 (U.S.) debenture
(特定资产作抵押的)债券 (Brit.) mortgage debenture, (U.S.) mortgage bond
(美)可换股票的债券 (U.S.) convertible bond, (Brit.) convertible debenture (stock)
政府公债 government bond
建国公债 national development bond
国防公债 defence bond
战时公债 war bond

(为征集资金)新发行的证券 **new issues**

有利息无期公债 **funded debt, bonded debt, fixed liabilities**

手上拥有的证券资产 **holdings**

股票持有人 **stock-holder, share-holder**

优先股票持有人 **preference holder**

投资者拥有的各种有价证券 **portfolio**

股票持有证 **stock certificate**

证券转让证 **transfer deed**

证券交易所 **stock exchange**

股票买卖 **buying and selling of stock**

通过股票经纪人的交易 **over-the-counter transaction**

通过证券交易所的交易 **transaction on stock exchange**

股票交易额 **turnover**

股票经纪人 **stock broker**

股票公司 **jobbing firm**

股票商人 **stock jobber**

佣金 **commission, brokerage**

固定利息 **fixed interest**

不固定的利息 **variable interest**

股票行市 **stock market**

股票行市普遍看涨 **bullish market**

股票行市普遍看跌 **bearish market**

股票报价 **quotation for stock**

升值(高于票面值) **appreciation in value (above par)**

降值(低于票面值) **depreciation in value (below par)**

(股票)投机商 **(stock) speculator**

债券还本 **bond refunding**

提前给定息证券还本 **retiring debenture before final maturity**

(债券)到期不予清还本息 **default in redemption (of bonds) at maturity**

金融指数 **financial index**

股票指数 **share index, stock index**

道·琼斯指数 **Dow Jones Index**

《金融时报》指数 **Financial Times Index**

恒生指数 **Hang Seng Index**

清偿债款, 收回证券 **liquidating securities**

褫夺股权 **divestiture**

## 资本、资金与利润 Capital, Fund and Profit

资本 **capital**

资金,基金 **fund**

固定资本 **fixed capital**

流动资本 **floating capital, circulating capital**

不变资本 **constant capital**

可变资本 **variable capital**

周转资本 **working capital**

专用资本 **special capital**

财政资本 **financial capital**

商业资本 **commercial capital**

信贷资本 **loan capital**

社会资本　social capital

资本核定　assessment of capital

资本集中　concentration of capital

提供资本　capital financing

投资资金　investment goods, money capital

资金周转　circulation of funds

资金积累　accumulation of funds, accumulation of capitals

资本价值与产值的系数　capital coefficient

资产升值的收益　capital gain

资产贬值的损失　capital loss

投资　investment

长期投资　long-term investment

直接投资　direct investment

股票证券投资　portfolio investment

资本资产(固定资产与专利权等)　capital assets

(有形)固定资产　fixed assets

流动资产　current assets

动产　personal property, chattel personal

准不动产　chattel real

不动产　real property

债务　liabilities

提前拨出的开支　deferred charge, prepaid expense

折旧开支　depreciation charge, amortization charge

折旧储备金　depreciation provision, depreciation fund

红利, 股息　dividend, yield

年中红利　interim dividend

年终红利　final dividend

总红利　total dividend

红利储备金　dividend cover

股息单(领取股息通知书)　dividend warrant

清算资金,发还股本　liquidating dividend

毛利　gross profit

净利　net profit

一般利润　normal profit

最高利润　maximum profit

最低利润　minimum profit

巨额利润　huge profit

超额利润　superprofit

平均利润　average profit

利润幅度　profit margin

利润率　rate of profit

增加盈利　increasing profits

追求利润　chasing profits

生意正在赢利(亏本)　business running at a profit(loss)

扭亏转盈　switch from loss to profit

分配利润制度　profit sharing system

上缴利润　forwarding profits to the state

## 金融与货币　Money and Currency

金融　money, finances

金融政策　monetary policy

金融管理　monetary management

货币单位 **monetary unit**

金融制度 **monetary system**

货币改革 **monetary reform**

纯金 **fine gold, pure gold**

〔纯度（英）.9166,（美）.900的〕标准铸币黄金 **standard gold, coin gold (.900 fine in the U.S. and .9166 or 11/12 fine in the U.K.)**

金条 **gold bullion**

金砖, 金锭 **gold ingot**

金本位制 **gold standard**

金条本位制 **gold bullion standard**

金汇兑本位制 **gold exchange standard**

脱离（废弃）金本位制 **abandoning the gold standard, leaving the gold standard**

含金量 **gold content, gold parity**

黄金双价 **dual gold price**

黄金总库 **gold pool**

地下金库 **gold cache**

黄金储备 **gold reserve**

储存的黄金 **deposited gold**

黄金外汇储备 **gold and foreign currency reserves**

黄金条款 **gold clause**

黄金保值条款 **gold guarantee clause**

黄金保留条款 **gold value reserve clause**

特别提款权 **Special Drawing Rights (SDRs), paper gold**

白银 **silver**

〔纯度（英）.500,（美）.900 的〕标准铸币白银 **standard silver, coin silver (.900 fine in the U.S. and .500 fine in the U.K.)**

银本位制 **silver standard**

货币 **currency**

世界货币 **world currency**

基本货币 **key currency, basic currency**

金本位货币 **gold currency**

银本位货币 **silver currency**

以银代金作为法定货币 **demonetizing gold and monetizing silver**

金券 **gold certificate**

银券 **silver certificate**

国库发出的本票 **treasury note**

国库发行的货币 **treasury currency**

（发行银行仅以自己的资产作保证所发行的）资产货币 **asset currency**

（受金融管理当局）管理的货币 **managed currency**

（不受金融管理当局管理而）自由伸缩的货币 **automatic currency**

十进制货币 **decimal currency**

外国货币 **foreign currency**

储备货币 **reserve currency**

占领军发行的货币 **occupation currency**

法定货币 **legal tender, lawful money**

兑换铸币的票据 **coin note**

可兑黄金的货币 **convertible currency**

不能兑换外汇的货币 **blocked currency**

干预货币 **intervention currency**

周转货币 vehicle currency

硬通货 hard currency, hard money

金属货币 metallic currency, metallic money

金(银、铜、镍等)币 gold (silver, copper, nickel, etc.)coin

铸硬币厂 mint

贝币 shell-money, monetized shell

软通货 soft currency, soft money

纸币 paper money, representative money, fiduciary issue

电子货币 electronic currency

本位货币,货币单位 standard money, monetary unit

辅币 subsidiary money, fractional currency

(不作为法定货币的)小额辅币 facultative money

零钱 small money

假钞票 counterfeit note

货币条款 currency clause

欧洲货币 Euro-currency

欧洲英镑 Euro-pound

欧洲美元 Euro-dollar

欧尔康 European Composite Unit (Euro)

游资 idle (inactive) money

吸收游资 absorbing idle money (inactive money)

(银根紧缩时期)以高利率出贷的货币 dear money, tight money

同美元挂钩来确定一货币与黄金的比价 determining the parity of a currency with gold by linking it to U.S. dollar

流通货币量 volume of money in circulation

黄金担保纸币流通 circulation of paper money under gold guarantee

纸币发行过多 over-issue of paper currency

货币区(集团) monetary area (bloc)

英镑区 sterling area

法郎区 franc area

美元区 dollar area

货币购买力 purchasing power of currency

世界金融要求 world monetary demand

世界金融供应 world monetary supply

基本货币供应额 basic money supply

通货膨胀 monetary inflation

隐蔽的通货膨胀 repressed inflation

通货膨胀的恶性循环 vicious spiral of inflation

通货膨胀率 rate of inflation

通货膨胀消减 disinflation of currency

收缩通货(收紧银根) deflation of currency (money squeeze)

货币贬值 currency devaluation, currency depreciation

货币升值 currency appreciation, currency revaluation

货币战 currency war

货币危机 monetary crisis

美元危机 (U.S.) dollar crisis

(金融市场上)美元过多 dollar

glut

抛售美元　dollar sale

抢购黄金　gold rush

现金管理　cash control

金融资产　financial assets

货币的动荡和混乱　monetary upheavals and chaos

金融市场　money market, financial market

资金市场　capital market

黄金市场　gold market

白银市场　silver market

金融业居间人　financial intermediary

金融动态　financial trends

信贷可靠性　creditworthiness

国际信用　international confidence

## 国际收支　Balance of International Payments

国际收支　balance of payments, balance of international payments

国际收支平衡　equilibrium of balance of payments

国际收支不平衡　disequilibrium of balance of payments

国际支付手段　medium (means) of international payments

国际收支顺差　balance of payments surplus

国际收支逆差　balance of payments deficit

国际收支危机　balance of payments crisis

收支地位从顺差走向逆差(或相反)　payment position going from surplus to deficit (or vice versa)

对外贸易总额　total volume of foreign trade

进出口总额　total import and export figures

贸易入超(逆差)　trade deficit, unfavourable (adverse)

balance of trade

贸易出超(顺差)　trade surplus, favourable balance of trade

进口总值　gross import value

出口总值　gross export value

贸易平衡　balance of trade

贸易不平衡　imbalance of trade

有形贸易　visible trade, tangible trade

商品贸易　merchandise trade, commodity trade

商品进口　merchandise import, commodity import

商品出口　merchandise export commodity export

商品进口总额　total merchandise imports, total commodity imports

商品出口总额　total merchandise exports, total commodity exports

商品贸易结余　balance from merchandise (commodity) trade

无形贸易  invisible trade, intangible trade

无形贸易项目  invisible (trade) items

劳务进口  import of services

劳务出口  export of services

劳务收入  income from services

劳务收入净额  net return from services

技术进口 import of technology

技术出口  export of technology

无形贸易进口总额  total invisible imports

无形贸易出口总额  total invisible exports

有形贸易与无形贸易进口总额  total imports, visible and invisible

有形贸易与无形贸易出口总额  total exports, visible and invisible

有形贸易与无形贸易进、出口差额  balance of visible and invisible imports and exports

资金流动  capital movements

资金内流  capital influx

资金外流  capital efflux

黄金流动  gold movements

黄金输入  gold import

黄金内流  gold influx

黄金输出  gold export

黄金外流  gold efflux

政府对外经援和投资  government's foreign aid and investment

对外长期贷款  long-term loans to foreign countries

对外短期贷款  short-term loans to foreign countries

海外投资 overseas investment

私人投资  private investment

私人长期对外投资  private long-term foreign investment

私人短期资金外流额  efflux of private short-term capital

对外流动负债的增加 increase in overseas floating debts

对外流动负债的减少 decrease in overseas floating debts

汇出侨汇  immigrant remittance

汇入侨汇 emigrant remittance

国民海外旅游开支  overseas tourist expenditures

宗教与慈善捐款  missionary and charitable contributions

以黄金或外汇支付来填补的收支差额  gaps to be filled by payments in gold or foreign exchange

对储备金的压力  pressure on the reserves

对储备金的消耗  drain on the reserves

储备资产  reserve assets

## 海 关 (一)  Customhouse( I )

海关总署  Customs Bureau

海关  custom house, the (Maritime) Customs

海关关长  Customs commissioner

海关人员 customs officer, customs official

海关法 customs law

中华人民共和国暂行海关法 the Provisional Customs Law of the People's Republic of China

海关规章制度及法令 customs rules and regulations

海关监督 customs supervision

货运监管 supervision and control over freight transport

进出口货物监管 supervision and control over imports and exports

过境货物监管 supervision and control over transit cargo

转运货物监管 supervision and control over transhipment cargo

通运货物监管 supervision and control over through cargo

进出口展览品监管 supervision and control over imported and exported exhibition articles

进出国境运输工具及其服务人员所带物品的监管 supervision and control over transports arriving and leaving the country and their attendants' personal effects

货运事故的检查和处理 inspection and decision on incidents of freight transport

国际航行船舶的监管 supervision and control over vessels engaged in international navigation

国际列车的监管 supervision and control over railway trains on international service

国际民航机的监管 supervision and control over civil aircraft on international service

进出国境汽车的监管 supervision and control over incoming and outgoing motor vehicles

进出国境旅客行李物品的监管 supervision and control over personal luggage of passengers arriving and leaving the country

外国驻华使领馆, 外交官, 领事官公私物品的监管 supervision and control over articles for private and official use of foreign embassies and consulates, diplomats and consuls in China

进出口邮递物品的监管 supervision and control over imported and exported postal parcels

进出口礼品的监管 supervision and control over imported and exported gift articles

进出口货样、广告品的监管 supervision and control over imported and exported mercantile samples and advertising matter

关税税则　customs tariff

中华人民共和国海关进出口税则　the Customs Import and Export Tariff of the People's Republic of China

税率　tariff rate, duty rate

普通税率　normal tariff, normal rate

最低税率　minimum tariff, minimum rate

进出口货物的税则归类　classification of imports and exports under customs tariff

关税　customs duty

进口税　import duty

出口税　export duty

通过税　transit duty

免税进口　duty-free importation

船舶吨位税　tonnage dues

一般税率　general tariff

自主(国民)关税　national tariff

法定关税税率　statutory tariff

单一关税　single tariff

双档关税税率　double tariff

进出口货物的关税完税价格　dutypaying value of imports and exports

多档关税税率　multiple tariff

复式关税　complex tariff

协定关税　conventional tariff, agreement tariff

财政关税　revenue tariff

从价税　ad valorem duty

从量税　specific duty

混合(复合)关税　mixed duty, compound duty

选择关税　selective duty

保护关税　protective tariff

反倾销税　anti-dumping duty

加重关税　dual tariff

紧急关税　emergency tariff

滑动(伸缩)关税　sliding tariff, flexible tariff

反补贴税　countervailing duty, antisubsidy duty

进口附加税　import surtax

进口额外费　import surcharge

差价(额)税　variable import levy

国内税　internal tax

增值税　value added tax

海关代征工商统一税　consolidated tax to be collected through the Customs

特惠关税　preferential tariff

普通优惠关税　general preferential duties

现存特惠关税　existing preferential tariff

英国特惠税率　British Imperial Preferential Tariff

非歧视关税　nondiscriminatory tariff

歧视关税　discriminatory tariff, differential duties

报复关税　retaliatory tariff

关税水平　tariff level

关境　customs frontier

## 海　关 (二)　Customhouse(Ⅱ)

海关手续　customs formalities

通关港(进口港)　port of entry

船舶进口报告书　report of ship's entry

进口报关 customs entry (entering goods and vessel at the Customs)

收取船舶单据 collecting ship's papers

船舶执照 ship licence

所有权证明书 certificate of ownership

国籍证书 certificate of registry

吨位丈量证书 tonnage measurement certificate

载重线证明书 loadline certificate

离港证明书 certificate of departure from port

开船证明书 certificate of date of sailing

适航证明书 certificate of seaworthiness

航程证明书 certificate of itinerary

航行日志 log book

事实记录 statement of facts

船员清单 crew list

船员更动报告 crew replacement report

舱单 manifest

入境许可证 entry permit

登陆证 landing permit

报关 customs declaration

进口申报 import declaration

出口申报 export declaration

出口清单 export manifest

进口清单 import manifest

进出口货物明细单 specification of imports and exports

虚报 false declaration

报关费 customs declaration fee

征收关税 collection of duty

入境旅客行李物品和个人邮递物品的征税 collection of duty on luggage of incoming passengers and on personal postal matter

税单 duty memo (memorandum)

验货 cargo examination

海关验货单 particular paper for examination

口岸纳税 duty to be paid at port of import

集中纳税 duty to be paid by importer's head office

完税凭证 duty-paid proof

完税收据 duty receipt

海关发票 customs invoice

吨位税证书 tonnage dues certificate

关税的减免 exemption and rebatement of duty

依税则免税 duty exempted by tariff, duty-free by tariff

按外交豁免权免税 duty exempted in accordance with diplomatic immunity (protocol)

作为礼节而免税 duty exempted as a matter of etiquette

作为礼遇而免税 duty exempted as a matter of courtesy

特准减税 duty partially remitted

特准免税 duty remitted

补税(对短征而言) collection of duty short-paid

退税(对溢征而言) refund of

duty over-collected

退税证明书 debenture

放行 release

外交信袋和外交信使行李物品的放行 release of diplomatic pouches (mail-bags) and luggage of diplomatic couriers

免领许可证出(进)口物品验放申请书 application for the release of articles requiring no export (import) licence

文物出口证明书 certificate for export of cultural relics

外国货物转运准单 transhipment permit for foreign goods

外国驻华使领馆公私物品进(出)口清单 clearance record for importation (exportation) of articles of foreign embassies and consulates in China for private and official use ("clearance record")

退关 shut out

海关保税 customs bond

保税仓库 bonded warehouse

保税工场 bonded factory

关栈税 bonding fee

结关港(输出港) port of clearance

船舶出口申报书 application for customs clearance

出口结关 customs clearance (clearing goods and vessel at the Customs)

结关费 customs clearing fee

出港许可证 port clearance

出境许可证 exit permit, departure permit

查船 inspection of ships, search of ships

海关扣留 customs detention

船只扣留 detention of vessel

货物扣留 detention of cargo

海关查扣 customs seizure

查扣物品凭单 seizure ticket

海关关封 customs seal

对违禁品的没收 confiscation of contraband

违章案件的处理 decision on a case of infringement of regulations

违章案件的申诉 protest against Customs decision on a case of infringement of regulations

海关罚款 customs fine

查禁走私(缉私) prevention of smuggling

一般走私案件 ordinary case of smuggling

重大走私案件 serious case of smuggling

走私案件的处理 decision on a smuggling case

走私案件的申诉 protest against Customs decision on a smuggling case

宽大处理 lenient treatment

密报(告发) information

密报(告发)者 informant

# 保 险 (一) Insurance(Ⅰ)

保险人(保险公司) insurer, underwriter (insurance company)

最先承保的保险公司 direct-writing company, originating company

分保公司 ceding (insurance) company

共同保险公司 co-insurance company

投保 insurance application

投保人 insurance applicant

被保险人 insurant, the insured

保险经纪人 insurance broker

保险推销员 insurance canvasser

保险调解人 insurance adjuster

保险权益 insurance interest

保险标的物 insurable subject matter

保险物 interest insured

保险金额(值) amount insured, sum of insurance, insurance value

分担保值 contributory value

分保 ceding, retrocession (for reinsurance)

(人寿保险)委托协议 insurance trust

受托领管人寿保险金的人 insurance trustee

委托书 power of attorney, proxy

保险期 period of insurance

保险批单 insurance endorsement

退保注销 cancellation (of insurance)

保险索赔 insurance claim

保险赔偿 insurance indemnity (compensation)

赔保险金的最高限额 limit of indemnity

保险范围 insurance coverage, risks covered

不足的保险 insufficient coverage, narrow coverage

加保 increasing coverage, extending coverage

续保 renewing coverage

保险费率 premium rate

保险费 premium

额外保险费 extra premium

附加保险费 additional premium

保险费回扣 premium rebate

保险金(保险收入) insurance proceeds

(保险业)统计员 actuary

保险单据 insurance document

保险凭证 certificate of insurance

保险合同 insurance treaty

进口货物预约保险合同 general open insurance treaty for import cargo

出口货物预约保险合同 general open insurance treaty for export cargo

预约总保单 general open policy

保险证明书 cover note

保险担保书 guarantee of

insurance

保险单 insurance policy

航程保险 voyage policy

期限(定期)保险 time policy

单独保单(船名确定保单) specific policy

流动(预约)保单 floating policy, open policy

保险金额确定保单 valued policy

保险金额未确定保单(不定值保单) unvalued policy

可转让的保单 transferable policy

概保单(总括保单) blanket policy

保险单的修改 rectification of policy

分保条 reinsurance slip

保险费收据 premium receipt

委付 abandonment

代位权 right of subrogation

保险客户 policy-holder

按发票价(金额)加百分之十投保 insuring at invoice cost plus 10% (=at 110% of invoice value)

## 保 险 (二) Insurance(Ⅱ)

保险种类 kinds of insurance

双重(重复)保险 double insurance

超过货值的保险 over-insurance

限额以下不赔保险 excess insurance

相互保险 mutual insurance

自保 self-insurance

原始保险 direct-writing insurance

分保(再保险) re-insurance

随意分保 facultative reinsurance

超损失分保 excess-loss reinsurance

限额以下不赔分保 excess reinsurance

合同分保 treaty reinsurance

不可撤销改变的分保 flat reinsurance

联合保险 co-insurance

保险 insurance against risk

火险 fire insurance

一般保险 general insurance

商业保险(实业保险) business insurance

渔业保险 fishery insurance

飞机、船舶保险 hull insurance

航空保险 aviation insurance

物产保险 property insurance

失窃保险 burglary insurance

债务保险 liability insurance

社会保险 social insurance

劳动保险 labour insurance

雇主债务保险 employer's liability insurance

因公伤亡保险 worker's compensation insurance

失业保险 unemployment insurance

人寿保险 life insurance

养老保险 endowment insurance

团体(人寿)保险 group (life)

insurance

疾病保险　health insurance

汽车保险　auto insurance

出事即赔汽车保险　no-fault auto insurance

意外事故保险　accident insurance

第三保险　third-party insurance (insurance against injury to third parties)

运输保险　transportation insurance

陆上运输保险　overland transportation insurance, land transit insurance

航空运输保险　air transportation insurance, insurance against air risk

邮包运输保险　parcel post insurance

驳运保险　insurance against craft and/or lighter risks

仓库到仓库保险　warehouse to warehouse insurance

货物保险　cargo insurance

对货物(合同、订单等)的保险　insurance on goods (contract, order, etc.)

信用保险　credit insurance, fidelity insurance

分期付款售货保险　instalment sales insurance

旅行保险　traveller's insurance

购买人寿保险　buying life insurance

买了(一定金额的)保险　carrying (a certain sum of) insurance

## 保　险 (三)　Insurance(Ⅲ)

水险(海运货物保险)　marine insurance, ocean marine cargo insurance

承保险别　risk insured, risk covered

全损险　(insurance against) total loss only (TLO)

水渍险　(insurance) with particular average (WPA), basic risks

平安险(单独海损不赔)　(insurance) free of (from) particular average (FPA)

战争险　(insurance against) war risk

综合险　(insurance against) all risks

罢工,暴动,民变险　(insurance against) strike, riot and civil commotion (SRCC)

附加险　(insurance against) extraneous risks, (insurance against) additional risks

盗窃提货不着险　(risk of) theft, pilferage and non-delivery (TRND)

淡水雨淋险　(risk of) fresh and/or rain water damage (wetting)

渗漏险　(risk of) leakage

短量险　(risk of) shortage in

weight/quantity

钩损险　(risk of) hook damage

污染险　(risk of) contamination (tainting)

破碎险　(risk of) breakage

碰损险　(risk of) clashing

生锈险　(risk of) rust

受潮受热险　(risk of) sweating and/or heating

恶味险(变味险)　(risk of) bad odour, (risk of) change of flavour

发霉险　(risk of) mould

舱面险　on deck risk

变质险　(risk of) deterioration

包装破裂险　(risk of) packing breakage

内在缺陷险　(risk of) inherent vice

途耗或自然损耗险　(risk of) normal loss, (risk of) natural loss

自燃险　(risk of) spontaneous combustion

进口关税险(关税险)　(risk of) contingent import duty

发酵险　(risk of) fermentation

打凹险　(risk of) denting and bending

桐油异构险　(risk of) isomerization (wood oil, tung oil)

挥发险　(risk of) evaporation

氧化险　(risk of) oxidization

擦伤险　(risk of) scratching

升华险　(risk of) sublimation

海损分担保证　average bond

共同海损保证　general average bond

海损保证金　average deposit

共同海损保证金　general average deposit

共同海损分摊额　general average contribution

免赔率(额)　franchise

不计免赔率　I.O.P. (irrespective of percentage)

保险条款　insurance clause

海洋运输货物保险条款　ocean marine cargo insurance clauses

货物平安险(学会)条款　institute cargo (free of particular average) clause (FPA)

共同海损条款　general average clause (G/A clause)

单独海损全赔条款　with particular average irrespective of percentage (WPAIOP) clause

除外责任(除外保险)条款　exclusive clause

放弃条款　waiver clause

仓至仓条款　warehouse to warehouse clause

驳运险条款　craft and/or lighter (lighterage) clause

冰冻条款　ice clause

船舶互撞责任险条款　"both to blamecollision" clause

罢工险不保条款　strike, riot and civil commotion clause

兵险不保条款　free of capture and seizure clause (FC & S clause)

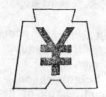

# 银行业　Banking

## 银　行　Bank

兑换货币　money changing
保管货币　custody of money
接受存款　taking money on deposit
贷款　loaning money
延长信贷　extending credit
利用期票或汇票划汇款项　transferring funds by drafts and bills of exchange
中央银行　central bank, national bank, banker's bank
发行货币银行　bank of issue, bank of circulation
商业银行　commercial bank
储蓄信贷银行　(Brit.) commercial bank, (U.S.) member bank, (W. Europe) credit bank
分期信贷公司　finance house, finance company
储蓄银行　savings bank
互助储蓄银行　mutual savings bank
邮局储蓄银行　post office savings bank

抵押银行　(U.S.) mortgage bank, (Brit.) building society
实业银行　industrial bank
家宅贷款银行　home loan bank
准备银行　reserve bank
特许银行　chartered bank
往来银行　corresponding bank
承兑银行　merchant bank, accepting bank
投资银行　(U.S.) investment bank
进出口银行　import and export bank (EXIMBANK)
贴现银行　discount bank
汇兑银行　exchange bank
委托开证银行　requesting bank
开证银行　issuing bank, opening bank
通知银行　advising bank, notifying bank
议付银行　negotiation bank
保兑银行　confirming bank
付款银行　paying bank
代收银行　associate banker of

collection

受托银行 consigned banker of collection

清算银行 clearing bank

本地银行 local bank

国内银行 domestic bank

国外银行 overseas bank

钱庄 unincorporated bank, money shop

银行分行 branch bank

银行支行 subbranch bank

信托储蓄银行 trustee savings bank

信托公司 trust company

金融信托公司 financial trust

信托投资公司 unit trust

(银行的)信托部 trust institu-tion

(银行的)信用部 credit depart-ment

商业信贷公司(贴现公司) commercial credit company (discount company)

街道储蓄所 neighborhood savings bank, bank of deposit

信用社 credit cooperative

合作银行 credit union

商业兴信所 credit bureau

票据交换所 clearing house

保管箱 safety-deposit box

保险柜(银柜) safe

保险库 strong room, vault

无人银行 self-service bank

## 存款与票据  Deposit and Bills

开帐户 opening an account

政府帐户 government account

清算帐户 clearance account

存款人与银行的来往帐 bank account

居民帐户 resident account

非居民帐户 non-resident account

结欠清单 account rendered

确定清单 account stated

开证申请人 accountee

帐目编号 account number

开支票帐户 opening a checking account

开户存款 opening an account, opening a deposit account

存户 depositor

活期存款 current account, demand deposit

特别活期存款 special current account

定期存款 (U.S.) time deposit, savings account, (Brit.) deposit account

定期存款单 saving certificate

储蓄存款 savings deposit

活期储蓄存款 current savings account

小额活期存款 petty current account

(不)生利存款 non-interest-bearing deposit

联名存款(帐户) joint account

机关团体存款 deposit by various institutions and social groups

储蓄印花 savings stamp

金库存款 treasury deposit

存折 passbook, bankbook

存款收据　deposit receipt

存入一笔款　making a deposit

提取存款　making a withdrawal of a deposit

取款单　withdrawal order

透支　overdraft, overdrawing

结帐　squaring an account

银行结单　bank statement

票证交换　clearing

银行借贷余额　bank balance

电脑控制的结帐系统　giro

银行票据(总称)　bank money

支票簿　cheque book

票根　counterfoil, stub

支票　cheque, check

不记名支票　bearer cheque

记名支票　order cheque

横线支票　crossed cheque

保付支票　certified cheque

空白支票　blank cheque

未付支票　outstanding cheque

已付支票　canceled cheque

伪(假)支票　forged cheque

旅行支票　traveller's cheque

空头支票　rubber cheque

银行本票　cashier's order, cashier's cheque

一般本票(约定期票)　promissory note

庄票(银票)　banker's note

汇票　draft, order, bill of exchange

进口汇票　import bill

出口汇票　export bill

票据附页　allonge rider

银行开的支票　banker's draft

银行与银行之间的汇票　bank draft

国内期票　inland bill of exchange

国外期票　foreign bill of exchange

即期汇票　sight draft, demand draft

短期汇票　short-term draft

远期汇票　usance time draft

长期汇票　long draft (bill)

单张汇票　sola draft (bill)

无追索权汇票　draft without recourse

银行承兑汇票　bank acceptance

部分承兑汇票　partial acceptance

商业承兑汇票　trade acceptance

来人汇票　bearer draft

通融汇票　accommodation bill

贴现的期票　discounted bill

未付汇票　outstanding bill

到期未付的票据　overdue bill

货到后提款汇票　arrival bill

退票　dishonoured bill

跟单汇票　documentary bill

进口押汇　inward documentary bill

出口押汇　outward documentary bill

光票(白票)　clean bill, white paper

托收汇票　bill of collection

应收票据　bill receivable

应付票据　bill payable

质押书　letter of hypothecation, hypothecation certificate

## 信用证 Letter of Credit

汇款 remittance

邮政汇款 postal remittance

邮政汇票 postal order, money order

旅行社汇票 express money order

信汇 mail transfer (M/T)

电汇 telegraphic transfer (T/T)

委托付款书 authority to pay

委托购买证 authority to purchase (A/P)

银行信用保证书(保函) letter of guarantee (L/G)

信用卡 credit card

信用证 letter of credit (L/C)

开证 establishment of L/C, opening of L/C

跟单信用证 documentary L/C

可撤销跟单信用证 revocable documentary L/C

不可撤销跟单信用证 irrevocable documentary L/C

光票信用证 clean L/C

旅行社信用证 traveller's credit, circular credit

偿付信用证 reimbursement credit

可撤销的信用证 revocable L/C

承兑信用证 banker's acceptance L/C

保兑信用证 confirmed L/C

不保兑信用证 unconfirmed L/C

议付信用证 negotiable L/C

公开议付信用证 general negotiable L/C

指定议付信用证 restricted negotiable L/C

可转让信用证 transferable L/C

无限制转让信用证 without restriction L/C

不可转让信用证 non-transferable L/C, non-assignable L/C

可分割信用证 devisible L/C

不可分割信用证 non-divisible L/C

对背(从属)信用证 back to back L/C, subsidiary L/C

对开信用证 reciprocal L/C

即期信用证 sight L/C

迟付即期信用证 deferred sight L/C

远期信用证 usance L/C, deferred payment L/C

预支信用证 anticipatory L/C

全部预支信用证 clean payment L/C

红条款信用证 red clause L/C

绿条款信用证 green clause L/C

循环信用证 revolving L/C

可积累使用的循环信用证 cumulative revolving L/C

不循环信用证 fixed L/C

带电汇条款信用证 with T/T reimbursement clause L/C

有追索权的信用证 with recourse L/C

无追索权的信用证 recourseless L/C

展延信用证　extended L/C

凭即期汇票支付的信用证　L/C available by draft at sight

当地信用证　local credit

开出信用证　issuance of L/C

审证　examination of L/C

信用证有效期　expiry date of L/C, validity of L/C

受益人　beneficiary

信用证条件　credit terms

让与书　letter of assignment

转让手续费　transfer com-mission

延期手续费　extension commission

承兑费　acceptance charges

通知手续费　advising commission

统一手续费　flat commission

托收手续费　collection commission

保兑手续费　confirmation commission

## 信贷、信托与抵押　Credit, Trust and Mortgage

信贷市场　credit market

分期付款信贷　(US) instalment credit, (Brit.) hire-purchase

(消费者购物)短期信贷　consumer credit

赊购信贷　(Brit.) credit account, (US) charge account

承兑信贷　acceptance credit

信用借款　open credit

冻结信贷　frozen credit

款项转户　credit transfer, Giro

信贷法　credit laws

借贷收缩　credit squeeze

贷款最高限额　credit line

信用地位　credit standing

信贷扩大　credit expansion

收紧信贷　tightening credit

信贷限制　credit restriction

信托　trust

商业信托　business trust, common-law trust

年金信托　annuity trust

投资信托　investment trust

遗嘱信托　testamentary trust

固定信托　fixed trust

灵活信托　flexible trust

信托财产　trust property

信托款项　trust money

信托资产　trust assets

信托帐户　trust account

信托文件　trust instrument

信托证　trust deed

信托协定　trust agreement

信托声明书　declaration of trust

信托人　truster

受托人(单位)　trustee

成立信托　setting up a trust, creating a trust

年金　annuity

延发的年金　deferred annuity

延期纳税的年金　tax-deferred annuity

到期的年金　annuity due

年金受惠人　annuitant

贷款(放贷)　loan

借贷来的资金　loan capital

供放款的资金　loanable funds

商业贷款 business loan

抵押贷款 mortgage loan

消费者购物贷款 consumer loan

学生贷款 (US) student loan

整借摊还贷款 self-amortizing loan

信用贷款 fiduciary loan

可偿还贷款 redeemable loan

个人贷款 personal loan

银行定期贷款 term loan

一夜(即还)贷款 overnight loan

应召即还的短期贷款 money at call and short notice

短期贷款 short-term loan

长期贷款 long-term loan

中期贷款 medium-term loan

无息贷款 interest-free loan

无息或低息贷款 soft loan

逾期未还债款 overdue loan

束缚性贷款 tied loan

商业贷款和存款 commercial loans and deposits

筹借债款 raising a loan

借出债款 taking out a loan

偿还债款 paying off a loan, making good a loan

贷款条件 terms of loan

银行借款最高限额 bank lending ceiling

利息(息金) interest

法定利息 legal interest

单利 simple interest

复利 compound interest

优待利率 prime rate

存款利率 savings account rate

贷款利息 interest on a loan

应付利息 payable interest

利率 interest rate

贷款利率 lending rate

本金 principal

本金连所生利息 principal with accrued interest

利率自由化 liberalization of interest rate

抵押 mortgage

第一次抵押 first mortgage

信托抵押 trust mortgage

动产抵押 chattel mortgage

买价抵押 purchase-money mortgage

住宅抵押 house mortgage

分期赎回的抵押 instalment mortgage

固定款额的抵押 closed mortgage

可增加贷款的抵押 open-end mortgage

抵押契约 mortgage deed

抵押利率 mortgage rate

赎回抵押 mortgage redemption

贷款的还款日期 redemption date

承受抵押人(贷方) mortgagee

抵押借款人(借方) mortgager

担保品 security, cover

## 外 汇 Foreign Exchange

汇兑换算表 exchange table, conversion table

汇价(汇率) rate of exchange

法定汇率 official exchange rate

现行汇率 current exchange

rate

固定汇率　fixed flat rate

银行买价　buying rate

银行卖价　selling rate

直接标价　direct quotation

直接汇率(应收汇率)　direct rate

间接标价　indirect quotation

间接汇率(应付汇率)　indirect rate

官价上下限　upper and lower intervention limits

浮动汇率　floating rate

中心汇率　central rate

双档汇率　dual exchange rate

复汇率　multiple rate

电汇汇率　rate of telegraphic transfer (T/T Rate)

信汇汇率　rate of mail transfer (M/T Rate)

开盘汇率　opening rate

收盘汇率　closing rate

中间汇率　mid-point rate, middling rate

即期汇兑　spot exchange

商业汇率　merchant rate

银行汇率　banker's rate

单汇率　single rate

自由汇率　free exchange rate

名义汇率　nominal rate

外汇期货交易　forward exchange transaction

远期外汇标价　forward exchange quotation

远期汇率　forward exchange rate

实际市场汇率　factual market rate

升水　premium

贴现(贴水)　discount

银行贴现　bank discount

真贴现(外贴现)　true discount

贴现率　discount rate, bank rate

贴现行市　discount market

再贴现(期票)　rediscounting (bills of exchange)

贴现经纪人　discount broker

汇兑平价　parity of exchange

外汇市场　foreign exchange market

外汇经纪人　exchange broker

外汇投机　exchange speculation

套汇　arbitration of exchange, cross exchange

直接(对角)套汇　direct exchange

间接(三角)套汇　indirect exchange

套汇汇率　cross rate, arbitrage rate

外汇储备　foreign currency (exchange) reserve

外汇管制(管理)　foreign exchange control

外汇管理制度　exchange control system

外汇管理法令　exchange control regulations

外汇管理机构　exchange control authorities

外汇限额制　exchange quota system

外汇限制　exchange restriction

外汇行情(挂牌)　exchange quotations

外汇折算率　foreign exchange coefficient, conversion rate

外汇平准基金　exchange stabilization fund

外汇移转证　exchange surrender certificate

外汇条款　exchange clause

外汇波动　exchange fluctuation

外汇危机　exchange crisis

外汇收支总额　total foreign exchange

结汇　settlement of exchange

外汇收支　balance of exchange

金点　gold point

黄金输出(入)点　gold export (import) point

浮动　float

自由浮动　free float

联合浮动　joint float

## 会计、簿记与审计　Accounting, Bookkeeping and Auditing

会计(学)　accounting

公共会计　public accounting

商业会计　business accounting

银行会计　bank accounting

成本会计　cost accounting

折旧会计　depreciation accounting

电脑化会计　computerized accounting

会计行业　accountancy

总审计局　general accounting office

公共会计服务处　public accounting service

会计员　accountant

公共会计(员)　public accountant

会计长　accountant general

持有特许状的会计师　(Brit.) chartered accountant, (US) certified public accountant

会计档案　accounting dossiers

审计员　comptroller of accounts

簿记　bookkeeping

单式簿记　single-entry

复式簿记　double-entry

簿记员　bookkeeper

记帐员　ledger clerk

帐本(帐簿)　ledger, account book

原始帐册　book of original entry

日记帐(流水帐)　journal, daybook

现金出纳帐　cash book, cash journal

总帐(簿)　general ledger

分类帐(簿)　subsidiary ledger

卡片分类帐　card ledger

活叶分类帐　loose-leaf ledger

帐目(帐户)　account

总帐　controlling account

分类帐　subsidiary account

实帐　real account

资本帐(股本帐)　capital account

资财帐　stock account

资产帐　asset account

负债帐　liability account

净产帐 proprietorship account, assets account

对物帐 impersonal account

货物帐 goods account

现金帐 cash account

名义帐 nominal account

收益帐 income account

支出帐 expense account

储备金帐 reserve account

混合帐 mixed account

工资帐 wage account

原材料消耗帐 cost of material account

劳动力开支帐 cost of labour account

捐税支出帐 cost of burden account

通常开支帐 overhead expenses account

折旧帐 depreciation account

销货帐 sales account

购货帐 purchase account

赊购帐 credit account, charge account

损益帐 profit and loss account

明细帐 itemized account

偿还帐(报销帐) reimbursement account

借、贷金额相抵销无余额的帐 closed account

假帐 dummy account

试算表 trial balance

借贷对照表 balance sheet

损益表 income statement, profit and loss statement

管帐 keeping accounts

记帐 making an entry in the account, entering an item in the ledger

记帐日期 date of entry

帐目事项 item of entry, particular of entry

借方(收入) debit (receipt)

贷方(支出) credit (payment)

过帐 transferring accounts

(帐目)转下页 (account) carried forward to next page

(帐目)承上页 (account) brought down from preceding page

暂停登帐 closing the books

凭证记帐法 voucher system

付款凭单 voucher

应付凭单 voucher payable

白头单 unauthenticated voucher

凭单据报销 being reimbursed on handing in vouchers

凭证原始登记簿 voucher register

纸条记帐法 slip system

贷方传票 credit slip, credit ticket

借方传票 debit slip

余额(结余) balance

借方余额 debit balance

贷方余额 credit balance

总结帐目 summarizing accounts

结帐 settling accounts

定期结帐 settling accounts at regular intervals

审计(学) auditing

核帐 auditing accounts

对全年帐表的审查 audit of a year's accounts

检查帐目 examining accounts

| | | | |
|---|---|---|---|
| 年终决算 | year-end auditing | 认可财务帐表 | certifying financial statements |
| 核实帐目 | verifying accounts | | |
| 审核财务帐据 | auditing financial statements | 核算员(审帐员) | auditor |
| 发现欺诈行为 | detecting fraud | 女核算员 | auditress |

## 杂 项 Miscellaneous

| | | | |
|---|---|---|---|
| 银行家 | banker | | check (draft) |
| 行长(总经理) | president | 退票通知 | note of dishonour |
| 银行经理 | bank manager | (金额)大写 | (amount) in words |
| 副经理(襄理) | assistant manager, sub-manager | (金额)小写 | (amount) in figures |
| 银行工作人员 | bank employee | 出票人 | maker, drawer |
| 出纳员 | teller, cashier | 受票人(付款人) | drawee (payer) |
| 存款出纳员 | deposit teller | 受款人 | payee |
| 收款员 | receiving teller | 签字式样 | specimen signature |
| 付款员 | paying teller | 回条(回贴) | signed delivery receipt |
| 电脑出纳 | electronic "teller" | | |
| 兑现 | cash in | 档案管理 | dossiers management |
| 现金运转 | cash transfer | | |
| 钞票 | bank note, bank paper | 应收帐 | account receivable |
| 银行的现钞和流动资产 | liquid assets of a bank | 应付帐 | account payable |
| | | 可对持票人付款 | payable to bearer |
| 票额(票值) | denomination | | |
| 银行储备金 | bank reserves | 可对抬头人付款 | payable to order of … |
| 冻结资金 | frozen fund, blocked fund | | |
| | | 印鉴核对书 | letter of indication |
| 周转资金 | revolving fund | | |
| 银行无支付能力 | bank failure | 背书 | endorsement |
| 银行营业时间 | banking hours | 有条件背书 | qualified endorsement |
| 银行贴现日 | discount day | | |
| 出票日 | date of draft | 无追索权背书 | endorsement without recourse |
| 金融票据到期日 | date of maturity | | |
| | | 特别背书 | special endorsement |
| 长远还本期 | long maturity | | |
| 支付汇票的习惯期限 | usance | 联合背书 | joint endorsement |
| 兑现支票 | honouring a check (draft) | 背书人 | endorser |
| | | 被背书人 | endorsee |
| 拒付支票 | dishonouring a | 银行定期刊物 | bank letter |

# 商 业 Commerce

## 一 般 General

发展经济,保障供给。 Develop the economy and ensure supply.

满足人民需求 satisfying the needs of the people

国营商业 state commerce, state trade

合作社商业 cooperative commerce, cooperative trade

私人商业 private commerce, private trade

行商业 transient business

营业执照 business licence

营业额 volume of business

商品交换 commodity exchange

商品等价交换 exchange of equivalent in commodity

货币交换 exchange through money

物物交换(以货易货) barter

活跃城乡交流 boosting the interflow of goods between town and country

互通有无 exchange of needs

商品流通 commodity circulation

商品损耗率 rate of loss and wastage of commodity

产销平衡 co-ordination of production and marketing

供销平衡 co-ordination of supply and marketing

供需平衡 co-ordination of supply and demand

供不应求 demand exceeding supply

缩小剪刀差 narrowing the price scissors

建立供给合同制度 instituting the supply contract system

定产、定购、定销 quota system for production, purchase and marketing

收购 purchase

销售 sale

交易(买卖) transaction

购物高潮 buying spree

购买力 purchasing power

批发 wholesale

零售 retail

惠顾 patronage

商业道德 commercial morality

商业法 business law, commercial law

商业诉讼 commercial litigation

商业动态 commercial trends

日夜服务 service round-the-clock

夜间售货制度 night shop system

经营费 working expenses, operating expenses

使用电脑营业 computerized service

(资金,商品)周转率 turnover rate (of funds, commodities)

分期付款购物方式 (Brit.) hire purchase, (U.S.) instalment plan

分期付款 payment by(in) instalments

分期付款的首次支付 down payment

一半付现,一半分期的支付方式 payment by half down and half in instalments

整笔支付 lump-sum payment

交货前付款 payment before delivery

货到付款 cash on (against) delivery (COD, CAD)

货款两清 collected and delivered

在习惯期限内支付 payment within usance

货源 source of supply

库存量很大 stock ample, stock large

库存量很少 stock light, stock small

无货(售空) stock exhausted, be all sold out

脱销 stock running out

经常有货 regular supply available

更多的品种和规格 more variety and a greater number of specifications

商业票据 trade bills

货价单 direction

估价单 estimate

收据 voucher, receipt

发货单(发票) bill of goods, invoice

定货单 contract for goods

取货单 order for goods

(印有企业名称地址的)空白发货单 billhead

定量供应票证 ration card

(粮、布等)票证 (rice, cotton cloth,…) coupon

陈列橱窗 show window

玻璃柜台 show case

货架 shelf

陈列商品 goods on display, displayed items

商标(牌子) trade mark, brand

标价签 price tag

邮购服务 postal purchase service

营业时间 business hours

服务态度 attitude towards customers

意见簿 book for comments and criticisms

服务态度好 gratifying service

服务态度恶劣 poor service,

service with a scowl

柜台守则　code of counter behaviour

百拿不厌, 百问不烦　ready answers to enquiries, tireless catering to customers' needs

送货上门　delivery at customers' doorsteps

包扎　wrapping up

放尺梢, 多量若干　long pull, overmeasure

如不满意, 原银奉还。Money back if goods fail to satisfy the customer.

退货　return of goods

磅称　scales

提称　steelyard, lever scales

短称, 短量　short in weight, giving short measure

按瓶金　bottle deposit

按金收条(卡片)　deposit receipt (card)

(商品)试用期……天　trial period of … days

保障消费者安全规章制度　consumer-safety rules

交款处　cash desk, cashier's

商品盘点, 暂停营业。Stock taking, business suspended.

这是按米(公斤)卖的。It's sold by the metre (kg).

这是成对卖的。It goes in pairs.

那只是陈列的(非卖的)。It's for show only (not for sale).

## 商业机构　Commercial Establishments

商业机构　commercial establishment

商业部　Ministry of Commerce

商业网　commercial network

商业网点　point of connection in the commercial network

商业区　commercial district

商业部门　commercial department

营业部　business department

收购站　purchase centre, purchase station

粮食收购站　grain-purchasing centre

代销店　marketing agency

代购代销店　purchase and marketing centre

供销合作社　supply and mar-

keting cooperative

消费合作社　cooperative store, consumer cooperative

超级市场　supermarket

商场(大百货商店)　emporium

百货商店　department store

(大店内的)专业零售部　shop (shoppe)

批发商店　wholesale shop

零售商店　retail shop

折扣商店　discount shop

彻夜(日夜)商店　all-night store, day-and-night store

布店　draper's (shop), dry goods store

服装店　(Brit.) toggery, clothing shop

成衣店　tailor's (shop)

男服装店　men's wear shop

女服装店 couturier, dress-maker's (shop)

儿童商店 children's shop

故衣店 second-hand clothing store

皮货店 furriery

皮革制品商店 leather product store

男帽店 men's hat store

女帽店 lady's hat store, millinery

鞋帽店 headwear and foot-wear shop

鞋店 shoemaker's (shop), shoe shop

缝纫用品店 haberdasher

五金店 hardware store, (Brit.) ironmongery

家具店 furniture and uphol-ster's shop

山货土产商店 forest and native products store

土特产商店 native and special products store, specialities store

瓷器店 china shop

玻璃店 glass shop

照相机商店 camera shop

化妆品店 toiletry shop

烟草店 tobacconist's store

钟表店 clock and watch shop

镜框商店 picture frame store

玩具店 toy shop

珠宝店 jeweller's (shop)

花店 florist shop

鸟店 bird shop

纪念品商店 souvenir shop, gift shop

古玩店 curio shop, antique shop

旧货店 second-hand store

药房 pharmacy, (U. S.) drug store

中药店 Chinese medicinal herbs store

成药店 compounded medicine store

面包店 bakery, baker's (shop)

糕饼店 pastrycook's shop

奶制品店 creamery

糖果店 confectionery, confectioner's shop

糖果摊 candy stall

鱼店 fish dealer's, (Brit.) fishmonger's

肉店 butcher's shop, meat shop

肉摊 butcher's stall

猪肉店 pork-butcher's shop

烧腊店 barbecuer and curer's shop

野味店 game store

菜店 vegetable store

蔬菜水果店 greengrocer's (store), (Brit.) greengrocery

水果店 fruit store, fruiterer's

水果摊 fruit stall

自动出售的杂货店 groceteria, self-service grocery store

书店 bookstore

外文书店 foreign language bookstore

旧书店 second-hand (antiqua-rian) bookstore

文教用品店 school supply and stationery store

体育用品店 sports store

办公室设备商店 office equipment store

报摊 newspaper stall (or kiosk)

眼镜店 optician's (shop)

背篓商店 wicker-basket shop

农村市集 rural fair

寄售商店 commission house

废品收购店(站) waste collecting shop (station)

废品回收 reclamation of waste and used materials

商品交易会 trade fair

商品交易所 commodity exchange house

新产品展销店 shop displaying and selling new products

样品陈列所(室) sample room, show-room

后勤部门 rear supply service department

## 商业人员 Commercial Personnel

商界 commercial circles, business community

商业人员 commercial worker

商人 businessman, merchant

董事长 director general

副董事长 vice-director general

董事 director

董事会 board of directors, directorate

合伙 partnership

两合公司 limited partnership

无限公司 unlimited partnership

有限公司 company limited (Ltd.)

股东 stockholder, shareholder

无限责任股东 active partner

有限责任股东 sleeping partner, limited partner

总经理 managing director, general manager

副总经理 assistant managing director

经理 manager

副经理 vice manager, assistant manager

襄理 assistant manager

营业部经理 sales manager, business manager

办事员 clerk

雇主 employer

雇员 employee

店主 proprietor, shopkeeper

柜台服务员 shop assistant

(商店)巡视员 floor walker, shop walker

推销员 salesman

旅行推销员 travelling salesman, commercial traveller, drummer

行商 transient vendor, transient merchant

旅行采购员 travelling buyer, touring buyer

挨户兜售物品的小贩 pedlar

沿街叫卖的小贩 hawker

伙食供应商 purveyor

(大商店的)勤杂人员 commissionaire

中间商 middleman, intermediary

经纪人(揞客) broker

包装商品工人 packer

搬运工人 porter

顾客 customer, client, patron

全体顾客 clientele

消费者 consumer

用户 enduser, user

## 商　品　Commodity

生产资料 means of production (capital goods)

辅助生产资料(中间商品) auxiliary means of production (intermediate or producer goods)

生活资料 means of livelihood (consumer goods)

经济商品 economic goods

出口商品 export goods

再出口商品 re-exported goods

出口转内销商品 export goods withdrawn for sale on home market

进口货 imported goods

内销商品 goods made for domestic market

中国货 Chinese goods

外国货 foreign goods

耐用商品 durable goods

耐用的消费商品 consumer durables

易变商品 perishable goods

定量配给的商品 rationed goods

免证供应的商品 non-rationed goods

统购统销商品 goods solely purchased and distributed by the state

高档商品 high-priced goods

低档商品 low-priced goods

特价商品 bargain-priced goods

议价商品 negotiated-priced goods

(减价出售的)处理商品 disqualified goods (disposed of at reduced prices)

高质产品 quality goods

低质产品 shoddy goods

奢侈商品 luxury goods, luxuries

华丽商品 tinsel goods

试产商品 trial-produced goods

再生商品 recycled product

复制商品 reproduction goods

一级商品 firstclass goods

次品 undergrade goods

级外产品 offgrade product, substandard goods

残缺商品 defective goods, flawed goods

脱销商品 out-of-stock commodity

畅销品 best seller, fast seller, salable item

滞销商品 slow seller, poor seller, unmarketable goods

积压商品 dead stock

旧货 used goods, second-hand goods

初级产品 primary goods

半成品 semi-finished product

成品 finished product

工业产品 industrial product

矿产与金属产品 minerals and metals

化工产品 chemical product

纺织品 textile goods, (U. S.) dry goods

轻薄衣料 dress goods

按尺码出售的布匹 piece goods, yard goods

液体商品 wet goods, liquid goods

新鲜蔬菜 green goods

加工产品 manufactured goods

手工产品 handmade product

五金商品 hardware

手工艺品 handicraft product

农业产品 agricultural product, farm product

商品粮 commodity grain, market grain

土产 native produce

山货 forestry produce, forest product

水产品 maritime product, aquatic product

副产品 byproduct, sideline product

名产(特产) speciality, (U. S.) specialty

主要商品 staple commodity, main item

流行商品 popular item, hot item

代用商品 substituting commodity, substitute

还原商品 reproduced commodity, reproduction

特种规格商品 goods of anomalous size

季节性商品 seasonal commodity

行情易起波动的商品 sensitive item

"需要密切注意"的商品 "requiring close attention" item

"引起直接关心"的商品 "causing immediate concern" item

出售时给以退款保证的商品 goods sold with money-back guarantee

现货 spot goods

期货 futures

展出品 exhibit

## 价 格（一） Price（Ⅰ）

价格理论 price theory

价格政策 price policy

计划第一、价格第二的原则 principle of giving first place to plan-execution and second place to pricing

价值规律(法则) law of value

货物价格与分配的自然过程

price mechanism, price system

单一价格制 single price system

两重价格制 two-tiered price system, dual price system

价格管制 price control

统一的价格政策 unified price policy

物价机构　price setting and regulating agency

价格制订　price setting

物价指数　price index

市价表　price current, price list

统一价格　unified price

单价　unit price

总价　total price

基价　basic price, base price

全价　full price

半价　half price

零售价　retail price

批发价　wholesale price

季节性价格　seasonal price

暂定价格　provisional price

公平价格　fair price, just price

平均价格　average price

合理价格　reasonable price

不合理价格　fancy price, unreasonable price

调整价格　adjusting a price, price adjustment

内定价格　administered price

比价　comparative price

差价　price differential, price difference, price gap

提价　raising a price

降价　lowering a price

减价　reducing a price, price reduction

最后价格　last price, final price

已调整的价格　adjusted price

新价　new price

旧价　old price

原价　original price

实价　actual price

公价(官价)　official price

议价　negotiated price

国内市场价格　domestic market price

国际市场价格　international market price

参考价格　reference price

(交易所的)报价　quoted price, quote

开盘价格　opening price

收盘价格　closing price

论价　price haggling

讨价还价　price bargaining

买方的还价　buyer's returned price

卖主的要价　seller's asking price

卖价　selling price

买价　buying price

黑市价格　black market price

昂价　long price, heavy price

交易所外价　street price

过高的价格　exorbitant price, prohibitive price

空前最高价　highest-ever price

空前最低价　lowest-ever price

贱价　giveaway price

最高限价　ceiling price, maximum price

最低价格　floor price, rock-bottom price

达记录水平价格　record-level price

消费价格　consumer price

转售价格　resale price

成本价格　cost price

低于成本的价格　below-cost price

处理价格 sales price, bargain rates

固定价格(实价) fixed price, set price

正常价格 normal price

估计价格 estimated price

推算价格 constructed price

行市价格 market value, market price

时价(现行价格) current price, prevailing price, market price

与市场一致的价格 in-line price

与市场不一致的价格 out-of-line price

现金付款价格 cash price

记帐付款价格 credit price

定价(虚价) nominal price

让步价格 concessional price

票面价格 call price, face value, par value

帐面价格 book value

同业卖价 trade price

拍卖价格 auction price

投标价格 price tendered, price bidded

抵押价 mortgaged price

含佣价格 price including commission, commission included price

竞争价格 competitive price

歧视价格 discriminatory price

倾销价格 dumping price

垄断价格 monopolistic price, monopoly price

维持价格 support price

公议价格 convention price

干预价格 intervention price

滑动价格 sliding-scale price

毛价 gross price

净价 net price

现货价格 spot price

期货价格 forward price

广告价格 advertised price

刊物价格 published price

商品目录价格(厂盘) catalogue price, list price

成交价格 concluded price

协定价格 agreement price

合同价格 contract price

规定价格 stipulated price

发票价格 invoice price

附加价格 extra price

特别价格 exceptional price

进口价格 import price

出口价格 export price

# 价　格（二）　Price（Ⅱ）

让价 price concession

价格冻结 price freeze

价格歧视 price discrimination

价格极限(保留价格) price limit (reserve price)

价格涨落变动范围 price range

物价水平 price level

价格意见 price idea

价格动态 price movements

价格战(一再削价的商业竞争) price war

示意性出价 indicating a price

估价 assessing a price, price

assessment

计算价格　calculating a price

开价, 定价　making a price, pricing, fixing a price

加高价格　marking up a price

减低价格　marking down a price

漫天讨价以致减少或没有销路　pricing goods out of the market

斗价　reasoning for a better price

略减价格　shading a price

弥合价格差距　bridging a price gap

数量诱因(价格低则数量相应增加)　quantity inducement

买得越多,价格越低　the larger the order, the lower the price

价格越低,买得越多　the lower the price, the larger the order

数量减价 (订购量大则价格相应减低)　quantitative reduction

停售以待价格上升　holding over (on) for a higher price

停购以待价格下降　holding off for a lower price

友好让价　amicable allowance in price

象征性的减价　symbolic reduction (of price)

价格很稳　price well maintained

价格无显著变化　price bearing no appreciable change

价格波动　price fluctuating, price fluctuation

价格盘旋于……与……之间　price hovering between…and…

价格有上涨趋势(价格看涨)　price taking an upward trend, price looking up

价格稳步上升　price advancing steadily

价格上升很快　price rising rapidly, price moving quickly upward

价格盘旋上升　price spiraling

价格直线上升　price rising perpendicularly

价格猛涨　price skyrocketing (soaring)

大涨之风(价格)　big bulge in prices

价格日疲　price sagging

价格正在软化　price easing off

价格呆滞且有更弱或下降的趋势　price dull with a weaker or downward tendency

价格突然下降　price tobogganing

价格下降　price declining

价格剧降　price falling rapidly, price plummeting

价格暴跌　price slumping, price nose-diving

价格趋平　price levelling off

价格回涨　rebound in prices

定价货币　price-setting currency

地区差价　regional price difference (discrepancy)

## 品质、数量与样品　Quality, Quantity and Sample

品质　quality
标准品质　standard quality
惯常的品质　usual quality
合销品质　good merchantable quality (GMQ)
头等品质　first class quality, first-rate quality
优良的品质　excellent quality
第一流的品质　prime quality, tip-top quality
优等品质　superior quality
最好的品质　best quality
上等品质　top quality
高品质　high quality
一批中最好的货物　the pick of the lot
精选的品质　choice quality, selected quality
精美的品质　fine quality
完好的品质　sound quality
好的品质　fair quality
一致的品质　uniform quality
受欢迎的(大众化的)品质　popular quality
一般(平均)的品质　average quality
一般品质　common quality
中等水平以上的品质　above average quality
一般水平以下的品质　below average quality
大路货品质　fair average quality
低品质　low quality
好的品质　good quality
质量不高的品质　indifferent quality

有问题的品质　questionable quality
劣品质　bad quality, poor quality
下等品质　inferior quality
装船品质　shipped quality
到货品质　landed quality
数量　quantity
总数量　total quantity
大的数量　large quantity
相当大的数量　considerable quantity
巨大的数量　enormous quantity, huge quantity
足够的数量　sufficient quantity
充足的数量　liberal quantity
可观的数量　sizable quantity
颇为巨大的数量　substantial quantity
实惠的数量　useful quantity
最大的数量　maximum quantity
最小的数量　minimum quantity
小的数量　small quantity
微不足道的数量　inconsequential quantity
平均数量　average quantity
中等数量　moderate quantity
适当的数量　reasonable quantity
足够装运的数量　shipment quantity
有限数量　limited quantity

相应的数量　**corresponding quantity**

同等数量　**equal quantity**

估计数量　**estimated quantity**

准确数量　**exact quantity**

追加数量　**additional quantity**

额外数量　**extra quantity**

后续的数量　**further quantity**

装船数量　**shipped quantity**

到货数量　**landed quantity**

等级　**grade**

高档　**high grade**

中等　**medium grade, middling grade**

低档　**low grade**

基准等级　**basis grade**

等外　**off-grade**

规格　**specification**

样品　**sample**

正货　**bulk of goods**

货样　**sample of goods**

回样(对等货样)　**counter sample**

复样　**duplicate sample**

装船样品　**shipping sample**

一般平均货样　**fair average sample**

有代表性的货样　**representative sample**

一套样品　**a sample set**

公司商行名称录　**business directory**

商品目录　**catalogue**

商品说明书　**descriptive literature, specifications**

商品插图说明书　**illustrated leaflet**

式样　**pattern**

复样　**return pattern**

样本(剪样)　**pattern book, sample cutting**

## 包　装　Packing

出口包装　**export packing, export packaging**

内包装　**inner packing, inner packaging**

外包装　**outer packing, outer packaging**

商业包装　**commercial packing**

中性包装　**neutral packing**

原始包装　**original packing**

一向使用的包装　**usual packing**

惯常(传统)包装　**customary packing**

特别(指定)包装　**special packing**

直接包装　**immediate packing**

迎合当地市场喜爱的包装　**packing (packaging) coming in line with local market preference**

适合海运包装　**seaworthy packing**

紧密的包装　**compact packing**

加固包装　**reinforced packing**

条形包装　**strip packing**

小型包装　**small packing**

供一次使用包装　**one-service packing**

防水包装　**water-proof packing**

防漏气包装　**air-tight packing**

防碎包装　**breakage-proof**

packing
防漏包装 leakage-proof packing
(喷塑料薄膜)封存包装法 cocoon packing
紧身包装法 contour packing
压缩包装法 squeeze packing
散装包装法 bulk packing
活动浅盘包装法 tray packing
分隔包装法 fractional packing
(容器)套上保护物 sheathing
(容器内周围)垫上保护物 lining
轻率的包装 imprudent packing
不合适的包装 inadequate packing
改装 re-packing, re-packaging
外表装潢 surface treatment
包装机器 packing machine, packaging machine

制纸板箱机 cartoning machine
捆扎机 bundling machine
粘合机 gumming machine
钉封机 wire-stitching machine, stapler
打孔机 perforating machine
加标记的机器 marking machine
包装条件 conditions of packing, terms of packaging
包装要求 packing instructions
包装技术 packing technology
包装费 packing expenses
包纸费 wrapping charges
装箱费 casing charges
装袋费 bagging charges
装潢费 making-up charges
改装费用 repacking charges
加工费 processing charges

## 包装材料 Packing Materials

包装材料 materials for packing (packaging)
(半)硬容器 (semi-)rigid container
折叠容器 collapsible container
一次使用的容器 throw-away container, single-use container
可再用的容器 reusable container
多次使用容器 returnable container
按钮式气密容器 aerosol container
集装箱 container
透明塑胶袋 polyethylene bag,

polythene bag
箔衬袋 foil bag
牛皮纸袋 kraft-paper bag
五层纸袋 five-ply paper bag
草袋 rush bag
布袋 cloth bag
粗麻袋 gunny bag, gunny sack
多层袋 multi-walled sack
草席包 rush mat bale
机器榨包 machine-pressed bale
捆扎 bundle
瓦楞纸盒 corrugated paper box
纸板盒 cardboard box
锦缎盒 brocade box

木箱　wooden case
纤维板箱　fibre board case
胶合板箱　veneer case (box)
三合板箱　ply-wood case
金属圆桶　metal drum
铁桶　iron drum
反白(厚纤维纸)桶　fibre drum
聚乙烯圆桶　polythene drum
桶　cask
小木桶　wooden keg
琵琶桶　wooden barrel
直圆铁桶　cylinder
板条箱　wooden crate
竹篓　bamboo basket
柳条筐　wicker basket
纸板箱　carton
可折叠纸板箱　folding carton
铁皮罐(听)　tin
瓶　bottle
长颈瓶　flask
球形玻璃瓶　carboy
针剂药水瓶　vial
(胶)囊　(gelatin) capsule
瓦坛　jar
粗麻布　burlap
麻袋片　gunny cloth
麻布　hessian cloth
油布　tarpaulin (tarred canvas)
席　mat

沥青纸　tar paper, asphalt paper
油纸　oil paper
蜡纸　wax paper
玻璃纸　cellophane paper
羊皮纸　parchment paper
铁丝　iron wire, steel wire
铁箍带　iron band, steel band
铁箍　iron hoop, steel hoop
尼龙丝　nylon twine
小绳　string
绳索　rope
填料　stuffing material
衬垫物　cushioning material
皱纹填塞物　crepe(d) wadding
木丝(刨花)　excelsior, wood shavings
碎纸　shredded paper
纸屑　paper scraps
纸条　paper wool
棉絮　cotton wool
木屑　sawdust
软绵纸　tissue paper
稻草　straw
泡沫塑料　foamed plastics
支撑物　bracing apparatus, holding apparatus
隔板　partition, divider
包封用胶乳　adhesive latex

# 库存与运输　Stock and Transportation

仓库　warehouse, storehouse, magazine
(东方)仓库　godown
油库　oil storage
水下油库　submerged oil storage

谷仓　granary
冷藏库　cold storage room
地窖　underground storage room
冷藏室　cool chamber
存仓　storing in warehouse

(货物)入仓与出仓　receiving and dispatching of goods

仓库管理　warehouse management, storekeeping

冷藏储存食物法　storing food by refrigeration

辐射储存食物法　storing food by irradiation

激光照射　laser irradiation

伽马射线处理　gamma ray irradiation

(果物储存)人工冬眠法　artificial hibernation (of fruits)

低压冷藏法　low-pressure storage

防腐蚀　anticorrosion

防燃　antideflagration

防潮　dehumidification

脱水处理　dehydration

消灭害虫　pest extermination

存仓费　warehousing costs

栈单(仓单, 码头收据)　warrant, warehouse receipt

库存　stock

货物清单　inventory

(年度)存货登记, 存货列册　(annual) inventory

存货已尽　stock depleted

充实存货　loading up on inventories

运输　transportation

陆运　land transportation

公路运输　road transportation

铁路运输　rail transportation, railway transportation

海运　sea transportation

空运　air transportation

管道运输　pipe transportation

提货单　bill of lading (B/L)

航空托运单　air transportation waybill, air consignment note

汽车公司提单　trucking company's B/L

陆运收据　cargo receipt

国际铁路联运单　international through rail service waybill

交货　delivery

遵守交货日期　meeting delivery date

依时运送货物　on-time delivery

迅速交货　early delivery

延期交货　late delivery, deferred delivery

即期交货　prompt delivery, immediate delivery

远期交货　forward delivery, future delivery

定期交付　delivery on term

出货单, 栈单　delivery order

送货簿　delivery book

送货回单　delivery receipt

帐目全清收据　acquittance

## 广　告　Advertising

广告　advertising

通知广告术　informative advertising

劝购广告术　persuasive advertising

登报广告　newspaper advertising

电影广告　cinema film advertising

广播广告　advertising on radio, wireless advertising

无线电台的广告节目　radio commercial

电视广告　advertising on television

空中广告　aerial advertising, sky-writing

电视台的广告节目　TV commercial

时装展览　fashion show

汽车展览　motor show

(商品)橱窗陈列　shop-window display

活广告(身前身后挂广告牌的人)　sandwich man

商业广告　commercial advertising

推销广告　sales promoting advertisement

分类广告　classified advertisement

为某商品(劳务)作广告　advertising certain goods (service)

宣传(商品、劳务)　giving publicity to (goods, service)

广告宣传活动　advertising campaign

广告价格　advertising rates

广告费　advertising fee

广告战　advertising war

登广告者　advertiser

广告设计师　advertisement designer

广告社　advertising agency

广告牌　advertisement sign

霓虹灯广告　neon sign

(舞台上的)广告幕　advertisement curtain

张贴广告　bill-posting

巨幅广告牌　huge advertisement boarding

招徕术　showmanship

## 拍卖与投标　Auction and Tender

拍卖　auction, auctioneering

拍卖市场　auction market

拍卖行　auction company, auction house

拍卖商品　auction goods

拍卖前看货　inspection of goods before auction

把……交付拍卖　putting … up to (for or at) auction

拍卖出售　selling by (at) auction

拍卖人　auctioneer

拍卖目录　auction catalogue

递盘(出价)　bid, bidding

送盘人　bidder

相竞递盘　bidding against each other

竞争性递盘　competitive bid

组合递盘　package bid, partial bid

密封递盘　sealed bid

混合递盘　joint bid

撤回递盘　withdrawing bid, retracting bid

投标 (Brit.) tender, (U.S.)
bid

公开投标 public tender,
public bid

标购 buying tender, buying
bid

标售 selling tender, selling
bid

招标 invitation for tender,
invitation for bid

投标(或承包)截止日期 tender
deadline, bid deadline

投标人 tenderer, bidder

招标通知 tender notice, bid
notice

招标条件 tender conditions,
bid conditions

提标(提出承包书) submission
of tender, submission of
bid

投标(或承包)文件 tender doc-
uments, bid documents

投标保证金 tender bond, pro-
visional bid guarantee

投标(或承包)建议书 tender
proposal, bid proposal

开标(开启承包书) opening
tender, opening bid

中标(得标) winning tender,
winning bid

中标人 successful tenderer,
winning bidder

未中标 losing tender, losing
bid

## 商业非法行为 Commercial Malpractice

商业非法行为 commercial
immorality

商场舞弊行为 commercial
wrongdoing, commercial
irregularity

不正派的勾当 shady dealings,
shady business

暗中交易, 走后门买卖 under-
the-counter transaction

"走后门" dealing at the
backdoor

故意少给找头 shortchanging

短秤 shortweighting

转手倒卖 buying and then
reselling for exorbitant
profit

开假发票多收款 overinvoicing

(为获得商业上的好处而)暗中付出
贿赂 undercover payment,

payola

以次货充好货 palming off
shoddy as quality goods

行贿 bribery

贩卖私酒 bootlegging

诈骗行为 fraud scheme

假商店(老千公司) phony com-
pany, bogus firm

拖欠付款 defaulting payments

非法报酬 illegal payoff

伪造票证 forging documents

涂改票证 falsifying documents

盗窃行为 ripoff

囤积 hoarding

投机倒把 speculation

黑市买卖货 black marketeer-
ing, black marketing

(商品)搀杂, 搀假 adulterating

放高利贷 practising usury

隐蔽贴水 concealed discount

金融、证券投机买卖 speculating on currencies and securities

商品的投机买卖 speculating on commodities

报假帐 making false financial statements

地下市场 clandestine market

操纵市场 market manipulation

"自由贸易" unauthorized trading

"自由生产" unauthorized production

地下工厂 clandestine factory

违反专利权 patent violation

违法私印书本、私制唱片、录音带 piration of books, records, tapes

套购外汇 illicit arbitration of foreign exchange

套购统购统销商品 illegal buying of goods to be bought and distributed solely by the state

贩卖毒品 drug trafficking

买卖赃物 fencing

诈骗银行行为 bank fraud

勾结进行商业舞弊 colluding to commit commercial misdeed

盗窃(偷听)秘密商业情报 stealing (intercepting) secret commercial information

以低质货品冒充高质货 deliberate misgrading

盗用注册商标 unauthorized use of registered trade-mark

偷税漏税 tax evasion, defrauding the revenue

违章 infringement of customs regulations

走私 smuggling

瞒税 concealing facts to avoid proper taxation

## 其他商业用语 Miscellaneous Commercialisms

商会 chamber of commerce

同业公会 trade association

垄断企业 monopoly

寡头企业 oligopoly

(多种行业的)联合大企业 conglomerate

联合企业 joint enterprise

合并企业 merger

卡特尔 cartel

国际卡特尔 international cartel

康采恩 concern

辛迪加 syndicate

托拉斯 trust

跨国公司 trans-national(multi-national) company

国际财团 consortium

父公司 parent company

附属公司(子公司) subsidiary company, affiliated company

姊妹公司 sister company

(自动售货商店)超级市场 supermarket

市郊大型百货商店 hypermarket

典当业 pawnbroking, pawnbrokerage

当铺 pawnbrokery, pawnshop

当铺主 pawnbroker

停业, 倒闭 closedown

(企业倒闭时的)清理 liquidation

破产 bankruptcy, insolvency

破产者 bankrupt

工商巨头 magnate

(不参与经营的)资本家 rentier

大亨 tycoon

暴发户 upstart, parvenu

富商 merchant prince

老板 boss

黑市商人 blackmarketeer

买卖赃物者 fence

放高利贷者 usurer, loan shark

卖空 selling short, short sale

买空 going long on the market, buying on margin

# 百 货 Wares of Commerce

## 衣 料 Drapery

衣料　suit material, dress material

纺织物(品)　textile

布匹　piecegoods, cloth

机织物　woven fabric

针织物　knit fabric, tricot

平针(单面)织物　jersey

提花织物　jacquard, broché

双面织物　double-knit

混纺织物　mixture fabric, blended fabric

无纺织物(粘合织物)　bonded-fabric

棉织物　cotton fabric

棉布　cotton cloth, cotton piece-goods

原布　grey shirting, grey cloth

白布(本布)　(Brit.) calico, (US) plain white cotton cloth

漂白布　bleached cotton fabrics

染色布　dyed shirting

标色(扣布)　T-cloth

印花布　cotton prints

色织布　yarn-dyed fabric

蜡染印花布　batik

斜纹布　drill, drilling

咔叽布　khaki drill

双面卡　reversible khaki

双经布　dosuti

阴丹士林布　indanthren cloth

蓝色工作服布　blue jean

(蓝经白纬的)劳动布(坚固呢)　denim

棉帆布　duck

粗帆布　canvas

棉府绸　cotton poplin

棉哔叽　cotton serge

棉茧绸　cotton pongee

白细布　long cloth

细薄布　cotton cambric

绉布　crape-cloth

泡泡纱　seersucker, plisse crepe

凹凸布　embossed fabric

格子布　check

柳条布　dimity

多色花布　chintz

土布　nankeen

绒布(毛布)　cotton flannel, canton flannel, flannelette

防水布　water-repellent cloth

夏布　grass cloth

细夏布　fine grass-cloth

被单布　sheeting

提花被单布　broché quilting

亚麻布　linen (cloth)

亚麻格子布　linen check

丝绸　silk

真丝　pure silk

印花丝绸　printed silk piece-goods

人造丝绸　rayon, artificial silk

人造纤维绸　man-made fibre piece-goods

柞蚕丝绸　tussah silk piece goods

交织绸　mixed silk-rayon piece goods

提花丝绸　jacquard silk

绫　damask silk

栲绸　gambiered canton silk

茧绸(山东绸)　pongee

塔夫绸　taffeta

全丝光亮塔夫绸　lustrine

熟绸　soft pongee

薯莨绸　rust-coloured sen-shaw

缎　satin

棉缎(贡缎)　sateen

织锦缎　tapestry satin

花缎　figured satin

锦　brocade

真丝织锦　pure silk brocade

古香缎　Suzhou brocade

绢　lutestring

羽纱　camblet

乔其纱　georgette

香云纱　gambiered canton gauze

广东绉纱　canton crepe

呢绒　woolen piece-goods

粗花呢　tweed

毛哔叽　wool serge

法兰绒　flannel

灯芯绒　corduroy

天鹅绒(丝绒)　velvet

虎皮丝绒　striped velvet

羊毛剪绒　woolen velvet

粗纺呢绒　woollen

精纺呢绒　worsted

开士米(精纺毛料)　cashmere

长毛绒　plush

马海呢　mohair

骆驼绒　camel hair

华达呢　garbadine

大衣呢　overcoating

海军呢　admiralty cloth, melton

格子呢　tartan, plaid

人字呢　herringbone

佩士利花呢　paisley

凡立丁　valetin

派力斯　palace

合成纤维织物　synthetic fabrics

化学纤维　chemical fabrics

尼龙(耐纶)　nylon

维尼纶　vinylon

涤纶(的确凉)　dacron, polyester, terylene

腈纶　chinlan

奥纶　orlon

卡普纶　capron

棉涤纶　trueran, cotton-polyester fabric

涤粘纶　trueran-viscose fabric

麻涤纶　mixed linen-polyester fabric

丝涤纶 blended fabric of silk and polyester
毛涤纶 modelon, wool-polyester blend
针织尼龙 nylon tricot
单封 single width
双封 double width
碎料(布头,布尾) small piece
织物质地(身骨) texture
缩水率 rate of shrinkage
手感 feel
耐磨性 abrasion resistance

均匀度 evenness
弹性 resilience
拒水性 water repellence
吸水性 water absorptivity
防起球 resistance to balling
免熨 no-iron
防皱 crease resistance
防缩水 shrink-proof
免晒(滴干) drip-dry
不褪色 fast colour
褪色 fading

## 服装　Clothing

服装 garments
男服 men's clothing
制服 uniform
中山装① Zhongshan-style tunic, Chinese tunic suit
干部服 cadre tunic
水兵服② jumper
普通西装 lounge suit, (US) business suit
上衣④ jacket, coat
(配套)长裤⑤ suit trousers
晚礼服 evening dress

大礼服(燕尾服)⑥ dress suit
小礼服 dinner-jacket, (US) tuxedo
长大衣 frock coat
短上衣(夹克)⑦ jacket
背心⑧ vest, waistcoat
长裤 pants, trousers
短裤 shorts, short pants
便裤 slacks
长内裤 drawers
短内裤 briefs, short pants, underpants

衬衣 shirt

短袖衬衣 sports shirt

假衬衣 dickey, dicky

内衣 underwear, undershirt

汗背心⑨ singlet

(圆领、反领)短袖汗衫⑩ T-shirt

长袖汗衫⑪ long-sleeved undershirt, sweat shirt

卫生衣 sweater, jersey

卫生裤 sweat pants

羊毛衣 woolen sweater

羊毛裤 woolen pants

拉毛羊毛衫 brushed wool sweater

毛背心 woolen vest

开胸羊毛衫 cardigan

套头毛衣 pullover, slipover

羽绒衫 down and feather-filled garments

睡衣裤 pyjamas, pajamas

睡衣 pyjama tops (jacket)

睡裤 pyjama bottoms

妇女或小孩睡衣 nighty

浴衣 bath robe

晨衣 dressing gown

运动服装 sportswear

球衣(运动衣) jersey

运动裤 sports pants

沙滩装 beach wear

游泳衣 swimsuit

游泳裤 swim trunks

滑雪衣 ski-wear

长袖紧身体操衣 leotard

防风衣 wind-jacket, (US) windbreaker

斗蓬(披肩) cape

雨衣 raincoat

雨披 rain-cape

风雪大衣(皮猴) parka

有带风大衣 ulster

皮大衣 fur overcoat

夹大衣 light overcoat

活动里子 detachable lining

工作服 overalls, fatigues

工装裤(牛仔裤) (blue) jeans

罩衣 smock frock

猎装 bush coat

卡装(卡曲) car coat

棉袄 cotton padded coat

棉背心 cotton-padded vest

棉紧身 cotton-padded hug-me-tight

女服 women's clothing

一套女西服⑫ suit dress (coat and skirt)

连衣裙⑬ dress

女短衫裙 short gown

女衬衫 blouse, waistcoat

中袖女衬衣 three-quarter blouse

无袖女衬衣 blousette

短外衣 coatee

袋形女服 sack

宽松女裤 slacks

百褶裙 pleated skirt

吊带裙 skirt with shoulder-straps

长衬裙 slip

衬裙 petticoat, underskirt

腰带(紧身褡) girdle

胸罩 bra(ssiere)

紧身胸衣 corset, bodice

胸衣 foundation garment, corselet

女短内裤 panties, knickers

紧身袜裤 stretch nylon tights

三角裤 briefs

室内穿的衣服　house dress
童服　children's clothing
女童服　dresses for girls
男童服　dresses for boys
学生装　school uniform
褶饰童装　smocking dress
儿童外衣　frock
妹裙　girl's frock
日光服　sunsuit
防脏围裙(罩衣)　pinafore
无袖肩扣套衣　gertrude
童内裤　panties
开裆裤　pants with open crotch
连袜童睡衣　sleeper
婴儿服　baby clothes, swaddling clothes
婴儿上衣　sacque, baby jacket
围涎　bib
尿布　(Brit.) napkin, nappy, (US) diapers
民族服装　national dress, national costume
纱笼(马来围裙)①　sarong
苏格兰男短裙②　kilt
旗袍③　Chinese-styled long gown

日本和服④　kimono
蒙古服⑤　Mongolian costume
西藏服⑥　Tibetan costume
维吾尔服⑦　Uigur costume
朝鲜服⑧　Korean costume
窄腿裤　tapering trousers
喇叭裤　bell-bottomed trousers, bell-bottoms
马裤　riding breeches
灯笼短裤　knickers, breeches
超短裙　miniskirt
缠腰布　breech clout, loincloth
裤腰带　belt
裤带扣　buckle
吊带　suspenders
领带　tie, necktie
领带针　tie-pin
穿衣镜　dressing glass
试衣室　fitting room
小号　small size
中号　medium size
大号　large size
特大号　extra large size
衣服剪裁款式　cut
服装式样, 时式　style, fashion
时装　fashionable dress

## 帽 类 Headdresses

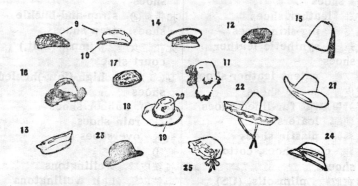

| | | |
|---|---|---|
| (无边有檐)便帽⑨ cap | 高顶礼帽 silk hat, top hat |
| 帽檐(帽舌)⑩ visor | 通帽㉔ topee, sun helmet |
| 带护耳皮帽⑪ fur cap with earflaps | 女帽,女头饰 millinery |
| 贝雷帽⑫ beret | 平顶女帽 platter |
| 橄榄帽⑬ garrison cap | 绒球女帽 tam-o'-shanter |
| 军帽⑭ service cap | 扣带女帽㉕ bonnet |
| 尖顶帽 peaked cap | 带缨童帽 child's cap with pompon |
| 室内便帽(瓜皮帽) skullcap | 头巾 kerchief |
| 睡帽 night cap | 三角头巾 babushka |
| 土耳其帽⑮ fez | 面纱 veil |
| 西藏毡帽⑯ Tibetan cap | 围巾(颈围) muffler, scarf |
| 维吾尔帽⑰ Uigur cap | 女披肩(方形围巾) shawl |
| 有边帽⑱ hat | (海员)防水帽 southwester |
| 帽边⑲ hat brim | 安全帽 safety helmet |
| 帽顶⑳ hat crown | 钢盔 steel helmet |
| 平顶卷边帽 porkpie hat | 冠冕 coronet |
| 锥顶内折呢帽 Homburg | 草帽 straw hat |
| 匈牙利利呢帽㉑ Kossuth | 藤帽 rattan hat |
| 墨西哥式帽㉒ sombrero | 竹帽 bamboo hat |
| 圆顶礼帽㉓ bowler-hat, derby | 圈头花串 chaplet |

## 鞋袜类  Footwear and Hosiery

鞋  shoes
皮鞋  leather shoes
猪皮鞋  pig-skin shoes
人革鞋  synthetic leather shoes
漆皮鞋  patent leather shoes
反皮鞋  suede shoes
毛衬里皮鞋  fur-lined shoes
皮便鞋  loafers
塑料鞋  plastic shoes
布鞋  cloth shoes, cotton shoes
帆布胶鞋  plimsolls, (US) sneakers, canvas shoes
棉鞋  cotton-padded shoes
绒鞋(毡鞋)  felt shoes
凉鞋  sandals
交叉皮条凉鞋  huaraches
拖鞋  slippers
无跟女拖鞋  babouches
缚带鞋  laced shoes
便鞋  casual shoes, slip-ons
松紧带便鞋①  low-cut congress shoes, elastic-sided shoes
扣带鞋②  strap-and-buckle shoes, strap shoes
无扣带女鞋  pumps, (Brit.) court shoes
高(低)跟鞋  high-(low-)heeled shoes
胶鞋③  rubber shoes
雨鞋  rain shoes
套鞋  overshoes
靴④  boots
长统皮靴  wellingtons
半统皮靴  half wellingtons
垫绒胶套靴  arctics
高统胶靴  hip boots
涉水胶靴  waders
尖头鞋  pointed(-tiped) shoes
运动鞋  sports shoes
体操鞋⑤  gym shoes, sneakers
篮球鞋⑥  basketball shoes
足球鞋⑦  football shoes
网球鞋⑧  tennis shoes
田径鞋⑨  track shoes

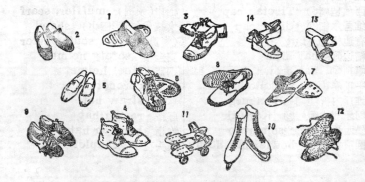

跑鞋　running shoes
冰鞋⑩　skates
旱冰鞋(雪屐)⑪　roller skates
滑雪鞋　ski boots
雪鞋　snow shoes
草鞋⑫　straw sandals
屐⑬　clogs, sabots
厚底鞋⑭　platform shoes
罩鞋　spats
鞋带　(Brit.) shoelace, (US) shoestring
绑腿套　gaiters
鞋的各部分　parts of a shoe
鞋面(鞋帮)　upper (vamp)
鞋头　tip, shoecap
鞋舌　tongue
鞋衬里　lining
鞋孔　eyelet
鞋底　sole
内底(鞋垫)　insole

贴边　welt
鞋跟　heel
鞋后跟马钉　heel plate
鞋拔　shoe horn
鞋楦　shoe tree, shoe last
量脚尺　size stick
试鞋凳　shoes trying stool
袜类　hosiery
长袜　stockings
吊袜带　garter
短袜　socks
反口袜　anklets
毛巾袜　terry socks
丝袜　silk socks
腈纶交织袜　acrylic-nylon socks
锦纶丝袜　sheer nylon socks
尼龙袜裤　stretch nylon tights

## 皮革与毛皮　Leather and Fur

牛皮　ox-hide
小牛皮　calf-skin
猪皮　pig-skin
羊皮　sheep-skin
山羊皮　goat-skin
麂皮　buck-skin, doe-skin
鲨鱼皮　shark-skin
鳄鱼皮　crocodile-skin
反皮　suede (leather)
人造革　synthetic leather, imitation leather, leather-cloth
漆皮　patent leather
毛皮　fur

貂皮(元皮)　kolinsky
水貂皮　mink
黑貂皮　sable
豹皮　leopard
虎皮　tiger
银狐皮　silverfox
鸡鼬皮(艾虎皮)　fitch
水獭皮　beaver
麝鼠皮　mustrat
黄羊皮　gazelle
羊皮　sheepskin, lambskin
皮大衣　fur overcoat
皮上衣(外套)　leather jacket
毛皮里手套　fur-lined gloves

## 床上用品　Bedthing

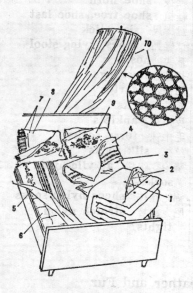

床单⑤　sheet, bottom sheet
床罩　bedspread, coverlet
床垫,褥垫⑥　mattress
羽绒床垫　feather bed
弹簧床垫　spring mattress
海绵胶床垫　foam rubber mattress
褥套　bedtick
木棉床垫　silk cotton mattress, kapok fibre mattress
藤丝床垫　rattan-fibre mattress
草垫　straw mattress
床下摆(床边下垂饰布)　valance
床上摆(床顶下垂饰布)　valance attached to canopy
帏帐　priscillas
枕头(枕芯)⑦　pillow
枕套⑧　pillow-slip, pillowcase
枕巾⑨　pillow sham
床篷　canopy
蚊帐　mosquito net
珠罗(纱)帐⑩　bobbinet mosquito net
蚊帐钩　tiebacks
席子　mat
草席　straw mat
软草席　fine straw mat
竹席　bamboo-strip mat
藤席　rattan mat
睡眠袋　sleeping bag
汤婆子　warming pan, bed warmer, foot warmer
铺卷　bedding roll

铺盖　bedclothes, covers
褥具　bed linen
被套①　quilt slip, quilt cover
棉胎②　cotton quilt
丝绵被　cocoon-fibre quilt
尼龙被　nylon quilt
鸭绒被　eiderdown
毛毯③　woollen blanket
棉毯　cotton blanket
毛巾被　terry blanket
电毯子　electric blanket
珠被(提花被单)　broché sheet
被单④　sheet, turn-down sheet

## 家　具　Furniture

木制家具　wood furniture
竹制家具　bamboo furniture
藤制家具　cane furniture, rattan furniture
钢制家具　steel furniture
塑料家具　plastic furniture
书橱　bookcase
书架　bookshelf
公文柜　filing cabinet
屏风　screen
书桌　desk
办公桌(写字台)　desk, writing-table
会议桌　conference table
餐桌　table, dinner table
圆桌　round table

纱柜(食橱)⑪　cupboard
餐具柜(酒柜)⑫　sideboard
壁柜　built-in cupboard
大立柜⑬　wardrobe
五斗柜⑭　chest of drawers
衣柜　clothes-cupboard, (US) linen closet
樟木箱　camphorwood chest
床头柜⑮　bedside table, night table, nightstand
长沙发⑯　sofa
长靠椅　settee
两用长靠椅(杠床)⑰　dual-purpose settee (couch)
折叠式躺椅(帆布椅)⑱　deck chair

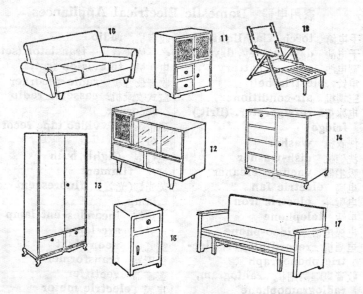

安乐椅　easy-chair
可拆拼沙发　sectional sofa
转椅　swivel chair
摇椅　rocking chair
藤椅　cane chair, wicker chair
椅垫　cushion
茶几　teapoy, tea table, coffee table
圆凳,方凳　stool
长凳(条凳)　bench
靠背椅　chair
折叠椅　collapsible chair, folding chair
扶手椅,单人沙发　armchair
梳妆台　dressing-table, (US) dresser
柱式衣帽架　clothes tree
单人床　single bed

双人床　double bed
折叠床　folding bed
沙发床　sofa bed
活动床　pulldown bed
双层床(碌架床)　double-deck bed, bunk bed
床架　bedstead
(有栏栅的)儿童床　child's cot, crib
帆布床　canvas cot
吊床　hammock
床垫(垫褥)　mattress
地毯　carpet
小地毯(挂毯)　rug
门前擦鞋棕垫　door-mat
一套卧室家具　a bedroom-suite
一套客厅家具　a parlour-suite
一套厨房家具　a kitchen-suite

## 家用电器　Domestic Electrical Appliances

手电筒　torch, flashlight
干电池　dry battery, dry cell
蓄电池　storage battery
电铃　electric bell
空调机　air-conditioner
电冰箱　refrigerator, (Brit.) fridge
洗衣机　washer
洗碗机　dish-washer
吸尘器　vacuum cleaner
电扇　electric fan
电熨斗　electric iron
电话　telephone
电视电话　video-phone
电唱机　record player, electric phonograph
收音电唱两用机　radiogram, radiogramophone

收音机　radio
半导体收音机　transistor (set)
电视机　television (set)
收音录音机　radio recorder
盒式收录机　cassette radio recorder
磁带录像机　video tape recorder
电灯泡　(light) bulb
灯丝　filament
荧光灯(光管)　fluorescent lamp
白炽灯　incandescent lamp
电弧灯　arc lamp
霓虹灯　neon light
变压器　transformer
整流器　rectifier
电表　electric meter

开关(电闸)　switch
按钮开关　press button
拉绳开关　pull switch
换向(旋转)开关　tumbler
　switch
插头　plug
三脚插头　three-pin plug
插座　socket
接合器　socket adapter

起辉器　starter
电线　electric wire
绝缘胶布　friction tape
保险丝　fuse
试电笔　test pencil
电工钳　combination pliers
电工刀　electrician's knife
电工剪　electrician's scissors
螺丝起子　screwdriver

## 小五金　Domestic Hardware

锁扣(锁牌)①　hasp
锁环②　staple
挂锁(扣锁)③　padlock
留匙锁　key-in-knob lock
弹簧锁　spring lock
榫式门锁④　mortise lock
橱柜抽屉锁⑤　cabinet drawer
　lock
数码锁　combination padlock
安全锁　safe lock
磁锁　magnetic padlock
钥匙圈　key-ring
钥匙链　key-chain

(门窗铰链)活页⑥　hinge
门窗插销⑦　bolt
(可从外面开的)门闩⑧　latch
铁钉　wire nail
螺钉　screw
螺栓　bolt
螺帽　nut
铆钉　rivet
开尾销　coffer pin
锯子　saw
锤子　hammer
钳子　pincers, pliers
刨子　plane
凿子　chisel
锉子　file
螺丝起子　screw driver
小刀　pocketknife
折刀　jackknife
弹簧折刀　clasp knife
指甲剪　nail clipper
指甲锉　nail file
拉链　zipper
衣领扣⑨　hook and eye
按扣(迫钮,揿钮)⑩　snap fast-
　ener, snapper
鞋眼(鸡眼)⑪　grommet

# 文 具 Stationery

文房四宝——纸、笔、墨、砚 the four stationery requisites ——paper, writing-brush, ink and ink-stone

信封 envelope

信纸 letter paper, writing paper

写字纸 writing paper

证卷纸 bond paper

打字纸 typing paper

便条纸 note paper

复写纸 carbon paper, duplicating paper

信笺 letter writing pad

笔记簿 notebook, notepad

便条簿 memo pad

活页本 loose-leaf notebook

活页夹 (loose paper) folder

练习簿 exercise book

日记本 diary

此纸化墨水。 This paper blots.

此墨水化纸。 This ink blots.

文具盒 stationery case

蘸水钢笔 pen

自来水笔 fountain pen

笔尖 nib, (US) point

墨水管 ink barrel

笔杆 penholder

笔套(笔帽) pen cap

金笔 fountain pen with gold nib

铱金笔 fountain pen with iridium-tipped nib

圆珠笔 ball pen, ballpoint pen

圆珠笔芯 refill

铅笔 pencil

软芯铅笔 soft pencil

硬芯铅笔 hard pencil

毛笔 writing brush

绘画毛笔 hair pencil

颜色铅笔 coloured pencil, crayon

墨条 ink-stick

墨汁 Chinese ink

墨砚(砚台) inkstone, inkslab

墨水瓶 inkpot, inkbottle

墨水台 inkstand

去墨水剂 ink eraser

吸墨水纸 blotter, blotting paper

吸墨水纸滚台 blotting pad

橡皮(铅笔擦) rubber, eraser

粉笔擦 blackboard eraser

粉笔 chalk

画笔 painting brush

画板 drawing board

调色板 palette

水彩颜料 water colour

油画颜料 oil colour

树胶水彩颜料 gouache colour

彩色盒 colour box

直尺 ruler

丁字尺 T-square

三棱尺 triangle scale

三角板 triangle, set square

曲线尺 French curve

量角器 protractor

圆规 compasses

计算尺 slide rule

缩放尺① pantograph

带夹书写板② clipboard

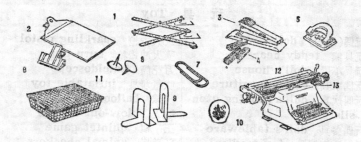

算盘 abacus

袖珍计算机 pocket computer

铅笔刀(铅笔刨) pencil sharpener

裁纸刀 paper knife

钉书机③ stapler

钉书钉④ staple

打孔机⑤ perforator, punch

铁皮夹子⑥ clip

回形针⑦ paper clip

大头针 pin

图钉(按钉)⑧ thumb tack, drawing pin

纸剪子 paper scissors

胶水 glue, mucilage

去胶剂 glue-dispenser

浆糊 paste

透明胶带 adhesive tape, scotch tape

封蜡(火漆) sealing wax

橡皮筋 rubber band

书挡(书立)⑨ bookend

镇纸(纸压)⑩ paper-weight

橡皮图章 rubber stamp

日期章 date stamp

印台 inkpad

钢印(凹凸印) embossed seal

海绵盒 damper, moisting sponge

公文柜 filing cabinet

卷宗 file

报纸夹 newspaper file

铁线篮(文件篮)⑪ wire basket, file basket, in-and-out basket

废纸篓 waste-paper basket

打字机⑫ typewriter, typing machine

打字色带⑬ copying ribbon

打字蜡纸 stencil paper

改正液 correction fluid

油印机 mimeograph

铁笔 stencil pen, stylus

刻写钢板(模板) stencil-plate

蜡纸 stencil paper

墨滚 inking roller

油墨 printing ink

复印机 duplicating machine, duplicator

拷贝机 copying apparatus

直接影印机 photostat, photocopying machine

书签 book-mark

## 玩 具 Toy

玩偶(娃娃)　**doll**
玩具熊　**teddy bear**
玩具小屋　**doll's house**
玩偶家具　**doll's furniture**
玩偶炊具　**doll's cooking utensils**
玩偶餐具　**doll's tableware**
玩偶医疗器具　**toy medical apparatus**
摇鼓　**shaker**
小铃鼓　**tambourine**
小喇叭　**toy trumpet**
玩具钢琴　**toy piano**
积木　**blocks, bricks**
六面画　**picture cubes**
算术方木　**arithmetic blocks**
字母方木　**alphabet blocks**
拼图板　**picture puzzle**
拼图胶粒　**plastic picture peg**
胶泥　**plasticine**
玩具小人(公仔)　**figurine**
不倒翁　**roly-poly, tumbler**
陀螺　**top**
惯性小汽车　**friction toy car**
发条式货车　**clockwork toy truck**
发条式火车　**clockwork toy train**
电动式轮船　**battery-operated toy ship**
惯性飞机　**friction toy plane**
喷水手枪　**water pistol**

发火手枪　**sparkling pistol**
喷火冲锋枪　**burp gun**
万花筒　**kaleidoscope**
吹气玩具　**inflatable toy**
气球　**balloon**
吹龙　**blow-out dragon**
王子棋　**quintet game**
斗兽棋　**animal checkers**
弹子跳棋　**marble checkers**
铁环　**hoop**
弹弓　**catapult**
跳绳　**skipping rope**
橡皮筋　**skipping rubber-band**
毽子　**shuttlecock**
摇马　**rocking horse**
叫鸭　**quacking duck**
儿童学步车　**go-cart, baby walker**
儿童三轮车　**child's tricycle**
跷板　**seesaw**
秋千　**swing**
滑梯　**children's slide**
七巧板　**tangram**
猪形储蓄罐　**piggy bank**
刺绣玩具　**embroidered toy**
泥塑玩具　**clay toy**
陶瓷玩具　**ceramic toy**
绒毛玩具　**plush toy**
棉鸟　**cotton bird**
通花玩具　**crocheted toy**
皮毛玩具　**fur toy**
电子玩具　**electronic toy**

## 珠 宝 Jewelry

珠宝首饰　**jewelry**
装饰品　**ornament**

宝石　**jewel, precious stone**
天然的　**genuine**

| | | | |
|---|---|---|---|
| 人造的 | artificial | 珍珠 | pearl |
| 仿制品 | imitation | 镀金的 | gilded |
| 假的 | fake | 镶金的 | inlaid with gold |
| 钻石 | diamond | 金饰 | gold jewelry |
| 红宝石 | ruby | 印章戒指 | signet ring |
| 蓝宝石 | sapphire | 手镯 | bracelet |
| 紫晶石 | amethyst | 耳环 | earring |
| 金星石 | golden star stone | 耳扣 | earclip |
| 虎眼石 | tiger-eye | 项链 | necklace |
| 松石 | turquoise | 袖扣 | cuff-link |
| 浮雕宝石 | cameo | 别针 | pin |
| 白玉 | white jade | 坠子 | pendant |
| 翡翠 | green jade, jadeite | 胸针 | brooch |
| 碧玉 | jasper | 饰钮 | stud |
| 绿玉 | emerald | 一串珠子(念珠) | beadroll |
| 黑玉 | jet | 珠袋 | bead purse |
| 珊瑚 | coral | 金银丝镶嵌珠宝 | filigree jewelry |
| 玛瑙 | agate | | |
| 玳瑁 | shell of hawksbill turtle | 鼻烟壶 | snuff bottle |

## 杂 项　Miscellaneous

| | | | |
|---|---|---|---|
| 玻璃器皿 | glassware | | hot-water bag |
| 搪瓷器皿 | enamelware | 痰盂 | spittoon |
| 瓷器 | porcelain | 盥洗用品 | toilet articles |
| 铝制品 | aluminium ware | 毛巾 | towel |
| 饭盆 | rice basin | 浴巾 | bath towel |
| 饭盒 | lunch box, (Brit.) mess-tin, (US) mess-kit | 手帕(手绢) | handkerchief |
| 手提多层饭盒(食篮) | food carrier | 香皂 | toilet soap |
| | | 药皂 | medicated soap |
| 热水瓶 | thermos bottle, vacuum flask | 洗发粉 | shampoo |
| | | 洗衣皂 | laundry soap |
| 冰瓶 | ice bottle | 海绵 | bath sponge |
| 保温杯 | vacuum cup | 脸盆 | wash-basin |
| 冷水瓶 | water bottle | 洗衣粉 | detergent |
| 旅行水壶 | traveller's water bottle, canteen | 去污粉 | cleanser |
| | | 牙刷 | tooth brush |
| 热水袋 | hot-water bottle, | 洁牙剂 | dentifrice |
| | | 牙膏 | tooth paste |

漱口剂　mouth-wash
香脂　cold cream
牙粉　tooth powder
雪花膏　vanishing cream
爽身粉　talcum powder
挎包(书包)　satchel
小背包　musette bag
背包　knapsack
手提包　handbag
网兜　string bag, net bag
旅行袋　travelling bag, carryall
旅行皮包　portmanteau
公文包　briefcase, portfolio
手提箱　suitcase
雨伞　umbrella, gamp
阳伞　parasol, sun umbrella

干湿两用雨衣　mackintosh
雨衣　rain coat
缩骨伞　telescopic umbrella
竹雨帽　bamboo rain hat
雨披　rain cape, poncho
自行车雨衣　rain coat for bicyclist
衣架　coat hanger
晾衣绳　clothesline
晒衣夹　clothes-peg
搔背(不求人)　back-scratcher
挖耳勺　earpick
羽毛掸子　feather-duster
煤油灯　kerosine lamp
马灯　barn lantern
汽灯　gas lamp

# 食品市场　Food Market

## 肉 类　Meats

肉店　the butcher's
(宰好的)牲畜躯体　carcass
猪肉　pork
肩肉　pork shoulder
后腿肉　ham
里脊(柳肉)　tenderloin, fillet
腰肉(上肉)　loin
排骨　spareribs
背板肥肉　fatback

腹肉(泡腩)　pork belly
软边　flank, side
五花腩条　bacon strip
上前胛　butt
肘肉(猪踭)　pork hock
猪脚(猪手)　pig's feet, trotter
猪头　pig's head
猪尾　pig's tail
板油　leaf fat

小猪　piglet, pigling
乳猪　suckling pig
羊肉　mutton
羊羔肉　lamb
山羊肉　goat meat
兔肉　rabbit meat
小牛肉　veal
牛肉　beef
前腿肉　shank
后腿肉　round
里脊(牛柳)　tenderloin, fillet
腰肉(腰窝头)　sirloin
打捧(臀肉)　rump
胸肉(牛腩)　brisket
软肋　beef flank
颈肉(花头)　chuck
牛尾　ox-tail
杂肉　variety meat
内脏　viscera, entrails
肝　liver
心　heart
肾(腰子)　kidney
大肠　intestines
小肠　chitterlings
肚　tripe
牛重瓣胃　manyplies (omasum)
胰　sweetbread

肉馅　meat filling
碎肉　mince, minced meat
肉丸　meat ball
肉片　meat slice
肉丝　shredded meat
肉丁　meat dice, meat cube
盘菜　portioned dish ingredients, dish ingredient set
罐头肉　canned meat
烧腊店　barbecuer and curer's shop
烧(烤的)全猪　barbecue
烧肉　roast pork
腊肉　cured meat
卤肉　marinated meat
烟肉(熏肉)　bacon
香肠　sausage
大红肠　Bologna sausage
猪牛肉混合香肠　frankfurter
色拉米香肠　salami
野味　game
野猪肉　wild boar meat
野兔肉　hare meat
狍子肉　roe deer meat
黄猄肉　muntjac meat
獐子肉　river deer meat
果子狸肉　masked civet meat

## 禽　类　Fowls

三鸟店　poultry dealer
家禽　poultry
鸡　chicken
母鸡　hen
小母鸡　pullet
公鸡　cock, rooster
阉鸡　capon
火鸡(吐绶鸡)　turkey

鸭　duck
番鸭(麝香鸭)　musk duck
泥鸭(菜鸭)　table duck
鹅　goose
鸽　pigeon
胸肉　white (breast) meat
腿肉　dark meat
(鹅、鸭)掌　web

翼　wing

鸡鸭杂　giblets

珍肝　gizzard and liver

猎禽　game bird

野鸡(山鸡,雉)①　pheasant

松鸡②　grouse

鹧鸪③　partridge

斑鸠④　turtledove

竹鸡⑤　bamboo

沙雏⑥　snipe

野鸭⑦　mallard

雁(野鹅)⑧　wild goose

鹌鹑⑨　quail

禾花雀　ricebird

麻雀　sparrow

蛋　egg

蛋白　egg white

蛋黄　egg yolk

鲜蛋　fresh egg

冻蛋　frozen egg

咸蛋　salt egg

皮蛋　preserved egg

## 鱼　类　Fish

鱼店　fishmonger's

淡水鱼　freshwater fish

鲤鱼⑩　carp

鲫鱼⑪　crucian carp

金鱼　goldfish

草鱼(鲩)⑫　grass carp

青鱼(黑鲩)　black carp

鲢鱼⑬　silver carp

鳙鱼(大头)⑭　bighead, fathead

鲮鱼⑮　mud carp

团头鲂(武昌鱼)　Wuchang black bream

鳊(北京鳊)⑯　Beijing bream

鳜鱼(桂鱼)⑰　Chinese perch

非洲鲫　bolti

乌鳢(生鱼)⑱　snakehead mullet

鳑鱼⑲　minnow

胭脂鱼(火烧鳊)　Chinese sucker

鲶鱼(总称)　catfish

欧洲鲶鱼　sheatfish

胡子鲶(塘虱)⑳　Chinese catfish

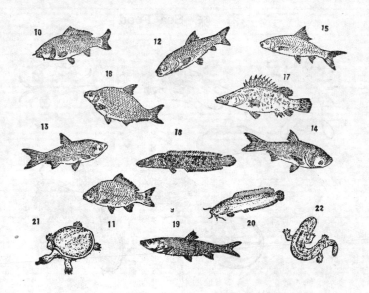

黄鳝　mud eel
泥鳅　loach
海鳝(白鳝)　white eel
甲鱼(水鱼，鳖)㉑　turtle
娃娃鱼(大鲵)㉒　giant salam-
　　ander
田鸡　meat frog
咸水鱼　saltwater fish
鲥鱼　Yangtze shad
鲈鱼　bass
石斑鱼　grouper
碟鱼　plaice, flounder
鲟鱼　sturgeon
鲑鱼　salmon
大马哈鱼　dog salmon
黄花鱼　yellow croaker
鲳鱼　pomfret
曹白鱼(鳓)　herring

青鱼(鲱)　Pacific herring
池鱼(圆鲹)　scad
沙鱼　shark
鲸鱼　whale
鳘,鳕　cod
凤尾鱼　long-tailed anchovy
沙丁鱼　sardine
金枪鱼　tuna
比目鱼(鲽、鳎、鲆的总称)　sole
狮子鱼(剥皮鱼)　snailfish
飞鱼　flying fish
鳟鱼　trout
带鱼　cutlass fish, hair tail
马鲛鱼　mackeral
银鱼　glass fish
蛇鲻(狗棍)　lizard fish
咸鱼　salt fish

# 海　味　Sea Food

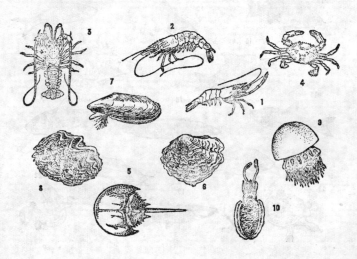

海味店　sea food store
虾蟹贝类　shellfish
青虾(沼虾)① shrimp
对虾(明虾)② prawn
龙虾③ lobster
虾仁　shelled shrimp
蟹④ crab
蟹膏(蟹黄)　crab roe, crab spawn
蟹钳　crab pincers
鲎(蟹鲎)⑤ king crab, horse-shoe crab
海螺　conch
牡蛎(蚝)⑥ oyster
贻贝(淡菜)⑦ dried mussel
鲍鱼　abalone
扇贝　scallop
江瑶柱(干贝)　dried scallop meat

蛤蜊　clam
蛏⑧ razor clam
蚶　ark shell
海蜇⑨ jellyfish
鱿鱼　squid
墨鱼(乌贼)⑩ cuttlefish
海参　sea cucumber, bêche-de-mer
章鱼　octopus
海龟　sea turtle
鱼肚　fish-maw
鱼翅　shark's fin
海星　starfish
海胆　sea urchin (sea hedge-hog)
燕窝　bird's nest
鱼子　hard roe
鱼白　soft roe
鱼子酱　caviar

海带 tangle, seaweed

紫菜 red laver, porphyra

石花菜(大菜) agar

发菜 star jelly

## 蔬 菜 Vegetables

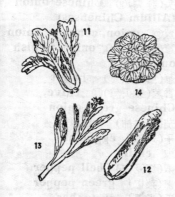

蔬菜店 greengrocer's

白菜⑪ Chinese cabbage, *pakchoi*

大白菜(黄芽白,绍菜)⑫ Beijing cabbage, *baicai*

菜心(菜苔)⑬ false *baicai* flowering cabbage

(上海)榻菜⑭ Shanghai cabbage

青菜(油菜) greens

甘蓝(卷心菜,椰菜)⑮ cabbage

皱叶甘蓝 savoy cabbage

花椰菜(椰菜花)⑯ cauliflower

芥蓝 cabbage mustard

球茎甘蓝(芥蓝头)⑰ kohlrabi

芜菁甘蓝(洋大头菜)⑱ rutabaga

芥菜 leaf mustard

芜菁 turnip

榨菜(茎用芥菜)⑲ tuber mustard

大头菜(根用芥菜,冲菜)⑳ globular root of mustard

菠菜 spinach

莴苣(生菜) lettuce

皱叶莴苣(玻璃生菜) crinkled lettuce

空心菜(蕹菜) *wengcai*, water spinach

西洋菜(豆瓣菜) watercress

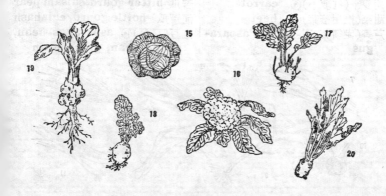

苋菜　**edible amaranth**
芹菜(旱芹)　**celery**
莙荙菜(叶用甜菜, 牛皮菜)　**chard, leaf beet**
茼蒿　**crown daisy**
枸杞菜　**leaf of matrimony vine**
芫荽(香菜)　**coriander**
欧芹(洋芫荽)　**parsley**
萝卜①　**radish**
圆长白萝卜②　**winter white radish**
胡萝卜(红萝卜)③　**carrot**
甜菜(根用恭菜)④　**beet**
芦笋(龙须菜, 石刁柏)⑤　**asparagus**

韭葱(洋大蒜)⑥　**leek**
韭菜⑦　**Chinese leek**
韭黄　**blanched Chinese leek**
蒜⑧　**garlic**
藠头(荞头)⑨　**Chinese onion (Allium Chinenses)**
洋葱⑩　**onion, common onion**
大葱⑪　**spring onion, Welsh onion**
青葱(白头葱)⑫　**shallot**
细香葱(红头葱)⑬　**chive, Chinese green onion**
番茄(西红柿)　**tomato**
茄子(矮瓜)　**eggplant**
辣椒　**chilli**
圆椒(灯笼椒)　**bell pepper**
青椒(菜椒)　**green pepper**
黄瓜(青瓜)　**cucumber**
白瓜　**white melon**
节瓜(毛瓜)　*jiegua*, **wax gourd**
冬瓜　**Chinese wax gourd**
南瓜　**Chinese squash**
美洲南瓜　**pumpkin**
棱角丝瓜(粤丝瓜)　**sponge gourd**
粤水瓜　**vegetable sponge**
苦瓜　**bitter gourd, balsam pear**
葫芦瓜　**bottle gourd, calabash**
豇豆(豆角)⑭　**asparagus bean, string bean, green bean**

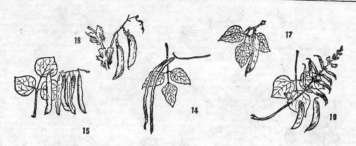

菜豆(玉豆、龙芽豆)⑮ lima bean
扁豆⑯ lentil
云豆(四季豆) kidney bean
刀豆⑰ sword bean
豌豆(麦豆)⑱ pea, garden pea
赤豆(小豆) adzuki bean
黄豆(大豆、毛豆) soya-bean,
　(Am.) soybean
绿豆 mung bean
蚕豆 broad bean
豆荚 bean pod
豆芽 bean sprouts
茭笋 wild rice shoots
莲藕 lotus root
慈姑 arrowhead
荸荠(马蹄) water chestnut

菱角 water caltrop
蘑菇 mushroom
木耳 fungus
竹笋 bamboo shoots
芋头 taro
姜 ginger
山药 yam
马铃薯(土豆) potato
甘薯(番薯) sweet potato
木薯 cassava
参薯(大薯) white yam, wing-
　ed yam
葛(粉葛) kudzu
竹芋 arrowroot
沙葛(豆薯) yam bean

## 水 果 Fruit

水果店 fruit shop (store)
苹果 apple
雪梨 snow pear
沙梨 sand pear
柑桔 orange
蜜柑 Chinese honey orange
甜橙(广柑) sweet orange
桔子 mandarin orange
金桔 kumquat
香橼 citron

柠檬 lemon
椰子 coconut
木瓜(番木瓜) papaya
杨桃(五敛子) carambola
桃 peach
蜜桃 honey peach
李 plum
梅 *mei*, plum
杨梅(香杨梅) bayberry
　(sweet gale)

| 香蕉① | banana | 蒲桃 | rose apple |
|---|---|---|---|
| 大蕉② | plantain | 石榴⑨ | pomegranate |
| 荔枝③ | litchi, lichi, lychee | 番石榴⑩ | guava |
| 龙眼④ | longan | 柿子 | persimmon |
| 黄皮⑤ | wampee | 海棠果 | crab apple |
| 菠萝⑥ | pineapple | 野生海棠果 | cherry apple |
| 木波罗(波罗蜜)⑥ | jack-fruit | 番荔枝 | sweetsop, custard apple |
| 柚子⑦ | pomelo | | |
| 佛手⑧ | finger citron | 芒果⑪ | mango |
| 佛手柑 | bergamot | 无花果⑫ | fig |
| 杏 | apricot | 人心果⑬ | sapodilla |
| 樱桃 | cherry | 山楂⑭ | haw |
| 葡萄 | grape | 枇杷⑮ | loquat |

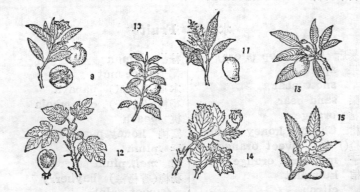

榴莲　durian
苹婆(凤眼果)　seed of the
　noble bottle tree
草莓　strawberry
枣子　Chinese date, jujube
橄榄　Chinese olive
葡萄柚　grapefruit (Toronja)
面包果　breadfruit

牛油果(鳄梨)　aquacarte
西瓜　water melon
香瓜　musk melon
哈蜜瓜　Hami musk melon,
　Hami cantaloupe
果蔗　sugar-cane
罐头水果　canned fruit

## 杂 货 Grocery

食品杂货店　grocery
干菜　dried vegetable
脱水菜　dehydrated vegetable
白菜干　dried Chinese
　cabbage
干姜粉　ginger powder
火蒜　toasted garlic
笋干　dried bamboo shoots
香菇(冬菇)　dried mushroom
竹荪⑯　bamboo fungus
黄花菜(金针)　dried day-lily
木耳　fungus
白木耳(银耳, 雪耳)　white
　fungus
百合　dried lily bulb
坚壳果　nut
栗子(板栗)⑰　chestnut
榛子　hazelnut

榄仁　olive kernel
花生　peanut
腰果　cashew nut
核桃(胡核)　walnut
杏仁　apricot kernel
椰子蓉　grated coconut
白果(银杏)⑱　ginko fruit
莲子　lotus seed
芡实(鸡头)　seed of gorgon
　plant, euryale seed
薏米⑲　Job's tears
瓜子　melon seed
葵花子　sunflower seed
槟榔⑳　betelnut
干果　dried fruit
红枣　dried red jujube
　(Chinese date)
葡萄干　raisin

16　17　18　19　20

无核葡萄干　currant, seedless raisin

杏干　dried apricot

李干(嘉应子)　dried plum

桂元肉　dried longan pulp

柿饼　dried persimmon

腌制果　preserved fruit

蜜枣　candied jujube

桔胚(桔饼)　candied orange

糖水荔枝　lichee in syrup

咸水杨梅　bayberry brine

话梅　preserved plum

李脯(梅脯)　prune

山楂脯　preserved haw

什锦蜜饯　assorted candied fruits

糖冬瓜片　sugared wax gourd slices

蜜饯芒果　candied mango

糖姜片　sugared ginger slices

五味榄　spiced Chinese olive

腌制菜(泡菜)　pickles

咸菜　salted vegetable

榨菜　pickled tuber mustarb

冬菜　preserved shreds of cabbage

什锦菜　assorted pickles

咸酸荞头　pickled Chinese onion

糖醋蒜头　sweet and sour garlic

酸黄瓜　pickled cucumber

莳萝腌黄瓜　drill pickle

酸萝卜　pickled radish

## 烟　店　The Tobacconist's

烟草　tobacco

烟丝　cut tobacco, pipe tobacco

鼻烟　snuff

卷烟　cigarette

手卷烟　hand-rolled cigarette

雪茄　cigar

方头雪茄　cheroot

过滤嘴香烟　filter-tipped cigarette

烟碱(尼古丁)　nicotine

烟的香味　aroma

特长的香烟　king-size(d) cigarette

一包香烟　a packet of cigarettes

一条香烟　a carton of cigarettes

烟纸　cigarette paper

烟盒　cigarette case

锡纸　tin-foil

玻璃纸　cellophane

烟嘴　cigarette holder

烟斗　pipe

水烟筒　water pipe, hubble-hubble

烟丝袋　tobacco-pouch

打火机　cigarette lighter

火石　flint

充气火机　gas lighter

火柴　match

烟头(香烟屁股)　cigarette end, cigarette butt

烟灰缸　ashtray

# 饮食业 The Restaurant Industry

## 饮食店 Restaurants

饭店(餐馆, 酒家) restaurant
餐厅(餐室) dining-room
宴会厅 banquet room
大众化饮食店 eating house, cookshop
食堂 canteen
素食饭店 vegetarian restaurant
清真饭店 Muslim restaurant
小食店 snack bar
(食品)小卖部 buffet
面食店 noodle bar
西餐馆 café
快餐饭店 quick-lunch bar, fast-food restaurant
自助饭店(食堂) cafeteria
酒吧 bar

咖啡馆 coffeehouse
茶室(茶馆) teahouse
冰室 ice-cream parlour
冷饮店(柜) soda fountain
地方风味 distinctive flavour of local cuisine
饭店经理 restaurant manager
厨师 cook
厨师长 chef, head cook
见习厨师 assistant cook
服务人员 service worker
男服务员 waiter
女服务员 waitress
收款员 cashier
素食者 vegetarian
食品鉴尝家 gourmet

## 餐厅业务 Dining-room Service

餐(一顿饭) meal
早餐 breakfast
午餐 lunch
晚餐 supper
主餐(正餐) dinner
午后茶点 afternoon tea

点心 refreshment(s)
丰盛的一餐 substantial meal, square meal
便餐 pot-luck, simple fare, light meal
斋戒 fast

开斋 breaking one's fast
戒口(忌口) dieting
吃特别规定的食物 being on special diet
客餐(包餐) table d'hote
散餐(零点菜) a la carte
订餐桌 booking (reserving) a table
摆桌开餐 laying the table for dinner
点菜 ordering
写点菜单 taking an order
菜谱 menu, bill of fare
介绍菜色 recommending dishes
上菜 serving
餐前小食 hors d'oeuvre
开胃品 appetizer
主菜 main course, (Am.) entrée
餐后甜品 sweet, (Am.) dessert
一份(食物) portion (of food)
胃口好 good appetite
胃口差 poor appetite
收餐具(清餐桌) clearing the table
吃剩的东西 leftover(s)
结帐(开单) making out the bill
分单结帐 separate bills
合单结帐 one bill for all
付帐 paying (the bill)
收款台 cashier's counter
收据 receipt
找头(零钱) change
宴会 dinner-party, banquet, feast

茶会 tea party
招待酒会 reception dinner
自助晚餐 buffet supper
鸡尾酒会 cocktail party
请帖 invitation card
祝酒词 toast
为……干杯 proposing a toast to…
干杯! Bottoms up!
主人 host
客人 guest
订餐 ordering in advance
预定每位付钱(标准)多少? What's the figure (payment) you have in mind? (How much would you like to pay for each plate?)
每位十元,酒水另计。 10 yuan a plate, drinks extra.
请摆四个位子。 Please set plates for four.
这个菜要隔日预订。 This dish is ordered one day in advance.
请多摆一个位。 Another plate (cover), please.
你要什么菜? What would you like (to take)?
我们不收小费。 We don't take tips.
对不起,算错了帐。 Sorry, there's a mistake in the bill.
你多付了一角钱。 It should be 10 fen less.
你少付了五毛钱。 It should be 50 fen more.

# 厨 具 Kitchen Equipment

厨房　kitchen
食橱(碗柜)　kitchen cupboard, kitchen cabinet
壁橱　built-in cupboard
炊具　cookware
炉灶　range
柴炉　firewood stove
炭炉　charwood stove
煤炉① coal stove

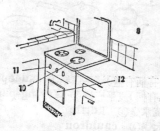

烤箱⑫ oven
电炉　electric stove
电子炉　electronic oven
微波烤箱　microwave oven
太阳灶　solar cooker
火锅(边炉)　chafing-dish
烹饪具　cooking utensils
锅(镬)具⑬ wok works
锅(镬)⑭ wok
锅盖⑮ cover
锅架⑯ wok stand
锅铲⑰ spatula, slice
长柄勺⑱ ladle
蒸架⑲ rack

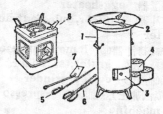

炉膛② fire box
通风门③ draught-door
煤球(蜂窝煤)④ briquette
通条⑤ poker
火钳⑥ tongs
煤灰铲⑦ ash-shovel
柴刀　wood chopper
风箱　bellows
酒精炉　spirit stove
煤油炉⑧ kerosene stove
煤气灶⑨ gas-range
煤气喷嘴⑩ gas-ring,
　gas-burner
煤气开关⑪ gas-stop, gas-cock

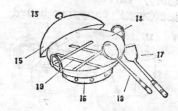

磨刀石　grindstone, knife sharpener

瓜刨⑫　peeler, paring knife

拔毛钳　clipper

切片机　slicer, slicing machine

绞肉机　meat grinder

去皮机　skinner

搅拌器　blender

打蛋器　egg-beater

榨汁器　juicer, juice extracter

柠檬挤汁器⑬　lemon squeezer

刨丝器⑭　grater, shredder

咖啡磨⑮　coffee grinder

(蒸汽加压)煮咖啡器　espresso machine

石磨　mill

过滤器　filter

容器　container

瓦器(陶器)　crockery

盆⑯　basin

提桶⑰　pail

木桶⑱　bucket

缸(瓮)⑲　vat

坛(广口瓶)⑳　jar

(小口有柄)水罐㉑　jug

(有柄有盖)深平底锅①　saucepan

(有柄)浅平底锅②　frying-pan

烧水壶③　kettle

大锅④　cauldron

砂锅　casserole

铝锅⑤　aluminium pot

蒸笼⑥　steamer

压力锅⑦　pressure cooker

胶圈⑧　rubber gasket

限压阀⑨　pressure control valve

安全阀⑩　fusible safety plug

电饭锅⑪　electric cooker

电热水器　electric heater

烤炉　roaster

烤架　grill

烤叉　spit

厨刀　chopping knife, kitchen knife

剁刀　mincing knife

切肉刀　carver

砧板(木墩)　chopping board

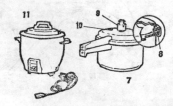

| | |
|---|---|
| 擀面杖 | rolling pin |
| 面板 | breadboard |
| 模子 | mould, form |
| 筛 | sieve |
| 粗筛 | screen |
| 箩斗(粉筛)㉜ | sifter |
| 揉面机(和面机) | kneader, mixer |
| 面条机 | noodle maker |
| 制面包机 | bread maker |
| 烤面包机 | toaster |
| 面包架 | toast rack |
| 包饺子机 | dumpling maker |
| 洗涤器具 | implements for washing |
| 洗碗机 | dish-washer, washing-up machine |
| 洗碗池 | washing-up sink |
| 漂清池(过碗池) | rinsing sink |
| 洗碗布 | dishcloth |
| 抹碗布 | dish-towel |
| 抹桌布 | duster |
| 洗瓶刷 | bottle-brush |
| 去污粉 | cleanser |
| 围裙 | apron |
| 瓶塞起子 | cork screw |
| 开瓶刀 | bottle opener |
| 罐头刀 | can opener |
| 坚果破壳器 | nut cracker |
| 提秤 | steelyard, lever scales |
| 磅秤 | scales |

| | |
|---|---|
| 大水罐㉒ | pitcher |
| 瓦壶㉓ | crock, earthenware pot |
| 金属圆罐㉔ | tin, (Am.) can |
| 水壶㉕ | water-bottle |
| 口盅㉖ | mug |
| 水勺㉗ | dipper |
| 瓢㉘ | gourd dipper |
| 漏斗㉙ | funnel |
| 漏勺㉚ | skimmer |
| 笊篱㉛ | strainer |
| 冰箱 | ice-box |
| 电冰箱 | refrigerator |

## 餐 具 Tableware

| | |
|---|---|
| 餐具柜 | sideboard |
| 一套餐具 | dinner set, dinner service |
| 瓷器餐具 | porcelain dinnerware |
| 银器餐具 | silver (plate) |
| 金器餐具 | gold plate |
| 餐巾 | table napkin, serviette |
| 餐纸 | paper napkin |
| 香巾 | towel |

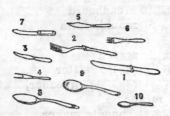

筷子　chopsticks
筷子架　chopsticks rest
餐刀①　table knife
餐叉②　table fork
肉刀③　carving knife
肉叉④　carving fork
鱼刀⑤　fish knife
鱼叉⑥　fish fork
水果刀⑦　dessert knife
餐匙⑧　tablespoon
汤匙⑨　soup spoon
茶匙⑩　teaspoon
汤勺　soup ladle
碟(浅碟)⑪　plate
汤碟⑫　soup plate
(有盖)汤盅⑬　tureen
碗⑭　bowl
奶酪罐　creamer, cream pitcher
五味架　cruet-stand
醋瓶　vinegar cruet

酱油瓶　soy cruet
胡椒瓶　pepper caster, pepper shaker
盐盅　salt cellar
芥末罐　mustard pot
豉油碟　soy dish
牙签筒　toothpick holder
茶具⑮　tea set, tea things
茶壶⑯　teapot
茶杯⑰　teacup
垫碟⑱　saucer
托盘⑲　tray
咖啡具⑳　coffee set
　咖啡壶㉑　coffee pot
　咖啡过滤壶㉒　percolator
　奶缸㉓　milk jug
　糖盅㉔　sugar-bowl
玻璃器皿　glassware
水瓶　carafe
玻璃杯　glass
耐热玻璃罐　pyrex canister

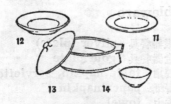

平底杯㉕ tumbler
(有耳)大杯㉖ mug
啤酒杯 beer mug
有脚器皿 stemware
高脚杯 goblet
烈酒杯㉗ liqueur glass
葡萄酒杯㉘ wine glass
甜酒杯㉙ cordial glass
香槟酒杯㉚ champagne glass

## 烹 调  Cookery

烹调书 cookbook
主料 main ingredient
配料 subsidiary ingredient
装饰料(配头) garnish
芡(调味汁) dressing, starchy sauce
芡粉 cooking starch
食料处理 processing of foodstuffs
屠宰(牲畜) slaughtering
褪毛弄净 dressing
光鸡 dressed chicken
去骨 boning
去骨鸭掌 boned duck web
去壳 shelling
虾仁 shelled shrimp
去皮 skinning
去皮田鸡 skinned frog
去鳞 scaling
切片 slicing
鱼片 sliced fish, fish slices
切丝 shredding
肉丝 shredded pork, pork shreds
切丁 dicing, cubing
鸡丁 diced chicken, chicken cubes
剁碎 mincing
剁碎的肉 minced meat, mince
捣烂 mashing
薯泥 mashed potatoes
泡浸 soaking
填(酿) stuffing
上浆 dipping in batter
上粉 rolling in starch
调味 seasoning
(加香料)调制 spicing
腌制 pickling
卤制 marinating
腊制 curing
烹调 cookery, culinary art
煮, 做, 调制 cooking, preparing
爆(快炒) sautéing
炒 (stir-) frying
煎 pan-frying
炸 deep-frying
炖, 焖 stewing
焖, 烧 braising, fricasseeing
红烧 braising
煨 simmering
扒 frying and simmering
蒸 steaming

白灼(烫) scalding
煮,滚 boiling
氽 pouring boiling soup into vessel containing ingredients
煮成半熟 parboiling
水煮荷包蛋 poaching
勾芡(打芡) pouring starchy sauce over the dish
烧,烤 roasting
(在烤架上)烤炙 grilling
熏 smoking
烘 baking
焙(炙) broiling
炸猪油 frying, rendering
掌握火候 fire (heat) control
武火 intense fire
文火 slow fire
文武火 moderate fire
不太熟 underdone
很嫩 rare
适中 medium
烧得恰到好处 done to a turn
熟透 well-done
过熟 over-done
烧焦 burned
五噬 five flavours
香 fragrant
脆 crisp
松(酥) short
肥(腻) rich

浓 thick
六味 six tastes
鲜(味美) delicious, tasty
甜 sweet
酸 sour
苦 bitter
辣 hot, peppery, pungent
咸 salty
无味 tasteless, flat
新鲜 fresh
陈腐 stale, tainted
未成熟(生) raw
成熟 ripe
嫩 tender
老(韧) tough
肥 fat
瘦(精) lean
硬 hard
软 soft
味浓 highly seasoned
清淡 light, mild
油腻 oily, greasy
难消化 heavy
涩 astringent
腥 rank smell of fish
膻(臊) rank smell of mutton
哈喇(油腐味) rancid
馊(变味) gone bad, spoiled, tainted
臭 stinking

## 调味品 Condiments

作料 seasoning
味精 gourmet powder, monosodium glutamate
盐 salt
精盐 table salt

食油 edible oil, (Am.) cooking oil
植物油 vegetable oil
花生油 peanut oil
茶〔籽〕油 tea (-seed) oil

菜〔籽〕油　rape oil
芝麻油　sesame oil
大豆油　soya-bean oil
椰子油　coconut oil
辣椒油　chilli oil
动物油　animal oil
猪油　lard
(牛羊)板油　suet
黄油(牛油)　butter
奶油　cream
干酪　cheese
人造奶油　margarine
调味汁　sauce
豉油(中国酱油)　soy sauce
蚝油　oyster sauce
鱼露　fish sauce
固体酱油　solid sauce
番茄汁　tomato sauce
辣酱油　worcester sauce
辣椒酱　chilli paste
番茄菜椒酱　chilli sauce
番茄酱　ketchup, catsup
酸辣酱　chutney
豆瓣酱(面豉)　soyabean paste
肉酱　meat paste
果酱　jam
菠萝酱　pineapple jam
桔子酱　marmalade
蛋黄酱　mayonnaise
醋　vinegar
香醋　aromatic vinegar
糖　sugar
红糖　brown sugar

砂糖　granulated sugar
方糖　cube sugar
冰糖　rock sugar
焦糖　caramel
糖酱　syrup
糖精　saccharin
麦芽糖　malt sugar, maltose
蜜糖　honey
香料　spice
香草　vanilla
香精油　essential oil
香料粉(五香粉)　spice powder
胡椒　pepper
芥末　mustard
咖喱　curry
薄荷　mint
桂皮　Chinese cinnamon, cassia bark
陈皮　dried orange peel
八角(大茴香)　Chinese aniseed, star aniseed
欧茴香　aniseed
茴香(小茴香)　fennel
胶料　gelatin
琼脂(大菜、石花菜)　agar
生粉　starch
豆粉　bean powder, pea-starch
色料　food colour
发酵粉　baking powder
面种　sourdough
酵母　yeast
碱水　lye
硼砂　borax

## 饮　料　Beverages

清凉饮料　cooling drink
冷饮　cold drink
冰冻饮料　iced drink

热饮　hot drink
饮用水　drinking water
中国茶　China tea

红茶　black tea
绿茶　green tea
〔香〕花茶　scented tea
茉莉花茶　jasmin(e) tea
乌龙茶　wulong tea
砖茶(茶砖)　brick tea
沏茶(泡茶)　brewing
头泡茶　first brew
浓茶　strong tea
淡茶　weak tea
柠檬茶　lemon tea
咖啡　coffee
牛奶咖啡　white coffee
净咖啡　black coffee
冰冻咖啡　iced coffee
速溶咖啡　instant coffee
可可　cocoa
麦乳精　malted milk
芝麻糊　sesame porridge
杏仁糊　almond porridge
牛奶　milk
酸牛奶　sour milk
奶制品　dairy product, milk product
奶油　cream
奶酪　cheese
奶粉　milk powder
炼奶　condensed milk
浓缩奶　evaporated milk
脱脂奶　skimmed milk
全脂奶　whole milk
冰奶　milk shake
奶油冻　mousse
羊奶　goat's milk
马奶　mare's milk
豆浆　soya milk
瓶装饮料　bottled drink
无酒精的饮料　soft drink
汽水(苏打水)　aerated water, soda water
矿泉水　mineral water
柠檬水　lemonade
桔子水　orangeade
菠萝汁　pineapple juice
柠檬汁汽水　lemon squash
橙汁汽水　orange squash, orangeade
姜汁汽水　ginger beer
可口可乐　coca-cola
啤酒　beer
苦啤酒　bitter
啤酒泡沫　beer froth
桶装散卖啤酒　draught beer
生啤　green beer
淡色啤酒　ale
浓烈黑啤酒　stout
汽酒　sparkling beer
红葡萄酒　red wine
白葡萄酒　white wine
玫瑰香葡萄酒　muscatel
绍兴花雕酒　Shaoxing wine
桂花陈酒　osmanthus wine
糯米酒(黄酒)　glutinous rice wine
苹果酒　cider
桔皮酒　curacao
樱桃酒　maraschino
玫瑰露　rose liquor
兰姆酒　rum
露酒　liqueur
开胃酒　aperitif
补酒　tonic wine
香槟酒　champagne
雪利酒(葡萄酒)　sherry
味美思苦艾酒　vermouth
金酒(杜松子酒)　gin
伏特加酒　vodka
白兰地　brandy

法国白兰地　cognac
鸡尾酒　cocktail
威士忌　whiskey
威士忌加苏打水　whiskey soda
清酒(日本米酒)　sake, saki
五加皮　Wu Jia Pi
竹叶青　bamboo leaf

莲花白　lotus white
茅台酒　maotai
烈酒　liquor, spirits
酒精　alcohol, spirit
六十度的酒　liquor containing
　60% alcohol

## 米面食品　Cereal Foodstuffs

主食　staple food
大米　rice
米粉　rice flour
粉条　rice noodles
排米粉　rice vermicelli
粉丝　bean vermicelli
通心粉　macaroni
米饭　cooked rice
糯米饭　cooked glutinous
　rice
饭焦(锅巴)　rice crust
桃花饭　rice crust with green
　peas and tomato sauce
八宝饭　babao rice
炒饭　fried rice
速煮饭(脱水米饭)　instant
　cooked rice
稀饭(粥)　congee, rice gruel
面粉　wheat flour
精面粉　super flour
面条　noodles
精面条　super noodles
方便面条(即席面条)　instant
　noodles, quick-served
　noodles
袋装食品　bag food
方便食品(即席食品)　instant
　prepared food, shelf-stor-
　age prepared meal

意大利圆面条　spaghetti
生面团　dough
馒头　*mantou* (steamed bun)
窝窝头　steamed corn bread
烧饼　baked wheat cake
油香饼(油条)　friedcake
面包　bread
面包块　loaf
烤面包片　toast
夹心面包片(三明治)　sandwich
鸡蛋三明治　egg sandwich
多层鸡肉火腿三明治　club
　sandwich
汉堡包(夹牛肉面包)　hamburger
热狗(夹香肠面包)　hot dog
煎饼　pancake
印度烙饼　chapati
黑面包　brown bread
裸麦面包(黑面包)　rye bread
面包干　rusk
面包皮　crust
面包屑　crumb
麦片　rolled oats
麦片粥　oatmeal, porridge
面花　Italian pâté
玉米饼　corn cake
小米粥　millet gruel
压缩饼干　condensed biscuit

## 中菜——汤类　Chinese Food—Soup

羹(浓汤)　thick soup

凤凰鱼蓉羹　thick soup of minced fish and egg

西湖牛肉羹　thick soup of minced beef and egg

蟹肉烩鱼翅　thick soup of shark's fin and crabmeat

鸡丝烩鱼翅　thick soup of shark's fin and shredded chicken

鳖肚烩鸡丝　thick soup of cod's maw and shredded chicken

鸭汁烩鱼唇　thick soup of fish-lips and duck essence

北菇烩鸭丝　thick soup of mushroom and shredded duck

鲜虾烩豆腐　thick soup of bean-curd and shrimp

鱼蓉烩豆腐　thick soup of bean-curd and minced fish

蟹肉烩冬蓉　thick soup of crabmeat and mashed wax gourd

龙虎凤大烩　thick soup of snake, cat and chicken

鸡丝浮皮羹　thick soup of puffed pig skin and shredded chicken

上汤燕盏　bird's nest soup

清汤散翅　clear soup of shark's fin

上汤虾丸　shrimp balls clear soup

蟹钳余北菇　clear soup of crabmeat and mushroom

鲜菇余鸡片　sliced chicken and fresh mushroom soup

雪耳余虾丸　shrimp balls soup with white fungus

竹荪余鸡片　sliced chicken soup with bamboo fungus

北菇炖鸡　steamed chicken and mushroom soup

清炖北菇　steamed mushroom soup

清炖子鸡　steamed spring chicken soup

陈皮炖鸭　steamed duck and orange peel soup

番茄蛋花汤　tomato and egg soup

时菜生鱼片汤　clear soup of snakehead mullet and greens

时菜牛肉片汤　clear soup of sliced beef and vegetable

时菜窝蛋汤　poached egg and vegetable soup

时菜猪肝汤　pork liver and vegetable soup

榨菜肉丝汤　shredded pork soup with pickled tuber mustard

紫菜虾米汤　dried shrimp and red laver soup

酸辣汤　sour-and-hot soup

木须汤　sliced pork soup with egg and fungus

三鲜汤　clear soup of three delicious ingredients

清炖凤吞燕　soup of steamed chicken stuffed with bird's nest

海南椰子盅　steamed whole coconut containing diced chicken and ham in soup

白玉藏珍　wax gourd with assorted meats in soup

八宝冬瓜盅　steamed whole wax gourd containing soup with various delicacies

甜芙蓉燕窝　sweet bird's nest soup with egg-white

## 中菜——三鸟类　Poultry

白切鸡　blanched chicken, plain chicken

蒸滑鸡　steamed chicken

炸子鸡　deep-fried spring chicken

红烧全鸡　stewed whole chicken in brown sauce

油淋鸡　boiling oil scalded chicken

茶香鸡　tea-scented chicken

栗子鸡　stewed chicken with chestnuts

砂锅鸡　chicken casserole

上汤浸鸡　boiled chicken in super soup

果汁鸡脯　fried chicken breast in fruit sauce

香滑鸡球　fried chicken fillet in gravy

云腿鸡片　fried sliced chicken with ham

芙蓉鸡片　sliced chicken with egg-white

笋炒鸡丝　fried shredded chicken with bamboo shoots

榄仁鸡丁　fried chicken cubes with olive kernels

宫保鸡丁　sautéd chicken cubes with chilli and peanuts

鲍鱼焖鸡　braised chicken with abalone

广州文昌鸡　sliced chicken with chicken liver and ham

江南百花鸡　chicken skin spread with shrimp paste

金华玉树鸡　sliced chicken and ham with greens

园林香液鸡　steamed chicken in spicy gravy

东江盐焗鸡　salt chicken, Hakka style

碧绿双色卷　chicken fillet and ham with greens

竹园椰奶鸡　chicken and bamboo fungus with cream and coconut juice

牡丹珠圆鸡　chicken and crab roe with shrimp balls

玉液煎鸡饼　fried chicken meat in cream sauce

香麻手撕鸡　shredded chicken in sesame sauce

韭黄炒鸽丝　fried shredded pigeon with blanched leek

木耳烧鸡片 **braised chicken slices with fungus**

木耳穿花鸡腿 **fried drumsticks with fungus**

云腿串鸡翼 **chicken-wing stuffed with ham**

脆炸片皮鸡 **deep-fried chicken with crisp skin**

北京烤鸭 **roast Beijing duck**

鱿鱼鸭片 **fried sliced duck with squid**

四式扒鸭 **braised duck**

香菇扒鸭 **braised duck with mushroom**

菠萝软鸭 **fried duck with pineapple**

茄汁软鸭 **fried duck in tomato sauce**

芝麻鸭肝 **fried duck liver with sesame**

脆皮鸳鸯鸭 **two-coloured crisp duck stuffed with minced shrimp**

东江窝全鸭 **simmered whole duck stuffed with glutinous rice and pork**

出水芙蓉鸭 **sliced duck with egg-white and ham**

百花酿鸭掌 **duck web stuffed with shrimp paste**

脆烤片皮鹅 **roast goose with crisp skin**

潮州烧雁鹅 **roast goose, Chaozhou style**

木耳炖全鸭 **stewed whole duck with fungus**

# 中菜——鱼虾类 Sea Food

清蒸鲩鱼 **steamed grass carp**

清蒸鳊鱼 **steamed bream**

五柳鲩鱼 **grass carp with pickles**

韭黄生鱼球 **fried snakehead mullet slices with blanched leek**

香滑山斑球 **fried mullet slices**

红烧鲤鱼 **braised carp in brown sauce**

姜葱焖鲤鱼 **braised carp with ginger and chives**

碧绿桂鱼卷 **Chinese perch rolls with greens**

菜蕗鲈鱼球 **fried bass slices with greens**

金腿三拼鲈 **steamed bass slices with ham and mushroom**

酥炸石斑块 **deepfried grouper slices**

豉汁石斑球 **fried grouper slices in soy sauce**

笋炒鲟鱼片 **fried sturgeon slices**

松子鱼 **cone-shaped deep-fried fish**

煎封鲳鱼 **fried pomfret**

糟溜鱼片 **stewed sliced fish in fermented rice sauce**

翡翠煎鲍脯 **fried abalone with greens**

鳖肚炖山瑞 **stewed turtle**

with cod's maw

生炒水鱼丝 **fried shredded turtle**

砂锅焗水鱼 **turtle casserole**

火腩焖大鳝 **braised eel with roast pork**

白灼海虾 **blanched prawns**

脆炸大虾 **deep-fried prawns**

干煎虾碌 **fried prawn with ketchup**

香汁焗龙虾 **fricasseed lobster in spicy gravy**

油泡虾仁 **fried shelled shrimps**

油泡虾九 **fried shrimp balls**

云腿虾茸夹 **fried ham sandwiched with minced shrimp**

百花酿香菇 **steamed mushroom stuffed with shrimp paste**

白灼海螺片 **blanched sliced conch**

冬笋炒螺片 **fried conch slices with bamboo shoots**

脆炸生蚝 **deepfried fresh oyster**

蛋煎虾饼 **fried shrimp-and-egg patties**

酥炸蟹盒 **deep-fried cases of** fat pork stuffed with crabmeat

清蒸膏蟹 **steamed crab**

蚝油网鲍片 **abalone slices in oyster sauce**

虾子扒海参 **fried and simmered beche-de-mer with shrimp roe**

蒜子挑柱脯 **stewed scallop meat with garlic**

石上鸣秋蝉 **steamed grouper slices spread with minced shrimp and mushrooms**

木耳炒虾仁 **fried shrimp with fungus**

百花玉环 **steamed fish-maw stuffed with shrimp paste**

芙蓉蟹片 **deep-fried slices of crabmeat and egg-white**

巧制金银鱼 **gold-and-silver fish**

白雪映红梅 **steamed patties of crabmeat and minced shrimp with crab roe on top**

百花酿蟹钳 **fried crab pincers stuffed with shrimp paste**

凉拌蜇皮 **cold jellyfish in soy sauce**

## 中菜——肉类 Meat Dishes

菜炒牛肉 **sliced beef sauté with greens**

蚝油炒牛肉 **sliced beef sauté in oyster sauce**

笋炒牛肉 **beef sauté with bamboo shoots**

茄汁煎牛柳 **fried beef fillet with tomato sauce**

滑蛋牛肉 **scrambled eggs and beef**

咖喱牛肉 **beef curry**

茄汁牛肉饼 **fried beef cake**

with tomato sauce

红焖牛腩 braised brisket of beef in brown sauce

椒子牛肉丝 fried shredded beef with chilli

炸牛肉丸 deep-fried beef balls

梅子蒸排骨 steamed pork ribs with pickled plums

香酥肉(咕噜肉) sweet-and-sour pork

韭黄肉丝 fried shredded pork with blanched Chinese leek

榄仁肉丁 fried diced pork with olive kernels

威化猪肝 fried pork liver with shrimp wafers

菠萝香酥肉 sweet-and-sour pork with pineapple

蛋煎猪脑 scrambled eggs and pig's brain

白云猪手 sweet-and-sour pig's feet

炒木须肉 fried shreds of pork, fungus and egg

笋炒腰花 fried pork kidney with bamboo shoots

炸肉丸 deep-fried pork balls

荔埔芋扣肉 steamed pork slices sandwiched with taro

菜炒肉片 fried sliced pork with greens

酥炸野鸡卷 deep-fried pork-and-ham rolls

脆皮三丝卷 crisp rolls of pork, sea-slug and bamboo shoots

东江春卷 egg rolls stuffed with minced meat and shrimp

回锅肉 boiled and fried pork slices in chilli sauce

北京涮羊肉 thin sliced mutton to be cooked at table in a chafing-dish

冬菇焖狗肉 stewed dog meat with mushrooms

八宝酿豆腐 stuffed bean-curd

什锦豆腐煲 bean-curd casserole

明炉叉烧 roast fillet of pork, Guangzhou style

烧全猪(广东烧肉) barbecued pork

卤水牛肉 spiced beef

卤水猪舌 spiced pig's tongue

卤眼润(肝) spiced liver stuffed with pork

野味山珍 game

五彩炒蛇丝 fried snake shreds

菠萝斑鸠片 fried turtle dove with pineapple

煎酿禾花雀 ricebirds stuffed with liver and sausage

红烧果子狸 braised masked civet

炖穿山甲 stewed pangolin

火腿穿田鸡腿 fried frog legs stuffed with ham

东江酿豆腐 stuffed bean-curd, Hakka style

大良炒牛奶 fried milk with chicken liver and shrimp

木耳凉拌三丝 mixed shreds of fungus, cucumber and vermicelli

鼎湖上素 assorted vegetarian dish, Dinghu style

七彩拼冷盘 assorted hors

d'oeuvres

象形拼冷盘(孔雀等形)　assorted

hors d'oeuvres (in shape of peacock, etc.)

## 中式点心　Refreshments (*Dimsum*)

饺子　*jiaozi*, Chinese ravioli (pocket or shell of noodle dough with fillings of meat, shrimp or vegetable, steamed or fried)

干蒸烧买　*shaomai* (filled-pocket of noodle dough, open and frilled on top, cooked by steaming)

包子　*baozi* (steamed bun with various fillings)

叉烧包　*chashaobao* (steamed bun filled with roast pork)

小笼包　steamed meat dumpling

汤圆　glutinous rice dumpling in soup

云吞　*wonton*, dumpling in soup

春卷　spring roll

荔埔芋角　deep-fried taro roll stuffed with meat

炸花卷　fried roll

虾蟹粉果　pocket of rice flour dough stuffed with shrimp and crabmeat

百花蛋黄角　shrimp turnover

鸡粒千层酥　chicken puff

核桃酥　walnut shortcake

杏仁豆腐　almond flavoured bean-curd

松糕　rice flour sponge cake

生磨马蹄糕　water-chestnut jelly

拔丝苹果　toffee apple

拔丝香蕉　toffee banana

油炸雪糕　fried ice-cream

冰糖雪耳　white fungus in sweet soup

白云奶露　almond cream

鲜奶雪耳　white fungus in milk

## 西餐——汤类　Western Food—Soup

肉类清(淡)汤　broth, thin soup

浓(稠)汤　thick soup

牛尾汤　oxtail soup

猪腰汤　kidney soup

咖喱肉汤　mulligatawny

法国肉汤　bouillon

俄罗斯甜菜汤　borsch

素菜浓汤　vegetable puree

茄蓉汤　tomato puree

薯蓉汤　potato soup

意大利菜汤　minestrone

鸡奶油汤　chicken cream soup

白菌奶油汤　mushroom cream soup

泡蛋清汤　poached egg clear soup

火腿丝清汤　sliced ham clear soup

面丝清汤　noodle clear soup

味浓肉类清汤　consomme

鸡粒青豆汤　consomme a la Reine

鸡丝火腿汤　consomme chicken and ham

鸡肝青豆汤　consomme Bavaroise

鸡腿菌丝汤　consomme trois fillet

露笋粒清汤　consomme

Windsor

奶油蟹肉汤　crab-meat potage with cream

(放入汤里的)炸面包粒　crouton

速煮汤料　instant soup mixes

## 西餐——肉类　Meat Dishes

牛排　beefsteak

煎牛肉饼(汉堡牛排)　Hamburg steak

牛肉饼托蛋　Hamburg steak with fried egg

扒牛柳洋葱　club steak and onion

牛柳(里脊)配酸汁　fillet steak with sour sauce

扒牛柳配菜　fillet mignon

扒牛柳白菌　beef fillet and mushroom

扒牛柳鸡肝　beefsteak a la Monte Carlo

铁扒牛排　grilled beefsteak

土豆烧牛肉　goulash

烩牛肉　beef a la mode

红烩牛肉　beef stew

咖喱牛肉　beef curry

小牛肉火腿卷　veal and ham rissole

炒牛肉丝　beef stroganoff

炸牛肉　schnitzel

炸牛肉托蛋　beef Holstem Schnitzel

奶汁牛柳丝　fillet stroganoff

炖小牛肉　fricandeau

烤牛肉卷　beef loaf

烩牛肚　tripe stew

煎薄牛肉　beef piccata

粉丝牛肉酱　spaghetti bolognaise

酥炸牛肉配菜　beef cutlet with vegetable

腿肉牛排　rump steak

菜焖肉片　ragout

铁扒猪排　grilled pork chop

酥炸(吉力)猪排　pork cutlet

焖猪排　braised pork chop

夏威夷猪排　pork chop a la Hawaii

铁扒猪排洋葱　grilled pork chop with onion

比吉打猪肉　piccata pork

猪肉串　pork a la brochette

火锅猪肉片　pork fillet Podjarka

烩猪肉　pork hotpot

黄油猪肉卷　pork a la Kiev

煎肉饼　Pojarsky cutlet

炸猪肉饼　pork croquettes

烤猪肉　roast pork

红烩猪肉丸　stewed quenelle (pork ball)

红烩羊肉　haricot mutton

烤羊肉串　mutton shashlik

烤羊脊　roast sadde of mutton

红烧家兔　rabbit stew

烧鸡　roast chicken

白煮鸡　boiled chicken

煎薄鸡片(比吉打鸡)　piccata chicken

咖喱鸡　chicken curry

酥炸鸡(吉力鸡) chicken cutlet

奶汁鸡排 chicken au gratin

奶汁鸡丝 chicken stroganoff

黄油鸡卷 chicken a la Kiev

番茄烩鸡 chicken and ham stew

葡国鸡 roast chicken a la Portugal

鸡王饭 chicken a la king

马里兰炸鸡 chicken Maryland

马林哥鸡 chicken Marengo

煎鸡肉饼 chicken croquettes

炸鸡肉丸 deep-fried chicken quenelle

铁扒子鸡 grilled spring chicken

罗马式鸡 Roman style chicken

白烩鸡饭 fricassee of chicken and rice

冻烧鸡 roast chicken, Guangdong style

冻烧鸡火腿 roast chicken and ham

牛油焖鸭 duck braised in butter

法国橙烩鸭 duck in orange zest and curacao sauce

酸烩火鸡 devilled turkey

苹果酿鹅 apple-stuffed goose

日本式火锅 sukiyaki

## 西餐——鱼类和其他 Fish and Other Dishes

炸鱼柳 fried fillet of fish

酥炸鱼(吉力鱼) fish cutlet

乳酪烤鱼 fish au gratin

蛋汁白煮鱼 boiled fish, egg sauce

鱼排 fish steak

熏鱼 smoked fish

奶油汁扒鱼 grilled fish, butter sauce

番茄烩鱼 fish stewed with tomatoes

煎鱼配酸豆(文也鱼) fish meunière

法国炖鱼 bouillabaisse

腌鲱鱼 keppered herring

冷醋鱼 cold sour fish

咖喱鱼 fish curry

红鱼子 red caviar

黑鱼子 black caviar

酥炸(吉力)大虾 prawn cutlet

乳酪烤蟹 crab meat au gratin

煎蛋 fried egg

清煮蛋(带壳) boiled egg

泡蛋 poached egg

乳酪蛋卷 cheese omelet

洋葱蛋卷 onion omelet

番茄蛋卷 tomato omelet

西班牙蛋卷 Spanish omelet

炒滑蛋 scrambled eggs

火腿炒蛋 scrambled eggs with ham

白菌炒蛋 scrambled eggs with mushrooms

鸡肝炒蛋 scrambled eggs with chicken liver

熏香肠 smoked sausage

煮香肠 boiled sausage

猪肝瘦肉香肠 liver sausage

舌肉香肠 tongue sausage

冻菜 cold dish

黄瓜(青瓜)色拉 cucumber

salad
洋葱色拉  onion salad
番茄色拉  tomato salad
大烩色拉  combination salad
生菜色拉  lettuce salad
白煮马铃薯  boiled potatoes

烤土豆  roast potatoes
酸汁蘑菇  pickled mushrooms
炸花生  fried peanuts
炸薯片  potato chips
炸薄脆  fried crisp chips
酸菜(酸瓜)  pickles

## 西餐——甜品  Confectionery

(正菜外的)附加点心  entremets
饭后水果甜食  dessert
面粉制的糕点  pastry
花色小蛋糕  petit-fours
蛋糕  cake
松糕  sponge cake
葡萄干糕  plum pudding
奶油蛋糕  cream cake
多层蛋糕  layer cake
牛奶蛋冻(炖蛋)  custard
果酱煎饼  jam pancake
糖浆煎饼  hot cake
奶油面包卷  cream bun
奶酪面包片  rarebit
烤软饼  crumpet
布丁(松软甜点)  pudding
馅饼  pie
苹果馅饼  apple pie
油煎馅饼  fritter
果馅饼  tart
杏仁馅饼  almond tart
姜饼  gingerbread
小馅饼  patty
软果糕  pastila, sweetmeat
  of fruit
果馅糕  soufflé sweetmeat
巧克力甜糕  chocolate trifle

饼干  biscuit
甜饼干  cookie
苏打饼干  soda biscuit
奶油薄脆饼干  cream cracker
奶盐苏打饼干  saltine
威化饼  wafer
奶油松饼  cream puff
蛋奶烘饼  waffle
小松饼  muffin
奶油冻  mousse
蛋奶酥  soufflé
乳冻(乳酥)  junket
甜食  sweetmeats
蜜饯  preserves
烩水果  stewed fruit
水果糖浆  compoto
果子冻  fruit jelly
冰棍(雪条)  ice lolly, ice
  sucker, popsicle
冰淇淋(雪糕)  ice-cream
紫雪糕  Eskimo pie
香草雪糕  vanilla ice-cream
巧克力雪糕  chocolate ice-
  cream
水果冰淇淋  sundae
菠萝冰淇淋  pineapple sundae

# 服务业 The Service Industry

## 旅 店 Hotel

旅馆(饭店、酒店) hotel
宾馆 guesthouse, hotel
客栈 inn, (Brit.) public-house
招待所 lodging house, hostel
汽车游客旅店 motel, (Am.)
　court
海滩旅店 beach hotel
温泉旅店 hotsprings hotel
别墅 villa
经理 manager
管理员 director
翻译 interpreter
总服务台职员 receptionist
服务员 service worker
勤杂服务员 page
搬行李服务员 porter
客房服务员 room attendant
客房女服务员 chamber-maid
餐厅男服务员 waiter
餐厅女服务员 waitress
旅客 guest
门厅 entrance-hall
前厅 lobby
休息室 lounge
总服务台(接待处) reception
　desk (office)

询问处 enquiries
登记住进旅馆 checking in
结帐离馆 checking out
旅客登记表 registration form
旅客登记册 hotel register
名字 given name
姓氏 surname
国籍 nationality
永久地址 permanent address
出生地点和时间 place and
　date of birth
从何处来 where from
到何处去 where to
拟住天数 length of stay
签名 signature
证件 documents
护照 passport
身份证,工作证 identity card
　(book)
旅游 travel, tour
出差 tour of duty, going on
　duty
行李 luggage, (U.S.) baggage
行李标签 luggage tag
提箱 suit-case
旅行袋 travelling bag

公事包　briefcase
楼面服务台　service counter
送酒菜到房间的服务　room service
房号卡　room number card
房间钥匙　room key
朝西的房间　room facing west
有浴室的房间　room with a bath
空房　vacant room
单人房　single (-bedded) room
双人房　double room
三套间　three-room suite
四套间　four-room suite
起居室(客厅)　sitting room
卧室　bedroom
餐室　dining room
书房　study
电话　telephone
叫人电钮　button for room service
衣柜(大衣橱)　wardrobe
阳台　balcony
纱窗　screen window
窗帘　curtain
气窗　upper casement (window)
浴室　bath (room)
浴缸　(bath) tub
洗手盆　basin
淋浴(装置)　shower
喷头(花洒)　shower nozzle
水厕(马桶)　water-closet
水箱　water tank, cistern
马桶坐圈　toilet seat
手纸　toilet paper
洗衣袋　laundry bag
空调机　air-conditioner
中央供暖(设备)　central heat-ing
暖气散热器　radiator
电梯　lift, (Am.) elevator
楼梯　stairs
电梯看管人　lift operator
电源开关　switch
插头　plug
插座　socket
门房(传达室)　gate-keeper's room, gate-house
庭院　grounds
走廊　corridor
屋顶花园　roof-garden
游艺室　recreation room
电影厅　cinema
阅览室　reading-room
旅馆餐厅　dining room, hotel restaurant
宴会厅　banquet room
会议室　conference room
客厅(沙龙)　saloon
酒吧间　bar
弹子房　billiard room
小卖部　shop, retail store
男盥洗室(男厕)　gentlemen's
女盥洗室(女厕)　ladies'
存衣处　cloak-room
杂物室　broom closet
邮政服务台　postal service counter
银行服务台　minibank
理发室　barber's
财务室　cashier's office
出租小汽车服务台　taxi counter
开帐单　making out the bill
房租　rent
收据　receipt
订房间　booking rooms
有空房间吗？　Have you any

accommodation (vacant rooms)?

能给我留一个双人房吗？ Can you reserve a double room for me?

我已预订二个双人房。 I've got a reservation of two double rooms.

这房间住一昼夜多少钱房租？ What's the price of the room?

包括膳宿在内，一天多少钱？ How much is boarding and lodging a day?

请换一换卧具。 Please change the bed clothes.

请明早七点叫醒我。 Please wake (ring) me up at seven a.m. tomorrow.

什么地方可以擦皮鞋？ Where can I have my shoes cleaned?

有位先生来找过你，给你留下一张字条。 Some gentleman asked for you and left this message.

这是额外服务帐单，不包括在一般规定之内的。 Here's the bill for additional services not included in the general provisions.

203 房吗？起床时间到了。 Room 203? It's time to get up.

离馆时请带齐东西。 Check your belongings before you leave.

## 洗衣店　Laundry

自动洗衣店　launderette
洗衣工　laundry worker
女洗衣工　laundress, washer-woman
脏衣服　soiled clothes, soiled linen
送去洗的衣服等　laundry
免烫衣服　non-press clothes
洗烫好的衣服等　laundry
洗好的湿衣服　wet wash
洗烫衣服　laundering
干洗　dry-cleaning
洗衣机　washing-machine
蒸汽洗衣机　steam washer
干燥机　drying-machine, laundry-drier
轧布机(轧干、烫平衣服)　ironer
烫衣机　laundry press

电熨斗　electric iron
烫衣板　ironing-board
浆衣服　starching
漂白　bleaching
软水　soft water
浓肥皂水　suds
漂清水　rinsing water
洗涤剂　detergent
肥皂　soap
洗衣粉　washing-powder
碱　alkali
漂白剂　bleach
去污剂　stain-remover
润湿剂　wetting-out agent
防水剂　water-repellent
上蓝剂　blue, washing-blue
浆粉　starch
洗衣板　wash-board, scrub-

bing-board

洗衣刷　scrubbing brush

木条垫脚板　duckboard

衣架　clothes (coat) hanger

晾衣绳　clothesline

晾衣夹　clothes-peg (pin)

晒衣架　clotheshorse

## 理发店　The Barbershop

理发店旋转招牌　barber's pole

男界理发店　the barber's

女界理发店　the hairdresser's

美容室　beauty parlour

理发师　barber, hairdresser

发式(发型)　style, hair-do

剪发　haircut

理平头　crew-cut

洗头　shampoo

修脸　shave

修胡子　moustache (beard)
　trimming

整发　hair-set

烫发　wave, curl

电烫卷发　permanent wave
　(perm)

热气卷发　marcel waving

化学卷发(冷波)　cold wave

卷出　curls outward

卷入　curls inward

吹干　drying of hair

染发　dyeing of hair,
　colour-rinsing of hair

染眉　tinting (dyeing) of
　brows

分头　parting

秃头　bald

发式手册　album of styles

理发椅　barber's chair

理发推子　clippers

理发剪子　scissors

剃刀　razor

电剃刀　electric razor

刀片　razor blade

革砥　leather strop

毛巾　towel

吹风机　hair drier

手风筒　hand drier

梳子　comb

镜子　mirror

发刷　hair-brush

发网　hair-net

发夹　hair pin

卷发夹　hair-curler

卷发钳　curling tongs

发蜡　pomade

发乳　hair cream

发油　hair oil, hair tonic

剃须膏　shaving cream

还原剂　neutralizer

冷气卷发剂　setting lotion

奎宁水　quinine

化妆品　cosmetics

化妆粉　face powder

粉盒　compact

胭脂　rouge

口红　lipstick

眼皮膏　eye-shadow

眉笔　eyebrow pencil

整容水　astrigent lotion

花露水　toilet water, florida
　water

科隆香水　eau-de-cologne

雪花膏　vanishing cream

香脂(冷霜)　cold cream

香水　scent, perfume

爽身粉　talcum powder

痱子粉(水)　prickly heat powder (lotion)

粉扑　powder puff

指甲剪　nail scissors

指甲锉　nail file

指甲油　nail polish

我要理发。　I need a haircut. (I want to have my hair cut.)

两边剪短些。　Cut it short at the sides.

通通剪短。Make it short all round, please.

后边留长些。Leave it long at the back.

头顶剪薄些。　Thin it at the top.

不要分头,请往后梳。　No parting, please. Just comb it straight back.

我要吹波。　I'd like to have my hair waved.

请平分。　Part in the middle, please.

请偏分。　Part at the side, please.

给我挽个髻。Do my hair in a knot (bun).

把我的头发编成辫子。Do my hair in braids (plaits).

我要修指甲。　Do my nails, please. (I'd like to have a manicure.)

我要前刘海。　I want to wear a fringe (bang).

请给我面部按摩。　I'd like to have a facial (massage).

## 裁缝店　The Tailor's

裁缝师　tailor

裁缝师(女服)　dressmaker

定做的衣服　clothes made to order, (Am.) custom clothes

定做衣服　ordering clothes

量尺寸　taking measurements

衣长　coat (shirt) length

衣领　collar

胸围　chest, bust

肩宽　width of shoulders

袖长　sleeve length

背长　neck-waist length

腰围　waist

臀围　hip

裤长　pants length

内裆　in-leg

裤脚口　hem of pants leg

式样　style, design

中式服装　garments in Chinese style

西式服装　garments in Western style

高领　high collar

尖领　pointed collar

直领　stand-up collar

方领　square-cut collar

硬领　stiff collar

圆领　round collar

反领　turndown collar

贴袋(明袋)　patch pocket

插袋(暗袋)　inset pocket

裤脚的反折部分　turn-up, (Am.) cuff

反折的裤脚　trouser legs turned up (cuffed)

不反折的裤脚　uncuffed

trouser legs

喇叭裤脚　flared legs
直筒裤脚　straight legs
宽裤脚　wide legs
试身(试穿)　fitting, trying on
合身　good fit
紧　tight fit
松　loose fit
(上衣)做得起皱　(jacket)
　sitting in wrinkles
裁剪　cutting
电动裁剪机　electric cutter
缝纫　sewing
针法　stitch
疏缝　basting
缝边　hemming
锁边　hemstitching
绣花　embroidering
缝补　mending
缝边裂开　burst seam
裤子臀部破了　worn trouser
　seat
从里面补上一块　patching from
　inside
改衣服　having clothes alter-
　ed
改短　taking up, making

shorter

改瘦　taking off
放长　letting down
改宽　letting out
翻新　having the coat turned
裁缝剪　tailor's shears,
　cutting out scissors
钮门剪　buttonhole scissors
带尺(软尺)　tape measure
手缝针　sewing needle
织补针　darning needle
安全扣针　safety-pin
别针(大头针)　pin
针顶　thimble
针插　pin cushion
锥子(钻子)　pricker, awl
线牌　card of mending thread
钮扣　button
揿扣(按扣, 迫钮)　snap, snap
　fastener
拉链　zipper, zip fastener
陈列服装的人体模型　tailor's
　dummy, dress-form
缝纫机　sewing machine
机头　sewing machine
机架　frame (stand)
脚踏　treadle

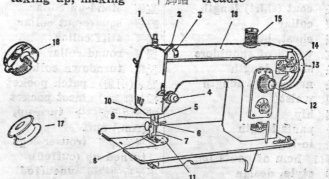

下带轮　driving wheel

电动缝纫机　electric sewing machine

压脚调压器①　presser foot adjuster

挑线杆②　thread taking-up lever

过线钩③　thread hook

夹线器④　tension disk

针杆⑤　needle bar

针夹⑥　needle clam screw

机针⑦　sewing machine needle

压脚⑧　presser foot

压脚杆⑨　presser bar

压脚扳手⑩　presser foot lifter

针板⑪　feed plate

针距旋钮⑫　regulator for setting stitch length

上轮⑬　balance wheel

绕线器⑭　bobbin-winder

线团⑮　reel of thread, spool of thread

面线　upper thread

梭床⑯　rotating shuttle

底线芯⑰　under-thread bobbin

机壳⑱　casing

## 照相店　Photo Studio

照相馆　the photographer's

照相　photo-taking, having one's picture taken

摆好姿势照相　posing for a photo

照片(相片)　photograph, photo, picture

半身相　half-length portrait

晕映(化白)照片　vignette

全身相　full-length portrait

合照　group photo

快照(生活相)　snapshot

全景照片　panorama

剪影(黑色轮廓像)　silhouette

相簿　photo album

相架　mount

摄影师　photographer

摄影术　photography

立体摄影　stereophotography

全息摄影　holography

胶卷　film roll

单张页片　film sheet

正片　positive

负片　negative

全色片　panchromatic film

彩色片　colour film

分色片　ortho (chrome)

胶卷感光速度　film speed

快速胶卷　fast film

暗室　dark room

显影冲洗　developing

定影　fixing

晒印　printing, making prints

放大　enlarging

放大的照片　enlargement

放大机　enlarger

切边机　print-trimmer

显影剂　developer

定影剂　fixer

底片　negative

晒相纸　printing paper

光面(纸)　glossy surface (paper)

无光面(绒面)　matte

绸纹面　silk (finish) surface

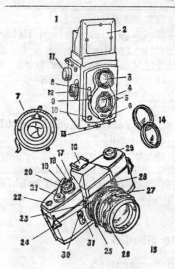

布纹面　textured surface
细绒面　semi-matte
照相机　camera
立体相机　stereo camera
即拍即印照相机　instamatic camera
小型照相机　miniature camera
折合式照相机　folding camera
双镜头反光相机①　twin-lens reflex camera
取景器盖②　viewfinder cover
取景镜头③　viewing lens
拍照镜头④　picture-taking lens
光圈调节钮⑤　diaphragm setting lever
自拍扳手⑥　self-timer lever
中心快门　between-lens shutter
焦面快门⑦　focal-plane shutter
快门扳手⑧　shutter lever

快门调节钮⑨　shutter speed adjusting lever
快门按钮⑩　shutter release button
胶卷轴顶钮⑪　film spool spring knob
卷片钮⑫　winding knob
调焦钮　focusing knob
对焦刻度表　focusing scale
后盖锁钩⑬　locking bolt of back cover
滤色镜⑭　filter
遮光光罩　lens hood
单镜头反光相机⑮　single-lens reflex camera
附件插座⑯　accessory shoe
焦平面标记⑰　focal plane mark
调速盘⑱　shutter speed dial
卷片扳手⑲　film winding lever
胶片感光度指示圈⑳　film-speed indicator
快门按钮㉑　shutter release button
计数窗㉒　exposure counter window
反光镜锁紧扳手㉓　reflex mirror locking lever
光圈调节圈㉔　diaphragm preselection ring
景深预测拨杆㉕　depth-of-field preview lever
调焦圈㉖　focusing ring
景深刻度圈㉗　depth-of-field scale
镜头拆卸钮㉘　lens change button
倒片钮㉙　film rewind knob

自拍器扳手㉚ self-timer lever
自拍按钮㉛ self-timer button
可换镜头 interchangeable lens
广角镜头 wide-angle lens
长焦距镜头 tele lens
可变焦距镜头 zoom lens
焦距 focal length
测距器 range finder
曝光表 exposure meter
快门线 shutter line

曝光不足 under-exposure
曝光过度 over-exposure
清晰度 sharpness, definition
顺光 frontlighting
侧光 sidelighting
逆光 backlighting
反射 bounce flash
闪光灯 flash light
三脚架 tripod
相版 trial print
相片样张 proof

## 钟表店 The Watchmaker's

计时器 timepiece
日晷(日规) sundial
手表 wrist watch
表带 watch strap, watch bracelet
表壳 watchcase
表把 button
表面 dial, face
表面玻璃 watch glass
表面刻度 chapter, figure
时针 hour hand
分针 minute hand
秒针 second hand
日历表 calendar watch
发条 mainspring
游丝 balance spring, hair spring
齿轮 wheel, pinion
轮轴 shaft
防震 shock-resistant
防水 water-proof
防磁 antimagnetic
防尘 dust-proof
防磨擦 scratch-proof
全钢 all steel

半钢 half steel
不锈钢 stainless steel
宝石轴承 jewel
自动表 self-winding watch
夜光表 watch with luminous dial
男装手表 man's watch
女装手表 woman's watch
电子石英手表① quartz watch
怀表 pocket watch

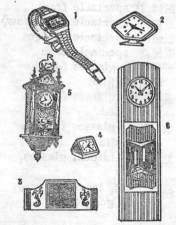

秒表　stop watch
闹钟(表)② alarm clock (watch)
座钟③ bracket clock
旅行闹钟④ travelling alarm clock
挂钟⑤ wall clock
塔钟 turret clock
自鸣钟 striking clock
落地大座钟⑥ grandfather clock
钟摆 pendulum
电钟 electric clock
母钟 primary clock
子钟 secondary clock
电子钟 electronic clock

标准时间 standard time
夏令时间 summer time, daylight saving time
时差 time difference
报时信号 time signal
校准手表 setting one's watch
这表很准。The watch is correct (exact). The watch keeps good time.
这表快(慢)一分钟。The watch is one minute fast (slow).
这表每天快(慢)两分钟。The watch gains (loses) two minutes a day.
倒拨一小时。Set the watch back one hour.

## 眼镜店　The Optician's

视力表 visual testing chart
视力计 optometer
验光配镜术 optometry
配镜师 optometrist
眼镜 spectacles, glasses
眼镜框 spectacle frame
眼镜脚 spectacle side (bow)
眼镜桥 spectacle bridge
眼镜盒 spectacle case
近视眼镜 glasses for the shortsighted
远视眼镜 glasses for the farsighted
散光眼镜 glasses for the astigmatic
双光眼镜 bifocal glasses, bifocals
激光防护镜 laserlight protective goggles

护目镜(风镜,平光镜) goggles
太阳镜(墨镜) sunglasses
水晶镜 crystal glasses
有色眼镜 tinted glasses
单片眼镜 monocle
放大镜 magnifying glass
双筒望远镜 binoculars, field glasses
望远镜 telescope
看戏望远镜 opera glasses
夹鼻眼镜 pince-nez
隐形眼镜 contact lenses
这眼镜多少度? What's the strength of the lenses of the spectacles?
这是浅度(中度,深度)近视眼镜。This is for the slight (medium, serious) shortsighted.

# 外 贸 Foreign Trade

## 国际贸易 International Trade

| | |
|---|---|
| 国际贸易纽带 nexus of international trade | 间接贸易 indirect trade |
| 国际贸易值 value of international trade | 间接进口 indirect import |
| | 间接出口 indirect export |
| 国际贸易量 quantum of international trade | 中介贸易 intermediate trade |
| 国际贸易地区分布 international trade by regions | 商品交易所贸易 commodity exchange |
| 国际贸易商品结构 international trade by commodities | 转口贸易 carrying trade |
| | 易货贸易 barter, bartering |
| 国际贸易活动 international trade activity | 直接易货 direct barter |
| | 间接易货 indirect barter |
| 对外贸易(国外贸易) external trade, foreign trade | 双边贸易 bilateral trade |
| | 有进有出的贸易 two-way trade |
| 贸易关系 trade relation | |
| 对外贸易惯例 custom of foreign trade | 双边主义 bilateralism |
| | 双边安排 bilateral arrangements |
| 贸易方式 mode of trade | 三角贸易 triangular trade |
| 总贸易 general trade | 多边贸易 multilateral trade |
| 总进口 general import | 多边主义 multilateralism |
| 总出口 general export | 多边安排 multilateral arrangements |
| 净进口 net-import | |
| 净出口 net-export | 单边进口 unilateral import |
| 直接贸易 direct trade | 单边出口 unilateral export |
| 直接进口 direct import | 专门贸易 special trade |
| 直接出口 direct export | 专门进口 special import |
| | 专门出口 special export |

复进口　re-import
复出口　re-export
过境贸易　transit trade
直接过境贸易　direct transit trade
间接过境贸易　indirect transit trade
水平贸易　horizontal trade
垂直贸易(南北贸易)　vertical trade (south-north trade)
边境贸易　frontier trade, border trade

补偿贸易　compensation trade
暂时进口　temporary import
暂时出口　temporary export
等价贸易　trade of equal values
不等价贸易　trade of unequal values
贸易渠道　trade channel
内外物资交流　flow of goods between domestic and foreign markets

## 世界贸易中常见的贸易政策和措施
## Policies and Measures Commonly Adopted in World Trade

自由贸易政策　free trade policy
贸易自由化　liberalization of trade
自由化措施　liberalization measures
自由(贸易)区　free (trade) zone
自由(贸易)港　free port
对外贸易区　foreign trade zone
互惠贸易政策　reciprocal trade policy
利益均等　equal opportunities
国民待遇　national treatment
优惠待遇　preferential treatment
普通优惠制　generalized preferential system

最惠国待遇　most favoured nation treatment
暂时防御性特惠制　temporary defensive preferential system
贸易歧视　trade discrimination
保护贸易政策　protective trade policy
超保护贸易政策　ultra-protective trade policy
保护关税政策　policy of protective tariffs
行政保护　administrative protection
财政保护　financial protection
间接保护　indirect protection
国家垄断　state monopoly
贸易管制　trade control
配额制　allocation system,

quota system

国家定额　state quota

数量限制　quantitative restriction

进口管制　import control

禁止进口　prohibition on importation

停止进口　import suspension

进口配额制　import quota system

绝对配额　absolute quota

全球配额　global quota

国别配额　allocated quota

关税及贸易总协定　General Agreement on Tariffs and Trade (GATT)

关税减让　tariff diminution

有秩序销售协定　orderly marketing agreement

进口许可证制　import licence system

特别许可证　special licence

技术签证　technical visa

免责条款　escape clause

国家安全条款　national security clause

危险点条款　dangerous point clause

保障条款　safeguard clause

抵制　boycott

封锁及禁运　blockade and embargo

出口管制　export control

禁止出口　prohibition on exportation

停止出口　export suspension

出口许可证制　export licence system

出口配额制　export quota

system

自动限制出口　voluntary restriction of export

抵偿贸易政策　compensation trade policy

出口补贴　export subsidy

出口奖金　export bonus, export bounty

出口信贷　export credit

出口信用国家担保　government guarantee of export credit

资本输出　export of capital

开发进口方式　importation under program of development

退税　drawback

出口退税　export refund

商品倾销　dumping of goods

财政援助　financial aid

外汇倾销　exchange dumping

关税合并,关税同化　mergence of tariffs, assimilation

协定贸易政策　agreement trade policy

共同体贸易政策　community trade policy

共同体基金　community fund

共同商议　collective discussion

关税同盟　customs union

建立对外共同税率　establishing common external tariffs

取消内部贸易障碍　removal of internal trade barriers

取消关税　elimination of tariffs

降低内部税率　reduction of internal tariffs

改善进入条件 **improved terms of access**

维持价格政策 **support price policy**

增补亏空支付制 **deficiency payment system**

特许权 **special concession**

农业保护主义 **agricultural protectionism**

关税配额 **tariff quota, customs quota**

关税壁垒 **tariff barrier, tariff wall**

非关税壁垒 **non-tariff barrier, non-tariff wall**

关税战 **tariff war**

## 对外贸易组织和人员 Foreign Trade Organizations and Personnel

外贸部 **Ministry of Foreign Trade**

外贸局 **Foreign Trade Bureau**

国营贸易机构 **state trading organ**

外贸公司 **foreign trade corporation**

进出口商行 **import and export firm**

出口代办行 **export commission house**

总公司 **head office, home office**

分公司 **branch office**

临时办事处 **temporary office**

联络处 **liaison office**

贸易访问团 **trade mission**

贸易团体 **trading body, trading group**

贸易代表机构 **trade representation**

常设采购代表（人） **resident buying representation (representative)**

贸易代表团 **trade delegation**

政府贸易代表团 **government trade delegation**

纺织品交易团 **textiles trade delegation**

工业展览会 **industrial exhibition**

农业展览会 **agricultural exhibition**

综合性的经济展览会 **comprehensive economic exhibition**

国际博览会 **international fair**

中国对外贸易中心 **China Foreign Trade Centre**

中国出口商品交易会 **China's Export Commodities Fair**

商务参赞 **commercial councillor**

商务专员 **commercial attaché**

谈判代表 **negotiating representative**

中国国际贸易促进会 **China Council for the Promotion of International Trade—C.C.P.I.T.**

贸易协商员 **trade consultant**

中国粮油食品进出口总公司

China National Cereals, Oils and Foodstuffs Import and Export Corporation

中国土产畜产进出口总公司 China National Native Produce and Animal By-products Import and Export Corporation

中国纺织品进出口总公司 China National Textiles Import and Export Corporation

中国轻工业品进出口总公司 China National Light Industrial Products Import and Export Corporation

中国化工进出口总公司 China National Chemicals Import and Export Corporation

中国机械进出口总公司 China National Machinery Import and Export Corporation

中国五金矿产进出口总公司 China National Metals and Minerals Import and Export Corporation

中国工艺品进出口总公司 China National Arts and Crafts Import and Export Corporation

中国技术进口公司 China National Technical Import Corporation

中国机械设备出口公司 China National Machinery Equipments Export Corporation

中国图书进口公司 China Publications Import Corp.

中国国际书店 China Publications Centre(Guozi Shudian)

中国电影发行放映公司 China Film Distribution and Exhibition Corporation

中国邮票出口公司 China Stamps Export Corporation

中国人民保险公司 People's Insurance Company of China

中国成套设备山口公司 China National Complete Plant Export Corporation

中国对外贸易运输总公司 China National Foreign Trade Transportation Corporation

中国远洋公司 China Ocean Shipping Company

中国租船公司 China National Chartering Corporation

中国外轮供应公司 China Ocean Shipping Supply Corporation

中国外轮代理公司 China Ocean Shipping Agency

中国打捞公司 China Salvage Company

## 市场调研 Market Research

国际市场 international market

国外市场 foreign market

国内市场 domestic market, home market

出口市场 export market

商品市场　commodity market

初级市场　primary market

市况调查　market survey

市场情况　market situation

市场分析　market analysis

市况报告　market report

市场的供销或价格情况(市气)
market tone

市场的潜在倾向　undertone of
market

市场正常(价稳)　market
healthy

行市兴隆　market brisk

行市活跃　market active,
(buoyant, lively)

行市坚硬　market strong

行市坚挺　market firm

行市十分坚挺　market very
firm

行市坚挺,趋势上涨　market
firm, tendency upwards

行市坚稳　market steady

行市大致坚稳　market about
steady

行市较坚稳　market rather
steady

行市勉强坚稳　market barely
steady

行市静稳　market quietly
steady

行市平静　market quiet

行市死寂　market still

行市稳静　market steady
quiet

行市不稳定　market unsettled,
market unsteady, market
uncertain, market queasy

行市反复不定　market erratic

市场混乱　market chaotic

行市涨落不定　market irreg-
ular

行市曲折上升　market irreg-
ular higher

行市较高　market higher,
market rather high

行市曲折下降　market irreg-
ular lower

行市较低　market lower,
market rather low

行市不振　market weak

行市不活跃(呆滞)　market
inactive, market dull

行市闲散　market idle

行市疲软　market easy

市软,趋势下降　market easy,
tendency downwards

行市上升　market picking up

行市好转(价格稳上)　market
improving

市上无货　market bare of
stocks

市场存货过多　market over-
stocked

市场货物充斥　market glutted

有利于买方的行市　buyer's
market

有利于卖方的行市　seller's
market

供求情况　demand and
supply situation

消费与库存的需求　demand
for consumption and stock

供不应求　demand exceeding
supply

供过于求　supply exceeding
demand

供求关系　relations between
supply and demand

商品供求关系的变化　change in relations between supply and demand

世界需求　world demand

国内需要　domestic requirement (demand)

很大的需求　thick demand, heavy demand

不大的需求　thin demand

实际需要　physical demand, actual demand

总需求　aggregate demand

需要越多就越缺货　goods in high demand being always in short supply

奇缺　acute shortage

消费者购买力　purchasing power of consumers

委托购货水平　mandatory buying levels

参加国际贸易的两国之间的价格比率　terms of trade

基本因素　fundamentals (fundamental factors)

技术性因素　technicals (technical factors)

技术性回升　technical rally

技术性回跌　technical reaction

季节性调整　seasonal adjustment

平衡表法　balance sheet method

比较类推法　comparative inference method

物价指数　commodity price index

商品价格的总指数　aggregate index of commodity prices

生活费指数　cost of living index

价格滑动条款　escalator clause

价格升降条款　rise and fall clause

加价或减价条款　up and down alteration of price clause

路透商品行情指数　Reuter's Index

## 询盘与发盘　Enquiry and Offer

询价　enquiry, enquiring

一般询价　general enquiry

特定(专门)询价　specific enquiry

具体需要的通知　advice of specific requirements

发盘(报价)　offer, offering

原发盘　original offer

专门发盘　special offer

特殊发盘　exceptional offer

独家发盘　exclusive offer

独家发盘人　exclusive offerer

被独家发盘人　exclusive offeree

实盘发盘　firm offer

虚盘(不受约束的发盘)　non-firm offer, offering without engagement

可撤销发盘　revocable offer

搭配发盘　combination offer

综合发盘　lump offer, offer on a lump basis

口头发盘(报价)　verbal offer

还盘(还价)　counter offer

反还盘 counter counter offer

附样发盘 sample offer

电报发盘 cable offer

买方发盘(发价, 递盘) buying offer

发盘的有效期限 duration of offer

以未售出为准的发盘 offer subject to (goods) being unsold

以第一艘便船为准的发盘 offer subject to shipment by first available steamer

以领得出口许可证为准的发盘 offer subject to export licence

以领得进口许可证为准的发盘 offer subject to import licence

以立即回电接受为准的发盘 offer subject to immediate acceptance by telegram

有权先售的发盘 offer subject to prior sale

以立即答复为准的发盘 offer subject to immediate reply

以有舱位为准的发盘 offer subject to shipping space available

按市价变动增减的发盘 offer subject to market fluctuation

以货到出口港为有效的发盘 offer subject to arrival of goods at port of shipment

卖方确认后有效的发盘 offer subject to seller's confirmation

如有变化, 无需另行通知的发盘 offer subject to change without notice

以买方看货后为有效的发盘 offer subject to buyer's inspection or approval

以答复于……日内抵达我处为有效的发盘 offer subject to reply received here by…days

在撤回前有效的发盘 offer good until withdrawn

发盘可以考虑(可以接受) offer entertainable, offer acceptable

接受发盘 acceptance of offer, accepting an offer

接受发盘, 但需作如下修改 offer accepted subject to following alterations

接受发盘, 请按……数量作新发盘 offer accepted, further for … (quantity) on same terms

发盘不能接受 offer unacceptable

婉拒发盘 declination of offer, declining an offer

再发盘(与前盘相同) repeat offer, repeating an offer

延盘 renewed offer, renewing an offer

重新发盘 re-offer, reoffering

按供应能力重新发盘 re-offer on basis of availability

确认发盘 confirmation of offer, confirming an offer

暂停发盘 withholding of offer, withholding an offer

撤回发盘 withdrawal of

offer, withdrawing an offer
撤销发盘　cancellation of offer, cancelling an offer
发盘人(报价人)　offerer
接盘人(被报价人)　offeree
递虚盘(不受约束的递盘) bidding without engagement
递实盘　firm bid, bidding firm
开价　quotation, quoting
低廉的开价　favourable quotation, quoting favourably
不受约束的开价　quotation without engagement
有竞争能力的开价　competitive quotation

以FOB(CIF)条件为基础的开价 quotation on FOB (CIF) basis
在有折扣的基础上开价　quotation on discount basis
以人民币(英镑,美元)开价　quotation in Renminbi (pound sterling, U.S. dollar)
开价低于所值　underquoting
开价表　quotation sheet
开价比较表(开价条件比较表) competitive list, comparative list
函电磋商　negotiation through letters and telegrams
一般商业惯例　common mercantile practice

## 价格条件　Price Terms

指定地点交货价格　franco render
买方住所交货价格　franco domicile
过境交货价格　franco border
送到进口国家的内地指定地点的价格　franco …(named inland point in country of importation)
生产地交货价格　ex port of origin
卖方仓库交货价格　ex (seller's) warehouse … (locality of seller's warehouse)
工厂(制造地)交货价格　ex factory (works, mill)… (place of manufacture)
农场(生产地)交货价格　ex plantation … (place of origin)

矿山(生产地)交货价格　ex mine … (place of origin)
(装运港)船边交货价格　F.A.S. (free alongside ship)… (port of shipment)
(装运港)离岸价格　F.O.B. (free on board) … (port of shipment)
装运港船上交货的离岸价格 F.O.B.… (named vessel at named point of shipment)
在国内指定的地点,送到指定的内陆运输工具上交货的离岸价格 F.O.B.… (named inland carrier at named inland point of departure)
在国内指定的发货地点,送到指定的出口地点,在指定的内地运输工具上交货的离岸价格　F.O.B. … (named inland carrier

at named point of exportation)

在国内指定的发货地点,送到指定的内陆运输工具上交货,运费预付到指定的出口地点的离岸价格 F.O.B. … (named inland carrier at named inland point of departure, freight prepaid to named point of exportation)

在国内的指定的发货地点,送到指定的内地运输工具上交货,减除到指定出口地点的运费的离岸价格 F.O.B. … (named inland carrier at named point of departure, freight allowed to named point of exportation)

(装运港)加理舱费的离岸价格 F.O.B.S. (free on board stowed) … (port of shipment)

(装运港)加理舱费和平舱费的离岸价格 F.O.B.S.T. (free on board stowed and trimmed) … (port of shipment)

(装运港)卡车上交货价格 F.O.T. (free on truck) … (port of shipment)

(装运港)火车上交货价格 F.O.R. (free on rail) … (port of shipment)

(装运港)飞机场交货价格 F.O.B. plane (airport), ex aerodrome … (port of shipment)

到岸价格 landed price

目的港船上交货价格 ex ship (free overside) … (port of destination)

成本加运费(目的港)价格 C. & F. (cost and freight) … (port of destination)

(目的港)到岸价格 C.I.F. (cost, insurance and freight) … (port of destination)

加佣金的(目的港)到岸价格 C.I.F.C. (cost, insurance, freight and commission) … (port of destination)

加利息的(目的港)到岸价格 C.I.F.I. (cost, insurance, freight and interest) … (port of destination)

加汇费的(目的港)到岸价格 C.I.F.E. (cost, insurance, freight and exchange) … (port of destination)

加战争险的(目的港)到岸价格 C.I.F.W. (cost, insurance, freight and war-risks) … (port of destination)

加佣金、利息的(目的港)到岸价格 C.I.F.C.I. (cost, insurance, freight, commission and interest) … (port of destination)

船边交货的(目的港)到岸价格 free overside, free overboard … (port of destination)

轮船舱底交货的(目的港)到岸价格 C.I.F. ex ship's hold … (port of destination)

轮船吊钩下交货的(目的港)到岸价格 C.I.F. under ship's tackle … (port of destination)

不包括佣金的(目的港)到岸价格
C.I.F. net … (port of destination)

加关税的(目的港)到岸价格
C.I.F. duty paid … (port of destination)

包括一切进口费用的(目的港)到岸价格 C.I.F. landed … (port of destination)

包括空运运费,保险费在内的(目的港)到岸价格 C.I.F. plane … (port of destination)

目的港保税仓库交货价格 in bond (duty unpaid) … (port of destination)

买方仓库交货价格 ex buyer's godown

目的港已完税交货价格 ex customs compound (duty paid) … (port of destination)

目的港码头未完税交货价格 ex quay (dock, wharf, pier) duty unpaid … (port of destination)

## 销售与购买 Sale and Purchase

销售(卖) sale

外销 external sale

单边(单面)销售 straight sale

直接销售 direct sale

间接销售 indirect sale

寄售 consignment sale

定销(定额销售) sale as per quota

包销 exclusive sale

公卖 government sale, public sale

当场看货交易 sale by (on) inspection

凭货样销售 sale by sample

凭规格销售 sale as per (by) specifications

凭标准品级销售 sale by standard or type

凭产地销售 sale as per origin

凭商标或牌子销售 sale by trade mark or brand

凭说明书销售 sale as per (by) description

凭指定式样出售 sale by pattern

区外销售(交易) extraterritorial sale

现款交易 cash sale, cash transaction

赊售 sale on account, credit sale, sale on credit

按市价出售 sale at market price

假售定 anticipatory sale (export now at a tentative price and settlement later based on agent's market defacto)

散装出售 sale in bulk

成批出售 sale by bulk

搭售 combination sale

销售(卖)现货 spot sale

销售(卖)期货 forward sale

销售(卖)路货 sale of goods afloat

按代理条件的销售 sale on agency basis

抽佣销售 sale on commission basis

估计销售 estimated sale

销售总额 gross sales

求售 offering for sale

征求订货 canvassing for sales

销售确认书 sales confirmation

购买 purchase, buy (buying)

单边(单面)购买 straight purchase

直接购买 direct buying

间接购买 indirect buying

政府大宗采购 government bulk buying

季节性购买 seasonal purchase

现金购买 cash buying

记帐购买 purchase on credit (account)

一时冲动性的购买 impulsive buying

按需要随时购买现货(随用随买) buying on a hand-to-mouth basis

货主与买主间的直接交易 principal-to-principal transaction

套头交易("海琴") hedging

征购 seeking to buy

购货确认书 purchase confirmation

交易单位(商品数量) trading unit

卖方 seller

买方 buyer, purchaser

国外联系户 liaison customer abroad

进口招(投)标 import tender

出口招(投)标 export tender

国际拍卖 international auction

减价拍卖(荷兰式拍卖) Dutch auction

## 订 单 Order

订货(订购) ordering, booking

买方直接开给卖方的订单 order

(中间商受买方委托代购货开出的)订单 indent

特定订单 specific indent (order)

非特定订单 open indent (order)

第一次订货 initial order (indent)

试订 trial order, tentative

order

确认的订单 firm order

可观的订单 substantial order

数量大的订单 large order, big order

数量小的订单 small order

长期订单 standing order

补充订购(单) additional order

尚未交货的订单 back order, outstanding order

样货订购,样品试购 sample

order, ordering against sample

邮购　mail order

新订单　new order, fresh order

订单格式表　order blank, order form

依照买家的设计和商标去制造的出口订单　export order for manufactures after buyer's own design and brand

用买家自己材料去制造的出口订单　export order for manufactures from buyer's own material

用买家自己材料去包装的出口订单　export order for manufactures packaged in buyer's own packing

向……(某人)订购……(某货)placing an order with… (sb.) for… (sth.)

再订(复订)　repeat order (repeating an order)

接受订单　taking an order, accepting an order

交付订货　execution of order, executing an order

确认订单　confirmation of order, confirming an order

确认书　letter of confirmation

确认通知书　confirmation note

订货确认条　confirmation slip

电报确认书　cable confirmation

缓冲库存　buffer stock

库存维持良好　stock well maintained

## 条约、协定与合同　Treaties, Agreements and Contracts

国际条约　international treaty

贸易条约　commercial treaty

通商航海条约　treaty of commerce and navigation

仲裁条约(协定)　arbitration treaty

贸易协定　trade agreement

自由贸易协定　free trade agreement

政府间贸易协定　inter-governmental trade agreement

民间贸易协定　non-governmental trade agreement

易货(交易)协定　barter agreement, business agreement

一般代理协议　agency agreement

配额协定　quota agreement

清算协定　clearing agreement

支付协定　payment agreement

价格协定　price agreement

贷款协定　loan agreement

关税协定　tariff agreement

赔偿协定　reparations agreement

货币协定　monetary agreement

试行协定　pilot agreement

口头协定　verbal agreement

书面协定 **written agreement**

双边协定 **bilateral agreement**

多边协定 **multilateral agreement**

委托(寄售)协议 **consignment agreement**

合同 **contract**

贸易合同 **commercial contract**

销售(销货)合同 **sales contract**

购货合同 **purchase contract**

离岸价合同 **FOB contract**

到岸价合同 **CIF contract**

期货合同 **forward contract**

经销合同 **distribution contract**

独家代理合同 **sole agency contract**

包销合同 **exclusive sales contract**

商业代理合同 **commission contract**

保险合同 **insurance contract**

分保合同 **reinsurance contract**

运输合同 **transportation contract**

租船合同 **charter party**

运载合同 **carriage contract**

运送合同 **affreightment contract**

保管合同 **storage contract**

草约 **draft agreement**

合同草案 **draft contract**

标准合同 **standard contract**

格式合同 **model contract**

有效合同 **valid contract, binding contract**

无效合同 **void contract**

贸易协定书 **trade protocol**

商品交换议定书 **protocol for exchange of goods**

批准书 **instrument of ratification**

合同正本 **negotiable copy of contract**

合同影印本 **photostatic copy of contract**

附件 **attachment**

附录 **appendix**

履约保证 **performance bond**

错误和遗漏不在此限 **errors and omissions excepted (E. & O. E.)**

合同条款与条件 **contractual terms and conditions**

协定有效期 **duration of agreement**

合同有效期 **duration of contract**

合同号码 **contract number**

合同金额 **contract value**

合同规定 **contract stipulation**

合同义务 **contractual obligations**

合同的约束力 **binding force of contract**

合同规定使用的货币 **contract currency**

合同一方 **a party of contract, the one party**

合同的另一方 **other party of contract, the other party**

合同双方 **both parties of contract**

合同各方 **all parties to contract, the contracting parties**

守约各方 observant parties of contract

有关各方 all parties concerned

有关双方 both parties concerned

缔结合同 concluding a contract

签订合同 signing a contract

履行合同 implementing a contract

更改合同 altering a contract

修改合同 amending a contract

修改通知书 amendment advice

延长合同 extending a contract

续约 renewing a contract

复订合同 repeating a contract

违反合同 violating a contract

破坏合同 breaking a contract

撤销合同 cancellation of contract, cancelling a contract

合同满期 termination of contract

否认合同有效 repudiating a contract

## 费 用 Fees and Charges

运费市场, 货载市场 freight market, cargo market

运费表 freight tariff

运费率 freight rate

平均(运费)率 average rate

水脚公会费率 conference rate

公会会员费率 member rate

基本运费率 basic rate

一般杂货运费率 general cargo rate

特定货运费率 particular commodity rate

特别储藏运费率 special storage rate

停埠船运费率 berth cargo rate

海运运费 ocean freight

起点运费(起点提单费) minimum freight (minimum charge per B/L)

整船计算的运费 lump sum freight

额外运费 extra freight

从价运费 freight ad valorem (treasure and valuable cargo freight)

回运货物运费 return cargo freight

附加费 surcharge

直航附加费 through service additional, direct additional

转船附加费 transhipment additional

变更卸货港费 alteration of destination

超长货物附加费 extra charge on long length

超重货物附加费 extra charge on heavy lifts

燃油附加费 bunker surcharge

装卸费 stevedorage

装货费 loading charges

卸货费 unloading charges,

landing charges

翻舱费　cargo shifting charges

垫舱物料费　dunnage charge

平舱费　trimming charge

理货费　tally charge

理舱费　stowage

搬运费　porterage

精选费　garbling charges

挑拣费　sorting charges

整理费　reconditioning charges

洗舱费　tank cleaning charge

扫舱费　sweeping fee

滞期费　demurrage

待时费　waiting charges

租赁设备费　charges for using dock facilities

刷标记费　marking charges

标纸费　labelling charges

仓租　godown charges, storage charges

保管及处理费用　keeping and handling expenses

进港手续费　port charges, inward

出港手续费　port charges, outward

货物港务费　cargo dues

码头费　wharfage, dockage

开关舱费　open and close hatch charges

吊车费　shore crane charge

绞车费　winch charge

驳船费　lighterage

港口附加费　port surcharges

港口拥挤附加费　port congestion surcharge

杂费　sundry charges, incidental expenses

零星用费　out-of-pocket expenses

灯塔费(灯塔税)　light fee (lighthouse dues)

运河税　canal dues

港务税　harbour dues

引水费(引航费)　pilotage

拖船费(牵引费)　towage

停泊费(泊位费)　berthage

移泊费　shifting charges (mooring and unmooring charges)

解系缆费　charges for casting and weighing anchor (tying and untying the hawser)

包装费在内　packing included

免费包装　packing free

另加包装费　packing extra

# 航　运　Shipping

海运市场　shipping market

航运界　shipping circles

航运业公会(水脚公会)　shipping conference

参加公会船只　conference steamer

运输业　forwarding business, transportation business

远洋航运　ocean shipping

部分陆运与部分海运运输　part land and part sea transit

水陆联运　through transport

by land and water, mixed traffic

运输公司 transportation company, transit company

航运公司 shipping company

转运公司 transfer company

定期班轮公司 regular shipping lines

载运轮船 carrying steamer, carrier

接运轮船,二程船 on-carrying steamer, connecting steamer

定期货船 cargo liner

定期客货船 passenger and cargo liner

定期邮船(班轮) liner, packet ship

不定期船 tramp

承运货物 consignment

发货人(出口方) shipper, consignor (exporter)

自负盈亏自办运输保险的中间商 merchant shipper

轮船代理人 shipping agent

运输代理人 forwarding agent

代运业务 forwarding operation

发货通知书 consignment note

收货人 consignee

押运人 supercargo

收货代理人 receiving agent

装货单(下货纸) shipping order

装运说明 forwarding instructions

运输委托书 forwarding order

收货单,大副收据 mate's receipt

舱位 shipping space

订舱 booking shipping space

船位拥挤 congestion of shipping space

货载船位 cargo accommodation

集装箱 container

固封舱 strong compartment

不透水舱 water tight compartment

冷藏厢 refrigeration compartment

因亏舱 broken stowage, broken space

深舱 deep tank

装船指示 shipping instructions

装船通知 shipping advice

公量 conditioned weight

理论重量 theoretical weight

运费吨 freight ton

重量吨 weight ton ("W"ton)

容积吨(尺码吨) measurement ton("M"ton)

超重 overweight

重量不足 underweight

发货地国家 country of delivery

收货地国家 country of destination

船期 sailing schedule

船期表 list of sailings

惯驶的航线 usual route

经由第三国过境 passage in transit through another country

绕航 deviation, change of voyage

在途中 en route, in transit

预离期 estimated time of

departure (ETD)

启程(出发)日期　date of sailing, date of departure

抵达时间　date and time of arrival

预计抵达日期　estimated time of arrival (ETA)

延滞日数　days of demurrage

出发港　port of departure

起航港　port of sailing

装运港　port of shipment, shipping port

装货港　port of loading

交货港　port of delivery

沿途停靠港　port of call

中途转运港　port of transhipment, intermediate port

卸货港　port of unloading, port of discharge

选择港　port of option, optional port

遇难港　port of distress

目的港　port of destination

到达港　port of arrival

抵港通知　notice of vessel's arrival

最后停泊港　last port, port of last call

装运条款　shipment clause

短溢装条款　more or less clause

班轮条款　liner terms, berth terms

提单条款　bill of lading clause

法律条款　legality clause

运费条款　freight clause

换装条款　change of steamer clause

改卸目的港条款　change of destined port of discharge clause

甲板货物条款　deck cargo clause

危险货物条款　hazardous cargo clause

税务条款　dues clause

延迟提货条款　delayed delivery clause

货物包装条款　packing clause

绕道险条款　deviation clause, change of voyage clause

承运人赔偿金额限制条款　limit of indemnity from the carrier clause

承运人权限条款　liberties clause

承运人责任条款　carrier's liability clause

不合理的海运运输条款　unreasonable shipping clause

限期运抵目的港条款　fixed date of arrival at port of destination clause

食品不准与危险品同装一船的条款　foodstuffs not allowed to be shipped with hazardous goods in one vessel clause

指定代理人条款　consignment clause

指定船舶条款　specifying vessel clause

指定装卸码头的条款　specifying docks for loading and unloading clause

限制配船部位的条款　restriction on shipping space clause

留置权书　letter of lien

赔偿保证书 letter of indemnity

海运运费罚金 freight indemnity

班轮舱位 liner space

运费已付 freight paid

费用已付 charges paid

运费已预付 freight prepaid

费用已预付 charges prepaid

运费由提货人支付 freight forward, freight collect

费用向收货人索取 charges collect

运费回扣 freight rebate

# 租　船　Ship Chartering

租船市场 chartering market

期租船 time charter

程租船 voyage charter

单程租船 single-trip charter, single-voyage charter

来回程租船 round-trip charter, return voyage charter

连续租船 consecutive voyage charter

光船租赁 bareboat charter, charter by demise

运输总额已定(包干)的租船 lumpsum charter

租船人 charterer

租船代理人(代表租船人) chartering agent

船东 shipowner

租船经纪人(代表船东) ship broker

租船委托书 chartering order

租金 charter hire

包运(租船)运费 affreightment

空舱费 dead freight

按日租赁 charter on per dium basis

按日(月)比例计算的运费 daily (monthly) pro-rata freight

程租船船方负担装卸费用条件 gross terms

装货费在外条件 free in (F.I.)

卸货费在外条件 free out (F.O.)

装卸费在外条件 free in and out (F.I.O.)

装卸理舱费在外条件 free in, out and stowed (F.I.O.S.)

起租检验 on-hire survey

退租检验 off-hire survey

验船师 marine surveyor, ship surveyor

受载期限 lay days

受载(备装)通知 notice of readiness

销约日期 cancelling date

撤销条款 cancellation clause

船级 classification of ship, ship's class

船只定级机关 classification society

配载不良 bad stowage

装载能力 loading capacity

(总)载重量 deadweight tonnage

总排水量 gross displacement tonnage

净排水量　net displacement tonnage

吃水　draft (draught)

吃水线　water line

吃水标　Plimsoll mark, load-line

吃水差　draft difference

吃水量很浅　very shallow draft

船舶吨位　tonnage

注册吨位　registered tonnage

注册总吨　gross registered tonnage ( Gr. R. T.)

注册净吨　net registered tonnage ( N. R. T. )

船舶周转率　turnround rate

杂货船　general cargo vessel

干货船　dry cargo vessel

散货船　bulk carrier

特别货船　special cargo vessel

装运整件货物的杂货船　packed cargo vessel

集装箱船　container ship

油槽船　oil tanker

重油船　dirty ship

劳埃德船舶动态日报　Lloyd's Daily Index

劳埃德船舶年鉴　Lloyd's Register of British and Foreign Shipping (Lloyd's Register)

劳埃德海事情报　Lloyd's List

波罗的海航运公会的"统一定期租船合同"　"Uniform Time Charter"

波罗的海白海船东公会的"统一杂货租赁合同"　"Uniform General Charter"

## 货运单据　Cargo Transportation Documents

货运单据　shipping documents, documents of despatch

货运单据副本　copy documents of shipment

运输凭证　transport documents

全套单据　full set of documents

(海运)提单　bill of lading (B/L)

海洋提单　marine B/L

提单正本(可议副提单）　negotiable copy of B/L (negotiable B/L)

提单副本(非议副提单)　non-negotiable copy of B/L (non-negotiable B/L)

装船提单　shipped B/L, on board B/L

收货待运提单　received for shipment B/L

直达提单　direct B/L

转运提单　transhipment B/L

联运提单　through B/L

舱面提单　on deck B/L

直运提单, (记名)提单　straight B/L, named B/L

不记名提单　bearer B/L,

| | | | |
|---|---|---|---|
| unnamed B/L | | 临时发票 | provisional invoice |
| 指示提单 | order B/L | 形式(预开)发票 | proforma invoice |
| 发货人指示提单 | shipper's order B/L | 商业发票 | commercial invoice |
| 收货人指示提单 | consignee's order B/L | 银行发票 | banker's invoice |
| 过期提单 | stale B/L | 签证发票 | certified invoice |
| 清洁提单 | clean B/L | 领事发票 | consular invoice |
| 不洁提单 | foul B/L, claused B/L | 政府签发的有关出口的证件 | governmental export authorization |
| 港口提单 | port B/L | 数量/重量证明书 | certificate of quantity / weight |
| 代管提单 | custody B/L | | |
| 班轮提单 | liner B/L | 产地证明书 | certificate of origin |
| 租船提单 | charter party B/L | | |
| 根据租船合同签发并受租船合同条件约束的提单 | B/L issued under and subject to the conditions of a charter party | 特许进口证明书 | certificate of import licence |
| | | 制造商证明书 | manufacturer's certificate |
| 以帆船装运的提单 | B/L covering shipment by sailing vessels | 领事公证 | consular certification, consular attestation |
| 运输代理人出立的提单 | B/L issued by forwarding agents | 保险单 | insurance policy |
| | | 装箱单 | packing list |
| | | 重量(磅码)单 | weight memo, weight list, weight note |
| 铁路及内河提单 | railway and inland waterway B/L | | |
| | | 重量规格单 | specifications of weight |
| 托运单 | waybill | 到货通知单 | notice of arrival |
| 发票 | invoice | 兽运及卫生证明书 | veterinary and sanitary certificate |

## 货　物　Cargo

| | | | |
|---|---|---|---|
| 进口货物 | import cargo | 裸装货 | nude cargo |
| 出口货物 | export cargo | 包装货物 | packed cargo |
| 杂货 | general cargo | 甲板货(舱面货) | deck cargo |
| 轻泡货(容积货物) | light cargo, measurement cargo | 舱内货 | under deck cargo |
| | | 冷冻货 | reefer goods, refrigerated goods |
| 散装货 | bulk cargo, cargo in bulk | | |
| | | 冷气货 | air-cooled cargo |

贵重货物　treasure and valu-
　able goods
笨大货物　bulky goods
重货　deadweight cargo
合同货物　contract goods
集装箱货物　container cargo
保价货物　insured cargo
在途中的货物　goods in transit
直达货　through cargo
过境货(转运货)　transit cargo
转船货(转口货)　transhipment
　cargo
(运费表上列举的)特定货物
　particular cargo
快运货　express goods, ex-
　press cargo
危险货　dangerous cargo,
　hazardous cargo
残损货物　damaged cargo
不合格货物　disqualified
　goods
待领货物　unclaimed cargo
回运货　return cargo
超重货物　heavy package,
　heavy lift
超长货物　long goods, lengthy
　goods

零批货　parcel of goods
多装的货物　overshipped
　cargo
短装货物　short-shipped cargo
误装货物　mis-shipped cargo
溢卸货物　overlanded cargo
短卸货物　shortlanded cargo
误卸货物　mis-discharged
　cargo
漏卸货物　over-carried cargo
超程货物　distance freight
(船舶遇险时)投弃的货物
　jetsam (lagan, ligan)
(遇难船只的)飘浮的货物
　flotsam (flotsan, flotson)
应税物品　dutiable goods
已完税货物　duty-paid goods
免税货物　duty-free goods
退关货物　shut out cargo
保税货物　bonded cargo
海关监管货物　goods under
　customs supervision
限制物品　restricted articles
违法(禁)物品　contraband
　(contraband articles)
货载动态　cargo movements

## 装卸船　Loading and Unloading

装船(上货)　loading
卸船(卸货)　unloading, dis-
　charging
装船能力　loading capacity
卸载能力　unloading capacity
装卸设备(条件)　loading and
　unloading facilities
装货率　rate of loading
卸货率　rate of discharge

靠码头装卸　loading and
　unloading alongside wharf
靠船边装卸　loading and un-
　loading alongside ship
满载　full load, full cargo
超载　overload
欠载　underload
港口习惯快速装卸　customary
　quick dispatch (CQD)

速遣费 dispatch allowance

晴天工作日 weather working day (W. W.)

连续工作日 running lay days

晴天工作日,但星期天,例假除外 weather working days, Sundays and holidays excepted (W. W. S. H. E.)

防止迟延 preventing delay

宽延日 day of grace

扫舱 sweeping

理舱 cargo stowing

混装 mixed loading

平舱 cargo trimming

翻舱 cargo shifting

理货 cargo tallying

理货人 tallyman, tally clerk

码头装卸工人 stevedore, longshoreman

装卸队组长 foreman

码头工人 docker

配载图(积载图) cargo plan, hatch list, stowage plan

配载(积载)系数 stowage factor

## 装运与交货 Shipment and Delivery

装运 shipment

交货 delivery

象征交货 symbolic delivery

实际交货 actual delivery

当场交货 spot delivery

随通知随装运 shipment on call

近期装运 early shipment, near shipment

试销货 trial shipment, sample shipment

第一次装船 initial shipment

分批装运 partial shipment, part shipment

分期装运 shipment in (by) instalments

固定的装运 regular sailing, regular shipment

即期装运 prompt shipment, immediate shipment

有机会即装运 shipment by first opportunity

直达轮装运 shipment by

direct steamer

第一艘便船装运 shipment by first available steamer

提前装运的货物 advanced shipment

准时装运 punctual shipment

定期(限期)装运 timed shipment

远期装运 distant shipment, forward shipment

迟误装运 delayed shipment

不定期装运 indefinite shipment

尽速装运 shipment as soon as possible, shipment soonest possible

发票多开价格的货物 over-invoiced shipment

发票少开价格的货物 short-invoiced shipment

未装运余额 balance of shipment

转运,转船装运 transhipment,

transfer

循例的转船装运　customary transhipment

转运量　volume of transhipment

再装船　reshipment

停装要求　instructions to hold shipment

装运条件　terms of shipment

公差　tolerance, allowance

无船时的延期装运　postponed shipment allowed in case of steamer unavailable

一次装运出去的货物　goods to be shipped in one lot

货物在(装船港)装船　goods to be loaded at (named port of loading)

货物在(卸船港)卸船　goods to be landed at (named port of unloading)

货物在(转运港)转运　goods to be transhipped at (named port of transhipment)

装运的准时性　punctuality of shipment

装船时间　time of shipment

装船日期　date of shipment

交货的基础　basis of delivery

装运时间表　shipment schedule

提前装运　advancing shipment

延期装运　extending shipment

加速装运　expediting shipment

中止装运　suspending shipment

保证交货　guaranteeing delivery

完成交货　fulfilling delivery

货物如期收到　shipment received in due course

通常交货地点　usual point for delivery

合同规定的交货地点　point of delivery as provided in contract

出栈凭证　delivery order

离岸重量　shipping weight, shipped weight

到岸重量　landing weight, landed weight

交货时重量　delivered weight

货物短装单　shortshipped cargo list

货物短卸单　shortlanded cargo list

## 结算与支付　Settlement of Payments and Payment

结算　settlement of payments

国际结算　international settlement (of payments)

结算单据　documents of settlement

现金结算　cash settlement

用人民币结算　settlement by means of Renminbi

清算手段　clearing medium

清算使用的货币　currency of

settlement

记帐结算 settlement on account

记帐货币 currency of account

双边结算 bilateral settlement

多边结算 multilateral settlement

相互冲帐 mutual compensation

支付 payment

支付地点 place of payment

支付条件 terms of payment

支付时间 time of payment

支付方式 mode of payment

支付票据 bill of payment

支付工具 means of payment

支付货币 currency of payment

全部付款 full payment

部分付款 partial payment

付现 cash payment

实物支付 payment in kind

易货偿付 barter payment

预先付款 payment in advance, forward payment

装船前付款 payment before shipment

立即付款 immediate (or prompt) payment

凭证付款 payment against presentation of shipping documents

货到付款 payment upon arrival (or receipt) of goods

累进付款(分批偿付货款) progressive payment

延付 deferred (or delayed) payment (payment on deferred terms)

回邮付现 cash by return mail (CRM)

回航付现 cash by return steamer

见票后付款(定期付款) payment after sight (date)

见票付款 payment at sight

见票后……天付款 payment … days after sight

订货款(押金) deposit, margin (earnest) money

偿付能力 solvency (paying capacity)

无支付能力(破产) insolvency (bankruptcy)

信用支付 payment by credit

用银行信用支付 payment by banker's credit

购买证支付方式 payment by (or against) A/P (authorlty of purchase)

银行保证书支付方式 payment by (or against) L/G (letter of guarantee)

信用证支付方式 payment by (or against) L/C (letter of credit)

用商业信用支付 payment by commercial credit

无证支付方式 payment without L/C (letter of credit)

汇付 payment through remittance

托收 collection (of payment)

托收委托书 collection order

货到收款 collection on arrival of goods

光票托收 collection on clean

bill (clean collection)

跟单托收 collection on documents, documentary collection

跟单承兑 documentary acceptance, acceptance on documents

承兑交单 documents against acceptance (D/A)

付款交单 documents against payment (D/P)

限期付款交单 documents against payment—sight (D/P—sight)

远期付款交单 documents against payment—after sight (—after date)

付款交单凭信托收据借货 documents against payment—trust receipt (D/P—T/R)

托收项下的凭单付款 payment against document through collection

(托收)需要时的代理人 referee in case of need

担保付款 aval

担保付款代理人 del credere agent

支取上的灵活限度 leeway in drawing

止付 withholding payment

拒付 refusing payment

止付通知单 stop payment order

开证申请书 application for L/C (letter of credit)

用电报安排信用证 arranging L/C telegraphically

拖延开信用证 procrastination of opening L/C

赎单 retiring a bill

零笔赎单 partial retirement

## 代理、经销与佣金 Agency, Distribution and Commission

销售代理(人) sales agency (agent)

订购代理 purchasing agency

出口商号代理 exporter's agency

商业代理 commercial agency

总代理 general agency, universal agency

独家代理 exclusive agency, sole agency

厂家代理 manufacturer's agency

直接经营又代理经营的代理 mixed agency

自费经营贸易的代理 merchant agency

寄售代理 consignment agency

自备仓库的代理 warehousing agency

无货存的代理 non-stock agency

特约代理 franchised agency

佣金代理 commission agency

分代理　sub-agency

经销　distribution

独家经销　sole distribution

优惠权利　preferential right

独家经营权利　exclusive right

直接代表　direct representative

代理地区　agent's territory

销售限额条款　quota clause

销售地区权利条款　territory rights clause

货主的权利与义务　principal's rights and duties

代理人的权利与义务　agent's rights and duties

申请代理　applying for agency

独家代理的条件　requirements for sole agency

经营方式　mode of doing business

经营能力　business capacity

经营范围　scope of business

经营规模　scale of business

交易额　volume of business

实际额　physical volume, actual volume

销售能力　sales ability

销售号召力　sales appeal

销售记录　record of sales

销售量　sales volume

销售计划　plan for sale promotion

保证每月销售量　guaranteed monthly sales

营业额　turnover

资金年周转额　annual turnover

支付能力　paying capacity, capacity for payment

现金头寸情况　cash position

信用调查报告　credit information

代理的聘定　agency appointment, appointing an agent

代理人佣金　agent's commission

佣金率　rate of commission

代销佣金　selling commission

代购佣金　buying commission

优厚的佣金　liberal commission

追加佣金　overriding commission

递加佣金(按实际情况或增或减)　commission on a sliding scale

同意代理按百分之……收取佣金　agency on the basis of… percent commission accepted

代理人的统计报告　agent's return

月报(统计)　monthly return

让供货人对某产品的行情保持经常了解　keeping suppliers constantly informed of the market development of a product

经营无力　incompetence, incapability

拒作代理　declining agency

进口许可证情况　import licence position (condition)

银行资料　bank reference

# 商　检　Inspection

中国商品检验局　**China Commodity Inspection Bureau**

输出输入商品检验暂行条例　**provisional regulations for the inspection of imported and exported commodities**

进出口商品法定检验　**legal inspection of imported and exported commodities**

进出口商品品质的检验和管理　**inspection, testing and control over the quality of imported and exported commodities**

联合检查　**joint inspection**

委托检验　**consignment inspection**

复验　**re-inspection**

复验权　**right of re-inspection**

残损检验　**inspection of damage**

进口商品的残损检验　**inspection on damage done to imported commodities**

积损(载货)鉴定　**inspection of cargo G.A. or P.A. (general average or particular average)**

包装检验　**packing inspection**

品质检验　**quality inspection**

核对货物品质　**checking quality of goods**

品质分析　**quality analysis**

干货舱清洁检验　**inspection on cleanliness of dry cargo hold**

油舱清洁检验　**inspection on cleanliness of tank**

油舱密固检验　**inspection on tightness of tank**

载损鉴定　**inspection on hatch and cargo**

船舱检查　**inspection on hold**

冷藏舱室检验　**inspection on refrigerating hold**

舱口检视　**hatch survey**

签封样品　**sampling**

封样　**sealing sample**

抽样办法　**method of sampling**

货载衡量　**measurement of cargo**

衡器计量　**weighing by scale**

水尺计重　**checking weight by draft**

容量计重　**checking weight by volume**

检验论断　**inspection findings**

监视卸载　**supervision of unloading**

监视装载　**supervision of loading**

检验费　**inspection fee**

品质检验费　**testing fee**

检验报告　**survey report**

检验证明书　**testing certificate, inspection certificate**

化验证明书(报告)　**analysis certificate, laboratory report**

样品报告　sampling report

货损检验报告　inspection report on cargo damage

货值证明　certificate of value (of goods)

公证行(商检人员)　surveyors

品质证明书　quality certificate

重量证明书　weight certificate, surveyors' report on weight

## 索　赔　Claim

要求赔偿　claim for compensation (damage)

索赔原因　cause for claim

品质索赔　quality claim

数量索赔　quantity claim

残损索赔　damage claim

残损赔偿　indemnity for damage

向保险商(公司)索赔　claim against the underwriters (insurance company)

保险商的责任　underwriters' liability

向承运人(船公司)索赔　claim against the carrier (shipping company)

向卖方索赔　claim against the sellers

卖方的责任　seller's liability

违约赔偿　compensation consequent on violation of contract

货物与样品不符　shipment not checking with sample

比原样低劣的品质　quality inferior to original sample

装运短少　short shipment

迟延装运　late shipment

错发错运　mis-shipment

不交货　non-delivery

随船单证不齐，或漏填错发　shipping documents incomplete, or not properly filled out and dispatched

损坏原因　cause of damage

卸货时受到的残损　damage inflicted during discharge

在途中造成的残损　damage received in transit

不合宜的包装引起的损坏　damage due to unsuitable packing

处理不慎引起的损坏　damage due to rough handling

重钉造成的残损　damage resulted from renailing

损害程度　extent of damage

损害额　amount of damage

恶意短量　shortage by ill-will

故意行为　wilful act

自然短量　shortage through natural loss

损耗　wastage

天然引起的损失　loss due to natural cause

残损证明　evidence of damage

商检人员的意见(证明书)　surveyors' comment (report)

海难(海事)　marine accidents,

perils of the sea

遇险性质 nature of occurence

战争行为 act of war

类似战争行为 warlike operations

天灾 "act of God"

不可抗力 force majeure

意外事故 contingency

偶然事故 casual mishap

海损 average

全损 total loss

全部货物全损 total loss of whole cargo

部分货物全损 total loss of partial cargo

实际全损 actual total loss

推定全损 constructive total loss

单独海损(部分损失) particular average (partial loss)

共同海损 general average

共同海损费用 general average expenditure

海损异议书 captain's protest

海事报告 sea protest, ship's protest

海损查勘人 average surveyor

联合检查小组 joint inspection party

事故证明书 certificate of accident

调查报告 investigation report

索赔调查人 claims investigator

索赔证件 papers in support of a claim

索赔清单 claim sheet

索赔文件 documents for claim

索赔通知 notice of claim

索赔有效时间(索赔时效) time of validity of claim

置索赔不理 ignoring a claim

拒赔 refusing a claim, rejecting a claim, declining a claim

使索赔无效 annulling a claim, invalidating a claim

放弃索赔 waiving a claim, dropping a claim

减轻索赔 qualifying a claim

考虑提赔 considering a claim

接受索赔 accepting a claim, entertaining a claim

承诺索赔 granting a claim

满足索赔 meeting a claim, satisfying a claim

清理索赔 clearing up a claim

理赔 settling a claim

理算 adjusting, adjustment

海损精算 average adjustment, average judgment

海损精算书 average statement

海损理算人 average adjuster

索赔理算人 claims adjuster

理赔代理人 claims settling agent

公证人(录事) notary public (public notary)

解决意见 proposal for settlement

立即解决 prompt settlement, immediate settlement

公正解决 equitable settlement, just settlement

友好解决 amicable settle-
ment, settling amicably

协商解决 settling through
negotiation

圆满解决 bringing matter to
a happy close

赔偿损失 making good a
loss, recouping for a loss

退回不合格的货物 returning
goods disqualified

换货 replacing goods,
replacement of goods

支付损害赔偿金 paying

damages

损失的赔偿额 compensatory
damages

全部赔偿 compensating fully

部分赔偿 compensating
partly

不合理的索赔 unreasonable
claim

反诉 counter claim

提赔权利 entitlement to
damages (compensation)

索赔悬案 outstanding claim

索赔者 claimant

受益人 beneficiary

## 争议与仲裁　Dispute and Arbitration

争议 dispute

争执点 point at issue, point
in question

未决问题 a moot point, a
debatable question

争议当事人 disputing parties

执行合同或与合同有关的争议
dispute arising from
execution of, or in
connection with, contract

争议的处理 treatment of
disputes

将案子提交仲裁 putting a
case to arbitration

打官司(诉诸法律) resorting
to litigation

责任 commitment, liability

责任范围 limitation of
liability

负法律责任 bearing legal
liability

负起责任 assuming

responsibility

转移责任 diverting
responsibility

推卸责任 shirking responsi-
bility, dodging responsibility

拒绝承认责任 disclaiming
responsibility

否认一切责任 denying all
responsibilities

撤回责任 relinquishing
responsibility

职责期限 period of
responsibility

责任终止 cesser of liability

仲裁 arbitration

商业仲裁 commercial
arbitration

仲裁法庭 arbitration tribunal

仲裁程序 arbitration proce-
dure

仲裁费用 arbitration fee

(expenses)

首席仲裁员　umpire

仲裁员　arbitrator

原告　plaintiff, accuser

被告　defendant, accused

证人　witness

承担裁判　assuming jurisdiction

受理案件　accepting a case

审理案件　hearing a case

裁决　arbitration award (decision)

胜诉方　winning party

败诉方　losing party

申诉(起诉)　suit, action

抗辩　pleading

诉状　writ

公正判断　impartial judgment

驳回案件　turning down a case

属船东或保险人职责范围的案件　a case for the underwriters (shipowner, etc.)

需要检查的案件　a case subject to examination

未决案件　a pending case, an outstanding case

长期未决的案件　a case of long standing

(委员会)受权调查范围　terms of reference

管辖权条款　jurisdiction clause

仲裁裁决终局论　theory of arbitration award being final and conclusive

法人　juridical person, legal person

自然人　physical person

法人团体　corporate body (body corporate)

属人法　lex personalis

物之所在地法　lex rei sitae

契约(合同)缔结地法　lex loci contractus

债务履行地法　lex loci solutionis

行为地法　lex loci actus

民法　civil law

商法　commercial law

海上法　marine law

海运法令　ordinance regulating carriage of goods by sea

公海　high seas, open seas

领海　territorial waters

商标权　ownership of trademark

专利权　patent

版权　copyright

追索权　recourse

船东留置权　shipowner's lien

对外贸易仲裁委员会　Foreign Trade Arbitration Commission—F.T.A.C.

海事仲裁委员会　Maritime Arbitration Commission—M.A.C.

# 附录(一)　Appendix（Ⅰ）

## 国际经济贸易组织　International Economic and Trade Organizations

中国国际贸易促进委员会　China Council for the Promotion of International Trade (C.C.P.I.T.)

美中贸易全国理事会　National Council for US-China Trade

日中经济协会　Japan-China Economic Association

日本国际贸易促进协会　Association for the Promotion of International Trade, Japan

英国国际贸易促进委员会　British Council for the Promotion of International Trade

国际商会　International Chamber of Commerce

国际海洋运输险协会　International Union of Marine Insurance

国际铝矾土协会　International Alumina Association

万国邮政联盟　Universal Postal Union (UPU)

关税合作理事会　Customs Co-operation Council (CCC)

联合国贸易与发展理事会　United Nations Trade and Development Board

经济合作与开发组织　Organization for Economic Cooperation and Development (OECD)

欧洲经济共同体(西欧共同市场)　European Economic Community (EEC), European Common Market (Europe)

欧洲自由贸易联盟(区)　European Free Trade Association (Area) (EFTA)

经济互助委员会(经互会)　Council for Mutual Economic Aid (CMEA)

欧洲集团　Eurogroup

十国集团　Group of Ten

二十国委员会　Committee of Twenty (Paris Club)

巴黎统筹委员会　Coordinating Committee (COCOM)

加勒比共同市场(加勒比自由贸易同盟) **Caribbean Common Market (CCM), Caribbean Free-Trade Association (CARIFTA)**

安第斯共同市场 **Andeans Common Market (ACM), Andeans Treaty Organization (ATO)**

拉丁美洲自由贸易联盟 **Latin American Free Trade Association (LAFTA)**

中美洲共同市场 **Central American Common Market (CACM)**

非洲与马尔加什共同组织 **African and Malagasy Common Organization (OCAM)**

东非共同市场 **East African Common Market (EACM)**

中非关税经济同盟 **Central African Customs and Economic Union (CEUCA)**

西非经济共同体 **West African Economic Community (WAEC)**

石油输出国组织 **Organization of the Petroleum Exporting Countries (OPEC)**

阿拉伯石油输出国组织 **Organization of Arab Petroleum Exporting Countries (OAPEC)**

英联邦特惠区 **Commonwealth Preference Area**

法国对外贸易中心 **Centre National du Commerce Exterieur (National Center of External Trade)**

中国人民银行 **People's Bank of China**

中国银行 **Bank of China**

国际复兴开发银行,世界银行 **International Bank for Reconstruction and Development (IBRD), World Bank**

国际开发协会 **International Development Association (IDA)**

国际货币基金协定(布里顿森林协定) **International Monetary Fund Agreement (Bretton Woods Agreement)**

国际货币基金组织 **International Monetary Fund (IMF)**

欧洲经济与货币同盟 **European Economic and Monetary Union**

欧洲货币合作基金 **European Monetary Cooperation Fund**

国际结算银行 **Bank for International Settlements (BIS)**

非洲开发银行 **African Development Bank (AFDB)**

美国进出口银行 **Export-Import Bank of Washington**

花旗银行 **National City Bank of New York**

美丰银行 **American Oriental Banking Corporation**

美国交通银行 **American Express Co. Inc.**

大通银行 **The Chase Bank**

泛美开发银行 **Inter-American Development Bank (IDB)**

欧洲投资银行 **European Investment Bank (EIB)**

米兰银行　Midland Bank, Ltd.

瑞士联合银行　United Bank of Switzerland

德累斯敦银行　Dresden Bank A. G.

(日本)东京银行　Bank of Tokyo, Ltd.

香港汇丰银行　Hongkong and Shanghai Banking Corporation

国际金融公司　International Finance Corporation (IFC)

非洲金融共同体　La Communauté Financiève Africane

(联合国)经济及社会理事会　(UN) Economic and Social Council (ECOSOC)

联合国开发计划署　United Nations Development Program (UNDP)

联合国资本开发基金　United Nations Capital Development Fund (UNCDF)

联合国工业发展组织　United Nations Industrial Development Organization (UNIDO)

联合国贸易与发展会议　United Nations Conference on Trade and Development (UNCTAD)

(联合国)粮食与农业组织　(UN) Food and Agricultural Organization (FAO)

(联合国)欧洲经济委员会　(UN) Economic Commission for Europe (ECE)

(联合国)拉丁美洲经济委员会　(UN) Economic Commission for Latin Amerca (ECLA)

(联合国)亚洲及远东经济委员会　(UN) Economic Commission for Asia and Far East (ECAFE)

(联合国)西亚经济委员会　(UN) Economic Commission for Western Asia (ECWA)

(联合国)非洲经济委员会　(UN) Economic Commission for Africa (ECA)

华侨投资公司　Overseas Chinese Investment Company

纽约证券交易所　New York Stock Exchange

伦敦股票市场　London Stock Market

波罗的海商业和航运交易所　Baltic Mercantile and Shipping Exchange

# 附录(二)　Appendix（Ⅱ）

## 常用商业略语　Commercial Abbreviations in Common Use

| | | |
|---|---|---|
| **Al** | 一等的 | **firstclass** |
| **a.a.r.** | 一切险(水险) | **against all risks (marine insurance)** |
| **a/c** | 往来帐 | **account current; current account** |
| **a/c** | 帐(目) | **account** |
| **acc.** | 承兑, 接受, 帐目或会计员 | **acceptance, accepted, account or accountant** |
| **accrd.** | 自然增长的 | **accrued** |
| **acct.** | 帐目, 帐户或会计员 | **account or accountant** |
| **acpt.** | 承兑 | **acceptance** |
| **a/cs pay.** | 应付帐 | **accounts payable** |
| **a/cs rec.** | 应收帐 | **accounts receivable** |
| **A.d.; A/d** | 在指定日期后 | **after date** |
| **ad.** | 广告 | **advertisement** |
| **ad init.** | 开始 | **(ad initium) at or to the beginning** |
| **ad int.** | 暂时, 临时 | **(ad interim) in the meantime** |
| **adj.** | 调停人, 理算人 | **adjuster** |
| **ad fin.** | 最终, 最后 | **(ad finem) at or to the end** |
| **ad inf.** | 永远, 无限 | **(ad infinitum) to infinity** |
| **ad lib.** | 随意 | **at pleasure** |
| **adv.** | 按值或广告 | **(ad valorem) according to value or advertisement** |
| **ad val.** | 按值 | **according to value** |
| **advert. (advt.)** | 广告 | **advertisement** |
| **a.f.** | 如下: | **as follows:** |
| **A.F.B.** | 空运单 | **air freight bill** |
| **agcy.** | 代理 | **agency** |
| **agrd.** | 同意 | **agreed** |

| | | |
|---|---|---|
| **agt.** | 代理人 | **agent** |
| **amt.** | 金额 | **amount** |
| **a.n.** | 到货通知书 | **arrival notice** |
| **ans.** | 回复 | **answer or answered** |
| **A/P** | 追加保险费, 应付帐或购买证 | **additional premium, account payable or authority to purchase** |
| **Approv.** | 同意;批准 | **approval** |
| **approx.** | 大概,大约 | **approximately** |
| **A.R.** | 应收帐 | **accounts receivable** |
| **arr.** | 抵达 | **arrived or arrival** |
| **art.** | 条款,项目 | **article** |
| **A/S** | 销售帐,见票后或见票 | **account sales, after sight or at sight** |
| **atten.(attn.)** | 注意 | **attention** |
| **Av. (av.)** | 平均 | **average** |
| **a/w** | 实际重量 | **actual weight** |
| **a.w.b.** | 空运单 | **air way bill** |
| **bal.** | 余额;结余 | **balance** |
| **B/C** | 托收汇票 | **bill for collection** |
| **B/D** | 贴现汇票, 银行汇票 | **bills discounted, or bank draft** |
| **b/d** | 接上页 | **brought down** |
| **B/E** | 报关通知单或汇票 | **bill of entry (customs), bill of exchange** |
| **b/f** | 转下页 | **brought forward** |
| **B/G** | 关栈货物 | **bonded goods** |
| **Bk** | 银行 | **bank** |
| **bkg.** | 银行业或簿记 | **banking or bookkeeping** |
| **bkpr.** | 簿记员 | **bookkeeper** |
| **bkpt.** | 破产者 | **bankrupt** |
| **B/L** | 提货单 | **bill of lading** |
| **B/P** | 包裹单或应付票据 | **bill of parcels or bill payable** |
| **B/R** | 应收票据 | **bill receivable** |
| **B/S** | 卖据或资产负债表 | **bill of sale or balance sheet** |
| **b.t.** | 班轮条件 | **berth terms** |
| **b.v.** | 帐面价值 | **book value** |
| **C.A.** | 资本帐或信贷帐 | **capital account or credit account** |
| **C.A.D.** | 凭单付现 | **cash against documents** |
| **c.a.f.** | 成本,保险加运费(价格) | **cost, assurance, freight (price)** |
| **c.&d.** | 银货两讫 | **collection and delivery** |

**c.&f.**　成本加运费价格　cost and freight

**Cash B/L**　凭提单付现　cash against bill of lading

**C/B**　现金帐　cash book

**C.B.D.**　交货前付现　cash before delivery

**C.C.**　现金信贷, 商会, 银行本票或(包括暴动的)民变险　cash credit, chamber of commerce, cashier's cheque or civil commotion (including riots)

**C/D**　付现折价, 存款证明书, 交货证明书, 凭单付现, 分期收款出售　cash discount, certificate of deposit, certificate of delivery, cash against documents or conditional sale

**c/d**　接上页　carried down

**cum div.**　带红利　with dividend

**c.f.**　成本加运费的到岸价格　cost and freight

**c/f**　转入下页　carried forward

**cf.**　比较　(confer) compare

**c.h.**　海关或票据交换所　customs house or clearing house

**chges.pd.**　费用已付　charges paid

**chges.ppd**　费用预付　charges prepaid

**c/i**　保险证明书　certificate of insurance

**c.i.a.**　交货前付现　cash in advance

**c.i.f.**　成本, 保险费加运费的到岸价格　cost, insurance and freight

**c.i.f.&c.**　成本, 保险, 运费加佣金(或费用)的到岸价格　cost, insurance, freight and commission (or charges)

**c.i.f.&e.**　成本, 保险, 运费加外汇的到岸价格　cost, insurance, freight and exchange

**c.i.f.&i.**　成本, 保险, 运费加利息的到岸价格　cost, insurance, freight and interest

**C.I.F.C.&I.**　成本, 保险, 运费, 佣金(或托收)加利息的到岸价格　cost, insurance, freight, commission(or collection)and interest

**C.I.F.C.E.&I.**　成本, 保险, 运费, 佣金(或托收), 贴水加利息的到岸价格　cost, insurance, freight, commission (or collection), exchange and interest

**CL. B/L**　光票信用证　clean bill of lading

**C/M**　出厂证明　certificate of manufacture

**C/N**　贷方通知单　credit note

**C.O.D.**　货到付现　cash on delivery

| coins. | 共同保险 co-insurance |
| conf'd | 确认 confirmed |
| c.o.s. | 装船付现 cash on shipment |
| c/p | 租船合同 charter party |
| CR. | 信贷 credit |
| Cr. | 债权人 creditor |
| C.R.M. | 回信付现或货到付现 cash by return mail or cash on receipt of merchandise |
| C.R.S. | 回航付现 cash by return steamer |
| c.t.l. | 推定全损 constructive total loss |
| c.t.l.o. | 推定全损险 constructive total loss only |
| D/A | 承兑交单或定期存款 documents against acceptance or deposit account |
| D/B | 流水帐 day book |
| Dbk. | 退税 drawback |
| D/D | 即期汇票 demand draft |
| Deb. | 退税证明书或借方 debenture or debit |
| deb. bal. | 借方结余 debit balance |
| d.f. | 空舱费 dead freight |
| Dft. | 汇票 draft |
| dft/c. | 光票 clean draft |
| Dis. | 折扣 discount |
| Div. | 红利 dividend |
| D/N | 借方通知单 debit note |
| d(do.) | 同上, 同前 ditto, the same |
| D.O. | 出货单, 栈单 delivery order |
| docs. | 单据, 文件 documents |
| D/P | 付款交单 documents against payment |
| D/R | 存款收据 deposit receipt |
| Dr. | 欠债人 debtor |
| Ds. dft. | 见票即付汇票或即期汇票 sight draft or day draft |
| d.t. | 交货时间 delivery time |
| d.w. | 总载重量 deadweight |
| ea. (@) | 每(件、个、只等) each |
| E.&O.E. | 错误和遗漏不在此限 errors and omissions excepted |
| e.e. | 错误不在此限 errors excepted |
| encl. | 附件 enclosure or enclosed |
| ETA | 预计的到达时间 estimated time of arrival |
| et al. | 以及其它地方或以及其它等等 (et alibi) and elsewhere |

| | | |
|---|---|---|
| | | or (et alii) and others |
| etc. | 等等 | (et cetera) and so on, and so forth |
| ETD | 预计的启程时间 | estimated time of departure |
| et seq(q). or et sq(q) | 以及下列等等 | (et sequentes or et sequentia) and those that follow |
| exps. | 开支或出口货物 | expenses or exports |
| ex whse. | 卖方仓库交货价格 | ex warehouse |
| F.a.a. | 一切海损不赔 | free of all average |
| F.&D. | 运费与滞期费 | freight and demurrage |
| F.A.Q. | 大路货或码头交货价格 | fair average quality or free at quay |
| F.A.S. | 离岸价格 | free alongside ship |
| F.B. | 运费单 | freight bill |
| F.C.&S. | 兵险不保 | free of capture and seizure |
| Fco. | 指定地点交货价格 | franco |
| f.f.d. | 无残损或免税 | free from damage or free from duty |
| F.I. | 装货费在外条件 | free in |
| F.I.O. | 装卸费在外条件 | free in and out |
| F.I.O.S. | 装卸理舱费在外条件 | free in, out and stowed |
| F.O. | 卸货费在外条件 | free out |
| f.o. | 目的港船边交货的到岸价格或实盘 | free overside, free overboard or firm offer |
| F.O.B. | 离岸价格 | free on board |
| f.o.c. | 免费 | free of charge |
| f.o.i. | 免息 | free of interest |
| F.O.R. | 火车上交货价格 | free on rail |
| F.O.S. | 离岸价格 | free on steamer |
| f.p. | 火险,保单,流动保单或全部款项已付讫 | fire policy, floating policy or fully paid |
| F.P.A. | 平安险 | free of particular average |
| frt.pp. | 运费已预付 | freight prepaid |
| frt.fwd. | 运费由提货人支付 | freight forward |
| f.w.d. | 淡水雨淋残损 | fresh water damage |
| f.x. | 外汇 | foreign exchange |
| G.A. | 共同海损 | general average; gross average |
| G.M.Q. | 上好可销品质 | good merchantable quality |
| G.M.T. | 格林威治平时 | Greenwich Mean Time |
| GR.R.T. | 注册总吨 | gross registered tonnage |
| gr.wt. | 毛重 | gross weight |

| | | |
|---|---|---|
| hrs. | 小时 | **hours** |
| i.e. | 即 | **(id est) that is, that is to say** |
| Id. | 同上 | **(idem) the same** |
| imps. | 进口货物 | **imports** |
| inst. | 本月的 | **instant (this month)** |
| Int. | 利息 | **interest** |
| In trans. | 在途中 | **in transit, on the way** |
| Inv. | 发货单 | **invoice** |
| I.O.U. | 借据 | **I owe you (memorandum for a debt)** |
| I.P.A. | 水渍险 | **including particular average** |
| J/A | 联名存款帐 | **joint account** |
| L.&D. | 损失与残损 | **loss and damage** |
| L/C | 信用证 | **letter of credit** |
| loco | 当地 | **on the spot** |
| ltg. | 驳船费 | **lighterage** |
| max. | 最高限度 | **maximum (the most)** |
| memo | 备忘录 | **memorandum** |
| M.I. | 水险 | **marine insurance** |
| min. | 最低限度 | **minimum (the least)** |
| M.I.P. | 水险保单 | **marine insurance policy** |
| M.O. | 小额汇票或邮函订货 | **money order or mail order** |
| M.R. | 收货单 | **mate's receipt** |
| MS. | 手稿 | **manuscripts** |
| M/T | 信汇 | **mail transfer** |
| n.a. | 无帐或不承兑 | **no account or non-acceptance** |
| N.B. | 注意,留心 | **(nota bene) note well, take notice** |
| neg. | 可议付 | **negotiable** |
| n.e.i. | 不包括在其它地方或它处并无表明 | **not elsewhere included or not elsewhere indicated** |
| n.e.m. | 它处并无提及 | **not elsewhere mentioned** |
| N/F;n/f | 无现金 | **no funds** |
| n/m/ | 无标记 | **no mark (markings), not marked** |
| No. | 号码 | **number** |
| n.o.s. | 别无其它规定或别无其它指定 | **not otherwise stated or not otherwise specified** |
| N.P. | 公证人 | **notary public** |
| n.p.f. | 并无规定 | **not provided for** |
| N.R.T. | 注册净吨 | **net registered tonnage** |
| n.s. | 并无指定 | **not specified** |

| | | |
|---|---|---|
| **nt.wt.** | 净重 | net weight |
| **o.a.** | 接受时，由于或我们的帐 | on acceptance, on account or our account |
| **o.e.** | 疏漏不在此限 | ommissions excepted |
| **O.K.** | 一切都妥或批准 | all correct, approved |
| **o.p.** | 船名未确定保单 | open policy |
| **p.a.** | 每年或单独海损 | per annum (per year, annually) or particular average |
| **P.A.** | 单独海损，委托书或收购代理人 | particular average, power of attorney or purchasing agent |
| **Par** | 等值 | equal value |
| **p.c.** | 百分率或价格表 | per cent (%) or price current |
| **pd.** | 已付(款) | paid |
| **per an.** | 每年 | yearly |
| **per capita** | 每人 | by the head |
| **per pro.** | 由……所代表，根据代理权 | per procuration (by power of authority) |
| **P/N** | 期票 | promissory note |
| **P.O.** | 邮政汇票或邮局 | postal order or post office |
| **prox.** | 下月的 | proximo (next month) |
| **P.S.** | 书后；再者 | postscriptum; postscript |
| **P.T.O.** | 请翻到反页 | please turn over |
| **r.c.c.&s.** | 暴动，民变和罢工险 | riots, civil commotion and strikes |
| **ref.** | 关于或有关事项 | referring to or reference |
| **R.I.** | 分保险(再保险) | re-insurance |
| **S.S.** | 轮船 | steamship |
| **T.L.O.** | 全损险 | total loss only |
| **S.d.** | 无限期地 | (sine die) indefinitely |
| **T.T.** | 电汇 | telegraphic transfer (cable transfer) |
| **ult.** | 上月 | ultimo (last month) |
| **V.** | 对(抗) | versus; against |
| **viz.** | (亦)即 | videlicet; namely |
| **via** | (途)经 | by way of |
| **W.A.** | 海损照赔险 | with average |
| **w.b.** | 全库帐簿 | warehouse book |
| **W/B** | 运货单或世界银行 | way bill or World Bank |
| **Whf.** | 码头 | wharf |
| **Whse.** | 货仓 | warehouse |

W/R 战争险 war risk

W.R.&S.R.&C.C. 战争险加罢工,暴动和民变险 war risk and strikes, roits and civil commotion (insurance)

wt. 重量 weight

& 与;同 and

& c. 等等 and so forth

# 附录（三） Appendix（Ⅲ）

## 各国货币 moneys of the world

| 货币名称 | name of currency | 简写 symbol | 国　名（地区名） | country (region) |
|---|---|---|---|---|
| 人民币元 | yuan | RMB￥ | 中　　国 | China |
| 圆 | won | W | 朝　鲜 | Korea |
| 圆 | won | W | 南　朝　鲜 | South Korea |
| 盾 | dong | D. | 越　　南 | Vietnam |
| 图格里克 | tugrik | | 蒙　　古 | Mongolia |
| 日　元 | yen | ￥ | 日　　本 | Japan |
| 比　索 | peso | P or P | 菲　律　宾 | the Philippines |
| 基　普 | kip | K | 老　　挝 | Laos |
| 瑞　尔 | riel | 于 or CR | 柬　埔　寨 | Cambodia |
| 铢 | baht | B | 泰　　国 | Thailand |
| 元 | kyat | K | 缅　　甸 | Burma |
| 元 | dollar | M $ | 马　来　西　亚 | Malaysia |
| 元 | dollar | S $ | 新　加　坡 | Singapore |
| 元 | dollar | B $ | 文　　莱 | Brunei |
| 卢比、盾 | rupiah | Rp. | 印度尼西亚 | Indonesia |
| 卢　比 | rupee | PRe(复) Rs | 巴　基　斯　坦 | Pakistan |
| 卢　比 | rupee | Re(复) Rs | 印　　度 | India |
| 塔　卡 | taka | Tk | 孟　加　拉 | Bangladesh |
| 卢　比 | rupee | NRe(复) Rs | 尼　泊　尔 | Nepal |
| 卢　比 | rupee | SLRe (复) Rs | 斯　里　兰　卡 | Sri Lanka |
| 卢　比 | ruepe | MRp | 马　尔　代　夫 | Maldive |
| 尼 | afghani | Af | 阿　富　汗 | Afghanistan |
| 里亚尔 | rial | Rl | 伊　　朗 | Iran |
| 里拉(镑) | lira (pound) | LT (£T) | 土　耳　其 | Turkey |

| 货币名称 | name of currency | 简 写 symbol | 国 名 (地区名) | country (region) |
|---|---|---|---|---|
| 镑 | pound | £C | 塞 浦 路 斯 | Cyprus |
| 第 纳 尔 | dinar | ID | 伊 拉 克 | Iraq |
| 镑(里拉) | pound | £s (LS) | 叙 利 亚 | Syria |
| 镑 | pound | (L£) LL | 黎 巴 嫩 | Lebanon |
| 第 纳 尔 | dinar | JD | 约 旦 | Jordan |
| 镑 | pound | I£ | 以 色 列 | Israel |
| 里 亚 尔 | riyal | YR (I) | 阿 拉 伯 也门共和国 | The Yemen Arab Republic |
| 第 纳 尔 | dinar | (S) YD | 南 也 门 | South Yemen |
| 里 亚 尔 | riyal | SR | 沙特阿拉伯 | Saudi Arabia |
| 第 纳 尔 | dinar | KD | 科 威 特 | Kuwait |
| 第 纳 尔 | dinar | BD | 巴 林 | Bahrain |
| 里 亚 尔 | rial | QR | 卡 塔 尔 | Qatar |
| 迪 拉 姆 | dirham | DH | 阿拉伯联合 酋 长 国 | The United Arab Emirates |
| 里 亚 尔 | rial | R(O) | 阿 曼 | Oman |
| 元 | dollar | HK$ | 香 港 | Hongkong |
| 元 | pataca | Pat; P | 澳 门 | Macao |
| 镑 | pound | LE £E | 埃 及 | Egypt |
| 镑 | pound | LSd(£S) | 苏 丹 | Sudan |
| 第 纳 尔 | dinar | LD | 利 比 亚 | Libya |
| 第 纳 尔 | dinar | D | 突 尼 斯 | Tunis |
| 第 纳 尔 | dinar | DA | 阿尔及利亚 | Algeria |
| 迪 拉 姆 | dirham | DA | 摩 洛 哥 | Morocco |
| 乌 吉 亚 | ouguiya | VM | 毛里塔尼亚 | Mauritania |
| 法 郎 | franc | CFAF | 塞 内 加 尔 | Senegal |
| 达 拉 西 | dalasi | DG | 冈 比 亚 | Gambia |
| 法 郎 | franc | MF | 马 里 | Mali |
| 西 里 | syli | Syli | 几 内 亚 | Guinea |

| 货币名称 | name of currency | 简 写 symbol | 国 名 (地区名) | country (region) |
|---|---|---|---|---|
| 新塞地 | new cedi | N₵ | 加 纳 | Ghana |
| 法 郎 | franc | CFAF | 象牙海岸 | Ivory Coast |
| 法 郎 | franc | CFAF | 上沃尔特 | Upper Volta |
| 法 郎 | franc | CFAF | 贝 宁 | Benin |
| 法 郎 | franc | CFAF | 尼日尔 | Niger |
| 元 | dollar | L(ib)$ | 利比里亚 | Liberia |
| 利 昂 | leone | Le | 塞拉利昂 | Sierra Leone |
| 法 郎 | franc | CFAF | 多 哥 | Togo |
| 奈 拉 | naira | ₦ | 尼日利亚 | Nigeria |
| 法 郎 | franc | CFAF | 喀麦隆 | Cameroon |
| 埃奎勒 | ekuela | | 赤道几内亚 | Equatoria Guinea |
| 法 郎 | franc | CFAF | 乍 得 | Chad |
| 法 郎 | franc | CFAF | 中非共和国 | The Central African Republic |
| 法 郎 | franc | CFAF | 加 蓬 | Gabon |
| 法 郎 | franc | CFAF | 刚 果 | the Congo |
| 扎伊尔 | zaire | Z | 扎伊尔 | Zaire |
| 法 郎 | franc | FBu | 布隆迪 | Burundi |
| 法 郎 | franc | RF | 卢旺达 | Rwanda |
| 元 | dollar | Eth $ | 埃塞俄比亚 | Ethiopia |
| 先 令 | shilling | So. Sh. | 索马里 | Somali |
| 先 令 | shilling | K sh | 肯尼亚 | Kenya |
| 先 令 | shilling | U sh | 乌干达 | Uganda |
| 先 令 | shilling | T sh | 坦桑尼亚 | Tanzania |
| 卢 比 | rupee | Mau Rs (MR) | 毛里求斯 | Mauritius |
| 法 郎 | franc | CFAF | 科摩罗 | Comoros |
| 法 郎 | franc | FMG | 马达加斯加 (马尔加什) | Madagascar Malgache (Malagasy) |

| 货币名称 | name of currency | 简 写 symbol | 国 名 (地区名) | country (region) |
|---|---|---|---|---|
| 埃斯库多 | escudo | Esc | 安 哥 拉 | Angola |
| 埃斯库多 | escudo | Esc | 莫 桑 比 克 | Mozambique |
| 埃斯库多 | escudo | Ese | 几内亚比绍 | Guinea-Bissau |
| 埃斯库多 | escudo | Ese | 佛 得 角 | Cape Verde |
| 埃斯库多 | escudo | Ese | 圣多美和普林西亚 | Sao Tome and Principe |
| 元 | dollar | R$ | 罗得西亚 | Rhodesia |
| 克 瓦 查 | kwacha | K | 赞 比 亚 | Zambia |
| 克 瓦 查 | kwacha | MK | 马 拉 维 | Malawi |
| 兰 特 | rand | R | 南 非 | South Africa |
| 兰 特 | rand | R | 博茨瓦纳 | Botswana |
| 兰 特 | rand | R | 莱 索 托 | Lesotho |
| 里兰吉尼 | lilangeni | E | 斯威士兰 | Swaziland |
| 卢 比 | rupee | SRp. | 塞 舌 耳 | Seychelles |
| 法 郎 | franc | | 吉 布 提 | Djibouti |
| 列 克 | lek | Lek | 阿尔巴尼亚 | Albania |
| 列 伊 | leu | L;Leu, (复)Lei | 罗马尼亚 | Romania |
| 第 纳 尔 | dinar | Din | 南斯拉夫 | Yugoslavia |
| 卢 布 | rouble | R; Rub; Rbl | 苏 联 | U.S.S.R. |
| 兹 罗 提 | zloty | Zl | 波 兰 | Poland |
| 福 林 | forint | Ft. | 匈 牙 利 | Hungaria |
| 克 朗 | koruna | Kcs. | 捷克斯洛伐克 | Czechoslovakia |
| 列 弗 | leva | Lv;(复) Le Va | 保加利亚 | Bulgaria |
| 马 克 | mark | M | 东德(GDR) | East Germany |
| 马 克 | mark | DM | 西德(GFR) | West Germany |
| 法 郎 (新法郎) | franc | FF(NF) | 法 国 | France |

| 货币名称 | name of currency | 简　写 symbol | 国　　名 (地区名) | country (region) |
|---|---|---|---|---|
| 里　　拉 | lira (复) lire | Lit | 意　大　利 | Italy |
| 盾 | florin; guilder | f. (Fl) | 荷　　兰 | Netherlands |
| 法　　郎 | franc | BF | 比　利　时 | Belgium |
| 法　　郎 | franc | Lux F | 卢　森　堡 | Luxembourg |
| 镑 | pound | £; £stg. | 英　　国 | U.K. |
| 镑 | pound | £ Ir | 爱　尔　兰 | Ireland |
| 马　　克 | markka | Fmk | 芬　　兰 | Finland |
| 克　　朗 | krona (复) kroner | SKr | 瑞　　典 | Sweden |
| 克　　朗 | krona (复) kroner | NKr | 挪　　威 | Norway |
| 克　　朗 | krone (复) kroner | DKr | 丹　　麦 | Denmark |
| 克　　朗 | kronar (复) kronur | IKr | 冰　　岛 | Iceland |
| 法　　郎 | franc | SF | 瑞　　士 | Switzerland |
| 先　　令 | shilling schilling | Sch | 奥　地　利 | Austria |
| 德拉克马 | drachma | Dr | 希　　腊 | Greece |
| 镑 | pound | £M | 马　耳　他 | Malta |
| 比塞塔 | peseta | Ptas | 西　班　牙 | Spain |
| 埃斯库多 | escudo | Esc | 葡　萄　牙 | Portugal |
| 里　　拉 | lira (复) lire | Lit | 圣马力诺 | San Marino |
| 法　　郎 | franc | FF | 摩　纳　哥 | Monaco |
| 瑞士法郎 | Swiss franc | S.F. | 列支敦士登 | Liechtenstein |
| 元 | dollar | Can $ | 加　拿　大 | Canada |
| 元 | dollar | US $ | 美　　国 | U.S.A. |
| 比　　索 | peso | Mex $ | 墨　西　哥 | Mexico |
| 格　查　尔 | Quetzal | Q | 危地马拉 | Guatemala |

| 货币名称 | name of currency | 简　写 symbol | 国　　名 (地区名) | country (region) |
|---|---|---|---|---|
| 伦 皮 拉 | lempira | L | 洪 都 拉 斯 | Honduras |
| 科　　郎 | colon | ₡ | 萨 尔 瓦 多 | El Salvador |
| 科 多 巴 | córdoba | C $ | 尼 加 拉 瓜 | Nicaragua |
| 科　　郎 | colon | ₡ | 哥 斯 达 黎 加 | Costa Rica |
| 巴 波 亚 | balboa | B | 巴 拿 马 | Panama |
| 比　　索 | peso | Cub $ | 古　　巴 | Cuba |
| 古　　德 | gourde | G | 海　　地 | Haiti |
| 比　　索 | peso | RD $ | 多 米 尼 加 | Dominican Republic |
| 　　元 | dollar | B $ | 巴 哈 马 | Bahamas |
| 　　元 | dollar | J $ | 牙 买 加 | Jamaica |
| 　　元 | dollar | TT $ | 特 立 尼 达 和 多 巴 哥 | Trinidad and Tobago |
| 　　元 | dollar | BDS $ | 巴 巴 多 斯 | Barbados |
| 　　元 | dollar | Ec $ | 格 林 纳 达 | Grenada |
| 博 利 瓦 | bolivar | Bs | 委 内 瑞 拉 | Venezuela |
| 比　　索 | peso | Col $ | 哥 伦 比 亚 | Colombia |
| 　　元 | dollar | G $ | 圭 亚 那 | Guyana |
| 　　盾 | guilder | Ant. f. | 荷属安的列斯 | Netherlands Antilles |
| 　　盾 | guilder | Sur. f. | 苏 里 南 | Surinam |
| 克 鲁 赛 罗 | cruzeiro dollar | Cr $ | 巴　　西 | Brazil |
| 苏 克 雷 | sucre | S/. | 厄 瓜 多 尔 | Ecuador |
| 索 尔 | sole | S/. | 秘　　鲁 | Peru |
| 比　　索 | peso | $b | 玻 利 维 亚 | Bolivia |
| 比　　索 | peso | Ch$ | 智　　利 | Chile |
| 瓜 拉 尼 | guarani | ₲ | 巴 拉 圭 | Paraguay |
| 比　　索 | peso | $a | 阿 根 廷 | Argentina |
| 新 比 索 | new peso | Ur $ | 乌 拉 圭 | Uruguay |

| 货币名称 | name of currency | 简　写 symbol | 国　　名 （地区名） | country (region) |
|---|---|---|---|---|
| 元 | dollar | Bda $ (BD $) | 百　慕　大 | Bermuda |
| 美　　元 | dollar | U.S. $ | 波多黎各 | Puerto Rico |
| 元 | dollar | $ A | 澳大利亚 | Australia |
| 元 | dollar | NZ $ | 新　西　兰 | New Zealand |
| 塔　　拉 | tala | WS $ | 西萨摩亚 | Western Samoa |
| 澳　　元 | Australiàw dollar | $ A | 瑙　　鲁 | Nauru |
| 潘　　加 | pa'anga | T $ | 汤　　加 | Tonga |
| 元 | dollar | F $ | 斐　　济 | Fiji |
| 基　　那 | kina | | 巴布亚新 几　内　亚 | Papua New Guinea |
| 新西兰元 | New Zealand dollar | NZ $ | 库克群岛 | The Cook Islands |

# 第四部分

# 工业、交通、通讯

## Part IV

### Industry, Transport and Communications

# 目 录

# Contents

496

498

# 总 类 General

## 企业管理 Management of Enterprises

现代化的科学管理 modernized scientific management

实行生产民主 practicing democracy in production

工人参加管理 worker participation in management

干部参加生产劳动 cadre participation in productive labour

改革不合理的规章制度 reform of irrational and outdated rules and regulations

开展劳动竞赛 developing labour emulation

学习外国的先进管理 learning from the advanced management of other countries

计划管理 plan control

国家计划 state plan

远景规划 long-term plan

现行计划 operative

各项经济技术指标 economic and technological target figures

按经济规律办事 acting according to the law of economy

经济核算 business accounting

班组核算 accounting in work groups

成本核算 cost accounting

降低成本 reduction of cost

生产投资 production investment

总产值 total value of output

劳动生产率 labour productivity

固定资产 fixed assets

流动资金 circulating funds

资金积累 accumulation of funds

资金周转 turnover of funds

上缴利润 profit handed over to the state

利润率 profit rate

机械设备折旧费 depreciation of machinery

非生产性开支 nonproductive expenditures

亏损 loss

补贴 subsidy

统一管理物资 unified management of materials

修旧利废 repairing old equipment and reclaiming scraps

合理利用原材料 rational use of materials

减少损耗 reduction of spoilage and waste

质量管理　quality control
产品检验　examination and test of products
成品　finished product
半成品　semifinished product
正品率　rate of standard product
次品　seconds
一等品　first grade product
二等品　second grade product
三等品　third grade product
等外品　offgrade product
废品　reject
原材料消耗　consumption of raw materials
燃料和动力消耗　consumption of fuel and power
考勤制度　system of checking work attendance

提高工时利用率　raising the utilization rate of working hours
技术责任制　system of technological responsibility
技术操作规程　regulations for technological operations
加强薄弱环节　strengthening the weak link
岗位责任制　the system of personal responsibility
设备维修　maintenance and repair of equipment
安全措施　safety measures
奖惩制度　system of reward and penalty
物质奖励　material reward
精神鼓励　spiritual inspiration
经济制裁　economic sanctions

## 技术革新和技术革命　Technical Innovation and Technical Revolution

解放思想　emancipating the mind
发明创造　innovation and creation
苦干加巧干　working hard and resourcefully
敢想敢干　daring to think and act
攻破技术难关　solving knotty problems (cracking hard nuts) in technology
排除生产中主要障碍　breaking through a bottleneck in production
引进外国先进技术　introducing advanced techniques from

other countries
合理化建议　rationalization proposal
技术协作　technical cooperation
现场会议　on-the-spot meeting
参观评比　public inspection and appraisal
改革陈旧设备　revamping outmoded equipment
改进操作方法　improving operating methods
革新工艺　renovating the technology
简化工序　simplifying the working process

实现自动化 attaining automation

提高工作效率 raising the work efficiency

提高设备利用率 raising the equipment utilization rate

提高生产率 raising productivity of the workers

科研走在生产前面 scientific research anticipating production

厂办技术学校 factory-run technical school

在实践中培养技术人才 training technical personnel through practice

大胆实验 bold experimentation

积累第一手资料 accumulating first-hand data

中间试验厂 pilot plant

试制(试产) trial production

成批生产 batch production

投产 put (go) into production

## 工业废料的综合利用 Multiple Utilization of Industrial Wastes

废气 gaseous waste

废水 liquid waste

废渣 residual solid waste

"三废" "three wastes"

固体废料 solid waste

放射性废料 radioactive waste

工厂尘雾 factory fumes

光化学烟雾 photochemical smog

漂浮油膜 floating oil slicks

大气污染 air pollution

水质污染 water pollution

环境污染 environment pollution

污染区 polluted area

污染物 pollutant

污染物浓度 concentration of pollutant

最高容许浓度(百万分之) maximum permissible concentration (ppm:parts per million)

造成公害 posing hazards to the public

污染控制 pollution control

环境保护 environmental protection

废料处理 waste disposal

回收有价值的副产品 recovering valuable by-products

溶剂回收 solvent recovery

有毒成份的回收 recovery of toxic components

再循环 recycling

再用 reuse

粉尘控制和回收 dust control and recovery

煤灰尘处理 fly ash handling

重力降尘室 gravity dust settling chamber

撞击除尘器 impingement dust separator

静电集尘器 electrostatic precipitator

旋风除尘器 cyclone dust extractor

离心除尘器 centrifugal dust separator

惯性除尘器 inertial dust separator

滤尘袋 bag filter

布袋滤尘室 baghouse

吸附 adsorption

洗涤 scrubbing

喷淋塔 spray tower

污水三级净化法 A-B-C process for sewage treatment

过滤 filtration

离心分离 centrifugation

沉降池 settling lagoon

消解 digestion

掺气 aeration

加菌淤渣 activated sludge

淤渣气 sludge gas

声波臭氧 sonozone

絮凝 flocculation

浮选 flotation

澄清 clarification

电渗析 electrodialysis

离子交换 ion-exchange

中和 neutralization

煅烧 incineration

高压压实 high-pressure compaction

分解蒸馏 destructive distillation

废热回收 recovery of waste heat

废热锅炉 waste heat boiler

废气能 exhaust gas energy

能量提取 energy extraction

# 劳动保护 Labour Protection

劳动保险条例 labour insurance regulations

劳动安全 labour safety

安全生产 safety in production

安全操作 safety in operation

安全操作规程 safety code

安全保障措施 safety precautions

安全措施 safety measures

安全设施 safety installation

安全哨 danger-warning post, look-out post

安全检查 safety inspection

高空作业 working on high

高温作业 working at high temperature

低温作业 working at low temperature

水下作业 working under water

带电作业 hot-line work

危险性作业 hazardous work

夏季洒(喷)水降温 sprinkling (spraying) water to allay the summer heat

空气调节 air-conditioning

防一切有害物质 protection against all harmful substances

防瓦斯爆炸 prevention of gas explosion

防火措施 fire prevention measures

减少噪音的办法 noise reduction means

劳动保护用品 labour protection appliances

安全帽　safety helmet

荧光安全灯　fluorescent safety lamp

安全服　protective clothing

安全带　safety belt

手套和手袖　gloves and sleeve-lets

防止事故　accident prevention

保健措施　health protection measures

工厂卫生　factory hygiene

调整工作时间　adjustment of working hours

八小时工作日　eight-hour work-day

三班制　three-shift workday system

日班　day shift

夜班　night shift

中班　swing shift

休息日　off day

转做较轻工作　change to light-er work

退休年龄　retiring age, pensionable age

退休老工人　retired veteran worker

退休金　pension

产假　maternity leave

保健食品(营养品)　nourishing food to maintain health (nutritives)

营养补助　nourishment subsidies

清凉饮料　cool drink

健康检查　physical examination, (Am.) checkup

定期健康检查　periodical physical examination, periodical checkup

## 职工生活福利　Welfare of Workers and Staff

福利基金　welfare fund

厂办卫生福利事业　factory-run health and welfare services

公费医疗　free medical care

工厂(分科)医疗室　factory (poly-) clinic

工厂急救站　factory first-aid station

特约医院(合同医院)　hospital under contract to a factory

免费住院治疗　free hospital treatment

工人疗养院　workers' sanatorium, workers' convalescent home

工人休养所　workers' rest home

女工休息室　rest room for women workers

因工伤事故死亡　death from an industrial accident

工伤　injury sustained in the performance of duty

因职业病死亡　death from an occupational disease

对死者家属的抚恤金　death benefit

对病残人员的抚恤金　disability pension

治丧费补助　subsidy for funeral expenses

保健费　subsidies for health, health subsidies

交通补助　traffic allowance

对女工规定的照顾　provisions for women workers

产假工资照发　maternity leave with full pay

难产或双胞胎延长假期　extended leave in case of abnormal delivery or birth of twins

规定喂奶时间　time allowed for baby-nursing

工厂田间托儿所　factory crèche

解放前的苦难　workers' sufferings before liberation

包身工　indentured labour

童工　child labour

没有安全设备　lack of safety equipment

伤亡事故频繁　serious casualties from frequent accidents

受机器、受监工、受厂主资产者本人的奴役　being enslaved by the machine, by the overseer and by the bourgeois manufacturer himself

不足温饱的工资　starvation wages

衣不蔽体　going in rags

贫民窟　slum

破烂房子　dilapidated house

交不起房租　being unable to pay rent

被房东迫迁　being evicted by the house-owner

破烂窝棚　ramshackle shanty

"滚地龙"　extremely low matshed

工资被克扣　wages illegally docked

被无理开除　being fired for no reason

找不到职业　being unable to find a job

长期失业　remaining unemployed for a long-drawn period

## 工业名称　Names of Industries

基础工业　basic industry

原材料工业　raw material industry

加工工业　processing industry

重工业　heavy industry

轻工业　light industry

采矿工业　mining industry

燃料工业　fuel industry

化学工业　chemical industry

石油工业　petroleum industry

石油化学工业　petrochemical industry

电力工业　power industry

原子能工业　atomic energy industry

冶金工业　metallurgical industry

黑色金属工业　ferrous metal industry

有色金属工业　non-ferrous metal industry

稀有金属工业　rare metal industry

金属加工工业　metal-working industry

机械(机器制造)工业　machinery (machine-building) industry

仪表工业　meter industry

电机工业　electric machinery industry

无线电工业　radio industry

建筑工业　building industry

纺织工业　textile industry

服装工业　clothing industry, garment industry

食品工业　food industry

乳品工业　dairy industry

罐头工业　canning industry

制革工业　leather industry

陶瓷工业　ceramics industry

地方工业　local industry

街道工业　neighbourhood industry

农村"五小工业"　"five small industries" in the countryside

小煤窑　small coal mine

小水电　small hydropower industry, minihydro

小农机　small agricultural machinery industry

小化肥　small chemical fertilizer industry

小水泥　small cement industry

手工业　handicraft

# 职　工　Workers and Staff

劳动英雄　labour hero

先进生产者　advanced production worker

模范工人　model worker

技术革新能手　technical innovator

突击手　shock worker

积极分子　activist

老工人　veteran worker

熟练工人　skilled worker

青年工人　young worker

学徒工　apprentice

季节工　seasonal worker

临时工　temporary worker

合同工　contract worker

职工家属　families of workers and staff

工人技术员　worker technician

机械师　mechanic

建筑师　architect

设计师　designer

总工程师　chief engineer

助理工程师　assistant engineer

见习工程师　student engineer

工人工程师　worker engineer

化验员　chemical analyst

检验员　inspector

管理人员　managerial staff

科室人员　office personnel

厂长　managing director

车间主任　workshop manager

工段长　section chief
工长(作业班长)　foreman
仓库管理员　storekeeper

非生产人员　nonproductive personnel

# 钢 铁 Iron and Steel

## 炼 铁 Iron Smelting

钢铁联合企业 iron and steel complex
铁矿石 iron ore
磁铁矿 magnetite
赤铁矿 hematite
褐铁矿 limonite
菱铁矿 siderite
脉石 gangue
选矿 ore dressing
粉碎 comminution
粗破碎 coarse crushing
中破碎 intermediate crushing
细破碎 fine crushing
颚式破碎机 jaw crusher
旋回破碎机 gyratory crusher
圆锥破碎机 cone crusher
筛分 screening
磨细 fine grinding
球磨机 ball mill
棒磨机 rod mill
砾磨机 pebble mill
磁选法 magnetic separation process
重选法 gravity concentration

process
浮选法 flotation process
精矿 concentrate
中矿 middlings
尾矿 tailings
脱水 dewatering
浓缩 thickening
过滤 filtering
干燥 drying
造块 agglomeration
烧结 sintering
粉矿 fine ore
熔剂 flux
自熔性烧结矿 self-fluxing agglomerate
球团 pellet
焙烧 roasting
还原〔作用〕 reduction
造渣〔作用〕 slag formation
渗碳〔作用〕 carburization
生铁 pig iron
白口铁 white iron
灰口铁 grey iron
斑驳铁 mottled iron

## 高　炉　Blast Furnace

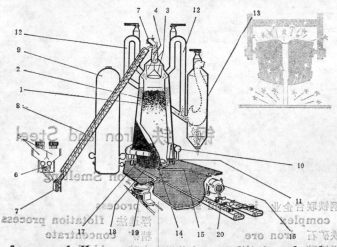

| 炉壳 | furnace shell | 燃烧室 | combustion chamber |
|---|---|---|---|
| 炉衬① | furnace lining | 格子砖室 | chequer chamber |
| 炉缸 | hearth | 热风管⑩ | hot blast main |
| 炉腹 | bosh | 风口⑪ | tuyère |
| 炉身 | stack | 煤气导出管⑫ | downcomer |
| 上料 | charging | 重力除尘器⑬ | gravity dust catcher |
| 固体原料 | solid materials | | |
| 料批 | batch | 涤气塔 | scrubbing tower |
| 料柱② | charge column | 静电除尘器 | electrostatic precipitator |
| 料线 | stock line | | |
| 料钟③ | bell | 放液 | tapping |
| 料斗④ | hopper | 放液口 | taphole |
| 布料器 | distributor | 出铁口⑭ | iron notch |
| 贮矿槽⑤ | ore bunker | 铁沟⑮ | iron runner |
| 称量车⑥ | scale car | 铁水罐⑯ | hot metal ladle |
| 卷扬机 | hoist machine | 出渣口⑰ | slag notch |
| 料车⑦ | skip | 渣沟⑱ | slag runner |
| 料车坑 | skip pit | 渣罐⑲ | slag ladle |
| 斜桥⑧ | inclined bridge | 撇渣器 | skimmer |
| 汽轮鼓风机 | steam-driven turboblower | 铸铁机 | pig casting machine |
| | | 铸铁模⑳ | pig mould |
| 热风炉⑨ | hot blast stove | | |

## 铁合金 Ferroalloys

| 硅铁 | ferrosilicon | 钒铁 | ferrovanadium |
| 锰铁 | ferromanganese | 磷铁 | ferrophosphorus |
| 铬铁 | ferrochromium | 硼铁 | ferroboron |
| 钨铁 | ferrotungsten | 镍铁 | ferronickel |
| 钼铁 | ferromolybdenum | 铌铁 | ferrocolumbium |
| 钛铁 | ferrotitanium | 锆铁 | ferrozirconium |

## 耐火材料 Refractories

耐火粘土 fireclay

高岭土 kaolin

水铝石 diaspore

铝矾土 bauxite

硅石 quartzite, ganister

镁石(菱镁矿) magnesite

白云石 dolomite

镁橄榄石 forsterite

刚玉 corundum

锆石 zircon

氧化锆 zirconia

耐火砖 firebrick

粘土砖 fireclay brick

硅砖 silica brick, ganister

brick

高铝砖 high-alumina brick

镁砖 magnesite brick, magnesia brick

铬砖 chrome brick

镁铬砖 chrome-magnesite brick

碳化硅(金刚砂)砖 carborundum brick

碳(石墨)砖 carbon (graphite) brick

测温锥 pyrometric cone

熔锥比值 pyrometric cone equivalent value

## 炼焦 Coking

回收化学产品的炼焦炉 chemical-recovery coke ovens

炼焦用煤 coking coal

配煤 blending

混合煤槽 mixing bins

运输皮带 conveyer belt

成排炼焦炉室 battery of coke ovens

装料门 charging door

碳化室 carbonization chamber

燃烧室 heating flue

蓄热室 regenerator

出焦 discharge of the coke

推焦机 pusher

推焦杆 ram

熄焦站 quenching station

筛焦站 screening station

冶金焦 metallurgical coke

筛余的焦炭 coke screenings

焦炭强度 coke strength

焦炭粒度　coke size
含硫量　sulphur content
含磷量　phosphorus content
灰分　ash content
挥发物　volatile matter
上升管　standpipe
集气总管　collecting main
荒煤气　raw gas
冷凝物　condensate
初步冷却器　primary cooler
煤气　gas
澄清槽　separator tank
氨釜　ammonia still
酚塔　phenol tower

电力脱焦油器　electric tar catcher
再热器　reheater
饱和器　saturator
硫酸　sulphuric acid
硫酸铵　ammonium sulphate
酸分离器　acid separator
最终冷却器　final cooler
洗涤塔　scrubber
储气器　gas holder
脱苯器　benzene still
粗苯　crude benzene
吡啶车间　pyridine workshop
甲基吡啶　picolines

## 焦化产品　Coke Chemicals

氨加工　ammonia processing
硫酸铵　ammonium sulphate
轻吡啶　light pyridine
粗苯加工　crude benzene processing
环戊二烯　cyclopentadiene
纯苯　pure benzene
甲苯　toluene
二甲苯　xylene
重溶剂石脑油　heavy-solvent naphtha
香豆酮(古马隆)—茚树脂　coumaroneindene resin
三甲基苯　trimethylbenzene
噻吩　thiophene
煤焦油加工　coal tar processing
中性产品　neutral products
萘　naphthalene
蒽　anthracene
咔唑　carbazole
菲　phenanthrene

苊　acenaphthene
芘　pyrene
䓛　chrysene
氧芴　dibenzofuran
芴　fluorene
荧蒽(萘嵌芴)　fluoranthene
联苯　diphenyl
α-甲基萘　alpha-methylnaphthalene
沥青　pitch
沥青焦　pitch coke
柏油　road tar
β-甲基萘　beta-methylnaphthalene
酸性产品　acid products
酚　phenol
邻位甲酚　o-cresol
间位甲酚　m-cresol
对位甲酚　p-cresol
二甲苯酚　xylenol
苯甲酸　benzoic acid
碱性产品　basic products

吡啶 pyridine
α-甲基吡啶 alpha-picoline
β-甲基吡啶 beta-picoline
γ-甲基吡啶 gamma-picoline
喹啉 quinoline
吲哚 indole

吖啶 acridine
煤气加工 coal gas processing
二氯乙烷 dichloroethane
氯乙醇 chloroethanol
尿素 urea

# 炼 钢 Steel Melting

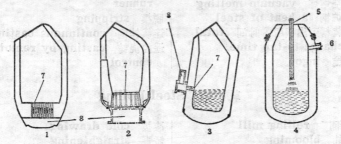

炼钢厂 steel mill
海绵铁 sponge iron
搅拌法 puddling process
熟铁 wrought iron
渗碳法 cementation process
坩埚法 crucible process
平炉炼钢法 open-hearth process
补炉 repairing the furnace
装料 charging
熔化 melting
精炼 refining
氧化 oxidizing
脱氧 deoxidizing
出钢 tapping
钢水 molten steel
废钢 steel scrap
铁水 molten pig iron
造渣剂 slag forming agent
石灰 lime
萤石 fluorspar

氧化剂 oxidizer
脱氧剂 deoxidizer
转炉炼钢法 converter process
底吹转炉 bottom-blown converter
酸性底吹转炉① bottom-blown acid converter (Bessemer converter)
碱性底吹转炉② bottom-blown basic converter (Thomas converter)
侧吹转炉③ side-blown converter
氧气顶吹转炉④ top-blown oxygen converter (L-D converter)
水冷却氧枪⑤ water-cooled oxygen lance
出钢口⑥ taphole
风口⑦ tuyère
风箱⑧ wind box

吹炼 blowing
炉衬 vessel lining
炉子倾动设备 device for tilting vessel
电炉炼钢法 electric process
电弧炉 electric-arc furnace
石墨电极 graphite electrodes
感应电炉 induction furnace
真空熔炼 vacuum melting
一炉钢 a heat of steel
从装料到出钢所需时间 total charge-to-tap time
钢锭 ingot

浇注 teeming
盛钢桶 teeming ladle
塞棒 stopper
钢锭模 ingot mould
保温帽 hot top
底盘 stool
中心注管 central runner
流钢砖槽 refractory-lined runner
脱模 stripping
连续铸钢 continuous casting
遥控浇铸 casting by remote control

# 轧 钢 Steel Rolling

轧钢厂 rolling mill
初轧 blooming
初轧机 bloomer
初轧方坯 bloom
热轧 hot rolling
冷轧 cold rolling
粗轧 rough rolling
精轧 finish rolling
钢材 rolled steel
方坯 square billet
薄板坯 sheet billet
薄钢板 steel sheet
中厚钢板 steel plate
镀层钢板 clad steel sheet
焊管坯 skelp
直缝焊 straight welding
螺旋缝焊 spiral welding
焊管 welded pipe
实心圆坯 solid round billet
挤压 extrusion
穿孔 piercing
穿孔芯棒 piercing mandrel
旋压 screw pressing

冷拔 cold drawing
矫直 straightening
无缝钢管 seamless steel tube
异形管 special section steel tube
波纹管 corrugated steel tube
型钢 section steel, shape steel
冷弯型钢 formed section steel
方钢① square bar
圆钢② round bar
扁钢③ flat bar
六角钢④ hexagonal section bar
角钢⑤ angle bar
不等边角钢 L-bar
工字钢⑥ I-bar
宽边工字钢 H-bar
槽钢⑦ channel bar, U-bar
丁字钢 T-bar
乙字钢 Z-bar
竹节钢 ribbed bar
带钢 strip steel

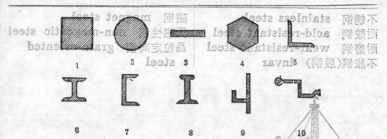

钢轨钢⑧　rail steel
窗框钢⑨　casement section steel
钢板桩⑩　steel sheet piling
拉丝　wire drawing
拉丝机　drawbench
钢丝　steel wire

锻造　forging
模锻　die forging
锻压机　forging press
液压机　hydraulic press
冲压　punching
冲压机　punch press

## 钢的热处理　Heat Treatment of Steel

铁的晶体结构　crystal structure of iron
体心立方结构　body-centred cubic structure
铁素体　ferrite
渗碳体　cementite
珠光体　pearlite
面心立方结构　face-centred cubic structure
奥氏体　austenite

马氏体　martensite
贝氏体　bainite
相变　phase change
退火　annealing
正火　normalizing
淬火　quenching
分级淬火　martempering
等温淬火　austempering
回火　tempering

## 钢的种类　Types of Steel

沸腾钢　rimmed steel
镇静钢　killed steel
半镇静钢　semikilled steel
普通碳素钢　plain carbon steel
低碳钢　low carbon steel
中碳钢　medium carbon steel
高碳钢　high carbon steel

低合金钢　low alloy steel
中合金钢　medium alloy steel
高合金钢　high alloy steel
结构钢　structural steel
工具钢　tool steel
高速钢　high-speed steel
易切削钢　free-cutting steel

| | |
|---|---|
| 不锈钢 stainless steel | 磁钢 magnet steel |
| 耐酸钢 acid-resistant steel | 无磁性钢 non-magnetic steel |
| 耐磨钢 wear-resistant steel | 晶粒定向钢 grain-oriented |
| 不胀钢(殷钢) invar | steel |

# 石 油 Petroleum

## 石油的生成和储集 Origin and Accumulation of Petroleum

| | |
|---|---|
| 遥远的地质年代 remote geologic age | 海底沉积 sea-bottom deposit |
| 陆上有机物 continental organic matter | 沉积盆地 sedimentary basin |
| | 海盆 sea basin |
| 海中有机物 marine organic matter | 湖盆 lake basin |
| | 有机淤泥 organic mud, slime |
| 浮游生物 plankton | 海相岩层—海洋沉积岩 marine rock formation—sea sedimentary rock |
| 海底生物 benthos | |
| 硅藻 diatom | |
| 轮藻 charophyta | 陆相岩层—湖泊沉积岩 continental rock formation—lake sedimentary rock |
| 腕足动物 brachiopoda | |
| 化石 fossil | |
| 化石燃料 fossil fuel | 地壳运动 earth movement, diastrophism |
| 沉积〔作用〕 sedimentation | |
| 大陆沉积 continental deposit (sediment) | 大地构造学 tectonics |
| | 地质变迁 geologic(al) change |
| 陆相沉积 land sediment | 绝氧、缺氧的环境 anaerobic and reducing environment |
| 海相沉积 marine deposit (sediment) | |
| | 细菌作用造成的分解 decomposition by bacterial action |

复杂的化学变化　complex chemical changes

初次迁移　primary migration

二次迁移　secondary migration

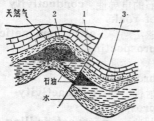

储油构造　reservoir structure

断层①　fault

褶皱　fold

背斜②　anticline

向斜③　syncline

圈闭　trap

不渗透层　non-permeable formation

断层露头　fault outcrop

地层褶皱　stratigraphic fold

地层超覆　stratigraphic overlap

岩性封闭　lithologic confining

大陆架(陆棚)　continental shelf

储集层(油储)　reservoir

储集岩石　reservoir rock

油床　oil pool, oil reservoir

天然气　natural gas

石油储藏量　petroleum reserve

## 石油勘探　Petroleum Exploration (Prospecting)

地质调查　geological survey

普查　reconnaissance survey

详查　detailed survey

地质图　geological map

石油显示标志　evidence of oil occurrence

油苗　oil seepage

气苗　gas seepage

油砂　oil sand

地蜡　earth wax

天然沥青　natural bitumen

地球物理勘探　geophysical prospecting

地震反射勘探　seismic reflection prospecting

地震仪器车④　seismic instrument car

爆炸⑤　detonation, explosion

地震检波器⑥　seismic detector

地震仪　seismograph

磁带地震仪　magnetic tape seismograph

地震波⑦　seismic event

折射波　refraction wave

反射波⑧　reflection wave

放大器　magnifier

示波器　oscillograph, oscilloscope

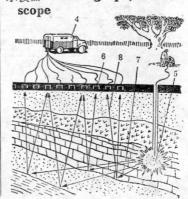

| | |
|---|---|
| 岩石的致密性 **compactness of rocks** | 电地球物理法 **electrical geophysical method** |
| 重力仪 **gravimeter** | 电阻率法勘探 **resistivity prospecting** |
| 重力勘探法 **gravimeter method** | 岩石的电导性 **conductivity of rocks** |
| 重力异常 **gravity anomaly** | 电磁法勘探 **electromagnetic prospecting** |
| 毫伽 **milligal** | |
| 磁力勘探 **magnetic prospecting** | 地球化学勘探 **geochemical prospecting** |
| 航空磁力勘探(航空磁测) **aeromagnetic prospecting (aeromagnetic survey)** | 放射性勘探 **radioactivity prospecting** |
| 磁力仪 **magnetometer** | 钻井勘探 **prospect drilling** |
| 岩石的磁性变化 **magnetic changes of rocks** | 新区预探钻井 **new-field wildcatting** |

# 石油钻井　Petroleum Drilling

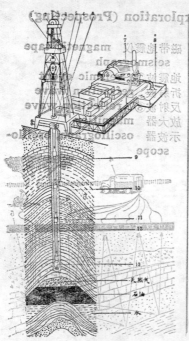

| | |
|---|---|
| | 完成钻井装置 **rigging up** |
| | 开钻 **spudding in** |
| | 旋钻 **rotary drill** |
| | 旋钻钻井 **rotary drilling** |
| 井架① | **derrick; rig** |
| 天车② | **crown block** |
| 游动滑车③ | **loose pulley** |
| 方钻杆 | **square drill rod** |
| 绞车④ | **winch** |
| 转盘⑤ | **rotary table** |
| 防喷器⑥ | **blow-off preventer** |
| 动力机⑦ | **power unit** |
| 泥浆泵 | **mud pump** |
| 气囊 | **air sac** |
| 泥浆池⑧ | **mud pool** |
| 表层套管⑨ | **surface casing** |
| 井眼⑩ | **well** |
| 钻柱⑪ | **drill stem** |
| 钻井泥浆⑫ | **drilling mud (drilling fluid)** |
| 钻头⑬ | **bit** |
| 冲击钻机 | **percussion drill** |

| | |
|---|---|
| 冲击钻井　percussion drilling | core bit |
| 涡轮钻具　turbo-drill | 金刚石钻头　diamond bit |
| 电钻钻井　electrical boring | 孔隙度　porosity |
| 海上钻井　offshore drilling | 渗透性　permeability |
| 定向钻井　directional drilling | 油饱和率　oil saturation |
| 初探浅井　trial pit | 碳酸盐含量　carbonate content |
| 钻孔　bore hole | 钻井岩屑　drilling cuttings |
| 井位选定　location of well | 泥浆循环　mud recirculation |
| 钻孔间距(井距)　spacing of wells | 井下首次现油　oil show |
| 钻井记录　driller's log | 钻出石油　striking oil |
| 钻速记录　rate-of-penetration log | 电测井　electrical logging |
| | 感应测井　induction logging |
| 岩心　core | 放射性测井　radioactivity logging |
| 取岩心　coring | (以旧井为中心向外扩展的)新钻井 |
| 岩心分析　core analysis | step-out well, delayed |
| 岩心筒　core barrel | development well |
| 筒式取心钻头　barrel-type | |

## 海上钻井　Offshore Drilling

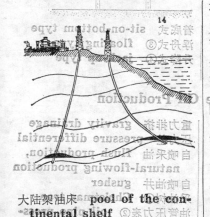

| | |
|---|---|
| | 地下测井仪器　subsurface well-surveying instrument |
| 14 | 定向钻井⑭　directional-drilling |
| | 海上油田　offshore field |
| | 海上钻井作业　offshore drilling operations |
| | 陆上后勤基地　base of operations on land |
| | 海上钻井装置　offshore drilling unit, rig |
| | 可移动的装置　mobile device |
| | 系泊设备　mooring equipment |
| 大陆架油床　pool of the continental shelf | 动力定位　power locating |
| 水下油储　oil reservoir under water | 自动推进　self-propelling |
| | 自给的平台　self-contained platform |

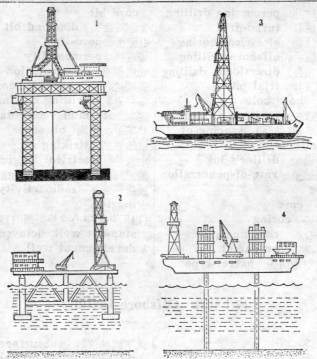

固定式平台① **fixed platform**
潜水式 **submersible type**
半潜式② **semi-submersible type**

着底式 **sit-on-bottom type**
浮舟式③ **floating type**
升降式④ **jack-up type**

## 采 油 Crude Oil Production

岩层中排挤石油的压力 **oil-expelling pressure in the rock strata**
水压力(水驱) **water drive**
气顶压力(气帽驱动) **gas-cap drive**
溶解气压力(溶解气驱) **solution gas drive, dissolved gas drive**

重力排挤 **gravity drainage**
压力差 **pressure differential**
自喷采油 **flush production, natural-flowing production**
自喷油井 **gusher**
采油树① **Christmas tree**
油管压力表② **oil pipe pressure meter**
修井闸门③ **valve for well**

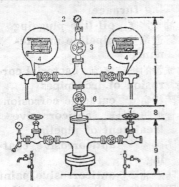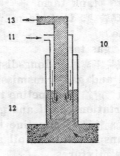

**repair**

油嘴④ **oil nozzle**

生产闸门⑤ **production valve**

总闸门⑥ **general valve**

套管闸门⑦ **casing valve**

油管头⑧ **oil pipe head**

套管头⑨ **casing head**

机械采油 **mechanical production**

气举采油⑩ **gas-lift production**

压气⑪ **gas repressuring**

压气机 **gas compressor**

抽油井⑫ **pumping well**

抽油机⑬ **oil pumping unit**

保持油层压力 **maintenance of oil-pool pressure**

注水 **water injection**

注气 **gas injection**

压回气 **repressuring gas**

提高油层的渗透性 **improving the permeability of the reservoir**

降低石油的粘度 **lowering the viscosity of petroleum**

二次采油 **petroleum secondary recovery**

含油带 **oil zone**

薄油层 **oil sheet**

油储层性能 **reservoir behaviour**

气田 **gas field**

油气 **combination gas**

气油比 **gas-oil ratio**

油井生产潜力 **well's potential**

桶/天 **barrels per day (bpd)**

气井每天喷气量 **deliverability of a gas well**

## 油、气贮存和运输 Storage and Transportation of Oil and Gas

贮油 **oil storing**

油库 **oil store**

原油库 **crude storage**

贮油槽 **oil storage tank**

贮油罐 **oil storage vessel**

油桶 **oil drum**

汽油箱　petrol tank

油罐场　tank farm

油罐场管线　tank farm pipe-line

气槽　gas tank

油、气长距离输送　long-distance oil and gas transmission

油、气管道输送　pipeline transportation of oil and gas

油、气混输管道　pipeline for transportation of oil and gas mixtures

油管干线　oil trunk pipeline

油管支线　oil branch pipeline

管道铺设　pipe laying, pipe-lining

管线通讯　pipeline communication

管线电子通讯设备　pipeline electronics

石油泵送系统　oil pumping system

管道泵站　pipeline pumping station

石油加热、加压站　oil heating and booster station

干线加热炉　trunk line heat-ing furnace

油管堵塞　oil-line plugging

管道维护　pipeline maintenance

铁管的细菌腐蚀　bacterial corrosion of iron pipes

阴极腐蚀　cathodic corrosion

管道防腐处理　anticorrosive treatment of pipeline

防腐涂料　anticorrosive coating

防腐油漆　anticorrosive paint

阴极防蚀　cathodic protection

油槽船　oil-tanker

运油船　oil-carrying ship, oil-carrier

油舱　oil hold

石油驳船　oil storage barge, oil hulk

原油船舶输送　shipping crude oil by water

石油码头　oil jetty

铁路油槽车　tank car, tank wagon

油罐汽车　tank truck

用汽车运石油　oil trucking

# 石油精制　Petroleum Refining

炼油厂　oil refinery

炼厂贮油槽①　refinery storage tank

气体分离器　gas separator

泵油站②　pump(ing) station

管式加热器③　tubular heater

馏分　cuts

冷凝器　condenser

吸收装置　absorption plant

稳定器(稳定装置)　stabilizer (stabilization plant)

汽提塔　stripper

烷化工厂　alkylation plant

裂化厂　cracking plant

脱蜡厂　dewaxing plant

沥青厂　bitumen plant

蒸馏塔④　distillation tower

沥青吹制设备　bitumen blow-

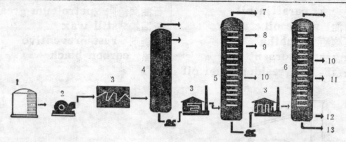

ing plant

提取塔 extraction column

真空蒸馏设备 vacuum distillation plant

浓缩柱 evaporating column

闪蒸塔 flash column

润滑油工厂 lubricating oil plant (lube plant)

脱硫设备 desulphurization plant

硫回收车间 sulphur recovery plant

催化裂化器 catalytic cracker (cat cracker)

催化重整装置 catalytic reformer

临氢重整装置 hydroformer

立式贮油罐 vertical storage tank

球形油罐 spherical tank

压力罐 pressure tank

常压精馏塔⑤ normal pressure fractionating tower

铂重整 platforming

铂重整反应 platforming reaction

铂催化剂 platinum catalyst

芳〔族〕烃抽提 extraction of aromatic hydrocarbons

加氢精制 hydrofining

汽油加氢精制 gasoline hydrofining

减压精馏塔⑥ reduced-pressure fractionating tower

催化裂化 catalytic cracking

丙烷脱沥青 debituminization of propane

## 原油产品 Crude Oil Products

液化石油气 liquefied petroleum gas

航空汽油⑦ aviation gasoline (aviation spirit)

车用汽油⑦ petrol (motor spirit), (Am.) gasoline

煤油⑧ kerosene

气油(瓦斯油) gas oil

烃气(气态烃) hydrocarbon gas

柴油⑨ diesel oil

燃料油⑩ fuel oil

润滑油⑪ lubricating oil

石油焦炭⑫ petroleum coke

沥青⑬ bitumen

石蜡 paraffin

石蜡油　paraffin oil
白油　white oil
石脑油　naphtha
吸收油　absorbent oil
残余燃料油　residual fuel oil

石油润滑脂　petroleum grease
釜馏蜡　still wax
防锈剂　rust preventive
炭黑　carbon black

# 石油化工　Petrochemicals

## 主要原料　Principal Raw Materials

石油中的烃类　hydrocarbons in petroleum
气体烃　gaseous hydrocarbon
液体烃　liquid hydrocarbon
固体烃　solid hydrocarbon
有机组分　organic constituent
非烃类　non-hydrocarbons
含硫、含氧、含氮的非烃类有机化合物　organic compounds of nonhydrocarbons containing sulphur, oxygen or nitrogen
炼油厂废料　refinery wastes
酸渣　acid sludge
碱性熔渣　basic slag

炼油厂气　refinery gases
粗汽油　crude gasoline
丁烷　butane
液化石油气　liquefied petroleum gas
石蜡　paraffin
地蜡　earth wax
乙烯　ethylene
丙烯　propylene (propene)
丁烯　butylene
苯　benzene
甲苯　toluene
二甲苯　xylene
乙炔　acetylene

## 生产技术　Production Technique

乙烯的生产　production of ethylene
烃类高温裂化　high-tempera-

ture cracking of hydrocarbons
裂解方法　cracking method

管式炉法　pipe-still process

移动床法　moving-bed process

流化床法　fluidized-bed process

部分燃烧法　partial combustion process

熔盐法　fused-salt process

催化裂化法　catalytic cracking process

乙烯的回收　recovery of ethylene

吸附分离　adsorption stripping

化学吸收　chemical absorption

在石油裂化过程中生产丙烯　producing propylene from petroleum cracking

石油馏分的裂化气　cracking gas of petroleum cuts

丁二烯和异丁烯的分离法　process for the separation of butadiene and isobutylene

硫酸法　sulphuric acid process

离子交换法　ion-exchange technique

催化脱氢　catalytic dehydrogenation

氧化脱氢　oxidative dehydrogenation

丁烷氧化脱氢制取丁二烯　preparing butadiene from oxidative dehydrogenation of butane

制取芳〔族〕烃　preparing aromatic hydrocarbons

铂重整　platforming

石油馏分的高温裂解　high-temperature cracking of petroleum cuts

从烃类裂解反应中得到乙炔　obtaining acetylene from cracking reaction of hydrocarbons

利用合成气制造氨　making ammonia from synthetic gas

## 基本石油化工产品　Primary Petrochemicals

甲烷产品　products from methane

氨　ammonia

炭黑　carbon black

甲醇　methanol

氯代甲烷　chloromethane

氰化氢　hydrogen cyanide

乙烯产品　products from ethylene

环氧乙烷　ethylene oxide

乙醇　ethyl alcohol

聚乙烯　polyethylene

苯乙烯　styrene

氯乙烷　ethyl chloride

二氯化乙烯　ethylene dichloride

二溴化乙烯　ethylene dibromide

丙烯、丁烯产品　products from propylene and the butylenes

异丙醇　isopropyl alcohol

异丙基苯(枯烯)　cumene

烯丙基氯　allyl chloride

环氧丙烷　propylene oxide

丁二烯　butadiene

异丁烯橡胶　butyl rubber

异戊二烯　isoprene

酚　phenol

## 基本石油化工产品的应用　Use of Primary Petrochemicals

合成橡胶　synthetic rubber
塑料　plastics
合成纤维　synthetic fibre
合成氨　synthetic ammonia
尿素　urea
杀虫剂　insecticide
洗涤剂　detergent
合成染料　synthetic dyestuff
涂料　coating
药品　medicine
甲醛　formaldehyde
防冻剂　antifreeze
抗爆液　antiknock fluid

刹车油　brake fluid
炸药　explosive
溶剂　solvent
冷冻剂　refrigerant
增塑剂　plasticizer
粘合剂　adhesive
密封剂　sealant
电气绝缘材料　electric insulating material
油漆　paint
化妆品　cosmetics
润滑油添加剂　lubricating oil additive

# 化工　Chemicals

## 化工厂和化工设备　Chemical Plant and Equipment

盐厂　salt refinery
纯碱厂　soda plant
硝酸厂　nitric acid plant
硫酸厂　sulphuric acid plant
化肥厂　chemical fertilizer plant

漂白粉厂　bleaching powder plant
农药厂　pesticide plant
制药厂　pharmaceutical plant
塑料厂　plastics factory
合成橡胶厂　synthetic rubber

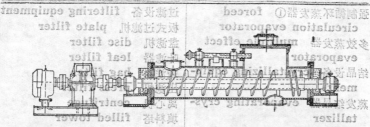

factory

人造纤维厂　artificial fibre factory

电石和氰氨化钙厂　calcium carbide and calcium cyanamide plant

石棉厂　asbestos factory

输送机械　conveying machinery

液体输送机械　liquid conveying machinery

气体输送机械　gas conveying machinery

轴流式通风机　axial fan

回转式鼓风机　rotary blower

往复压缩机　reciprocating compressor

多级压缩机　multistage compressor

真空泵　vacuum pump

管道　pipeline

固体输送机械　solid conveying machinery

斗式升降机　bucket elevator

螺旋运输机①　screw conveyor

固体粉碎机械　solid pulverizing machinery

传热设备　heat transfer equipment

套管式换热器　double-pipe heat exchanger

平行管换热器　flat-tube heat exchanger

板型换热器　plate exchanger

冷却塔　cooling tower

干燥设备　drying equipment

箱式干燥器　loft drier

转筒干燥器　revolving drier

喷雾干燥器　spray drier

冷冻设备　refrigerating equipment

氨气压缩致冷机　ammonia compression refrigerating machine

深冻设备　deep refrigeration equipment

冷凝槽　condensate trap

分离设备　separating equipment

旋风分离器　cyclone separator

离心筛　centrifugal screen

重介质分选机　heavy media separator

湿磁选机　wet magnetic separator

机械洗涤器　mechanical scrubber

沉降设备　settling equipment

重力沉降器　gravitation settler

蒸发设备　evaporating equipment

强制循环蒸发器① forced circulation evaporator

多效蒸发器 multiple effect evaporator

结晶设备 crystallizing equipment

蒸发结晶器 evaporating crystallizer

塔式结晶器 tower crystallizer

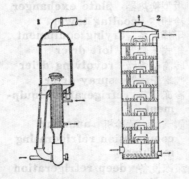

过滤设备 filtering equipment

板式过滤机 plate filter

盘滤机 disc filter

叶滤器 leaf filter

袋滤器 bag filter

压滤机 press filter

离心机 centrifuge

填料塔 filled tower

泡罩塔② bubble-cap tower

筛板塔 sieve-plate column

泡沫发生塔 foam column

化学反应设备 chemical reaction equipment

搅拌式反应锅 agitator reaction still

固定层反应设备 fixed bed reaction equipment

管式炉 pipe still

容器 container

贮槽 storage tank

料斗 hopper

气柜 gas tank

## 化工原料 Chemical Raw Materials

起始原料 starting material

基本原料 basic raw material

中间产品 intermediate material (intermediate)

无机原料 inorganic raw material

硫酸 sulphuric acid

亚硫酸 sulphurous acid

盐酸 hydrochloric acid

硝酸 nitric acid

磷酸 phosphoric acid

氢氧化钠(烧碱) sodium hydroxide (caustic soda)

氢氧化铵 ammonium hydroxide

氢氧化钙(熟石灰) calcium hydroxide (slaked lime)

碳酸钠(纯碱) sodium carbonate

苏打灰 soda ash

碳酸氢钠 sodium bicarbonate

氯化钠(食盐) sodium chloride (common salt)

硫酸钠 sodium sulphate

碱性氧化物 basic oxide

氧化钙(生石灰) calcium ox-

ide (quicklime)
酸性氧化物 acidic oxide
二氧化碳 carbon dioxide
三氧化硫 sulphur trioxide
空气 air
氮 nitrogen
氢 hydrogen
氧 oxygen
惰性气体(稀有气体) inert gas (rare gas)
氩 argon
氖 neon
氦 helium
氪 krypton
氙 xenon
硬水 hard water
软水 soft water
岩盐 rock salt
碳酸钙 calcium carbonate
石灰石 limestone
荧石(氟石) fluorite (fluorspar)
钠硝石 sodium nitre
磷灰石 phosphatic rock
孔雀石 malachite
方解石 calcite (calcareous spar)
滑石 talc
高岭土 kaolin
有机原料 organic raw material

含淀粉植物 starch yielding plant
葛根 kudzu root
栎实 acorn
稻草 rice straw
玉米芯 corncob
甘蔗渣 bagasse
芦苇 reed
芒草 Chinese silvergrass
桐子 tung seed
蓖麻籽 castor bean
蚕蛹 silkworm chrysalis
鱼肝 fish liver
胶乳 latex
漆树汁 lacquer-tree sap
松脂 rosin
脂族烃 aliphatic hydrocarbon
甲烷 methane
环烃 cyclic hydrocarbon
环己烷 cyclohexane
芳〔族〕烃 aromatic hydrocarbon
有机中间产品 organic intermediate
甲醇 methanol
丙酮 acetone (propanone)
醋酸 acetic acid
苯磺酸 benzene sulphonic acid
苯胺 aniline
氯化乙烯 ethylene chloride

## 单元过程 Unit Processes

化学变化(化学反应) chemical change (chemical reaction)
化合 chemical combination
分解 decomposition
取代(置换) displacement
双分解(复分解) double de-

composition
化学方程式 chemical equation
反应速率 reaction rate, speed of reaction
温度 temperature
压力 pressure

| | | | |
|---|---|---|---|
| 浓度 | concentration | 缩聚 | condensation polymerization |
| 催化剂 | catalyst | | |
| 氧化 | oxidatiun | 发酵 | fermentation |
| 还原 | reduction | 催化作用 | catalysis |
| 还原剂 | reducing agent | 试剂 | reagent |
| 氢化 | hydrogenation | 提纯 | purification |
| 脱氢 | dehydrogenation | 定性测定 | qualitative determination |
| 水解 | hydrolysis | | |
| 水合(水化) | hydration | 定量测定 | quantitative determination |
| 脱水 | dehydration | | |
| 脱蜡 | dewaxing | 元素分析 | elementary analysis |
| 卤化 | halogenation | 氨解 | ammonolysis |
| 卤素 | halogen | 芳构化 | aromatization |
| 硝化 | nitrification | 煅烧 | calcination |
| 磺化 | sulphonation | 燃烧 | combustion |
| 胺化 | amination | 重氮化 | diazotization |
| 加碱熔化 | alkaline fusion | 偶合 | coupling |
| 烷基化 | alkylation | 电解 | electrolysis |
| 脱烷基 | dealkylation | 氢解作用 | hydrogenolysis |
| 酯化 | esterification | 异构化 | isomerization |
| 聚合 | polymerization | 中和 | neutralization |

## 单元操作　Unit Operations

| | | | |
|---|---|---|---|
| 物理变化 | physical change | 冷凝 | condensation |
| 流体输送 | fluid transport | 凝结 | coagulation |
| 流体化 | fluidization | 凝固 | solidification |
| 过滤 | filtration | 热交换 | heat exchange |
| 沉淀 | precipitation | 材料高温加热 | high-temperature heating of materials |
| 混合 | mixing | | |
| 搅动 | agitating | 沸腾 | boiling |
| 澄清 | clarification | 冷却水 | cooling water |
| 稠化过程 | thickening | 质量传递 | mass transfer |
| 沉降 | sedimentation | 气体吸收 | gas absorption |
| 分类 | classification | 蒸馏 | distillation |
| 热传递 | heat transfer | 干馏 | dry distillation |
| 干燥 | drying, desiccation | 分馏(精馏) | fractional distillation, fractionation |
| 蒸发 | evaporation | | |
| 升华 | sublimation | 萃取 | extraction |

| | | | |
|---|---|---|---|
| 吸附 | adsorption | 粉碎 | pulverization |
| 溶解 | solution | 筛分 | screening |
| 稀释 | dilution | 分离 | separation |
| 气体液化 | liquefaction of gases | 离心分离 | centrifugal separation |
| 冷冻 | refrigeration | | |
| 结晶 | crystallization | 磁力与静电分离 | magnetic and electrostatic separation |
| 沥滤 | leaching | | |
| 吸收 | absorption | 浮选 | flotation |
| 解吸 | desorption | 连续法 | continuous process |
| 增湿 | humidification | 活化 | activation |
| 减湿 | dehumidification | 电化法 | electrochemical process |
| 气体扩散 | diffusion of gases | | |
| 固体输送 | solid transport | 高温分解 | pyrolysis |
| 腐蚀 | corrosion | 离子交换 | ion exchange |

# 煤炭　Coal

## 煤系和煤矿开采法　Coal Series and Mining Method

| | | | |
|---|---|---|---|
| 煤田 | coalfield | 半烟煤 | semi-bituminous coal |
| 煤层 | coal seam | 无烟煤 | anthracite |
| 煤的储量 | coal reserve | 石墨(笔铅) | graphite, plumbago |
| 泥炭 | peat | | |
| 褐煤 | brown coal (lignite) | 地蜡 | earth wax (ozokerite, ozocerite) |
| 煤玉(煤精) | jet | | |
| 烛煤 | candle coal (cannel) | 沥青煤 | asphaltic coal |
| 暗煤 | dull coal (durain) | 油页岩 | oil shale |
| 亮煤 | bright coal (clarain) | 炼焦煤 | coking coal |
| 纯木煤 | anthraxylon | 琥珀(煤黄) | amber |
| 烟煤 | bituminous coal | 泡沸石(沸石) | zeolite |

天然气 natural gas

露天开采① opencast mining, (Am.) opencut mining, strip mining

地下开采(井工开采) underground mining

竖井开采矿② shaft mine

斜井开采矿③ slope mine

平峒开采矿④ drift mine

人工开采 hand mining

钻爆法(打眼放炮) drilling and blasting

电钻打眼 electric drilling

填进炸药 inserting the charge

填塞炮泥 stemming the hole

放炮 firing the blast

机械凿岩 machine drilling

水力凿岩 hydraulic drilling

热力凿岩 jet piercer drilling

房柱式开采法 room-and-pillar method, board-and-pillar method

房柱式留煤开采法 battery breast method

分层开采法 slicing method

后退式开采法 retreat method

长壁开采法 longwall method

后退式长壁开采法 longwall retreat method

倒台阶开采法 overhand stope method

钢丝绳锯开采法 "cable-saw" method

单巷开采法 single entry method

拉底回采煤柱法 undercut-pillar method

掩护支架开采法 shield method

废石充填开采法 waste-fill method

不用支柱的倾斜分层开采法 untimbered rill method

水力开采法 hydraulic method

# 地面设备和井下布置　Surface Installations and Underground Layout

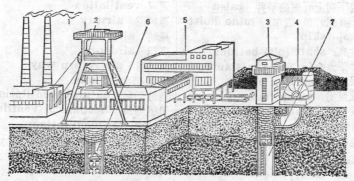

| 卷扬机房① | hoisting house |
| 卷扬机② | hoisting engine |
| 井架③ | head frame |
| 矿用扇风机④ | mine fan |
| 矿井口浴室和餐厅 | pithead bathroom and messhall |
| 选煤厂⑤ | coal preparation plant |
| 洗煤厂 | coal washery |
| 机修厂 | machine repair shop |
| 发电厂 | power plant |
| 矿山矿石堆 | mine dump |
| 脉石(矸石) | gangue |
| 倒煤厂 | coal yard, tipple |
| 煤坑 | coal pit |
| 主井⑥ | main shaft |
| 副井⑦ | auxiliary shaft |
| 罐笼⑧ | cage |
| 矿车⑨ | tub, mine car |
| 井底车场⑩ | shaft station |

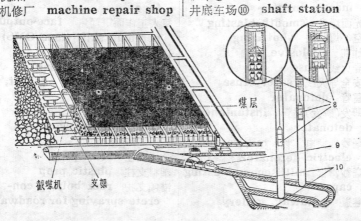

煤层

截煤机　支架

8

9

10

出风井 upcast shaft, discharge air shaft
进风井 downcast shaft
自上向下开掘的暗井 winze
自下向上开掘的暗井 raise
矿井提升机(绞车) mine hoist
箕斗 skip
井底 shaft (pit) bottom
井下水仓(水窝) shaft sump
吸水管 suction pipe
水泵房 pump room
变电所 transformer substation
电机车库 electric locomotive garage
调度室 dispatching room
绞车房 hoisting room
矿灯房 lamp room
通风 ventilation
通风道 airway
风墙 airlock
风门 airdoor
回风道 air return way
通风孔 air hole
自然通风 natural ventilation
机械通风 mechanical ventilation, fan ventilation
空气压缩机 air compressor

## 井巷工程 Shaft Sinking and Roadway Drivage

凿井吊盘 sinking platform
吊桶 kibble, shaft bucket
安全梯 safety ladder
泛光灯(探照灯) floodlight
通风管道 ventilation duct
激光导向测量 laser guide measurement
光面爆破 smooth blasting
空心爆炸法 shotfiring
炸药 explosive
导火线 fuse
安全导火线 safety fuse
雷管 detonator
即发(瞬发)雷管 instantaneous detonator
毫秒延发电雷管 millisecond electric detonator
毫秒雷管 millisecond blasting cap
巷道 roadway, gallery
巷道掘进 tunnelling, roadway drivage
巷道掘进指标 tunnelling quota
采场 stope
工作面 work-face
回采工作面 recovery work-face
每人工作面班产量 face output per man shift (face OMS)
顶板 roof
悬臂梁 cantilever bar
巷道支护 roadway support, roof support
支柱 prop
木支柱 wooden prop
刹杆 lagging
金属支柱 steel prop
塑料支柱 plastic prop
锚喷支护 roof bolting concrete spraying for roadway

support
钢筋混凝土支柱 reinforced concrete prop
喷射混凝土支护 shotcrete support
回柱 prop recovery
液压支架 hydraulic support
液压千斤顶 hydraulic jack

垛式液压支架 powered support of chock type, hydraulic chock
自移式液压支架 self-advancing hydraulic support
掩护式自移支架 self-advancing shield support

## 运 输 Haulage

井筒提升 shaft hoisting
主巷 mine haulage roadway
电机车 electric locomotive
蓄电池电机车 battery locomotive
架线蓄电池两用电机车 trolley-cum-battery locomotive
重车道 track for full tubs
空车道 track for empty tubs
人员运输车(斜井人车) manriding car, "man-trip" train
卷扬机(提升机) hoisting engine, hoister
皮带运输机 belt conveyor
槽形皮带运输机 troughed belt conveyor
刮板运输机 scraper conveyor
链板运输机① chain-scraper conveyor

自行矿车 shuttle car
斗式提升机 bucket hoist conveyor
可伸缩皮带运输机 extensible belt conveyor
可弯曲铠装运输机 armoured flexible conveyor
顺槽转载机 stage loader
运煤机(电溜子) conveyor
工作面运输 coal-face haulage
机械化盾构 mechanized shield unit
爬斗装岩 scraper loading

## 矿山机械 Mining Machinery

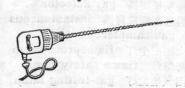

风镐 pneumatic pick
风钻 pneumatic drill
凿岩机 rock drill, hammer drill
电钻② electric drill
台钻 bench drill
气腿凿岩机 airleg rock drill

联合采煤机　coal combine

连续采煤机　continuous mining machine

截煤机　coal-cutting machine, cutter-loader

滚筒式截煤机　drum cutter

双滚筒可调高采煤机　double-ended ranging shearer

露天采煤机械　opencut mining machinery

迈步式挖掘机　walking excavator

轮斗式挖掘机(轮斗铲)　bucket wheel excavator

履带式挖掘机　crawler-mounted excavator

绳斗电铲　drag-line excavator

攉煤机　mechanical coal loader

硬质合金截煤机　carbide miner

硬质合金多头转割机　carbide-tipped multiple-rotating cutter

水力采矿机械　hydraulic mining machinery

水力爆破　hydraulic blasting

水枪①　hydraulic giant

隧道掘进机　tunneller

矿山生产自动化　automation in mining production

## 安全生产　Safety in Production

保安规程　safety regulations

矿山事故　mine hazard

沼气　firedamp

窒息性空气(碳酸气)　blackdamp (chokedamp)

一氧化碳　carbon monoxide

爆炸后气体　afterdamp

臭气(硫化氢)　stinkdamp (hydrogen sulphide)

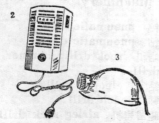

瓦斯和煤尘爆炸　explosion of gas and coal dust

顶板压力计　roof pressure gauge

瓦斯分布　distribution of gas

排放瓦斯法　gas draining method

瓦斯浓度测量　measurement of gas concentration

瓦斯量　amount of gas

瓦斯报警器②　gas alarm

瓦斯探测器　gas detector

瞬息瓦斯取样器　instantaneous gas sampler

火焰安全灯　flameproof lamp

防爆灯　flame safety lamp

沼气检验灯　gas-testing lamp

火灾　fire hazard
自燃　spontaneous combustion
采空区火灾(老塘火灾)　gob fire
防火墙　firebreak
灭火器　fire extinguisher
泡沫堵塞技术　"foam plug" technique
泡沫剂　foam agent
消防龙头　hydrant
喷洒泡沫溶液　spraying of foam-agent solution
密闭　sealing up
矿区水灾　flooding of mine
突发水灾　flash flood
水渗透　infiltration of water
排水　drainage
水仓(聚水坑底)　water sump
井筒管子格间　pump compartment
输水管道　water pipe
矿井水净化站　mine water purifying station

矿工装备　miner's outfit
矿工安全帽　miner's safety helmet
帽灯③　cap-lamp, head lamp
电池　battery
手灯　hand lamp
氧气面具　oxygen respirator
吸氧装备　oxygen apparatus
一氧化碳过滤面具　carbon monoxide filter respirator
氧气发生器全套装备　self-contained oxygen generator
紫外线灯(太阳灯)　ultraviolet lamp(artificial sun)
汞汽灯　mercury-vapour lamp
职业病的预防　prevention of occupational disease
风湿病　rheumatism
矿工眼球震颤病　miner's nystagmus
矽肺病　silicosis
肺尘埃沉着病　pneumoconiosis

# 电　力　Power

## 发　电　Electric Power Generation

发电站　power station
水力发电站　hydroelectric power station, hydropower station(hydro)

火力发电站　thermal power station
地热电站　geothermal power station

潮汐电站 tidal power station
风力发电站 wind power station
原子能电站 atomic power station
太阳能电站 solar power station
发电设备制造厂 power equipment plant
十五万千瓦成套水力发电设备 150,000 kilowatt hydroelectric power generating plant
装机容量 installed capacity
总发电量 total generation
总容量(总功率) aggregate capacity
额定功率 rated capacity
单机功率 unit capacity
输入功率 input power
输出功率 output power
功率因数 power factor
频率 frequency

效率 efficiency
额定转速 rated speed
高峰负荷时间 peak-load period, peak hours
正常负荷时间 off-peak period, off-peak hours
基本负荷 basic load
马力 horse power
千瓦 kilowatt(KW)
千瓦〔小〕时(度) kilowatt-hour(KWH)
电压 voltage
伏特 volt
电流 current
交流电 alternating current(AC)
直流电 direct current(DC)
安培 ampere
电阻 resistance
电容 capacitance
电抗 reactance

## 水力发电 Hydroelectric Generation

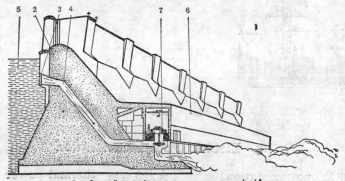

水力发电工程 hydroelectric scheme
引水式水电站 run-of-river power station
抽水蓄能式水电站 pump-storage power station

日调节水力发电站 pondage station

堤坝式水电站① dam-type power station

水工建筑物 hydraulic structure

大坝② dam, dike

围堰 cofferdam

进水闸门③ intake gate

引水隧洞④ intake tunnel

集蓄的河水⑤ river water impounded

发电厂房⑥ powerhouse

水轮发电机组⑦ turbogenera-tor unit

高水头 high head

低水头 low head

有效落差(有效水头) effective head

水情 regimen

水力参数 hydraulic conditions

流量 flow discharge

流量率——立方米/秒 rate of flow——cubic metres per second

溢流 overflow

涡轮机(透平) turbine

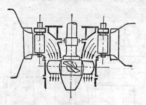

8

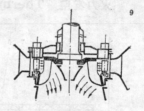

9

水轮机 water(hydraulic) turbine

冲击型水轮机 impulse water turbine

反击型水轮机 reaction water turbine

水泵水轮机 pump-turbine

轴流式水轮机⑧ axial-flow water turbine

混流式水轮机⑨ mixed-flow water turbine

蜗壳 spiral casing, volute chamber

转轮 runner

主轴 shaft

导叶 guide blade, guide vane

顶盖 head cover

联轴器 coupling

尾水管 draft tube, discharge tube

尾水渠 tailrace

前池 forebay

进水管 penstock

上下式水闸 vertical-lift gate

水轮发电机 hydraulic generator

立式 vertical type

卧式 horizontal type

伞型 umbrella type

定子 stator

定子机座 frame

定子铁芯 core

定子绕组 stator winding

叠绕组 lap winding

波绕组　wave winding
转子　rotor
转轴　shaft
转子中心体　core
轮毂　hub
支臂　hub spider
磁轭　magnetic yoke
叠片磁极　laminated pole
极靴　pole shoe
阻尼绕组　damper winding
旋浆式风扇　paddle-wheel fan
上机架　upper generator bracket

下机架　lower generator bracket
上导轴承　upper guide bearing
下导轴承　lower guide bearing
推力轴承　thrust bearing
制动器　brake
空气冷却器　air cooler
辅机　auxiliary set
励磁机　exciter
永磁发电机　magneto generator, permanent magnet generator

## 火力发电　Thermal Power Generation

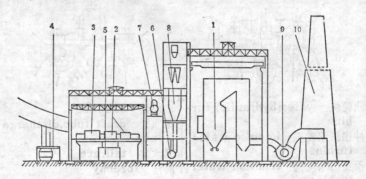

锅炉①　boiler
汽轮机②　steam turbine
发电机③　generator
主变压器④　main transformer
冷凝器⑤　condenser
磨煤机⑥　pulverizer, coal grinder
除气器⑦　de-aerator
原煤仓⑧　coal bunker
吸风机⑨　induced-draft fan
烟囱⑩　chimney
汽轮机　steam turbine

高压汽缸　high pressure cylinder
中压汽缸　intermediate pressure cylinder
低压汽缸　low pressure cylinder
喷嘴　nozzle
汽轮机转子⑪　turbine rotor
叶片⑫　blade, vane
叶轮⑬　blade wheel
导叶　guide blade, guide vane

主轴⑭ shaft

整体锻件 solid forging

中间再热 reheating

主汽门 stop valve

蒸气总管 steam main

调速器 governor

调速系统 speed-governing system

危急保安器 emergency stop protection

蒸气发生能力(蒸气发生率)——每小时——吨 steam raising

capacity (live steam rate) ——tons per hour

表面式冷凝器 surface condenser

冷凝水 condensate

冷凝水泵 condensate pump

喷水抽气机 water-jet air ejector

临界转速 critical speed

亚临界转速 sub-critical speed

飞逸转速 runaway speed

汽轮发电机组 turbogenerator

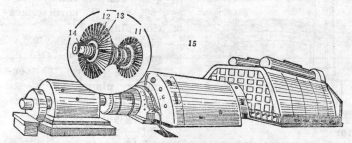

15

双水内冷汽轮发电机⑮ turbo-generator with a double internal water-cooling system

空心铜线圈 hollow copper wire coil

绝缘水管 insulation pipe

定子和转子均用水内冷 internal water-cooling for both stator and rotor

配套运转 operating on the unit principle

发电机主断路器 generator main circuit breaker

断开容量——千伏安 inter-rupting capacity——KVA

集电弓式隔离开关 pantograph

isolators

架空电路接线结构 overhead line terminal structure

过电压吸收器 surge arrester

不接地中性点 insulated neu-tral point

备用机组 standby unit, emer-gency set

燃气轮机发电机组 gas-turbo-generator

自由活塞燃气发生器 free-pis-ton gasifier

空气加热器 air boiler

轴流式压气机 axial compress-or

离心式压气机 centrifugal compressor

燃烧室 combustion chamber
增压装置 charging set
扩压器 diffuser
换热器 heat exchanger
中间冷却 intercooling
开式循环 open cycle
闭式循环 closed cycle

半闭式循环 semi-closed cycle
平衡活塞 dummy piston
自动起动 automatic starting
接触断路螺线管 contact breaker solenoid
周转减速齿轮 epicyclic reduction gear

## 原子能发电站 Atomic (Nuclear) Power Station

原子核反应堆① nuclear reactor
气冷石墨慢化天然铀反应堆 gascooled, graphite-moderated natural uranium reactor
筒形堆心 cylindrical reactor core
双壁耐压容器 double-shell pressure vessel
燃料管道 fuel-element channel

铀棒 uranium rod
控制棒 control rod
活性区分离装置 core separation plant
一回路装置（蒸气发生装置）primary plant
二回路(汽轮机)动力装置 secondary plant
混凝土生物防护屏 concrete biological shield
初级（一次）屏蔽 primary shield
次级（二次）屏蔽 secondary shield
净化中心站 decontamination centre
热交换器 heat exchanger
核电力 nuclear-generated electric power

## 地热电站 Geothermal Power Station

地热钻孔 geothermal borehole
蒸气冒涌装置 flashing steam plant
总管 main
控流阀 flow control valve
中压涌流器 intermediate

pressure flash vessel
低压涌流器 low pressure flash vessel
蒸气滤净器 steam scrubber
排水池 water discharge tank
低压汽轮机 low pressure turbine

## 控制系统　Control System

中央控制室　central control room

控制台　control desk, control board

监视信号盘　supervisory panel

调节开关柜　regulator cubicle

辅助开关设备　auxiliary switchgear

数据自动检测装置　data logger

模拟电路图　mimic diagram

远距离操作设备　remote operating equipment

信号装置　signal device

报警装置　alarm device

(自动控制的)扰动　disturbance

开动　starting up

停机　shutdown

厂用电系统　station service system

对部分地区暂停供电　load shedding

开关设备　switchgear

露天开关场　outdoor switchyard

露天油断路器　outdoor oil circuit-breaker

隔离开关　isolator

气中开关设备　air-break switchgear

气吹式断路器　air-blast circuit-breaker

灭弧　arc suppression(quenching)

配电室　switch room

配电盘　switchboard

自动重合闸继电器　automatic circuit recloser

瓷绝缘子　porcelain insulator

装脚绝缘子　post insulator

耐张绝缘子　strain insulator

旋转开关　rotary switch

插塞开关　plug switch

载流容量　current-carrying capacity

合闸顺序　switching order

合闸力　switching force

合闸　switching on

开闸　switching off

转接　switching over

断电(停电)　supply interruption (suspension)

## 变电输电 Power Transformation and Transmission

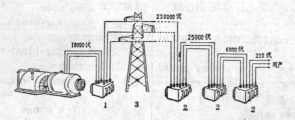

变电所 transformer station, substation

输电变压器 transmission transformer

升压变压器① step-up transformer

降压变压器② step-down transformer

高压电缆箱 high voltage cable end box

低压电缆箱 low voltage cable end box

变压器箱 transformer tank

油箱 oil tank

带荷自动抽头变换开关 automatic on-load tap-changer

全绝缘氮封变压器 fully-insulated nitrogen-sealed transformer

自耦变压器 auto transformer

冷还原取向性硅钢片芯 cold-reduced grain-oriented silicon steel core

入地变压器 buried transformer

接地变压器 grounding transformer, earthing transformer

防潮材料 non-hygroscopic material

变压器亭(配电亭) kiosk

整流 rectification

直流发电机 dynamo

可控硅整流器 silicon-controlled rectifier

高压电网 grid

超高压电网 supergrid

网络接合点 network junction point

输电线(电源线) powerline

架空电线 overhead line, aerial cable

高压电路 high tension line

低压电路 low tension line

高压电线塔③ pylon

地下电缆 buried cable

纸绝缘铅皮线 paper-insulated lead-sheathed cable

铝包电缆 aluminium-sheathed cable

氯丁橡胶包电缆 neoprene sheathed cable

硅橡胶绝缘 silicon rubber insulation

三芯电缆 three-core cable

电缆沟 cable duct

电缆暗道　cable gallery
接地线芯　earthing core
胶皮线　rubber insulated wire
漆包线　enamel insulated wire
带电线芯　live core
中性线芯　neutral core
单芯充油电缆　single-core oil-filled cable
双层铠装电缆　double-armoured cable
电缆架　cable stand
电缆槽　cable tank
电缆夹　cable clip, cable clamp
压合接头　compression fittings
电缆剪　cable cutter

母线系统(汇流条系统)　busbar system
架线工　overhead line worker
装线配件　line accessories
紧线钳　draw tongs
电线杆上操作台　pole platform
配电干线　distribution main
动力干线　power main
照明干线　lighting main
环形干线　ring main
主干线(中途干线)　trunk main
分压电路　bleeder circuit
网络保护装置　network protector
高压高遮断容量保险丝　high-voltage high rupturing capacity fuse (high-voltage HRC fuse)
保险丝盒　fuse box

# 机 械　Machinery

## 机械厂　Machine-Building Plants

通用机器厂　general machines plant
机床厂　machine tools plant
重型机床厂　heavy machine tools plant
冶金、矿山机械　metallurgical and mining machinery
石油、化学工业机械　machin-

ery for the petroleum and chemical industries
农业机械　farm machinery
电力机械　electric machinery
建筑机械　building machinery
筑路机械　road-building machinery
运输机械　transport machinery

轻工业机械 light industry machinery

铸工车间(翻砂车间) foundry

锻工车间 forge

机工车间 machine shop

辅助车间 auxiliary shop

修配车间 repair shop

装配车间 assembly shop, fitting shop

装配线 assembly line

制模工 moulder

铸工 founder

锻工 hammersmith, hammerman

车工 lathe operator, turner

钳工 bench worker, fitter

刨工 planer

铣工 miller

钻工 driller

焊工 welder

铆工 riveter

装配工 assembler

修理工 repairman

电工 electrician

生产成套设备 producing complete plants

用一般设备制造达到现代标准的新机械 using ordinary equipment to make new machinery up to modern standards

采用先进工艺技术 adopting advanced technologies and techniques

## 机床(一)　Machine Tools ( I )

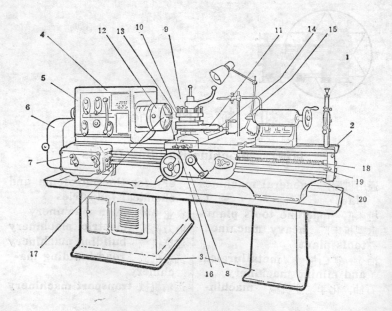

| | |
|---|---|
| 车床 lathe | 万能工作夹具 universal fitxure |
| 皮带车床 belt driven lathe | 机动车床(普通车床)① engine lathe |
| 万能车床 universal lathe | 床身② bed |
| 立式车床 vertical lathe | 床座③ base |
| 卧式车床 horizontal lathe | 床头箱④ headstock |
| 丝杠车床 leading screw lathe | 变速齿轮箱⑤ speed gear box |
| 多刀车床 multi-tool lathe | 交换齿轮箱⑥ change gear box |
| 高速车床 high speed lathe | |
| 仿形车床 copying lathe | 进给齿轮箱⑦ feed gear box |
| 自动六角车床 automatic turret lathe | 溜板箱⑧ apron |
| | 刀架⑨ carriage, tool post |
| 全齿轮马鞍车床 gear-head lathe with gap bed | 上刀架(小拖板)⑩ top rest |
| | 横刀架(横拖板)⑪ cross slide |
| 车刀 lathe tool | 夹盆⑫ chuck |
| 粗车刀 roughing tool | 刀夹⑬ tool holder |
| 精切刀 finishing tool | 刀架滑台⑭ tool slide |
| 高速车刀 high speed turning tool | 尾座顶尖⑮ tailstock centre |
| | 活顶夹⑯ live centre |
| 切削工具(刀具) cutting tool | 花盆⑰ face plate |
| (刀具的)切削寿命 working durability, service life (of cutting tool) | 导螺丝杠⑱ lead screw |
| | 进刀轴⑲ feed shaft |
| 夹具 jig | 回动轴⑳ reverse shaft |

## 机床(二)  Machine Tools (II)

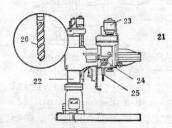

| | |
|---|---|
| | 排钻床 gang drill |
| | 灵敏钻床 sensitive drill press |
| | 摇臂钻床㉑ radial drill, drilling machine with pivoted arm |
| | 立柱㉒ column |
| | 传动电动机㉓ driving motor |
| | 手轮㉔ hand wheel |
| 钻床 drilling machine | 钻轴㉕ drill spindle |
| 多轴钻床 multiple-spindle drilling machine | 钻头㉖ drill |
| 回转式钻床 rotary drilling machine | 双刃钻 double cutting drill |
| | 麻花钻 twist drill |

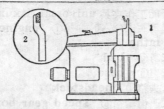

刨床① planer, planing machine
牛头刨床 shaper
龙门刨床(双柱刨床) double-housing planer, double-column planer
双面刨床 double face planer
液压刨床 hydraulic planer
粗刨刀② roughing planing tool
切断刨刀 parting planing tool

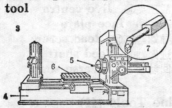

镗床③ boring machine
床身④ base
镗杆⑤ boring spindle
镗床工作台⑥ boring table
镗孔刀具⑦ boring apparatus

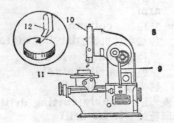

插床⑧ slotting machine
传动轴⑨ driving spindle
冲头⑩ punch
工作台⑪ work table
插刀⑫ slotting tool
冲模插床 die slotting machine
槽铣刀 slotting cutter

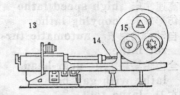

拉床⑬ broaching machine
拉刀⑭ broach
滑块⑮ slide block
平面拉刀 surface broach
整体拉刀 solid broach
组合拉刀 built-up broach
细齿拉刀 serration broach

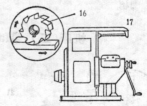

铣床⑯ milling machine
铣刀⑰ milling cutter
万能升降台式铣床 universal knee-and-column miller
齿轮铣床 gear milling machine
螺纹铣床 thread milling machine
立体仿形铣床 three-dimensional copy milling machine

滚齿机　gear hobbing machine
花键轴铣床　spline shaft hobbing machine
齿轮滚铣刀　gear hobber

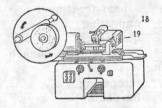

磨床　grinding machine, grinder
内圆磨床　internal grinding machine
外圆磨床⑱　external grinding machine, cylindrical grinder
砂轮座　grinding wheel head
球磨床　ball grinder

坐标磨床　jig grinder
磨轮(砂轮)⑲　grinding wheel
导轮　guide wheel
轮轴　wheel spindle
金刚砂　emery

组合机床　aggregate machine tool
组合万能机床　combined universal machine tool
连续自动工作机床　transfer machine
电解加工机床　electrolytic machine tool
电火花加工机床　electric spark machine tool
超声波加工机床　ultrasonic machine tool
程序控制机床　programme control machine tool
数字程序控制机床　digital process control machine tool

## 铸造和锻造　Casting and Forging

铸型　mould
砂型　sand mould
湿型　green sand mould
金属铸模　metal mould
模型　pattern
砂箱　mould box, flask
上箱　cope
下箱　drag
型芯　core
型砂　moulding sand
面砂　precoated sand
合成砂　synthetic sand
冒口　riser
抛砂机　sand slinger

化铁炉(冲天炉)　cupola
直接电弧炉　direct arc furnace
电感应炉　electric induction furnace
坩埚　crucible, fire pot
熔化锅　melting pot
高温计　pyrometer
浇铸　pouring, casting
压铸　pressure casting
离心铸造　centrifugal casting, rotary casting
熔模精密铸造　precision-investment casting
失蜡铸造　lost-wax casting

| | |
|---|---|
| 壳型铸造　shell moulded casting | 反击锻　counterblow forging |
| 压力硬模铸造　pressure die casting | 冲压　stamping |
| | 挤压　squeezing |
| 粉末冶金　powder metallurgy | 拉拔　drawing |
| 锤锻　hammer forging | 挤出　extruding |
| 自由锻造　smith forging | 热处理　heat treatment |
| 铁砧　anvil | 退火　annealing |
| 镦锻　upsetting | 淬火　quenching |
| 镦锻机　upsetter | 功频淬火　frequency quenching |
| 摇锤锻造　helve hammer forging | 回火　tempering |
| 模锻　drop forging | 硬化　hardening |
| 水压机锻造　hydraulic forging | 表面硬化　surface hardening |
| 夹板落锤　board drop hammer | 时效硬化　age hardening |
| 气锤　air hammer | 冷加工　cold working |
| 汽锤　steam hammer | 冷锻　cold forging |
| 滚锻　roll forging | 冷拔　cold drawing |
| 冲击锻　impact forging | 冷压　cold pressing |
| | 冷弯　cold bending |

## 加工方法　Working Process

| | |
|---|---|
| 车削　turning | 攻〔螺〕丝　tapping |
| 切削　cutting | 铰孔　reaming |
| 高速切削　high-speed cutting | 铣槽　channeling |
| 无屑加工　chipless machining | 冲孔　punching |
| 电解切削　electrolytic cutting | 拉削　broaching |
| 刨　planing, shaping | 超声波加工　ultrasonic machining |
| 铣　milling | |
| 螺纹铣削　thread milling | 电火花加工　electroarcing process |
| 磨削　grinding | |
| 镜面磨削　mirror face grinding | 铆接　riveting |
| 钻孔　drilling | 焊接　welding |
| 镗孔　boring | 电焊　electric welding |
| 磨光(抛光)　polishing | 乙炔焊　acetylene welding |
| 滚花　knurling | 溶化　fusing |
| 倒棱　chamfering | 喷漆　spray-painting |
| 去毛刺　burring | |

# 机 件 Machine Parts

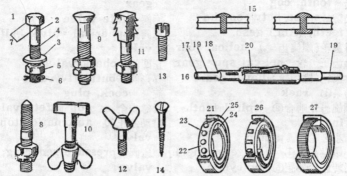

部件　unit, component part
备件　spare part
配件　fitting
螺栓①　bolt
　螺栓杆②　shank
　垫圈③　washer
　螺纹④　thread
　螺母⑤　nut
　开尾销⑥　split pin
　扳手钳口宽度⑦　width of
spanner jaw
双头螺栓⑧　stud
埋头螺栓⑨　countersunk-head
bolt
丁字头螺栓⑩　T-head bolt
棘螺栓⑪　rag bolt, stone bolt
螺钉　screw
翼形螺钉⑫　thumb (wing)
screw
有槽螺钉⑬　slotted screw
木螺钉⑭　wood screw
钉子　nail
平头钉(图钉)　tack
铆钉⑮　rivet
轴⑯　shaft

倒棱⑰　chamfer
斜面　bevel
轴颈⑱　journal
座⑲　seat
键槽⑳　keyway
锥形座　conical seat
滚珠轴承㉑　ball bearing
　轴承罩㉒　bearing cage
　钢珠㉓　steel ball
　内座圈㉔　inner race
　外座圈㉕　outer race
滑动轴承(普通轴承)　plain
bearing
减摩轴承(滚动轴承)　anti-fric-
tion bearing
滚柱轴承㉖　roller bearing
滚针轴承㉗　needle bearing
经向轴承(横力轴承)　radial
bearing
微型轴承　micro bearing
单列向心球轴承　single-row
centripetal ball bearing
推力球轴承　thrust ball bear-
ing
双列球面滚子轴承　double-row

spherical roller bearing
齿轮　gear
齿　tooth, cog
齿隙　space between the teeth, (Am.) gash
斜齿轮(螺旋齿轮)　helical gear
斜齿正齿轮　helical spur gear
伞齿轮(锥齿轮)　bevel gear
齿条①　rack
螺旋齿轮啮合②　spiral tooth-ing
　小齿轮③　pinion
　圆盘齿轮④　disc gear wheel
周转齿轮装置⑤　epicyclic gearing
　行星轮⑥　planet wheel

中心轮⑦　sun wheel
人字齿轮　double helical spur gear
闸阀　gate valve
球阀　spherical valve, ball valve
止回阀　check valve
蝶形阀　butterfly valve
旋塞　cock, plug
紧急安全阀　pop safety valve
自动停止阀　automatic stop valve
减压阀　pressure reducing valve
单向阀　one-way valve

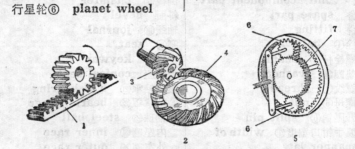

## 锅炉、泵、空气压缩机等　Boiler, Pump, Air Compressor, etc.

锅炉　boiler
水管锅炉　water tube boiler
　水冷壁　water wall
　燃烧室(炉膛)　combustion chamber
　水软化装置　demineraliza-tion plant
　给水泵　feed pump
　汽包　steam pocket
　饱和压力　saturation pressure

过热器　superheater
烟道　flue pass
再热器　reheater
中间再热锅炉　reheat boiler
蒸汽管道　steam line
弯头　bend
弯接管　bend connector
离心喷射器　cyclone
磨煤机　pulverizer
送风机　forced-draft fan

| | | | |
|---|---|---|---|
| 吸风机 | induced-draft fan | | pump |
| 离心泵 | centrifugal pump | 回转泵 | rotary pump |
| 叶轮 | impeller | 涡轮泵 | turbine pump |
| 蜗壳 | volute | 压力泵 | force pump |
| 往复泵 | reciprocating pump | 柱塞泵 | plunger pump |
| 进口 | inlet | 多级泵 | stage pump |
| 出口 | outlet | 空气压缩机 | air compressor |
| 止回阀 | check valves | 气锤 | air hammer, pneumatic hammer |
| 连杆 | connecting rod | | |
| 曲柄 | crank | 磨擦压力机 | friction press |
| 筒 | cylinder | 机动压力机 | power press |
| 活塞 | piston | 水(液)压机 | hydraulic press |
| 轴流泵 | axial-flow pump | 包装机 | baling press |
| 混流泵 | mixed-flow pump | 压片机 | tablet press |
| 齿轮泵 | gear pump | 制砖机 | brick press |
| 转子泵 | rotor pump | 榨油机 | oil press |
| 螺旋泵 | screw pump, volute | | |

## 发动机　Engine

| | | | |
|---|---|---|---|
| 蒸汽机 | steam engine | 柴油机 | diesel engine |
| 汽轮机(蒸汽透平) | steam turbine | 陆用柴油机 | stationary diesel engine |
| 水轮机 | hydraulic turbine | 船用柴油机 | marine diesel engine |
| 燃气轮机 | gas turbine | | |
| 核动力燃气轮机 | nuclear powered gas turbine | 汽缸盖 | cylinder head |
| | | 汽缸 | cylinder |
| 喷气发动机 | jet engine | 活塞 | piston |
| 核能透平喷气发动机 | nuclear turbojet | 活塞环 | piston ring |
| | | 连杆 | connecting rod |
| 内燃机 | internal combustion engine | 进气歧管 | intake manifold |
| | | 排气歧管 | exhaust manifold |
| 汽油机 | gasoline engine | 曲轴 | crankshaft |
| 转缸式发动机 | rotary engine | 凸轮 | cam |
| 四冲程 | four-stroke-cycle | 曲柄 | crank |
| 吸气 | intake | 挺杆 | tappet |
| 压缩 | compression | 正时齿轮 | time gear |
| 作功 | power (work) | 惰轮 | idling gear |
| 排气 | exhaust | 喷油泵 | injection pump |

离心调节器　centrifugal governor

散热器　radiator

汽缸数　number of cylinders

汽缸内径　cylinder bore

汽缸排量　cylinder displacement

活塞行程　stroke, travel of piston

piston

额定速度　rated speed

额定功率　rated output

最大功率　maximum output

持续功率　continuous output

燃油消耗率　fuel consumption

外型尺寸　overall dimensions

总重量　total weight

## 电动机　Electric Motor

感应电动机(异步电动机)　induction motor

同步电动机　synchronous motor

同步感应电动机　synchronous induction motor

换向器电动机　commutator motor

滑环电动机　slipring motor

直流电动机　direct current motor

motor

单相　single phase

三相　three phase

开敞式　open type

封闭式　enclosed type

全封闭式　totally enclosed type

鼠笼式　squirrel-cage type

立式　vertical type

卧式　horizontal type

## 手工具和量具　Hand Tool and Measuring Tool

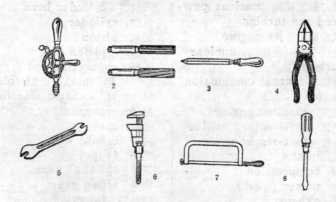

手锤　hammer
圆头铲　round spade
方铲　square spade
手虎钳　hand vice
手摇钻①　hand drill
手铰刀②　hand reamer
刮刀　scraper
三角刮刀③　three-cornered scraper
手钳　pliers
剪钳④　combination cut pliers

平头钳　flat nose pliers
扳手⑤　spanner, wrench
活扳手⑥　monkey wrench
锉　file
扁锉　flat file
凿　chisel
弓锯(钢锯)⑦　hack saw
螺丝起子(改锥)⑧　screwdriver
螺丝攻　screw tap
螺旋扳手　screw wrench
钢尺　steel rule

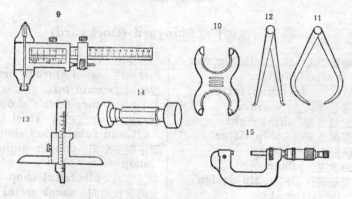

卷尺　tape measure
金属卷尺　metallic tape
折尺　folding pocket measure
丁字尺　T square
三角板　set square
游标卡尺⑨　vernier caliper
卡钳(卡尺)⑩　caliper(s)
外卡钳⑪　outside caliper
内卡钳⑫　inside caliper
千分尺,(分厘卡)⑬　micrometer
螺纹千分尺　crew micrometer
千分表, 校表　dial indicator
圆规　compasses

量角器　protractor
分线规　divider(s)
组合角尺(万能角尺)　combination set
角规　angle gauge
中心规　centre gauge
齿轮规　gear tooth gauge
螺距规　screw pitch gauge
线规　wire gauge
水平仪　level gauge
测深计⑭　depth gauge
圆柱塞规⑮　plug gauge
隙规　gap gauge

# 造　船　Shipbuilding

## 造船厂　Shipyard (Dockyard)

造船工人　shipbuilding worker, shipbuilder

放样工　loftsman, lofter

造船号料工　marker

造船木工　shipwright

船体装配工　ship fitter

装配工　erector

细木工　joiner

船舶设计部门　ship design department

船体建造部门　hull fabrication department

装备部门　outfitting department

压缩空气系统　compressed-air system

丙烷气系统　propane-gas system

运输系统　transport system

滚轴传送系统　roller conveyor system

气垫传送系统　hover-transport system

电动绞车　electric winch

起重绞车　crab

钢料堆场　steel storage area

放样间　mould loft

木工车间　carpenter's shop

钢料放样、加工车间　steel lay-off and fabrication shop

管子铜工车间　copper piping shop

电工车间　electrical shop

金属薄板车间　sheet metal shop

索具车间　rigging shop

俯仰式起重机　luffing crane

高架移动式起重机(桥式吊车)　overhead travelling crane

机工车间　machinist shop

电镀车间　galvanizing shop

船台　building slipway, building berth

造船架　stock

脚手架　staging

龙骨墩　keel-block

液压边墩　hydraulic bilge-block

胎架 cradle for hull section
剪切机 shearing machine
弯板机 plate-bending and forming machine
校平机 straightening rolls
自动化滚轧机 automatic rolling mill
型钢弯曲机 profile (frame) bender
光电跟踪气割机 photo-electric-tracing flame cutting machine
自动跟线气割机 automatic line-following gas-cutter
干船坞 dry dock, graving dock
浮船坞 floating dock
湿〔船〕坞 wet dock
船坞灌了水 dock flooded, dock filled
船坞抽干了水 dock pumped-out, dock emptied

## 造船工艺 Technology of Shipbuilding

造船学 naval architecture
轮机工程 marine engineering
室内造船 shipbuilding in hall
串联造船 tandem ship construction
分段建造 section fabrication
总段建造 module fabrication
两段法造船 ship construction in two parts
船体建造 hull fabrication
放样 mould lofting
实尺样板 full-scale template
比例放样 scale lofting
号料 plate marking
光学号料① optical marking, photo marking
电印号料 electro-print marking
船体钢料切割 hull steel cutting
水下切割 underwater cutting
钢板边缘加工 plate edge planing
爆炸成型 explosive forming
火工矫正 plate fairing by hot

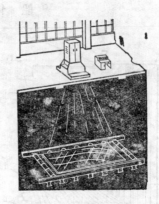

working
肋骨弯曲 frame bending
铺设龙骨 laying the keel
船体装配 hull assembly, hull erection
船台装配 erection on building berth
机械除锈 mechanical de-rusting
化学除锈 chemical de-rusting
高压水除锈 high-pressure water de-rusting

喷丸除锈　**shotblasting**
船体焊接　**hull welding**
垂直自动焊接　**vertical automatic welding**
横向自动焊接　**horizontal automatic welding**
水下焊接　**underwater welding**
安装机器　**installing the machinery**
装备　**fitting-out**
预装备　**fitting-out in advance**
单元装备　**unit fitting-out**
分段装备　**block fitting-out**

安装轴系　**installing the shafting**
装管　**pipe fitting**
铺设电线　**wiring**
安装电器设备　**installing electrical equipment**
喷漆　**spray painting**
船下水　**launching**
纵向下水　**end launching**
横向下水　**side launching**
系泊试验　**dock trial**
航行试验(试航)　**sea trial (trial run)**

## 船　体　Hull

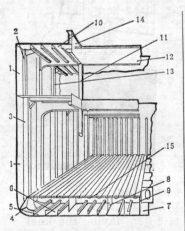

上层建筑　**superstructure**
主船体　**main hull**
球鼻型船首　**bulbous (bulb-nosed) bow**
货舱　**hold**
舱壁　**bulkhead**
气密舱壁　**airtight bulkhead**

防火舱壁　**fireproof bulkhead**
水密舱　**watertight compartment**
外板①　**shell plating**
舷缘列板②　**sheer strake**
舷侧列板③　**side strake**
舭龙骨④　**bilge keel**
舭板⑤　**bilge plate**
船底外板⑥　**bottom plating**
龙骨板⑦　**keel plate**
舷侧纵桁　**side stringer**
旁桁材⑧　**side girder**
双层底中桁材⑨　**centre girder**
甲板板⑩　**deck plating**
甲板支柱⑪　**deck pillar (stanchion)**
甲板横梁⑫　**deck beam**
肋骨⑬　**frame**
舱口围板⑭　**hatch coaming**
货舱护条　**cargo batten**
垫货板　**dunnage board**
舱底板⑮　**ceiling**

# 电 子 Electronics

## 电子设备 Electronic Equipment

电子仪器 electronic instrument

电子医疗仪器 electronic medical instrument

无线电器材 radio tools and equipment

无线电元件 radio component

无线电测量仪表 radio measuring instrument

电信器材 telecommunications equipment

半导体元件 semiconductor component

电视广播器材 television broadcasting equipment

导体 conductor

电路 electric circuit

安培计 ammeter

电压表 voltmeter

电阻 resistor

电感 inductor

电容器 capacitor, condenser

电子管 electronic tube, valve

二极管 diode

灯丝 filament

二极管 triode

栅极 grid

四极管 tetrode

五极管 pentode

六极管 hexode

七极管 heptode

八极管 octode

晶体管 transistor

单晶硅 monocrystal silicon

多晶硅 multicrystal silicon

控制栅极 control grid

帘栅极 screen (grid)

抑制栅极 suppressor grid

晶体二极管(半导体二极管) diode transistor, semiconductor diode

结 junction

PN结 PN junction

NP结 NP junction

晶体三极管 triode transistor

PNP型晶体管 PNP transistor

NPN型晶体管 NPN transistor

空穴传导 hole conduction

电子传导 electron conduction

发射极 emitter

集电极　collector
基极　base
线圈　coil
线圈组　coil assembly
振荡器　oscillator
检波器　detector
放大器　amplifier
整流器　rectifier

硅可控整流元件(可控硅)　silicon controlled rectifier
变压器　transformer
滤声器　acoustic filter
变频器　converter
电位计　potentiometer
光电管(光电池)　photocell, photoelectric cell

## 无线电收音机　Radio Receiver (Radio Set)

交流电收音机　mains set
直流电收音机　battery set
立体声收音机　stereo receiver
矿石收音机　crystal radio
汽车收音机　auto radio, car radio
超外差式收音机　superhet (erodyne) radio set
〔时〕钟控〔制〕收音机(时钟收音机)　clock radio
按钮调谐收音机　push-button-type receiver
晶体管收音机(半导体收音机)　transistor radio, semiconductor receiver
调幅收音机　AM (amplitude modulation) receiver
调频收音机　FM (frequency modulation) receiver
印刷电路　printed circuit
集成电路　integrated circuit
固体电路　solid circuit
薄膜电路　membrane circuit
微波集成电路　microwave integrated circuit
收音机外壳　cabinet
隔板　baffle board
电眼(阴极射线管)　magic eye

(cathode-ray tube)
扬声器(喇叭)孔　loudspeaker aperture
低音标尺　bass tone scale
高音标尺　treble tone scale
低音控制　bass tone control
高音控制　treble tone control
调频转钮　tuning knob
长波波段　long-wave band
中波波段　medium-wave band
短波波段　short-wave band
高保真度　high-fidelity, hi-fi
射频　radio frequency (RF)
中频　intermediate frequency (IF)
声频　audio frequency (AF)
高频　high frequency (HF)
甚高频(特高频)　very high frequency (VHF)
超高频　ultra high frequency (UHF)
超短波　ultra short-wave
微波　microwave
电源开关与音量控制　power switch and volume control
自动音量控制　automatic volume control (AVC)
波段转换开关　band switch

波段选择按钮　push-button wave band selector

电动主扬声器　main loudspeaker (electro-dynamic loudspeaker)

高音扬声器　treble frequency loudspeaker (tweeter)

保险丝　fuse

电压选择开关　voltage selecting switch

铁氧体棒状天线　ferrite-rod antenna

铁氧体棒状天线控制　ferrite-rod antenna control

电源变压器　mains transformer

低频变压器(输出变压器)　low-frequency (LF) transformer (output transformer)

机内特高频天线　built-in VHF antenna

偶极天线　dipole antenna

磁带录音机插孔　socket for tape recorder

附加扬声器插孔　socket for additional loudspeaker

特高频天线插孔　socket for VHF antenna

中长波天线插孔　socket for medium and long wave aerials

电唱机插孔　socket for pick-up

天线转换开关　antenna switch

耳机　earphone

## 电视〔接收〕机　Television Receiver (Teleset)

黑白电视机　monochrome (black-and-white) television receiver (TV set)

彩色电视机　colour television receiver, colour TV set

投影式电视接收机　projection television receiver

偶极天线　dipole antenna, doublet antenna

频道选择开关　channel selector

频率微调　frequency fine tuning

音量调整　audio volume control

音调调整　tone control

亮度调整　brightness control

对比度调整　contrast control

水平同步(行同步)控制　horizontal hold control

垂直同步(幅同步)控制　vertical hold control

图象宽度调整　width control

图象高度调整　height control

线性调整　linearity control

色度调整　chroma control, colour-saturation control

色调调整　hue control

会聚调整　convergence control

自动增益控制　automatic gain control (AGC)

自动频率控制　automatic frequency control (AFC)

自动亮度控制　automatic brightness control (ABC)

自动相位控制　automatic phase control

显像管　picture tube

像点(像素)　picture elements

浓淡点　half-tone elements

黑白显像管　monochrome picture tube

电子枪　electron gun

偏转系统　deflection yoke

第二阳极　second anode

电子束　electron beam

荧光屏　fluorescent screen

彩色显像管　colour picture tube, colour kinescope

单枪彩色显像管　single-gun colour picture tube, single-gun tube

单枪三束彩色显像管　trinitron

三枪彩色显像管　tri-gun colour picture tube, tri-gun tube

三支电子枪　three electron guns

荫罩　shadow mask

三色荧光屏　tricolour phosphor screen

重像(幻像)　ghost image

(荧光屏上)"雪花"干扰　snow

蜂音　buzz

## 电子计算机　Electronic Computer

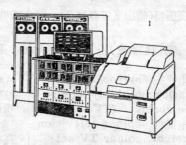

数字计算机① digital computer

模拟计算机　analogue computer

串行计算机　serial computer

并行计算机　parallel computer

实时计算机　real-time computer

分时计算机　time-sharing computer

小型计算机　minicomputer

台式计算机② desk computer

微型计算机　microcomputer

电子计算器　electronic calculator

袖珍计算机　pocket calculator

电子天平　electronic scale

第一代计算机　first generation computer

第四代计算机　fourth generation computer

计算机系列　computer family, computer series

双工系统　duplex system

多机系统　multi-computer system

主机　main frame

外部设备　external equipment

外围设备 peripheral equipment
硬件 hardware
软件 software
固件 firmware
机器语言 machine language
计算机语言 computer language
汇编语言 assembly language
编译程序语言 BCY language
公式翻译程序 FORmula TRANslator (FORTRAN)
汇编程序 assembler
目标程序 object program
翻译程序 translator
编译程序 compiler
程序库 routine library
二进〔数〕制 binary number system
二—十进制转换 binary-to-decimal conversion
二—十进制记数法 binary-coded decimal notation
浮点表示法 floating-point representation
定点表示法 fixed-point representation
定点制数的表示法 fixed-point representation of a number
代码 code
原码〔形式〕 code true form
补码 complement
溢出 overflow
逻辑代数(布尔代数) Boolean algebra
人—机联系 man-computer interaction
人—机通信 man-machine communication
运算速度 operational speed

## 电子数字计算机 Electronic Digital Computer

运算器(运算装置) arithmetic unit
存储器 memory, storage
磁心存储器 magnetic core memory
半导体存储器 semiconductor memory
随机存取存储器 random access memory
控制器 control unit
输入设备 input device
输出设备 output device
控制台 console, control desk
纸带输入机 paper tape reader
穿孔带 punched tape
穿孔卡〔片〕 punched card
绘图机 plotter
X—Y绘图仪 X-Y plotter
门电路 gate circuit
"与"门 AND gate
"或"门 OR gate
"非"门 NOT gate
触发器 flip-flop
寄存器 register
加法器 adder
逻辑电路 logical circuit
微型电路 microcircuit
固态电路 solid state circuit
集成电路 integrated circuit
集成电路片 silicon chip
硅基片 silicon chip
中规模集成〔电路〕 medium-

scale integration (MSI)

大规模集成〔电路〕 large-scale integration (LSI)

双极集成电路 bipolar integrated circuit

金〔属〕氧〔化物〕半导体集成电路 metal-oxide semiconductor integrated circuit

全薄膜化集成电路 all-thin-film integrated circuit

中断 interruption

程序 program

程序设计系统 programming system

微程序设计 microprogram-

ming

原始数据 initial data

中间结果 intermediate result

指令 instruction

信息 information

数据处理 data processing

位(比特) bit (binary digit)

字长 word length

字节 byte

字组 block

反馈 feedback

操作程序 sequence of operations

联机操作 on-line operation

脱机操作 off-line operation

# 雷 达 Radar

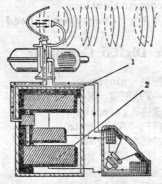

米波雷达 metrewave radar

微波雷达 microwave radar

激光雷达 laser radar

脉冲雷达 pulse radar

三座标雷达(空间雷达) three-dimensional radar (space radar)

多卜勒雷达 Doppler radar

跟踪雷达 tracking radar

制导雷达 guidance radar

导航雷达 navigation radar

卫星监视雷达 satellite surveillance radar

地面监视雷达 ground surveillance radar

航海雷达 marine radar

航天雷达 spaceborne radar

雷达发射机① radar transmitter

调制器 modulator

激励器 exciter

雷达接收机② radar receiver

滤波器 filter

混频器 mixer

振荡器 oscillator

自动增益控制 automatic gain control (AGC)

自动频率控制 automatic frequency control (AFC)

限幅器 limiter

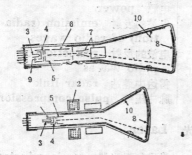

检波器　detector
解调器　demodulator
监测器　monitor
扫描器　scanner
磁控管　magnetron
中频放大器　IF amplifier
射频放大器　RF amplifier
视频放大器　video amplifier
显示器　indicator (display)
阴极射线管(高速电子管)①　cathode-ray tube
聚焦线圈②　focusing coil
电子束　electron beam
旁热丝③　heater
控制栅④　control grid
第二栅⑤　second grid
聚焦电极⑥　focusing electrode
偏转板极⑦　deflecting plate
荧光屏⑧　luminescent screen (radarscope)
阴极⑨　cathode
阳极⑩　anode
荧光屏上尖头信号　blip
记录速度　writing speed
收发转换开关　transmit-receive switch (TR switch)
天线收发转换开关　anti-TR switch (ATR)

旋转天线　rotating antenna
反射器天线　reflector antenna
抛物面天线⑪　parabolic antenna
赋形波束天线　shaped-beam antenna
余割平方天线　cosecant-squared antenna
单脉冲天线　monopulse antenna
龙伯透镜天线　Luneberg lens antenna
雷达信号　radar signal
雷达信息录取　extraction of radar information
方位角录取　azimuth angle extraction
仰角录取　elevation extraction
距离录取　range extraction
高度录取　height data extraction
波门录取　gate extraction
雷达覆盖空域　zone of radar coverage
噪声　noise
杂波　clutter
门限电压　threshold voltage
目标捕获　target acquisition

回波　radio echo
回波脉冲　echo pulse
机械扫描　mechanical scanning
电扫描　electronic scanning
扫描角　scan angle
扫描空域　scan sector

电源　power
电波的发射　emission (radiation) of radio waves
电波的反射　reflection of radio waves
雷达中继站　radar link
脉冲压缩　pulse compression

## 激 光　Laser

发光物质　luminescent substance
激励装置　exciter unit
光学谐振腔　optical resonant cavity
激光器　gas laser
气体激光全息摄影术　gas laser holography
氦氖激光器　helium-neon laser, He-Ne laser
离子激光器　ion laser
氩离子激光器　argon ion laser
二氧化碳激光器　carbon dioxide laser
固态激光器　solid state laser
光激励　light excitation
红宝石激光器①　ruby laser

半导体激光器　semiconductor laser
PN结激光器　PN junction laser
激光准直仪　laser collimator
激光测距仪　laser rangefinder
激光通讯　laser communications
激光导航　laser navigation
卫星跟踪激光器　satellite tracking laser
空间目标跟踪激光器　space tracking laser
相干性　coherence
干涉仪　interferometer
探鱼仪　fish detector
超声波探伤仪　ultrasonic flaw detector
可控硅充电机　silicon controlled rectifier battery charger
自动程序控制装置　automatic program control device
时间继电器　time relay
心电图机　cardiograph
灭虫紫外线灯　ultraviolet lamp for insect extermination
电子扫描显微镜　electronic scanner microscope

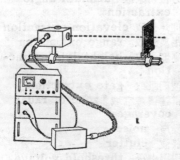

# 自动化　Automation

自动控制　automatic control

自动控制系统　automatic control system

自动调节　automatic regulation

自动调节系统　automatic regulating system

反馈　feedback

反馈控制系统　feedback control system

被控制量　controlled variable, regulated variable

控制量　manipulated variable

稳定性　stability

品质指标　index of quality, criterion of control quality

衰减度　degree of decay

静态精度　static accuracy

动态精度　dynamic accuracy

开环控制　open-loop control

前馈控制　feedforward control

闭环控制　closed-loop control

定值调节　constant value control, fixed set-point control

程序控制　program control

随动系统　servo system

伺服机构　servomechanism

伺服机械手　servo manipulator

自动机(机器人)　robot

脉冲系统　pulse system

计算机控制系统　computer control system

数字控制　numerical control

数字顺序控制　digital process control

数据处理　data processing

传感器　sensor, sensing element

集中检测系统　contralized monitoring system

自动化技术工具　automation equipment

半导体开关元件　thyristor

工业自动化　industrial automation

化工生产过程自动化　automation of chemical processes

油气田自动化　automation of oil and gas field

冶金生产自动化　automation of metallurgic processes

选矿生产过程自动化　automation of mineral processing

高炉自动化　automation of blast furnace

转炉自动化　automation of converter

轧钢自动化　automation of steel rolling

带钢热轧机计算机控制　computer control of narrow strip hotrolling mill

电力系统自动化　automation of electric-power system

电力系统安全控制　security control on electric-power system

水力发电站自动化　automation of hydroelectric power station

火力发电站自动化　automation of thermal power station

数字程序控制机床 numerically controlled machine tool

连续自动工作机床 transfer machine

铁路编组站自动化 automation of railway marshalling yard

铁路行车指挥自动系统 automatic system for railway traffic control

遥控 remote control

遥调 remote regulating

遥控力学 telemechanics

指令遥控系统 command remote control system

指令信号 command signal

数字指令 digital command

预警指令 alarm command

遥控编码 remote control coding

指令码 command code

信息码 information code

前导码 lead code

同步码 synchronous code

地址码 address code

开门码 opening code

保密码 secret code

执行码 actuating code

频率码 frequency code

译码矩阵 decoding matrix

编码矩阵 encoding matrix

指令监控台 command monitor

电视监视系统 television observation system

雷达监测系统 radar observation system

导航监测系统 navigation observation system

遥测监测系统 telemetry observation system

指令发射机 command transmitter

指令接收机 command receiver

编码器 encoder

解算器 resolver

无线电制导 radio guidance

红外制导 infrared guidance

激光制导 laser guidance

遥测 telemetry, telemetering

遥测系统 telemetry system

医用遥测 medical telemetry

空间遥测 space telemetry

远距信号 remote signalling

同步定点控制 synchro-position control

安全遥控设备 safety remote control equipment

射流技术 jet techinque

射流 jet

射流元件 jet component

单喷口 single jet

双喷口 double jet

空气喷射 air jet

液体喷射 fluid jet

可压缩射流 compressible jet

电子射流 electron jet

水枪射流 giant jet

高速射流 high speed jet

# 建　筑　Building Construction

## 建筑业工种人员　Building Trades

工班　work(ing) shift
起重机班组　crane team
装配工　assembler, assembly-man
混凝土班组　concrete team
混凝土工　concreter
拌和机司机　mixer-driver
钢筋工　steel fixer, steel bender
焊工　welder
设备安装工　fitter
泥水工(砖石工)　mason
石工　stonemason, mason
脚手架工　scaffolder
砌砖工　bricklayer
瓦工　tiler
灰泥工　plasterer
营造木工　carpenter
饰面工　facing worker

花饰铅条窗安装工　lead-light glazier, fret glazier
油漆工　painter
玻璃工　glass fitter
装饰工　decorator
电工　electrician
管子工(水暖工)　plumber
小工　assistant
修理工　repairman
仓库管理员　storekeeper
技术检查员　inspector
工长　foreman
工段长　section chief
工段工程师　section engineer
工地主任　site director, building director
设计人员(制图人员)　designer
承建者　builder, contractor
建筑师　architect

## 建筑材料 Building Materials

粘结材料 cementing materials

生石灰 quicklime

熟石灰 slaked lime

石灰膏(石灰乳) lime putty

生石膏 gypsum (plaster stone)

熟石膏 plaster of Paris

粉饰用石膏粉 gypsum plaster

水泥 cement

水泥标号 strength of cement

高标号水泥 high-strength cement

硅酸盐水泥(普通水泥) portland cement

快硬硅酸盐水泥(超级水泥) accelerated portland cement (supercement)

高铝水泥(矾土水泥) high alumina cement

膨胀水泥 expansive cement

钢渣水泥 slag cement

水泥灰浆 cement mortar

石灰灰浆 lime mortar

石膏灰浆 gypsum lime mortar, gypsum mortar

薄浆 grout

水泥砂浆 cement grout

灰泥 plaster

草筋灰 chopped-straw reinforced lime mortar

混凝土 concrete

粗骨料 coarse aggregate

细骨料 fine aggregate

掺合料(外加剂) admixture

水灰比 water-cement ratio

模板(模壳) forms, formwork

混凝土砌块 concrete block

钢筋混凝土 reinforced concrete

无节钢筋(光面钢筋) plain bar reinforcement

竹节钢筋① deformed bar reinforcement, ribbed bar reinforcement

钢丝网② wire fabric

预制混凝土元件 precast concrete unit

预应力混凝土 prestressed concrete

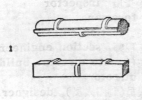

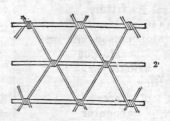

红砖　red brick
青砖　blue brick, sewer brick
墙面砖　face brick
瓷砖　glazed brick, enamelled brick
空心砖　hollow tile, cavity tile
多孔砖　perforated brick
阶砖　floor tile
花阶砖　encaustic tile
粉煤灰砖　fly-ash brick
灰沙砖　sand lime brick
土坯砖(泥砖)　adobe
瓦　roofing tile
板瓦和筒瓦　pan-and roll roofing tiles
板瓦(平瓦)　plain tile
凹瓦　concave tile
凸瓦　convex tile
搭接瓦　shingle-lap tile
瓦楞板　corrugated sheet
玻璃瓦　glazed roofing tile, enamelled terra-cotta tile
木料　wood
木材　timber
板材(制材)　sawn timber, (Am.) lumber
松杉板材　deal
湿材(生材)　greenwood
干燥木材　seasoned wood
压缩木材　compressed wood, compression wood
纤维板　fibreboard, wallboard, composition board
蔗渣纤维板　celotex
防腐材料　anti-rot material

绝缘材料　insulating material
装饰材料　finishing material
石料　building stone
花岗石　granite
片麻岩石　gneiss
大理石(云石)　marble
白云石　dolomite
云母大理石　cipolin(o)
彩花石　brocatello
珍珠岩制品　perlite products
铺路石板　flagstone
石米水泥制成的铺地石　granolith
大卵石　cobblestone
小卵石　pebble
窗玻璃　window glass
磨沙玻璃　frosted glass
雕花玻璃　cut glass
彩花玻璃　stained glass
磨口玻璃　ground glass
双重保温玻璃　thermopane
吸热玻璃　heat-absorbing glass, anti-actinic glass
有机玻璃(塑料玻璃)　plexiglass, organic glass
钢化玻璃　toughened glass
油毡　asphalt felt
沥青纸　asphalt paper
钢窗〔框〕　steel casement
油灰　putty
预制件　precast member, precast element, prefab
预制板件　precast panel
预制大面积轻型墙板　curtain walling

## 建筑机械和手工工具　Builder's Machinery and Hand Tools

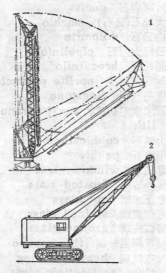

塔式吊杆起重机① **tower crane**

履带式起重机② **caterpillar crane**

旋臂起重机 **jib crane**

天顶吊车 **overhead crane**

万能吊车 **universal crane**

塔式吊架起重机 **tower hoist**

拖运吊架起重机 **mobile hoist**

手动滑车组 **hand pulley block**

桅杆起重机 **derrick**

电动螺旋起重机组 **power-driven screw-jack sets**

液压起重机组 **hydraulic jack sets**

喷枪 **spray gun**

气锤 **pneumatic hammer**

排除积水泵 **sump pump**

混凝土破碎机 **concrete breaker**

旋转式钻孔机 **rotary drill**

拖拉机式铲土机 **tractor shovel**

挖沟机 **trench excavator, trenching machine, trencher**

推土机 **bulldozer**

斜角推土机 **angledozer**

水力挖土机 **hydraulic excavator**

动力挖掘机 **power digger**

水力打孔机 **hydraulic thrust boring machine**

碎石和筛选联合作业车 **mobile stone crushing and screening plant**

冲击式碎土机 **impact grinder**

回转式碎石机 **gyratory crusher**

混凝土搅拌机 **concrete mixer**

混凝土浇注机 **concrete pouring machine**

按重量配料拌和机 **weigh batching mixer, weigh batcher**

打桩机 **pile-driver**

打桩机架 **pile-driver tower**

振动打桩机 **vibrating pile-driver**

砂浆拌和机 **mortar mixer**

车载砂浆拌和机 **truck-mounted mortar mixer**

沥青熔锅 **asphalt cauldron**

钢筋弯折机 **bending machine,**

angle-bender

钢筋调直机　bar straightener
钢筋剪切机　bar cutter
铲装车　loading shovel
底卸斗　hopper
混凝土载运车　concrete cart, buggy
水泥喷枪　cement gun
混凝土泵　concrete pump
滑模　sliding form
升模　climbing form
混凝土摊铺机　concrete spreader
振捣机　vibrating tamper, vibrator
开隧道机　tunnelling machine
脚手架　scaffold
工作便桥　gantry
梯凳　stepladder
梯子　ladder
伸缩梯　extending ladder
临时支架　falsework
拱架　centres, centering
基础支撑　shoring of foundation
吊斗　ship
架空运料索道　aerial ropeway,

(Am.) aerial tramway
测锤　plumb-bob
钢尺　steel tape
粉线　chalk line
粉线盒　chalk line case
镘刀（泥刀，抹子）　trowel
砌砖镘刀　bricklayer's trowel
抹灰镘刀　plasterer's trowel (float)
托灰板　hawk
砌砖手锤　bricklayer's hammer
灰沙斗　hod
水平仪　level
木锤　mallet
凿石锤　mason's hammer
铆钉锤　riveting hammer
灰浆槽　mortar trough
石灰池　lime pit
筛板　screen
混凝土推平耙　come-along
起钉钳　nail puller
手力剪铁刀　hand iron-cutters, hand iron-shears
木夯　beetle
油灰刀　putty knife

## 建筑工程　Construction Project

设计（制图）　designing
草图　preliminary drawing
简图　schematic drawing
详图（大样图）　detail drawing
立面图　elevation
平面图　plan
剖面图　cross-section
建筑透视图　architectural perspective

蓝图　blueprint
安全系数　factor of safety
工程造价　construction cost
单位造价　unit price, unit cost
担保期限　guarantee period
建筑许可证　building permit
施工进度计划　program(me), schedule
施工进度表　progress chart

施工总平面图 layout of construction work

依时竣工 timely completion, keeping to program(me)

误期 delay

最后验收 final acceptance

建筑声学 architectural acoustics

建筑力学 architectural mechanics

楼面面积 floor space

建筑面积 building area

建筑密度 building density

不合格 below proof

修复 restoration

整修 refurbishment

改建 alteration

扩建 extension

增建 addition

侧面伸建部分 wing

附加建筑物 annex

墙外附属建筑物 appendage

拆除〔钢架骨架结构〕 unbuttoning

退缩线 receding line

建筑工地 construction site

场地清除 site clearing

推平施工地址 bulldozing of the site

破土 ground breaking

奠基 laying the foundation stone

工地临时围板 hoarding, boarding

进出道 access road

轻便运输路 pioneer road

工地办事处 building office

材料库(贮料堆) stock of materials (stock pile)

废料场 spoil area, waste area

工地设备 site facilities

工地组织 site organization

工地轻便铁道 field railway

工地试验 field test

工地工作通知 field work order

现场校正图 record drawing, as-built drawing

施工详图 working drawing

## 房屋构造 Building Construction

基础 foundation, substructure

基脚(底脚) footing

桩基础 pile foundation

底岩 bed-rock

填成的地基 made ground

木桩 wood pile, timber pile

预制混凝土桩 precast concrete pile

现浇混凝土桩 cast-in-place concrete pile

灌浆 grouting up

防地震结构 earthquake resistant structure

挡土墙 retaining wall

地下室 basement

地下室墙 basement wall

骨架承重结构 skeleton construction

柱子 column

大梁 girder

拱 arch

拱座 abutment

斗拱 bracket

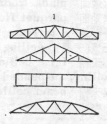
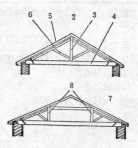

桁架① truss
单柱桁架(金字架)② king post truss
桁架中柱③ king post
系梁④ tie-beam
主椽⑤ principal rafter
支柱(斜撑)⑥ strut
双柱架⑦ queen post truss
双柱⑧ queen posts
承重墙 bearing wall
完幅隔火墙 fire wall
空心墙 hollow wall
墙体面板条层 wall furring
砌砖法 brick bond
露头砖(丁砖)⑨ header
露侧砖(顺砖)⑩ stretcher
露头半砖(假丁砖) half header (false header)
竖身丁砖⑪ bull header
竖身顺砖⑫ bull stretcher
立砌砖 soldier
屋角丁砖⑬ quoin header
装潢砌砖 decorative bond
涂泥篱笆墙 wattle and daub
夯土墙 rammed earth wall
半砖墙 half-brick wall
单砖墙 one-brick wall, whole-brick wall
一砖半墙 brick-and-a-half wall, one-and-half brick wall
砖层 course of bricks
盖顶砖层 coping course, barge course
毛粉饰(毛批荡) stucco
粗毛粉饰(石米粗砂批荡) rough-cast
水磨批荡(意大利批荡) scagliola
抹灰(批荡) plastering, plaster-work
两道抹灰工作 two-coat work (render and set)
刷石灰水 whitewashing
色粉涂饰 distempering
层压塑料墙板 laminated plastics wall panel
楼盖结构 floor construction

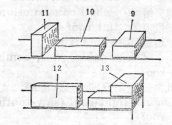

| | |
|---|---|
| 梁板结构楼盖 **beam-and-slab floor** | 木板地面 **plank floor** |
| 搁栅楼盖 **joint floor** | 镶木地面 **parquet floor** |
| 光板楼盖 **flat slab floor, girderless floor** | 水磨石地面 **terrazzo floor** |
| 地板 **flooring** | 天花板(天棚) **ceiling** |
| 阶砖地面 **tiled floor** | 空心天棚 **false ceiling, drop ceiling, suspended ceiling** |
| | 露梁天棚 **beam ceiling** |

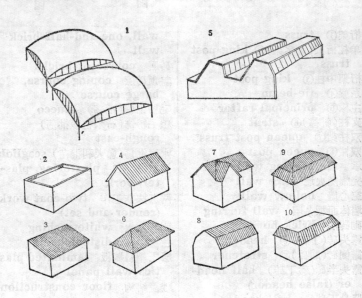

| | |
|---|---|
| 屋面结构 **roof construction** | 屋谷⑦ **valley** |
| 薄壳结构① **shell construction** | 斜折线形屋顶⑧ **gambrel roof** |
| 平屋顶② **flat roof** | 复折形屋顶⑨ **mansard roof, curb roof** |
| 单坡屋顶③ **shed roof** | 平台四坡屋顶⑩ **deck roof** |
| 人字屋顶④ **gable roof, comb roof** | 曲线屋顶 **curved roof** |
| 北窗采光屋顶(锯齿形屋顶)⑤ **north-light roof (saw-tooth roof)** | 扇形屋顶 **ribbed roof** |
| | 拱形屋顶 **arched roof** |
| | 扇形穹顶 **fan vault** |
| 四坡屋顶⑥ **hip roof** | 大屋顶 **overhanging roof** |

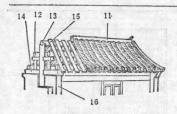

屋脊⑪　ridge
檩(桁)⑫　purlin
脊檩⑬　ridgepole
梁⑭　beam
椽子　rafter
角椽⑮　angle rafter
柱⑯　column
望板　sheathing
屋檐　eaves
飞檐　upturned eaves
雨水斗　roof drain
水落管　downpipe, down-
　　sprout
大沟(檐槽)　gutter
屋顶采光塔楼　clerestory
屋顶小棚屋　penthouse
避雷针　lightning conductor,
　　lightning rod
组合结构　composite con-
　　struction
镶面结构　veneered construc-
　　tion
分件装运现场装配结构　knocked
　　down system of construc-
　　tion
预制全面板装配结构　large
　　panel construction
充气临时建筑　inflatable build-
　　ing
工业化建筑体系　industrialized
　　building system

## 楼梯、窗、门　Stair, Window, Door

楼梯　stairway
一段梯级　a flight of stairs
两段梯级间平台　landing
楼梯栏杆　stair railing, banis-
　　ters
梯级平板　stair tread
楼梯井　stair well
直上楼梯　straight flight
分叉楼梯　bifurcated stair,
　　double-return stair
两边傍墙楼梯　box stair, en-
　　closed stair
单边傍墙楼梯　semihoused stair
螺旋式楼梯　spiral stair,
　　winding staircase
升降机(电梯)　lift, (Am.)
　　elevator
升降机井　lift well, (Am.)
　　elevator shaft
升降机舱　lift cabin
运货电梯　goods lift, (Am.)
　　freight elevator
自动扶梯　escalator
窗框　window frame
窗扇(窗扉)　sash, window
　　pane
窗台　windowsill
外推内拉(竖铰链)窗　casement
两重竖铰链窗　double-case-
　　ment window
双层玻璃窗　double-glazed
　　window
篷式窗(上撑窗)　awning win-
　　dow (top-hung window)
旋转窗　pivoted casement
中旋窗　centre-hung sash

上下扯窗　double-hung window, sash window

内向仰开窗　hopper light, hopper casement

横推窗　sliding sash

楣窗(气窗)　fanlight

天窗　skylight

地下室采光窗　vault light, pavement light

屋顶窗(老虎窗)　dormer window, dormer

风景窗　picture window

百叶窗　blinds, shutters

纱窗　window screen

窗格玻璃　windowpane

窗插销　window bolt, casement fastener

旋钮门　turn button

窗风撑　casement stay

法国式窗(落地长窗)　French window

连排窗　ribbon windows, window band

彩花玻璃窗　stained-glass window

门过梁(门楣)　door lintel

门框　doorcase, doorframe

门槛　threshold, doorsill

门扇　door

木栅门①　batten door, ledged and braced door

拼板门　board-and-brace door

夹板门(镶面门)②　flush door, hollow-core door

折门③　folding door, accordion door

单扇门　single door

双扇门　double door, two-leafed door

铰链门 hinged door

旋转门 revolving door

推拉门(滑动门)④ sliding door

弹簧门 swinging door

玻璃窗门 sash door

百叶门 shutter door

纱门 door screen

屋外围墙门(大门) gate

大门中的小门 wicket

楼板、屋顶上落梯口 hatch, hatchway

门阶 doorsteps

门台阶 stoop

门自动关闭器 door closer

门闩 bolt

门闩锁 latch

外门锁 vestibule latch, night lock

门扣 door catch

门上外窥孔 judas

铁栅门 iron gate

可折铁栅门 collapsible gate

装甲门 armoured door

横门门 barred door

## 浴室、厨房、排水系统 Bathroom, Kitchen and Drainage System

供水 water supply

总水管 water main

用户水管 service pipe

龙头 tap, faucet

冷、热水供应 hot and cold running water

浴室 bathroom

浴盆 bathtub

淋浴喷头 shower nozzle

脸盆 washbasin

抽水马桶 lavatory bowl, water closet bowl

水箱 flush tank

化粪池 septic tank

厨房 kitchen

洗涤盆 rinsing sink

洗碗碟盆 ashing-up sink

煤气管开关 gas-tap, gas-cock

灶 kitchen range

烟囱 chimney, smokestack

煤气炉 gas cooker

煤气表 gas meter

水表 water meter

排水系统 drainage system

建筑物内排水管 building drain

屋内污水渠 domestic sewage

建筑物外排水管 building sewer

渗井 absorbing well

地面水集水井 inlet well

污水渗井 cesspool, cesspit

暗渠 concealed gutter

檐下雨水槽 eaves gutter, eaves trough

污气管 vent pipe

## 空气调节、隔音和照明 Airconditioning, Soundproofing and Lighting

通风过道 breezeway
通气管道(风道) air duct
地下室通风采光井 areaway
地下层通气防湿沟 air drain
空气调节机 airconditioner
送气系统 plenum system
送气风扇 plenum fan
间接供暖 indirect heating
集中供暖 central heating
供暖管 caliduct
暖气供暖系统 warm air heating system
热水供暖 hot-water heating
冷却装置 cooling unit
热空气供暖器 hot-air heater
蒸气散热器 steam radiator
室内恒温器 room thermostat
湿度调节器 humidistat
壁炉 fireplace
壁炉面饰 mantelpiece, mantel shelf, chimney piece
壁炉柴架 andiron
隔音构造 sound-proof(ing) construction, acoustic construction

吸音砖 sound-proof tile
吸音板 sound-proof board
吸音涂料 anti-noise paint
生活用电设施 domestic electrical installation
街道地下电缆 street cable
引入用户电缆 service cable
引入用户电线 service line
进线口 service entrance
穿墙套管 wall bushing
断路闸板 circuit-breaker panel
保险丝盒 fuse-box
电源插座 outlet
室内照明 indoor lighting
顶棚灯 ceiling lamp
吊灯 pendant lamp
顶棚照明槽 ceiling lighting trough
流明化顶棚 luminated ceiling
日光灯(光管) fluorescent lamp, fluorescent tube
壁灯 wall lamp
枝形灯架 chandelier
吊扇 ceiling fan

## 建筑物各部分　Parts of a Building

住宅　house, residence, dwelling

(房屋)正面　facade

门廊　porch

会客厅　reception room

起居室　living-room

饭厅　dining-room

卧室　bedroom

起居兼卧室　living-bedroom

书房　study

厨房　kitchen

厕所　toilet, water closet, lavatory

储藏室　storeroom, lumber-room

用具室　utility room

地下室(地窖)　cellar

车房　garage

楼下　ground floor, (Am.) first floor

二楼　first floor, (Am.) second floor

楼上　upstairs

楼下　downstairs

阁楼　attic, garret

夹层楼　mezzanine

阳台　balcony

骑楼　veranda(h), (Am.) porch, piazza

骑楼底人行道(拱廊)　arcade

柱廊　colonnade

(有排窗)廊道　gallery

过道　passage, passageway

走廊　corridor

院子　courtyard

围墙内空地　grounds

大院　compound

前院　forecourt

花园　garden

后院　backyard

花藤架(凉亭)　arbour, bower

假石山　rock-garden, rockery

室外厕所　privy, (Am.) out-house

小便处　urinal

公寓楼　block of flats, (Am.) apartment house

套间　suite of rooms

两房(三房)公寓间　two-room (three-room) flat

屋顶公寓间　penthouse apartment

公共建筑物　public building

门房　gatehouse

阶前路　entry, entryway

进门大厅　entrance hall, foyer

门厅　vestibule

访客候见厅　anteroom, ante-chamber

文娱室　recreation room

休息室　lounge

膳堂　dining hall

集体宿舍　dormitory

家属宿舍　married quarters

(公共场所的)小食亭　refreshment pavilion

天台花园　roof-garden

伞篷花园　pavilion garden

撑伞式天盖　umbrella roof

## 建筑物类型　Types of Building

多层楼房　multistorey building

三十三层大楼　33 storey tower block

六层以上高楼　high-rise

六层以下矮楼　low-rise

摩天楼　skyscraper

无电梯楼房　walk-up

平房　single-storey building

一幢两户住层　two-family house, duplex house

错层式房屋　split-level house

独立建筑　free-standing building

行列式房屋　row houses

城镇行列式两层住房　town houses

附建单坡屋　lean-to

侧翼建筑　wing

四合院　quadrangle dwellings, courtyard dwellings

四合院中的一幢房　pavilion

避暑别墅　summer house

别墅　villa

村舍　cottage

窑洞　cave house

风雨板屋(鱼鳞板屋)　clapboard house, weatherboard house

夯土建筑　rammed earth construction

泥砖建筑　adobe construction

圆木建造的屋　log cabin

木板屋　shack, shanty

棚　shed

水上棚屋　pile dwelling

茅屋　thatched house

简陋小屋　hut

草泥屋　cobwall hut

## 建筑物名称　Names of Some Buildings

纪念堂　memorial hall

礼堂(会堂)　auditorium (assembly hall)

巍峨大厦　edifice

豪华第宅　mansion

宫　palace

殿　hall, palace

亭　pavilion, kiosk

台　platform, stage

阁　pavilion (storeyed)

牌楼　*pailou*, archway

纪念建筑物　monument

官邸　official residence

伊斯兰教堂(清真寺)　mosque

寺庙　temple

修道院　monastry

教堂　church

大教堂　cathedral

城堡　castle

金字塔　pyramid

小方尖塔　pyramidion

塔　tower

教堂尖塔　steeple

佛塔　pagoda

舍利塔　dagoba

伊斯兰教堂的塔　minaret

钟楼　bell tower, belfry

角楼　corner tower, turret

照壁　entrance screen
公厕　public lavatory, public conveniences, (Am.) comfort station
殡仪馆　funeral parlour

火葬场　crematorium
陵墓　mausoleum
公墓　cemetery
衣冠冢　cenotaph

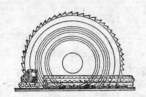

# 木材加工　Timber Processing

## 木　材　Timber

新伐木材　green timber
普通用材　common timber
高级用材　select timber
硬材(硬木)　hardwood
轻材(含脂材)　lightwood
原木　log
圆材　round timber
方材　squared timber, square
风干木材　air-dried timber (AD)
(按所需湿度)风干的木材　air-seasoned timber (AS)
已加工的木材　worked timber
规格板　dimension board
薄板(片木)　veneer
层压板(胶合木)　plywood, laminated wood
三夹板　three-plywood

合成树脂粘结层压板　resin-bonded plywood
隔热板(防火板)　insulating board
绝缘纤维板　masonite
木丝板(刨花板)　wood-wool slab
厚木板　plank
板条　lath, batten, strip
方木条(小方木)　rail
木材性质　qualities of timber
坚实性　hardness
韧性(耐朽性)　toughness
挠性　flexibility
翘曲　warping
收缩　shrinkage
木纹　woodgrain
缺陷　defect

心裂　heartshake
心腐　heart rot
风裂(环裂)　windshake
星状裂　starshake
幅裂　check
干燥开裂　season crack

袋腐(朽包)　pocket rot
湿朽　wet rot
粉蠹(木蠹虫)　powder post beetle
白蚁　termite, white ant
船蛆(凿船贝)　shipworm

## 制材和木工　Lumber Manufacture and Woodworking

锯木场(制材厂)　sawmill, lumber mill
制材(锯制材)　lumber
木材精加工　wood finishing
贮木场　wood yard (bay)
木工机械　woodworking machinery
木材运送链带　bulb-chain
剥皮机　barking drum, barker
铡柴机(碎木机)　hog, hogger
带锯　bandsaw machine
圆锯　circular saw machine, (Am.) buzz saw
链锯　chain saw
木工车床(造型车床)　pattern maker's lathe
木工铣床　wood milling machine
木工钻床　wood boring machine
木工刨床　wood planing machine
木工压刨床　wood planer and thicknesser
超光制刨床　super surfacer
压板机　veneer press
旋板机　rotary veneer lathe
制榫机　tenoning machine
榫眼机　mortising machine

开槽机　grooving machine
薄板剪切机　veneer clipper, clipper
防腐处理　preservative treatment
干燥处理　seasoning
蒸汽干燥　steam seasoning
热风干燥　hot-air seasoning
水养护　water seasoning
增加密度　densifying
化学压弯法　chemical bending
叠板压弯法　laminated bending
接合　joint
平接　butt joint
斜角接　mitre joint
嵌接　scarf joint
拼接(镶接)　splice
半嵌接合(子口接合)　halved joint (ship lap)
榫卯接合　mortise and tenon joint, mortise joint
榫眼　mortise
榫头　tenon
凹凸槽拼接　tongue-and-groove joint
鸠尾榫(马牙榫)　dovetail joint
胶合　glue joint
动物胶　animal glue
骨胶　bone glue

皮胶　hide glue
乳胶　emulsion
填缝料　crack filler
油灰　putty
〔油漆前〕打粉底　chalking
紫胶(虫胶)　shellac (lac)
清漆(光油)　varnish
紫胶清漆　shellac varnish
油树脂清漆　oleo-resinous
　varnish
漆　lacquer
漆稀释剂("天拿水")　lacquer thinner, thinner
木焦油(杂酚油)　creosote
木糠　sawdust
木粉(木屑)　wood flour
刨花(木丝)　wood wool

## 木工工具　Woodworking Tools

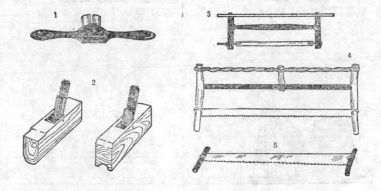

斧　ax
小斧　hatchet
横口斧　adze
手摇钻和钻头　brace and bit
木螺钻　auger bit
麻花钻　twist drill
弓转钻　bow drill, fiddle drill
平刨　bench plane
轴刨(弯刨)①　spokeshave plane
槽刨　rebate (rabbet) plane, fillister
卡角刨(摩角刨)②　angle plane

平口凿　chisel
圆口凿　gouge
榫眼凿　mortise chisel, framing chisel
角錾　corner chisel
木锉　wood rasp
三角锉　triangle file
架锯③　framed saw
双人大锯④　two-man framed saw
龙锯("过江龙")⑤　two-handled saw
拔钉锤　claw hammer

| | | | |
|---|---|---|---|
| 大榔头 | sledge hammer | 曲尺(角尺) | square |
| 撬杆 | crowbar | 活动曲尺 | bevel square |
| 撬棍 | pinch bar | 圆规 | compasses |
| 拔钉撬棍 | wrecking bar | 分规 | dividers |
| 钉头栓 | nail set | 木工用水准仪 | carpenter's level |
| 老虎钳 | vise | 划线规 | marking gauge |
| 螺丝起子 | screwdriver | 准线 | guideline |
| 锯齿磨 | handsaw sharpening tool | 墨斗线 | carpenter's ink box and line |
| 油石 | oilstone | 木工铅笔 | carpenter's pencil |
| 砂纸 | sandpaper | 排笔 | combination brush pen |
| 刮刀 | scraper | 油漆刷 | paint brush |
| 折尺 | zigzag rule | | |
| 钢卷尺 | steel tape | | |

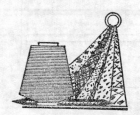

# 纺　织　Textiles

## 纺织工人　Textile Workers

| | | | |
|---|---|---|---|
| 落纱工 | doffer | 落布工 | cloth doffer |
| 络筒工 | winder | 挡车工 | operator |
| 纺纱工 | spinner | 漂白工 | bleacher |
| 摇纱工 | reeler | 染色工 | dyer |
| 缫丝工 | silk reeler | 印花工 | cloth-printing operative, printer |
| 拈丝工 | throwster | 配色工 | colourist |
| 整经工 | warper | 保全工 | maintenance worker |
| 穿经工 | enterer | | |

# 棉 纺 Cotton Spinning

清花 blowing (opening)
  原棉 raw cotton
  棉包 cotton bale
  锯齿棉 saw-ginned cotton
  皮辊棉 roller-ginned cotton
  开棉机 opener
  开清棉联合机 blowing room machinery
  棉箱给棉机 hopper feeder
  拆包机(抓棉机) bale breaker
  混棉 mixing
  自动混棉机① automatic blender
  清棉机 scutcher
  棉卷 lap
  滤尘器 dust chamber
  气流配棉器 air-flow distributor
梳棉 carding
  梳棉机② carding machine, card
  盖板梳棉机 flat card
  棉结 nep
  盖板(针帘)③ flat
  针布 card clothing
  圆筒(锡林)④ cylinder

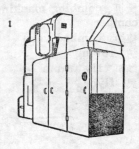

  小滚筒(道夫)⑤ doffer
  刺毛辊⑥ taker-in
  棉卷辊(罗拉)⑦ lap roller
  给棉辊(罗拉)⑧ feed roller
  棉卷均匀度仪 lap evenness tester
  棉条(梳条)⑨ sliver
  棉网 cotton-fleece
  棉条筒⑩ sliver can
  圈条器 coiler
  落棉 droppings
  回花 cotton waste
并条 drawing
  并条机 drawing frame
  紧压辊 calender roller
  皮辊 leather roller

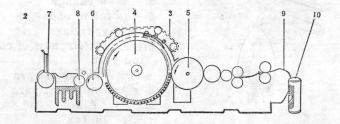

精梳　combing
条卷机　sliver lap machine
钳　clamp
精梳机　combing machine, comber
精梳纱　combed yarn
粗纺　roving
粗纱机　fly frame
锭翼　flyer

头道粗纱机　slubbing frame
式道粗纱机　intermediate frame
三道粗纱机　roving frame
粗纱　roving
粗纱头　roving waste
纱架　creel
粗纱筒管　roving bobbin

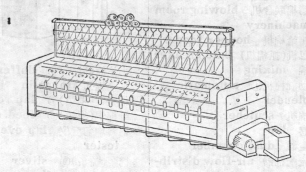

精纺　spinning
　细纱机①(环锭纺纱机)　ring spinning frame
　纱锭②　spindle
　高速分离锭子　high-speed separating spindle
大(小)牵伸　high (low) draft
超大牵伸　supper high draft

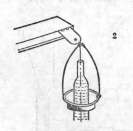

每分钟转数　revolutions per minute (RPM)
气流纺纱　open-end spinning
条子直接纺纱　sliver-to-yarn spinning
落纱机　doffing machine
棉纱(细纱)　cotton yarn
短纤纱　spun yarn
接头数　piece-ups
断头率　breakage
断头　broken ends
飞花　fly, flyings
棉纱的粗细　fineness of cotton yarn
低支纱　low count yarn
高支纱　fine count yarn
四十支纱　40s
十号纱　10 Tex

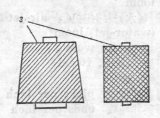

络纱 winding
　络纱滚筒 winding drum
　并纱机 doubling winder
　拈线机 twisting frame

环锭拈线机 ring doubling frame
络纱机 winding machine
筒子纱③ cheese
宝塔筒子 cone core
自动络纱 automatic winding
摇纱 reeling
　摇纱机 reeling machine
　绞纱 reeled yarn
打包 baling
　小包机 bundling press
　液压打包机 hydraulic baling press

# 棉 织 Cotton Weaving

整经 warping (beaming)
　经轴(织轴) beam
　轴经整经机 beamer
　整经筘(分纱筘) spacing reed
　整经机 warping machine
　分段整经机 sectional warping machine
浆纱 sizing, slashing
　浆纱机④ sizing machine
　浆槽⑤ size box
　煮浆桶 size boiling kettle
　调浆桶 size mixing kettle
　齿轮输浆泵 gear type size pump
　浆液循环装置 size circular unit
　烘筒式浆纱机 cylinder sizing machine
　热风式浆纱机 hot air sizing machine
　轴经上浆 beam warp sizing
　经纱上浆 slashing sizing

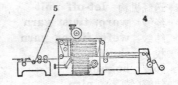

浆料助剂 sizing agent
上浆成份 sizing ingredients
上浆率 sizing percentage
化学浆料 sizing chemicals
合成浆料 synthetic size
淀粉〔浆〕 starch
穿经(穿筘) drawing-in
　综框 heald shaft
　综片 heald
　钢筘 reed, picker
　停经片 dropper
　穿筘架 drawing-in frame

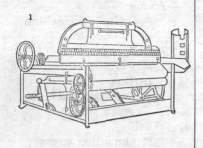

织布 weaving
织机 loom
自动织机① automatic loom
开口机构 shedding unit
投梭机构 picking unit
打纬机构 beating-up unit
卷取机构 take-up unit
送经机构 let-off unit
经纱 warp, twist yarn
纬纱 weft, filling yarn
梭子 shuttle
纱管 bobbin
纬管(纡管) pirn
自动换纬 automatic pirn change
换梭箱 shuttle change box
自动卷纬机 automatic pirn winder
光电提花织机 photo-electric jacquard loom
提花织造花板 pattern card
踏盘织机 tappet loom
多臂织机 dobby loom
无梭织机 shuttleless loom
剑杆织机 rapier loom
多梭箱织机 multiple box loom
喷气(水)投纬织机② air-jet (water-jet) loom
平纹 plain weave
斜纹 twill, tweel
缎纹 satin
每英寸纬数 picks per inch
每英寸经数 ends per inch
坯布幅宽 width of grey cloth
成品幅宽 width of finished cloth
布边 selvage
验布机③ cloth inspecting machine

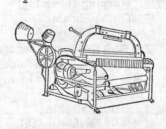

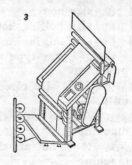

## 印　染　Printing and Dyeing

织物的预处理　pre-treatment of fabric
　准备　preparation
　烧毛　singeing
　退浆　desizing
　煮布锅　kier
　丝光机　mercerizing machine
　水洗　rinsing
　洗布机　cloth washing machine
　漂白　bleaching
　脱水机　hydroextractor
　J形箱　J-box
印花　printing
　印花机　printing machine
　套色印花　multicolour printing
　防染印花　reserve printing, resist printing
　滚筒绢网印花　rotary screen printing
　双面绢面印花　duplex screen printing
　平板印花　plate printing
　拔染印花　discharge printing
　辊筒印花　calender printing
　彩色印花　colour printing
　静电印花　electrostatic printing
染色　dyeing
　染色间　dye-house
　分批染色　batch dyeing
　染色样本　pattern card
　绳状染色机　winch dyeing machine
开幅卷染　jig dyeing
绞纱染色　hank dyeing
脉动染色　pulsator dyeing
喷射染色　jet dyeing
匹染　piece dyeing
间格染色　space dyeing
单色(本色)　self shade
交染　cross dyeing
印染一步法　printing and dyeing in a single process
荧光增白剂　fluorescent brightening agent, fluorescer
染色亲和力　dyeing affinity
吸色率(上染率)　dye-uptake
色泽坚牢度　fastness to colour
耐洗坚牢度　fastness to washing
耐白光坚牢度　fastness to light
耐汗渍坚牢度　fastness to perspiration
耐摩擦坚牢度　fastness to rubbing
耐烟气坚牢度　fastness to fumes
褪色　fading
渗色　bleeding
比色法　colorimetric method
色彩(色调)　hue
色泽　shade
颜料　pigment
染料　dyestuff
　天然染料　natural dye
　靛蓝　indigo

姜黄素 turmeric
茜素 alizarin
胭脂红 carmine
合成染料 synthetic dye
直接染料 direct dye
酸性染料 acid dye
碱性染料 basic dye

硫化染料 sulphur dye
还原染料 vat dye
冰染染料 glacial dye
活性染料 reactive dye
分散性染料 disperse dye
媒染染料 polygenetic dye

## 织物后整理 After-Treatment of Fabrics

干热定形 dry-heat set
汽蒸定形 steam set
永久定形 permanent set
退光 delustring
干整理 dry finishing
圆筒干燥机 cylinder drier
悬挂式干燥机 festoon drier
拉幅机 tenter frame,stenter
轧光整理 calender finish
蒸气轧光机 steam calender
轧花(拷花，压花) embossing
轧花辊 embossing roller
起绒(拉绒) raising
刮布 shearing
刷布机 cloth brushing machine
打褶机 pleating machine
码布机 folding machine
卷布机 cloth rewinder
堆布机 piling machine
化学处理 chemical finishing
　树脂整理 resination,resin finishing
　防皱整理 crease-resist finishing
　耐久压烫整理 permanent pleating
　拒水整理 water repellent finishing

"洗可穿" "wash and wear"
防水整理 waterproof treatment
防蛀整理 anti-moth treatment
阻燃整理 flame-proof treatment
防污整理 anti-soiling finishing
防静电整理 anti-static finishing
防起毛整理 anti-napping finishing
防起球整理 anti-pilling finishing
防熔整理 anti-fusing finishing
试验 testing
原棉分析机 raw cotton analyser
梳片式长度分析仪 comb-type fibre length sorter
束纤维强力机 fibre tuft strength tester
纤维切断器 staple fibre cutter
棉卷均匀度仪 lap evenness tester
条子粗纱测长器 sliver and

roving length sampler

捻度试验机 twist tester

纱线捻度机 yarn twist counter

单纱强力机 single strand tester

绞纱强力试验机 hank yarn strength tester

纤维杂质分离机 fibre and impurity analyser

纱线均匀度检查器(摇黑板器) yarn evenness tester

电感测湿仪 induction moisture meter for textiles

绞纱圈长测长器 hank circumference measuring apparatus

八篮恒温烘箱 8-basket conditioning oven

气候牢度试验 weathering test

织物磨损试验机 cloth wear testing machine

## 丝 织 Silk

缫丝厂 reeling mill

选茧车间 cocoon sorting workshop

开茧 cocoon opening

茧衣 cocoon's outer floss

双宫茧 doupion, cocoon double

薄皮茧 cocoon foible

煮茧车间 cocoon cooking workshop

膨化天然丝胶 natural gum softening

天然丝胶 sericin

缫丝车间 reeling workshop

缫丝机 reeling machine, filature

索绪机 cocoon beater, grouping end machine

理绪 cocoon picking

给茧装置 cocoon supplier

落绪 dropping end

出丝率 silk yielding

生丝 raw silk

熟丝 degummed silk, scoured silk

缫丝锅 reeler's trough

解舒 reeling quality

缫丝下脚 reeling waste

添绪 end feeding

绞丝 skein

但尼尔(简称"旦") denier (den. or d.)

复摇机(扬返机) hank reeling machine

绞纱烘燥机 hank drier

切断检验 winding test

脱胶 degumming

脱胶剂(练丝液) degumming agent

丝素 fibroin

洗涤 scouring process

绢纺(丝纺) silk spinning

绢丝 spun silk

绢纺工艺 schappe spinning

绢纺厂 waste silk spinning mill

精梳绢丝　schappe silk
绢绸　schappe voile
柞蚕绢丝　spun tussah yarn
加捻丝线　thrown silk
并丝机　doubling winder

丝绒(天鹅绒)　velour
丝棉　floss silk
绉织物　crepe
双面缎纹织物　double faced
　satin

## 麻 织 Linen

韧皮纤维　bast fibre
亚麻　flax
黄麻　jute
大麻　hemp
苎麻　ramie
剑麻(波罗麻)　sisal
亚麻短纤维(短麻屑)　tow
麻纺织机器　linen textile
　machinery
剥纤维机　fibre extracting
　machine
打麻机　scutcher
梳麻机　carding machine
链式粗梳机　chain bar spread-

er
链式并条机　chain bar draw-
　ing frame
亚麻精纺机　flax spinning
　frame
湿纺机　wet frame
半干精纺机　half-dry spinning
　frame
半干纺亚麻纱　half-dry spun
　flax yarn
亚麻纱　linen yarn
黄麻纱　jute yarn
苎麻纱　ramie yarn
亚麻织机　linen loom

## 毛 织 Woollens

粗梳毛纺厂　woollen mill
羊毛　wool
原毛　raw wool
死毛(抢毛)　kemp
中国羊毛　Chinese wool
中国羔羊毛　China lamb's wool
海宁羊毛　Haining wool
西宁羊毛　Xining wool
安哥拉山羊毛(马海毛)　mohair
开士米羊绒　cashmere
硬再生毛(短弹毛)　mungo
轻再生毛(长弹毛)　shoddy

剪毛　wool shearing
洗毛　wool washing, scouring
混毛　wool mixing
梳毛　carding
选毛　wool sorting
毛织机　woollen loom
缩呢机　felting machine
钢丝起绒机　card raising
　machine
剪毛机　cropping machine
开毛机　wool opener
蒸呢机　decatizing machine

洗涤机　rinsing machine
(毛条)复洗　backwashing
热风烘燥机　hot-air drier
粗梳毛纱　woollen yarn

精梳毛纱　worsted yarn
粗梳毛纺织物　woollen
精纺毛织物　worsted

# 针　织　Knitting

针织厂　knitting mill
针织机　knitting machine
经编机　warp knitting machine
经编整经机　tricot warper
纬编　weft knitting
圆形针织机　circular knitting machine
平机(横机)　flat knitting machine
大罗纹机①　rib machine
棉毛机(双面机)　interlock knitting machine
自动织袜机　automatic hosiery machine
缝袜头机　lockstitch looper
袜子定形机　hose setting machine
三色电子羊毛衫提花机　tricolour electric woollen jacquard knitting machine
光控手套自动机　photo-electric automatic glove knitting machine
积极式喂纱　active knitting feed
定形机　boarding machine
圆形针织物　circular web

针织绒布　double plush
电子针织机　electronic knitting machine

脱套自停装置　press-off detector
经编衬纬　warp knitting with weft insertion
经编针织物　warp-knitted fabric
纬编针织物　weft-knitted fabric

## 化 纤 Chemical Fibres

人造纤维 man-made fibre, artificial fibre

合成纤维 synthetic fibre

纤维素纤维 cellulose fibre

粘胶人造纤维 viscose rayon fibre

粘胶短纤维 viscose staple fibre

高湿模量纤维 high wet-modulus fibre

醋酯纤维 acetate fibre

三醋酯纤维 triacetate fibre

蛋白纤维 protein fibre

海藻纤维 alginate fibre

聚乙烯醇纤维 polyvinyl alcohol fibre

维尼纶 vinylon

聚氯乙烯纤维(氯纶) polyvinyl chloride fibre

聚丙烯腈纤维(腈纶) polyacrylonitrile fibre, polyacrylic fibre (orlon)

聚酰铵纤维(锦纶) polyamide fibre

耐纶(尼龙) nylon

聚酯纤维 poly-ster fibre

涤纶("的确良") dacron

聚丙烯纤维(丙纶) polypropylene fibre

长丝 filament

人造短纤维 staple fibre

无光人造丝 delustred rayon yarn

纺液染色(纺前染色)纱线 solution-dyed yarn

单根长丝(单纤维丝) monofilament

复丝(多纤维) multifilament

弹性织物 elastic fabric

弹力耐纶(弹力尼龙) elastic nylon

膨体纱 bulk yarn

干纺 dry spinning

湿纺 wet spinning

熔融纺丝 melt spinning

树脂切片 resin flake

真空干燥 vacuum drying

螺杆挤压机 screw-extruder

纺丝机 spinning machine

联苯箱 biphenyl box

纺丝泵 spinning pump

喷丝头 spinneret (nozzle)

绕丝机 take-up machine

浸渍 dip

压榨 pressing

磨碎 grinding

老化(老成) ageing

黄化 xanthating

过滤 filtration

压滤机 filter press

脱泡〔作用〕 de-aeration

凝固浴(纺丝浴) coagulating bath

上油 oiling

卷曲 crimping

卷曲机 crimping machine

纺丝溶液 spinning solution

缩聚作用 polycondensation

纤维物理性能 physical properties of fibre

强力(强度) strength

打节强度 knot strength

| | |
|---|---|
| 圈结强度　loop strength | 收缩率　shrinkage percentage |
| 伸长　elongation | 防水性　waterproofing |
| 弹性　elasticity | 　property |
| 含水量　moisture content | 防皱性　resistance to creasing |
| 公定回潮率　official regain | 防霉性　mould resistance |
| 卷曲数　number of crimps | 防蛀性　resistance to insects |
| 卷曲率　percentage of crimp | 耐晒性　resistance to sunlight |
| 残余卷曲率　residual crimp | 耐磨(耐穿)性　resistance to |
| 　percentage | 　wear |

# 橡　胶　Rubber

## 炼　胶　Rubber Processing

| | |
|---|---|
| 胶乳　latex | 　(ADS) |
| 凝胶　coagulum | 皱胶片　crepe |
| 生胶　crude rubber | 白皱片　pale crepe |
| 生胶块　rubber block, rubber | 软化　softening, maceration |
| 　biscuit | 热水缸　vat containing hot |
| 生胶片　sheet rubber | 　water |
| 烟胶片　smoked sheet (SS) | 洗涤　cleaning, washing |
| 风干胶片　air-dried sheet | 洗涤机　washing machine |

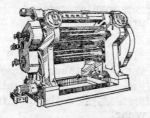 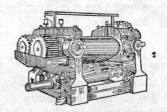

槽纹辊洗涤机　corrugated (grooved) roll washing machine

烘干　drying

真空烘干机　vacuum drier

烘胶房　drying loft, hot box

切胶机　cutting machine, cutter

破胶机　breakdown mill

粗碎机　grinding mill

加入配料　adding ingredients

开炼(混炼)　mixing, compounding

开炼机　stock blender (mixer)

压延　calendering

三辊压延机①　three-roll calender

压出机　extruder

混炼压出机　compounder-extruder

辗胶机　rolling mill

塑炼机　plasticator

压皱片机　crêping machine

切片机　slicing machine, slicer

精炼机　refining mill

硫化　vulcanizing

半硫化　set cure

硫化罐　vulcanizer

硫化橡胶(熟胶)　vulcanized rubber

塑炼(捏炼)　kneading

蜗杆塑炼机　worm kneading machine

开放式塑炼机　open roll mill

密闭式塑炼机②　closed roll mill

成形机　make-up machine

压出　extrusion

蜗杆压出机　worm (screw) extruder

带滤网的压出机　screw cleaning machine

涂胶机　rubber coating machine

轮胎翻新硫化机　tyre reconditioning vulcanizer

## 炼胶配料　Ingredients Used in Rubber Processing

乳化剂　emulsifying agent, emulsifier

熟化剂　curing agent

凝聚剂　coagulant

脱水剂　dehydrating agent

硫化剂　vulcanizing agent

软化剂　softening agent, macerating agent

防老化剂 antioxidant; age-resisting agent

催化剂 catalyst

活性剂 activating agent, activator

增塑剂 plasticizing agent, plasticizer

塑解剂 peptizing agent, peptizer

发泡剂 blowing agent, aerating powder

助发泡剂 blowing promotor

还原剂 reducing agent

防日光老化剂 sun-screening material

着色剂(颜料) colouring agent, pigment

融合剂 fluxing agent

香豆酮(古马隆) coumarone

湿润剂 humectant

补强剂 reinforcing agent

酚类防老剂 phenolic antioxidant

芳香剂(除臭剂) odorant, odor control agent

油剂 oiling agent

芳族烃油 aromatic hydrocarbon oil

高芳族油 highly aromatic oil

环烷油 naphthenic oil

锌钡白(立德粉) lithopone, crypton

炭黑 carbon black

白炭黑(二氧化硅) silica white (silicon dioxide)

添加填充剂(吃粉) absorb fillers

滑石粉 talc

填料 filling material, filler

## 橡胶种类 Types of Rubber

天然橡胶 natural rubber

巴拉橡胶 para rubber

接枝橡胶 graft rubber

泡沫胶 foam rubber

海绵胶 sponge rubber

恒粘度门尼橡胶 constant Mooney rubber

抑制结晶胶 crystallization-inhibited rubber

除蛋白橡胶 deproteinized rubber

再生胶 reclaimed rubber (reclaim)

超级橡胶 super rubber

海南橡胶 Hainan rubber

巴拉塔胶 balata

杜仲胶(古塔波胶) gutta-percha

节路顿胶 gutta-jelutong

合成橡胶 synthetic rubber

氯丁橡胶 chlorobutadiene rubber

异丁烯橡胶 isobutene rubber

丁腈橡胶 acrylonitrile butadiene rubber

顺丁橡胶 cis-butadiene rubber

乙丙烯橡胶 ethylene-propylene rubber

硅橡胶 silicone rubber

氟橡胶 fluorine rubber

异戊橡胶 isoprene rubber

丁基橡胶 butadiene rubber

丁苯橡胶　styrene butadiene rubber

丁钠橡胶　sodium rubber

丁锂橡胶　lithium polybutadiene rubber

高顺式聚异戊二烯橡胶　cis-rich polyisoprene rubber

高顺式聚丁二烯橡胶　cis-rich polybutadiene rubber

聚硫橡胶　polysulphide rubber

聚丙烯酸酯橡胶　polyacrylate (polyacrylic) rubber

聚氨酯橡胶　polyurethane rubber

聚硅氧烷橡胶　polysiloxane rubber

氟硅橡胶　fluorinated silicone rubber

聚炭弹性体　fluorocarbon elastomer

环化橡胶　cyclic (cyclized) rubber

无环弹性体　acyclic elastomer

油充橡胶　oil-extended rubber

油软化橡胶　oil-softened rubber

耐滑橡胶　high hysteresis rubber

## 橡胶性能　Properties of Rubber

粘弹性能　viscoelasticity, viscoelastic properties
　粘弹计　viscoelastometer

粘度　viscosity
　粘度计　viscosimeter, viscometer

回弹性　elastic resilience
　弹性计　elastometer, resiliometer

抗张性能　tensile properties
　抗张强力试验机　tensile testing machine
　张力计　tensi(o)meter, tension gauge

可塑性　plasticity
　(门尼)可塑计　(Mooney) plastometer

屈挠性　flexibility
　屈挠试验计　flexometer
　硬度计　durometer
　硫化仪　vulkameter

耐候性　resistance to weathering

耐药品性　resistance to chemical reagents

耐压强度　resistance to compression

耐龟裂性　resistance to cracking

抗破裂强度　resistance to rupture

# 塑 料 Plastics

## 塑料的拼份 Ingredients of Plastics

石油 petroleum
天然气 natural gas
液化石油气 liquefied petroleum gas
炼油厂气 refinery gas
煤油 kerosene
粗汽油 crude gasolene
气态烃 gaseous hydrocarbon
液态烃 liquid hydrocarbon
固态烃 solid hydrocarbon
脂族烃 aliphatic hydrocarbon
链烷 alkane
丁烷 butane
链烯 alkene (olefin)
乙烯 ethylene
丙烯 propylene
丁烯 butylene (butene)
炔 alkyne
乙炔 acetylene
芳族烃 aromatic hydrocarbon
苯 benzene (benzol)
甲苯 toluene
二甲苯 xylene

聚合烃 polymeric hydrocarbon
合成树脂 synthetic resin
高分子化合物 high molecular compound
单体 monomer
聚合物(聚合体) polymer
高聚物 high polymer
均聚物 homopolymer
共聚物 copolymer
等规聚合物 isotactic polymer
线型聚合物 linear polymer
网状聚合物 network polymer
配料 compounding ingredients
增塑剂 plasticizer
稳定剂 stabilizer
润滑剂 lubricant
发泡剂 foaming agent
填料(填充剂) filler
有机填料 organic filler
无机填料 inorganic filler
硬化剂 hardening agent
固化剂 curing agent
着色剂(颜料) dye, pigment

## 制造方法和工艺　Manufacture Methods and Technology

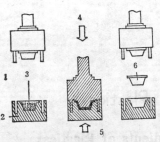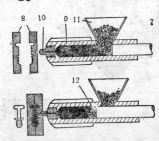

加成聚合 addition polymerization, polyaddition

游离基聚合 free radical polymerization

阳离子催化聚合 cationic polymerization

阴离子催化聚合 anionic polymerization

定向聚合 oriented polymerization

缩合聚合(缩聚) condensation polymerization

环化聚合 cyclopolymerization

聚合方法 method of polymerization

本体聚合〔法〕 mass polymerization

溶液聚合〔法〕 solvent (solution) polymerization

悬浮聚合〔法〕 suspension polymerization

乳液聚合〔法〕 emulsion polymerization

固定床聚合〔法〕 fixed bed polymerization

流化床(沸腾床)聚合〔法〕 fluidized bed polymerization

加工方法 technological process

模制(模塑) moulding

模压法① compression moulding

压缩塑模② compression mould

酚醛塑料粉③ phenolplast powder

加压④ pressing

加热⑤ heating

制成品⑥ finished product

注模法⑦ injection moulding

注射塑模⑧ injection mould

注模机⑨ injector

注射喷嘴⑩ injecting nozzle

加料仓⑪ stock bunker

活塞⑫ piston

挤出(挤压) extrusion

吹塑模制 blow moulding

真空成形 vacuum forming

冷塑 cold moulding

板材冲压 flat sheet punching

压延 calendering

涂覆  coating
离心(旋转)浇注成形  centrifugal (rotational) casting

发泡  foaming
脱模  knockout, ejection

## 塑料种类  Varieties of Plastics

热固性塑料  thermosetting plastics
酚醛塑料(电木)  phenolplastics (bakelite)
热塑性塑料  thermoplastic plastics
聚氯乙烯  polyvinyl chloride (PVC)
聚合树脂  polymerization resin
缩聚树脂  condensation resin
常用塑料  general purpose plastics
工程塑料  engineering plastics
改性塑料  modified plastics
软质塑料  flexible plastics
硬质塑料  rigid plastics
泡沫塑料  foam(ed) plastics
聚(二)苯醚塑料  polydiphenyl ether plastics
聚酰胺塑料  polyamide plastics
聚酰胺—1010  polyamide-1010
环氧树脂  epoxide (epoxy) resin
硝化纤维素塑料  nitrocellulose plastics
丙烯酸塑料  acrylic plastics
等规聚合物塑料  isotactic polymer plastics
乙烯类塑料  vinyl group of plastics

聚醛树脂  aldehyde resin
聚异丁烯塑料  polyisobutylene plastics
聚乙烯  polyethylene (polythene)
聚乙烯甲基醚塑料  polyvinyl methyl ether plastics
全卤塑料  perhalogenated (perhalogeno-) plastics
聚乙烯咔唑  polyvinyl carbazole
聚炭酸酯塑料  polycarbonate plastics
聚氨酯塑料  polyurethane plastics
丙酮树脂  acetone resin
氨树脂  amino resin
甲酚树脂  cresol resin
乙氧基醋酸树脂  ethoxyline resin
呋喃树脂  furan resin
糠醛树脂  furfural resin
聚乙烯亚胺树脂  polyethylene imine resins
可熔酚醛树脂  resol resin
硅酮树脂  silicone resin
磺酰胺树脂  sulphamide resin
二甲苯酚树脂  xylenol resin
香豆酮树脂  coumarone resin

## 塑料性能  Properties of Plastics

抗霉性  resistance to mildew
介电强度  dielectric strength

电绝缘性  insulation characteristics

抗电弧性　resistance to electric arc
耐磨性　resistance to abrasion
吸水性　water absorption power
着色性　ability to take on colours
耐化学腐蚀性　resistance to chemical corrosion
尺寸稳定性　dimensional stability

冲击强度(耐冲击性)　impact strength
表面强度　surface strength
不易燃性　non-inflammability
透光性　ability to transmit light
弹性　elasticity
韧性　toughness
脆性　brittleness
硬性　hardness

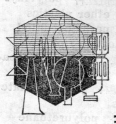

# 玻　璃　Glass

## 玻璃制造　Glass-Making

玻璃工厂　glassworks
原料分批混合　batch mixing of raw materials
硅石　silica
水晶　rock crystal
石英岩　quartzite
石英砂　quartz sand
长石　feldspar
石灰石　limestone
白云石　dolomite
硼砂　borax
硼酸　boric acid
碳酸钡　barium carbonate, witherite
铅丹　red lead
磷酸　phosphoric acid

砒霜　white arsenic
芒硝　Glauber('s) salt
纯碱　sodium carbonate
破碎废玻璃　callet
助熔剂　melting promoter
着色剂　pigment, colouring agent
脱色剂　decolouring agent, decolourizer
加速剂　accelerant
熔炼　melting
坩埚　crucible
槽炉(池炉)　tank furnace
温度梯度　temperature gradient

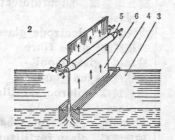 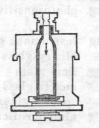

成形 forming
吹制① blowing
(取熔融玻璃用的)铁杆 punty, pontil
铁杆供料器 punty feeder
料滴供料机 gob feeder
形坯(料泡) parison
自动制瓶机 automatic bottle-making machine
槽子砖垂直引上法② the Four-cault process
玻璃液③ molten glass
槽子砖④ trough with a long slit

引上机⑤ upward drawing machine
玻璃板⑥ sheet-glass
水平拉制法 horizontal drawing
研磨 grinding
抛光 polishing
铁丹 rouge
退火 annealing
退火窑 annealing kiln
退火温度 annealing temperature
消除热应力 relieving of thermal stress

## 玻璃种类 Types of Glass

片玻璃 sheet glass
平板玻璃 plate glass
图案玻璃 figured plate glass
磨光玻璃 polished glass
乳白玻璃 milk glass, opal glass
磨砂玻璃 frosted glass
磨口玻璃 ground glass
彩花玻璃 stained glass
安全玻璃 security glass
三层安全玻璃 triplex glass
夹丝玻璃 wire(d) glass
叠层玻璃 laminated glass

硬质玻璃 hard glass
钢化玻璃 toughened glass, tempered glass
镜玻璃 mirror glass
雕花玻璃 cut glass
浮雕玻璃 cameo glass
压花玻璃 embossed glass
光学玻璃 optical glass
透镜〔片〕 lens
眼镜片 eyeglass
滤光玻璃 filter glass
荧光玻璃 fluorescent glass

透紫外线玻璃　sunalux glass

光敏玻璃　photosensitive glass

仪器玻璃　instrument glass

二元玻璃　binary glass

石灰玻璃　lime glass

石英玻璃　quartz glass

特种玻璃　special glass

铝硅玻璃　aluminosilicate glass

硼硅玻璃　borosilicate glass

高硅氧玻璃　vycor glass

吸热玻璃　heat-absorbent glass

防火玻璃　fire-resisting glass, fireproof glass

防弹玻璃　bulletproof glass

焊接用玻璃　solder glass

激光玻璃　laser glass

磁性玻璃　magnetic glass

半导电玻璃　semiconducting glass

导电玻璃　conductive glass

高介电玻璃　superdielectric glass

电极玻璃　electrode glass

玻璃纤维　glass fibre

玻璃棉　glass wool

玻璃丝　spun glass

微晶玻璃　microcrystalline glass

玻璃微珠　glass microballoon

玻璃肥料　glass fertilizer

粘性(粘滞度)　viscosity

脆性　brittleness

炸裂　cracking

耐腐蚀性　resistance to corrosion

透明性　transparency

半透明性　translucency

不透明性　opaqueness

透光率　light transmission rate

折射　refraction

反射　reflection

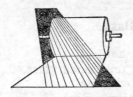

# 造　纸　Paper

## 造纸的原材料　Papermaking Materials

棉花　cotton

麻类纤维　bast-fibre

稻麦秆　straw

棉秆　cotton stalk

玉米秆　corn stalk

芒草　Chinese silvergrass

芦苇　reed

西班牙草　esparto grass

蔗渣　bagasse
纸莎草　papyrus
竹子　bamboo
破布　rags
废纸　wastepaper
造纸木材　pulp wood
针叶树　conifer
马尾松　Masson pine
红松　Korean pine
云杉　spruce
铁杉　hemlock

胶冷杉　balsam fir
杨　poplar
桦　birch
染料　dyestuff
矿物颜料　mineral pigment
胶料　sizing material, sizing
化学药品　chemicals
填充料　filling material, filler
涂布料　coating material

## 原料处理　Treatment of Raw Materials

拣出无用和有害的物质　sorting out useless and harmful materials
杂质　extraneous components
除尘　dusting
除墨　de-inking

浸透　macerating
清洗　washing
破碎　crushing
打散　thrashing
剥树皮　barking
切碎　chopping, chipping

## 制纸浆　Pulping

木料的成份　composition of wood
纤维素　cellulose
半纤维素　semicellulose
木素　lignin
碳水化合物　carbohydrate
树胶树脂　gum resin

化学制浆　chemical pulping
碱法制浆　alkaline process, sulphate pulping
碳酸钠(纯碱)　sodium carbonate (soda)
氢氧化钠(烧碱)　sodium hydroxide (caustic soda)
硫酸钠　sodium sulphate

酸法制浆　acid process, sulphite pulping
亚硫酸氢钙　calcium bisulphite
硫磺　sulphur
石灰　lime
亚硫酸氢镁　magnesium bisulphite
氧化镁　magnesium oxide
蒸煮器　digester, boiler
蒸煮液　cooking liquor
泄料池　blow pit
木质素溶解　lignin dissolved
树胶水解　gum hydrolyzed
洗浆　washing
筛浆　screening
半制浆　half stuff

氯化处理　chlorination

漂白粉(次氯酸钙)　bleaching powder (calcium hypochlorite)

漂白机　bleacher

稀释　diluting

漂洗槽　potcher

脱水　dewatering

增稠　thickening

机械制浆　mechanical pulping

纸浆制造机　macerator

磨木机　grinding machine, grinder

磨石　grindstone, pulpstone

磨纹　pattern

剥皮木料　barked wood

送料链条　feed chain

螺旋挤浆机　screw press

浆池　vat

筛浆机　screen

旋涡精选机　vortex action pulp cleaner

匀浆机　refiner

连续化学机械制浆　continuous chemical-mechanical pulping

连续蒸煮器　continuous digester

盘磨机　disc grinder

微生物制浆　bacterial pulping

微生物　bacterium

酶　enzyme

木质素被酶分解　lignin enzymolyzed

纸浆的种类　kinds of pulp

木浆　wood pulp

草浆　straw pulp

化学浆　chemical pulp

机械浆　mechanical pulp

精制浆　refined pulp

## 打浆和施胶　Beating and Sizing

备料　preparation of stock

打浆机　beater

旋转飞刀　rotating fly-bar

底刀　bed-plate

浆槽　beater tub

分丝帚化的小纤维　hairlike fibril

纤维悬浮液　suspension of fibre

施胶　sizing

添加料　additive

松香　resin

明矾　alum

石膏　gypsum

滑石　talc

纸土　paper clay

白垩　chalk

磨浆机　refiner

浆团　knot, cluster

结筛(除节机)　knotter

沉砂槽　riffler

浆度　beating degree

稠度　consistency

均匀状态　homogeneous state

## 抄 纸 Paper Making

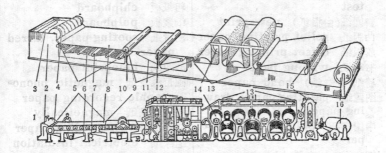

3 2 4  5 6 7  8  10 9 11 12  14 13  13  15
1  16

湿法造纸 **wet process of papermaking**

抄纸机① **paper machine**

流浆箱② **stock chest**

纸浆③ **papermaking pulp**

浆料进口 **stock inlet**

出浆口(浆堰)④ **sluice**

铜网部⑤ **wire section, fourdrinier section**

铜网⑥ **bronze wire (screen)**

铜网导辊⑦ **wire guide roll**

形成湿纸页⑧ **forming wet sheet**

压榨部⑨ **press section**

吸水压榨 **suction press**

真空吸水箱⑩ **suction box,** **vacuum couch**

毛毡带⑪ **felt web**

湿压辊⑫ **wet press roll**

干燥部⑬ **drying section**

蒸气烘缸⑭ **steam heated cylinder**

干燥毛毡 **dryer felt**

冷缸 **cooling cylinder**

压光 **finishing**

压光机⑮ **calender**

卷纸机⑯ **winder, reel**

复卷机 **rewinder**

切纸机 **cutter, trimmer**

三边切纸机 **trilateral paper trimming machine**

令 **ream**

## 造纸厂及其产品 Paper Mill and Its Products

造纸厂 **paper mill**

纸板厂 **paperboard mill**

备料车间 **raw material treatment department**

配料车间 **furnishing department**

制浆车间 **pulp making department**

抄纸车间 **papermaking department**

成品车间 **finishing department**

| | |
|---|---|
| 耐破度试验　bursting test | 建筑纸板　building paper-board |
| 耐折度试验　folding test | 纤维板　fibreboard |
| 拉力试验　tensile strength test | 粗纸板　chipboard |
| 新闻纸(白报纸)　newsprint | 纸浆板　pulpboard |
| 凸版纸　relief printing paper | 沥青纸　roofing paper, tarred paper |
| 胶版纸　offset printing paper | 晒图纸　blueprint paper |
| 书写纸　writing paper | 磁带录音纸　magnetic phonographic recording paper |
| 磅纸(证券纸)　bond paper | 磁感记录纸　magnetically sensitive recording paper |
| 图画纸　painting paper, drawing paper | 绝缘纸　electrical insulation paper |
| 中国宣纸　Chinese Xuan paper | 涂布纸　coated paper |
| 打字纸　manifold paper | 砂纸　sandpaper |
| 复写纸　carbon paper | 发光纸　luminous paper |
| 钢板(打字)蜡纸　stencil paper | 不燃纸　incombustible paper |
| 蜡光纸　glazed paper | 易燃纸　combustible paper |
| 皱纸　crêped paper | 防水纸　waterproof paper |
| 凹凸纸　embossed paper | 防锈纸　rustproof paper |
| 纱纸(薄纸)　tissue paper | 钢纸　vulcanized paper |
| 金纸　tinsel | 合成纤维纸　synthetic fibre paper |
| 锡纸　tinfoil | 塑料涂布纸　plastic-coated paper |
| 包装纸　wrapping paper | |
| 牛皮纸　kraft paper | |
| 瓦楞纸　corrugated paper | |
| 玻璃纸　cellophane | |

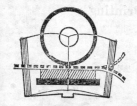

# 印　刷　Printing

## 印刷的起源和发展　Origin and Development of Printing

纸的发明　invention of paper

印章的使用　use of seal

印泥　cinnabar ink

石碑雕刻文字　stone inscription

拓印　ink rubbing, squeeze

拓石　squeeze from stone inscription

刻版印刷发明于隋朝，公元 600 年左右　block printing invented in about 600 A.D. in the Sui Dynasty

《金刚经》——世界最早的印刷物，印于唐朝，公元 868 年　Indra Sūtra—the oldest printed book in existence, printed in 868 A.D. in the Tang Dynasty

毕升于宋朝公元 1041—1048 年间发明活字印刷　Bi Sheng invented movable type printing in the Song Dynasty between 1041 and 1043 A.D.

木刻活字　movable wooden type

胶泥活字　fired earthenware type

中国印刷术向外国传播　spreading of Chinese printing technique to foreign countries

现代印刷术　modern printing

印刷术的新发展　new developments in printing

照相排字机　photosetting machine

自动电子排字机　automatic electronic photosetting machine

电子刻版机　electronic engraving machine

电子分色机　electronic colour analyser

感光树脂印版　sensitive resin plate

电子印刷机　electronic printing machine

## 印刷的种类　Kinds of Printing

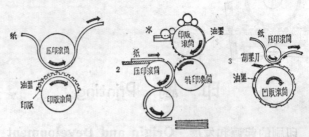

刻版印刷　**block printing**

活版印刷　**typography, movable type printing**

凸版印刷① **relief printing, letterpress**

平版印刷——石印和胶印② **planography—lithography and offset printing**

凹版印刷③ **gravure, intaglio printing**

孔版印刷　**stencil printing**

特种印刷　**special printing**

木刻水印　**coloured woodblock printing**

彩色印刷　**multicolour printing**

珂罗版印刷　**collotype, photogelatin printing**

橡皮版印刷(苯胺印刷) **flexography, aniline printing**

丝网印刷　**silk screen printing**

静电印刷　**xerography**

磁性印刷　**magnetic printing**

蜡版油印　**mimeography**

贴花印刷　**decal printing**

手摇印刷　**hand press printing**

报纸印刷　**newspaper printing**

美术印刷　**fine arts printing**

书籍印刷　**book printing**

铁皮印刷　**steel plate printing**

软管印刷　**soft tube printing**

胶版眷写版印刷　**hectographic printing**

凹凸印刷　**embossing**

影印　**photographic reprinting**

直接影印　**photostating**

## 排版(排字)　Type Setting (Composing)

排字工人　**type setter, compositor**

印刷工人　**printer**

字模　*character (letter) matrix*

铸字　*character casting,* **letter founding**

铸字厂　**type foundry**

活字架　**type case**

排字手盘　**composing stick**

排字尺　**setting rule**

捆版绳 page cord

衬垫物(铅条) furniture (lead)

校样活字盘 galley

校样(小样) galley proof

手稿 manuscript

手写体 script

印刷体 print

黑体 boldface

斜体 italic

宋体 Song style character

美术字 artistic character

废字 obsolete character

排字机 composing machine,
type setter

单字铸排机 monotype

行型活字铸排机 linotype

拼版 assembling

铅空 space

拼好的活字版 lockup form

活字版架 chase

垫版 laying

垫版楔子 quoin, wedge

大样(机样) press-proof

校对 proofreading

校对符号 proofreader's
marks

## 制 版 Plate Making

印版 printing form, plate

活字版 printing form of
movable type

复制版 duplicate plate

制铅版 stereotype making

压制纸型 making mould (ma-
trix) by pressing

纸型用纸 papier mâché

浇铸铅版 stereotype casting

镀镍 nickel plating

平铅版 flat stereotype

圆铅版 curved stereotype

电版 electrotype, electro

制电版(电解法制铜版) electro-
typing

蜡模 wax mould

石墨粉 graphite powder

电解槽 electrobath

硫酸铜溶液 solution of cop-
per sulphate

电解 electrolysis

线条图版 line cut, line en-
graving

网点图版(照相铜版) halftone

照相法制图版 photoengrav-
ing, photoetching

色调 tone

滤色镜 ray filter lens

网屏 halftone screen

网线 thread

网点 dot

阴图底片 negative

晒印照片 photoprinting

阳图 positive

腐蚀溶液 etching solution

腐蚀空白部分 etching non-
printing parts

防蚀蜡层 etching-proof wax
coating

保护图文部分 protecting
image parts

塑料版 plastic plate

石版 litho plate

照相法制平版 photolithogra-
phy

金属平版(胶印版) offset plate

拒水性 tendency to repel water
亲墨性 affinity for ink

照相法制凹版 photointaglio etching

## 印 刷 Printing

印刷厂 printing house
付印 going to press
在印刷中 in the press
印刷好了 off the press
大印量印刷 long run
小印量印刷 short run
装版 mounting
印刷物检查 checking of printed stock
印刷错误 misprint
印刷物污迹 workup
印版磨损 press batter
印刷机的四大部分 the four units of a printing press
进纸部分 feeding unit
施墨部分 inking unit
印刷部分 printing unit
出纸部分 delivery unit
凸版印刷机 letterpress, relief press
平压式印刷机 platen press
平台印刷机(辊压式印刷机) flat-bed press, cylinder press
二回转印刷机 two-revolution

press
轮转印刷机 rotary press
卷筒进纸印刷机 web-fed (roll-fed) press
单页进纸印刷机 sheet-fed press
胶版(平版)印刷机 offset press
压印滚筒 impression cylinder
印版滚筒 plate cylinder
油墨滚筒 ink roller
橡皮滚筒(转印滚筒) rubber blanket cylinder (offset cylinder)
湿润滚筒 damping roller
多色胶印机 multicolour offset press
凹版印刷机 intaglio press
轮转凹印机 rotogravure press
凹印机刮墨刀 doctor blade
复印机 duplicating press, duplicator
快干油墨 fast drying ink
热固油墨 heatset ink

## 书籍装订 Bookbinding

人工装订 hand binding
机械装订 machine binding
折叠成书帖 folding into signatures
缝合 sewing

涂胶水 applying adhesive, gluing
压实 pressing
修切 trimming, cutting
装入书封 casing in

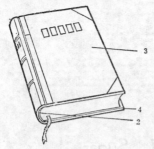 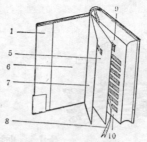

| 裱里 | lining | 金边 | gilt edge |
|------|--------|------|-----------|
| 饰边 | edge-decorating | 对开 | folio |
| 加护封 | jacketing | 四开 | quarto |
| 铁线装订 | wire stitching | 八开 | octavo |
| 散装本 | unbound | 十六开 | sixteen mo, 16 mo |
| 合订本 | bound volume | 三十二开 | thirty-two mo, 32 mo |
| 活页 | loose leaf | | |
| 平装本 | paperback edition | 袖珍本 | pocket edition |
| 精装本 | hardback edition | 缩微本 | microcopy |
| 高级精装本 | de luxe edition | 护封① | jacket, dust cover |
| 标准本 | library edition | 书脊纱布② | back (spine) gauze |
| 缩印本 | compact edition | 封面③ | front cover |
| 影印本 | photographic reprint edition | 封底④ | back cover |
| 普及本 | popular edition | 书名页⑤ | title page |
| 拓本 | rubbing edition | 卷首插画 | frontispiece |
| 改装本 | rebind | 环衬页⑥ | end paper |
| 线装书 | old-type thread-stitched book | 扉页(衬页)⑦ | flyleaf |
| 毛边书 | rough edge edition | 正文 | body of the work |
| 皮面 | leather binding | 奇数页 | recto |
| 硬纸板面 | pasteboard binding | 偶数页 | verso |
| 硬纸面 | stiff paper binding | 书签带(丝带)⑧ | bookmark (ribbon) |
| 玻璃纸面 | cellophane cover | 天头空白⑨ | head (upper) margin |
| 塑料面 | plastic cover | 地脚空白⑩ | foot (lower) margin |
| 布面 | cloth binding | | |
| 色边 | coloured edge | | |

# 制　糖　Sugar

## 糖类名称　Names of Sugars

| | |
|---|---|
| 蔗糖　cane sugar | 葡萄糖　grape sugar, glucose |
| 甜菜糖　beet sugar | 丁维葡萄糖　D-glucose |
| 红糖　brown sugar | 麦芽糖　maltose |
| 白糖　white sugar | 阿拉伯糖　arabinose |
| 粉糖　powdered sugar | 果糖　fruit sugar, fructose |
| 砂糖　granulated sugar | 还原糖　reducing sugar |
| 片糖　tablet sugar | 非还原糖　non-reducing sugar |
| 方糖　cube sugar | 转化糖　invert sugar |
| 冰糖　rock sugar | 右旋糖　dextrose |
| 冰片糖　rock sugar in tablets | 左旋糖　levulose |
| 细白糖　castor sugar | 糖膏　massecuite |
| 白绵糖　confectioner's sugar | 糖精　gluside, sacharin |

## 糖厂副产品　By-products of Sugar Refinery

| | |
|---|---|
| 蔗蜡　sugarcane wax | 酒精　alcohol |
| 蔗脂　sugarcane fat | 药用酵母　medicinal yeast |
| 纤维原料　crude fibre | 饲用酵母　yeast for animal feeds |
| 合成纤维　synthetic fibre | |
| 纸浆　pulp for papermaking | 甘油　glycerin |
| 糖醛　furfural | 丙酮　acetone |
| 谷氨酸　glutamic acid | 乙醇　ethanol |
| 谷氨酸钠(味精)　monosodium glutamate | 丁醇　butanol |
| | 柠檬酸　citric acid |
| 发酵原料　ferment | |

## 取 汁 Juice Extraction

精制糖厂 sugar refinery

土法制糖 indigenous methods of sugar extraction

现代方法制糖 modern methods of sugar extraction

蔗糖厂 cane mill

糖蔗 sugarcane

理平 compacting

切断 chopping

撕碎 shredding

撕碎机 shredder

压榨 crushing

三辊压榨机 three-roller crushing mill

蔗汁 cane juice

筛分 screening

蔗渣 bagasse

甜菜糖厂 beet mill

洗涤机 washer

滑槽 chute

盘式切丝机 disc slicer

鼓式切丝机 drum slicer

人字形甜菜丝 V-shaped chip, cossette

浸提 diffusion

浸提器组 diffusion battery

甜菜浆 beet pulp

甜菜汁 beet juice

贮汁箱 receiving tank

加热 heating

热汁器 juice heater

## 清 汁 Juice Purification

蔗汁澄清 clarifying cane juice

石灰处理 liming

石灰乳(氢氧化钙) milk of lime (calcium hydroxide)

中和 neutralization

亚硫酸法 sulphitation process

二氧化硫 sulphur dioxide

亚硫酸晶体沉淀 precipitation of calcium bisulphite crystals

清除被吸附的杂质 removal of adsorbed impurities

非糖沉淀物的凝聚 condensation of nonsugar precipitates

压滤机 filter press

甜菜汁澄清 clarifying beet juice

二碳饱充法 carbonation process

二氧化碳 carbon dioxide

碳酸钙沉淀 precipitation of calcium carbonate

测定最佳碱度 measuring optimum alkalinity

去色 decolorization

漂白 bleaching

浓缩 concentration

糖浆 syrup, concentrated juice

糖浆纯度 purity of syrup

滤泥 filter mud

转光度检糖汁 polarimeter

## 煮 炼  Boiling Until Crystallization

三系煮糖法 three-series sugar extraction

多效蒸发罐 multiple-effect evaporator

真空蒸发罐(煮糖罐)① vacuum boiling pan

超饱和 supersaturation

晶种法 seeding

助晶槽② seeding trough

晶种(籽晶) seed crystal (grain)

离心分蜜机③ centrifugal separator

晶粒 crystal, granule

母液 mother liquor

糖蜜 molasses

甲糖④ first sugar

甲蜜⑤ first molasses

乙糖 second sugar

乙蜜⑥ second molasses

丙糖⑦ third sugar

废糖蜜⑧ final molasses, blackstrap

振动筛⑨ vibrating screen

原糖 raw sugar

精制糖 refined sugar

旋转式干燥机 revolving drier

自动称重包装机 automatic weighing and packing machine

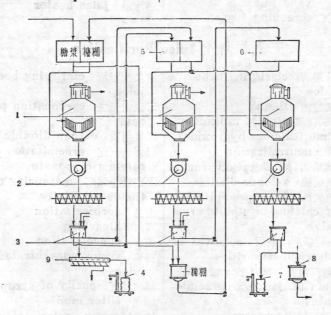

# 食品加工 Food Processing

## 罐头厂 Cannery

食品原料 raw-food material

水洗 water washing

高压喷水机 high-pressure water spray

清洗浮选机 flotation washer

干洗 dry cleaning

空气喷净 air blasting

预处理 preparatory operations

分选 sorting

按大小分级 size grading

按成熟程度分级 maturity grading

剪削修整 trimming

(豌豆)去蔓 vining (peas)

(豌豆)脱荚 shelling (peas)

(玉米)去衣 husking (maize)

(玉米)除须 silking (maize)

(玉米)脱粒 shelling (maize)

(水果)去皮 peeling (fruits)

(水果)去心 coring (fruits)

(柑桔)分瓣 sectioning (citrus fruits)

去核 pitting

切片 slicing

切丁 dicing

浸泡 soaking

去渣 straining

取汁 extracting the juice

均质 homogenization

预煮 precooking

电介质加热 dielectric heating

填装 filling

自动填料机 automatic filling machine

排气(空罐) exhausting

热排气 thermal exhausting

排气箱 exhaust box

自动真空封罐机 automatic vacuum-can sealing machine

热灭菌 heat sterilization

冷却 cooling

加贴标签 labelling

## 饼干面包厂　Bakery

硬质面粉(面筋含量高)　hard flour (high gluten content)

软质面粉(面筋含量低)　soft flour (low gluten content)

压榨酵母(鲜酵母)　pressed yeast

活性干酵母　active dried yeast

碳酸氢钠(小苏打)　sodium bicarbonate (baking soda)

碳酸氢铵(食臭粉)　ammonium bicarbonate

酒石酸氢钾　cream of tartar

砂糖　granulated sugar

饴糖　malt syrup

葡萄糖浆　glucose syrup

起酥油　shortening

奶油　butter

猪油　lard

植物油　vegetable oil

氢化油　hydrogenated oil

乳化剂　emulsor

磷脂　phospholipid

香料(香精)　essence

色素　colouring matter

强化剂　enrichment ingredients

饼干制造　biscuit manufacture

连续式和面机　continuous mixer

折叠型压片机　laminator

滚印式成型机　rotary moulder

甜饼干　sweet biscuit, (Am.) cookie

苏打饼干　soda cracker

夹心饼干　sandwich biscuit

维夫(威化)饼干　wafer

面包制造　bread manufacture

一次发酵法　straight dough method

二次发酵法　sponge dough method

发酵室　fermentation chamber

切块机　divider

搓圆机　rounder

醒发　quick rising

醒发室　proofer

烘烤炉　oven

烤盘　tray

冷却　cooling

包装　packaging

包装机　wrapper

## 糖果厂　Confectionery Manufactory

糖果　sweets, (Am.) candy

原辅料　ingredients

蔗糖　cane sugar

甜菜糖　beet sugar

麦芽糖　malt sugar

枫糖　maple sugar

蜂蜜　honey

糖蜜　molasses

糖浆　syrup

焦糖　caramel

淀粉　starch

乳品　milk products

蛋品　egg products

明胶　gelatin

果仁　nut

调香 flavouring
增色 colouring
硬糖 hard sweets, caramel
水果糖 fruit drops
花生脆糖 peanut brittle
太妃糖 toffee, (Am.) taffy
软糖 soft sweets
牛奶巧克力软糖 fudge
夹心糖 filled sweets
巧克力糖 chocolate

乳脂夹心巧克力 chocolate cream
乳脂心 cream filling, cream centre
棉花糖 marshmallow
蛋白牛奶果仁糖 nougat
条糖 candy bar
棒糖 lollipop
口香糖 chewing-gum

## 啤酒厂 Brewery

酿造啤酒的原料 brewing materials
大麦芽 barley malt
啤酒花 hops
辅料 adjuncts
捣碎 mashing
芽浆桶(糖化桶) mash tub
淀粉分解酶 amylolytic enzymes
麦芽汁 wort
煮沸 boiling
酿造锅 brew kettle
渗滤系统 percolating system
发酵槽 fermentation tank

底发酵 bottom fermentation
顶发酵 top fermentation
生啤酒 green beer
熟化 aging
熟啤酒 mature beer
装桶机 racking machine
啤酒桶 beer cask
桶装啤酒 draught beer
装瓶机 bottle filler
瓶装啤酒 bottled beer
罐装啤酒 canned beer
储藏啤酒 lager beer
黑啤酒 dark beer
苦啤酒 bitter beer

## 蒸酒厂 Distillery

蒸馏酒的生产 production of distilled spirits
粉碎粮谷 grinding the grain
糊化 gelatinizing the starch
加曲(加入霉菌生的淀粉酶) addition of fungal amylase
糖化 converting the starch into sugars
糊精 dextrin

麦芽糖 maltose
葡萄糖(右旋糖) glucose (dextrose)
加酒母 addition of yeast
酿酶(酒化酶) zymase
酒醅 wash
蒸馏 distillation
甑(蒸馏器) still
柱馏器 column still

酒槽　spent grain
白酒　plain spirit
色酒　flavoured spirit
浸制法　infusion process
酒精强度　alcoholic strength
六十度烧酒　potable spirit containing 60% alcohol by volume
英美标准酒精强度　proof

英国标准强度100%的酒含酒精57.3%（容量比）British 100 proof spirit contains 57.3% alcohol by volume
美国标准强度100%的酒含酒精50%（容量比）U.S. 100 proof spirit contains 50% alcohol by volume

# 陶　瓷　Ceramics

## 中国早期陶器　Early Chinese Pottery

新石器时代中期陶器　mid-neolithic pottery
仰韶彩陶　Yangshao painted pottery
新石器时代晚期陶器　late neolithic pottery
龙山黑陶　Longshan black pottery
印纹陶　stamped pottery
灰陶　grey pottery
赤陶　terra-cotta
商代白色刻陶　incised white pottery of the Shang Dynasty
手制　shaping by hand
模制　shaping in a mould
轮制　shaping on a potter's wheel
纹饰　ornamental pattern
绳纹　cord mark
席纹①　mat mark
篦纹　comb mark
几何形纹②　geometric pattern
螺纹　spiral pattern

回纹　fret pattern, meander pattern

方格纹　chequered pattern

彩绘　colour painting

（彩绘的）颜料　pigment

陶罐③　pottery jar

陶尊④　pottery vase

陶豆⑤　pottery stemmed bowl

陶鼎⑥　pottery tripod

陶鬲⑦　pottery tripod with bulbous hollow legs

陶鬶⑧　pottery pitcher

陶片　pottery shard

釉陶　glazed pottery

半瓷质器物　semi-porcelain ware

原始瓷器　protoporcelain ware

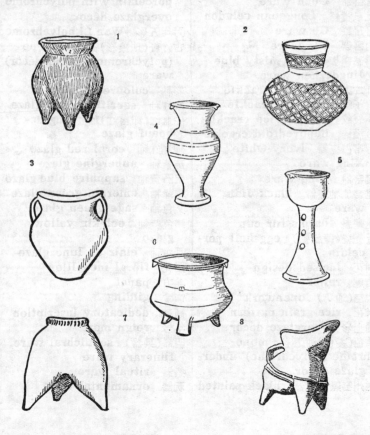

## 中国古瓷 Old Chinese Porcelain

青瓷　celadon
越窑器　Yue ware
秘色越器　Yue ware specially made for imperial use
汝窑器　Ru ware
官窑器　Guan ware
龙泉青瓷　Longquan celadon
哥窑器　Ge ware
钧窑器　Jun ware
景德镇影青瓷器　misty blue Jingdezhen ware
开片大小　size of crackle
鱼子纹　fish roe crackle
冰裂纹　cracked ice crackle
百圾碎　hundredfold crackle
邢窑白瓷器　ivory-white Xing ware
定窑器　Ding ware
建窑黑釉瓷器　black Jian ware
兔毫盏　hare's fur cup
蛋壳瓷(薄胎瓷)　eggshell porcelain
刻花　incised design
凸雕　relief
镂空(通花)　openwork
米花　rice-grain pattern
釉上彩　overglaze décor
单色(多色)釉下彩　monochrome (polychrome) underglaze décor
磁州窑黑白瓷器　black-painted cream-white Cizhou ware
青花瓷　blue and white porcelain
釉里红　underglaze red
釉上斗彩　blue and white porcelain with polychrome overglaze décor
万历五彩　Wan Li polychrome
古月轩(珐琅彩)瓷器　Gu Yue (polychrome enamel décor) ware
彩釉　coloured glaze
祭红釉　sacrificial red glaze
牛血红(郎窑红)釉　sang-de-boeuf glaze
珊瑚红釉　coral red glaze
茄紫釉　aubergine glaze
宝石蓝釉　sapphire blue glaze
翠绿釉　emerald green glaze
艾色釉　sage green glaze
鳝鱼黄釉　eelskin yellow glaze
月白釉　clair de lune glaze
团花　floral medallion
斗方　panel
饰金　gilding
题款　dedicatory inscription
年号　reign mark
明器(冥器)　sepulchral ware, funerary ware
祭器　ritual ware
玩器　ornamental ware

## 现代陶瓷工艺　Modern Ceramic Technology

粘土　clay
瓷土(高岭土)　china clay (gaolin)
球土　ball clay
瓷石　china stone (petuntse)
石英　quartz
长石　feldspar
蒙脱石　montmorillonite
陶瓷混合料(坯料)　ceramic mix (body)
设计　designing
成形　forming, shaping
可塑成形　plastic forming
拉坯　throwing
盘车拉坯　jiggering
干压　dry pressing
流体静压　hydrostatic pressing
热压　hot pressing
注浆成形　casting
粘土浆　slurry
粘土悬浮剂　deflocculant
石膏模　plaster mould

干燥　drying
干燥炉　drying oven
修整　polishing
未经烧制的生陶瓷器　green ware
烧制　firing
间歇窑　periodic kiln
隧道窑　tunnel kiln
蒙烰窑(隔焰窑)　muffle kiln
装窑　placing
加热　heating up
徐热　soaking
冷却　cooling
出窑　drawing
初次焙烧　preliminary firing, biscuit firing
素坯　biscuit
绘画　painting
施釉　glazing
贴花　transfer printing
烧釉　glost firing
釉皿　glost ware

## 陶瓷种类　Types of Ceramics

硬瓷　hard porcelain
软瓷　soft porcelain
骨灰瓷　bone china
块滑石瓷　steatite porcelain
烘炙陶瓷　frit porcelain
缸瓷　stoneware
乳白瓷　opalescent porcelain
金属陶瓷　cermet
电子陶瓷　electronic ceramics
热电陶瓷　thermoelectric

ceramics
压电陶瓷　piezoelectric ceramics
超高介电常数陶瓷　ultra-high-dielectric-constant ceramics
高频陶瓷　radio ceramics
光学陶瓷　optical ceramics
耐火陶瓷　refractory ceramics
耐酸陶瓷　acid-proof ceramics

耐腐蚀陶瓷 corrosion-resistant ceramics
加固陶瓷 reinforced ceramics
磁性陶瓷 magnetic ceramics
日用陶瓷器 ceramic ware for daily use
宜兴紫砂陶器 Yixing red stoneware
广彩瓷器 Guangzhou décor porcelain ware
陶瓷洁具 ceramic sanitary ware
美术陶瓷 art pottery and porcelain, artistic ceramics

## 美术陶瓷 Art Pottery and Porcelain

陶瓷雕塑 ceramic sculpture
白釉陶半身像 bust in white-glazed pottery
彩瓷小人像 polychrome porcelain statuette
表现社会主义新风尚的群像 new genre groups representative of socialist life
唐马(仿唐三彩陶马) Tang horse (three-colour glazed pottery horse patterned after the Tang model)
熊猫小塑像 panda figurine
结晶釉 crystalline glaze
结晶釉花瓶 flower vase with crystalline glaze
花盆 jardinière, ornamental flower pot
花插 flower holder
瓷屏 porcelain plaque
笔筒 cylindrical brush box
笔洗 tray for washing brushes
笔架 brush rest
水注 tiny pot to hold water for ink slab
注子 ewer
鸣鸟酒具 chirping bird wine set

# 美术工艺 Arts and Crafts

## 象牙雕刻 Ivory Carving

象牙雕刻艺术品 art ivory
浮雕 bas-relief, low relief

深雕　high relief

通雕　pierced work

立体圆雕　sculpture in the round

完整一块的雕刻　monobloc sculpture

多层象牙球　ivory balls within balls

将象牙块削成正圆球形　making a piece of ivory perfectly spherical

在象牙球中钻圆锥形孔若干个　boring several conical holes into the ivory ball

圆锥形孔的尖端在球中心会合　apices of conical holes meeting at the centre of the ball

在每一孔内按要求切出的层数画线　marking the inside of each hole with lines to indicate the number of balls to be cut out

用弯刃雕刻刀先将中心球切出　first cutting out the central ball by means of a graver with a curved blade

将中心球磨光雕花　polishing and carving the central ball

由内到外依次切出并雕刻其余各层　cutting out and carving the other balls successively from the inside out

乌木座象牙插屏　ivory plaque mounted in ebony

彩色象牙雕像　tinted ivory figure

## 其他手工艺　Other Handicrafts

漆器　lacquer ware

银丝螺钿漆托盘　lacquer tray inlaid with silver and mother-of-pearl

雕漆(剔红)　carved lacquer

脱胎漆雕刻品　objects carved out of solid lacquer

玉雕　jade carving

石雕　stone carving

石雕窗格　stone tracery

角雕　horn carving

木雕　wood carving

金木雕　gilt wood carving

竹根雕　bamboo-root carving

椰雕　coconut-shell carving

榄雕　olive-stone carving

墨鱼骨雕　cuttle-bone carving

雕花墨砚　carved ink-stone

贝雕画　picture in carved shell

羽毛画　picture in plume

麦秸画　picture in straw

树皮画　picture in bark

木画　picture in cork

蛋壳画　eggshell painting

掐丝珐琅　cloisonné

北京景泰蓝　Beijing cloisonné

料器　glass artware

玻璃小饰品　glass trinkets

草编织品　straw plaited work

藤编织品　rattan basketwork

竹编织品　bamboo basketwork

柳条编织品 **wickerwork**
刺绣 **embroidery**
抽纱 **drawn-work**
挂毯 **tapestry**
绒贴 **patchwork**
绒鸟 **chenille bird**
通草花 **rice-paper flower**
剪纸 **papercut**
佛山秋色 **Foshan papier mâché work**
盆景 **miniature landscape,**

mini-scape
套盒 **Chinese boxes**
灯色 **decorative lanterns**
走马灯 **shadow-picture lantern**
彩绘绢扇 **painted silk fan**
檀香扇 **carved sandal-wood folding fan**
泥人 **clay figurine**
面人 **dough figurine**

## 珠宝首饰 Jewelry

项链 **necklace**
项圈 **circlet**
坠子 **pendant**
小盒坠子 **locket**
戒指 **ring**
印章戒指 **signet-ring**
耳环 **earrings**
镯子 **bracelet**
别针 **brooch**
簪 **hairpin**
领带夹 **tie-clip**
袖扣 **cuff-links**
金银丝细工饰品 **filigree**
浮雕宝石 **cameo**
宝石 **gem**
金刚钻(钻石) **diamond**
珍珠 **pearl**
玉 **jade**
翡翠 **true jade, jadeite**
软玉 **nephrite**
红宝石 **ruby**
蓝宝石(蓝刚玉) **sapphire**
纯绿宝石(祖母绿) **emerald**
绿刚玉 **oriental emerald**

黄玉 **topaz**
黄宝石 **oriental topaz**
紫水晶(紫石英) **amethyst**
东方紫水晶 **oriental amethyst**
碧石(碧玉) **jasper**
水蓝宝石 **aquamarine**
绿柱石 **beryl**
金绿玉 **chrysoberyl**
猫儿眼 **cat's eye**
蛋白石 **opal**
绿松石 **turquoise**
石榴石 **garnet, carbuncle**
青金石 **lapis lazuli**
玛瑙 **agate**
苔纹玛瑙 **moss agate, Mocha stone**
缟玛瑙 **onyx**
缠丝玛瑙 **sardonyx**
玉髓 **chalcedony**
绿玉髓 **chrysoprase**
肉红玉髓 **cornelian**
血滴石 **bloodstone, heliotrope**
琥珀 **amber**

# 民 航 Civil Aviation

## 民航服务处 Civil Air Transport Service

国内航空线　**internal air route**

国际航空线　**international air route**

航班时刻表　**flight schedule**

航班号　**flight number**

原机直达航班　**through flight**

中途不停站的直达航班 **non-stop flight**

夜间航班　**night flight**

头等座　**first class**

经济座(旅游座) **economy class (tourist class)**

不定日期客票　**open date ticket**

定日期客票　**confirmed date ticket**

货物空运　**airwaybill, airbill**

合同货物　**cargo under contract**

免领进口许可证验放凭单 **application for release of articles without import licence**

退票手续费　**cancellation charge**

民航旅客集散站　**air terminal**

民航机场交通车　**airport bus**

"旅客退票，不迟于开航前＿小时办理者，仍需付手续费。" **"In the event of bookings cancelled anytime up to＿ hours before scheduled departure, a cancellation charge will be made."**

"旅客迟至开航前＿小时以内才要求退票，我们就有权将已付票款全部或部分扣下，不予退还。" **"We reserve the right to retain the whole or part of the fare in the case of bookings cancelled within ＿ hours of scheduled departure."**

"不定日期客票要在开航前＿天落实。" **"Open date tickets must be firmed up ＿ days in advance."**

"票价随时可能变更，未必事先通告。" **"All fares are subject to change with or without notice."**

# 民航机场　Airport

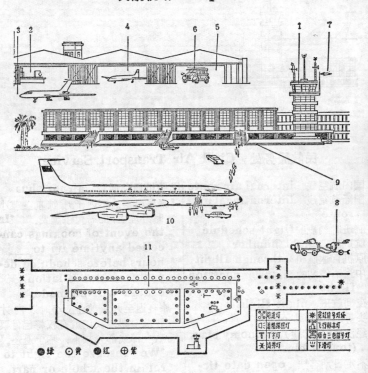

| | | | |
|---|---|---|---|
| ⊙絵 | ○黄 | ⊙红 | ⊕紫 |

| 喷气客机场 | jetport |
|---|---|
| 指挥塔台① | control tower |
| 航修厂② | aircraft repair and maintenance workshop |
| 维修场③ | service apron |
| 例行维修 | routine maintenance |
| 飞行前维修 | preflight maintenance |
| 飞行后维修 | postflight maintenance |
| 飞机库④ | hangar |

| 全天候机库 | all-weather hangar |
|---|---|
| 可控气候机库 | climatic hangar |
| 伸缩式机库 | telescopic hangar |
| 充气式机棚 | inflatable hangar |
| 消防站⑤ | fire station |
| 消防车⑥ | fire truck |
| 泡沫灭火车 | foam tender |
| 气象站 | meteorological station |
| 风向袋⑦ | wind sock |

加油服务　refuelling service
加油车⑧　refuelling tender
充气车　air servicer
机场救护车　crash tender
雷达扫描器　radar scanner
候机大楼⑨　terminal building
停机坪⑩　parking apron, tarmac
装卸场　loading apron
进入场　approach apron
滑行道　taxiway
跑道⑪　runway
滑行道灯　taxiway lights
跑道灯　runway lights
齐地面跑道灯　flush runway lights

移动式跑道灯　B-2 runway lights
地平线标志灯　horizon lights
进场角信号灯　angle-of-approach light
进场灯　approach light
下滑道灯　glide path lights
降落方向指示灯　landing direction light
降落信号灯　landing light
标灯　beacon light
边界灯　boundary lights
水上飞机碇泊灯　anchor light
水上机场航道灯　channel lights
水上机场滑行水道灯　taxi-channel lights

## 航空旅行　Air Travel

报到办手续　check-in
行李过磅托运　having the luggage weighed in
免费运送行李限额　free luggage allowance
超重行李　excess luggage
登机牌　boarding card
舷梯　ramp
客机设备　airliner accommodation
装有空气调节和增压设备的机舱　air-conditioned and pressurized cabin
减少炫光的偏振玻璃舷窗　cabin window polarized to reduce glare
中央过道　centre aisle
每排六座布置　six-abreast seating
座位间隔　seat pitch

座椅　armchair seat
卧椅　sleeperette chair
衣帽架　coat rack
衣帽间　wardrobe
盥洗室　toilet
饮食柜　buffet
配餐柜　pantry
厨房　galley
旅客供应品　catering stores
行李舱　luggage compartment
货舱　cargo hold
驾驶舱　flight deck
机组　flight crew
驾驶员　pilot
副驾驶员　co-pilot
领航员　navigator
随机机械员　flight engineer
服务组　cabin crew
领班服务员　purser
男服务员　steward

女服务员  stewardess

对旅客广播系统  passenger address system

起动  revving up

滑行上跑道  taxiing onto the runway

起飞  take-off

高空飞行  high altitude flying

平稳飞行  smooth flight

不平稳飞行  bumpy flight

颠簸  rocking, tossing, bumping

爬升  climbing

降低  losing height

盘旋  circling

空中加油  air refuelling, flight refuelling

气穴  air pocket

进入机场  homing in

降落  landing

着地  touchdown

空中爆炸  mid-air explosion

飞机坠毁  plane crash

劫持飞机  hijacking

迫降  forced landing

"一路平安!"  "Happy landings!"

"起飞(降落)时请不要吸烟,并系好安全带。"  "No smoking while taking off(landing), and fasten your seat belts."

"不要在空中拍照。"  "No photos from the air."

## 飞机类型  Types of Aircraft

单翼飞机①  monoplane

双翼飞机②  biplane

陆上飞机  landplane

滑橇起落架飞机  skiplane

水上飞机  seaplane

船式水上飞机③  flying boat

浮筒式水上飞机④  floatplane

水陆两用飞机  amphibian

短距起落飞机  STOL (short take-off and landing) aircraft

垂直起落飞机  VTOL (vertical take-off and landing) aircraft

旋翼飞机⑤  autogyro

直升飞机⑥  helicopter

亚音速运输机  subsonic transport

跨音速运输机  transonic transport

超音速运输机  supersonic transport (SST)

超高音速运输机  hypersonic transport

航天飞机  space shuttle

远程运输机  long-range transport

短程运输机  short-range transport

航空支线运输机  feederline transport

洲际航班飞机  intercontinental airliner

巨型喷气客机  jumbo jet

长期票乘客运输机  commuter transport

货运机  cargo transport

航空邮政运输机  airmail transport

护航飞机  escort aircraft

可改装运输机 convertible transport

通用飞机 general-purpose aircraft, utility aircraft

农用飞机⑦ agricultural aircraft

救护飞机 ambulance aircraft

搜寻营救飞机 search and rescue aircraft

测量飞机 survey aircraft

气象观测飞机 meteorological aircraft

游览飞机 touring aircraft

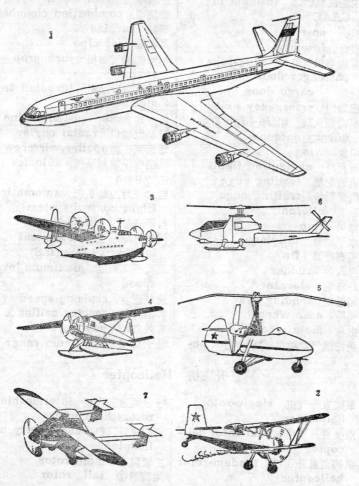

## 运输机 Transport Plane

四台喷气发动机的客货运输机 **four-jet passenger-cargo transport**

中国民航标志 **insignia of CAAC**

机头 **nose**

机身 **fuselage**

塞式密封客舱门 **plug-type passenger door**

货舱门 **cargo door**

应急门 **emergency exit**

超高频天线 **ultra-high frequency antenna**

机翼 **wing**

航行灯 **navigation lights**

机翼前缘 **leading edge**

机翼后缘 **trailing edge**

副翼 **aileron**

襟翼 **flap**

水平尾翼 **tailplane**

垂直尾翼 **fin**

方向舵 **rudder**

升降舵 **elevator**

起落架 **landing gear**

前轮 **nose wheels**

主轮 **main wheels**

涡轮喷气发动机 **turbojet engine**

进气道 **air intake**

压气机 **compressor**

燃料喷嘴 **fuel nozzle**

燃烧室 **combustion chamber**

涡轮 **turbine**

尾喷管 **jet pipe**

涡轮螺桨发动机 **turboprop engine**

涡轮风扇发动机 **turbofan engine**

活塞式发动机 **piston engine**

星型发动机 **radial engine**

螺旋桨 **propeller, airscrew**

航空电子控制系统 **avionics system**

自动飞行控制系统 **automatic flight control system**

自动驾驶仪 **autopilot**

仪表着陆系统 **instrument landing system (ILS)**

最大平飞速度 **maximum level speed**

巡航速度 **cruising speed**

实用升限 **service ceiling**

有效载荷 **payload**

最大航程 **maximum range**

## 直升飞机 Helicopter

单桨直升飞机 **single-rotor helicopter**

双桨直升飞机 **dual-rotor helicopter**

纵列桨直升飞机 **tandem-rotor helicopter**

啮合桨直升飞机 **intermeshing-rotors helicopter**

重型直升飞机 **heavy-duty helicopter**

主旋翼① **main rotor**

尾旋翼② **tail rotor**

反扭矩旋翼 anti-torque rotor

可折旋翼 folding rotor

旋翼旋转面 rotor disc

旋翼支架 rotor pylon

桨叶 rotor blade

铰接桨叶 hinged blade

扑动桨叶 flapping blade

桨距 blade pitch

总桨距 collective pitch

总桨距操纵杆 collective pitch lever

周期变距 cyclic pitch change

周期变距操纵杆 cyclic pitch control stick

尾桁 tailboom

水平安定面 horizontal stabi-lizer

三轮式起落架③ tricycle-type landing gear

滑橇起落架 skid-type landing gear

充气浮筒 pneumatic float

应急浮筒式起落架 emergency flotation gear

涡轮轴发动机 turboshaft engine

飞行起重操作 flying crane operation

起重能力 hoisting capacity

悬停升限 hovering ceiling

直升飞机场 heliport

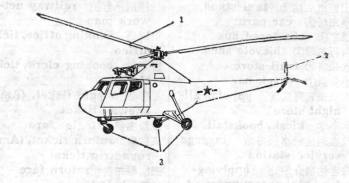

# 铁路交通运输 Railway Transport

## 火车站(一) Railway Station (Ⅰ)

火车站广场　station square

钟楼　clock tower

公共汽车候车亭①　bus shelter

出租汽车站②　taxi stand

停车场③　car park

包车④　chartered bus

自行车棚⑤　bicycle shed

水果店⑥　fruit store

小食店⑦　snack bar

大众通宵商店⑧　popular all-night store

书亭⑨　kiosk, bookstall

代客运送行李服务站　luggage service station

旅客住宿介绍处　applying-for-hotel-accommodation office

市内交通图⑩　city traffic map

天气预报⑪　weather bulletin

问讯处　inquiry office

"旅客留言"　"Left Messages"

火车时刻表　railway timetable

列车到达时刻表　arrival time-table, (Am.) arrival sched-ule

列车离站时刻表　departure timetable, (Am.) departure schedule

铁路网示意图　railway net-work map

售票处　booking office, ticket office

售票员　booking clerk, ticket clerk

单程票　single ticket, (Am.) oneway ticket

单程车费　single fare

来回票　return ticket, (Am.) roundtrip ticket

来回程车费　return fare

半票　half ticket

月台票　platform ticket

预订到____的直达车票　booking through to ____

"买去北京的票吗？请到左边第一个窗口。"　"Booking to Bei-jing? First window on the left."

"第62次快车14点20分到。"　"Number 62 Passenger

Express is due in at four-teen twenty."

"前往___的下一列车是第43次快车，23点33分从___开出，5点47分到达___。" "The next train to ___ is Number 43 Express, depart ___ twenty-three thirty-three, arrive ___ O-five forty-seven."

"可以提早___天订票。" "Tickets may be booked___ days in advance."

"到___没有直达车，要在___转车。" "There's no through train to___. You'll have to change at___."

"去___的单程票价是___元，卧铺另计。" "Single fare to___ ¥ ___, berth extra."

"车票有效期是___天。" "The ticket is good for___days."

"1米20以下的儿童才能买半票。" "Half fare for children under one metre twenty only."

## 火车站(二)  Railway Station (Ⅱ)

候车大厅  **waiting hall**

车次与站台指示牌  **train and platform indicator**

自动扶梯  **escalator**

外宾候车室  **waiting room for foreign guests**

贵宾候车室  **VIP room**

母婴候车室  **mother-and-child room**

餐室  **refreshment room**

糖果糕点小卖部  **confectionery**

纪念品柜台  **souvenier counter**

小银行  **minibank**

外币兑换柜台  **money exchange desk**

电话间  **telephone booth**

急救站  **first-aid station**

行李托运处  **luggage office**

磅秤  **weighing machine**

托运的行李  **registered luggage**

行李标签  **luggage tag, luggage label**

行李票(收据)  **luggage check**

超重行李收费单  **excess (overweight) luggage voucher**

大型衣箱  **trunk**

手提箱  **suitcase**

铺盖卷  **bedroll**

小件行李寄存处  **left-luggage office, (Am.) checkroom**

旅行袋  **travelling bag**

挂包  **sling bag**

网袋  **string bag**

手提袋  **carryall**

柳条篮  **wicker basket**

背囊(帆布背包)  **rucksack, knapsack**

意见箱  **suggestion box**

"欢迎批评建议"  **"Suggestions and Comments Welcome."**

广播器  **loudspeaker**

广播通知  **announcement over the public address system**

"布朗先生,布朗先生,____公司的罗伯特·布朗先生,请即到问讯处,有急事。"  **"Calling for Mr. Brown, calling for Mr. Brown. Mr. Robert Brown, of____Company, please come to the inquiry office. Urgent!"**

"请注意:乘坐第20次快车去北京的旅客,现在可以上车。"  **"Attention, please. Number 20 Passenger Express to Beijing is ready for immediate boarding."**

"就要开车啦,快上车!"  **"All aboard!"**

## 火车站(三)  Railway Station (Ⅲ)

站台(月台)  **platform**

站长  **stationmaster**

铁路警察  **railway policeman**

搬运工人  **porter**

列车员  **conductor**

验票员  **ticket collector**

剪票铗 ticket punch
出发站台 departure platform
离站指示器 departure indicator
到达站台 arrival platform
电动站台运货车 electric platform truck
到站指示器 arrival indicator
终点牌 destination plate
天桥 footbridge, platform bridge
桥下通道 underpass

出口处 exit
栅门 barrier
快车(普通快车) express
特别快车 special express
直达快车 through express
慢车 stopping train, (Am.) local train
客货混合列车 mixed train
终点站 terminus, terminal
中途小站 way station
联轨站(枢纽站) junction

## 客 车 Passenger Train

车厢 carriage, coach
连廊 vestibule
车厢内部设备 interior accommodation
中央过道两旁双座席 seats in pairs on each side of centre aisle
单人躺椅座席 individual reclining seat
内嵌烟灰缸的扶手 armrest with built-in ashtray
软垫座席 cushioned seat
旋转座席 swivel seat
背靠背的长椅硬座 back-to-back bench seats
座旁小灯 reading light
双层玻璃窗 double-glazed window
行李架 luggage rack
空气调节器 air-conditioner
灭火器 fire-extinguisher
通风装置 ventilator
蒸气散热器 steam radiator
车厢内的警报索 communica-

tion cord
厕所 lavatory, toilet
卧车 sleeping car, sleeper
走廊 corridor
卧室 sleeping compartment
上铺 upper berth
下铺 lower berth
折叠式小桌 folding table
翻椅 tip-up seat
餐车 dining car, diner
餐车服务员 table attendant
小食部 buffet
行李车 luggage van
包乘组 train crew
列车长 chief conductor
"往____的 ____ 快车还有三分钟就要开出. 不是乘这一班的, 请离开列车." "Number ____ Express to ____ is leaving in three minutes. Those who are not going on this train, please step off."

"买了直达 ____ 车票的旅客, 可在任何中途站下车停留, 于车票有效期内随时乘坐其他列车继续行程。" "Passengers booked through to ____ may stop over at any intermediate station and resume their journey on another train any time within the validity of the ticket."

"旅客中途下车, 不按所购车票坐完全程,票价差额概不退还。"
"No refund will be made to passengers who choose to break their journey at an intermediate station."

"旅客乘坐本列车, 超过 原票所规定旅程的,请补票。" "Passengers who choose to extend their journey on this train can do so on payment of the excess fare."

"这是郑州站。去西安的旅客在这里转乘西行列车。" "Zhengzhou. Passengers for Sian change here to westbound train."

"列车停 站时, 不得使用车上厕所。" "Do not use the toilet when the train is at a stop."

## 机车(一)　Locomotive ( I )

内燃机车① diesel locomotive

内燃机械力传动 diesel mechanical power transmission

内燃液力传动 diesel hydraulic power transmission

流体传动装置 fluid gear

内燃电传动 diesel electric power transmission

柴油发电机组 diesel-electric set

交直流电传动 AC-DC electric power transmission

主发电机 main generator

牵引电动机 traction motor

操纵台 control stand

仪表板 instrument panel

冷却水温度计 cooling water temperature gauge

油压表 fuel pressure gauge

空转控制钮 idling control knob

撒沙装置操纵杆 sander control knob

充电控制灯 control lamp for battery charge

燃料泵进给踏板 fuel injection pump feed pedal

电力机车② electric locomotive

架空接触导线 overhead contact wire

受电弓 bow current collector, pentograph

主断路器 main switch, main circuit breaker

引入线绝缘子 lead-in insulator

压缩空气断路器 compressed-air circuit breaker

篷顶切断开关 roof disconnecting switch

变压器　transformer
硅整流装置　silicon-controlled rectifier
驱动电动机　driving motor
制动器电动机　brake motor
电动机风扇　motor ventilator
风喇叭　air whistle
电力机车司机室　electric locomotive driver's cabin
司机台　driver's control desk
位置指示器　position indicator
信号灯　signal light
牵引电机电流　traction motor current

牵引电机电压　traction motor voltage
励磁电流　exciting current
仪表灯　instrument light
按钮开关　push-button switch
司机驾驶盘　driver's control handwheel
副司机台　assistant driver's control desk
警铃　alarm bell
紧急制动器　emergency brake
燃气轮机车　gas turbine locomotive
蒸汽机车③　steam locomotive

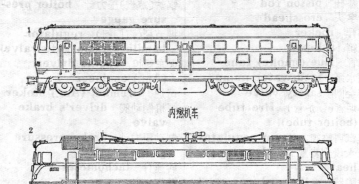

内燃机车

电力机车

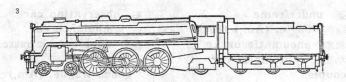

蒸汽机车

## 机车(二)　Locomotive（II）

蒸汽机车　steam locomotive
锅炉　boiler
火箱　fire box
连杆　connecting rod
汽包　steam dome
沙箱　sand box
沙管　sand tubes
风力撒沙装置　pneumatic sand-
　ing gear
烟囱　chimney
汽室　steam chest
汽缸　steam cylinder
活塞杆　piston rod
十字头　crosshead
摇杆　rocker
灰箱　ash-pan
烟管　flue (smoke) tube
注水泵　feed-water pump
安全阀　safety valve
小烟管(锅炉管)　fire tube
　(boiler tube)
蒸汽调整阀　steam regulator
给水预热装置　feed-water pre-
　heater
排障器　rail guard (cowcatch-
　er)

支承轴　carrying axle
连动轴　coupled axle
主动轴　driving axle
汽笛　steam whistle
煤水车　tender
自动润滑泵　automatic lubri-
　cant pump
预热压力计　preheater pres-
　sure gauge, manometer
加热压力计　heating pressure
　gauge
水位表　water gauge
锅炉(蒸汽)压力计　boiler pres-
　sure gauge
调节杆(汽门阀)　regulator
　handle (steam gate valve)
火车司机　engine driver,
　(Am.) engineer
司炉　fireman, (Am.) stoker
司机制动阀　driver's brake
　valve
制动压力计　brake pressure
　gauge
转速计　tachometer
截汽　steam cut-off
遥测温度计　telethermometer

## 铁路车辆　Rolling Stock

车架　underframe
转向架　bogie, (Am.) truck
风刹车　pneumatic brake
自动车钩　automatic car
　coupler
车轮　coach wheel
轮缘　wheel flange

了望车　observation car
救护车　ambulance car
双层客车　double-deck passen-
　ger coach
货车　goods wagon, (Am.)
　freight car
敞车①　open goods wagon

篷车② **covered goods wagon**
高边车 **high-sided wagon**
低边车 **low-sided wagon**
行李车 **luggage van**
邮车 **mail car**
罐车(液柜车)③ **tank wagon**
冷藏车④ **refrigerator wagon**
牲畜车 **livestock wagon**
多层间隔运禽车 **multi-deck partitioned wagon for the transport of fowl**
集装箱平车 **container flatcar**

矿石车 **ore transport wagon**
木材车 **timber transport wagon**
漏底车 **hopper wagon**
倾卸车 **tipping wagon**
侧倾车 **side-tipping wagon**
倾斗车 **trough tipper, (Am.) dump car**
查道车 **rail inspection car**
救险起重车 **breakdown crane wagon**

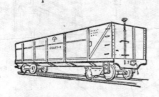

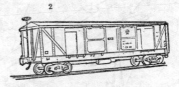

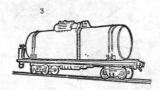

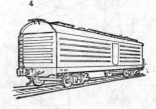

## 登山铁路　Mountain Railways

齿轨铁路〔系统〕① **rack and pinion railway system**

登山齿轨② **rack (mountain) railway (cog railway)**

电力机车③ **electric railway locomotive**

齿轨车辆④ **rack railway coach**

承重齿轮⑤ **running wheel**

主动轮⑥ **driving pinion(s)**

导轨(齿条)⑦ **rack**

铁轨⑧ **rail**

双导轨 **double rack**

缆索铁道⑨ **funicular railway**

缆索铁道车辆(缆车)⑩ **funicular railway coach, (Am.) cable car**

牵引索⑪ **haulage cable**

缆车索道(架空索道)⑫ **suspension cable railway (aerial cableway)**

单线索道⑬ **monocable rope-**

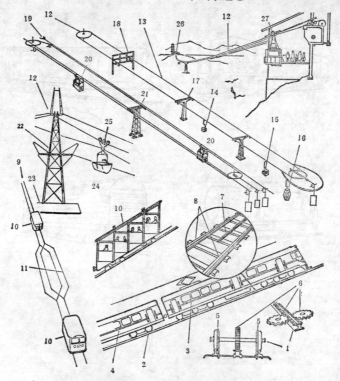

way

架空滑车单座⑭ lift chair (single chair)

双人座⑮ two-seater lift chair (double chair)

小舱⑯ small cabin

循环索缆 circulating rope, circulating cable

支柱⑰ one-mast support

龙门架⑱ gantry support

双线索道⑲ bi-cable ropeway

承载钢缆 standing cable (carrying cable)

客舱⑳ passenger cabin, (Am.) shuttle car

中间支架㉑ intermediate sup-port, intermediate mast

双线架空索道 double cable suspension railway

花架铁塔㉒ lattice mast

铁塔基座㉓ tower base foundation

牵引索滑轮 haulage-cable pulley

翻转式装料斗㉔ tipping bucket, dumping bucket

挡块 tip stop

滚轮滑动架㉕ pulley cradle

山谷站㉖ valley station

山顶站㉗ mountain station (top station)

## 铁路交通管理 Railway Traffic Control

调度室 dispatching room

调度员 train dispatcher

中心控制台 console of centralized control

编组站 marshalling yard, (Am.) classification yard

驼峰调车场 hump

转车台 turntable

圆形修车房(圆形车库) roundhouse

红外线探伤仪 infrared detector

编组轨道 classification tracks

调轨机车 shunting engine, (Am.) switcher

车辆缓行器 retarder

指挥塔(信号楼) yard (control) tower, (Am.) switch tower

编组站站长 yardmaster

轨道模型盘 track diagram

双向通话设备 two-way speaking appliance

信号员 signalman

信号旗 signal flag

号志灯 signal lantern

路签 key

自动闭塞色灯信号 automatic block signalling with colourlight signals

机车色灯信号机 ATC (automatic train control)

转辙信号 switch signal

列车近站信号 distant signal, approach signal

臂板信号 semaphore

减速信号 reduce-speed sign

停车信号 stop sign

司机鸣笛标 whistle sign

公里标 kilometre post

## 货运站　Freight Terminal

货棚　freight shed
货棚侧线　shed siding
装货站台　loading dock
装运标尺　load gauge
桥秤　weighbridge
电动货车和拖车　electric truck with trailer
货运列车　freight train
棚车　boxcar
敞车　open-top car
平车　flatcar
货箱　packing-case
板条箱　crate
货盘　pallet

零担货物　LCL (less-than-car-load) freight
货运单　consignment note, way-bill
公路铁路联运　coordinated road-rail transport
平车载拖车的运输方式　piggy-back
运费　freight rates
铁路货运量　volume of railway freight
日装车数　daily loading of freight wagons

## 铁路定线　Railway Location

测量　surveying
测量经纬仪　surveyor's transit
测量罗盘仪①　surveyor's compass
平板仪②　surveying plane table
水准仪③　surveyor's level
标尺　surveying rod
标杆　surveyor's pole
山岭　mountain ridge
河谷④　river gorge
地震区　earthquake zone
地下河⑤　underground river, subterranean river
断层⑥　fault
溶洞　karst cave
流沙⑦　drifting sand
泥石流⑧　mud-rock flow
瓦斯层　gasfilled layer

岩浆爆发　magmatic explosion
粉砂　silt
滑坡(山崩)　landslide, landslip
塌方　cave-in
铁路桥　railway bridge
隧道⑨　tunnel
涵洞　culvert
路堤　embankment
路旁水沟　ditch, trench
暗沟　underdrain
铁路示意图　diagrammatic map of railway
高架铁路　elevated railway
悬索铁路　cable railway
地下铁路　underground railway, tube, (Am.) subway
活动道路　travolator
单轨铁路　monorail
标准轨距　standard gauge

宽轨　broad gauge
窄轨　narrow gauge
单轨线　single-track line
双轨线　double-track line

焊接长轨　long welded rail
无缝长轨　continuous welded rail

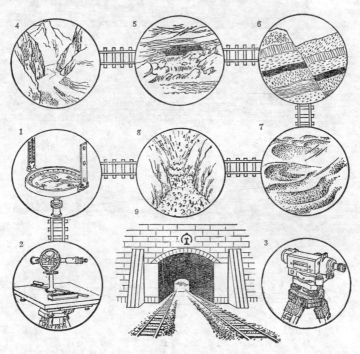

## 铺　轨　Track Laying

铺轨队　rail gang
工长　gang foreman, ganger
道床　roadbed

铁路路堤　railway embankment

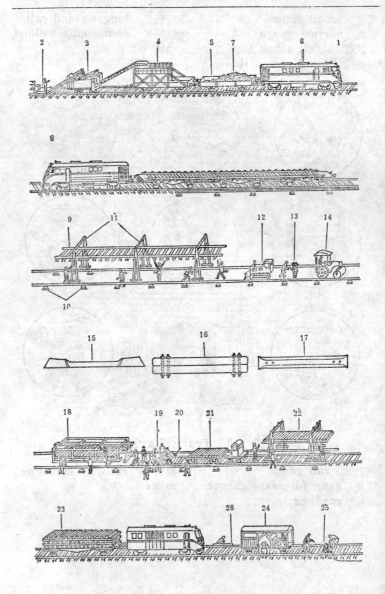

工程列车① **track construction train**

指挥车② **control truck**

筛碴机③ **ballast-washing machine**

料斗车④ **hopper truck**

弃土车⑤ **waste truck**

道碴机车⑥ **ballast train locomotive**

筛过的道碴 **cleaned ballast**

挖出的弃土⑦ **waste**

载轨列车(工程车)⑧ **track carrying train**

轨节⑨ **section of track**

轨座⑩ **rail chair**

龙门吊车⑪ **travelling portal crane**

推土机⑫ **bulldozer**

内燃夯土机⑬ **power rammer**

道床碾压机⑭ **ballast-roller**

轨枕 **sleeper, (Am.) crosstie**

混凝土轨枕⑮ **concrete sleeper**

双轨枕⑯ **double sleeper**

钢轨枕⑰ **steel sleeper**

杂酚油(木馏油) **creosote**

轨枕铺设机⑱ **sleeper-layer**

铺路工⑲ **platelayer, tracklayer**

起轨器(钢轨钳)⑳ **rail tongs**

轨道平车(养路小车)㉑ **sleeper truck**

轨枕输送机㉒ **sleeper conveyor truck**

轨枕输送机车㉓ **sleeper transport train**

轨枕捣固机㉔ **ballast-tamping machine**

焊工组㉕ **welding team**

铝热焊料斗 **thermite welding funnel**

道轨水准仪㉖ **rail level**

# 钢 轨 Rail

轨头 **rail head**

轨腰 **rail web**

轨底 **rail bottom**

钢轨垫板 **sole plate, base plate**

钢轨垫片 **washer**

螺纹道钉 **sole plate screw**

弹簧垫圈 **spring washer**

钢轨扣件 **clip**

丁字头螺栓 **hook bolt**

轨缝 **rail joint**

鱼尾板 **rail fish-plate, (Am.) joint bar**

鱼尾板螺栓 **fish bolt**

接头轨枕 **coupled sleeper**

接头轨枕螺栓 **coupling bolt**

就地操纵道岔 **hand switch, hand-operated point**

握柄架 **hand switch box**

平衡锤 **switch weight**

道岔表示器(道岔表示灯) **switch signal (switch lamp)**

转辙杆 **stretcher bar**

尖轨 **switch toe**

道岔滑床板 **slide chair**

护轨 **inner check rail**

辙叉 **frog**

辙叉翼轨 **wing rail**

道岔连接轨 **closure rail**

遥控道岔 **remote-controlled**

point

平交道口　level crossings, (Am.) grade crossings

道口栏杆　lattice barrier

道口看守工　gatekeeper, (Am.) crossing watchman

道口预告信号　warning cross

道口看守房　gatekeeper's cabin

养路领工员　line inspector

呼叫自动栏木　microphone operated barrier

内话机　electric speaking-tube appliance

无人看守道口　unprotected crossing

交通管理色灯　traffic warning light

# 公路交通运输　Road Transport

## 道路、街道　Roads, Streets

公路　highway, highroad

公路容量　highway capacity

国家公路　national highway

地方公路　local highway, local road

乡村公路　country road

公路干线　arterial highway, trunk road

公路支线　secondary road, feeder road

高速公路　motorway, (Am.) superhighway, expressway, freeway

偏僻道路　back road

禁止中途停车的直通道路　clearway

高架道路　elevated road

低于地面的道路　depressed road

双层道路　double-deck road

辐射式公路　radial road

环心式公路　orbital road

侧绕公路　bypass highway (bypass)

支路　byroad

环行公路　ring road, (Am.) belt road

辅助道路　relief road

征税道路　toll road

路〔线〕　route

单向行车路　one-way road

双向行车路　two-way road

驮运道路　pack road

临时绕行道　detour

马车路  coach road
大车路(牛马车路)  cart road
通道  thoroughfare
林荫大道  boulevard
大街  avenue
街道  street
横街  side street
巷(里,坊)  lane
由街道通到房舍的车道  drive,
  (Am.) driveway
石板街  flagged path, flag-
  stone path
胡同(屋间巷,窄巷)  alley
死胡同  blind alley, dead
  end, cul-de-sac
走道  walkway
人行小道  footpath
小径  path, track, trail
山径  mountain path
泥路  earth (dirt) road
铺木路  wood block road
卵石路  cobbled road

陶砖路  vitrified brick road
碎石路  gravel road
柏油路  macadam road,
  asphalt road, blacktop road
水泥混凝土路  cement con-
  crete road
道路结构  road structure
路冠(路顶)  road crown
路面  road surface, pavement
沥青路面  asphalt surface,
  bituminous layer
混凝土路板  concrete slab
路面下层  sub-surface
路基  subgrade, foundation
路床(路基面)  road base, road-
  bed
副基  subbase
石碴层  ballast layer
压实的粒料层  compacted
  aggregate
路肩  shoulder
排水渠  drainage ditch

## 筑路和清道机械  Road-Making and Street-Cleaning Machines

挖土机①  power navvy,
  power shovel, (Am.) shovel-
type excavator
平地机②  road grader

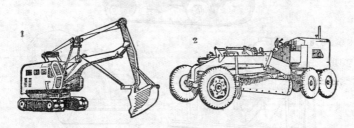

推土机① **bulldozer**

斜角推土机 **angledozer**

夯锤(夯具)② **ram, earth tamper, compactor**

撒石机 **stone spreader, macadam spreader**

石片散布机 **chippings spreader**

铲运机 **scraper**

混凝土搅拌机③ **concrete mixer**

钢筋敷设机 **steel reinforcement laying machine**

混凝土散布机④ **concrete spreading machine, concrete spreader**

焦油炉 **tar heater**

焦油浇注机⑤ **tar sprayer**

沥青铺面机 **asphalt layer**

混凝土路面接缝切削机⑥ **concrete surface joint cutter**

压路机⑦ **road roller**

扫路机(清道机) **road sweeping machine**

清道手推车 **road sweeper's barrow**

街道冲洗车 **street and gully cleanser**

渠道渗井清理车 **gully and**

**cesspool emptier**

清粪车 **nightsoil collector**

垃圾车 **refuse lorry, (Am.) garbage truck**

洒水车 **watering lorry, flushing truck, sprinkler**

扫雪车 **snow plough**

## 高速公路 Motorway (Superhighway)

分离道路 **divided road**

非分离道路 **undivided road**

中央分离带 **median strip**

行车方向分离带 **directional separator**

外侧分离带 **outer separator**

路侧带 **margin, verge, side strip**

自行车道 **cycle path, bikeway**

镶石路边 **curb**

路边石 **curbstone**

行人道 **pavement, (Am.) sidewalk**

路面 **roadway**

行车线范围 **travelled way**

车线 **traffic lane**

第一(外)车道 **first (outside) lane**

第二(内)车道 **second (inside) lane**

中心车道 **centre lane**

路边车道 **curb lane**

辅助车道 **auxiliary lane**

变速车道 **speed change lane**

分离转向车道 **separated turning lane**

停车候车道 **waiting bay, (Am.) turn-out lane**

回车道 **turnaround**

路上停车道 **parking lane**

超车或避车车道 **lay-by**

道路立体枢纽 **traffic interchange, (interchange)**

立体交叉 **grade separation, flying junction**

丁字型立体交叉 **T-grade separation**

Y字型立体交叉 **Y-grade separation**

菱形立体交叉 **diamond interchange**

苜蓿叶式立体交叉 **cloverleaf**

立体环行交叉 **bridged rotary intersection**

直联式立体交叉 **directional interchange**

立体交叉上叉道 **flyover, (Am.) overpass**

立体交叉下叉道 **underpass**

平面交叉 **intersection, junction**

十字交叉(十字路口) **right-angle intersection (crossroads)**

铁路与公路平交道 **level crossing, (Am.) grade crossing**

三枝交叉 **three-way intersection, three-leg intersection**

四枝交叉　**four-way intersection, four-leg intersection**

丁字型交叉　**T-intersection**

Y字型交叉　**Y-junction, (Am.) Y-intersection**

叉式交叉　**fork junction**

剪刀式交叉　**scissor junction, (Am.) oblique intersection, skew intersection**

错列交叉　**right left/ left**

right staggered junction, (Am.) offset intersection

多枝交叉　**multiway intersection, multiple intersection**

环行交叉　**roundabout, (Am.) traffic circle**

导流式交叉　**channelized intersection**

非导流式交叉　**unchannelized intersection**

## 道路状况　Road Conditions

全国公路规划　**national highway program**

道路网　**road network**

公路局　**road board, highway bureau**

筑路　**road making, road construction**

道路养护(养路)　**road maintenance**

修路　**road mending**

道路改良　**road improvement**

重铺路面　**resurfacing**

平稳的道路　**smooth road**

崎岖的道路　**rough road, bumpy road**

路面上的凹凸　**potholes and bumps**

条坑路面　**washboard**

宽度收缩(交通拥挤)路段　**bottleneck**

坡度　**gradient**

慢坡　**easy grade**

陡坡　**steep grade**

坡度变更点(纵坡转折点)　**break in grade**

上坡路　**upgrade**

下坡路　**downgrade**

路弯　**bend, turn**

U字形转弯　**hairpin bend, hairpin turn**

Z形路　**zigzag route**

路边服务站　**roadside service**

路边询问站　**roadside information centre**

路边加油站　**roadside filling station, service station**

公路行车旅馆(附有停车场设施的)　**motel**

"此路不通"　**"No thoroughfare"**

"不得在公路上乱扔杂物。"　**"Do not litter the highway."**

"修路"　**"Road under repair"**

"道路施工"　**"Road under construction"**

"小心障碍"　**"Beware obstruction"**

"提防危险"　**"Beware dangers"**

"此路通行"　**"Road clear"**

"此处修路，请转左行"　**"Road closed for repair. Turn left"**

"路边禁止停车"　**"No curb-**

parking"

"禁止摄影" "Photographing
prohibited"

"外国人未经许可，不得逾越此线"

"Out of bounds to for-
eigners without special
permit"

## 桥 梁 Bridges

双线、双层铁路和公路两用桥①
**double-track, double-deck
rail and road bridge**

引桥② **approach to the
bridge, approach span**

混凝土路面③ **concrete road
surface**

四股车道的公路④ **four-lane
highway**

人行道⑤ **footway, pavement**

桥栏杆⑥ **bridge railing**

钻石形桁架⑦ **diamond-shaped
truss**

桥塔⑧ **bridge tower**

桥墩⑨ **pier**

石拱桥⑩ **stone arch bridge**

桥面(路面) **bridge floor**

主拱⑪ **main arch**

拱肩拱(小拱)⑫ **spandrel
arch (minor arch)**

桥台⑬ **abutment**

斜坡道⑭ **ramp**

拱跨⑮ **span of arch**

连拱桥 **multiple arch bridge**

多跨桥 **multiple span bridge**

十七孔桥 **seventeen-arch
bridge, bridge of seventeen
spans**

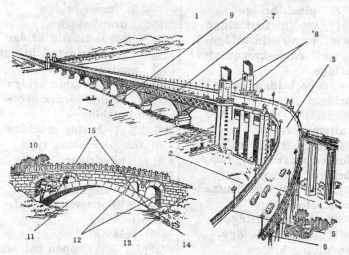

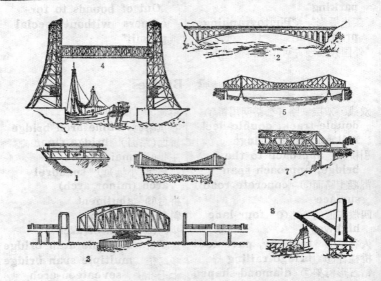

双曲拱桥　**two-way curved arch bridge**

木板桥　**plank bridge**

小桥(行人桥)① **footbridge**

铁索桥　**iron-chain bridge**

索拉钢桥　**cable-braced steel bridge**

索桥　**rope bridge, cable bridge**

钢结构铁路桥　**steel lattice railway bridge**

钢筋混凝土公路桥② **reinforced concrete highway bridge**

预应力混凝土桥　**prestressed-concrete bridge**

开合桥　**bascule bridge**

旋转桥③ **swing bridge, revolving bridge**

升降桥④ **lift bridge**

悬臂桥⑤ **cantiliver bridge**

悬索桥⑥ **suspension bridge**

桁架桥⑦ **truss bridge**

吊桥⑧ **drawbridge**

高架桥(栈桥)　**trestle bridge**

预制桥　**prefabricated bridge**

浮桥　**pontoon bridge**

轻便活动桥　**portable bridge**

架桥机　**bridge girder erection machine**

冲击式钻机　**boring machine of the percussion type**

打桩机　**piledriver**

管柱钻孔法　**tubular column drilling method**

气压沉箱法　**pneumatic caisson method**

沉箱　**caisson**

沉井(开口沉箱) **open caisson**

围堰　**cofferdam**

## 交通安全　Traffic Safety

防止事故　prevention of accidents

交通调查　traffic study

交通现象　traffic behaviour

交通容量　traffic capacity

车道容量　lane capacity

驻车容量　parking capacity

交通规则　traffic regulations

公路巡逻队　highway patrol

交通巡逻队　traffic patrol

交通警察　traffic policeman

摩托车巡逻警察　motor traffic policeman, (Am.) motor patrolman

交通安全教育运动　educational movement for traffic safety, traffic safety campaign

治安纠察队　public security patrol

安全设施　safety installations

安全地带　safety zone

交通岛　traffic island

中央分离岛　medial island, divisional island

转向诱导岛　directional island

安全岛　refuge, pedestrian island

乘客上下车安全岛　loading island

中央岛　rotary island, central island

导流岛　channelizing island

交通岗　traffic point

交通岗亭　traffic control box

交通指挥塔　raised control tower

交通指挥台　podium

警笛　police whistle

唇式扩音器　lip microphone

手持式扩音器　hand microphone

警察指挥棒　police baton

车辆感知器　vehicle detector

车辆感知板　vehicle detector pad

道路安全防护栏　road guard, road fence

路障　road block

行人防护栏　pedestrian guard rail

路面反光镜(猫眼)　cat's eye

呼援电话亭　telephone rescue box

援救站　rescue service

修理救援车　break-down vehicle, (Am.) wrecker

乘客座位安全带　seat belt, safety belt

驾驶技术考核　driving test

驾驶汽车者　motorist

驾驶员(司机)　driver

实习驾驶员　learner driver

汽车实地试验　road test

实习驾驶员执照　learner driver's provisional licence

司机执照　driver's licence

机动车行驶证　vehicle registration certificate

机动车车牌　number plate

交叉路口交通规则　regulations for crossing

停放车辆规则　**regulations for parking**

速度限制　**speed limit**

速度监视所　**speed-trap**

行驶时两车前后距离限制　**restricted clearance**

侧方车距　**lateral clearance**

## 交通标志和信号　Traffic Signs and Signals

转向限制标志　**turn-control signs**

直行①　**NO TURNS; GO STRAIGHT THROUGH**

直行和右转弯②　**NO LEFT TURN; GO STRAIGHT THROUGH or TURN RIGHT**

直行和左转弯③　**NO RIGHT TURN; GO STRAIGHT THROUGH or TURN LEFT**

向右转弯④　**TURN RIGHT ONLY**

向左转弯⑤　**TURN LEFT ONLY**

靠右(行驶)　**KEEP RIGHT**

向左或右转弯⑥　**TURN; TURN LEFT or RIGHT ONLY**

单行线　**ONE-WAY TRAFFIC**

禁令标志　**prohibitory signs**

禁止驶入⑦　**NO ENTRY; DO NOT ENTER, WRONG WAY**

禁止停车⑧　**NO STOPPING**

禁止车辆停驻　**NO PARKING**

禁止通行⑨　**ROAD CLOSED**

禁止汽车通行⑩　**ROAD CLOSED TO CARS; NO MOTORCARS; AUTOS NOT PERMITTED**

禁止大型卡车通行⑪　**NO HEAVY TRUCKS**

禁止汽车及摩托车通行⑫　**NO CARS and MOTORCYCLES**

禁止超车⑬　**NO PASSING; DO NOT PASS; NO OVERTAKING**

禁止汽车调头⑭　**NO U-TURN**

禁止人力货车通行⑮　**NO HANDCARTS**

禁止载客三轮车通行⑯　**NO PEDICABS**

禁止畜力车通行⑰　**NO BEAST-DRAWN CARTS**

禁区　**AREA CLOSED; RESTRICTED AREA**

(车辆)重量限制⑱　**MAXIMUM WEIGHT…**

载重限制　**LOAD LIMIT…**

(车辆)高度限制⑲　**MAXIMUM HEIGHT…**

(车辆)速度限制⑳　**MAXIMUM SPEED…; SPEED LIMIT…**

禁止鸣喇叭㉑　**NO HORN; NO HOOTER**

警告标志　**warning signs**

交叉路口㉒　**CROSSROADS**

急转弯或回转弯㉓　**BEND**

铁路与公路交叉㉔　**CROSSBUCK**

铁路道口　**RAILWAY CROSSING**

危险㉕　**DANGER!**

陡坡㉖　**STEEP HILL**

雨天路滑 **SLIPPERY WHEN WET**

傍山险路㉗ **BRINK OF PRECIPICE**

慢驶 **SLOW**

隧道㉘ **TUNNEL**

渡口㉙ **FERRY**

注意行人㉚ **BEWARE PEDESTRIANS, PEDESTRIANS AHEAD**

预告人行横道 **ADVANCE PEDESTRIAN CROSSING**

准备停车 **BE PREPARED TO STOP**

停车 **STOP**

让路 **YIELD**

人行横道 **PEDESTRIAN CROSSING**

工人施工 **DANGER! MEN WORKING; MEN AT WORK**

速度提示牌(排档提示牌) **advisory speed tab**

路标 **informatory signs, (Am.) guide signs**

指路牌 **signpost, finger-post, (Am.) guide-post, destination sign**

道路汇合 **MERGE**

入市区路线 **CITY ROUTE**

自行车路线 **BICYCLE ROUTE**

公里里程碑 **kilometre stone**

英里里程碑 **milestone**

地方处所介绍标志 **information signs**

路面标示 **carriageway markings, (Am.) road markings**

嵌钉人行横道 **studded crosswalk**

斑马条纹人行横道 **zebra crossing**

交通指挥灯 **traffic lights, traffic guide lights**

绿灯——直行或右转弯 **green—through, or turn right**

黄灯——注意,禁止一切车辆通行 **yellow—caution, stop**

红灯——禁止通行,可以右转弯 **red—stop, or turn right**

绿、黄灯——左转弯,掉头,直行,或右转弯 **green-and-yellow—turn left, U-turn, through or turn right**

柱式信号灯 **pedestal signal**

悬吊式信号灯 **pendant signal**

座式信号灯 **support signal**

车辆促动交通信号 **vehicle-actuated signal**

## 交通事故 **Traffic Accidents**

机动车辆肇事 **motor accident**

机动车辆交通事故 **motor traffic accident**

行人被撞倒 **pedestrian knocked down**

骑自行车者被撞下车 **cyclist knocked off the bike**

两车对撞 **head-on collision**

撞到路灯柱上 **hitting a lamppost**

后车撞前车 **running into the back of the preceding car**

汽车翻转 **car overturned**

汽车撞毁 **car smashed up**

汽车陷入沟里 **car ditched**

汽车事故伤亡 **road toll**

事故原因 cause of accident

无执照驾驶 driving without a licence

驾驶作风恶劣 reckless driving

酒后驾驶汽车 driving under the influence of alcohol

超速 speeding, violation of speed limit

违反交通规则 violation of traffic regulations

违反交通规则行为 traffic offence

违章驾驶行为 motoring offence

违反停放规定行为 parking offence

高速转弯 cornering at speed

直穿环行交叉 cutting across the roundabout

逆行驶入单向行车街道 driving anti-wise into a one-way street

不顾交通信号灯 ignoring traffic lights

冲红灯 running the red light

不遵守交通规则走路 jaywalking

疲劳驾驶 fatigue driving

驾驶能力衰退 impaired driving

炫目的车头灯光 glaring headlight

道路失修 road neglect

交通拥塞 traffic congestion, traffic jam

急刹车 sudden braking

作一百八十度转弯 making a U-turn

突然转向 swerving

侧滑 skidding

保护现场痕迹 securing the traces

度量刹车印 measuring the skid marks

检查车辆证件 examining car documents

交通事故现场图 condition-collision diagram

事故地点档案 accident location file

呼吸分析器测醉试验 breathalyser test

损伤赔偿 damages for injury

违反交通规则罚款 traffic violation fine

警告 caution

违章行为记入执照 endorsement of licence

吊销执照 revocation of licence

纪律处分 disciplinary action

## 公共汽车交通 Bus Service

公共汽车市线 urban bus service

公共汽车郊线 suburban bus service

城乡间公共汽车 country bus

市际公共汽车 interurban bus, intercity bus

公共汽车队 bus fleet

带拖卡的公共汽车 bus with trailer

伸缩连接　concertina con-
　nection
双层公共汽车　double-deck
　bus, double-decker
中途上落站　bus-stop
中途上落站牌　bus-stop plate
候车亭　bus shelter
终点站　bus terminal
路线指示牌　route indicator
气动折门　air-operated fold-
　ing door
电动滑门　power-operated
　sliding door
让乘客上车　picking up
　passengers
让乘客下车　dropping off
　passengers
司机驾驶室　driver's cabin, cab
司机座位　driver's seat
左座驾驶　left-hand drive
右座驾驶　right-hand drive
通道　gangway, aisle
站立位置　standing space,
　(Am.) standee space
站立乘客　standing passenger,
　(Am.) standee
拉手吊带　strap
拉着吊带站立的乘客　strap-
　hanger
座位靠背上的扶手铁杆　grab-
　rail
扶手铁柱　stanchion
让座　offering one's seat to
　another
乘务员　conductor
检票员　inspector
购票(付车费)　paying one's
　fare
售票　collecting fares

按段站收费办法　zonal fare
　system
一个票价路段　fare-stage
远近一律的车费　uniform
　fare for any distance
月票　monthly ticket
持月票乘车者　commuter
过段站下车　overriding
过段站补票　paying due fare
　for overriding
全线行车时间　overall running
　time
开车频率　frequency of service
每隔五分钟开一辆车　a five-
　minute frequency, buses
　running on a five-minute
　headway
交通拥挤时刻(高峰时间)　rush
　hours, peak hours
非交通拥挤时刻　off-peak
　hours
高峰交通量　peak traffic
通宵车　all-night service
交通运输调度　accommodation
　of traffic
更改行车路线　rerouting
公共汽车运行表　bus table
"请买票!"　"All fares,
　please!"
"禁止不购票乘车。"　"No fare
　dodging," "No bilking."
"下车请跟着!"　"Step along,
　please!" "Step lively,
　please!"
"不要让孩子踏上座位。"　"Don't
　let children put their feet
　on the seat."
"梯口禁止站立。"　"No travel-
　ling on the steps."

## 汽车总站 Central Bus Station

旅客大厅 passenger concourse

候车室 waiting hall

询问处 inquiry office

询问处服务员 inquiry clerk

票房 booking office, ticket office

售票窗口 ticket window

票房售票员 ticket clerk, booking clerk

电话订票 booking by phone

预售三天票 selling tickets three days in advance

退订购票 cancelling one's booking

临近开车时退订票 last-minute cancellation

退票付还价款 redeeming a ticket

请求签票延长有效期限 request for ticket validity extension endorsement

包裹行李处 parcels and luggage office

超重行李收费 overweight charge

托运行李 having luggage registered

小件行李寄存处 left luggage office, (Am.) checkroom

寄存行李 depositing luggage

取出行李 withdrawing luggage

汽车站站长 local traffic supervisor

各线班车离站站台 main service departure bays

长途班车 long-distance service

加班车 special bus

同班加开车 duplicate vehicle

包车(专车) chartered bus

终点站橱窗牌 destination blind

中途站 way-stop

(乘务员)叫站 calling out the stops

到站 arrival

卸客 discharging (dropping off) passengers

卸乘客行李 discharging (unloading) passengers' luggage

洗车场 washing bay, wash area

洗车装置 washing plant

保养场 servicing bay, maintenance bay

汽车站总停车库 depot

车房 garage

停车空位 parking gap

## 货车运输 Trucking

公路货运 freight road transport

总重 total weight

毛重 gross weight

皮重 tare

净重 net weight

容积 volume

体积 bulk, dimensions

货车装载 truck loading

载重量 load-carrying capacity

| | | | |
|---|---|---|---|
| 有效负载 | payload | 装卸坡台 | loading ramp |
| 装载高度 | loading height | 长距离运输 | long haul |
| 装载面积 | loading area | 短距离运输 | short haul |
| 装载限度 | loading limit | 无载行程 | dead mileage |
| 装满 | loading to capacity | 运输调度 | movement control |
| 轻载 | light loading | 急运(抢运) | rush transport |
| 超载 | overload | 运输车场 | transport park |
| 超载能力 | extra load-carrying capacity | 公路尽头 | roadhead |
| | | 清卸地点 | emptying point |
| 货物装卸 | freight handling | 送达地点 | delivery point |
| | | 卸载台 | discharging platform |

## 机动车辆　Motor Vehicles

| | | | |
|---|---|---|---|
| 运输车辆 | transport vehicle | 自卸卡车② | tip lorry, tipper, dump truck |
| 运输卡车① | lorry, truck | | |
| 重型运输卡车 | heavy-duty truck | 侧向自卸车③ | side-tip dumper |
| 中型运输卡车 | medium-duty truck | 三向自卸车 | three-way tipper |
| | | 底卸拖运车 | bottom-dump hauler |
| 轻型卡车 | light truck | 低架卡车 | low loader |
| 柴油机运输车辆 | diesel engine road vehicle (DERV) | 平台式运输车 | platform truck |
| 柴油机卡车 | diesel truck | 垂放边栏运输车 | dropside truck, dropsider |
| 自动装卸机械化运输车 mechanized lorry | | 牵挂式运输车④ | tractor-trailer |
| | | 搭挂式运输车 | semi-trailer |

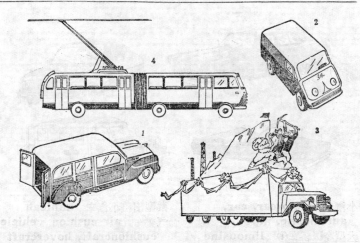

铰接式挂车  articulated trailer

铰接式六轮车  articulated six-wheeler

长型货物挂车  pole trailer, pole carrier

载重牵引车  prime mover

无车厢运货车  goods chassis

快速运货车  express freight car, express freighter

客货运输车  carryall

车后开门运输车①  estate car, shooting-brake, station wagon

全篷轻型运输车  van

轻型送货②  delivery van

无篷低栏小型运送车  pickup

公路运输集装箱车  frameless road haulage container

散装货物运输车  bulk carrier

救火车  fire engine

油槽车  petrol tanker

水槽车  drinking water tanker

冷藏车  refrigeration van, (Am.) reefer

邮车  mail van

广播宣传车  loudspeaker van, sound truck

汽车行列  motorcade

彩车(游行表演展览车)③  float

运输汽车队  caravan of trucks

载客车辆  passenger vehicle

无轨电车④  trolley-bus

架空接触电线  trolley wire, overhead contact line

聚电杆  trolley pole, contact pole

触轮  trolley wheel

有轨电车  tram, (Am.) streetcar

大型长途旅游客车  motor coach

小型客车  minibus

微型客车  microbus

工人上下班车  workers carrier

校车  school bus

教练车  training car

| | |
|---|---|
| 小汽车 motorcar, car, automobile, auto | 微型出租小汽车 minicab |
| 大型高级轿车① limousine | 气垫车 air cushion vehicle, cushioncraft, hovercraft |
| 小轿车② saloon (car), (Am.) sedan (car) | 活动房屋〔车〕 mobile home |
| 双座小汽车 coupé | 旅行用的大篷车 caravan |
| 折篷小汽车③ convertible (car) | 野营用车辆 camper |
| 硬顶小汽车 hard-top (car) | 救护车④ ambulance |
| 带天窗的小汽车 sun-roof car | 警车 police van, police car |
| 敞式汽车 open car | 摩托车 motorcycle, motor-bike |
| 蚬壳形汽车 fastback (car) | 小轮摩托车 motor scooter |
| 跑车 sports car | 机器脚踏两用车 moped, auto-cycle |
| 小型汽车 compact | 机动三轮车 motor cabin, cy-clecar, tricar |
| 微型汽车 minicar, bubble car | |
| 出租小汽车 taxi (cab) | 轻型越野车(吉普) jeep |

## 汽 车 Motorcar (Automobile)

| | |
|---|---|
| 发动机系 power system | 活塞 piston |
| 　汽油发动机⑤ petrol (gaso-line) engine | 活塞环 piston ring |
| 　柴油发动机 diesel engine, heavy oil engine | 连杆 connecting rod |
| 　汽缸体 cylinder block | 曲轴 crankshaft |
| 　汽缸盖 cylinder head | 飞轮 flywheel |
| | 凸轮轴 camshaft |
| | 进气阀 intake (inlet) |

valve
排气阀 exhaust valve
排气管 exhaust pipe
消声器 silencer, (Am.)
　muffler

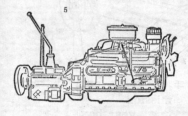

润滑系 lubrication system
　机油泵 oil pump
　机油盘(油槽) oil sump,
　　(Am.) oil pan
　机油滤清器 oil filter
供油系 fuel supply system
　油箱 fuel tank
　燃油滤清器 fuel filter
　空气滤清器 air filter
　汽油泵 fuel pump
　供油泵 fuel feed pump
　汽化器 carburettor
　喷油泵 injection pump
　喷油嘴 atomiser, injection
　　valve, injection nozzle
冷却系 cooling system
　散热器 radiator
　水泵 water pump
　风扇 cooling fan
　风扇皮带 V-belt, fan belt
电系 electric system
　发电机 dynamo (generator)

起动机 starter motor
分电器(配电盘) distributor
　(timer)
火花塞(火嘴) spark-plug
点火开关(点火钥匙) ignition
　switch (ignition key)
起动机开关(起动机按钮) start-
　er switch (starter button)
喇叭按钮 horn (hooter)
　button
头灯 head lamp, headlight
大灯(远距灯) driving light
小灯(近距灯) anti-dazzle
　(short range) light
翼子板灯 wing lamp, fender
　light
刹车灯 stop light, brake
　light
尾灯(后灯) taillight (rear
　lamp
雾灯 fog light
车侧标志灯 side marker
　light
方向指示灯 trafficator blink-
　er, (Am.) direction indica-
　tor, turn signal light
车厢内顶灯 dome light
仪表板照明灯 panel light,
　dash lamp
减光器开关(小灯开关) dimmer
　switch, dipswitch, (Am.)
　dimswitch
倒车灯 reversing light,
　backup light
机油警灯 oil warning light
顶篷灯 roof light
牌照灯 number plate light

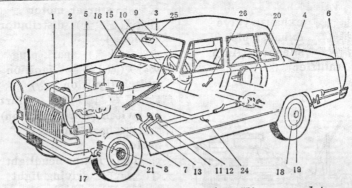

车体　**car body**

散热器护栅① **radiator grille**

发动机罩② **engine bonnet, (Am.) engine hood**

车篷③　**car roof**

汽车后部行李箱④　**car boot, luggage boot (Am.) baggage trunk**

后部车门　**tailgate**

车门与手把　**car door and handle**

前保险杠⑤　**front bumper**

后保险杠⑥　**rear bumper**

保险杠护垫　**bumper guard**

防护板(挡泥板)⑦　**wing, fender (mudguard)**

脚踏板　**running board**

车架　**chassis frame**

横梁　**cross-member**

前桥(前轴)　**front axle**

后桥(后轴)　**rear axle**

螺形弹簧⑧　**helical (coil) spring**

板簧　**leaf (laminated, plate) spring**

自动变速〔器〕　**automatic transmission**

手控变速〔器〕　**manual transmission**

变速箱　**gear box**

传动轴　**drive shaft, propeller shaft**

万向轴　**cardan shaft**

万向带(十字轴)　**universal joint**

离合器机组　**clutch assembly**

减振器　**damper, shock absorber, (Am.) snubber**

方向盘(驾驶盘)⑨　**steering wheel**

变速杆(换档杆)⑩　**gear shifting lever, gear change rod**

脚踏制动板(脚闸)⑪　**brake pedal, foot brake, (Am.) service brake**

离合器脚踏板⑫　**clutch pedal**

加速踏板(油门)⑬　**acceleration pedal, accelerator**

手闸⑭　**hand brake**

停车制动器　**parking brake**

紧急制动器　**emergency brake**

挡风玻璃⑮　**windscreen, (Am.) windshield**

风挡刮水器⑯　**windscreen wiper, (Am.) windshield**

wiper

车轮 wheel

轮辋⑰ wheel rim (wheel band)

轮盘⑱ wheel disc (wheel dish)

轮盖 wheel cover (wheel cap)

轮毂 wheel hub (wheel nave)

轮毂盖⑲ hub cover (hub cap)

双胎车轮 dual (double) wheel

备用车轮⑳ spare wheel

车轮制动器 wheel brake

制动鼓 brake drum

制动盘 brake disc

轮胎㉑ tyre

充气轮胎 pneumatic tyre

单管(无内胎)轮胎 tubeless tyre

白边轮胎 white-wall tyre

内胎 tyre tube

内胎气门和盖 tyre tube valve and cap

轮胎防滑链 tyre chain

仪表板㉒ dashboard, instrument panel

仪表㉓ instruments

安培表(电流表) ammeter, battery indicator

油温计 oil temperature gauge

油压表 oil pressure gauge

水温表 water temperature indicator

气压表 pressure gauge

油位表 fuel level gauge, petrol gauge, (Am.) gasoline level gauge

速度与里程表 speedometer with mileometer (mileage recorder, odometer)

车用时钟 car clock

车用无线电收音机 car radio

车内设备与装潢 interior trim and appointments

遮日板 sun shield, (Am.) sun visor

圆背坐椅 bucket seat

可折合坐椅 jump seat

可调靠背坐椅 reclining seat

坐椅调整手把㉔ seat adjusting handle

地毯 floor mat, auto carpet

后视镜㉕ driving mirror, rear view mirror

车门固定按钮 door lock knob

车窗升降器手把㉖ window riser (window raiser) handle

车顶通风装置 roof ventilation

导管通风装置 duct ventilation

司机个人用具匣㉗ cubby-hole, (Am.) glove compartment

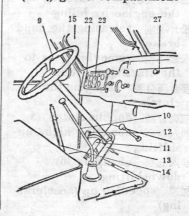

## 汽车驾驶　Driving

总的性能　overall perform-ance

操纵灵敏性　manoeuvrability

方向稳定性　directional stabi-lity

对路面的附着能力　road-hold-ing ability, grip

全面能见度　full (panoramic) visibility

前面能见度　forward visibility

后面能见度　backward visibil-ity

有限视界　restricted visibility

转弯半径　turning circle

爬坡能力　gradeability, climb-ing ability

底盘轴距　chassis wheelbase

汽车驾驶　car driving

入空档　placing gear in the neutral position

起动发动机　starting the en-gine

空转发动机加温　warming up the engine by idling

松开手闸　releasing the hand brake

入起动档　removing gear to the starting position

接合离合器　engaging the clutch

双离合器　double clutch

换入高档　changing high, up-shifting

换入低档　changing low, downshifting

加速　speeding up (accelerat-ing)

减速　slowing down (decelera-ting)

前进　going forward

超车　overtaking

用高速档经济车速行驶　cruising

开慢车　clocking over

全速行驶　driving at full speed

正常速度　normal speed

恒速　constant speed

快车道速度　expressway speed

向左转　turning left

向右转　turning right

掉头　turning round (turn-about)

倒车　backing, reversing

刹车　braking

停车　stopping

停放汽车　parking

新发动机磨合运转　running in of a new engine

通过障碍物　negotiating an obstacle

停车后重新起动　re-starting

驶入车房　garaging

上坡起动　uphill starting

下坡制动　downhill braking

加油(踏油门)　bending the throttle, stepping on the gas

前轮驱动　front-wheel drive

后轮驱动　rear-wheel drive

四轮驱动　four-wheel drive

汽车对方向盘反应迟钝　under-steer

汽车对方向盘反应过敏　over-steer

推车起动　push starting

## 汽车维修　Car Maintenance and Repair

汽车修理工　car repairman (auto-mechanic)

日常维修　routine maintenance

调整发动机　tuning up

故障检查和排除　troubleshooting, troublehunting

全面检修　overhaul

发生故障　breakdown

故障　failure, stoppage

故障部位　trouble spot

发动机毛病　engine trouble

发动机滞行　sluggish engine

发动机停顿　engine stalling

发动机失灵　engine seized up

发动机积垢　engine sludging

活塞积碳　carbon on piston

火花塞塞嘴变质　deteriorated spark plug tip

离合器打滑　clutch slipping

离合器发抖　clutch jerky

刹车不紧　brake not holding well

挂档困难　trouble in gearshift

汽化系统有毛病　trouble in the carburetion system

点火系统有毛病　trouble in the ignition system

电气系统有毛病　trouble in the electric system

后桥有敲击声　knocks in the rear axle

车轮打滑　wheel skidding

车轮定位不准　wheels not in alignment

发动机爆震　pinking

左右偏离　yawing

左右(横向)颠簸　rolling

前后(纵向)颠簸　pitching

空转　wheel spinning

机械故障　mechanical defect, mechanical bug

轮胎穿孔　tyre puncture

漏气轮胎　flat tyre

爆胎　tyre blowout, tyre break

燃油汽管渗漏　fuel and vapour line leaking

轮胎翻修　tyre soling

胎冠翻修　tyre recapping

补胎　tyre patching

换胎　tyre changing

去碳　carbon removing

去锈　rust removing

车身镶板矫正　body panel straightening

加油站　filling station, petrol station, (Am.) gasoline station

加油泵　petrol (gasoline) filling pump

维修车间　maintenance shop

检修坑　repair pit

车用千斤顶　car jack

洗车机　car washer

轻便车台　portable car ramps

楔形车轮垫块　wheel chock

黄油枪　grease gun

润滑油罐　lubricant (oil) can

喷枪　spray gun

铆枪　riveting gun

发动机清洗枪　engine cleaning gun (engine cleaner)

机动打气机　motor driven air

pump

脚踏打气机　foot-operated air pump

气焊气割机　gas welding and cutting outfit

轻便空气压缩机　portable air compressor

发动机修理架　engine repair stand

转车台　turntable

齿轮与轴承拆卸器　gear and bearing puller

小齿轮拆除工具　pinion removal tool

轮胎拆装杆　tyre lever

轮胎撑开器　tyre spreader

橡皮木槌　rubber mallet

丝锥板牙套具　tap and die set

老虎钳　vice

电池充电机　battery charger

头灯灯光定位器　headlight beam setter

麂皮　chamois leather

废棉纱　cotton waste

## 摩托车　Motorcycle

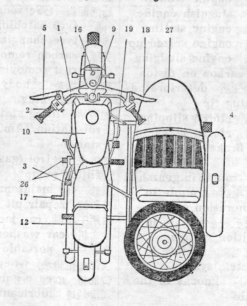

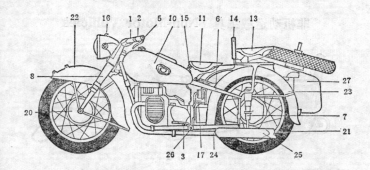

两缸四冲程发动机 **two-cylinder four-stroke motor**
单缸二冲程发动机 **single cylinder two-stroke motor**
车把① **handlebar**
变速转把② **gear twist grip (handlebar gear change)**
脚控变速杆③ **foot-operated gear lever**
节流阀转把(油门转把)④ **throttle twist grip**
离合器握把⑤ **clutch lever**
车架⑥ **frame**
缓冲器⑦ **telescopic springing**
可伸缩筒式前叉⑧ **telescopic fork**
转向减振器⑨ **steering damper**
汽油箱⑩ **fuel tank, petrol tank, (Am.) gasoline tank**
机油箱 **oil box**
悬臂式鞍座⑪ **cantiliver saddle**
双座鞍⑫ **dual seat**
后座⑬ **pillion**
鞍座手把⑭ **saddle grip**
鞍座支架⑮ **saddle bracket**

点火开关⑯ **ignition switch**
电起动器 **dynastarter**
脚踏起动器⑰ **kickstarter**
前闸手柄(手闸)⑱ **front brake hand lever (hand brake)**
后闸踏板(脚闸)⑲ **rear brake pedal (foot brake)**
轮毂闸⑳ **hub brake**
车轮㉑ **wheel**
前挡泥板㉒ **front fender**
后挡泥板㉓ **rear fender**
挡泥瓣 **mud flap**
排气管㉔ **exhaust pipe**
消声器(排气箱)㉕ **silencer, muffler (exhaust box)**
脚垫㉖ **foot-rest**
蓄电池存放匣 **battery compartment**
工具箱 **tool box**
摩托车撑架 **motorcycle stand**
风挡 **windscreen(Am.) windshield**
行李架 **luggage rack**
鞍形袋 **saddle bag, panniers**
边车㉗ **sidecar**
拖车(挂车) **trailer**

## 非机动运载工具　Non-Motor Vehicles

三轮车　**tricycle**
载客三轮车　**pedicab**
轮椅①　**wheel chair,invalid carriage**
手推童车　**stroller**
手推婴儿车　**perambulator (pram), (Am.)baby carriage**
手推车　**push-cart, hand-cart**
两轮手推车　**hand barrow**
独轮手推车　**wheelbarrow, single-wheel barrow**
脚轮小台(小台车)②　**trolley**
人力车　**rickshaw**

轿子　**sedan chair**
担架　**stretcher, litter**
畜力车　**beast-drawn cart**
马车　**horse carriage**
牛车　**ox-cart**
雪橇③　**sleigh, sledge, (Am.) sled, cutter**
长雪橇　**bobsleigh, bobsled**
滑橇　**sledge runner**
驮畜　**pack animal**
驮畜队　**pack train**
骆驼队　**caravan of camels**

## 自行车　Bicycle

车架④　**frame**
前管⑤　**head tube**
上管⑥　**top tube(cross bar)**
下管⑦　**down tube**
立管⑧　**seat tube**
立叉⑨　**seat stays(rear fork)**
平叉⑩　**chain stays(bottom fork)**
前叉⑪　**front fork**
前叉锁母⑫　**head lock ring**
前叉立管⑬　**front fork tube**
叉腿⑭　**fork blade**

灯架⑮　**lamp bracket**
车把⑯　**handlebar**
把套⑰　**handlebar grip**
后闸手把⑱　**rear brake hand lever**
前闸手把⑲　**front brake hand lever**
把立管⑳　**handlebar stem**
翘把　**rise handlebar**
车轮㉑　**wheel**
轮胎(外胎)㉒　**tyre (outer cover)**

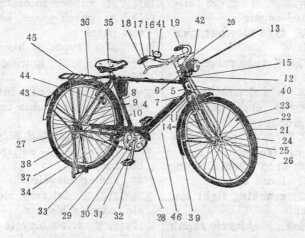

内胎　tube
内胎气门阀(气嘴)㉓ tube valve
轮圈(轮箍)㉔ rim (band)
轮辐条㉕ wire spoke
轮毂㉖ wheel hub
轮轴　wheel axle
飞轮㉗ free wheel, gear
　wheel
飞轮轮缘(飞轮外套) free
　wheel sprocket
飞轮千斤(棘轮爪) ratchet pawl
链条传动装置 chain drive
链轮㉘ chain wheel, chain
　sprocket
传动链(滚子链条)㉙ drive
　chain, bushed chain
链条调整装置 chain adjuster
中轴㉚ bottom bracket bear-
　ing axle
曲柄㉛ crank
脚蹬㉜ pedal
车闸　brake
蹬形闸㉝ stirrup brake

闸拉杆　pull rod, brake rod
闸皮㉞ brake shoe
钳形闸　caliper brake
钢闸绳(带套) bowden cable
涨闸　internal expanding
　hub brake
附件　accessories
弹簧鞍座㉟ spring seat sad-
　dle
尾架㊱ carrier
撑架㊲ cycle stand
单撑架　kick-stand
全链罩　full chain guard
半链罩㊳ partial chain guard
挡泥板㊴ mudguard
保险叉㊵ safety fork
车铃㊶ bicycle bell
车灯㊷ bicycle lamp
尾灯㊸ rear reflector
摩电机㊹ dynamo
车锁㊺ bicycle lock
打气筒㊻ bicycle air pump,
　tyre inflater

自行车故障与维修　cycle failure and repair

轮胎爆裂　tyre blowout, tyre break

车胎阀门漏气　tube valve leaking

车轮摇晃　wheel wobbling

链条滑离链轮　chain slipping off sprocket

链条滑离飞轮外套　chain slipping off free wheel rim

飞轮打滑　free wheel slipping

曲柄松滑　loose crank

蹬转困难　cranking tight and difficult

自行车修理工具　bicycle repair kit

自行车扳手　bicycle wrench set

橡皮胶　rubber cement

橡皮胶水　rubber solution

内胎补片　patch piece, blow-out patch

自行车种类　types of bicycle

旅行用轻便自行车　touring bicycle

双梁载重自行车　heavy-duty bicycle with double top tubes

折叠式自行车　folding bicycle

伸缩式小轮径自行车　collapsible bicycle

赛车　racing bicycle

送货用自行车　delivery bicycle, carrier bicycle

特技自行车　trick bicycle

儿童用自行车　child's bicycle

女用自行车　woman's bicycle

多档自行车　multi-speed bicycle

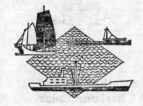

# 航 运 Shipping

## 港 口 Port

商港　commercial port
自由港　free port
出发港　port of departure
停泊港　port of call
目的港　port of destination
到达港　port of arrival
避难港(避风港)　port of distress
不冻港　ice-free port, warmwater port
天然港　natural harbour
人工港　artificial harbour
港口结构　harbour accommodation

航道　navigation channel
激光航道标　laser channel marker
引水站　pilot station
引水船　pilot boat
港口导航系统　harbour navigation system
防波堤　breakwater, mole
柱形浮标①　spar (pillar) buoy
罐形浮标②　can buoy
球形浮标③　spherical buoy
鼓形浮标(浮鼓)④　drum buoy
鸣笛浮标　whistle buoy

灯浮标 light buoy①
港池 harbour basin
锚地 anchorage
港外泊地 roadstead (roads)
泊位 berth
系泊处 moorings
系泊浮筒② mooring buoy
系缆桩 bollard, dolphin
灯塔 lighthouse, beacon
灯船③ lightship
微波航道信标 microwave course beacon
码头 dock, wharf, quay
顺岸码头 wharf
突堤码头 pier
栈桥 jetty
浮码头 floating pier, pontoon
旅客码头 passenger pier
包装货码头 packed cargo wharf
散装货码头 bulk cargo wharf
集装箱码头 container wharf
油码头 oil wharf
船坞 dock
港口轮渡 harbour ferry
货仓 warehouse, godown
货棚 storage shed
堆场 store space
港口铁路侧线 harbour railway siding

气象站 weather station
港口雷达 harbour radar
信号台 signal tower
避风所 storm shelter
港务局 port administration bureau
港务机关 port authority
海关 customs
检疫 quarantine
燃料供应船 bunkering tanker
杂货供应船 chandlering launch
淡水船 freshwater tanker
供应和补给 supply and replenishment
检修设备 servicing and repair facilities
货运 freightage
吞吐量 volume of freight traffic
转运量 volume of transhipment

# 机动船舶 Powered Vessels

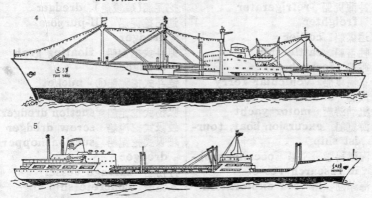

蒸汽机船 steamship (SS), steamer
内燃机船 motor vessel (MV)
汽轮机船 turbine steamer
电力推进船 electric (propulsion) ship
柴油机电动船 diesel-electric ship
核动力船 nuclear-powered ship
喷水推进船 hydrojet-propelled ship
机帆船 motor junk
客船 passenger ship
定期航船(班船) liner
定期远洋船 ocean liner
邮船 mail liner
沿海船 coasting vessel, coaster
不定期不定线船 tramp
内河轮船 river steamer
客货船 passenger-cargo ship
货船 freighter, cargo ship

五万吨级远洋货轮④ 50,000-ton-class ocean-going freighter
油船⑤ oil tanker
超级油船 super tanker
巨型〔原〕油船 very large crude oil carrier (VLCC)
拖船 tugboat
载驳母船(子母船)⑥ lighter aboard ship (LASH)
载驳货船 barge carrier
干货船 dry cargo ship

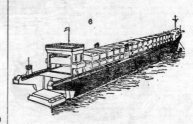

散装货船 bulk carrier
集装箱船 container ship
冷藏货船 refrigerator freighter
运煤船 collier
牲畜船 cattle ship
渡船 ferry (boat)
车辆渡船 vehicular ferry
汽艇 motorboat
机动游艇 motor yacht
游览船 excursion boat, tourist ship
海洋科学研究船 oceanographic research vessel
海洋勘探船 sea exploration vessel
石油钻井船 drilling platform, rig
顶推船① pushboat, pusher
破冰船② ice-breaker

测量船 surveying vessel
航标船 buoy tender
挖泥船(疏浚船) dredger
通用挖泥船 all-purpose dredger
抓斗式挖泥船 floating grab dredger
链斗式挖泥船③ bucket (ladder) dredger
吸扬式挖泥船 suction dredger
绞吸式挖泥船 screw dredger
耙吸式挖泥船 suction hopper dredger
打捞船 salvage vessel
水泥船 concrete ship
气垫船④ hovercraft, air cushion craft, surface effect ship (SES)
水翼船⑤ hydrofoil
双体船 twin-hull vessel

## 非机动船 Non-powered Vessels

驳船　barge, lighter
帆船　sailing vessel
单桅纵帆船　sloop
双桅横帆船　brig
三桅帆船　bark, barque
张帆小游艇⑥　sailing dinghy
中国式帆船⑦　junk
　　船桅　mast
　　船帆　sail
　　翼帆　studding sail
　　船首三角帆　flying jib, jib
　　帆桁　yard
　　索具　rigging
　　支索(稳正索)　stay
　　船篷　awning
　　船舵　rudder
　　舵柄　tiller

撑篙船　punt
篙　pole
用篙撑船　punting
帆布艇　canvas canoe
橡皮艇　rubber dinghy
独木舟　dugout
浮桥舟　pontoon
木筏　raft

竹筏　bamboo raft
羊皮筏　sheepskin raft

舢板(舢舨)　sampan
短桨　paddle
划桨(无桨叉支撑)　paddling
荡桨(有桨叉支撑)　rowing
划艇　rowboat
桨　oar
桨叉　rowlock, oarlock
摇橹船⑧　sculling boat
橹⑨　scull
摇橹　sculling

## 客货船 Passenger and Cargo Ship

船身 hull
船头 bow
船尾 stern
舷(船边) side
左舷① port (side)
右舷② starboard (side)
船首旗杆③ jack staff
船尾旗杆④ ensign staff
公司旗 house flag
开船旗 blue peter
两脚桅 bipod mast
锚和锚链⑤ anchor and cable
起锚机⑥ windlass
水尺 draught, draft
载重线标志 Plimsoll mark
吃水线 water line
前桅 foremast

主桅 main mast
后桅 mizzen mast
前甲板⑦ fore deck
后甲板⑧ aft deck, after deck
装卸吊杆⑨ cargo derrick
吊杆柱(将军柱)⑩ Samson post, king post
装卸绞车⑪ cargo winch
救生艇吊艇柱⑫ lifeboat davit
舱口⑬ hatch (way)
舱壁 bulkhead
烟囱⑭ funnel
通气筒⑮ ventilator, vent
栏杆⑯ railing
系船缆索 hawser, mooring rope

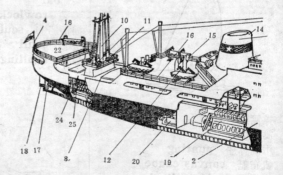

| | |
|---|---|
| 系缆桩　**bitt, bollard** | 主甲板㉔　**main deck** |
| 挡鼠隔　**rat guard** | 后甲板㉕　**quarter deck** |
| 舷门　**gangway** | 甲板间　**tween decks** |
| 舷梯　**accommodation ladder** | 甲板室　**deck house** |
| 绳梯　**Jacob's ladder** | 旅客舱室　**passenger cabin** |
| 舷窗　**porthole** | 特等客舱套间　**stateroom suite** |
| 探照灯　**searchlight** | 豪华套间　**de luxe suite** |
| 左舷灯——红色　**port light——** | 餐厅　**dining saloon** |
| 　**red** | 休息室　**lounge** |
| 右舷灯——绿色　**starboard** | 会议室　**conference room** |
| 　**light——green** | 海图室　**chart room** |
| 驱动系统　**driving unit** | 船员食堂　**crew's mess room** |
| 螺旋桨⑰　**screw propeller** | 厨房　**galley** |
| 螺旋桨轴　**shaft** | 厨具室　**pantry** |
| 舵⑱　**rudder** | 厕所　**toilet, head** |
| 主机⑲　**main engine** | 货舱㉖　**hold** |
| 辅机⑳　**auxiliary engine** | 行李舱　**luggage locker** |
| 船首楼㉑　**forecastle** | 贵重货舱　**treasure room** |
| 船尾楼㉒　**poop** | 备用燃料舱　**reserve bunker** |
| 桥楼(驾驶楼)㉓　**bridge** | 压载舱　**ballast tank** |

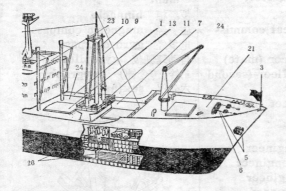

污水舱 bilge
燃料柜(燃料舱) fuel tank
淡水柜(淡水舱) freshwater tank
制淡水设备 freshwater distilling plant
容积吨位 capacity tonnage
总登记吨位 gross registered tonnage

净登记吨位 net registered tonnage
净排水量(空船排水量) net displacement tonnage
总排水量(满载排水量) gross displacement tonnage
载重吨位 deadweight tonnage

## 航 海 Navigation

远洋航行 ocean voyage
初航 maiden voyage
船队 fleet
护航队 convoy
商船队 merchant fleet
船只 vessel
国产船 China-built ship
外籍船 foreign-nationality ship
租用船 chartered ship
海员 seaman
全体船员 crew
船长 captain, master, skipper
政治委员 political commissar
大副 chief officer (mate)
二副 second officer (second mate)
三副 third officer (third mate)
事务长 purser
轮机长 chief engineer
二管轮 second engineer
三管轮 third engineer
大管事 chief steward
二管事 second steward
导航员 navigator

舵手 quartermaster, helmsman
水手长 boatswain (bosun)
水手 sailor
船上理货员 supercargo
船上木工 ship's carpenter (Chips)
驾驶室 wheelhouse
航海日志 logbook
海图 chart
舵轮 steering wheel, helm
航海仪器 navigation instrument
罗经柜 binnacle
磁罗经 magnetic compass
电罗经 gyro compass
自动驾驶仪 gyropilot
车铃(传令钟) telegraph
六分仪 sextant

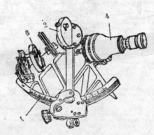

刻度盘① calibrated scale
指标镜② rotating mirror
地平镜③ fixed mirror
望远镜④ telescope
拖曳式计程仪 patent log
陀螺稳定器 gyro stabilizer
回声测深器 echo sounder
无线电测向仪 radio direction-finder
电子导航仪定位 ascertaining position by electronic navigator
船位显示器 plan position indicator (PPI)
航海时计 marine chronometer
雷达导航 radar pilotage
雷达装置 radar unit
扫描器 scanner
显像装置 display unit
"多普勒"测距仪 Doppler ranger
汽笛 siren, whistle
航行灯 navigation light
航道 fairway
航向 course
起锚启航 weighing anchor
解缆开航 unmooring, slipping the moorings
在航行中 under way
全速 full speed
中速 moderate speed
慢速 slow speed
微速 dead slow speed
全速前进 full speed ahead
微速后退 dead slow astern
航速18节(海里/小时) speed of 18 knots (nm/hr)
顶流航行 sailing against the current
顺流航行 sailing with the current
涟波(1级海况) rippled sea
小浪(2级海况) smooth sea
轻浪(3级海况) slight sea
中浪(4级海况) rather rough sea
强浪(5级海况) rough sea
波峰 crest
波谷 trough
浪花 spray
暴风 storm
飓风 hurricane
台风 typhoon
旋风 cyclone
轻雾 mist
大雾 thick fog
能见度好 visibility good
能见度差 visibility poor
涨潮 flood tide
落潮 ebb tide
航线正确 on the right course
航线偏误 on the wrong course
方位 bearing(s)
航行顺利 plain sailing
抛锚 dropping (casting) anchor
系缆 mooring
港岸停泊 in port
靠码头 in dock
出港证 clearance permit
航海健康申明书 marine declaration of health
检疫合格证 health clearance papers
海事报告 sea protest
发送信息(发送信号) sending a message (sending a signal)

接收信息(接收信号) acknowledging a message (acknowledging a signal)

检疫通信(检疫信号) pratique message signal

判定位置 locating

无线电报 radiotelegraphy

高频无线电话 VHF radiotelephony

声号 sound signal

摩氏信号灯 Morse signalling lamp

摩氏手旗信号 Morse signalling by handflags

摩氏手臂信号 Morse signalling by arms

航海手旗信号 semaphore

## 海难救助 Salvage

公海事故 accident on the high seas

碰撞 collision

失火 on fire

爆炸 explosion

操纵装置失灵 steering gear damaged

搁浅 run aground

触礁 hit a submerged reef

发动机故障 engine trouble

危险船倾 dangerous list

出现漏水 sprung a leak

漂浮 adrift, drifting

操纵失灵 disabled

遇险 in distress

下沉 sinking

船只遇难 shipwreck

弃船 abandon ship

生存者求援 survivors require assistance

呼救电报 distress call

呼救信号 SOS

声音信号 sound signal

视觉信号 visual signal

烟雾信号 smoke signal

救助队 rescue party

打捞队 salvage party

救火船 fireboat

遇险位置在北纬＿＿度, 东经＿＿度 position of distress at latitude ＿＿ degrees north, longitude ＿＿ degrees east

救助船① salvage vessel

沉船② wreck, sunken ship

浮筒打捞法③ lifting a wreck by pontoons

压气抽水法④ refloating a wreck by using compressed air to blow out the water

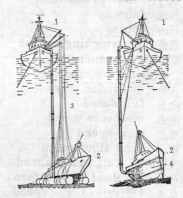

潜水员 diver

蛙人⑤ frogman

救生火箭　**life rocket**
救生衣⑨　**life jacket**
空气救生衣　**air jacket**
救生圈⑩　**life buoy**
救生带　**life belt**
伤亡人数　**casualties**

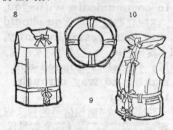

水中呼吸器⑥　**aqualung**
橡皮脚掌⑦　**flipper**
救生设备　**life-saving apparatus, life-saving kit**
救生衣物⑧　**life preserver**
救生艇　**lifeboat**
救生筏　**life raft**

## 国际通语信号旗　International Code Flags

信号旗　**code flag, signal flag**
字母旗①　**letter flag**
回答旗②　**answering pennant (answering flag)**
数字旗③　**numeral flag**
代旗④　**substitute flag**
单字母信号　**single-letter signals.**

A　我下面有潜水员；请慢速远离我。　**I have a diver down; keep well clear at slow speed.**

B　我正在装、卸或载运危险货物。　**I am taking in, or discharging, or carrying dangerous goods.**

C　是（肯定或"前组信号的意义应理解为肯定的"）。　**Yes (affirmative or "The significance of the previous group should be read in the affirmative").**

D　请让开我；我操纵困难。　**Keep clear of me; I am manoeuvring with difficulty.**

E　我正在向右转向。　**I am altering my course to starboard.**

F　我操纵失灵；请与我通信。　**I am disabled; communicate with me.**

G　我需要引水员。（在渔场由邻近一起作业的渔船使用时，它的意思是"我正在收网"。）　**I require a pilot. (When made by fishing vessels operating in close proximity on the fishing grounds, it means: "I am hauling nets.")**

H　我船上有引水员。　**I have a pilot on board.**

I　我正在向左转向。　**I am altering my course to port.**

J 我船失火，并且船上有危险货物，请远离我。 **I am on fire and have dangerous cargo on board, keep well clear of me.**

K 我希望与你通信。 **I wish to communicate with you.**

L 你应立即停船。 **You should stop your vessel instantly.**

M 我船已停，并且没有对水速度。 **My vessel is stopped and making no way through the water.**

N 不(否定或"前组信号的意义应理解为否定的")。(这个信号仅可以用视觉或用音响信号发出。在用话音或无线电发送这个信号时应该用"NO"字。) **No (negative or "The significance of the previous group should be read in the negative").(This signal may be given only visually or by sound. For voice or radio transmission the signal should be "NO".)**

O 有人落水。 **Man overboard.**

P (在港内)本船将要出海，所有人员应立即回船。 **(In harbour) All persons should report on board as the vessel is about to proceed to sea.**
(在船上，当由渔船使用时,意为:) 我的网缠在障碍物上。 **(At sea, it may be used by fishing vessels to mean:) My nets have come fast upon an obstruction.**

Q 我船没有染疫，请发给进口检疫证。 **My vessel is "healthy" and I request free pratique.**

R 你可谨慎地驶过我船。 **You may feel your way past me.**

S 我的机器正在开倒车。 **My engines are going astern.**

T 请让开我，我正在对拖网作业。 **Keep clear of me; I am engaged in pair trawling.**

U 你正在临近危险中。 **You are running into danger.**

V 我需要援助。 **I require assistance.**

W 我需要医疗援助。 **I require medical assistance.**

X 中止你的意图，并注意我发送的信号。 **Stop carrying out your intentions and watch for my signals.**

Y 我正在拖走锚。 **I am dragging my anchor.**

Z 我需要一艘拖轮。(在渔场由邻近一起作业的渔船使用时，它的意思是"我正在放网"。) **I require a tug. (When made by fishing vessels operating in close proximity on the fishing grounds it means: "I am shooting nets.")**

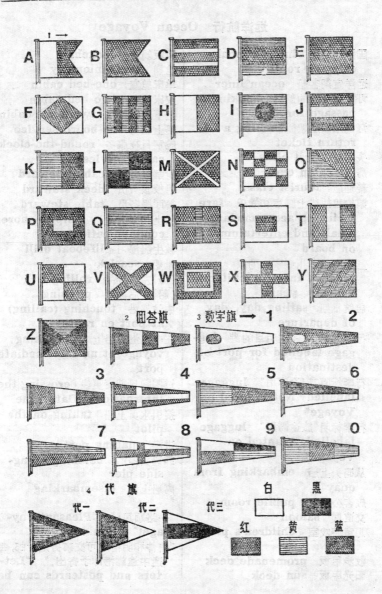

## 远洋航行 Ocean Voyage

国际航海线 international shipping route

远洋定期客船 ocean liner

订购到____的船票 booking a passage for____

订购来回船票 booking a return ticket

头等舱 first class

房舱 cabin class

普通舱 tourist class

票价包括船上膳宿和娱乐 fare including accommodation, meals and entertainment on board

____岁以下儿童票价酌减 reduced fare for children under____years

启航日期 sailing day, day of departure

行李贴上标签,注明目的港 luggage labelled for port of destination

行李标明"旅途不用" luggage labelled "Not Wanted on Voyage"

行李标明"旅途需用" luggage labelled "Wanted on Voyage"

从码头上船 embarking from quay

旅客公用室 public room

交谊厅 saloon

儿童游戏室 children's playroom

散步甲板 promenade deck

阳光甲板 sun deck

甲板躺椅 deckchair

舱梯 companionway

单床舱室 one-bed cabin

双床舱室 two-bed cabin

上下双铺舱室 two-berth cabin

船上服务 on-board service

舱室日夜服务 round-the-clock cabin service

舱室服务员 cabin steward

甲板服务员 deck steward

餐厅服务员 table steward

船上和岸上通讯 ship-to-shore communication

救生艇演习 lifeboat drill

晕船 seasick

(船)左右摇晃 rolling

(船)前后颠簸 pitching

中途靠港 touching (calling) at port en route

在中途港离船上岸 breaking voyage at an intermediate port

过国际日期变更线 crossing the International Date Line

接引水员上船 taking on the pilot

进港 making port

靠码头停泊 berthing alongside pier

离船上岸 disembarking

"一路顺风!" "Pleasant voyage!" ("Bon voyage!")

"信件和明信片可交事务处付邮,每逢中途靠港即予寄出。" "Letters and postcards can be

mailed through the purser's office and will be forwarded from each port of call."

"航行途中可用无线电话和电报与岸上通讯。" "Radio telephone and telegraph facilities are available while at sea."

"贵重物品可寄存事务处保险箱。" "Valuables may be deposited in safe deposit boxes at the purser's office."

"停膳概不退款。" "No refund will be made for meals not taken."

"不要惊慌,这是演习。" "Don't panic! This is a drill."

"旅客可在船上接待亲友,费用自付。" "Guests may be entertained on board at the passenger's expense."

"请来访者离船返岸。" "All visitors ashore!"

"东(西)行过国际日期变更线,加(减)一天。" "One day is gained (lost) on crossing the International Date Line eastward (westward)."

## 货物处理　Cargo Handling

货物种类　cargo classification
过境货物　transit cargo
转运货物　transshipment cargo
运往____的货物　cargo in transit to____
通运货物　through cargo
包装货　packed cargo
散装货　bulk cargo
杂货　general cargo
甲板货　deck cargo
冷气货　air-cooled cargo
尺码货,轻泡货　measurement cargo
笨大货物　bulky cargo
超长货物　lengthy cargo
超重货物　heavy lift cargo
贵重货物　precious (valuable) cargo
货物运输　cargo transport
进口货物　import cargo
出口货物　export cargo
空运　air transport
陆运　overland transport
海运　sea transport
水运　water transport
水陆联运　coordinated water-land transport
运输保险　transportation insurance
订舱位　booking shipping space
提货单　bill of lading (B/L)
发货人(发货单位)　shipper, consignor
收货人(收货单位)　consignee
码头工人　docker
装卸工人　stevedore, (Am.) longshoreman
领班　foreman
理货员　tallyman, cargo-checker
码头管理员　wharfinger
仓库管理员　warenouse (godown) keeper

商品检查员 cargo surveyor

熏烟消毒员 fumigation officer

称货员 weighman

吊车司机 craneman

装货 loading, pickup

卸货 unloading, discharging

积载图(船图) stowage (cargo) plan

积载系数 stowage factor

水尺 draft

舱单(货物清单) manifest, cargo list

检舱 hold inspection

清舱 hold cleaning

地脚货 sweepings

熏舱消毒 hold fumigation

垫舱 dunnaging, padding

垫舱板 dunnage plank

防擦板 chafing plate

装载(码垛) cargo stowing

隔票 cargo separation

混装 mixed loading

翻舱 cargo shifting

平舱 cargo trimming

超载 overload

纠正左(右)舷倾 correcting a port (starboard) list

压舱物 ballast

货物多溢 cargo overlanded

货物短缺 cargo shortlanded

索赔 claim for compensation

延滞费 demurrage

驳运费 lighterage

堆存费(仓库费) stowage

空舱费 dead freight

## 装卸机具 Loading and Unloading Gear

门座起重机(龙门吊车)① gantry crane

搬运吊车 transfer crane

旋臂转柱起重机 slewing portal crane

桥吊(装卸桥)② bridge crane

塔吊 tower crane

电吊 electric crane

浮吊③ floating crane

伸臂起重机④ cantilever crane

岸吊 shore crane

斜槽煤吊 coal chute crane

流动式吊车 mobile crane

移动式吊车 travellift

锤头式吊车 hammer-head crane

汽车式起重机⑤ truck crane

叉车(铲车)⑥ forklift

斗式铲车⑦ bucket lift truck

跨道车⑧ straddle truck

台式升降装卸车 elevating platform truck

货盘车 pallet truck

底盘车 chassis

台车 bogie

自动倾卸卡车 tipper

牵引车(拖头) tractor, hustler

拖车(挂车) trailer

皮带输送机⑨ belt conveyor

吸粮机 grain elevator (sucker)

吸铁吊具 lifting magnet

堆货机 stacking machine

抓斗 grab

漏斗 funnel

摇臂吊杆　derrick
滑车⑩　block, pulley
吊货钢丝绳　cargo runner

吊杆负荷　capacity of derrick
卷扬机(绞车)⑪　winch
链式起重机(葫芦)⑫　chain hoist

网络　**cargo net**
装卸扣(钩环)　**shackle**
装卸钩(手钩)　**cargo hook**
撬杠　**crowbar**
吊货盘　**cargo tray**
索具　**tackle**
吊索　**sling**
帐篷　**tent**
油布　**tarpaulin**
帆布　**canvas**
集装箱装卸桥　**gantry container crane, portainer**

装卸桥轨道　**gantry container crane rail**
移动式集装箱吊运车　**transtainer**
外伸框架吊运车　**outrigger**
轨道式船用桥吊　**shipboard gantry crane**
堆装吊车　**stack crane**
堆装跨道车　**stacking straddle carrier**
装箱机　**container loader**

## 集装箱运输　Containerized traffic

集装箱化　**containerization**
集装箱船①　**container ship**
半集装箱船　**semi-container ship**
集装箱两用船　**convertible container ship**
集装箱专用列车　**container unit train**
集装箱港　**container port**
人工岛港　**port island**
集装箱集散站　**container terminal**
集装箱仓库　**container depot**
吊上吊下　**lift on/lift off (Lo/Lo)**
开上开下　**roll on/roll off (Ro/Ro)**

(车辆)开上开下船　**roll on/roll off ship**
载驳货船　**lighter aboard ship (LASH)**
集装箱场　**container yard (CY)**
集装箱货运站　**container freight station (CFS)**
整箱货　**full container load (FCL)**
拼箱货　**less than container load (LCL)**
密封集装箱　**sealed container**
开顶集装箱　**open top container**
侧开门集装箱　**side door container**
侧壁全开式集装箱　**open side**

container

通风集装箱 ventilated container

干货集装箱② dry cargo container

散装货集装箱 bulk container

汽车集装箱 car container

牲畜集装箱③ pen container

罐状集装箱 tank container

板架集装箱 flat rack container

冷藏集装箱 refrigerated container

保温集装箱 insulated container

内柱式集装箱 interior post type container

外柱式集装箱 outside post type container

折叠式集装箱 collapsible container

薄壳式集装箱 monocoque container

装箱 vanning

拆箱 devanning

门到门运输 door-to-door transportation

门到场 door to CY

门到站 door to CFS

紧固作业 lashing operation

集装箱运输方式 container transport systems

底盘车方式 chassis system

海——陆公司方式 Sea-Land system

跨运车方式 straddle carrier system

麦逊公司方式 Matson system

搬运吊车方式 transfer crane

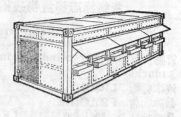

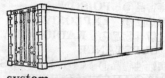

system

集装箱海上运输公司方式 Container Marine Lines system, (CML system)

场内搬运车方式 internal transfer vehicle system (ITV system)

快速集装箱装卸方式 speedtainer system

劳托维克装卸方式 Loutovick system

场地起重机装卸方式 yard crane system

集装箱码头 container wharf

(集装箱)堆场 marshalling yard

集装箱货运站 container freight station (CFS)

箱位 slot

集装箱出入口 dock

间档 bay

装货跳板 dock leveler

地秤 platform truck scale

# 货物标志和货物残损　Cargo Marks and

## Cargo Damage

货物指示标志 **cargo indication marks**

液体货物 **LIQUID**

易碎物品 **FRAGILE**

易燃物品① **IMFLAMMABLE**

易腐物品 **PERISHABLE**

危险物品 **DANGEROUS**

毒害品② **POISON**

爆炸品③ **EXPLOSIVES**

放射性物品④ **RADIOACTIVE SUBSTANCE**

腐蚀性物品⑤ **CORROSIVES**

小心⑥ **HANDLE WITH CARE**

小心玻璃 **GLASS (HANDLE WITH CARE)**

请勿倒置⑦ **KEEP UPRIGHT**

此端向上 **THIS END UP**

必须平放 **KEEP FLAT**

切勿平放 **NOT TO BE LAID FLAT**

切勿投掷 **NO DUMPING**

切勿挤压 **DO NOT CRUSH, NO CRUSHING**

切勿坠落 **DO NOT DROP, NO DROPPING**

禁止用手钩⑧ **USE NO HOOKS**

由此吊起⑨ **SLING HERE**

用滚子搬运 **USE ROLLERS**

保持干燥 **KEEP DRY**

保持冷藏 **KEEP FROZEN**

防湿⑩ **GUARD AGAINST DAMP**

防冻⑪ **PROTECT AGAINST COLD**

防热⑫ **PROTECT AGAINST HEAT**

防光⑬ **KEEP IN DARK PLACE**

由此开启⑭ **OPEN HERE**

货物残损 **cargo damage**

箱子破 **case broken**

箱子裂 **case plank split (case cracked)**

箱子磨损 **box chafed (box frayed)**

箱子擦损 **box scratched**

箱子切损 **box chipped**

虫损 **damage by insects**

碰坏 **damage by clashing**

撞坏 **damage by collision**

挤坏 **damage by squeezing**

压坏 **damage by crushing**

拖坏 **damage by towing**

袋破 **bag torn**

袋漏 **bag leaky**

袋口松散(散包) **bag seam slack**

袋子油渍 **bag oil-stained**

袋子污渍 **bag dirt-stained**

袋子霉渍 **bag mildew-stained**

袋子潮湿 **bag wet with moisture**

桶漏 **drum leaky**

桶瘪入 **drum dented**

桶凸出 **drum bulged**

桶生锈 **drum rusty**

包箍失落 **bale hoop missing**

包胀破(炸包) **bale burst**

散捆 **bundle off**

請勿倒置 7

由此吊起 9

由此开启 14

防热 12

防光 13

防湿 10

防冻 11

禁止用手钩 8

小心 6

爆炸品 3

易燃物品 1

毒害品 2

腐蚀性物品 5

一级放射性物品（浅蓝色）4

红色

内货外露　contents exposed

内货发霉　contents mouldy

内货霉烂　contents rotten

内货变味　contents rancid

内货变质　contents deteriorated

内货虫蛀　contents worm-eaten

内货发芽　contents sprouting

内货渗出　contents oozing

内货收缩　contents shrunken

内货蒸发　contents evaporated

内货腐蚀　contents attacked

内货自然融化　natural melting of contents

内货自然损耗　natural (normal) loss of contents

内货数量不足　shortage or loss of contents in weight

## 内河交通　River Traffic

内河　inland river

内河航运　inland water transport

河道(水道)　watercourse

可航水道　navigable channel, waterway

主航道　main channel

顺流交通　downstream traffic

逆流交通　upstream traffic

河港　river port

河源　riverhead, source

上游　upper reaches

中游　middle reaches

下游　lower reaches

河口　estuary, mouth of river

三角洲　delta

支流　tributary

浅滩　ford, shallows

河中小岛　river islet

潮〔水〕河　tidal river

边界河　border river

运河　canal

河闸, 船闸　lock(s)

升船机　ship lift (ship elevator)

使船通过河闸驶向上(下)游　locking a ship up (down)

河堤保护　bank protection

防洪堤　flood dike, flood bank

分洪工程　flood diversion project

护堤工程　dike fortification work

排水闸　drainage lock, sluice

排水渠　draining ditch, outfall ditch

木桩　pile, stake

沙包　sandbag

堆石护坡　rock facing

草皮　turf

河道疏浚　river dredging

# 邮 电 Post and Telegraph

## 邮政系统 Postal System

人民邮政 People's Post
邮局 post office
邮务所 postal agency
流动邮务所 mobile postal agency
邮票代售处 stamp sales agency
原寄局(寄发局) office of origin (despatching office)
寄达局 office of destination
投递局 office of delivery
邮区 postal district, postal zone
邮区号码 number of postal area, (Am.) ZIP code number
邮政局长 postmaster
邮务员 postal clerk
柜台值勤邮务员 counter clerk
拣信员 sorter
邮递员 postman, (Am.) mailman, mail carrier
一八七四年国际邮政公约 International Postal Convention of 1874
万国邮政联盟 Universal Postal Union

## 邮政业务 Postal Service

邮件 post, (Am.) mail
国内邮件 inland mail, domestic mail
国外邮件 foreign mail
国外寄来的邮件 incoming foreign mail
寄往国外的邮件 outgoing foreign mail
国际邮件 international mail
国际邮件互换 exchange of international mail
(车船递送的)普通邮件(平邮) surface mail
航空邮件 airmail
航空信 airmail letter, air letter

航空签条　airmail label, airmail sticker

航空邮寄　by airmail, par avion

挂号邮件　registered mail

挂号签条　registered mail label

挂号信　registered letter

保价邮件　insured mail

保价信　insured letter

保价费　insurance

回执　signed delivery receipt

遗失或损坏赔偿　compensation for loss or damage

快递　express delivery, (Am.) special delivery

快递邮件　express mail

快信　express letter

露封信件　unsealed letter

改寄邮件　redirected mail

邮资不足的信件　understamped letter

欠资信　postage-due letter

无法投递的邮件　undeliverable mail

死信　dead letter

待领邮件业务〔处〕　poste restante, (Am.) general delivery

留局待领信件　poste restante letter

邮政信箱　post-office box (PO box)

用户到局认领邮件的邮政信箱　call box

用户自行开箱取邮件的邮政信箱　lockbox

明信片　postcard

双明信片　reply-paid postcard, (Am.) double postal card

美术明信片　picture postcard

封缄信片　lettercard

邮简　letter sheet

航空邮简　aerogram(me), air letter

包裹邮务〔处〕　parcel post

邮政包裹　postal parcel, (Am.) package

保价包裹　insured parcel

小件邮包　postal packet, small parcel

大宗包裹　bulky parcel

包裹柜台　parcel counter

包裹秤重机　parcel-weighing machine

最高重量　maximum weight

包裹详情单　parcel form

领取包裹通知　notice of arrival

寄件人　sender

收件人　addressee

邮汇业务　postal remittance service

邮政汇票　money order

电汇汇票　telegraph money order

汇费　commission

汇款通知　advice of payment

指定兑付局　designated office of payment

接受订阅报刊　accepting subscriptions for newspapers and periodicals

分发报刊　distributing newspapers and periodicals

印刷品　printed matter

邮箱　post box, (Am.) mailbox

邮筒　pillar box

投信口　letter slot (drop)

航空信箱　airmail box
邮袋　postbag, (Am.) mailbag
邮戳　postmark
信件秤　letter scales
收信(收箱)　collection from the post box
拣信　sorting
自动拣信机　computerized sorter
盖上日戳　datestamping
管道风力输送　pneumatic dispatch

"无法投递时, 退回寄件人。"　"In case of non-delivery, return to the sender."
"收件人已死亡。"　"Addressee deceased."
"无人认领。"　"Unclaimed."
"无此地址。"　"No such address."
"地址不详。"　"Address incomplete."
"已搬迁, 地址不明。"　"Moved, address unknown."

## 邮资、邮票　Postage and Stamps

邮资　postage, postal rates
国内邮资　inland postage
国际邮资　international postage
邮资标准　postal tariff
附加邮资　surcharge
欠资　postage due
挂号邮资　additional postage for registration
包裹邮资　parcel postage
邮资免付　post-free
邮资已付　post-paid
自动邮资盖印机　frankingmachine
超重　overweight
超重费　overweight charge
手续费　service charge
查询费　service charge for tracing item of mail
撤回信件或更改收件人地址申请费　service charge for letter recall or change in addressee's address
进口欠资函件处理费　service charge for notification of inward postage-due letter
邮票　(postage) stamp
航空邮票　airmail stamp
特种邮票　special stamp
纪念邮票　commemorative stamp
印在明信片或邮简上的邮票　imprinted stamp
作废邮票　invalid stamp
注销邮票　cancelled stamp
各种资额的邮票　stamps of various denominations
各种图案的邮票　stamps of various designs
新发行的邮票　newly released stamp
崭新邮票　mint stamp
一套邮票　a set of stamps
自动售邮票机　automatic stampvending machine
贴邮票机　stamp affixer
(代替邮票的)邮戳　indicia

## 集　邮　Philately (Stamp Collecting)

邮票目录(邮票一览) stamp catalog(ue)

集邮簿　stamp album

邮票钳　stamp tongs

放大镜　magnifying glass

私人收藏　private collection

公家收藏　public collection

集邮展览　philatelic exhibition

集邮者　philatelist, stamp collector

集邮团体(集邮者协会) philatelic society (philatelic association)

集邮者〔代表〕大会　philatelic congress

集邮邮票　philatelic stamp

旧邮票　used stamp

未用过的邮票　unused stamp

珍贵邮票　rare stamp

缺损邮票　spoilt stamp

伪造的邮票　counterfeit stamp, forgery

复制品　duplicate

首日邮戳　first-day issue postmark

首日封　first-day cover

末日邮戳　last-day postmark

纪念邮戳　cachet, commemorative postmark

特别盖销　special cancellation

有纪念邮戳的信封　cacheted envelope

## 电　报　Telegraph

长途电信局　long-distance tele-communications bureau

电报局　telegraph office

发报局　sending office, office of origin

收报局　receiving office, office of destination

电报大楼　telegraph building

电报柜台　telegraph counter

国际报房　international telegraph room

报房　telegraph apparatus room, traffic room

莫尔斯电报系统　Morse telegraph system

高频无线电　high-frequency radio

打字电报机　teletypewriter

载波设备　carrier equipment

传真机室　facsimile room

快速电报系统　rapid telegraphic system

数据传输机　data-transmitting unit

报文格式器　telegram format setter

光电发报机　photo-electric transmitter

快速凿孔机　rapid card-puncher

中文译码机　Chinese code-converter

十二路电信传真机 **12-channel telephoto**

气敏半导体电缆查漏仪 **gas-sensitive semiconductor cable leak detector**

报务员 **telegrapher, telegraphist**

电报 **telegram**

海底电报 **cable(gram)**

政务电报 **government telegram**

明语电报 **telegram in plain language**

密码电报 **telegram in cipher, cipher telegram**

阿克米商品成语电码 **ACME code**

业务(公务)电报 **service telegram**

私务电报 **private telegram**

新闻电报 **press telegram**

天文电报 **astronomical telegram**

气象电报 **meteorological telegram**

致意电报 **greetings telegram**

贺电 **telegram of congratulations, congratulatory telegram**

唁电 **telegram of condolence**

普通电报 **ordinary telegram**

加急电报 **urgent telegram**

书信电报 **lettergram**

日间书信电报(日信电) **day letter**

夜间书信电报(夜信电) **night letter**

传真电报 **phototelegram**

分送电报 **multiple telegram**

已付回报费的电报 **reply paid telegram**

已付回报费凭单 **reply paid voucher**

话传电报 **telephone telegram**

跟转电报 **telegram to follow the addressee**

改发电报 **redirected telegram**

校对电报 **collated telegram**

专送 **express delivery**

亲启 **personal delivery**

指定在某日投送 **delivery on a specified date**

送妥通知 **telegraphic notification of delivery, telegram with notice of delivery**

邮局留文 **poste restante**

邮局挂号留文 **poste restante registered**

国际转帐电报 **international transferred account telegram**

国际转帐电报业务凭证 **international transferred account telegraph service card**

电报挂号 **cable address**

挂号期限 **registration period**

收报人付费国际私务电报 **international collect private telegram**

国际电报信用卡 **international credit card for telegraph services**

凭信用卡拍发收报人付费电报 **sending a collect telegram against a credit card**

收报人付费卡 **collect card**

电报纸 **telegraph form**

报头 **preamble**

纳费业务标志 paid service indication

收报地名 destination

收报人姓名住址 addressee's name and address

电文 text, message

发报人署名 sender's signature

收据 receipt

收报时间 time of receipt

计字 word counting

计费 calculating charges

计费字数 number of chargeable words

电报每字资费 telegraph rate per word

资费表 tariff, schedule of rates

少收资费 undercharging

多收资费 overcharging

退款 refunding

数字 figure

字母 letter

符号 sign

缩写 abbreviation

斜划 fraction bar

连字号 hyphen

破折号 dash

省略号 apostrophe

印刷体书写 writing in block letters

大写(用文字表达的)数字 figures in longhand writing

发送电报 dispatching a telegram, transmitting a telegram

接收电报 receiving a telegram

接受顾客交发的电报 accepting a telegram for dispatch

译成电码 coding

译电 decoding

"请填写电报纸。" "Please fill-in the telegraph form."

"拍加急吗?" "Send urgent?"

"加急收费加倍。" "Urgent telegrams cost double."

"书信电报收费减半。" "Letter-grams are charged at half the ordinary rate."

## 用户电报 Telex

用户电报交换机 telex exchange

发报间 punching room

电传打字电报机 teleprinter

凿孔纸条 punched tape, perforated tape

凿孔机 puncher

计时器 time meter

自动发报机头 autohead

用户电报交换台值机员 telex switchboard operator

主叫用户 caller, calling subscriber

被叫用户 called subscriber

有关人命安全的用户电报 safety of life telex call

政务用户电报 government telex call

普通私务用户电报 ordinary private telex call

用户电报挂号单 booking form for telex service

公众用户电报挂号单　booking form for telex call through public booth

数码键　figure key

字母键　letter key

回车键　"carriage return" key

换行键　"line-feed" key

D键　"D" key

"你是谁?"键　"Who are you?" key

拆线键　clearing button

你停止发送　PO (Stop your transmission.)

你已与被叫用户接通　DF (You are in communication with the called subscriber.)

请复述　COL (Collation, please./ I collate.)

我复述　I collate.

符号　sign

"R"信号(已收到)　signal R (received)

等一等　MOM (wait,waiting)

间隔信号　signal "space"

错误　E (error)

回呼密语　answer-back code, back code

变码　garbled code

呼叫信号　calling signal

呼叫号码　call-number

凿孔　punching a tape

挂号　booking a telex call

发报　running a tape, sending off a message

拆线　cutting the line

准备好凿孔纸条　preparing a message in the form of a punched tape

电传机号码　telex number

## 电　话　Telephone

电话局　telephone office

电话总机　telephone exchange

自动交换机　automatic switchboard

纵横制交换机房　crossbar telephone exchange room

专用小交换机　private branch exchange (PBX)

国际终端交换所　international terminal exchange

中继线　trunk line

电话分机　extension telephone

公共电话间　telephone kiosk, (Am.) telephone booth

电话号码簿　telephone directory, (Am.) telephone book

自动桌式电话机　automatic desk telephone

拨号盘　dial

指孔盘　finger plate

送受话器　handset

送受话器叉簧　cradle

受话器(听筒)　receiver

送话器(口承)　mouthpiece

商业电子电话机①　electronic

business telephone

录音电话机，书写电话机 **dictograph (dictaphone)**

按钮电话 **push-button telephone**

键盘电话机 **key telephone**

电视电话(机) **picture (tele) phone, video-phone, view phone**

可移动无线电话机 **cordless portaphone**

头带受话器(耳机) **earphone**

无塞绳受话器 **cordless earphone**

电话号码 **telephone number**

分局号码 **area code, district code**

查号台 **directory enquiry**

话务员 **telephone operator, telephonist**

发话人 **calling party, caller**

受话人 **called party, person receiving the call**

长途电话 **trunk call, (Am.) long distance call**

长途电话台 **long-distance exchange (operator)**

市内电话 **urban telephone**

郊区电话 **suburban telephone**

国际无线电话 **international radio telephone**

国际转话 **international transit call**

直接拨号长途电话 **direct distance dialing call**

遇险电话 **distress call**

急用电话 **emergency call**

叫号电话(局间电话) **number call (station-to-station call)**

叫人电话 **person-to-person call, personal call**

通知通话时间和通话费用 **advise duration and charge (ACD)**

传呼电话 **messenger call**

政务电话 **government telephone**

预约电话(定时电话) **sequency call (fixed time call)**

公务(业务)电话 **service (business) telephone**

受话人付费电话 **collect call, reverse charge call**

普通电话 **ordinary call**

加急电话 **urgent call**

公共电话 **public telephone**

会议电话 **conference telephone**

销号费 **cancellation fee**

通话计时器 **telephonometer**

通话占用分钟数 **call minutes**

通话总消耗时间 **total elapsed time**

"喂，总机吗？请接五局二八二三。" **"Hullo, operator? Get me 5-2823, please."**

"等一等。" **"Hold the line, please."**

"占线！" **"Line engaged!"**

"打错了。" **"Wrong number."**

"没人接。" **"No answer."**

"接通了！请讲话！" **"You're in connexion. Please go ahead."**

"时间到了，要不要延长？" **"Time's up. Are you extending?"**

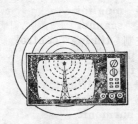

# 无线电和电视 Radio and Television

## 无线电通讯 Radio Communication

| | | | |
|---|---|---|---|
| 无线电报 | radiogram | 滤波器 | filter |
| 天线 | aerial, antenna | 低通滤波器 | low pass filter |
| 音频 | audio frequency | 高通滤波器 | high pass filter |
| 高频放大器 | audio-frequency amplifier | 带通滤波器 | band pass filter |
| | | 振荡器 | oscillator |
| 显示器 | indicator | 调谐器 | tuner |
| 自动音调调整 | automatic tone correction | 电容器 | capacitor, condenser |
| | | 电阻器 | resistor |
| 自动调谐 | automatic tuning control | 二极管 | diode |
| | | 三极管 | triode |
| 发射机 | transmitter | 晶体管 | transistor |
| 发射台 | transmitting station | 变压器 | transformer |
| 步谈机 | walkie-talkie | 电感 | inductance |
| 载波(载频) | carrier | 导体 | conductor |
| 频率 | frequency | 线圈 | coil |
| 超高频 | ultra high frequency | 电路 | circuit |
| 甚高频 | very high frequency | 基群 | basic group |
| 高频 | high frequency | 指示灯 | indication (indicator) lamp |
| 中频 | medium frequency | | |
| 低频 | low frequency | 告警指示器(报警信号设备) alarm | |
| 微波 | microwave | | |
| 超短波 | ultra short wave | 衰减器(增益调整器) attenuator | |
| 短波 | short wave | 电源 | power |
| 中波 | medium wave | 电平 | level |
| 长波 | long wave | 电压 | voltage |

电流　current
交流电　alternate current (AC)
直流电　direct current (DC)
输出　output
输入　input
保险丝　fuse
拾音器　pick-up
电缆　cable
插头(塞子)　plug
插座(塞孔)　jack, socket
额定电流(标称电流)　nominal current
额定电压(标称电压)　nominal voltage
U形插塞　U-link
导频　pilot
继电器　relay
调制器　modulator

解调器　demodulator
监视器　monitor
扫描器　scanner
同步控制　timing control
脉冲　pulse
测试　test
放大器　amplifier
计数器　counter
谐波　harmonic
发生器　generator
增音机　repeater
阻抗　impedance
按钮　button
耦合　coupling
阈　threshold
塞绳　cord
电容　capacitance
电容量　capacity

## 无线电广播　Radio Broadcasting

广播电台　broadcasting station
播音室　studio
播音室广播　studio broadcast
实况广播　live broadcast
国内广播　home broadcast
国际广播　international broadcast
联播　network broadcast, chain broadcast
转播　relay broadcast
重播　repeat
双重广播　dual broadcast
定向广播　directional broadcast
立体声广播　stereophonic broadcast
两路立体声广播　binaural

broadcast
照原稿宣读的广播　scripted broadcast
不用稿子的广播　unscripted broadcast
无线电广播节目　radio program(me)
播音室广播节目　studio program(me)
室外广播节目　remote program(me), nemo
实况广播节目　live program(me)
录音广播节目　pre-recorded program(me), taped program(me)
联播节目　network program(me)

全国广播网　national network
呼号　call sign, call signal
信号调(信号曲)　signature tune
新闻广播　news broadcast
实况广播报道　running commentary
广播剧　radio drama
广播讨论会　panel discussion
广播讨论小组　panel
专题讲座节目　forum
(电子学)广播课程　radio course (in electronics)
广播体操　broadcast callis-thenics
天气预报　weather forecast
答问比赛节目　quiz program- (me)
行情报告　market report
报时信号　time signal
广播时间　air time
播音员　announcer
实况广播员　commentator
广播稿　script
广播节目撰稿者　scriptwriter
广播节目间的简短通知　spot announcement

## 广播技术　Broadcasting Technique

无线电传输　radio transmission
无线电发射机　radio transmitter
微音器(话筒)　microphone, mike
录音室　recording studio
录音车　recording van
多声道录音　multichannel recording
多声道录音机　multichannel recorder
立体声录音机　stereo recorder
磁带录音机　tape recorder
循环磁带录音机　endless tape recorder
盒式磁带录音机　cassette recorder
收录两用机　radio cassette
磁带　magnetic tape
带盘　tape reel
盒式磁带　cassette tape
放音　playback
消音　erasure
前置放大器　preamplifier
混频　mixing
混频和音量控制　mixer and volume control
控制间　control booth
监听扬声器　monitoring loudspeaker
回声室　echo chamber
放大器　amplifier
主控制室　master control room
调制　modulation
调制器　modulator
调幅　amplitude modulation (AM)
调频　frequency modulation (FM)
调相　phase modulation (PM)
压电振荡器　piezoelectric oscillator
射频放大器　radio-frequency amplifier
天线　antenna

垂直天线　vertical antenna
多振子天线　multi-element antenna
电磁波　electromagnetic wave
广播信道　broadcast channel
专用广播信道　clear channel
地方广播信道　regional channel
本地广播信道　local channel
频率容限　frequency tolerance
载波功率　carrier power
信号强度　signal strength

射电场强　radio field intensity
天空电波(天波)　sky wave
地面电波(地波)　ground wave
衰落　fading
广播有效作用区　broadcast service area
噪声　noise
静电干扰　static interference
人为干扰　jamming
有线转播　rediffusion on wire
有线广播　wire broadcasting

# 电视广播　Telecasting

电视　television (TV)
黑白电视　monochrome TV, black-and-white TV
彩色电视　colour television
兼容制彩色电视系统　compatible colour television system
电视〔广播〕台　television broadcast(ing) station
电视塔　television tower
电视发射机　television transmitter
电视频道　television (frequency) channel
全频道彩色电视机　all-channel colour TV set
频带宽度　bandwidth
音频载波　sound carrier
图像载波　picture carrier
远距离电视摄像　remote pickup
电视车　television mobile unit
电视摄像机　television camera, telecamera

电视摄像管　television camera tube, (Am.) pickup tube
超正析摄像管　image orthicon
光电摄像管　iconoscope(ico)
移像光电摄像管　image iconoscope
光导摄像管　vidicon
氧化铅光导摄像管　plumbicon
析像管　image dissector
扫描　scanning
同步信号　synchronizing signal
消隐信号(消隐脉冲)　blanking signal (blanking impulse)
频率调制音频信号　frequency modulated sound signal
图像信号　picture signal
彩色传输　colour transmission
彩色信号　colour signal
电视录像　television recording
录像器　video recorder
录像磁带　video tape
磁带录像　video tape recording (VTR)

磁盘录像 magnetic disc recording

屏幕录像 kinescope recording

屏幕录像机 kinescope recorder

电子束录像 electron beam recording (EBR)

激光录像 video recording by laser

单像管 monoscope, monotron

电视节目监控器 television program(me) monitor

电视演播室 television studio

电视电影 telecine

电视广播剧 teleplay

电视实况转播 livc telecast, televising

电视课程 telecourse

电视讲话 televised speech

电视记者招待会 televised news conference

马拉松式电视广播节目 telethon

电视观众 televiewers

电视转播 television relay

国际电视现场转播 live international television coverage

微波中继 microwave relay

同轴电缆 coaxial cable

闭路电视 closed-circuit television (CCTV)

手术示范室① operation theatre

反射镜② mirror

微音器(话筒)③ microphone (mike)

电视摄像机④ television camera, telecamera

控制台⑤ control desk

接收机⑥ receiver

艾多福投影机⑦ Eidophor projector

工业电视 industrial television (ITV)

单管式彩色工业电视摄像机 single-tube colour ITV camera

水下电视 underwater television

微光电视 low light level television

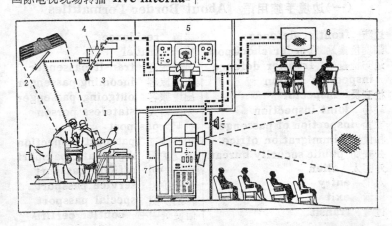

## 卫星通讯　Satellite Communications

火箭　rocket
通讯卫星　comsat (communications satellite), telstar
静止卫星(同步卫星)　geostationary satellite (synchronous satellite)
位置控制　position control
姿态控制　attitude control
天线　antenna
转发器　repeater, translator
遥测　telemetering
指令　command
电源　power
地面站　ground station

卡塞格伦天线　Cassegrain antenna
发射机　transmitter
接收机　receiver
终端设备　terminal equipment
控制设备　control equipment
可靠性　reliability
频分多路(FDM)　frequency-division multiplexing
调频(FM)　frequency modulation
频分多址(FDMA)　frequency-division multiaddress

# 附　录　Appendices

## (一)边境手续用语　About Border Formalities

边防　frontier defence
国境检查站　border checkpost
边防检查站　frontier defence inspection station
检查员　inspector
联检　joint inspection
旅检　inspection of passengers
移民局　immigration office
公安局　public security bureau
外国人　alien
入境　entry
出境　exit
过境　transit

居留　residence
旅行　travel
过境旅客　transit passenger
入境旅客　incoming passenger
出境旅客　outgoing passenger
无国籍人　stateless person
护照　passport
护照检查　passport inspection
外交护照　diplomatic passport
官员护照　official passport
公务护照　service passport
特别护照　special passport
信使证明书　courier certifi-

cate

| 入境签证 | entry visa |
| --- | --- |

出境签证　exit visa

过境签证　transit visa

一次入境签证　single entry visa

多次入境签证　multiply entry visa

旅游签证　tourist visa

居留签证　resident visa

办理签证　applying for a visa

办理居留登记　applying for residence registration

申报户口　reporting for entry in the domiciliary register

办理迁移证件　applying for removal permit

入境许可证　entry permit

出境许可证　departure permit

居留证　residence permit

旅行证　travel permit

通行证　pass

登陆证　landing permit, shore pass

登轮证　boarding (embarking) permit

住宿证　lodging permit

海员证　seaman's book

身份证　certificate of identity, identity book (card)

离职证　discharge book

拒发签证　refusal to issue a visa

拒绝入境　entry disallowed

违反规定　contravention of provisions

警告　warning

罚款　fine

拘留　detention

吊销签证　cancelling a visa already issued

宣布签证作废　annulling a visa already issued

限令某人出境　ordering a person to leave the country within a time limit

驱逐出境　expulsion from the country

逮解出境　deportation

偷越国境　surreptitious (clandestine) crossing of the border

边境事件　border incident

外交豁免权　diplomatic immunity

通过外交途径处理　to be dealt with through diplomatic channels

海关　customs

海关规则　customs regulations

海关检查　customs inspection

海关监管　customs supervision and control

海关登记　customs registration

办理海关手续　going through (completing) customs formalities

报关　making a customs declaration

海关人员　customs officer

海关文件　customs papers

外币申报单　foreign currencies declaration form

旅行支票　traveller's cheque

证券　security

票据　bill

兑换水单　exchange memo

行李申报单　luggage declara-

tion

武器申报单 **declaration of firearms**

进口许可证 **import licence**

出口许可证 **export licence**

外国货物转运准许证 **foreign goods conveying permit**

免验证 **PWE authority, laissez-passer**

免验放行 **release without customs examination**

登记放行 **release upon registration**

发货票 **invoice**

收据 **receipt**

行李票 **luggage check**

行李票签 **luggage tag**

随身携带的行李 **hand luggage**

托运的行李 **registered luggage**

分离运输行李 **unaccompanied luggage**

个人用品 **personal effects**

本人身上所带物品 **articles carried on one's person**

代别人携带的物品 **articles carried on behalf of others**

应申报物品 **articles to be declared**

关税 **customs duty**

税单 **duty receipt**

普通税率 **general tariff**

最低税率 **mininum tariff**

特惠关税 **preferential tariff**

纳税物品 **dutiable articles**

免税物品 **duty-free articles**

免税定额 **duty-free allowance**

减税物品 **duty-rebated articles**

国际惯例 **international practice**

缉私队(抄关队) **search party**

走私行为 **act of smuggling**

违章行为 **act of violation of regulations**

谎报 **false declaration**

听候处理 **pending decision**

海关处分通知书 **customs decision**

没收违禁品 **confiscation of contraband**

扣留物品 **articles under detention**

海关加封物品 **articles under customs seal**

外交信袋放行 **passing of diplomatic mailbag**

外交信使行李物品放行 **passing luggage of diplomatic courier**

退关 **shut out**

结关 **getting customs clearance**

办完海关手续 **customs formalities completed**

检疫所(检疫站) **quarantine service (station)**

防疫检查 **quarantine inspection**

检疫锚地 **anchorage for health clearance**

卫生检查 **sanitary inspection**

港口医务官员 **port medical officer**

检疫对象 **quarantine object**

检疫证书 **quarantine certificate**

种痘 **vaccination against**

smallpox

预防霍乱接种 vaccination against cholera

预防注射 inoculation

鼠疫 plague

斑疹伤寒 typhus

回归热 relapsing fever

天花 smallpox

黄热病 yellow fever

感染区 infected area

黄皮书 yellow book

健康证 health certificate

航海健康申明书 maritime declaration of health, declaration of physical fitness for voyage

疑是传染病例 suspected case of epidemic

病情 full particulars of the case

症状 symptoms of the case

发病日期 date of the onset

反常死亡 abnormal mortality

隔离〔检疫〕三天 being under quarantine for 3 days

黄色旗 Q flag, yellow flag, (Am.) yellow jack

检疫通行证(进口检疫证) pratique

消毒 disinfection

除鼠 deratization

除虫 disinsecting, disinsectization

动植物检疫所 animal and plant quarantine service

## （二）外国港口 Foreign Ports

元山(朝鲜) Wonsan (Korea)

清津(朝鲜) Ch'ongjin (Korea)

金策(朝鲜) Kimch'aek (Korea)

兴南(朝鲜) Hungnam (Korea)

南浦(朝鲜) Namp'o (Korea)

釜山(朝鲜) Pusan (Korea)

仁川(朝鲜) Inch'on (Korea)

东京(日本) Tokyo (Japan)

横滨(日本) Yokohama (Japan)

川崎(日本) Kawasaki (Japan)

千叶(日本) Chiba (Japan)

横须贺(日本) Yokosuka (Japan)

大阪(日本) Osaka (Japan)

神户(日本) Kobe (Japan)

名古屋(日本) Nagoya (Japan)

北九州(日本) Kitakyushu (Japan)

下关(日本) Shimonoseki (Japan)

佐世保(日本) Sasebo (Japan)

长崎(日本) Nagasaki (Japan)

鹿儿岛(日本) Kagoshima (Japan)

函馆(日本) Hakodate (Japan)

胡志明市(越南) Hô Chi Minh City (Viet Nam)

海防(越南) Haiphong (Viet Nam)

岘港(越南) Da Nang (Viet Nam)

磅逊(柬埔寨) Kompong Som (Cambodia)

曼谷(泰国) **Bangkok (Thailand)**

槟城(马来西亚) **Penang (Malaysia)**

瑞天咸港(马来西亚) **Port Swettenham (Malaysia)**

马六甲(马来西亚) **Malacca (Malaysia)**

古晋(马来西亚) **Kuching (Malaysia)**

亚庇(马来西亚) **Kota Kinabalu (Malaysia)**

山打根(马来西亚) **Sandakan (Malaysia)**

新加坡 **Singapore**

文莱(文莱) **Bandar Seri Begawan (Brunei)**

雅加达(印尼) **Djakarta (Indonesia)**

丹戎不碌(印尼) **Tandjungpriok (Indonesia)**

三宝垄(印尼) **Semarang (Indonesia)**

苏腊巴亚(泗水)(印尼) **Surabaja (Indonesia)**

棉兰(印尼) **Medan (Indonesia)**

巨港(巴邻旁)(印尼) **Palembang (Indonesia)**

巴东(印尼) **Padang (Indonesia)**

马辰(印尼) **Bandjarmasin (Indonesia)**

坤甸(印尼) **Pontianak (Indonesia)**

巴厘巴板(印尼) **Balikpapan (Indonesia)**

马尼拉(菲律宾) **Manila (Philippines)**

宿务(菲律宾) **Cebu (Philippines)**

三宝颜(菲律宾) **Zamboanga (Philippines)**

仰光(缅甸) **Rangoon (Burma)**

毛淡棉(缅甸) **Moulmein (Burma)**

吉大港(孟加拉) **Chittagong (Bangladesh)**

加尔各答(印度) **Calcutta (India)**

孟买(印度) **Bombay (India)**

马德拉斯(印度) **Madras (India)**

科伦坡(斯里兰卡) **Colombo (Sri Lanka)**

亭可马里(斯里兰卡) **Trincomalee (Sri Lanka)**

卡拉奇(巴基斯坦) **Karachi (Pakistan)**

阿巴丹(伊朗) **Abadan (Iran)**

巴士拉(伊拉克) **Basra (Iraq)**

科威特(科威特) **Kuwait (Kuwait)**

亚丁 (也门民主人民共和国) **Aden (People's Democratic Republic of Yemen)**

荷台达(阿拉伯也门共和国) **Hodeida (Yemen Arab Republic)**

吉达(沙特阿拉伯) **Jidda (Saudi Arabia)**

亚喀巴(约旦) **Aqaba (Jordan)**

特拉维夫——雅法(以色列) **Tel Aviv-Jaffa (Israel)**

海法(以色列) **Haifa (Israel)**

埃拉特(以色列) **Elath (Israel)**

贝鲁特(黎巴嫩) **Beirut (Leba-non)**

拉塔基亚(叙利亚) **Latakia (Syria)**

伊斯坦布尔(土耳其) **Istanbul (Turkey)**

伊兹密尔(土耳其) **Izmir (Tur-key)**

亚历山大(埃及) **Alexandria (Egypt)**

塞得港(埃及) **Port Said (Egypt)**

苏伊士(埃及) **Suez (Egypt)**

的黎波里(利比亚) **Tripoli (Libya)**

班加西(利比亚) **Benghazi (Libya)**

卜雷加港(利比亚) **Marsa el Brega (Libya)**

托卜鲁克(利比亚) **Tobruk (Libya)**

突尼斯(突尼斯) **Tunis (Tuni-sia)**

阿尔及尔(阿尔及利亚) **Algiers (Algeria)**

瓦赫兰(奥兰)(阿尔及利亚) **Oran (Algeria)**

卡萨布兰卡(摩洛哥) **Casa-blanca (Morocco)**

丹吉尔(摩洛哥) **Tangier (Mo-rocco)**

拉斯帕耳马斯(加那利群岛) **Las Palmas de Gran Canaria (Canary Islands)**

圣克鲁斯(加那利群岛) **Santa Cruz de Tenerife (Canary Islands)**

努瓦克肖特(毛里塔尼亚) **Nouakshott (Mauritania)**

达喀尔(塞内加尔) **Dakar (Senegal)**

巴瑟斯特(冈比亚) **Bathurst (Gambia)**

比绍(几内亚(比绍)) **Bissau (Guinea(Bissau))**

科纳克里(几内亚) **Conakry (Guinea)**

弗里敦(塞拉利昂) **Freetown (Sierra Leone)**

蒙罗维亚(利比里亚) **Monrovia (Liberia)**

阿比让(象牙海岸) **Abidjan (Ivory Coast)**

阿克拉(加纳) **Accra (Ghana)**

塔克腊迪(加纳) **Takoradi (Ghana)**

洛美(多哥) **Lomé (Togo)**

科托努(贝宁) **Cotonou (Benin)**

拉各斯(尼日利亚) **Lagos (Ni-geria)**

哈尔科特港(尼日利亚) **Port Harcourt (Nigeria)**

杜阿拉(喀麦隆) **Douala (Cameroon)**

巴塔(赤道几内亚) **Bata (Equa-torial Guinea)**

利伯维尔(加蓬) **Libreville (Gabon)**

让蒂尔港(加蓬) **Port-Gentil (Gabon)**

黑角(刚果) **Pointe Noire (Congo)**

马塔迪(扎伊尔) **Matadi (Zaire)**

罗安达(安哥拉) **Luanda (Angola)**

洛比托(安哥拉) **Lobito (Angola)**

苏丹港(苏丹) **Port Sudan**

(Sudan)

马萨瓦(埃塞俄比亚)　**Mesewa** (Ethiopia)

吉布提(吉布提)　**Djibouti** (Djibouti)

摩加迪沙(索马里)　**Mogadishu** (Somali)

蒙巴萨(肯尼亚)　**Mombasa** (Kenya)

达累斯萨拉姆(坦桑尼亚)　**Dar es Salaam** (Tanzania)

桑给巴尔(坦桑尼亚)　**Zanzibar** (Tanzania)

坦噶(坦桑尼亚)　**Tanga** (Tanzania)

洛伦索——马贵斯(莫桑比克)　**Lourenco Marques** (Mozambique)

贝拉(莫桑比克)　**Beira** (Mozambique)

莫桑比克(莫桑比克)　**Mozambique** (Mozambique)

塔马塔夫(马达加斯加)　**Tamatave** (Madagascar)

马任加(马达加斯加)　**Majunga** (Madagascar)

路易港(毛里求斯)　**Port Louis** (Mauritius)

圣但尼(留尼汪)　**Saint-Denis** (Réunion)

开普敦(南非)　**Cape Town** (South Africa)

伊丽莎白港(南非)　**Port Elizabeth** (South Africa)

德班(南非)　**Durban** (South Africa)

康斯坦萨(罗马尼亚)　**Constanta** (Romania)

里耶卡(南斯拉夫)　**Rijeka** (Yugoslavia)

斯普利特(南斯拉夫)　**Split** (Yugoslavia)

瓦尔纳(保加利亚)　**Varna** (Bulgaria)

布加斯(保加利亚)　**Burgas** (Bulgaria)

都拉斯(阿尔巴尼亚)　**Durrës** (Albania)

发罗拉(阿尔巴尼亚)　**Vlorë** (Albania)

雅典——比雷埃夫斯(希腊)　**Athens —— Piraeus** (Greece)

萨洛尼卡(希腊)　**Salonika** (Greece)

瓦莱塔(马耳他)　**Valletta** (Malta)

热那亚(意大利)　**Genoa** (Italy)

威尼斯(意大利)　**Venice** (Italy)

那不勒斯(意大利)　**Naples** (Italy)

里窝那(意大利)　**Leghorn** (Italy)

塔兰托(意大利)　**Taranto** (Italy)

的里雅斯特(意大利)　**Trieste** (Italy)

巴塞罗那(西班牙)　**Barcelona** (Spain)

毕尔巴鄂(西班牙)　**Bilbao** (Spain)

巴伦西亚(西班牙)　**Valencia** (Spain)

直布罗陀(英占)　**Gibraltar** (British occupied)

里斯本(葡萄牙)　**Lisbon** (Portugal)

波尔图(葡萄牙)　**Oporto** (Portugal)

马赛(法国) **Marseilles (France)**

土伦(法国) **Toulon (France)**

尼斯(法国) **Nice (France)**

波尔多(法国) **Bordeaux (France)**

勒阿弗尔(法国) **Le Havre (France)**

加来(法国) **Calais (France)**

敦刻尔克(法国) **Dunkirk (France)**

安特卫普(比利时) **Antwerp (Belgium)**

阿姆斯特丹(荷兰) **Amsterdam (Holland)**

鹿特丹(荷兰) **Rotterdam (Holland)**

伦敦(英国) **London (UK)**

利物浦(英国) **Liverpool (UK)**

南安普敦(英国) **Southampton (UK)**

朴次茅斯(英国) **Portsmouth (UK)**

普利茅斯(英国) **Plymouth (UK)**

布里斯托尔(英国) **Bristol (UK)**

加的夫(英国) **Cardiff (UK)**

塔尔伯特港(英国) **Port Talbot (UK)**

斯温西(英国) **Swansea (UK)**

多佛尔(英国) **Dover (UK)**

赫尔(英国) **Hull (UK)**

纽卡斯尔(英国) **Newcastle-on-Tyne (UK)**

格拉斯哥(英国) **Glasgow (UK)**

阿伯丁(英国) **Aberdeen (UK)**

贝尔法斯特(英国) **Belfast (UK)**

都柏林(爱尔兰) **Dublin (Ireland)**

科克(爱尔兰) **Cork (Ireland)**

奥斯陆(挪威) **Oslo (Norway)**

卑尔根(挪威) **Bergen (Norway)**

特隆赫姆(挪威) **Trondheim (Norway)**

斯德哥尔摩(瑞典) **Stockholm (Sweden)**

哥德堡(瑞典) **Göteborg (Sweden)**

马尔默(瑞典) **Malmö (Sweden)**

哥本哈根(丹麦) **Copenhagen (Denmark)**

汉堡(西德) **Hamburg (W Germany)**

不来梅(西德) **Bremen (W Germany)**

威廉港(西德) **Wilhelmshaven (W Germany)**

罗斯托克(东德) **Rostock (E Germany)**

格但斯克(波兰) **Gdańsk (Poland)**

格丁尼亚(波兰) **Gdynia (Poland)**

赫尔辛基(芬兰) **Helsinki (Finland)**

土尔库(芬兰) **Turku (Finland)**

雷克雅未克(冰岛) **Reykjavik (Iceland)**

列宁格勒(苏联) **Leningrad (USSR)**

维堡(苏联) **Vyborg (USSR)**

摩尔曼斯克(苏联) **Murmansk (USSR)**

敖德萨(苏联) **Odessa (USSR)**

符拉迪沃斯托克(海参崴)(苏联)

Vladivostok (USSR)

悉尼(澳大利亚) Sydney (Australia)

墨尔本(澳大利亚) Melbourne (Australia)

阿得雷德(澳大利亚) Adelaide (Australia)

布里斯班(澳大利亚) Brisbane (Australia)

纽卡斯尔(澳大利亚) Newcastle (Australia)

弗里曼特尔(澳大利亚) Fremantle (Australia)

达尔文(澳大利亚) Darwin (Australia)

霍巴特(澳大利亚) Hobart (Australia)

惠灵顿(新西兰) Wellington (New Zealand)

奥克兰(新西兰) Auckland (New Zealand)

莫尔兹比港(巴布亚新几内亚) Port Moresby (Papua New Guinea)

阿批亚(西萨摩亚) Apia(W Samoa)

帕果——帕果(东萨摩亚) Pago Pago (E Samoa)

苏瓦(斐济) Suva (Fiji)

努美阿(新喀里多尼亚岛) Nouméa (New Caledonia)

帕皮提(塔希提岛) Papeete (Tahiti)

韦腊克鲁斯(墨西哥) Veracruz (Mexico)

坦皮科(墨西哥) Tampico (Mexico)

曼萨尼略(墨西哥) Manzanillo (Mexico)

马萨特兰(墨西哥) Mazatlán (Mexico)

阿卡普尔科(墨西哥) Acapulco de Juárez (Mexico)

巴拿巴城(巴拿马) Panama City (Panama)

科隆(巴拿马) Colón (Panama)

哈瓦那(古巴) Havana (Cuba)

西恩富戈斯(古巴) Cienfuegos (Cuba)

金斯敦(牙买加) Kingston (Jamaica)

蒙特哥贝(牙买加) Montego Bay (Jamaica)

太子港(海地) Port-au-Prince (Haiti)

圣多明各(多米尼加) Santo Domingo (Dominica)

威廉斯塔德(库腊索岛) Willemstad (Curacao)

西班牙港(特立尼达和多巴哥) Port of Spain (Trinidad and Tobago)

巴兰基利亚(哥伦比亚) Barranquilla (Colombia)

卡塔赫纳(哥伦比亚) Cartagena (Colombia)

布韦那文图拉(哥伦比亚) Buenaventura (Colombia)

瓜亚基尔(厄瓜多尔) Guayaquil (Ecuador)

卡亚俄(秘鲁) Callao (Peru)

瓦尔帕来索(智利) Valparaiso (Chile)

塔尔卡瓦诺(智利) Talcahuano (Chile)

阿里卡(智利) Arica (Chile)

安托法加斯塔(智利) Antofagasta (Chile)

彭塔阿雷纳斯(智利)　Punta A-renas (Chile)

马拉开波(委内瑞拉)　Maracaibo (Venezuela)

拉瓜伊拉(委内瑞拉)　La Guaira (Venezuela)

乔治敦(圭亚那)　Georgetown (Guyana)

帕拉马里博(苏里南)　Paramaribo (Surinam)

里约热内卢(巴西)　Rio de Janeiro (Brazil)

圣多斯(巴西)　Santos (Brazil)

累西腓(巴西)　Recife (Brazil)

蒙得维的亚(乌拉圭)　Montevideo (Uruguay)

布宜诺斯艾利斯(阿根廷)　Buenos Aires (Argentina)

罗萨里奥(阿根廷)　Rosario (Argentina)

布兰卡港(阿根廷)　Bahia Blanca (Argentina)

蒙特利尔(加拿大)　Montreal (Canada)

魁北克(加拿大)　Quebec (Canada)

哈利法克斯(加拿大)　Halifax (Canada)

圣约翰(加拿大)　St. John (Canada)

温哥华(加拿大)　Vancouver (Canada)

彻奇尔(加拿大)　Churchill (Canada)

纽约(美国)　New York (USA)

费城(美国)　Philadelphia (USA)

巴尔的摩(美国)　Baltimore (USA)

波士顿(美国)　Boston (USA)

波特兰(美国缅因州)　Portland, Maine (USA)

迈阿密(美国)　Miami (USA)

新奥尔良(美国)　New Orleans (USA)

休斯敦(美国)　Houston (USA)

圣弗兰西斯科(旧金山)(美国)　San Francisco (USA)

洛杉矶(美国)　Los Angeles (USA)

长滩(美国)　Long Beach (USA)

圣迭戈(美国)　San Diego (USA)

西雅图(美国)　Seattle (USA)

波特兰(美国俄勒冈州)　Portland, Oregon (USA)

火奴鲁鲁(檀香山)(美国)　Honolulu (USA)

## (三)民航机构　Civil Aviation Organizations

中国民用航空总局　General Administration of Civil Aviation of China (CAAC)

巴基斯坦国际航空公司　Pakistan International Airlines (PIA)

法国航空公司　Air France (AF)

加拿大航空公司　Air Canada

加拿大太平洋航空公司　Canadian Pacific Airlines (CPA)

日本航空公司　Japan Air Lines (JAL)

全日本航空公司　All Nippon Airways (ANA)

英国航空公司　British Airways

泛美航空公司 Pan American World Airways (Pan Am)

环球航空公司 Trans-World Airlines (TWA)

西德汉莎航空公司 Lufthansa

荷兰皇家航空公司 Royal Dutch Airlines (Koninklijke Luchtvaart Maatschappij, KLM)

斯堪的纳维亚航空公司 Scandinavian Airlines System (SAS)

比利时世界航空公司 Belgian World Airlines (Société Anonyme Belge d'Exploitation de la Navigation Aérienne, SABENA)

意大利国际航空公司 Italian International Airlines (Aerolinee Italiane Internazionali, ALITALIA)

瑞士航空公司 Swissair

爱尔兰国际航空公司 Irish International

康达斯帝国航空公司(澳大利亚) Qantas Empire Airways LTD (QEA)

国泰航空公司 Cathay Pacific

印度航空公司 Air India

泰国航空公司 Thai Airways International LTD

孟加拉航空公司 Bangladesh Biman

塞浦路斯航空公司 Cyprus Airways

印度尼西亚鹰记航空公司 Garuda Indonesian Airways (GIA)

伊朗航空公司 Iran Air

伊拉克航空公司 Iraqi Airways

黎巴嫩航空运输公司 Lebanese Air Transport

马来西亚航空公司 Malaysian Airline System (MAS)

新加坡航空公司 Singapore Airlines

中东航空公司 Middle East Airlines

蒙古航空公司 Mongolian Airlines

菲律宾航空公司 Philippine Air Lines (PAL)

阿富汗皇家航空公司 Royal Afghan Airlines

约旦皇家航空公司 Royal Jordanian Airlines (ALIA)

沙特阿拉伯航空公司 Saudi Arabian Airlines

土耳其航空公司 Turkish Airlines (Turk Haval Yollari AO, THY)

缅甸联邦航空公司 Union of Burma Airways

也门航空公司 Yemen Airlines

非洲航空公司 Air Afrique

阿尔及利亚航空公司 Air Algérie

科摩罗航空公司 Air Comores

加蓬航空公司 Air Gabon

几内亚航空公司 Air Guinée

马达加斯加航空公司 Air Madagascar

马拉维航空公司 Air Malawi

马里航空公司 Air Mali

毛里塔尼亚航空公司 Air Mauritanie

扎伊尔航空公司 Air Zaire

埃塞俄比亚航空公司　Ethiopian Airways

加纳航空公司　Ghana Airways

刚果航空公司　Lina Congo

埃及航空公司　Misrair (Egypt Air)

尼日利亚航空公司　Nigeria Airways

泛非航空公司(坦桑尼亚)　Pan African Air Services (Tanzania)

南非航空公司　South African Airways

苏丹航空公司　Sudan Airways

佛得角航空运输公司　Cape Verde Air Transport (Transportes Aereos de Cabo Verde)

突尼斯航空公司　Tunis Air

赞比亚航空公司　Zambian Airways

阿根廷航空公司　Aerolineas Argentinas

哥伦比亚中央航空公司　Aerolineas Centrales de Colombia (ACES)

墨西哥航空公司　Aeromexico

秘鲁航空公司　Aeroperu

巴哈马航空公司　Bahamasair

古巴航空公司　Cubana

多米尼加航空公司　Dominicana

巴西航空运输公司　Tramsbrasil

苏联民航　Soviet Air Line (AEROFLOT)

巴尔干保加利亚航空公司　Balkan Bulgarian Airlines

捷克斯洛伐克航空公司　Czechoslovak Airlines (Ceskoslovenske Aerolinie, CSA)

芬兰航空公司　Finnair

伊比利亚航空公司　Iberia

东德国际航空公司　Interflug

波兰航空公司　LOT

卢森堡航空公司　Luxair

匈牙利航空公司　Malev Hungarian Airlines

罗马尼亚航空公司　Tarom

葡萄牙航空运输公司　Transportes Aereos Portugueses (TAP)

南斯拉夫航空运输公司　Yugoslav Air Transport (Jugoslovenski Aerotransport, JAT)

瑙鲁航空公司　Air Nauru

新西兰航空公司　Air New Zealand

澳大利亚安塞特航空公司　Ansett Airlines of Australia

# 第五部分

# 农 业

## Part V

## Agriculture

# 目　录

# Contents

728

# 农村人民公社 Rural People's Commune

中国农村的基层单位 **basic unit of China's countryside**

三级所有制 **three levels of ownership, ownership on three levels**

以(生产)队为[所有制]基础 **with production team as the basic level of ownership**

基本核算单位 **basic accounting unit**

大队所有部分 **brigade-owned sector**

公社所有部分 **commune-owned sector**

社办事业 **commune-run undertaking**

社办企业 **commune-run enterprise**

公社党委会 **commune Party committee**

公社党委书记 **secretary of commune Party committee**

大队党支部 **brigade's Party branch**

大队党支书 **brigade's Party branch secretary**

副书记 **deputy secretary**

(生产)大队长 **brigade leader**

生产队长 **team leader**

副队长 **deputy leader**

生产队委员会 **team committee**

生产队委 **team committee member**

妇女工作组主任 **head of the women's work group**

民兵营长 **militia battalion leader**

贫下中农群众代表 **rank-and-file representative of the poor and lower-middle peasants**

贫下中农协会 **poor and lower-middle peasants' association**

社员代表大会 **commune members' representatives assembly**

生产管理委员会 **committee for the management of production**

计划生育委员会 **committee for the promotion of family-planning**

大队干部 **brigade cadre**

公社(机关所在) **commune office, headquarters of the commune**

大队部 **brigade office**

生产队部 **team office**

农业办公室 **office of agricul-**

ture

文教办公室　office of culture and education

知青办公室　office in charge of educated youth work

政治处　political work department

武装部　people's military department

保卫组　security group

财务组　section for financial affairs

农村人口　rural population

农业人口　agrarian population

非农业人口　non-agrarian population

农户　peasant household

军属　PLA man's family

烈属　revolutionary martyr's family

侨眷　family of overseas Chinese

困难户　needy family

五保户　household who enjoys the "five guarantees"

城市下乡知识青年　educated youth from town

农业科技人员　agro-technician

"赤脚医生"　"barefoot doctor"

拖拉机站　tractor station

拖拉机手　tractor driver

管水员　irrigation supervisor, irrigator

仓库保管员　storehouse keeper

会计员　accountant

记账员　bookkeeper

出纳员　cashier

犁手　ploughman

记分员　work-point recorder,

work-point bookkeeper

渔民　fishermen

牧民　herdsmen

农业机械化　mechanization of agriculture

提高农业劳动生产率　raising labour productivity in agriculture

土地规划　plan of land utilization

开荒　land reclamation

开发山区　developing mountain areas

耕山队　mountain-cultivating team

开发新土地　bringing new land under cultivation

生产计划　production plan

国家计划　state plan

生产指标　production target

生产定额　fixed production quota

单位面积产量　unit yield, per unit-area yield

平均亩产　average yield per mu

总产量　total output, total yield

生产管理　production management

生产责任制　system of production responsibility

包产到组　fixing output quotas on a production group basis

三包一奖制　system of fixed quotas for workdays, output and costs, with part of the extra output as reward

联系产量计报酬 calculating payment (workpoints) on the basis of the output

生产进度 rate of production

农忙季节 busy farming season

农闲季节 slack farming season

高产稳产田 land of high and stable yields

旱涝保收田 land of stable yield even in case of drought or waterlogging

因地制宜 suiting local conditions

水稻生产现场会议 on-the-spot meeting on rice growing

"三夏"生产现场会议 on-the-spot meeting on summer harvesting, planting and field management

粮食空前丰收 record grain harvest

粮食生产超过历年最高水平 surpassing the record year in grain output

比去年大大增产 making a sizable increase over the last year

比去年同期增加百分之… …per cent higher than in the same period of the last year

比19___年增加百分之… rising by…per cent over 19___

…产量超过19___年 output of… surpassing that for 19___

比19___年(该产量)相应数字增加百分之…以上 more than…

per cent above that for the corresponding figure for 19___

…倍增加 ___fold increase

多种经济 diversified economy

副业生产 sideline production

家庭副业 household sideline production

集体养猪场 collective pig farm

公养 collective raising

私养 raising by individual households

(猪)公有私养 raising collective-owned pigs by individual households

公栏私养 raising pigs on a collective pigsty by individual households

自留畜 private livestock

自留地 private plot

零星果树 scattered fruit trees

零星树木 small holding of trees

农村集市 rural fair

国营商业的补充 supplement to state commerce

议价贸易 buying and selling at negotiated prices

分配 distribution

各尽所能 按劳分配 from each according to his ability, to each according to his work

多劳多得 more income for those who work more

照顾国家、集体和个人利益 attention to the interests of the state, the collective and the individual

秋收分配 distribution after autumn harvest, autumn distribution

粮食分配 distribution of grain

收入分配 distribution of income

分配方案 distribution plan

公粮 agricultural tax in grain, public grain

余粮 surplus grain

减征公粮 reduction of tax quota in grain

免交公粮 exemption from agricultural tax in grain

集体收入 collective income

生产队收入 production team's income

社员收入 income of the commune members

全年总收入 gross annual income

支出数字 figures on expenditure

生产队账目 production team's accounts

劳动定额 work quota

男(女)全劳动力 able-bodied man (woman)

辅助劳动力 auxiliary manpower

出勤率 rate of attendance

评工记分 evaluation of work and allotment of workpoints

劳动日 man-day, work-day

工分值 work-point value

补贴工分 subsidiary workpoints

口粮依人定量 basic food rationing according to the capacity of each

商品粮 commodity grain

救济粮 relief grain

农业信用贷款 agricultural credit

粮所 grain station

粮仓 granary

晒谷场 grain-sunning ground, sunning ground

分配草案 drafted distribution plan

逐步积累生产队的公积金 building up the team's accumulation fund

扣除 deduction

补助金 subsidy

合作医疗资金 cooperative medical fund

敬老院 home for the aged

兽医站 veterinary station

农科站 agro-technical station

农业技术推广站 centre for the popularization of advanced agrotechnics

公社卫生院 commune hospital

大队卫生站 brigade's medical and health centre

合作医疗 cooperative medical service

大队办小学 brigade-run primary school

文化室 centre of cultural activities

灯光球场 floodlit playground

有线广播 wire-broadcasting

流动放映队 mobile film projection team

电视室　television room, TV room

科学种田　scientific farming

科学实验小组　scientific experiment group

农忙托儿所　busy season nursery

男民兵　militiaman

女民兵　militiawoman

基干民兵　core member of the militia, core militia-man

普通民兵　ordinary militiaman

征兵站　conscription station, draft centre

农业八字宪法——水、肥、土、种、密、保、管、工　The Eight-Point Charter for Agriculture——water, fertilizer, soil, seeds, rational close planting, plant protection, management, tools

# 农业气象学　Agricultural Meteorology

生物气象学　biometeorology

生物气候学　bioclimatology, bioclimatics

植物与气候的相互作用　plant-climate interaction

气候环境资料　climatic environmental data

植物小气候　phytoclimate

小气候的人工调控　artificial modification of microclimates

农业地形气候学　agrotopoclimatology

生物气候律　bioclimatic law

树线　tree-line, (Am.) timber line

等始花线　isanthesic line

农业气候区划　agroclimatic classification

农业气候区　agroclimatic region

农业气象站　agricultural me-

teorological station, agro-
meteorogical station

农业气象辅助站(观测站) aux-
iliary agricultural meteorological station

农业气象预报 agrometeoro-
logical forecast

农业天气预报 agricultural
weather forecast

简明〔天气〕预报 forecast
bulletin

当天天气预报 short-range
forecast

近期天气预报 medium-range
forecast, extended forecast

数值天气预报 numerical
weather predication
(NWP), numerical forecast

天气报告 weather report

天气图 weather map (chart),
synoptic map (chart)

传真天气图 facsimile chart

地面〔观测〕天气图 surface
chart, surface synoptic
chart

高空气象图 upper-air chart

(气象图用)气象符号 plotting
symbol

日射 insolation

日照可能最长度 maximum
possible solar duration

净辐射平衡 net radiation
balance

直接日射强度表 pyrheliometer

电位表 potentiometer

勒〔克司〕(米烛光) lux (metre-
candle)

照度计(勒〔克司〕计) luxmeter

呎烛光 foot-candle

韦斯顿照度计 Weston Illumi-
nometer

光强度 light intensity

克卡 gram-calorie (gm-cal)

英国热单位 British thermal
unit (BTU)

最适光强度较差 optimum
light intensity range

光饱和点 light saturation
point

补偿点 compensation point

周期性 periodicity

光周期性 photoperiodism

临界光周期 critical photo-
period

光给充足的地区 region with
an abundant light supply

光黑时间相对长度 relative
length of the light and
dark periods

日夜兼适植物 day-night neu-
tral plant

短日照长夜植物 short-day-
long-night plant

长日照短夜植物 long-day-
short-night plant

日曝 solarization

光〔的〕质〔量〕 quality of light

温度效率 thermal efficiency

温效指数 temperature effi-
ciency index

生长期有效积温 growing
degreeday

最高温度 maximum tem-
perature

最低温度 minimum tem-
perature

最适温度 optimum tempera-
ture

平均温度　mean temperature

昼夜气温　diurnal temperatures

日气温较差　diurnal temperature range

对作物的温度较差　temperature range for crop plants

最适温度较差　optimum temperature range

最适夜间温度较差　optimum night temperature range

能交换调节　regulation of the energy exchange

地温　ground temperature

土温(土壤温度)　soil temperature

土温的日变化　daily fluctuations in soil temperature

土温的年变化　annual variation in soil temperature

改变地温性质　altering the thermal properties of the ground

热害　heat damage

温室气候　class-house climate, greenhouse climate

热浪　heat wave

冷空气　cold air

寒潮　cold wave (current)

高压　anticyclone, high cyclone

高压脊　ridge of high pressure

脊线　ridge line

低压　depression, low cyclone

低压槽　trough

槽线　trough-line

冷锋　cold front

暖锋　warm front

风暴　storm

台风　typhoon

风级(风力)　windscale

风速表　anemometer

风向指示器　wind direction indicator

风向标　wind vane

台风警报　typhoon warning

尘暴　dust-storm

沙暴　sandstorm

防风带　shelterbelt

风障　windbreak

大气中的水汽含量　moisture content of the atmosphere

空气湿度　humidity of the air

绝对湿度(水汽浓度)　absolute humidity, vapour concentration

相对湿度　relative humidity

湿度表　hygrometer

饱和差　saturation deficit

温湿指数　moisture-temperature index, hydrothermal index

蒸发表　atmometer, atmidometer, evaporimeter

水汽凝结体　hydrometeor

降水量　precipitation

有效降水量　effectiveness of precipitation, effective precipitation

晴天　clear sky

少云天　sky slightly clouded

多云天　cloudy sky

多云近阴天　very cloudy sky

阴天　overcast sky

高云　high cloud

中云　medium cloud, middle cloud

低云　low cloud

平均云量　mean cloudiness

轻雾　mist

霾　haze

雾　fog

雾滴　fog-drip, fog-droplet

树挂雾凇　rime

云的调控　cloud modification

云的催化　cloud seeding

人工造雨　rainmaking

降雨　rainfall

全年降雨分布　distribution of rainfall throughout the year

雨量强度　rain intensity, raininess

雨带的变移　shifting of the rain belt

雨量器　raingauge, pluviometer, udometer

毛毛雨　drizzle, mizzle

冻毛毛雨　freezing drizzle

雨滴　rain drop

冻雨　freezing rain

雨凇　glaze

极微雨　very light rain, trace

小雨　light rain

中雨　moderate rain

大雨　heavy rain

阵雨　rain shower

暴雨　cloudburst

暴风雨　rainstorm

雷暴　thunderstorm, lightning storm

雷区　region of thunderstorm activity

雷阵雨　thunder shower

雨〔夹〕雪　sleet

露　dew

地面霜　ground frost

严霜　killing frost

辐射霜　radiation frost

风霜(平流霜)　wind frost, advection frost

防霜　frost protection

风机(防霜风扇)　wind machine, frost fan

降雪量　snowfall

米雪　snow grains

雪暴　snowstorm

低吹雪　drifting snow

高吹雪　blowing snow

积雪　snow cover, snowpack

测雪板　snowboard

测雪桩　snowstake

冰雪面消融　ablation

雪的水当量　snowpack water equivalent

冰日　ice day

冰暴　ice storm, silver storm

〔冰〕雹　hail

冰丸(小雹)　ice pellet, small hail

雹块　hailstone

雹暴　hailstorm

冻害　winter injury

冰点下气温　subfreezing temperature

径冻不足　insufficient cold

植物生长季节　vegetation season, growing season

农作季节　agricultural season

季节性迟后　seasonal lag

仲春　the middle of spring

盛夏　the height of summer

仲秋　midautumn

隆冬　depth of winter

二十四节气　twenty-four solar terms

立春 First Spring Day, Spring Begins

雨水 Rain Falling Day, Rain water, the Rains

惊蛰 Torpid-Arousing Day, Insects Excited

春分 Vernal Equinox

清明 Clear and Bright Day, Clear and Bright

谷雨 Rain-for-Grain Day, Grain Rains

立夏 First Summer Day, Summer Begins

小满 Prime Fill-Up Day, Grain Fills

芒种 Grain-in-Ear Day, Grain in Ear

夏至 Summer Solstice

小暑 Mid-Heat Day, Slight Heat

大暑 Scorching-Heat Day, Great Heat

立秋 First Autumn Day, Autumn Begins

处暑 Limit of Heat Day, Limit of Heat

白露 Pearl Dew Day, White Dew

秋分 Autumnal Equinox, Autumn Equinox

寒露 Cold Dew Day, Cold Dew

霜降 Frost Descending Day, Hoar Frost Falls

立冬 First Winter Day, Winter Begins

小雪 Little Snow Day, Little Snow

大雪 Heavy Snow Day, Heavy Snow

冬至 Winter Solstice

小寒 Moderate Cold Day, Little Cold, Slight Cold

大寒 Acute Cold Day, Severe Cold

生长期中气温 growing-season temperatures

无霜生长期 frost-free growing season

不合季节的高气温 unseasonably high temperature

气温突降 sudden drop in temperature

二分雨 equinoctial rains

梅雨 plum rains

霪雨 excessive rain

干旱 drought

伏天 dog days

湿润的大气兼有低速风 moist atmosphere accompanied by winds of low velocity

秋老虎 autumnal summer heat

寒露风 cold-dew wind

干冷的冬天 cold climate with dry winter

冬旱 winter drought

干燥的大气兼有高速风 dry atmosphere accompanied by winds of high velocity

湿冷的冬天 cold climate with moist winter

天气谚语 weather lore, weather proverb

# 土 壤 Soil

自然土壤　natural soil

农业土壤　agricultural soil, soil well suited to agriculture

可耕土壤　arable soil

原生矿物　primary mineral

次生矿物　secondary mineral

母质　parent material

母岩　parent rock

火成岩　igneous rock

原生岩　primary rock

花岗岩　granite

玄武岩　basalt

沉积岩　sedimentary rock

运积岩　transported rock

砂岩　sandstone

页岩　shale

变质岩　metamorphic rock

大理石　marble

石英岩　quartzite

岩石的风化　weathering of rocks

生物风化　biological weathering

化学风化　chemical weathering

物理风化　physical weathering

风蚀　wind erosion

土壤形成　soil formation

成土过程　soil-forming proces

农业土壤发生　genesis of agricultural soil

成土因素　soil-forming factor

土壤生物　soil organism

生物系列　biosequence

土壤绝对年龄　absolute age of soil

土壤相对年龄　relative age of soil

地质循环　geocycle, geological cycle

生物群落　biocoenosis, biotic community

生物循环　biological cycle

土壤微生物区系　soil microflora

土壤肥力　soil fertility

自然肥力　natural fertility

人为肥力　anthropogenic fertility

有效肥力　effective fertility

土壤发育　soil development

熟化作用　maturation

生土、未成熟土　immature soil

熟土　mature soil

肥沃土　fertile soil

疏松土　loose soil

瘦瘠土　infertile soil, lean soil

结壳土壤　incrusted soil
固结土壤　consolidated soil
土粒　soil particle
土块　clod
土壤质地　soil texture
粗质土壤　coarse-textured soil
细质土壤　fine-textured soil
细土　fine soil
致密质地　close texture
早发土　early soil
中等质地土壤　medium-textured soil
机械组成　mechanical composition
机械分析　mechanical analysis
砾石　gravel
砂　sand
砂质土　sandy soil
砂壤土　sandy loam
砂砾质壤土　sandy gravelly loam
砂质粘壤土　sandy clay loam
粉砂　silt
粉砂壤土　silt loam
粉砂粘土　silty clay
粘粒　clay particle
粘土　clay
重粘土　heavy clay
轻粘土　light clay
粘壤土　clay loam
壤土　loam
壤砂土　loam sand
土壤结构　soil structure
土壤组成　soil constitution
土壤团粒　soil granule
单粒结构　single-grain structure
片状结构　platelike structure
块状结构　blocklike structure

棱柱状结构　prismlike structure
角块状结构　angular blocky structure
团粒状结构　granular structure
团块状结构　crumb structure
土壤团聚体　soil aggregate
土壤水　soil water, water in soil
土壤水分　soil moisture
土壤湿度　soil humidity
含水量　moisture content, water content
持水量　moisture-holding capacity, water retaining capacity
凋萎系数　wilting coefficient
永远致萎点　permanent wilting point
暂时致萎点　temporary wilting point
变干，失去水分　drying out
蒸腾率　transpiration ratio
自由水　free water
毛管运动　capillary movement
毛〔细〕管水　capillary water
最大毛管持水量　maximum capillary capacity
悬着水分　suspended moisture
田间持水量　field capacity
有效水分　available water
无效水分　unavailable water
重力水　gravitational water
吸湿水，吸着水　hygroscopic water
最适水分　optimum moisture
持水当量　moisture equivalent
地面水　surface water

地下水 subterranean water

地下渗流 percolation

土壤密度 soil density

土壤比重 specific gravity of soil

土壤容重 volume weight of soil

土壤孔隙度 soil porosity

毛管孔隙 capillary pore, capillary space

非毛管孔隙 non-capillary pore

好气性细菌 aerophile bacterium (pl. bacteria)

嫌气性细菌 anaerobic bacterium (pl. bacteria)

土壤空气 soil air

容气量 air capacity

透气性,透气度 air permeability

土壤通气性 soil aeration

通气良好的土壤 well-aerated soil

通气不良的土壤 poorly-aerated soil

土壤温度 soil temperature

土壤热量平衡 heat balance of soil

土壤热容量 heat capacity of soil

容积热容量 heat capacity per unit volume

土壤比热 specific heat capacity of soil

土壤导热性(或导热率) heat conductivity of soil

导热率 thermal conductivity

土壤温度表(土温计) soil thermometer

土壤的机械施用率 soil workability

脱粘点 sticky point

临界含水量 critical moisture content

土壤的塑性指数 plasticity index of soil

液态极限 liquid limit

塑性极限 plastic limit

土壤渗透性 soil permeability

比表面积 specific surface area

孔隙 pore

膨胀 swelling

收缩 shrinking

龟裂,坼裂 fissure

裂纹 crack

结皮,结壳 crust

土壤结持度 soil consistence, soil consistency

土壤结持常数 soil consistence constant

粘结性 coherence

分散 dispersion

絮凝作用 flocculation

粘粒絮凝 clay flocculation, flocculation of clay

无机物质 inorganic matter

盐基 base

盐基交换 base exchange

盐基代换量 base-exchange capacity

盐基饱和度 degree of base saturation

土壤溶液 soil solution

土壤胶体 soil colloid

土壤盐渍度 soil salinity

盐化〔作用〕,盐渍〔作用〕 salinization

返盐 uprise of salt

土壤反应 soil reaction

土壤酸度 soil acidity

交换性酸度 exchange acidity

活性酸度 active acidity

潜性酸度 potential acidity

水解性酸度 hydrolytic acidity

土壤碱度 soil alkalinity

土壤酸碱度值(pH值) pH value of the soil

土壤缓冲作用 soil buffer action

吸收性能(吸收能力) absorbing power

交换量 exchange capacity

阳离子交换量 cation exchange capacity

阴离子交换量 anion-exchange capacity

有机物质 organic matter

离子的代换能力 ion exchange power

有机质的矿质化 mineralization of orgainc matter

有机质的腐殖化 humification of organic matter

腐殖质 humus, humic substance

腐殖酸 humic acid

吸收表面 absorption surface

腐殖质粘土复合体 humus-clay complex

土壤吸收性复合体 absorbing complex of soil

碳氮比 carbon-nitrogen ratio (c/N)

土壤剖面 soil profile

土层 soil horizon

土被(地被物) soil covering

植被 plant cover, vegetation

表土 surface soil, topsoil

亚表土 subsurface soil

松软表土 mould

耕作层土 ploughed soil

底土, 心土 subsoil

犁底层, 犁磐 plough (Am.plow) sole pan, plough pan

土层, 土体 solum

淋溶层(A层) eluvial horizon, zone of leaching (A horizon)

灰化层 podzolic horizon, spodic horizon

淀积层(B层) illuvial horizon, zone of deposition (B horizon)

淹育层 submergenic horizon

渗育层 percogenic horizon

潜育层 gley horizon

不透水层 impervious layer

埋藏土层 buried soil horizon

粘磐 clay pan

石灰结核(砂姜) lime concretion

铁锰结核 iron-manganese concretion

泛域土, 非地带性土壤 azonal soil

土壤地带性 soil zonality

土色 soil colour

淡色土 light-coloured soil

暗色土 dark-coloured soil

土壤的分布 distribution of soil

土壤分类 soil classification

土纲 soil order

土壤亚纲 soil suborder

土类 soil great group

土壤亚类 soil sub-group

土族　soil family
土系　soil series
土型　soil type
冰沼土　tundra soil
冰川土　glacial soil
冻土　frozen soil
灰化土　podzolic soil
黑钙土(黑土)　chernozem, black earth
栗钙土　chestnut soil
灰钙土　sierozen
灰色土　grey soil
漠境土　desert soil
半漠境土　semi-desert soil
棕钙土　brown soil
棕色森林土　brown forest soil
褐土, 褐色土　cinnamon soil
红壤, 红土　red earth, red soil
黄壤　yellow earth, yellow soil
黄土　loess
黄土性土　loessial soil
紫色土　purple soil
砖红壤　laterite
沼泽土　marshy soil, boggy soil
草甸土　meadow soil
草原土　steppe soil
水稻土, 水田土壤　paddy soil, rice soil
菜园土　vegetable soil
盐〔渍〕土　saline soil
含盐土壤　salty soil
碱土　alkali soil
白碱土　white alkali soil
黑碱土　black alkali soil
碱化土　alkalized soil
盐碱土　saline-sodic soil, saline-alkali soil

冲积土　alluvial soil
森林土　forest soil
森林-草原土　forest-steppe soil
青藏高原土壤　Qinghai-Tibet plateau soil
山地森林土　mountain-forest soil
山地草甸草原土　mountain meadow-steppe soil
山地半漠境土　mountain semi-desert soil
土壤调查　soil investigation
流域规划　basin planning
大地整理　land preparation
土壤制图　soil mapping
土样　soil sample
土壤采样钻　soil auger
土壤三相　three-phase of soil
土壤固相　solid phase of soil
土壤液相　liquid phase of soil
土壤气相　gaseous phase of soil
土壤详图　detailed soil map
土壤概图　reconnaissance soil map
剖面描述　description of profile
肥力鉴定　fertility characterization
土壤改良　soil amelioration, soil improvement
盐碱土改良　saline-sodic soil amelioration, saline-alkali soil amelioration
土壤侵蚀　soil erosion
正常侵蚀　normal erosion
地质侵蚀　geological erosion
自然侵蚀　natural erosion

加速侵蚀　accelerated erosion
水蚀　water erosion
雨滴侵蚀　raindrop erosion
表面侵蚀　surface erosion
沟蚀，沟状侵蚀　gully erosion
土崩　landslide
风积土　wind-blown soil

侵蚀率　erosion ratio
土壤流失　soil loss
防止土壤侵蚀　soil erosion control
土壤保持　soil conservation
水土保持　soil and water conservation

# 肥　料　Fertilizer

## 一般用语　General Terms

简单肥料　straight fertilizer
混合肥料　mixed fertilizer, fertilizer mixture
多种混合肥料　multicomponent fertilizer
复合肥料　compound fertilizer
完全肥料　complete fertilizer
不完全肥料　incomplete fertilizer
直接肥料　direct fertilizer
间接肥料　indirect fertilizer
颗粒肥料(粒肥)　granular fertilizer, granulated fertilizer, pelletized fertilizer
液体肥料(液肥)　liquid fertilizer
粉状肥料(肥田粉)　powdered fertilizer
细菌肥料　bacterial fertilizer
抗菌素肥料　antibiotic fertilizer
速效肥　quick-acting fertilizer, active fertilizer
长效肥(迟效肥)　slow-release fertilizer, controlled-release fertilizer, controlled-availability fertilizer
残积肥　residues of previous fertilizer applications
矿质肥料(无机肥料)　mineral fertilizer, inorganic fertilizer
有机肥料　organic fertilizer
积肥　manure storage,

manure accumulation

堆肥 compost, composted manure

肥料要素 fertility element

植物养分 plant nutrient

主要养分 major nutrient

次要养分 minor nutrient

微量养分 micronutrient

肥料需要量,需肥量 fertilizer requirement

肥料等级(以氮、磷、钾肥比率表示)

fertilizer grade (designated by the percentage of N.P.K.)

有效养分 available nutrient

肥料配合式 fertilizer formula

肥料保证成分 fertilizer guarantee

肥料载送剂 fertilizer carrier

肥料盐指数 fertilizer salt index

肥源 fertilizer source

### 天然有机肥料 Natural Organic Fertilizers

骨肥 bone fertilizer

生骨粉 raw bone meal

蒸制骨粉 steamed bone meal

脱脂骨粉 bone tankage

过磷酸钙骨粉 bone super-phosphate

酸化鱼粉 acidulated fish scrap

干鱼粉或鱼粉 dried fish scrap or meal

蹄骨粉 hoof-and-horn meal, hoof and horn

干血粉 dried blood

杂肉干粉 animal tankage

动物粪肥 barnyard manure, stable manure, (Am.) manure

腐熟厩肥, 沤肥 rotted manure, decomposed manure

农家肥 farmyard manure (F.Y.M.), muck

腐熟农家肥 well-rotted farm-yard manure

稿秆拌和的农家肥 strawy farmyard manure

粪肥 faecal manure

干粪肥 poudrette

液体厩肥 liquid manure

猪牛粪水 pig and cattle slurry

猪(牛)粪 pig (cattle) dung

干牛粪 dried cow manure

干羊粪 dried sheep manure

粪肥堆 dung heap, manure pile

家禽粪 poultry-dung, fowl manure

干家禽粪肥 dried poultry manure

秘鲁海鸟粪 Peruvian guano

蚯蚓 earthworm

蚯蚓粪 earthworm cast, cast

蚕粪(蚕沙) silkworm faeces, silkworm excrements

三鸟毛(鸡、鸭、鹅毛) feathers

根瘤菌 root nodule bacteria

固氮根瘤菌 nodular nitrogen-fixing bacteria

塘泥　pond silt
河泥　river mud, river silt
干污泥　dried sewage sludge
垃圾　refuse, garbage
泥炭粪肥　peat fertilizer
泥炭藓　peat moss
绿肥　green manure
黄花苜蓿　sickle alfafa, sickle lucerne
紫云英　astragalus, Chinese clover, milk vetch
苕子　vetch
田菁　sesbania
白芥　white mustard
草木樨　sweet clover
柽麻属　crotalaria
海草肥　seaweed fertilizer
绿藻　green algae
红萍　Azolla pinata

木棉籽麸　kapok seed press pulp
椰干麸　copra press pulp
蓖麻油渣　castor pomace
棉籽粉　cotton seed meal
饼肥　cake fertilizer
菜籽饼　rapecake
豆饼粉　ground beancake
可可豆饼粉　ground cocoa cake
灰肥　ash fertilizer
草木灰　plant ashes
椰壳灰　coconut shell ash
亚麻籽粉　linseed meal
花生麸　peanut press pulp
烟草梗　tobacco stems
花生秸　peanut stems
稻秆　rice straw
作物残茬　crop residues

## 化学肥料　Chemical Fertilizers

氮肥　nitrogen fertilizer, nitrogenous fertilizer
无水氨（液），液态氨　anhydrous ammonia
粗氨水　ammonia liquor
煤气厂氨水　gas liquor
氨水（氢氧化铵）　aqua ammonia, ammonia water, ammonium hydroxide
尿素（脲）　urea
乙烯双脲　ethylene diurea (EDV)
甲醛尿素　urea formadehyde
硝酸铵　ammonium nitrate
硫酸铵　ammonium sulphate, sulphate of ammonia
混酸铵（路那硝）　Leuna salt-

peter
碳酸铵　ammonium carbonate
碳酸氢铵　ammonium bicarbonate
硝酸钠（智利硝）　sodium nitrate
硝酸钙　calcium nitrate
硝酸钠钾　nitrate of soda-potash
石灰氮（氰氨化钙）　calcium cyanamide
硝酸铵钙　cal-Nitro, A-N-L, Ammonium nitrate-limestone mixture
氯化铵　ammonium chloride
氨化泥炭　ammoniated peat
磷肥　phosphate fertilizer,

phosphatic fertilizer

安福粉（磷酸一铵） Ammophos (monoammonium phosphate)

磷酸钙 calcium phosphate

过磷酸钙 superphosphate, calcium superphosphate

重过磷酸钙 triple super (phosphate), concentrated superphosphate

熔合磷肥 fused tricalcium phosphate

硝酸磷肥（"过磷酸铵"） nitraphosphate, "ammonium superphosphate"

氨化过磷酸钙 ammoniated superphosphate

磷酸二钙 dicalcium phosphate

钢渣磷肥（托马斯磷肥） basic slag, Thomas phosphate

莱纳磷肥 Rhenania phosphate

磷灰石 rock phosphate

硝酸过磷酸钙 nitric superphosphate

偏磷酸钾 potassium metaphosphate

钙镁磷肥 fused calcium-magnesium phosphate

钾肥 potash fertilizer, potassium fertilizer

钾碱 potash

钾盐（天然氯化钾） sylvite

粗钾盐 manure salt (KCL)

氯化钾 muriate of potash (M/P), potassium chloride

硫酸钾 potassium sulphate

硝酸钾 potassium nitrate

钾镁硫酸盐 Sul-Po-Mag, sulphate of potassium-magnesia, potassium magnesium-sulphate

氮磷钾肥 azophoska

光卤石，杂盐 carnallite

钾盐镁矾 kainite

氧化钾 potassium oxide

氧化钾当量 potassium oxide equivalent

钙肥 calcium fertilizer

土壤改良剂 soil amendment

石灰 lime, burnt lime, quicklime

消石灰 hydrated lime

石膏 gypsum

镁肥 magnesium fertilizer

白云石 dolomite

烧白云石 calcined dolomite

白云石质消石灰 dolomitic hydrated lime

烧水镁矾 calcined kieserite

镁氧矿 magnesia

菱镁矿 magnesite

## 其他肥料 Other Fertilizer Materials

硫酸铝 aluminum sulphate

硬石膏 anhydrite

硫酸铜 copper sulphate, cupric sulphate

绿矾 copperas

硼砂 borax

硫酸亚铁 ferrous sulphate

硫酸锰 manganese sulphate

大量需要的营养元素　**macronutrient**

微量需要的营养元素　**micronutrient**

含有最适度的溶解养分的　**eutrophic**

溶解养分增加过程　**eutrophication**

植物生长调节剂　**plant-growth regulator**

植物生长激素　**plant-growth substance, plant hormone, phytohormone**

促进生根粉剂　**root-inducing powder**

促进生根激素　**root-inducing hormone**

成花诱导　**floral induction**

开花后用激素喷洒　**postbloom spray with hormone**

九二〇激素　**920 plant hormone**

萘乙酸　**naphthalene acetic acid**

异芏长素, 吲哚乙酸　**indole acetic acid**

吲哚丁酸　**indole butyric acid**

## 施　肥　Fertilizer Application

土壤施肥　**fertilization of the soil**

合理施肥　**rational application of fertilizer**

普遍施用　**general application**

局部施用　**local application**

护养施肥　**maintenance application**

培养肥力　**building up fertility**

潜在肥力　**inherent fertility, potential fertility**

肥效　**effect of fertilizer**

肥料的残留值　**residual value of fertilizers**

基肥　**basal manure**

施基肥　**basal dressing**

深耕施肥法(全层施肥法)　**deep tillage with fertilizer application**

分层施肥法　**different applications at different depths**

施混合肥　**application of mixed fertilizers**

种肥　**starter fertilizer**

种肥溶液　**starter solution**

种子拌肥　**seed dressing**

分两次施肥　**application in two dressings**

追肥　**topdressing**

分期追肥　**topdressing at different stages**

后期追肥(抽穗后追肥)　**postearing topdressing**

飞机追肥　**aerial topdressing**

施肥量　**application rate, rate of manure**

中和值　**neutralizing value (N.V.)**

补偿地力作物, 补肥作物　**restorative crop**

表施　**surface application, topdressing**

撒施法　**broadcast method, broadcast application**

表施氮肥　**nitrogen top-**

dressing

表面施肥淋水　surface application of fertilizers combined with surface watering

稀释　dilution

免耕直播表施法　surface application under a system of zero tillage and direct seeding

灭茬掺肥　fertilizer incorporation by stubble-ploughing

施过肥的田　manured plot

未施肥的田　unmanured plot

侧施法　side-placement method, side dressing

条施法　row method, row application, drilling

穴施法　perforated method, application in the planting hole

液施法　liquid method, liquid application

肥水拌和后施用　manure and water applied premixed

槽车撒布　tanker distribution

随水灌肥　application with irrigation water

叶面喷洒　foliage spray, foliar spray

根外施肥　ex-root nutrition

压青(施用绿肥)　green manuring

有机物质　organic matter

施灰泥　marling

施石灰　liming

养分平衡　nutrient balance

吸持量　sorption capacity

过度吸收　luxury uptake

营养缺乏　nutrient stress, nutrient deficiency

叶片诊断　foliar diagnosis

营养吸收度　nutrient content, nutrient uptake

营养浓度(百分)　nutrient concentration (%)

# 水　利　Water Conservation

## 水利工程　Water Conservancy Project

抗旱　resisting drought

防洪　flood prevention

排涝　draining water-logged areas

水利工程学　hydrotechnics

土方工程　earthworks

石方工程 rock excavation

坍方 landslide, slide

塌陷 collapse, cave-in

年流量 annual discharge

支流 tributary

(河道)分叉 forking

河流汇合点 confluence, junction

潮区(感潮河段) tidal reach

三角洲上受咸水侵入的河汊 delta reaches being contaminated by salt water

河口湾 estuary

海堤 seawall

防波堤 breakwater

增加陆地 land accretion

海中收回陆地 winning land back from the sea

新增的陆地 innings

圩田 polder

冲去土地盐分 leaching land of salt

(开运河使)河道取直 (digging a canal) to cut the meanders of a river

防洪 flood protection, flood control

洪水痕迹 flood level mark

最大洪水 maximum flood

特大洪水 catastrophic flood, superflood

骤发洪水 flash flood

空前未有的洪水 record flood

洪峰 peak flood, flood peak, crest

堤 bank, embankment

泛滥，淹没 inundation, flooding

冲坍，冲崩 washing out

护堤 bank protection

折流坝 groyne, (Am.) groin

防洪警报装置 flooding warning system

水尺 water level gauge

自记水位计 water-level recorder, automatic water-level recorder

水情 regimen

水位上升速率 rate of rise of water level

平均水位(平水) mean water

高水位线 high water mark

低水位 low water

最低水位(枯水) minimum flow, lowest flow

分洪 flood diversion

治河 harnessing of a river

淤塞 silting up

疏浚 dredging

上游 upstream

下游 downstream

土坝(土石坝) earth dam

迎水面(上游面) upstream face

背水面(下游面) downstream face

水位抬高 raising of water level

正常高水位 normal top water level

非常水位 exceptional water level

最高壅水位 maximum water level, top water level

泄洪 flood discharge

溢洪道 spillway

溢流堰 weir

自由式溢流堰 uncontrolled

weir, open spillway

浸水式溢流堰(潜堰) controlled weir, controlled spillway

溢流坝(滚水坝) spillway dam, overflow dam

重力式溢流坝 gravity spillway dam

分水坝分水堰 diversion dam, diversion weir

拱坝 arch dam

连拱坝 multiple arch dam

堆石坝 rockfill dam

乱石堆筑 randam rubble fill

水闸 sluice, sluice gate

鼓形水闸门 drum gate

坝体加高 raising of dam

超水高度 freeboard

坝体加固 strengthening of dam

围堰 cofferdam

上游围堰 upstream cofferdam

下游围堰 downstream coffer-

dam

水上(上游水) headwaters

引水渠(前渠) headwater channel, headrace

进水口 water intake, water inlet

引水隧洞 intake tunnel

水头 head, pressure head

压力水入口 pressure intake port

压力水管 penstock, pressure pipe-line

回水区 backwater zone, backwater area

回水长度 backwater length

泄水道 tailrace

尾水 tailwater

静水池(消力池) stilling pool

人工湖，人工蓄水池 artificial lake

水库 reservoir

## 农田基本建设　Farmland Improvement Groundwork

农田给水工程 farm water supply engineering

给水水源 water supply sources, sources of water supply

给水系统 water supply system

灌溉水源 sources of irrigation water

灌溉工程 irrigation project

灌溉区 irrigation district

排水计划 scheme for irrigation and drainage, water management scheme

水流集贮 water harvesting

集水区 catchment area, (Am.) watershed

径流 run-off

拦蓄水 intercepted waters

农田蓄水坝 farm dam

蓄水库 impounding reservoir

水库总容量 total storage capacity, total reservoir storage

水库有效库容 usable storage of a reservoir

蓄水量/挖方比率 storage ratio, storage/excavation ratio (S/E ratio), water-to-earth ratio

供水水库 service reservoir, distribution reservoir

农田水库 farm reservoir

(水库)充水 filling

(水库)放水(消落) draw-off

水位下降 drawdown

放空，排空 emptying

泄漏 leakage

侧边泄水道 by-wash, by-channel

水道 watercourse

山塘围堰 hillside dam

山沟堰 gully dam

环山渠 winding canal along the hillsides

梯田 terraced fields

梯田排水道 terrace outlet channel

梯田系统 terrace system

蓄水围 ring dam

农用水塘 farm pond

地下水 underground water, subsurface water

潜水(地下水) ground water

地下径流 groundwater runoff

潜水位(地下水位) groundwater table, water table

降低地下水位 lowering of water-table

地下水流 ground water flow

凿通，打通 making an opening through

水井 well

管井 tube well, wellpoint

机钻井孔 borehole

自流井 artesian well

解冻(冰雪融解) thawing

融雪水 snow melt

调节水闸 closing dike

涵洞 culvert

渡槽 aqueduct

渡水高垾 elevated ditch

沟 ditch

(稻)田水管理 water management (in paddy fields)

大田布局 field layout

灌溉需水总量 irrigation requirement, duty of water

公顷/米水量 hectare-metre of water

畂/呎水量 acre-foot of water

潜在蒸发蒸腾 potential evapotranspiration

补给土壤储水量 replenishing soil moisture reserve

土壤缺水度 soil moisture deficit (S.M.D.)

水质 water quality

水的处理 water treatment

碱性水的酸化 acidification of alkaline water

灌溉效率 irrigation efficiency, distribution efficiency

灌溉强度 irrigation intensity

灌溉结构 irrigation structure

灌溉系统图 irrigation layout plan

灌溉渠网 grid of irrigation channels

灌溉总渠 main irrigation artery

灌溉主渠(干渠) main (irrigation) canal

灌溉支渠 secondary canal, irrigation lateral

自流灌溉 irrigation by gravity flow

自流灌溉的农田 commanded land
自流水总管道 gravity main
抽上蓄水 pumped storage
机械提水灌溉 pumping irrigation
排灌站 pumping station
吸升水头 suction head
灌溉水头 irrigating head
低扬程泵 lowlift pump
高扬程泵 highlift pump

水泵抽水坑 sump
水下泵 submersible pump
涡轮泵 turbine pump
抽水井 suction well
过顶渠 summit canal
倒虹吸管 inverted siphon, sag pipe
灌溉龙头 irrigation hydrant
竖管 standpipe
输水管 main pipes
接水喉管 lateral pipes

## 灌溉方法 Irrigation Methods

地面灌溉 surface irrigation
方块灌溉 check-basin irrigation
畦灌 border-strip irrigation
田埂 border dike
畦沟(田边沟) border ditch
灌溉沟 irrigation ditch, field ditch
浸灌 flooding irrigation
漫灌 wild-flooding irrigation
冲洗 flushing
垅沟灌溉 corrugation irrigation
沟灌 furrow irrigation
地下渗灌 subirrigation
鼠道 mole
喷灌 sprinkler irrigation, spray irrigation
多种用途喷灌系统 multi-purpose sprinkler system
多孔管喷灌装置 perforated sprinkler
滴灌 drip irrigation, trickle irrigation
滴流出水管 emitter

固定喷灌系统 solid-set sprinkler system
固定喷头 stationary nozzle
活动喷灌装置 portable sprinkler
中枢灌溉系统 centre-pivot irrigation system
中央井 central well
活动支承塔 mobile support tower
注射肥料进入给水管 injecting fertilizers into the water supply line
定期换水 refreshing the water periodically
一层水 water layer
慢慢放水 letting the water down slowly
种前灌水 pre-sowing watering, pre-sowing irrigation
种后灌水 post-sowing irrigation
种时(或种后)植地浇水 spot watering at (or after) planting

定植浇水  setting-in watering

生长全期浇水  throughout-life watering

收割前浇水  pre-harvest watering

全面浇水  overall watering

防霜冻灌溉  irrigation for frost protection

预灌  advance irrigation, pre-wetting

连续空中喷灌  continuous overhead sprinkling

排水  drainage

地表排水  surface drainage

排水沟  drainage ditch

排水道  outlet

排出水  drained-off water

排干田  drained field

## 一些地理名词  Some Geographical Terms

山区  mountain region

山地  rough country

山腰  hillside, mountainside

峡谷  gorge, canyon

沟壑  ravine

溪流  brook, (Am.) creek

山溪  mountain stream

山洪  swollen mountain stream

旱谷  wadi, dry river bed

平原  plain

丘陵地  hilly land

起伏不平之地  rolling land

沼泽地区  marshland

三角洲  delta

沙漠  desert

草原  grassland

绿洲  oasis

泥石流  mud-rock flow

泥流  mud flow, mudstream

沙丘  sand dune

稳定沙丘  arrested dune

流沙  quick sand

干旱带  arid zone, arid region

临时山洪  arroyo-running

泛滥平原  flood plain

土岗  earth hummock

高原  plateau

高地  tableland

沼泽河  swamp stream

瀑布  waterfall

悬崖泉  cliff spring

涝  waterlogging

分水岭  water divide

瀑流  cataract

江水盆地  catch pit

地下泉  underground spring

伏流  underground stream

自喷井  gusher

喷泉  gushing spring

高地田  upland field

荒地  wasteland

# 选种和育种 Seed Selection and Breeding

## 种子和种 Seeds and Species

胚 embryo
胚茎 plumule
胚根 radicle
下胚轴 hypocotyl
上胚轴 epicotyl
胚乳 endosperm
子叶 cotyledon, seed leaf
种皮 seed coat
〔物〕种 species
种名 specific name
种型 specific type
原种 maternal seed, mother seed, pedigree seed, stock seed
原种种子 original seed
原始种 initial species, original species
端始种 incipient species
自生种(原生种) indigen(e)
基本种 elementary species
当地种(本地种、乡土种) native species, indigenous species, endemic species
外地种(外来种) exotic species
复合种 aggregate species

无性种 asexual species
无性种(无融生殖种) apomictic species
恒有种 constant species
世界种 cosmopolitan species
优势种 dominant species
杂交种 hybrid species
新种 novel species
伴生种 auxiliary species, companions
连生种 fast growing species
偶现种 casual species
栽培种 cultivated species, cultigen
姊妹种 dual species
群型种 cenospecies
兼用种 dual-purpose breed
次要种 secondary species, accessory species
亚种 subspecies
残遗种 relic species, deleted species
优良种子 elite seed
品系 strain, line
对照品系 check clone

系谱(谱系) line of descent, lineage

近交系(自交系) inbred strain, inbred line

远交系 outbred strain, outbred line

复合品系 composite strain

纯品系 pure strain

高产品系 high-yielding strain

生理小种 physiological form, physiological strain

品种 variety, breed

地方品种 local variety, native breed

改良品种(育成种) improved variety

推广良种 popularization of good strains

栽培品种 cultivar

对照品种 check variety

多系品种(混系种) composite variety

标准品种 standard variety

蔓性品种 vine variety

引进品种 introduced variety

大种 major species

小种 microspecies

纯育品种 pure-breeding variety

抗性品种 resistant variety

抗旱品种 drought-resistant variety

耐寒品种 hardy variety

早熟品种 early-maturing variety

中熟品种 midseason variety, mid-variety, medium variety

晚熟品种 late variety, late maturing variety

高秆品种 long-stalked variety

矮秆品种 short-stalked variety

无核品种 seedless variety

稀穗品种 lax-spiked variety

感温性品种 temperature response variety

光周期反应性品种 photoperiodic response variety

推广品种 popularized variety

推荐品种 recommended variety

夏季品种 summer variety

秋季品种 autumn variety

冬季品种 winter variety

综合品种 synthetic variety

稀有品种 rare variety

高产品种 high yielding seed

亚变种 subvariety

变劣品种 off-type variety

特征明显的变种 distinct variety

合格种子 certified seed

纯洁种子(不混杂种子) pure seed

不纯种子(混杂种子) mixed seed

杂种种子 hybrid seed

中间杂种 intermediate hybrid

天然杂种 natural hybrid

永久杂种 permanent hybrid

结构杂种 structural hybrid

三系杂种 ternary hybrid

回交种 comeback

自然播种种子 self-sown seed

败育种子(不稔种子) abortive seed

| | | | |
|---|---|---|---|
| 不育种子 | sterile seed | 处理过的种子 | treated seed |
| 成熟籽粒 | ripe seed | 未洗净的种子 | underwashed seed |
| 饱满籽粒 | plump seed | 注册种子 | registered seed |
| 消毒种子 | disease-treated seed | 烘干种子 | roasted grain |
| 染病种子 | infected seed | 多籽植物 | allseed |
| 萌芽种子 | germinating seed | 单籽果 | one-seeded fruit |
| 需暗种子 | dark seed | 等外谷粒 | off-grade grains |
| 破皮种子 | scarified seed | 农作物品种名称 | cultivar-name |
| 皱缩种子 | wrinkled seed | 育种家 | breeder |
| 发育不全种子 | rudimentary seed | 育种协会 | breeding association |

## 作物遗传学　Crop-plant Genetics

| | | | |
|---|---|---|---|
| 隐性性状 | recessive trait, recessive character | 一对基因杂种 | monohybrid |
| 显性性状 | dominant trait, dominant character | 双因子杂种 | dihybrid |
| | | 三因子杂种 | trihybrid |
| 母〔本植〕株 | mother plant | 连锁群 | linkage group |
| 父〔本植〕株 | father plant | 连锁基因 | linked genes |
| 基因 | gene | 交换 | crossing-over |
| 纯合基因 | homozygous genes | 单交换 | single crossing-over |
| 杂合基因 | heterozygous genes | 双交换 | double crossing-over |
| 有丝分裂 | mitosis | 雄性不育性 | male sterility |
| 减数分裂 | meiosis | 染色体型雄性不育性 | male sterility of the chromosomic type |
| 染色体 | chromosome | | |
| 嘧啶 | pyrimidine | 细胞质型雄性不育性 | male sterility of the cytoplasmic type |
| 嘌呤 | purine | | |
| 腺嘌呤 | adenine | | |
| 胸腺嘧啶 | thymine | 倍数性 | ploidy |
| 乌嘌呤 | guanine | 基因组 | genome |
| 胞嘧啶 | cytosine | 染色体基数 | x number, basic number |
| 键合 | bonding | | |
| 基因分离 | segregation of the genes | 单倍体染色体数 | n number, gametic number |
| 基因自由组合 | independent assortment of the genes | 二倍体数 | 2n number, diploid number, somatic number |
| 基因型〔遗传型〕 | genotype | 整倍体 | euploid |
| 表〔现〕型 | phenotype | 同倍体 | homoploid |

| | |
|---|---|
| 非整倍体　aneuploid | 基因突变　gene mutation |
| 异倍体　heteroploid | 从显性到隐性　from dominant to recessive |
| 单倍体　haploid | |
| 二倍体　diploid | 从隐性到显性　from recessive to dominant |
| 三倍体　triploid | |
| 四倍体　tetraploid | 从有生命力到死亡　from viable to lethal |
| 五倍体　pentaploid | |
| 六倍体　hexaploid | 致死基因　lethal gene |
| 七倍体　septaploid | 分开保留上级表现型　isolating and maintaining superior phenotype |
| 八倍体　octoploid | |
| 九倍体　nonoploid | |
| 双二倍体　double deploid, amphidiploid | 弃掉下级表现型　discarding inferior phenotype |
| | 群选　mass selection |
| 异源多倍体　allopolyploid | 单株选择　single plant selection |
| 芽〔的突〕变　bud sport, bud mutation | |
| | 综合育种　combination breeding |
| 嵌合体　chimaera, chimera | |
| 周缘嵌合体　periclinal chimera | 上级基因排代某一个体的下级基因　superior genes displacing the inferior genes of one individual |
| 周缘区分嵌合体(边缘嵌合体)　mericlinal chimera | |
| 扇形嵌合体　sectorial chimera | |

# 育　种　Seed Breeding

| | |
|---|---|
| 植物育种　plant breeding | 自由传粉　free pollination |
| 育种材料　breeding material | 蕾期授粉法　bud pollination |
| 原始材料(亲本材料)　parent material | 亲近授粉　close pollination |
| | 近缘授粉　sib-pollination |
| (具某一特征的)品种　race | 人工辅助授粉　artificial supplementary pollination |
| 抗锈病品种　rust-resistant race | |
| | 防止飘来花粉　protection against stray pollen |
| 种子改良　seed amelioration | |
| 定向培育　directive breeding | 返祖现象　atavism, reversion |
| 纯系选择　pure-line selection | 返祖性再生　atavistic regeneration |
| 纯育(同系交配)　pure breeding | |
| 纯育(纯一传代)　breed-tree, tree breeding | 世代交替　alternation of generations, metagenesis |
| 传粉　pollening | 杂交育种　cross-breeding |

创造新品种　**creation of a new variety**

种质　**germ plasm**

可遗传的特性　**heritable characteristic**

遗传组合　**genetic combination**

附加遗传物质　**additional genetic material**

不同基因型而表征相似的群体　**land race**

对遗传的人工操纵　**genetic manipulation**

人工杂交　**artificial crossing, artificial hybridization, controlled crossing**

有性杂交　**sexual hybridization**

有性杂种　**sexual hybrid**

无性杂交　**asexual hybridization**

无性杂种　**asexual hybrid**

品种间杂交　**interbreed**

种间杂交　**interspecific crossing, interspecific hybridization**

种间杂种　**interspecific hybrid, species hybrid**

品系间杂交　**line cross**

属间杂种　**bigeneric hybrid, bigener**

双杂交　**double cross(ing)**

复合杂交　**composite cross-(ing), composite hybridization**

正反交　**reciprocal cross**

交叉杂交(二品种交替杂交)　**criss-crossing**

三元杂交(三品种杂交)　**three-way cross**

杂交的演进　**sequence of hybridization**

级进杂交　**grading up**

杂交返祖　**reversion on crossing**

杂交优势　**heterosis**

杂交后代(子代)　**filial generation**

杂交一代　**F1, first filial generation**

杂交二代、三代…　**F2, F3…**

杂交亲和性　**cross-compatibility**

杂交不亲和性　**cross-incompatibility**

杂交结实性　**cross-fertility, cross-fruitfulness**

杂交不结实性　**cross-infertility**

杂交不育　**cross-sterility**

不可交配性　**incrossability**

A系(雄性不育系)　**A-line**

B系(保持系)　**B-line**

R系(恢复系)　**R-line**

绿色革命　**green revolution**

育种规划　**breeding program**

育种方案　**breeding project**

育矮种和半矮种　**breeding dwarf and semidwarf varieties**

广谱抗病　**broad-spectrum disease resistance**

甄别试验品种　**screening experimental varieties**

自然突变　**spontaneous mutation**

诱发突变　**induced mutation, directed mutation**

化学诱变　**chemomorphosis**

诱变剂　**mutagen**

化学诱变剂　**chemical mutagen**

辐射育种 radiation breeding
突变率 mutation rate
品系退化 standard aberration of seed strains, degeneration of seed strains
杂交育种工作者 hybridologist
植物育种站(选种站) plant breeding station
育种圃(育种区) breeding nursery
育种小区 breeding plot
原种圃 stock plot, elite plot
杂种圃 hybrid nursery
玻璃纸袋 glassine bag

## 种子测定 Seed Testing

种子检查 seed inspection
种子鉴定 seed certification
(种子)健全鉴定 score for soundness
鉴定表 score card, scoring card
品种试验 variety test
(品种)种子试验区 seed-trial ground
品种区 variety plot
品种试验小区 variety test plot
品系试验 strain test
对照试验 check test
比较试验 comparative test
田间试验 field test
保护区 protective plot
对照小区 check plot
种子纯度 purity of seeds
品种纯度 purity of variety, varietal purity
种子成活力 seed viability
种子(生)活力 seed vitality
成活率(存活率) survival rate
品种特征 varietal characteristic
抗病力 disease-resistant power
种子升重(1公升种子重量) seeds litre-weight
种子容量 seeds volume-weight
无籽性(无核性) seedlessness
种子传播的病害 seed-borne disease
种子管理站(种子检验站) seed control station
品种鉴定说明(品种检索表) key to varieties

# 耕作和栽植　Tillage and Planting

耕作　tillage
耕作作工　tillage action
耕作设备(耕作工具)　tillage equipment, tillage tools
耕作目的　tillage objective
耕作施工　tillage operation
耕作要求　tillage requirements
埋入　anchoring
覆埋　burying
密实　compaction
打碎　crushing
刨块　cutting
内翻　inversion
拌混　mixing
锄松　loosening
碎分　shattering
分劈　shearing
土壤的物理反应　soil physical reaction
碎劈　tearing
抛离　throwing
全面耕作　broadcast tillage, total surface tillage
条行耕作　strip tillage
分层耕作　zone tillage
出苗前耕作　pre-emergence tillage
出苗后耕作　post-emergence tillage
收割前耕作　pre-harvest tillage

收割后耕作　post-harvest tillage
种前耕作　pre-planting tillage
种后耕作　post-planting tillage
头轮耕作　primary tillage
次轮耕作　secondary tillage
起种植床(起平畦)　bedding
疏间　blocking, thinning, checking
錾土　chiseling
综合耕作施工　combined tillage operations
交叉十字犁耕　cross cultivation, cross ploughing
碎压(碎土与压密同时进行)　cultipack
中耕　cultivation
作蓄水坑　damming, pitting, basin listing
掘土　digging
荡平　dragging
耙田　harrowing
植株培土　hilling
锄土　hoeing
掺合　incorporating
土地整治　land forming
地面挖补　land planting
拔起(根茎)　lifting
双边开沟　listing, middle-

breaking

犁田 ploughing

残积物处理 residue processing

起垄 ridging

用滚杆除草 rod weeding

滚压 rolling

用旋转锄锄土 rotary hoeing

用旋转机具耕作 rotary tilling

耙松表土 scarifying

耕底土 subsoiling

深耕 deep tillage

垂直覆盖 vertical mulching

锄草 weeding

田间管理工作 field work

清耕法 clean tillage, clean culture, clean cultivation

全套耕作 complete tillage

水土保持耕作 conservation tillage

(对农机)通道限制 controlled traffic

常规耕作法(惯用耕作法) conventional tillage

非全套耕作(省略耕作) incomplete tillage

最省耕作(减省耕作) minimum tillage, reduced tillage

留残茬耕作(免犁耕作) mulch tillage, stubble mulch tillage, ploughless farming

免耕法 no-tillage system, zero tillage

一次完成耕作 once-over tillage

犁植结合法 plough-planting system

最适度的耕作 optimum tillage

取向耕作 oriented tillage

亚表土耕作 subsurface tillage

表土耕作 surface tillage

等高耕作 contour tillage

残茬处理 crop residue management

作物轮作 crop rotation

休闲 fallow

土壤管理 soil management

条行间种 strip cropping, strip farming

夏季休闲 summer fallow

苗床栽植 bed planting

撒播栽植 broadcast planting

保平栽植 flat planting

双边沟栽植 lister planting

窄行栽植 narrow row planting

垄植 ridge planting

缝栽 slit planting

草皮上栽植 sod planting

轮辙上栽植 wheel track planting

闭垄 back furrow

墒沟 dead furrow

泥盘 pans

犁翻层 plough layer

压成层(犁底层,机具行驶压实层) pressure plan, plough sole, traffic sole

根床 root bed

苗床 seedbed

可耕性 tillability

耕作面情况 tilth

(农机具转弯的)田头地 turnrow, turn strip, head land

单一作物经营 one-crop farming, monoculture

多种作物经营 diversified

farming

作物复种 succession of crop

连作 continuous cropping

五种作物轮作 five-crop rotation, five-course rotation

前作物 preceding crop, forecrop

后作物 succeeding crop, aftercrop

双作 double cropping

套种, 间种 undersowing

补充作物 catch crop, intercrop

伴种作物 companion crop

播种 interplanting

高秆植物下栽植 underplanting

坡地垦殖 hillculture

人工护养栽培 protected cropping

水栽法 hydroponics

灌溉农业经营 irrigation farming

旱地农业经营 dryland farming

集约农业经营 intensive farming

粗放农业经营 extensive farming

无灌溉农业经营 dry farming

烧垦(刀耕火种) shifting cultivation, swidden cropping, slash-burn-and-abandon process

开垦荒地 pioneering, land clearing (reclaiming)

先锋作物 pioneer plant

栽培试验 growing-on test

梯田种植 terrace cropping

种植面积 sown area

耕作总面积 total area under cultivation

种双行 sowing in paired rows

植距 sowing distance, planting distance, spacing

株距 seed spacing, plant spacing

行距 row spacing

密植 close planting

合理密植 rational close planting

宽行栽植 wide-row planting

窄行栽植 narrow-row planting

梅花形栽植① quincunx planting

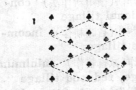

无保护播种(无覆盖物的播种) pure sowing

留株播种(屏障播种) coulisse planting, flap planting

按尺度索方形穴播 wire-row planting

# 农业机械与农具　Agricultural Machinery and Farm Implements

## 拖拉机　Tractors

农用拖拉机　agricultural tractor, farm tractor

万能拖拉机　universal tractor, general-purpose tractor

重型拖拉机　heavy-duty tractor

中型拖拉机　medium-sized tractor

小型拖拉机　small tractor, baby tractor

手扶式拖拉机　walking tractor

轮式拖拉机　wheeled tractor

标准型轮式拖拉机　standard-type wheeled tractor

两轮犁耕拖拉机　two-wheeled ploughing tractor

三轮型中耕拖拉机　tricycle-type row-crop tractor

钢轮拖拉机　steel-wheeled tractor

胶轮拖拉机　rubber-tyred tractor

气胎轮拖拉机　pneumatic-tyred tractor, air-tyred tractor

履带式拖拉机　caterpillar tractor, crawler tractor, tracklayer

窄履带式拖拉机　narrow-track tractor

半履带式拖拉机　half-track tractor

全履带式拖拉机　full-track tractor

小型履带式拖拉机　baby tracklayer

中耕(行间)拖拉机　row-crop tractor

柴油拖拉机　diesel tractor

汽油拖拉机　petrol tractor

前悬挂通用机架　front-mounted toolbar

中悬挂通用机架①　mid-mounted toolbar

后悬挂通用机架　rear-mounted toolbar

双向拖拉机(可逆式拖拉机) **reversible tractor**
串联式拖拉机 **tandem tractor**
水旱地两用拖拉机 **amphibious tractor**
山坡地拖拉机 **hillside tractor**
园圃拖拉机 **horticultural tractor, garden tractor**
后引擎拖拉机 **rear-engined tractor**
机引农具 **tractor-trailed implement**
拖拉机底盘 **tractor chassis**
拖拉机可调式座位 **adjustable tractor seat**
牵引装置 **hitch**
牵引杆 **draw bar**
联结钩 **hitch iron**

# 犁 Ploughs

铧式犁 **share plough**
轮式犁 **wheeled plough**
双轮双铧犁 **two-wheeled double-share plough**
多铧犁 **many-bottom(ed) plough gangplough, multishare plough**
圆盘犁 **disc plough, (Am.) disk plow**
垂直圆盘犁 **vertical-disc plough**
垂直多圆盘犁 **poly-disc, disc tiller**
多组圆盘犁 **gang disc plough**
跃障圆盘犁 **stump-jump disc plough**
垂直小圆盘犁 **harrow plough**
五铧圆盘犁 **five-share disc plough**
圆盘开沟铲 **disc furrower**
多组犁 **gang plough**
开沟犁 **digger plough**
中间悬挂式双向犁 **mid-mounted reversible plough**
起垄犁, 培土犁 **ridging plough, ridge plough**
单铧犁 **single-furrow plough**

双铧犁 **double-bladed plough, two-furrow plough, two-bottom plough**
锄式开沟器 **hoe furrow opener**
(带有前车架的)犁 **plough with forecarriage**
独轮犁 **one-wheel plough**
摆杆步犁① **swing plough**

双轮犁 **two-wheel plough**
高速犁 **high-speed plough**
双向立垡犁 **reversible plough of half-turn type**
双向四分之一翻转犁 **reversible quarter-turn plough**
双组犁 **two-gang plough**
单向犁 **run-round plough, two-way plough, (Am.) one-way plow**

双向型 **one-way plough, reversible plough, (Am.) two-way plow**

有壁型 **mouldboard plough**

无壁型 **mouldboardless plough**

悬挂式犁 **mounted plough**

双壁开沟犁 **double-breasted plough**

双层犁 **double-deck plough, double-cut plough, double-depth plough**

双壁起垄犁 **double-mould-board ridging plough**

牵引式犁 **trailed plough**

半悬挂式犁 **semi-mounted plough**

全悬挂式犁 **fully mounted plough**

深耕犁 **deep digging plough**

心土犁(深耕犁) **subsoil plough**

直接悬挂式心土犁 **direct-mounted subsoiler**

心土铲(深耕铲)① **subsoiling plough, subsoiler**

牵引犁 **drag plough**

重型拖拉机牵引犁 **heavy tractor plough**

架式犁 **frame plough**

开沟犁(起垄犁) **gutter-plough**

挖沟犁 **trench plough**

双壁开沟犁 **lister**

窄式开沟铲 **scooter**

暗沟犁 **mole plough**

暗沟排水犁 **mole drainage plough**

坡地排水沟犁 **hill drainage plough**

凿形松土犁 **chisel plough**

犁播机(条播犁) **drill plough**

长壁犁(草地犁) **lea plough**

坡地犁 **hillside plough**

机力升降犁 **power-lift plough**

犁铧(犁头) **plough-share**

犁辕(犁梁) **plough beam**

犁体 **plough body, (Am.) plow bottom**

犁壁 **mouldboard, (Am.) moldboard**

通用型犁壁 **general-purpose mouldboard**

深耕犁壁 **digger mouldboard**

犁刀 **plough coulter, (Am.) plow colter**

直犁刀 **knife coulter**

圆盘犁刀 **disc coulter**

副犁(小前犁) **skim coulter**

切角式小前犁 **fin cutter**

犁把手 **plough handle**

犁架 **plough stock**

犁柄 **stilt, (Am.) plow tail, plow neck**

犁螺栓 **ploughbolt**

犁耕机具装备 **ploughing outfit**

铧刃 **edge of share**

铧尖 **plough point**

车架 **wheeled carriage**

前车架 **forecarriage**

地轮 **land wheel**

沟轮 **furrow wheel**

牵引杆 **draught beam, draw beam, drawbar**

犁沟宽度调节器 furrow-width adjuster

犁侧板 landside

犁托 frog

步犁 walking plough

畜曳改良步犁 animal-drawn improved plough

# 耙 Harrows

机引之字耙 zigzag tractor harrow

播种耙 seeds harrow

轻型耙 light harrow

鸭掌式耙(牵引耙) duckfoot harrow, drag harrow

钉齿耙 tined harrow, toothed harrow, spike-tooth harrow

木架钉齿耙① wooden-framed spiked harrow

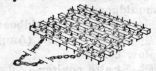

弹簧齿耙 spring-tined harrow

簧齿除草耙 spring-toothed weeder

簧齿式中耕机耙 spring-tined cultivator-harrow

旋转式除草机 rotary weeder

地轮传动旋转耙 ground-driven rotary harrow

链耙 chain harrow

旋转耙 rotary harrow

钉齿链耙 spiked link harrow

挠性链齿耙 flexible harrow

自净机引耙 self-cleaning tractor harrow

刀齿自净耙 pitchpole harrow

动力摆动耙 power-driven reciprocating harrow

动力驱动摆动式钉齿耙 recipro-

cating power-driven tine harrow

圆盘耙② disc harrow

重悬挂A型圆盘耙 heavy mounted A-type disc harrow

牵引式圆盘耙 trailed disc harrow

偏置式圆盘耙 off-set disc harrow

单列圆盘耙(灭茬圆盘耙) single-row disc harrow

双功圆盘耙(双列圆盘耙) double-action disc harrow

串联圆盘耙 tandem disc harrow

悬挂式串联耙 mounted tandem harrow

圆盘耙组 disc gang

调整杆 adjusting lever

用圆盘耙耙地 disking

绳索牵引双向耙 cable-towed two-way harrow

浅耕松土耙 pulverizing harrow

除草小耙 drill-harrow

草地耙 grassland harrow

刀耙 blade harrow

带齿拖耙(钉板耙) Dutch harrow

无齿拖板(板耢) toothless drag harrow

平地耙 smoothing harrow

平地拖板 planker, scrubber

匀土齿耙 spike tooth rake

水田耙 paddy field harrow

耙的刮刀 scraper

## 压土器 Rolls

光面压土器 flat roll

环面压土器 ring roll

机引压土器 tractor roller

滚压器 roll pack(er)

耕沟土垡压平器 furrow press

田面细平拖板 float

平地机 land leveller

平地滚压器 land roller

## 旋转耕作机 Rotary Cultivators

手扶旋耕机 walking rotary cultivator

旋锄机 rotary hoe

拖挂旋耕机 trailed rotary

cultivator

悬挂式螺旋挖掘机 mounted helical digger

## 条播机 Seed Drills

杯式排种装置 cup-feed mechanism

种子漏斗 seed hopper

圆盘排种装置 disc feed mechanism

外槽轮排种装置 internal double-run force feed mechanism

内槽轮排种装置 brush feed mechanism

刷式排种装置 brush feed mechanism

碟形排种装置 plate feed mechanism

销齿式排种轮 studded roller

条播开沟器 drill coulter

单圆盘条播开沟器 single-disc

drill coulter

双圆盘条播开沟器 double-disc drill coulter

划行器 marker

机挂条播机 tractor-mounted drill

半悬挂机引条播机 semi-mounted tractor drill

分组式条播机 unit drill

精密条播机 spacing-drill, precision drill

单粒排种条播机 single-seed drill

可逆式条播机 conversible seed drill

谷物条播机 corn drill

玉米条播机 maize drill, (Am.)

corn drill

蔬菜条播机　vegetable drill

棉花条播机　cotton drill

块根作物条播机　root drill

垄播机　ridge drill

手推转盘条播机　rotary hand drill

联合条播机(谷播肥料联合条播机)　combined drill, combined grain-and-fertilizer drill

## 撒播机　Broadcasting Machines

手推播种车　seed barrow

手摇撒播器　fiddle

机动撒播器　rotary seeder

流动撒播机　mobile seeder

机引撒播器　tractor-powered

broadcast seeder

下排式撒播器　drop-type broadcaster

全幅撒播机　full-width seed broadcaster

## 点播机　Dibblers

点播机①　dibbler

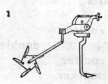
1

方形穴播机　checkrow planter, checkrow bunch planter,

hill-check planter, square-cluster planter

累积式穴播机(带穴播阀)　cumulative-drop planter

穴播机　hill planter

双行方形穴播机　two-row check row planter

多粒排种穴播机　hill-drop planter

## 种植机　Planters

鱼鳞坑田面播种机　basin planter

垄作播种机　bedder planter

重粘土田播种机　blackland planter

兼施液肥播种机　liquid fertili-

zer planter

沟播机　lister

除草覆盖撒播机　weeder-mulcher broadcast planter

水稻直播机　paddy planter

马铃薯种植机① potato planter

蔬菜播种机 vegetable(-seed) planter
块根种植机 tuber planter
球茎作物种植机 bulb planter
种茎作物栽植机 ratoon planter
耕耘播种机(留茬地播种机) tiller planter
花生播种机 peanut planter

## 移植机 Transplanting Machines

水稻插秧机 rice transplanter, paddy transplanter, rice planter
人力水稻插秧机 hand-operated rice transplanter
多用水稻插秧机 multi-purpose rice transplanter

双行插秧机 twin-row transplanter
三行插秧机 triple-unit transplanter
插秧船 floating seedling-container for rice-transplanting

## 中耕机具 Implements for Inter-cultivations

作垄器 ridger
牵引式三行作垄器 trailed three-row ridger
深耕中耕机② grubber

中耕通用机架 hoeing toolbar
无独立操向后悬挂机架 rear toolbar with no independent steerage

独立操向后悬挂机架 rear toolbar with independent steerage
中悬挂中耕机 midmounted hoe
中耕用自动底盘 self-propelled toolbar
动力输出轴传动转锄机 p.t.o.-driven rotary hoe
行间转锄机 inter-row rotary hoe
振动锄 vibro-hoe
间苗机 gapper, thinner
旋转盘刀式间苗机 rotary-head thinner
摆动式间苗机 oscillating thinner

顺行间苗机① down-the-row thinner

中耕机铲 cultivator shares

中耕机齿 cultivator teeth, cultivator tines

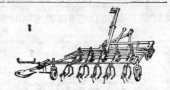

## 施肥机具 Manure Distributors

碟盘——搅杆式排肥装置 plate and flicker feed

辊式排肥装置 roller feed

搅拌轮式排肥装置 agitator feed

往复板式排肥装置 reciprocating plate feed

输送带——刷式排肥装置 conveyor and brush feed

机挂旋转式撒肥机 tractor-mounted spinner distributor

转盘式撒肥机 spinning disc distributor

振斗撒肥机 fertilizer distributor with oscillating spout

石灰撒布机 lime spreader

星轮排肥装置 star-wheel fertilizer feed

施肥附加装置 fertilizer (placement) attachment

农家肥撒布机 farmyard manure spreader

带水平辊农家肥撒布机 farmyard manure spreader

with horizontal rotors

粪沟清理机 mechanical gutter cleaner

行走轮驱动撒肥机 traction spreader

机引离心式撒肥车 tractor-drawn centrifugal spreader

双列击肥轮撒肥机 two-beater spreader

固肥液肥通用撒布机 universal spreader for solid and liquid fertilizers

真空罐式液肥洒布机 vacuum tank spreader

液肥罐 fertilizer tanker, liquid manure tanker

液肥撒布车 tanker-spreader

泥肥罐，粪水罐 sludge tank

液肥喷雾机 fertilizer sprayer

定点施肥(穴施肥) fertilizer placement

施肥开沟器 fertilizer placer

飞机撒肥 distribution of fertilizer by aircraft

## 收割机械　Harvesting Machinery

联合收割机① **combine harvester, combine**

自走式联合收割机　**self-propelled combine**
偏心拨禾轮　**pickup reel**
切割器　**cutterbar**
螺旋推运器(搅龙)　**auger**
升运器　**elevator**
喂入轮　**feeding beater**

脱粒装置　**threshing mechanism**
杂穗推运螺旋　**returns auger**
逐稿轮　**stripper beater**
杂穗升运器　**tailings elevator**
平台式逐稿器　**straw shaker**
杂穗盘(杂穗滑板)　**returns pan**
(筛孔)可调筛　**adjustable sieve**
谷粒筛(下筛)　**grain sieve**
谷粒升运器　**grain elevator**
粮箱　**grain tank**
粮箱卸载装置　**grain tank unloader**
发动机　**engine**
条铺检拾附加装置　**windrow picking attachment**

## 割捆机　Binder

拨禾轮　**reel**
分禾器(分茎器)　**divider**
鱼雷式分禾器　**torpedo divider**
旋转式分禾器　**revolving divider**
收割台帆布输送带　**platform**

**canvases**
打捆台　**binder deck**
打捆装置　**binding mechanism**
打结装置　**knotting mechanism**

## 脱粒机　Threshing Machines

清选脱粒机　**finishing thresher**
固定脱粒机　**stationary thresher**
移动式脱粒机　**travelling thresher, portable thresher**
脚踏脱粒机　**pedal thresher**
电动脱粒机② **power thresher**

自动喂入装置　self-feeder
脱粒滚筒　thresher drum
脱粒凹板　thresher concave
击杆式脱粒滚筒的凹板　beater-type drum and convave
钉齿式脱粒滚筒和凹板　peg-type drum and convave
逐稿器　straw shaker
颖糠(颖壳)　chaff
碎茎稿　cavingo

未脱粒穗　chobs
除芒器　awner
碎稿筛　cavings riddle
净粒器　chobber
颖糠碎稿吹风机　chaff and cavings blower
清粮室筛架　dressing shoe
旋转筛　rotary screen
装袋器　bagging apparatus

## 块根作物收割机械　Root Harvesting Machinery

马铃薯挖掘犁①　potato raising plough

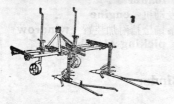

挖根机　rooter
掘薯抛掷机　potato spinner
升运式挖掘机　elevator digger
摇筛式马铃薯挖掘机②　swing-sieve potato digger
茎叶切碎机　haulm pulverizer
马铃薯分级机　potato sorter

甜菜挖掘机　sugar-beat lifter
甜菜切顶机　sugar-beat topper
切顶堆行机　topper-windrower
切顶装载机　topper-loader
甜菜联合收割机　complete beat harvester
甜菜清理装载机　beat cleaner loader

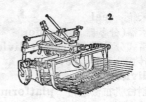

## 谷场谷仓用机械　Barn Machinery

预净机　pre-cleaner
种子清选机　seed cleaner
抖筛　reciprocating sieve
气吸风力清选机　aspirating cleaner

筛选机　sieve cleaner
塔式谷物干燥机　tower-type grain drier
风选机　winnower
旋转筛联合风选分级机　combined

winnower and grader with rotary screen

进料斗　deed hopper

筛　sieve

风扇　fan

滑槽(除砂和莠种子)　chute (for sand and weed seeds)

送谷滑槽　grain delivery chute

斗式升运器　bucket elevator

旋转筛　rotary screen

尾谷装袋口　tail corn sacking spout

头谷装袋口　head corn sacking spout

吸风塔(柱形吸风筒)　aspiration leg

窝眼式滚筒选种机　indented cylinder seed cleaner

风力清选机　pneumatic separator

比重清选机　specific gravity separator

干式种子消毒机　seed dusting machine

种子药物消毒机　chemical seed dresser

带清理滚笼的块根切碎机①　root cutter with cleaning cage

盘式石磨机　buhr-stone mill

对辊磨　roller-crushing mill

锤式粉碎机　hammer mill

压块机　cuber

制粒机　pelleter

## 作物干燥设备　Crop Drying Equipments

盘式干燥机　tray drier

环形输送带干燥机　endless belt conveyor drier

干燥室　drying chamber

高温干燥机　high temperature drier

旋转干燥筒　rotary drying drum

三级高温干燥机　three-stage high-temperature drier

多次通过式干燥机　multipass drier

连续式干燥机　continuous drier

间歇式干燥机(分批式干燥机)②　batch drier

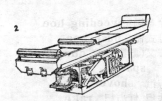

袋装干燥法　sack-drying method

送气室　plenum chamber

风扇式空气加热器　fan-heater

红外线干燥机　infrared drier

仓内干燥法　barn-drying method

轴流式风扇　axial-flow fan

隧道式干燥机　tunnel drier

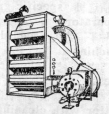

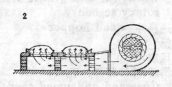

塔式谷物干燥机① **tower-type grain drier**

阶梯式谷物干燥机 **cascade grain drier**

倾斜盘式干燥机 **inclined tray drier**

袋装谷物平台干燥机② **platform drier for bagged grain**

通风谷物干贮塔 **ventilated silo grain drier**

辐射通风干贮塔 **radial-flow ventilated silo**

在谷仓地台上干燥谷物设备③ **drying grain equipment on the barn floor**

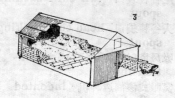

砖砌主管道 **brick main duct**

刷扫式输送螺旋 **sweep auger**

# 农　具　Farm Tools

除草锄 **weeding hoe**
推式锄 **push hoe**
粪叉(厩肥叉) **dung fork**
铲 **spade**
方锹 **shovel**
铁耙, 钉齿耙 **rake**
粪钩锄 **dung hoe**
长柄镰刀 **scythe**
钩镰 **sickle**
草耙 **hay rake**
连枷 **flail**

挖根锄 **grubbing hoe**
凹口锄 **crescent hoe**
行播器 **row-seeder**
点播器 **dibber**
牛轭 **yoke**
扁担 **carrying pole**
畚箕 **basket**
禾桶 **threshing tub**
谷拨 **grain scraper**
禾叉(干草叉) **pitchfork**

# 作物保护 Crop Plant Protection

## 一般用语 General Terms

预防和消灭植物病虫害 prevention and elimination of plant diseases and pests
综合防治 integrated control
化学防治 chemical control
生物防治 biological control
主动保护(积极保护) active protection
植物防病注射 vaccination of plants
植物杀除剂试验 phytocidal test
空气传染 air-borne infection
气中侵染 aerogenous infection
空中防治 aero-control
植物检疫 plant quarantine, plant sanitation
种子消毒 seed disinfection
土壤消毒 soil disinfection
消毒剂 disinfectant
制止植物疾病蔓延 checking the spread of plant disease

抗感染 anticontagion
抗虫害 pest-resistance
虫害防治 pest control
杂草防治 weed control
植物免疫性 phyto-immunity
药物喷射 chemical spray
喷雾(喷撒) spraying
空中喷雾 aero-spraying
喷粉 dusting
飞机喷粉 air-dusting
触杀剂喷雾 contact spraying
自动喷雾器 automatic sprayer
喷药伤害 spray injury
诱捕 trapping
诱虫灯 trap lamp
捕虫沟(诱杀沟) insect-trench, trap trench
抗药性(耐药性) drug-fast
(害虫的)天敌 natural enemy (of pests)
消灭病原体 eliminating the pathogen

## 植物病害　plant Diseases

植物流行病　epiphytotic disease

植物虫毒病害　phytotoxemia

植物病理检验　phytopathological inspection

感染密度(危害度)　density of infection

抗病力(抗病性)　disease resistance

植物病害防治　control of plant diseases

植物病害流行预测　forecast of epiphytotic diseases

受感染植物　attacked plant

病的起源　pathogenesis, pathogeny

病原体　pathogen

病原细菌　pathogenic bacteria

致病生物　pathogenic organism

土著细菌　autochthonous bacteria

病原菌　pathogenic fungi

接触传染　contagion

病毒　virus

发病　disease development

发病率　disease incidence

发作(发病)　attack

严重发病　bad attack

感染(侵染)　infection

大量感染　mass infection

感病性　susceptibility

媒介昆虫(传病昆虫)　insect vector

传递(传播)　transmitting

侵害(侵袭)　invasion, attack

潜伏期　incubation period, incubative stage, latent period

病征　symptom, sign

检查　examination

病害甄别(病害诊断)　disease screening

损伤(破损)　injury, break

损害(伤害)　lesion

愈合　coalescence, cicatrization

坏死　necrosis

坏死组织　necrotic tissue

环境条件　environmental conditions

营养缺乏病　deficiency disease

营养缺乏病症　deficiency symptom

耐病性　disease tolerance

病毒病　virus disease

枯萎病(凋萎病)　blight

抗凋萎素　antiblastion

萎缩症　atrophy

青枯病　bacterial wilt

叶斑病　leaf spot

花叶病　mosaic

霉病　mildew

霜霉病　downy mildew

炭疽病　anthracnose,anthrax

煤污病　sooty mould, black blight

穿孔病　shot hole

白粉病　powdery mildew

颈腐病　neck rot

根腐病　root rot

根肿病　clubroot

黑腐病　black rot

软腐病　soft rot
雪腐病　snow mould
斑萎病　spotted wilt
溃疡　canker
疮痂病　scab
疱疹(湿疹)　blister tetter
疱锈病　blister rust
黑斑病　black spot
白化病　albinism
黑穗病(黑粉病)　smut
黑穗病菌　smut fungus
感染黑穗病的　smutted

不感染黑穗病的　smut-free
圆葱黑粉病　smut of onion
镰刀菌萎蔫病　fusarium wilt
锈病　rust
锈病防治剂　rust preventer
螨病　acariasis
囊尾蚴病　bladder-worm disease
马铃薯早(或晚)疫病　early (or late) blight of potato
日灼　sun-scald, sunscorch

# 虫 害 Insect Pests

害虫防治　pest control
环阻法　banding
遭受虫害　insect infestation, being plagued by pests
害虫　injurious insect, destructive insect, pest, vermin
主要害虫　primary pests
咀嚼式口器害虫　chewing pests, insects with biting mouth parts
刺吸式口器害虫　sucking pests, insects with sucking mouth parts
澳洲蛛甲　Australian grain borer
象虫　weevil
豆象　bruchid weevil
虻害　warble fly pest
小地老虎　black cutworm
植物跳虱　plant lice
甲虫　beetle
红蜘蛛　red spider
龟甲虫　tortoise beetle

五月金龟子　May beetle
铁线虫　wireworm
卷叶虫　roller
卷叶蛾　tortrix moth
潜叶虫　leaf miner
锯蜂(叶蜂)　sawfly
根虫　rootworm
马铃薯瓢虫　potato beetle
水果食心虫　fruit worm
菜青虫　cabbage worm
豌豆象鼻虫　pea weevil
椿象　stink bug
天牛　long-horned beetle
跳甲　flea beetle
毛虫　caterpillar
蚜虫　aphid
蚱蜢　grass hopper
蝗虫　locust
蚧(介壳虫)　scale insect
蜻蜓　dragonfly
蛞蝓　slug
凤蝶　swallowtail
蜗牛　snail
白蚁　termite, white ant

虫口密度　population density
捕虫饵　insect bait

毒杀　poisoning

# 农　药　Agricultural Chemicals

农用杀虫剂　agricultural insecticide
胃毒剂　stomach poison, stomach insecticide
触杀剂　contact insecticide
接触性毒剂　contact toxicant, contact poison
后效杀虫剂　residual insecticide
内吸剂　systemics
内吸杀虫剂　systemic insecticide
熏蒸〔消毒〕剂　fumigant
驱虫剂　insect repellant
引诱剂(诱虫剂)　attractant
窒息剂　asphyxiant
窒息气　asphyxiant gas
敏感性　susceptibility
抗药性(对杀虫剂)　resistance to insecticide
剂量(药量)　dose, dosage
有效药剂　effective agent
剂量效应　dosage effect
农药污染　pesticide contam-

ination
残效　carry-over effect
残留毒性(残毒)　residual toxicity
农药残留标准　trace standard of agricultural chemicals
农药中毒　being poisoned by agricultural chemicals
粉剂　dust, powder
可湿性粉剂　wettable powder
悬浮液　suspension
乳剂　emulsion
油乳剂　oil emulsion
液剂　flowable
烟雾剂　smoking agent
补助剂　accessory agent
粉末载体　dust carrier
溶剂　solvent
润湿剂　wetting agent
分散剂　dispersing agent
增效剂　synergist
浓度　concentration
适期施药　proper timing of insecticide application

# 杀虫剂　Insecticides

无机杀虫剂　inorganic insecticide
有机杀虫剂　organic insecticide
有机含磷杀虫剂　organic phosphorous insecticide
滴滴涕　DDT

六六六(六氯化苯)　HCH, BHC
福美双(涕门涕滴)　Thiram, TMTD
甲氧滴滴涕　methoxychlor
敌百虫　dipterax
除虫菊　pyrethrum
除虫菊粉　pyrethrum powder,

| | |
|---|---|
| **Dalmatian insect powder** | 土壤杀虫剂　**soil insecticide** |
| 除虫菊酯　**pyrethrin** | 二嗪农　**diazinon** |
| 丙烯除虫菊　**allethrin** | 鱼藤酮　**rotenone** |
| 艾氏剂　**aldrin** | 胡椒荃丁醚　**peperonyl buto-** |
| 异艾氏剂　**Isodrin** | **xide** |
| 狄氏剂　**Dieldrin** | 砷酸铅　**lead arsenate** |
| 异狄氏剂　**endrin** | 砷酸钙　**calcium arsenate** |
| 六氯乙烷混合剂　**hexachlorae-** | 亚砷酸　**arsenolite** |
| **thane mixture** | 巴黎绿　**Paris green** |
| 氯化烃杀虫剂　**chlorinated hy-** | 氟化钠　**sodium fluoride** |
| **drocarbon insecticide** | 稻丰散　**ersan** |
| 氯丹　**chlordane** | 杀蚜剂　**aphidicide** |
| 七氯　**heptachlor** | 杀螨剂　**acaricide** |
| 巴丹　**Padan** | 阿拉散(一种杀螨剂)　**aratjame** |
| 三硫磷　**trithion** | 杀螨特　**aramite** |
| 甲拌磷(三九一一杀虫剂)　**thimet** | 三氯杀螨砜　**tedion** |
| 倍硫磷　**baytex** | 杀幼虫剂(杀蜎剂)　**larvicide** |
| 内吸磷(一〇五九杀虫剂)　**systox** | 杀蛾剂　**mothicide** |
| 1605(对硫磷杀虫剂)　**parathion** | 杀虱剂　**pediculicide** |
| 硫磺粉　**sulphur dust** | 杀虫毒剂　**poison insecticide** |
| 马拉松　**malathion** | 杀虫粉　**insect powder** |
| 八甲磷　**schradan** | 杀虫胶　**insect paste** |
| 杀螟松　**sumithion** | 无效杀虫剂　**inefficient insec-** |
| 罗纳丹　**ryanodine** | **ticide** |
| 硫丹　**thiodan** | 杀鼠剂　**raticide, rodenticide** |
| 乐果　**rogor** | 灭鼠　**deratization** |
| 杀螟腈　**cyanox** | 杀鼠灵　**warfarin** |
| 毒杀芬　**toxaphene** | |

## 杀霉菌剂　Fungicides

| | |
|---|---|
| 霉菌　**fungus (pl. fungi)** | 消毒(杀菌)　**disinfection** |
| 病原菌　**pathogenic fungi** | 抗菌活性　**antibiotic activity** |
| 疫菌　**blighting fungi** | 抑菌剂　**germifuge, bacterios-** |
| 土壤霉菌　**soil fungi** | **tat** |
| 霉菌对作物的危害　**ravage of** | 农用抗菌素　**agricultural anti-** |
| **fungi on crops** | **biotic** |
| 抗霉性(抗霉力)　**mold resis-** | 抗真菌素　**eumycin** |
| **tance** | 抗真菌剂　**antifungal** |

杀菌剂　germicide

杀真菌素　cabicidin

杀真菌剂　mycocide

保护性杀真菌剂　protective fungicide

无机杀菌剂　inorganic fungicide

有机杀菌剂　organic fungicide

抗霉素　antimycin

拒霉素　resistomycin

抗微生物剂　antimicrobic

抗寄生物药剂　antiparasitic

杀寄生物剂　parasiticide

多硫化钡　solbar

石硫合剂　lime-sulfur solution

福美双　arasan

二硝散　nirit

苯汞铵　puratized NSE

氰胍甲汞　panogen

福美砷　asomate

托布津　topsin

百菌清　Daconil

稻丰宁　rabcon

二氯萘醌　phygon

灭菌丹　phaltam

灭瘟素　blasticidin

萎锈灵　oxathiin

克瘟散　hinozan

稻瘟霉素　blastmycin

抗稻瘟素　antipiriculin

杀藻剂　algicide

杀菌剂的化学稳定性　chemical stability of fungicides

渗进作物内部　permeating the plant

消除感染　eliminating infection

粘附在叶片上　adhering to foliage

霉菌孢子　fungus spore

毒效　poisonous effect

飞机喷粉机　airplane duster

## 除草剂　Herbicides

杂草(莠草)　weed

稗①　tare (weed), barnyard grass

有害杂草　injurious weed

杂草丛生　overrunning weeds, invasion of weeds

杂草为害　weed encroachment

长满杂草的　weedy, infested with weeds

难根除的杂草　troublesome

weeds

危害大的杂草　ill weeds

寄生的杂草　parasitic weeds

非乡土性杂草　imported weeds

无杂草的　weed-free

接触除莠剂　contact weed-killer

选择性除莠　selective weeding

选择性除草剂　selective herbicide

非选择性除草剂(灭生性除草剂)　nonselective herbicide, sterilant

百草枯　Paraquat

敌草索　Dacthal

稗蓼灵　Bipc

八氯环乙烯酮 octane
莠去津 atrazine
敌稗 propanil
扑草净 prometryne
灭草隆 monuron
非草隆 femuron
敌草隆 diuron
燕麦灵 barban
除草油 weed oil
除莠油 deweeding oil
除草效力 herbicide action
(非)选择性触杀型叶片喷药 selective (nonselective) foliage contact spray
(非)选择性内吸传导型叶片喷药 selective (nonselective) translocated spray

(非)选择性根部施药 selective (nonselective) root application
出苗前(后)喷药 preemergence (postemergence) spray
原生质选择性 protoplasmic selectivity
酶作用 enzyme action
施药方法 application method
粘附强度 adhesion strength
影响除草剂药效的因素 factors influencing the action of herbicides
生长点的位置 location of growing point
叶的取向 orientation of leaves

# 禾谷类作物 Cereal Crops

## 稻谷生产 Rice Production

水稻① paddy rice, lowland rice

陆稻(旱稻) upland rice, dry rice
籼稻 *xian* rice, long-grain rice
粳稻 *jing* rice, short-grain rice
粘稻 *zhan* rice, non-glutinous rice
糯稻 glutinous rice

早稻　**early rice, early season rice**

中稻　**midseason rice, middle-season rice**

晚稻　**late rice**

单季稻　**single-cropping of rice**

双季稻　**double-cropping of rice**

三季稻　**triple-cropping of rice**

再生稻　**ratooning rice**

抗旱品种　**drought-resistant variety**

抗倒伏品种　**lodging-resistant variety**

抗稻瘟品种　**rice-blast-resistant variety**

耐寒性　**cold tolerance**

耐旱性　**drought tolerance**

伸穗力　**panicle exsertion**

分蘖力　**tillering ability**

秆力　**straw strength**

深水中的生长力　**elongation in deep water**

受浸后的复原　**recovery from submergence**

受旱后的复原　**recovery from drought stress**

谷粒的糖淀粉含量　**amylose content of the grain**

基础种　**foundation seed**

浸种　**seed soaking**

催芽　**accelerating germination**

炼芽　**hardening-off seeds**

播种量　**seeding rate**

秧龄　**seedling age**

秧田　**seedling bed**

泡田　**ponding**

发芽力　**germinating power**

发芽势　**germinating energy, vigour of germination**

稻苗绵腐病　**seedling blight of rice**

移植　**transplanting**

插秧　**setting out rice seedling**

直播　**direct seeding**

返青　**recovery from transplanting**

浆土　**puddled soil**

插秧密度　**density of transplants**

单位面积株数　**number of plants per unit area**

一次插下的株数　**number of plants per hill**

给田排灌几次　**flooding and draining the field several times**

持久灌水　**prolonged flooding**

中耕　**cultivation, intertillage**

已刮草的一块田　**scraped plot**

中耕机锄铲——齿式　**cultivator steel**

中耕器锄铲——刮式　**hoe blade**

拔节阶段(长茎阶段)　**stem elongation stage**

孕穗阶段　**booting stage**

抽穗阶段　**heading stage**

扬花阶段　**flowering stage**

灌浆阶段　**filling stage, milking stage**

蜡熟期　**dough stage**

成熟期　**ripening stage, maturing stage**

完熟作物　**ripened crop**

成熟不均匀　**uneven ripening**
倒伏　**lodging, falling over**
不结实的小穗　**sterile spikelet**
可脱粒度(落粒倾向)　**panicle threshability, shattering tendency**
稻秆的弯折角　**culm angle**
难脱粒水稻品种　**hard-to-thresh rice variety**
割幅　**swath**
收割(割禾)　**reaping rice**
打禾　**rice threshing**
手打　**hand threshing, manual threshing**
手打的稻谷　**hand-threshed paddy**
机打　**mechanized threshing**
禾桶和禾围　**threshing tub and a shield**
脱粒干净　**thorough threshing**
擦破谷壳　**peeling of the grain**
堆秆　**straw stacking**
簸谷　**winnowing**
晒干　**sun-drying**
机械干燥　**mechanical drying**
储藏干燥　**in-storage drying**

仓内干燥　**in-bin drying**
袋装干燥　**sack drying**
稻谷加工　**rice processing**
碾米　**rice milling**
清选　**cleaning**
去谷壳　**husking**
糙米　**husked rice, brown rice**
去麸皮　**bran removal**
糠　**bran flour**
米糠油　**rice bran oil**
分级　**grading**
包装　**packaging**
麻袋　**jute bag**
无包装储放　**bulk storage**
秤重　**weighing**
碾米机，碾米厂　**rice mill**
精碾程度　**degree of polishing**
磨粉　**flour milling**
干粒重　**1000 kernel weight**
谷粒大小　**grain dimensions, grain size**
碾出米量　**milling yield**
烹调品质　**culinary quality**
白米　**white rice, polished rice**
碎米　**broken rice**

## 水稻病虫害　Rice Pests and Diseases

蝗虫　**locust**
稻螟　**rice borer**
粘虫①　**armyworm**

地老虎②　**cutworm**
蜡蝉　**planthopper**
瘿蚊　**gall midge**

瘿蚊成虫① gall midge adult

青叶蝉 green leafhopper

铁甲虫 hispa

水稻病毒媒介昆虫 insect vector of rice virus

稻纵卷叶螟 rice leaf roller

稻纵卷叶螟成虫 adult rice leaf roller

蝼蛄 mole cricket

水稻二化螟 rice-stem borer

水稻二化螟的蛹② pupa of rice-stem borer

水稻二化螟幼虫③ larva of rice-stem borer

水稻二化螟成虫 stem borer adult

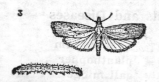

蓟马 thrips

叶蝉 leafhopper

稻叶黑粉病 leaf smut of rice

白叶枯病 bacterial leaf blight

细菌性叶条纹病 bacterial leaf stripe

稻纹枯病 sheath and culm blight of rice

稻条斑病 cercospora spot of rice

稻瘟病④ rice blast

稻麯病 false smut, green smut of rice

茎腐病 stem rot

黄矮病 yellow-dwarf

徒长 spindling

恶苗病(徒长病) Bakanae disease

叶的衰老 senescence of leaves

褪绿病 chlorosis

(对生长的)抑制 stress

性质不良的土壤 problem soil

飞蝗 migratory locust

群集度 gregariousness

蝗灾 plague of locusts

蝗虫防治 locust control

截捕沟 trap trench

独居蝗虫 solitary locust

蝗群 locust horde, locust swarm

不规则的周期性 irregular periodicity

爆发期 outbreak period

爆发地区 outbreak area

迁徙飞行　migration flight

蝗虫入侵　locust invasion

沙漠蝗虫　desert locust

毒饵诱杀法　poison bait method

砷类毒饵　arsenical poison bait

六六六　gammexane

组织蝗虫防治　organization of locust control

打蝗斗争　anti-locust battle

改变爆发地区的生态　altering the ecology of outbreak area

喷射最严重的蝗灾地区　spraying the worst locust-in-fested area

二硝磷甲酚喷射　spraying dinitro-ortho-cresol

对蝗虫主动防御　active defence against locusts

营养缺乏病　deficiency disease, deficiency disorder

营养缺乏检验　deficiency checking

营养缺乏症状　deficiency symptom

缺氮、磷等　nitrogen deficiency, phosphorus deficiency, etc.

## 小麦生产　Wheat Production

普通小麦①　common wheat

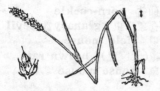

春小麦　spring wheat

冬小麦　winter wheat

将冬小麦转化为春小麦　converting winter wheat to spring wheat

种子春化　seed vernalization

面包小麦　bread wheat

硬质小麦　hard wheat

软质小麦　soft wheat

硬粒小麦　durum wheat, macaroni wheat

实茎小麦　solid stem wheat

密穗小麦　club wheat

斯卑尔脱小麦　spelt wheat

土耳其小麦　Turkish wheat

野生二粒小麦　wild emmer, wild wheat

栽培一粒小麦　einkorn wheat

二粒小麦　emmer

圆锥小麦　poulard wheat

波兰小麦　Polish wheat

杂交小麦种子　hybrid wheat seed

小麦杂交优势　heterosis in wheat, hybrid vigour in wheat

细胞质的雄性不育性　cytoplasmic male sterility

雄性不育品系　male-sterile line

复育因素　fertility-restoring factor

"诺林"种质　"Norin" germ plasm

"诺林"遗传特征　"Norin" heredity

墨西哥小麦　Mexican wheat

抗锈病的小麦　rust-resistant wheat

小麦生长带　wheat belt

种小麦地　wheatland

适应较严酷的环境　being a-dapted to harsher environ-ments

累积土壤湿度　accumulated soil moisture

防渍　prevention against waterlogging

适中的湿度　moderate mois-ture

着生分蘖　consolidative tillering

行侧追肥(行间追肥)　side dressing

防霜冻　frost prevention

雪栏　snow-fence

筛选机　screening-machine, sifter

麦子　wheat grain

谷朊　glutelin

麸朊　gliadin

全麦面粉　whole-wheat flour

小麦线虫　wheat nematode, wheatworm

麦种蝇　wheat bulb fly

谷蛾　wheat-flour moth, grain moth

小麦瘿　wheat galls

粉螨　flour mite

秆锈病　stem rust

叶锈病　leaf rust

赤霉病　scab

腥黑穗病　stinking smut

散黑穗病　loose smut

小麦黑粉病　flag smut of wheat

根腐病　root rot

禾谷花叶病　wheat mosaic

野燕麦　wild oat

麦仙翁　corn-cockle

谷仓象鼻虫　granary weevil

田鼠　field mouse

褐鼠(大家鼠)　brown rat

家鼠　house mouse

# 玉米生产　Maize Production

玉米(玉蜀黍)①　maize, (Am) Indian corn, corn

非甜质玉米　field corn

硬质种玉米　flint corn

粉质种玉米　flour corn, soft corn

马齿种玉米　dent corn

甜质玉米　sweet corn

爆裂种玉米　popcorn

蜡质玉米　waxy corn

玉米穗轴（玉米芯）　cob, ear

玉米雄花穗　tassel

玉米抽丝　silking

玉米苞叶　husk

雌雄〔花〕同株植物　monoecious

plant

玉米去雄　detasseling

自花授粉　self-pollination

手工去雄　manual detasseling

试验品系　tester line

遗传的灵活性　genetic flexibility

近交的适合性　inbred suitability

杂交优势株　plant exhibiting hybrid vigour

纯合种子　homozygous seed

异合种子　heterozygous seed

糖淀粉扩张基因　amylose extender gene, ae gene

行播作物　row crop

提早播种　earlier planting

缩短行距　reducing the row-spacing

精耕细作　intensive cultivation

最少耕作法　minimum tillage

等高耕作的玉米田　contour-ploughed cornfield

田间脱粒　field shelling

玉米摘芯脱粒机　picker-sheller

湿磨　wet-milling

玉米淀粉　cornstarch

胶淀粉　amylopectin

玉米糖　corn sugar

玉米油　corn oil

玉米粉　corn meal, corn flour

玉米象虫　maize billbug

玉米粘虫　maize armyworm

玉米根虫　maize rootworm

玉米根蚜　corn root aphid

玉米〔叶〕蚜　corn-leaf aphid

玉米穗夜蛾　corn earworm

玉米螟　corn borer

玉米条纹毒病　maize streak

玉米黑粉病　corn smut

## 大麦生产　Barley Production

大麦①　barley

裸〔大〕麦(青稞)　naked barley

春大麦　spring barley

冬大麦　winter barley

在温室用化学诱变雄性不育　chemical inducement of male sterility in the greenhouse

较密行距　closer row-spacing

割晒条铺　windrowing

搓成粉粒　pearling

麦芽　malt

制麦芽的大麦品种　malting variety of barley

优良的制麦芽品质　good malting quality

麦芽糖　maltose, malt sugar

## 高粱生产  Sorghum Production

高粱①  sorghum, *gaoliang*

食用高粱  grain sorghum
西非高粱  milo
南非高粱  kafir corn
苏丹草  Sudangrass
高粱苏丹草杂交种  sorghum-
  sudangrass hybrid, "Sordan"

芦粟(芦黍甜高粱)  sorgo,
  sweet sorghum, sugar
  sorghum
帚用高粱  broomcorn
青饲高粱(饲用高粱)  grass sor-
  ghum
密穗  dense panicle
散穗  loose panicle
茎秆的髓  pith in the stalk
脱粒后的穗子  brush
高粱醇溶朊  kaf(f)irin
加工制糖浆  processing for
  syrup
高粱饴  sorghum sweetmeat

## 次要禾谷类作物  Minor Cereals

燕麦②  oats

裸燕麦(油麦、莜麦)  naked oats
春燕麦  spring oats
冬燕麦  winter oats
燕麦粉  oat flour
(燕)麦片  oatmeal, oat-flakes
燕麦皮  oat hull
糠醛  furfural

黑麦  rye
黑麦稿秆  rye straw
荞麦  buckwheat
粟(谷子,小米)③  millet

珍珠稷  pearl millet, cattail
  millet
非洲稷(龙爪稷,鸭脚粟)  Afri-
  can millet

黍、稷、穄子① shu broom corn millet, proso millet

穇(湖南稷子) billion-dollar grass, Japanese millet

菰 wild rice

甜茅 mannagrass

# 油料作物 Oil Crops

## 落花生 Peanut

从生型 bushy type

蔓生型 trailing type

厚荚 thick-walled pod

薄荚 thin-walled pod

除草 weeding

培土 hilling

果针 peg

下针 pegging the entire fruit

饱满的果实 completely filled fruit

不饱满的果实 partially filled fruit

离壳 shrinking away from the shell

烘干花生 roasted peanut

花生油 peanut oil

花生麸 peanut-oil press cake

花生酱 peanut butter

细菌性萎蔫病 bacterial wilt

花生丛簇病 peanut tosette

叶斑病 leaf spot disease

## 大　豆　Soybean

黄〔大〕豆① yellow bean, yellow soybean

青〔大〕豆② green bean, green soybean

黑〔大〕豆③ black bean, black soybean

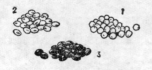

根瘤结核 nodule
长根瘤 nodulation
种子的接种 inoculation of seeds
接种体 inoculum
专用品种 variety tailor-made for specific use

炸荚 shattering
豆油 soybean oil
豆饼(豆麸) bean cake
豆粕 bean meal
豆腐 bean curd
豆浆 bean milk
酱油 soy sauce
炭疽病 anthracnose
基腐病 foot rot
细菌性斑点病 bacterial blight
大豆象 bean weevil
细菌性疱状斑 bacterial pustule
荚茎雕腐病 pod and stem blight
褐茎腐烂病 brown stem rot
大豆花叶病 soybean mosaic virus

## 椰　子　Coconut

椰树④ coconut palm, coconut tree

椰子园 coconut plantation
高种椰子 tall coconut palm
矮种椰子 dwarf coconut palm

芽眼 eye
吸器("椰饼") haustorium, "apple"
椰林 coconut grove
椰肉 coconut meat
椰子水 coconut water, coconut milk
椰干 copra
椰干炉 copra kiln
摘椰子 harvesting coconuts from the palms
椰油 coconut oil

皂化数 saponigication number

椰麸 coconut cake

椰衣 coconut husk

椰衣纤维 coir

浸解纤维(沤出纤维) retting the fibre

古铜叶萎病 bronze leaf wilt

尖茎病 tapering stem wilt, pencil point

二瘤犀岬 rhinoceros beetle

椰心叶岬 coconut hispid

椰园蚧 coconut scale

## 油 棕 Oil Palm

油棕① oil palm

1

油棕种植场 oil-palm plantation

人工授粉 artificial pollination

果皮 pericarp

类胡萝卜素 carotenoid

佛焰花序 spadix

果穗 fruit bunch

油棕白油种 albescens of oil palm

厚壳种(杜拉种) dura

薄壳种(丹那拉种) tenera

无壳种(比西夫拉种) pisifera

带土包扎移植 ball transplanting

酶活动 enzymatic activity

游离脂肪酸 free fatty

人造黄油 margarine

干棕仁 dried kernel

棕油 palm oil

棕仁干燥筒 kernel silo

油棕萎蔫病 fusarium will

橙斑病 orange spot

## 芝 麻 Sesame

芝麻② sesame

蒴果 capsule

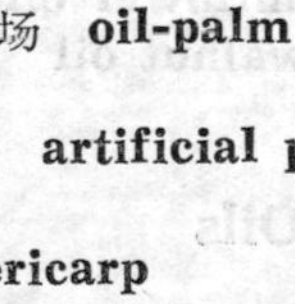

2

芝麻花 sesame flower

芝麻茎 stalk of sesame

芝麻油 sesame oil

芝麻酱 sesame soy

芝麻麸 sesame oil press cake

不裂的芝麻品系 strain of indehiscent sesame

不炸荚的品种 variety with nonshattering fruit

潜叶虫 leaf miner

## 油橄榄　Olive

橄榄园　olive orchard
橄榄枝①　olive branch
橄榄油　olive oil
油分离器　oil separator
除去苦糖甙　removing bitter
　glucoside
油橄榄甲虫　olive fruit fly
油橄榄实蝇　olive fruit fly

## 杂　类　Miscellany

油菜(芸薹)　rape
油菜籽　rapeseed
菜油　rape oil, rapeseed oil
菜籽饼　rape cake

茶油　tea oil, tea-seed oil
向日葵油　sunflower oil
葵籽饼　sunflower oil cake
核桃油　walnut oil

## 非食用油　Nonedible Oils

油桐树　*tong* tree
油桐园　*tong* orchard
早结果矮种　dwarf, early-bear-
　ing variety
晚结果大种　large-growing,
　late-bearing variety
接枝树　whip
骨籽枝　scaffold branch
桐籽　*tong* nut
桐油　*tong* oil, Chinese wood
　oil
木油树　*mu you shu*
木油　*mu* oil
日本木油　Japanese wood oil

石栗　candlenut, candle berry
　tree
石栗油(烛果油)　candlenut oil
亚麻籽　linseed
亚麻籽油　linseed oil
亚麻籽饼　linseed cake
蓖麻②　castor-oil plant

| | |
|---|---|
| 蓖麻籽　castor bean | 苏子油　perilla oil |
| 蓖麻油　castor oil | 乌柏油　Chinese tallow |
| 蓖麻籽饼　**castor pomace** | |

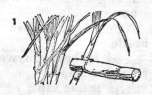

# 糖料作物　Sugar Crops

## 甘　蔗　Sugarcane

甘蔗①　sugarcane

薄壁细胞　**parenchyma cell**
薄壁基本组织　**parenchymatous**
　**ground tissue**

节　**node**
芽(芽眼)　**bud, eye**
根原基　**root primordium**
叶痕　**leaf scar**
叶舌　**ligule**
叶耳　**auricle**
垂皮　**dewlap**
叶鞘　**sheath, leaf sheath**
种根(临时根)　**set-root**
苗根(永久根)　**shoot root**
次生茎(分蘖茎)　**secondary**
　**shoot**

蔗头 rootstock of a cane stool

蔗茎插条(蔗"种") cane stem cutting, cane "seed"

穴植 planting in holes

沟植 planting in furrows

挖坑起畦种植法 planting fields to the "grand bank" system

补植(补苗) replanting

培土平垄 bedding

蔗糖含量 sucrose content

白利糖度(甘蔗锤度) degrees Brix

手提折光计 hand refractometer

低斩(傍地斩) cutting at the ground level

宿根蔗(旧头蔗) stubble cane, ratoon cane

宿根蔗栽培 ratoon cultivation

甘蔗枯叶残茎 trash and tops

开蔗垄 off-barring the cane

蔗渣 bagasse

吸涨作用 imbibition

离析作用 maceration

糖膏 massecuite, fillmass

糖蜜 molasses

结晶器 crystallizer

粗糖 raw sugar

脱色 decoloration

钻心虫(甘蔗螟虫) stalk borer

甘蔗绵蚜虫(蔗蟋) woolly aphid of the leaf

甘蔗金龟子(蔗龟、蛴螬) grub

凤梨病 pineapple disease

黑穗病 smut

## 其他糖料作物 Other Sugar Crops

糖用甜菜① sugar beet

成簇种子 seed cluster

单颗条播 single-seed drilling

新出地面苗 braird

间苗 singling, thinning

顺行间苗 down-the row thinning

横向分簇间苗 cross-blocking thinning

切顶 topping

带土成分低 low dirt tare

风干行 windrow

堆藏窖 clamp

甜菜缨 beet top

甜菜糖浆 beet molasses

甜菜糖 beet sugar

甜菜渣 beet pulp

甜菜废液 beet slop

甜菜网螟(草地螟) beet webworm

甜菜龟甲虫 beet tortoise beetle

甜菜夜蛾幼虫 beet armyworm

糖槭 sugar maple

槭树液汁 maple sap

槭糖浆 maple syrup

槭糖 maple sugar

糖棕 sugar palm, gomuti

亚塔椰子树 nipa palm

# 饮料作物　Beverage Crops

## 茶叶生产　Tea Production

茶树① **tea plant**

茶场　**tea plantation**

茶园　**tea garden**

无性繁殖系选择　**clonal selection**

母树选择　**selection of mother trees**

小叶品种　**small-leaved variety**

大叶品种　**large-leaved variety**

茶的自花受精　**selfing of tea**

临时遮阳棚　**temporary shade house**

构架(主干修剪)　**framing, stem pruning**

成型(成型修剪)　**shaping, shape pruning**

养护(养护修剪)　**maintenance pruning, production pruning**

复原　**rehabilitation**

整形(泲修剪)　**reshaping, deep pruning**

再构架(根颈修剪)　**reframing, collar pruning**

采茶　**tea plucking**

顶芽　**terminal bud**

托叶　**stipule**

采茶法　**plucking system**

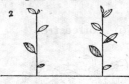

"一芽二(三)叶"②　**"two (three) leaves and a bud, [B+2(3)]"**

采摘周期　**plucking cycle**

采摘剪　**plucking shears**

茶厂　**tea factory**

干缩　**withering**

揉茶　**rolling of green tea leaves**

揉茶机　**rolling machine, roller**

发酵室　**fermentation chamber**

烘焙炉　**drying oven**

防止外干里湿　**preventing casehardening**

精筛　**sorting by screens**

| | |
|---|---|
| 香气　aroma | 乌龙茶　Wulong |
| 泡茶　infusing tea | 祁门红茶　Qimen black |
| 香味　flavour | 龙井茶　Longjing |
| 品茶员　tea taster | 碧螺春　Biluochun |
| 叶茶类　leaf teas | 毛茶　crude tea |
| 白毫　pekee (P) | 熙春　Xichun |
| 小种　souchon (S) | 珠茶　gunpowder tea |
| 橙黄白毫　orange pekoe (OP) | 花茶类　scented teas |
| 白毫小种　pekoe souchon (PS) | 茉莉花茶　jasmine tea |
| 碎茶类　broken teas (BT) | 玫瑰红茶　rose black tea |
| 花香　fannings (F) | 砖茶　brick tea |
| 茶末　dust tea (D) | 根腐病　root rot |
| 武夷茶　Wuyi, *bohea, boei* | 立枯病　damp (ing) -off |
| 拼配　blending | 红锈病　red rust |
| 红茶　black tea | 麻点病　bird's eye spot disease |
| 绿茶　green tea | 灰斑病　grey blight |

# 咖啡生产　Coffee Production

咖啡树① 　coffee tree

| | |
|---|---|
| 小粒种咖啡　Arabian coffee | 摘顶　capping |
| 中粒种咖啡　robusta coffee | 第一次剪枝　first pruning, finca |
| 高种咖啡　excelsa coffee | 多干修枝法　multiple-stem system |
| 大粒种咖啡　Liberian coffee | 咖啡浆果　coffee berry |
| 荫蔽管理　shade management | 独豆咖啡　peaberry |
| 遮阳棚　slathouse | 咖啡豆　coffee bean |
| 荫蔽树　shade tree | 银皮,种皮　silverskin, parchment coat |
| 覆盖作物　cover crop | 剥肉　pulping |
| 咖啡树整形　training coffee | 发酵池　fermenting tank, fermenting vat |
| | 安全点(转黑点)　punto-negro, black point |
| | 硬质咖啡　hard coffee |
| | 带壳咖啡　parchment coffee |
| | 咖啡针锈病　Hemilcia rust |

## 可可生产　Cocoa Production

可可树① cacao tree, cocoa tree

薄皮种可可(甜可可) Criollo cocoa, sweet cacao

厚皮种可可(苦可可) Forastero cocoa, bitter cacao

薄皮厚皮杂交种 Criollo-Forastero hybrid

无性繁殖 clonal propagation, vegetative propagation

有性繁殖 generative propagation

压条法 marcottage

嵌木芽接法 chip budding

改良福科特芽接法 modified Forkert's method of budding

可可插条 cacao cutting

可可插条繁殖箱 propagation bin for cacao cuttings

可可斑螟 cacao moth

鬼帚病(丛枝病) witches' broom disease

肿枝病 swollen shoot virus disease

可可黑果腐病 black pod disease of cacao

可可豆 cocoa bean

发酵箱 fermentation bin

焙过的可可豆 roasted cocoa bean

可可脂 cocoa butter

可可碱 theobromine

# 香料作物　Spice Crops

胡椒 pepper

胡椒粒 peppercorn

黑胡椒 black pepper

白胡椒 white pepper

辣椒 chil(l)i, red pepper

灯笼椒 sweet pepper, bell pepper

芫荽 coriander

肉桂 cinnamon

白豆蔻 cardamon

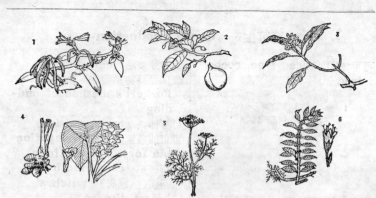

| | |
|---|---|
| 小豆蔻　**cardamon** | 花椒　**prickly ash** |
| 香草兰①　**vanilla** | 八角　**star anise** |
| 香草醛　**vanillin** | 茴香⑤　**fennel** |
| 肉豆蔻②　**nutmeg** | 莳萝　**dill** |
| 肉豆蔻衣　**mace** | 薄荷⑥　**mint** |
| 丁香③　**clove, clove tree** | 留兰香(绿薄荷)　**spearmint** |
| 丁香油　**clove oil** | 胡椒薄荷　**peppermint** |
| 姜　**ginger** | 多香果　**allspice, piments,** |
| 姜黄④　**turmeric** | 　**Jamaican pepper** |

# 烟草生产　Tobacco Production

普通烟草(红花烟草)⑦　**tobacco,
common tobacco**
黄花烟草　**Aztec tobacco**
弗吉尼亚烟叶　**Virginia (to-
bacco)**
布赖特烟叶　**Bright (tobacco)**
伯利烟叶　**Burley (tobacco)**

土耳其烟叶　Turkish tobacco

苏门答蜡烟叶　Sumatra tobacco

古巴烟叶　Havana (tobacco)

马里兰烟叶　Maryland tobacco

路易斯安那上等黑烟叶　perique (tobacco)

均匀撒种　uniform distribution of seeds

去劣去杂　roguing the weak, sickly, and off-type plants

打顶　topping

抹腋芽(抹赘芽)　removing the axiliary buds

分批采收　harvesting by the "priming" system

连茎收割　cutting entire stalks

上部叶(顶叶)　leaf

中部叶(腰叶)　seconds, cutters

下部叶(脚叶)　lugs

烟叶梗　tobacco stick

烟叶干燥室　tobacco barn, tobacco shed

热气烤干　flue-curing

烟熏烤干　fire-curing

室内吹干　dark air-curing

晒干　sun-curing

〔烟叶〕发酵　fermentation, sweating

发酵室　fermentation barn

烤烟　flue-cured tobacco, fire-cured tobacco

尼古丁含量(烟碱含量)　nicotine content

焦油含量　tar content

雪茄烟心　cigar filler

雪茄外包烟叶　cigar wrapper

雪茄内包烟叶　cigar binder

口嚼烟草　chewing tobacco

口嚼烟块　plug cut

卷烟　cigarette

混合烟丝　pipe blend

香料配制烟　aromatic tobacco

剥除叶中脉　stripping out the midrib

黑胫病　black shank

烟草花叶病　tobacco mosaic (virus)

烟草环斑病　tobacco ring spot virus

烟草夜蛾幼虫　tobacco budworm

# 蔬 菜 Vegetables

菜园 vegetable garden, kitchen garden

商品菜园 market garden

卷心菜(椰菜、甘蓝、洋白菜) cabbage

抱子甘蓝 Brussels sprouts

花椰菜(花菜、菜花) cauliflower

软化栽培 blanching culture

嫩茎花椰菜 green brocedi

球茎甘蓝("芥蓝头") kohlrabi

大白菜(黄芽菜) Beijing cabbage, *baicai*

白菜 *pakchoi*, Chinese cabbage

菜心 flowering cabbage, mock *pakchoi*

芥蓝 cabbage mustard

茼蒿 garland chrysanthemum

芥菜 leaf mustard

菠菜 spinach, spinage

莴苣(生菜) lettuce

直立莴苣 cos lettuce

散叶莴苣 loose-headed lettuce

结球莴苣 head lettuce

水蕹菜(西洋菜) watercress

枸杞 Chinese matrimony vine

苋菜 Chinese spinach, edible amaranth

蕹菜 water spinach

马齿苋 purslance

芹菜(旱芹) celery

水芹 water dropwort

芜菁 turnip

芜菁甘蓝 rutabaga

莙荙菜(叶甜菜) chard, leaf beet, spinach beet

石刁柏(芦笋、龙须菜) asparagus

莼菜 water shield

韭菜 *jiucai*, Chinese leek

荞头(藠) *jiaotou*, Chinese onion

洋葱(圆葱) onion, common onion

葱(大葱) spring onion, stone leek

小玉葱 Chinese green onion, chive

姜 ginger

辣椒 chilli

灯笼椒(圆椒) bell pepper, sweet pepper

大蒜(蒜头) garlic

火蒜 roasted garlic

香芹菜(芫荽) parsley

芫荽 coriander

萝卜 radish

胡萝卜 carrot

茄子 eggplant

西红柿(番茄) tomato

苦瓜 balsam pear, bitter cucumber

丝瓜 sponge gourd, dishcloth gourd

水瓜 vegetable sponge

黄瓜(青瓜) cucumber

冬瓜 wax gourd, white gourd

甜瓜 muskmelon

节瓜(毛瓜) *jiegua*, hairy squash

南瓜(番瓜) Chinese squash

葫芦瓜 bottle gourd

西葫芦 pumkin

笋瓜 winter squash

竹笋 bamboo shoot

冬笋 winter bamboo shoot

茭白(茭笋) *jiaobai*, wild rice shoots

慈姑 arrowhead

莲藕 lotus root

荸荠(马蹄) water chestnut

白豆角 white string bean

青豆角 green string bean

四季豆 kidney bean

木薯 cassava

马铃薯 potato

甘薯(番薯) sweet potato

芋(芋头) taro, dasheen

参薯(大薯) greater yam, yampi

葛(竹芋) arrowroot

沙葛 *shage*, yam bean

菱角(龙角) water caltrop

豌豆 garden pea

嫩豌豆 green pea

菜豆 lima bean

刀豆 Jack bean, sword bean

豇豆 string bean

豆芽 bean sprouts

# 水果作物　Fruit Crops

## 柑桔类　Citrus

无性繁殖　asexual propagation

接穗的选择　selection of scionwood

实生苗砧木　seedling stock, seedling rootstock

幼苗行植　lining out

休眠芽接　dormant budding

春季芽接　spring budding

倒 T 形盾状芽接法　budding on inverted-T shield-bud method

〔芽接用〕带片芽　bud with wood

〔芽接用〕去片芽　bud without wood

劈接　cleft-grafting the stub

高接　top-working

压条枝　marcot(te)

剪枝　topping

摘心(打尖)　pinching

除徒长枝　removal of water sprouts

品种衰老　varietal senescence

定期复壮老品系　periodic rejuvenation of the old-line variety

汁囊　juice sac

酸果　tart fruit

柑桔外果皮　flavedo

全采　clean picking

选采　spot picking

脱青　degreening

上腊　waxing

干桔渣　dried citrus pulp

桔子油　citrus seed oil

果胶　pectin

橙皮素　hesperidin

橙(甜橙)　orange, sweet orange

酸橙　sour orange, bitter orange

柑　king orange

蜜柑(椪柑)　Chinese honey orange, Ponkan

宽皮桔　mandarin

红橘(朱砂桔)　tangerine

四季桔　Citrus microcarpa

金橘　Kumquat

毛柑　Mauritius papeda, kabuyao, porcupine orange

citrus red spider

白柑① white-sapote
柠檬 lemon

粗皮柠檬② rough lemon
莱檬 lime
柚子 pomelo, pumello
沙田柚 pear-shaped pomelo
葡萄柚 grapefruit
香橼（枸橼）③ citron
佛手柑④ finger(ed) citron, "Hand-of-Buddha"
黄皮 wampee
桔蚜 citrus aphid
桔小实蝇 citrus fruit fly
柑桔红蜘蛛 citrus red mite,

桔锈螨 citrus rust mite
黑点蚧 citrus black scale
桔粉虱 citrus whitefly
桔粉蚧 citrus meolybug
盖氏桔粉蚧 citrophilus mealybug
柑桔绿霉病 green mo(u)ld of citrus
柑桔青霉病 blue mo(u)ld of citrus
柑桔溃疡病 citrus canker
柑桔疮痂病 citrus scab
柑桔细菌性火疫病 citrus blast
柑桔衰退病 citrus decline

## 香蕉 Banana

香牙蕉 common banana
大蕉 plantain, cooking banana
幼剑芽 young sword sucker
（从老株切取的）地下茎块 rhizome pieces (cut from old stool)

雄花簇 male flower cluster
两性花 perfect flower
雌花 female flower
单性结实 parthemocarpy
除无用芽 removing unwanted sprouts
留结实芽 retaining fruiting

suckers

香蕉花蕾　male bud

断蕾　cutting off male flower clustero

用竿支撑蕉树茎　propping up banana stems with poles

一梳香蕉　comb

一轴香蕉①　bunch

易腐水果　perishable fruit

防湿袋(防潮袋)　moistureproof bag

大蜜啥(兰田种)　Yros Michel

香蕉萎蔫病(巴拿马病)　banana with Panama disease

香蕉叶斑病(芭蕉瘟)　banana leaf spot, sigatoka disease

香蕉〔根〕象甲　banana root borer, banana weevil, banana beetle

香蕉茎象甲　banana stem borer weevil

香蕉细菌性萎蔫病　moko disease, bacterial wilt

香蕉痂蛾　banana scab moth

香蕉黑蚜虫　banana aphid

香蕉锈蓟马　banana rust thrip

束顶病(萎缩病)　bunchy top disease

# 苹果和梨　Apple and Pear

仁果类　pome fruit

苹果园　apple orchard

短果枝　fruit spur

混合芽　mixed bud

短化栽培　dwarf culture, dwarfing

短化砧〔木〕(短性砧)　dwarf(ing) stock

东茂林砧木　East Malling (EM) stock

短型芽变　dwarf bud sport, dwarf bud mutation

早熟非贮藏类型　early non-storage type

中熟贮藏类型　mid-season storage type

晚熟贮藏类型　late storage type

萘基乙酰胺　NAD (alphanaphthaleneacetamide)

附果(假果)　accessory fruit

苹果汁　cider, apple juice

火疫病　fireblight

苹果蠹蛾　codlin(g) moth

苹绵蚜　woolly apple aphid

苹果天牛　apple longicorn beetle

苹果潜叶虫　apple leaf miner

苹蓟马　apple thrips

改良闭心式整枝　modified leader training

截短枝条　heading-back

疏芽　disbudding

生长调节剂 growth regulators
细胞动素 cytokinin
赤霉素 gibberellin
大小年结果习性 biennial habit, alternate habit
大收年 on year
小收年 off year
萘乙酸 NAA (naphthaleneacetic acid)
防止采前落果 preventing preharvest fruit drop
离层 abscission layer

苹果锈病 apple rust
苹果白粉病 apple mildew
苹果树腐烂病 apple-tree canker
梨 pear, common pear
砂梨 Chinese pear, sand pear
雪梨 snow pear
梨枝干枯病 pear-blight
梨瘿蚊 pear midge
梨黑星病 pear scab
梨枝小蠹 pear-twig beetle

# 菠萝（凤梨） Pineapple

菠萝① pineapple
主株茎 stem of main plant
蘖芽(块茎芽) ratoon
(地上)吸芽 (aerial) sucker
果柄 fruit stem
基生裔芽 basal slip
复果(聚花果) multiple fruit
鳞状果皮 scaly rind
冠裔芽 crown slip
冠芽 crown
无刺卡因种 Smooth Cayenne

黄色果肉品种 variety of the yellow-fleshed group
白色果肉品种 variety of the white-fleshed group
单一作物经营 single-crop plantation
成花诱导 floral induction
季节外开花 out-of-season flowering, extraseasonal flowering
季节外结果 out-of-season fruiting, extraseasonal fruiting
菠萝红蜘蛛 pineapple red mite
菠萝粉蚧 pineapple mealybug
菠萝坚盾蚧 pineapple scale
菠萝发酵病 yeasty fermentation
菠萝水泡病 Thielaviopsis soft rot

# 葡 萄 Grape

葡萄① grape
葡萄栽培 viticulture
葡萄园 vineyard, grapary
欧洲种葡萄 vinifera, wine grape
美洲种葡萄 labrusca
圆叶葡萄 muscadine
玫瑰香葡萄 muscat, muskat
无核品种 seedless variety
葡萄藤 grapevine
主蔓 arm
支柱栽培 stake culture
葡萄棚 trellis

单干形整枝 cordon training
短枝修剪 spur pruning
种蔓修剪 cane pruning
直立雄蕊 upright stamen
有效花粉 functional pollen
弯曲雄蕊 reflexed stamen
无效花粉 impotent pollen, nonfunctioning pollen
环状剥皮 girdling
葡萄串 grape cluster
发育不良的〔葡萄〕浆果 shot berry
葡萄干 raisin
小粒葡萄干 currant
葡萄根瘤蚜 grape phylloxera, vine louse
葡萄霜霉病 grape downy mildew
葡萄透翅蛾 grape clearwing moth
葡萄叶蜂 grape sawfly

# 木 瓜 Papaya

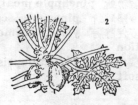

木瓜② papaya, papaw
公木瓜树(雄株) staminate papaya tree, male plant
两性木瓜树(两性株) hermaphrodite papaya tree, bisexual plant, perfect plant
母木瓜树(雌株) pistillate papaya tree, female plant

苏劳种　Solo variety

短种木瓜　dwarf strains of papaya

碧地种　Betty variety

蓝茎种　Blue Stem variety

木瓜乳　papaya latex

木瓜酶(木瓜素)　papain

木瓜碱　carpaine

山木瓜　mountain papaya, mountain papaw

## 草莓　Strawberry

长匍茎　runner

草莓梗　crown

瘦果　achene

需要地面覆盖　needing mulching

草莓蚜虫　strawberry aphid

## 核果类　Drupe Fruits

桃　peach

杏　apricot

杏仁　almond

苦杏仁(北杏)　bitter almond

甜杏仁(南杏)　dessert almond

扁桃　almond

李　plum

樱桃　cherry

开心式整枝　open-centred training

粘核种　clingstones

离核种　freestones

催熟　accelerating maturity

## 其他果类作物　Other Fruit Crops

1

鳄梨①　avocado, alligator pear

芒果　mango

芒果的镶接　veneer grafting of mango

芒果花序枯萎病　blossom blight of mango

香芒　kuwini, kaweni

臭芒果　batjang, gray mango

腰果(槚如)　cashew

腰果梨　cashew apple

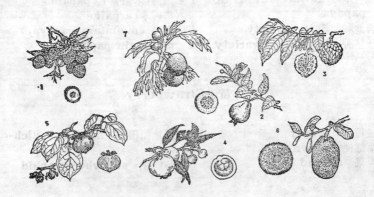

| 荔枝① lychee, litchi | 红毛榴莲 soursop |
| 龙眼 longan | 面包树⑦ breadfruit tree |
| 杨桃 carambola | 有核面包树 breadnut tree |
| 香杨桃 bilimbi | 枣椰子 date, date palm |
| 番石榴② guava | 芒枣树 otaheite-apple, amberella |
| 番荔枝③ sugar-apple | 人心果 sapodilla |
| 高山番荔枝 cherimoya | 树番茄 tree tomato |
| 蒲桃④ rose apple | 红毛丹 rambutan |
| 枇杷 loquat | 金毛丹 pulasan |
| 柿⑤ Kaki, persimmon | 曼密果 mamey-apple |
| 软柿 seeded kaki fruit | 鸡蛋果 passion fruit, purple granadilla |
| 水柿 seedless kaki fruit | 山竹子 mangosteen |
| 柿饼 dried persimmon | 蛇果 gandaria |
| 石榴 pomegranate | 异叶果 ilama |
| 杏 apricot | 牛心梨 bullock's-heart, custard-apple |
| 红果仔 pitanga, surinam cherry | 枣 Chinese date, jujube |
| 无花果 fig | 猕猴桃 Chinese gooseberry, "monkey" peach |
| 无花果虫媒 caprifer | 罗汉果 *luohanguo* |
| 无花果授粉 caprification | |
| 波罗蜜(木波罗)⑥ jack-fruit | |
| 香波罗蜜 champedak | |
| 榴莲 durian | |

# 纤维作物 Fibre Crops

## 棉 花 Cotton

棉田 cotton field

中棉(树棉)① Chinese cotton, tree cotton

草棉② Levant cotton

陆地棉③ upland cotton

海岛棉④ sea-island cotton

埃及棉 Egyptian cotton

巴西棉 Brazilian cotton, kidney cotton

岱字棉 Deltapine

爱字棉 Acala

珂字棉 coker

二形性 dimorphism

叶枝(单轴枝) vegetative branch, monopodial branch

果枝(合轴枝) fruiting branch, sympodial branch

回交 backcrossing

棉铃(棉桃)⑤ cotton ball

落铃 boll shedding

棉绒⑥ lint

摘心(打尖) top removal

化学脱叶剂 chemical defoliant

轧棉(轧花) ginning

原棉 raw cotton

籽棉　unginned cotton, seed-cotton

皮棉(去籽棉花)　ginned cotton, lint

衣分率(衣分指数)　lint percentage, lint index

棉短线　linters

纤维〔平均〕长度　staple

长绒棉　cotton of long staple

超级长绒　extra long staple

短绒棉　cotton of short staple

纤维整齐度　fibre uniformity

纤维细度　fibre fineness

纤维强度　fibre strength

纤维成熟度　fibre maturity

棉纤维转曲度　spirality of cotton fibre

棉籽　cottonseed

棉籽油　cottonseed oil

棉籽饼　cotton cake, cottonseed cake

棉毒素(棉籽毒)　gossypol

棉蚜①　cotton aphid

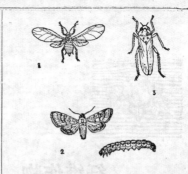

棉铃虫②　bollworm

红铃虫　pink bollworm

〔棉〕金刚钻虫　diamond bollworm

棉铃象虫　cotton boll weevil

棉叶跳蝉③　leaf hopper

棉卷叶螟　cotton leaf roller

棉蝽(污棉虫)　cotton stainer

〔叶〕角斑病　angular leaf spot, black arm

棉炭疽病　cotton anthracnose

# 亚 麻 Flax

纤维亚麻④　fibre flax

亚麻田　flax field

亚麻田除草　flax weeding

拔麻　flax pulling

拔麻机　flax puller

沤麻　flax retting

沤麻池　retting dam

夹榨滚筒　rollers

捣麻机　paddling-machine

亚麻稿秆　flax straw

手工梳理　hand combing

麻梳　flax comb

〔梳出的〕麻屑　flax tow

打麻　flax dressing

亚麻碎屑　flax waste

亚麻锈病　flax rust

亚麻萎蔫病　flax wilt

# 黄 麻 Jute

圆果种黄麻① round-pod jute
长果种黄麻② cylindrical-pod jute
〔从沤过的黄麻〕分离纤维 separating fibres (from retted jute stems)

田间撕分 field ribboning
麻袋 gunny sack
打包麻布 burlap cloth
根瘤线虫 root-knot nematode

## 苎麻和大麻 Ramie and Hemp

苎麻③ ramie, China grass
刮麻机 raspador, decorticator
收割打麻机 harvester-ribboner
韧皮纤维剥除机 bast-fibre decorticator
煮炼 scouring
一绞 hank
梳整 carding
果胶含量 pectin content

青苎麻 green ramie
黄苎麻 yellow ramie
夏布 grass linen
丝核菌 Rhizoctonia solani

大麻④ hemp, true hemp
雌雄异株植物 dioecious plant
雄麻 staminate hemp
雌麻 pistillate hemp
麻线 twine

大麻屑 hemp tow, hemp combings

碎茎打麻机 hemp-breaker-and-scutcher

# 其 他 Miscellany

槿麻(洋麻)① Kanaf, Deccan hemp

适应异花授粉 adaptation for cross-pollination

感光性品种 photoperiodic response variety

喷雾沤(室沤) mist retting, chamber retting

堆沤 stack retting

蕉麻(马尼拉麻) abaca, Manila hemp

剑麻(菠萝麻)② sisal (green agave)

灰叶剑麻 henequen, Mexican sisal hemp

马盖麻 cantala, Manila maguey

虎尾兰麻 bowstring hemp, sansevieria

青麻(苘麻)③ qingma, China jute

木棉树④ kapok, capok, silk-cotton tree

# 橡胶生产  Rubber Production

1

橡胶树① **rubber tree**

橡胶纵剖苗 **split Hevea seedling**

芽接桩 **budded stump**

高截干实生树 **high stumped seedling**

橡胶树的芽接 **budding of hevea**

芽片 **bud-patch**

芽接位 **budding panel**

街道式栽植法 **avenue planting system**

篱笆式栽植法 **hedge planting system**

疏伐 **thinning**

试割胶乳 **testatex**

胶苗试割分级器 **testatex grader**

轮式分级器 **wheel grader**

乳管 **latex vessel**

〔乳管〕网结系 **anastomosing system, anastomosing networks**

鲱骨形割线 **herringbone tapping cut**

胶乳合成 **latex formation**

连续割胶制 **continuous tapping system**

周期割胶制 **periodic tapping system**

排胶面 **latex flow area**

割面 **tapping panel**

涨压 **turgor pressure**

渗出 **exudation**

爆皮流胶 **bark burst, bark splitting and bleeding**

树皮消耗量 **bark consumption**

树皮再生 **bark renewal**

割胶过度 **overtapping**

褐皮病(死皮) **brown bark (BB) disease**

多割线 **multiple tapping cuts**

死皮树 **dry (rubber) tree**

干胶含量 **dry rubber content of the latex**

收胶桶 **latex collecting bucket**

收胶杯 **collecting cup**

胶舌 **spout**

割胶刀 **tapping knife**

收胶站 **collecting station**

稀释胶乳 **diluting the latex**

凝固　coagulation
抗凝固剂　anticoagulant
胶杯加氨　cup ammoniation
凝固池　coagulating tank
烟房　smokehouse
洞道式烟房　tunnel smoke-
　house
场设工厂　plantation factory
皱片　crepe rubber
生胶片　sheet rubber
保存胶乳(浓缩胶乳)　conserved
　latex, concentrated latex
喷雾法橡胶(散片橡胶)　Hopkin-
　son sprayed rubber
橡胶粉　rubber powder
混合皱片　compo crepe

泥皱胶　earth crepe
白斑　virgin patch
白根病　white root rot, white
　root disease
条溃疡　stripe canker
斑溃疡　patch canker
块溃疡　lump canker
南美叶疫病　South American
　leaf blight
霜霉病　downy mildew of
　rubber
白蚁　termite
橡胶疫霉菌　phytophthore
　heveae
季风性落叶病　phytophthora
　leaf blight

# 林 业  Forestry

## 一般用语  General Terms

热带雨林带　tropical rain
　forest region
季雨林带　monsoon forest
　region
亚热带林带　subtropical
　forest region
温带混交林带　temperate
　mixed forest region
阔叶针叶混交林带　mixed
　broadleaf-conifer forest
　region
西南部针叶林带　southwest

　conifer forest region
草原和沙漠地带的森林　forests
　in grasslands and deserts
全国林业会议　national
　forestry conference
林业资源普查　comprehensive
　survey of forest resources
森林航测　forest aerial photo-
　grammetry
大规模造林规划　large-scale
　afforestation program
普遍造林运动　general affor-

estation movement

重新造林 reafforestation, reforestation

森林综合利用 integrated forest utilization

多种利用林业 multiple-use forestry

森林监督管理 forest supervision

森林经营管理 forest management

森林行政管理 forest administration

增加森林生产率 increasing forest productivity

保续生产经营 sustained yield management

短轮伐期 short(-term) rotation

长轮伐期 long(-term) rotation

粗放林业 extensive forestry

集约林业 intensive forestry

农业间作 combination of forest and field crops

农场式林业 farm forestry

林业部 ministry of forestry

林业局 forestry bureau

林业站 forestry centre

大队林场 woodland of a production brigade

森林护养 forest conservation

封山育林 forest conservation

护林队 forest guards

森林法 forest law

滥伐森林 destructive cutting of forest

盗伐林木 theft of trees from a forest

伐除森林 deforestation

林木全光 forest denudation

林管区 forest district

林班 forest compartment

林班线 compartment line

原始森林 primeval forest, virgin forest

经济林 economic forest

建筑用材 construction timber

工业原料用材 wood as industrial raw material

用材林 timber forest

竹林 bamboo groves

防护林 protection forest, protective forest

水源涵养林 forest for conservation of headwaters

水土保持林 forest for water and soil conservation

防风林 windbreaks

防沙林 sand-breaks

护田林带 shelterbelt

海岸防护林 protective coastal forest

固砂林 protection forest for stabilization of sand dunes

护坡林 forest for protecting slopes from soil erosion

海防林 shelter belt for protecting sea coasts

泛区森林 forest on land liable to inundation

风景林 forest for scenery, ornamental plantation

森林地面 forest floor

活地被物 living mulches, living covers

死地被物(枯枝落叶层) litter, vegetable remains

林分　forest-stand

主林木　major forest tree, chief species

副林木　subsidiary species

林木组成(森林结构)　species composition of a forest, constitution of a forest

单纯林　pure forest

混交林　mixed forest

引进种　exotic species

林龄　age of stand

龄级　age class

同龄林分　even-aged stand

异龄林分　uneven-aged stand

林相　forest form

生长量　growth, increment

树高生长量　height increment

直径生长率　diameter increment percent

林冠　canopy

树冠　crown, tree-crown

林冠层　stor(e)y

郁闭度　canopy density, degree of closeness

林分林冠郁闭　canopy closing of a stand

后生树林分　second growth stand

林分底面积　basal area of a stand

单层林　single-storeyed forest, single-storied forest

两层林　two-storeyed forest

多层林　multi-storeyed forest

上层木　overstorey, overwood

下层木　understorey, underwood

阴性树　shade-bearing tree, shade-bearer

阳性树　light-demanding tree, light-demander

喜温树种　thermophilic tree species

干材　bole

硬材(阔叶树材)　hardwood

软材(针叶树材)　softwood

早材(春材)　early wood (spring-wood)

晚材(秋材)　late wood (autumn-wood)

材积增长量　volume increment

立木蓄积　growing stock

尖削　taper, fall-off

木质组织　xylem tissue

心木　corewood

应力木　reaction wood

应拉木　tension wood

应压木　compression wood

节　knot

根段原木　butt log

树根生长周期性　growth periodicity of tree roots

根的软木化　root suberization, root suberification

根的更新　root regeneration

簇叶　foliage

伪年轮　false ring

压坏(压缩破坏)　compression failure

风倒(拔树)　windthrow

风倒木　windfall

风扭木　windblown tree

冻裂　frost splits, frost cracks

冻轮　frost ring

天然脱枝　natural pruning

落叶期　abscission period

# 造林学　Silviculture

采种　seed collecting, seed collection

种苗原产地　provenance

留种树　seed tree

改良树种　genetically improved strain of tree

选种圃　selective nursery

繁殖苗圃　propagating nursery

"双"苗床　"double" nurseries

移植苗圃　transplant nursery

修苗移植　trimming transplanting

移植成活率　transplant survival percent, transplanting success

增殖苗圃　multiplication nursery

穴植　hole-planting

带土栽植　ball planting, planting with root ball

假植　heeling-in

移植机　transplanting machine

丛植　bunch planting, massive planting

下木栽植(树下栽植)　underplanting

定植苗　planting stock

苗木密度　stocking, degree of stocking

密植距　close spacing

疏植距　wide spacing

适中的植距　intermediate spacing

补植树　replacement tree, "beat-up"

抚育　tending, after-care

幼林抚育　tending of young growth

树冠抚育　crown tending

幼树(大苗)　sapling

攀树器　climbing iron

打枝(修枝)　pruning

修剪枯枝　dry pruning

晚期修剪　late pruning

修剪高度　pruning range

人工繁殖　artificial propagation

插条繁殖　cutting propagation

茎插条　stem cutting

根插条　root cutting

压条法　marcottage, marcotting layerage

堆土压条法　mound layering, stool layerage

空中压条法　air layerage, marcottage

波状压条法(重复压条法)　serpentine layerage (compound layerage)

连续压条法　continuous layerage

嫁接　grafting

劈接　cleft graft

皮下接　rind graft, bark graft

根接　root graft

鞍接　saddle graft

腹接　side graft

舌状腹接　side tongue graft

搭接　splice graft, whip graft

镶接　veneer graft

楔接　wedge graft

舌接 whip-and-tongue graft, whip graft

根靠接 root grafting by approach

靠接 inarching, approach grafting

袋育植株 polybag plant

袋育芽接法 polybag budding

接穗 scion

矮化栽培 dwarf culture

树木矮化法 nanigation

矮壮树 dumpy tree

矮壮素 ccc (cycocel)

林木繁殖 forest tree propagation

实生树 seedling-plant

实生树群 seedling population

实生苗 seedling sprout

实生树林带 seedling strip

实生树植区 seedling clearing

萌生林 coppice

矮林作业 coppice-method

乔林作业 high forest system

下层林丛 underbrush

保护带 boundary belt

保护行(边行) quard row, boundary row

天然更新 self-restoration, natural regeneration

人工更新 artificial regeneration

更新修剪 renewal pruning, rejuvenating pruning

间种更新 periodic rejuvenation

择伐更新法 selection system of natural regeneration

上方天然下种更新法 natural regeneration under shelterwood

更新伐 reproduction-cutting, reproduction-felling

伞伐 shelterwood cutting

伞伐择伐作业 shelterwood selection system

划伐作业 shelterwood group system

择伐式间伐 selection cutting

择伐作业 selection method

疏伐 thinning

选择疏伐 selective thinning

抚育性疏伐 improvement thinning, improvement cutting

支配木 dominant tree, dominant

被支配木 suppressed tree

解放伐 release cutting

解除伐 disengagement cutting, liberation cutting

解放被压木 release of overtopped trees (from overtopping trees)

强度疏伐 heavy thinning

除伐 cleaning

后伐(终伐) removal cutting, removal felling

皆伐 clear cutting, clear felling

皆伐地面上栽植造林 plantation on clear felled area

控制的焚烧 controlled burn

采伐迹地 clearing, cutover

倒树机 treedozer

拔树起重器 monkey jack

横切动力锯 dragsaw

采运木轨道 tramway for felling

伐前更新　preregeneration

伐后更新　regeneration after removal of old growth

伐后残余林木　residual stand

更新间隔期　regeneration interval

植被重建　revegetation

林地保护树　soil-protection wood

定期保续收获　sustained annual yield working

连年保续作业　deterioration

indicator

恶化指标　damage (done) by severe frost cator

严重霜害　damage (done) by severe frost

野兽食害　damage by game

冻死　winter-killing

苗木立枯病　damping-off of seedling

梢枯病　top drying

落叶病　wilt disease

## 森林试验站　Forest Experiment Station

试验区　test block

划定栽培区　regional assignment

分散的区组试验　distributed block trial

对照小区　check plot

重复单株小区试验　replicated tree-plot experiment

苗木培育圃　plant school

根实验室　root laboratory

品系甄别苗圃　clone-screening nursery

谱系栽培　pedigree culture

系比试验　clone trial

测树器　dendrometer

树高测定器　hypsometer

生长计　auxanometer

生长锥　accretion borer, increment borer

生长记录器　auxograph

比重计　densitometer

树木直径尺　tree calipers

树围卷尺　circumference tape

测容器　xylometer

树皮规　bark-gauge

剥皮器　bark spud, barking iron

分光光度计　spectrophotometer

照度计　lightmeter

露光计　actionometer

蒸腾计　potometer

生长(激)素　auxin

种植钵(营养钵)　culture pan

盆栽试验　pot incubation test

附签条(标牌)　tagging

林相图　stock map

产量等级指标　yield class indication

产量曲线图　production pattern

种植材料推荐　planting recommendations

树木园　arboretum

示范林　demonstration forest

示范区　demonstration plot

实验单元　experimental unit

指标林分　index stand

## 森林气象学 Forest Meteorology

森林小气候 **forest microclimate**

森林能量预算 **energy budget of a forest**

森林热量预算 **forest heat budget**

森林能量平衡 **forest energy balance**

森林热量平衡 **forest heat balance**

树干的热流 **heat flow in tree trunks**

温度梯度 **temperature gradients**

蒸散作用 **evapotranspiration, fly-off**

日辐射强度 **intensity of solar radiation**

(森林的)阳光返照率 **solar albeds (of a forest)**

林冠透光率 **transmissivity of a canopy to light**

森林内阳光的可变性 **variability of light in a forest**

短波辐射 **short-wave radiation**

长波辐射 **longwave radiation**

(白天多云时的)阴光 **shade light (on cloudy days)**

森林积雪 **forest snowpack**

## 森林除草 Weeding in the Forest

灌丛清除 **scrub clearance and cleaning**

机械除草 **machine weeding**

手工除草 **hand weeding**

除莠剂除草 **weeding with herbicides**

轻便除草机① **portable clearing saw, portable brushcutter**

手扶除草机 **pedestrian controlled weeding machine**

自动铲草机② **autoscythe**

背负式机动鼓风弥雾器 **motorised knapsack mistblower**

背负式手动喷射器 **hand-operated knapsack sprayer**

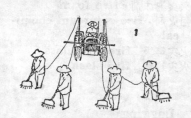

拖拉机除草机　tractor-powered weeding machine

拖拉机悬挂喷射器①　tractor-mounted sprayer

树木注射器　tree injector

自动树木注射器　tree ject

修枝砍刀　billhook

修枝钩刀②　brush(ing) hook

飞机喷施除莠剂　aerial application of herbicides

超低剂量喷药　ULV spray (ultra-low-volume spray)

护面罩　face shield

呼吸罩　respirator

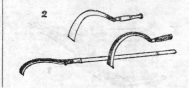

## 森林火灾防救　Forest Fire Control

火灾危险　fire hazards

火灾季节　fire season

火险天气预报　fire weather forecast

防火线　fire control line, firebreak, fire lane

防火沟　fire line

防火植物带　living firebreak

常绿防火林　green break, evergreen firebreak

保火险母树　fire insurance tree

消防营地　fire camp

消防人员　fire fighter, fireman

防火巡逻队员　fire patrolman

防火了望塔　fire tower

防火了望员　fire lookout, towerman

防火监视哨　fire guard

救火调度员　dispatcher

火灾定位仪　fire-finder

火势　fire behaviour

火情扫描　fire scan

蔓延速率计算器　rate-of-spread meter

野火　wildfire, free-burning fire

顺风火　head fire

飞火　spot fire, jumping fire

地表火　grass fire, ground fire

伏地火　creeping fire

树冠火　crowning fire

树干火　stem fire

闷火　smouldering fire

休眠火　hangover fire

雷击火　lightning-caused fire

扑灭林火　extinquishing a forest fire

围控火势　containing a fire, corraling a fire

迎头打火　backfiring

空中降水(飞机泼水)　water dropping

飞机投水弹　water bombing

空降灭火员　smoke jumper

灭火直升飞机　helitanker

灭火泡沫剂　fire foam

阻火剂　fire retardant chemical

火灾等级　fire size class

火灾迹地　fire slash

## 木材采运作业　Logging

林内运木道　clearing road

滑材道　log slip

板滑道　board-chute

运材车①　log-waggon, log tractor

高轮集材车　logging wheels, katydid

低轮集材车　bummer

架空集材机　aerial skidder, cableway skidder

楞场　forest depot

原木楞台　log deck

原木起运装置　log hoist, log haul-up

翻木机　log turner, hook lever

木材装车场　log landing

运材火车　log train

贮木场　timber-yard, lumber-yard

流送材　drift-wood

流材道　timber-floating channel

集送流材工　log driver

流材堵塞　logjam

留场　capturer

放排　rafting

木排　raft

贮材河缆　log-holding boom

曳材上水链槽　haul-up

## 常见树木名称　Names of Some Common Trees

红松　Korean pine (Pinus Koraiensis)

落叶松　larch (Larix)

赤松　Japanese red pine (Pinus densiflora)

油松　Chinese pine (Pinus tabulaeformis)

水松②　water pine (Glyptostrobus pensilis)

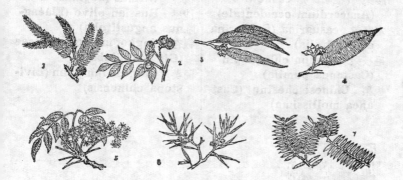

冷杉 fir (Abies)

云杉 spruce (Picea)

水杉 dawn redwood (Metasequoia glyptostroboides)

杉木(沙木) China fir (Cunninghamia lanceolata)

落羽杉① bald cypress (Taxodium distichum)

柏木 mourning cypress (Cupressus funebris)

侧柏(扁柏) Chinese arborvitae (Biota orientalis)

桧(桧柏) Chinese juniper (Sabina chinensis)

柳杉 Chinese cryptomeria (Crytomeria fortunei)

楠(柟) nanmu (Phaebe nanmu)

杨 poplar (Populus)

紫檀② padauk (Pterocerpus)

黄檀属 rosewood (Dalbergia)

柠檬桉③ lemon eucalyptus (Eucalyptus citriodora)

蓝桉 Tasmanian blue eucalyptus, blue gum (Eucalyptus globulus)

大叶桉④ swamp mahogany, beakpod eucalyptus (Eucalyptus robusta)

白千层 cajeput tree, paperback tree (Melaleuca quinquenervia)

栎 oak (Quercus)

檫木 Chinese sassafras (Sassafras tsumu)

苦楝⑤ chinaberry tree (Melia azedarach)

樟树 camphor tree (cinnamomum camphora)

鹅掌楸 Chinese tulip tree (Liriodendron chinense)

泡桐(白花种) fortunes paulownia (Paulownia fortunei)

泡桐(紫花种) Paulownia imperials (Paulownia tomentosa)

台湾相思树⑥ Taiwan acacia (Acacia confusa)

毛竹 moso bamboo (Phyllostachys pubescens)

香榧(榧)⑦ Chinese torreya (Torreya grandis)

824

腰果树(槚如树) cashew (Anacardium occidentale)
木麻黄 casuarina (Casuarina equisetifolia)
毛枝栗 common chinquapin (Castanea pumila)
板栗 Chinese chestnut (Castanea mollissima)

核桃 walnut (Juglans)
沙枣 Russian olive (Elaeagnus angustifolia)
银杏 gingko, maidenhair tree (Gingko biloba)
蒲葵 Chinese fan-palm (Livistona chinensis)

# 牧畜业 Animal Husbandry

## 牧区畜牧业 Pastoral Industry

牛羊业 pastoralism
草原 grassland, (Am.) rangeland
牧草地 sward, meadow
放牧地 pasture, (Am.) range
畜牧场 stock farm, (Am.) ranch
半农半牧区 mixed pastoral farming area, agricultural-pastoral area
草田轮作 ley farming
放牧 grazing, pasturing, depasturing
(草原)载畜量 carrying capacity, stocking density
载畜率 stocking rate
放牧育成 rearing on pasture
放牧肥育 grass finishing

放牧场出入口 bumper gate
放牧法 grazing system
定区放牧法 set-stock grazing
换区放牧法 mob-stock grazing
分区轮牧法 rotational grazing
划片轮牧法 paddock grazing
限界放牧法 strip grazing
后篱笆 back fence
前沿电篱笆 forward electric fence
过栏补饲放牧 forward creep grazing
青刈喂饲 green soiling
食腐羊群 scavenger sheep
再生草 silage aftermath
待期放牧 deferred grazing
早春放牧 early bite

放牧　herding the cattle
定居畜群　sedentary herd
游牧畜群　nomadic herd
行走中畜群，被赶畜群　drove
无人放牧的牲畜　unherded
　animals
离群牲畜　straggler

牛鼻圈　bull ring
曲柄牧羊棍　crook
套索　lasso
打号　marking
打耳标　earmarking
角上烙印　horn branding
冷冻打号　freeze branding

## 综合畜牧场　Animal Husbandry Complex

畜舍　barn
普通畜舍　general-purpose
　barn
养马场　horse range
马厩　horse barn, stables
栓系分隔栏　tie stall
无栓分隔栏　loose-box, box
　stall
厩旁小牧场　paddock
饲料箱　feedbox
干草槽　hay manger, hayrack
饲喂过道　feedway, feed alley
清粪过道　litter alley
饲槽档栏　feeding rack
排水沟，粪尿沟　gutter
奶牛场房舍　dairy housing
分栏舍饲法　stall-barn system
散放舍饲法　loose-housing
　system
奶牛房　dairy shed, dairy
　barn
牛房　cow shed, cow barn,
　byre
对头式栓牛　facing cows in,
　faced-in cows
对尻式栓牛　facing cows out,
　faced-out cows
下犊牛栏　maturity pen
犊子栏　calf pen
干草捆架　hayloft

挤奶室　milk room, milking
　parlour
挤奶台　elevated milking
　stall
敞壁畜棚　open shed
室外牛栏　cow pen
活动场地　exercise yard
幼畜补饲栏　creep
幼畜隔栏补饲　creep feeding
自动控制畜舍　controlled
　house
简易畜舍　climatic housing
活动栅栏　hurdle
按钮操纵喂饲　push-button
　feeding
饲料输送管道　feed line
自动送料饲槽　feed conveyor
　trough
饲料分送器　bunk feeder
输送链式饲料分送器　bunk
　feeder with chain con-
　veyor
连续饲槽　continuous manger
吊挂饲槽　hanging feeder
干碎料饲斗　dry-mash hopper
饲料计量　feed metering
精饲料计量箱　concentrate
　metering hopper
省饲料的家畜　easy keeper
多吃饲料的家畜　hard keeper

自动饲喂器　**automatic feeder**

自动饮水器　**autodrinker,
automatic livestock waterer**

畜舍清扫机　**barn cleaner**

耙粪器　**dropping board
scraper**

除粪道　**dunging passage**

粪尿沟清扫机　**gutter cleaner**

冲洗器　**flasher**

粪尿池　**lagoon**

氧化沟　**oxidation ditch**

畜舍污水　**barn sewage**

流出物处理　**effluent disposal**

牛体拭刷吸尘器　**cattle groom-
ing machine**

家畜卫生　**animal sanitation**

熏烟消毒　**fumigation**

熏烟消毒器　**fumigator**

熏蒸剂　**fumigant**

药浴池　**dipping bath, dipping
pit, dipping vat**

滴溜栏　**draining pen**

浸泡药浴　**plunge-dip**

喷雾药浴①　**spray-dip**

待浴栏　**forcing pen**

浴羊剂　**sheepdip, sheepwash**

养羊场地　**sheep run**

养羊场　**sheep station**

舍饲养羊　**indoor sheep pro-
duction**

羊栏　**sheepfold, sheepcot(e)**

种畜饲养场　**stud**

畜圈　**corral**

产羔圈　**drop corral**

产羔栏　**lambing pen**

产羔棚　**lambing shed**

母子圈　**mothering corral**

母羊认羔栏　**claiming pen**

临时羊栏　**chatching pen**

分群狭道　**cutting chute**

分群狭道活门　**dodge gate**

羊群放牧场　**sheepwalk**

养猪场　**pig farm, piggery,
pigsty**

集中猪舍　**permanent pig
house, (Am.) central hog
house**

通用猪舍　**general-purpose
pig house**

专业养猪场　**specialized pig
farm**

完全圈养法　**total confine-
ment system**

舍饲肥育猪圈　**pig parlour,
pig corral**

单列式猪舍　**single-row pig
house**

矮小型猪舍　**kennel-type
piggery**

敞开式猪圈　**open-fronted pig-
pen**

母猪分娩栏　**farrowing stall**

母猪分娩房　**farrowing house**

初生猪篮　**farrowing basket**

自动哺乳器　**automatic sow**

(母猪圈中的)护仔栏　**farrowing
rail, guard rail**

断奶猪群饲栏　**weaner pool
and yard**

断奶仔猪　**weanling pig, runner**

猪浴池　**pig wallow**

## 饲料和饲养 Feeds and Feeding

饲养标准 feeding standard
采食量 feed intake capacity
能量平衡 energy balance
饲料转化率 feed conversion, feed efficiency
饲料到乳转化率 feed-to-milk conversion efficiency
干物质 dry matter (DM)
消化率 digestibility
平衡饲料 balanced feed, balanced diet
平衡用混合料 balancer
配制饲料 formula feed
饲料添加剂 feed additive
用电子计算机计配的饲料 computer formulated diet
平衡日粮 balanced ration
限量饲料 controlled feeding
自由采食饲养 cafeteria feeding, free-choice feeding
人工饲养 artificial feeding
饲喂时间表 feeding schedule
粗饲料 roughage, coarse fodder

混成精饲料 concentrate mixture
青绿饲料 green feed
预干青饲料 wilted green
青贮饲料 silage, ensilage
低水分青贮饲料 drylage, haylage
干粗饲料 dry fodder
散装饲料 bulk feed
整体饲料 bundle feed
小麦麸 wheat bran
油饼 oil cake
豆饼粉 soybean meal (SBM)
亚麻籽油饼粉 linseed oil meal
棉籽油饼粉 cotton-seed oil meal
干啤酒槽 brewer's dried grains
舐盐砖 salt-lick
微量矿物质添加剂 trace mineral supplement
家厨弃料 home-waste
泔水 swill
强化饲料 fortified feed

## 肥 育 Fattening

舍饲肥育 yard finishing, yard fattening
场饲肥育 drylot finishing, drylot feeding
放牧肥育 grass finishing
肥育场 feedlot, drylot, fattening unit
水泥地面肥育场 paved feedlot
肥育牲畜 fattening stock, fattener(s)
肥育幼畜 fatling(s)
待肥育牲畜 store stock
未经肥育牲畜 unfattened stock
高度肥育牲畜 highly-finished stock
肥育不足牲畜 under-finished stock

肥育过度牲畜　overfinished stock

膘情(肥度)　condition, finish, degree of fatness

膘情系数　coefficient of condition

膘情好　in good (high) condition, in good (high) flesh

上等膘(肥膘)　show condition, prime condition

膘情差　lacking in condition, in thin flesh

增膘　conditioning

掉膘　losing condition, loss of flesh

满膘　highly-finished

肥育期　finishing stage

(活)体重　liveweight, body weight

空腹体重　empty body weight

成年体重　mature weight

(肥育终期)体重　final weight

定期秤重　routine weighing

校正重　adjusted weight

增重　liveweight gain, liveweight increment, gaining in weight

断奶后增重　postweaning gain

秤重日期　date weighed

预期日增重　expected daily gain

平均日增重　average daily gain

增重率　rate of liveweight growth, rate of body weight gain

增重能力　gaining ability

增重效率　efficiency of gain

快速增重　fast-gaining

减重　liveweight loss

净增重　net gain

肥育配制饲料　fattening ration

饲料的营养成分　feedstuff

热敏探示器　thermistor probe

## 家畜繁育　Animal Breeding

品种　breed

品系　strain of breed

检定卓越畜系祖畜　proved stock getter

检定合宜品种祖畜　proved sire of an appropriate breed

祖畜后代　get-of-sire

繁育方法　breeding system

近亲繁育　inbreeding

品系繁育　linebreeding

品系杂交　outcrossing

杂交繁育　crossbreeding

级进杂交　grading-up

用纯种与本地种级进杂交　upgrading the local breed by pure breeds

杂交优势　heterosis

培育新种　evolving new breeds

遗传工程　genetic engineering

分子遗传学　molecular genetics

细胞遗传学　cytogenetics

数量遗传学　quantitative genetics

遗传密码　genetic code

自然选择　natural selection
遗传隔离　genetic isolation
选择配种用畜　selection of mating stock
生产性能特征　performance traits
出生重量　birth weight
妊娠期日数　gestation days
一窝产子数　litter size
一窝一子　singleton
一窝二子　twins
一窝三子　triplets
一窝四子　quadruplets
一窝多子　multiple young at a birth

泌乳期产乳总量　milk yield in L.P. (lactation period)
奶油脂肪(量)　butter fat
繁育季节　breeding season
发情　coming in(to) heat, being in season
发情探测　heat detection
人工授精　artificial insemination
孕马血促性腺激素　pregnant mare serum gonadotrop (h) in (P.M.S.G.)
妊娠中隔期　gestation interval
谱系家畜育种(纯种繁殖)　pedigree breeding

# 家　畜　Domestic Animal

马① horse
公马 stallion
母马 mare
驹 foal
公驹 colt
母驹 filly

驴② ass, donkey
小驴 burro
公驴 jackass
母驴 jenny
骡③ mule
驴骡(驮骔) hinny

斑马 zebra
纯种马 clean-bred horse, pure-blooded horse
种母马 broad mare, producing mare
种公马 stud horse

乘用马　hack, saddle horse, mount

矮脚乘用马　cob

驮马　pack horse

挽车马　harness horse, draught horse

重挽马　heavy draught horse, (Am.) drafter

农用重挽马　farm draught horse, (Am.) farm chunk

一套挽马　horse team, (Am.) horse hitch

小挽马　harness pony

力役马　work horse

军马　army horse

家用驯马　family broken horse

未驯马　green horse

难驯马　restive horse

赛跑用马　racehorse, racer

越障马　fencer

跳高马　jumper

娱乐用马　pleasure horse

伊犁马　Ili horse

蒙古马　Mongolian Pony

大通马(浩门马)　Tatung Pony

阿拉伯马　Arab horse

纯血马　Blood Horse

牛(总称)　oxen, cattle

黄牛①　common ox

公牛　bull

母牛　cow

犊子　calf

阉公牛(犍)　bullock, ox

(成年去势的)阉公牛　stag

(幼龄去势的)阉公牛　steer

公犊　bull calf

未产犊母牛　heifer

产犊母牛　calver

肉用牛(菜牛)　beef cattle, meat cattle

奶牛②　cow, dairy cattle

役用牛　draft cattle, work cattle

纯种牛　purebred cattle

水牛③　buffalo

印度水牛　Indian buffalo

非洲水牛　African buffalo

野黄牛(羭)　gaur

牦牛④　yak

犏牛(牦牛黄牛杂种)　*pianniu*, cattle yak

大额牛　gayal
蒙古牛　Mongolian cattle
秦川牛　qinchuan cattle
南阳牛　Nanyang cattle
北京黑白花牛　Beijing Black-and-White cattle, Beijing Black Pied cattle

绵羊①　sheep
公羊　ram, tup
母羊　ewe
羔羊　lamb
老公羊　aged ram, aged tup
阉公羊　gelded ram, wether
家绵羊(金蹄兽)　domestic sheep, Ovis aries, golden hoof

山羊②　goat
公山羊　billy goat, he-goat
母山羊　nanny goat, she-goat
山羊羔　kid
乳用山羊　dairy goat
肉用羊　mutton sheep
粗毛羊　coarse-wooled sheep
细毛羊　fine-wooled sheep
长毛羊　long-wooled sheep
齐口羊　full-mouthed sheep

淘汰的老母羊　cast-for-age (CFA) ewe
羊群　flock
农区羊群　farm flock
领头羊　bellwether
领头(去屠场)羊　Judas goat
种羊　breeding sheep
大角野羊　mountain sheep
东方盘羊　Urial Group, red sheep
湖羊　*huyang* sheep
滩羊　*tanyang* sheep
成都麻羊　*ma* goat
藏羊　Tibetan sheep
中卫山羊　Zhongwei goat
美利奴羊　Merino sheep
新疆毛肉兼用细毛羊　Xinjiang Merino sheep
澳洲美利奴羊　Australian Merino sheep
克什米尔山羊　Kashmere goat
猪　pig, (Am.) hog, swine
家猪　swine
公猪　boar
阉猪　hog, (Am.) stag, barrow, castrated pig
小母猪　gilt
成年母猪　sow
种公猪　stock boar
种母猪　brood sow
一窝新产猪　farrow
同窝仔猪　littermate
仔猪　piglet, pigling
烤用仔猪　roaster
生猪　live hog, hog on foot
肉用型猪　meat-type hog, pork-type hog
腌用猪　baconer
鲜肉用猪　pork pig, porker

小型肉猪　small pork, light porker
中型肉猪　medium porker, porket
大型肉猪　cutter
大肥猪　heavy pig
生长肥育猪　store pig
猪群　swine herd
野猪　wild boar
广东猪　Guangdong pig
文昌猪　Wenchang pig
上海白猪　Shanghai White pig
北京黑猪　Beijing Black pig
昌黎猪　Changli pig
淮猪　Huai pig

哈白猪　Harbin White pig
吉林黑猪　Jilin Black pig
东北民猪　Min pig
宁乡猪　Ningxiang pig
沙子岭猪　Shaziling pig
新金猪　Xinjin pig
垛山猪　Duoshan pig
波中猪(黑猪)①　Poland China pig
大白猪②　Large White pig, Large Yorkshire pig
梅花猪③　spotted pig
家兔　rabbit
狗　dog
猫　cat
豚鼠(洋鼠)　guinea pig

## 驯化野生动物　Domesticated Wild Animal

麝香鹿　musk deer (Moschus moschiferus)
驯化麝香鹿　domesticating musk deer
麝鹿围场　musk deer pen
外分泌腺　exocrine glands
麝香提取　musk extraction
梅花鹿　sika deer, Japanese deer (Cervus nippon)
印度象　elephant (Elephas maximus)
(野兽)踪迹　spoor
跟踪(野兽)　spooring

獠牙　tusk
有獠牙的动物　tusker
象牙　ivory
幼象　baby elephant
受教驯象　trained elephant
象群　herd of elephants
象屋　elephant house
水貂　Eastern mink, little black mink (Mustela vison)
紫貂(黑貂)　sable (Martes zibellina)
大灵猫　civet (Viverra zibetha)
陷阱诱捕　trapping

# 副 业 Side-line Occupation

## 综合养鸡场 Poultry-farming Complex

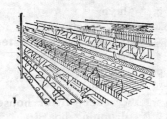

蛋用鸡 **egg-laying poultry**

排笼(养鸡法) **battery system**

排笼鸡舍① **battery house**

多层鸡笼 **multideck battery, multideck cage**

倾斜铁丝网地面 **sloping wire floor**

斜面产蛋箱 **roll-away nest**

自动集蛋系统 **automatic egg pickup system**

集蛋槽 **egg collecting trough**

传送带清粪鸡笼 **belt-cleaned poultry cage**

自流饮水器 **drinking fountain**

饲养员出入口 **service passage**

鸡笼清扫器 **cage cleaner**

饲养员过道 **service passage**

铺草运动场 **straw-yard, hen-yard**

(鸡舍)日浴廊 **sun porch**

(鸡舍)日浴台 **sun balcony**

产蛋工厂 **egg factory**

产蛋记录卡片 **egg record card**

产蛋期 **laying cycle**

平均产蛋量 **average egg yield**

产蛋强度 **laying intensity, laying rate**

产蛋力 **egg-laying capacity**

产蛋性能 **egg-laying performance**

母鸡只日产蛋率 **hen-day egg production**

母鸡第一产蛋年 **pullet year**

生物年度 **biological year**

硬壳蛋 **hard-shelled egg**

软壳蛋 **soft-shelled egg, membraneous egg**

无精蛋 **infertile egg, clear egg**

受精蛋 **fertile egg**

双黄蛋 **double-yolked egg**

(日产)双蛋　egg-pair
照蛋　candling eggs
照蛋灯，验蛋器　egg candler,
　egg tester
鸡蛋分级机　egg grader
臭蛋，孵不成的蛋　addle egg
可孵成的蛋　hatching egg
产蛋困难　egg bound
窝外蛋　floor egg
抱窝　sitting, brooding
一窝蛋　clutch of eggs
孵化季节　hatching season
人工孵化　artificial incuba-
　tion
每批孵化数　hatching eggs
　per setting

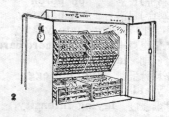

电孵器②　electric incubator
孵化器蛋盘　incubator tray,
　hatcher tray
生理零点　physiological zero
预孵　preincubation
翻蛋　egg turning
(孵化器)报警系统　alarm
　system
出雏盘　hatcher tray
雏鸡盒　chick box
天然孵化雏鸡　hen-hatched
　chick
人工孵化雏鸡　incubator-
　hatched chick

初生雏鸡　day-old chick
孵化率　hatchability
分层育雏笼　tier brooder
育雏室　brooder, brooder
　house
笼架式育雏室　battery brooder
肉用仔鸡鸡舍　broiler house
烤用仔鸡　roaster
食用鸡　table bird, table
　poultry
幼雏鸡　starter, started chick
中雏鸡　grower
中雏母鸡　started pullet,
　range-size pullet
产蛋鸡　layer
公鸡　cock, rooster
阉鸡　capon, castrated rooster
肥育阉母鸡　spayed hen,
　poulard
养鸡场　hennery
厚褥草鸡舍　deep-litter house
承粪板　dropping board
家禽饮水器　poultry drinker
栖木　perch, roost
全进全出制　all-in, all-out
　system
鸡群放养法　free-range poultry
　keeping
活动鸡舍　colony house
临时鸡笼　catching crate
家庭副业养鸡　backyard
　poultry raising
鸡笼　hen coop
开放式鸡舍　open-side poultry
　house
限量饲喂　restricted feeding
隔日饲喂　alternate-day feed-
　ing, skip-a-day restriction
每周五日饲喂制　skip-two-days-

per-week feeding program

填饲 forced feeding

饲鸡槽 poultry feeder

饲槽添料漏斗 hopper

撒喂 scratch feed, litter feeding of grain

阶段饲养 phase feeding battery laying

笼养产蛋鸡饲料 battery laying feed

中雏日粮 growing ration

肉用仔鸡日粮 broiler ration

雏鸡生长素 chick growth factor

颗料饲料 pellet feed

饱饲 full feeding, being fed to appetite

顶点代谢 summit metabolism

嗉囊 crop

种用小母鸡 breeder pullet

种用小公鸡 breeder cockerel

群配 flock mating, mass mating

近交系小鸡 inbred line chick

近交杂种小鸡 inbred hybrid chick

(种用)后备母鸡 replacement pullet

来航鸡① Leghorn

澳洲黑鸡 Australorp

澳洲黑来航杂种鸡 Austra-White cross

小型来航鸡 Mini Leghorn

芦花洛克鸡② Barred Plymouth Rock

白洛克鸡③ White Plymouth Rock

九斤黄 cochin

狼山鸡④ Langshan

丝毛鸡(竹丝鸡)⑤ Silky (silkie) fowl

小种鸡 Bantam

大种鸡 Large fowl

珠鸡 Guinea fowl, Guinea hen

雌相公鸡 hen-cock

雄相母鸡 cock-hen

火鸡(吐绶鸡)⑥ turkey

雄火鸡 gobbler, tom turkey, turkey-cock

雌火鸡 turkey-hen

火鸡雏 turkey poult, squab turkey

## 水 禽 Waterfowl

水鸭　fresh water duck
公鸭　drake
小鸭　duckling
雏鸭　green duck
养鸭塘　duck-pond
养鸭者　ducker
叫鸭笛　duck call
浮萍　duckweed
龙须眼子菜　duck grass
填鸭　duck-cramming, forced feeding of ducks
填肥鸭　forced-fed duck
绿头鸭　mallard
黄鸭　ruddy sheldrake
麻鸭①　sheldrake

北京鸭②　Beijing duck
番鸭③　perching duck
半番鸭(泥鸭)④　hybrid perching duck
杂种鸭　male duck
养鹅场　goosery
养鹅者　gooseherd
填鹅　goose noodling, goose cramming
填鹅饲条　noodle
中国鹅⑤　Chinese goose
非洲鹅　African goose
天鹅⑥　swan
野鹅　wild goose

## 鸽与其他 Pigeon and Others

鸽　pigeon, dove
雏鸽　squab
养雏鸽　squab raising
鸽舍　pigeon-house, pigeonry
鸽栏, 鸽圈　pigeon pen
鸽棚　dove-cot
鸽饲料　pigeon feed
鸽乳　pigeon milk
信鸽　homing pigeon, carrier pigeon

军用鸽(信鸽)教养员　pigeoneer
卡诺鸽　carneau pigeon
法国孟登鸽　French Mondein pigeon
荷麦鸽　Homer pigeon
野禽　wild fowl
鹧鸪　partridge
鹌鹑　quail
斑鸠　turtledove

## 蚕丝业　Sericulture

桑蚕(家蚕)① Chinese silkworm (Bombyx mori)
蚕卵 silkworm egg
桑叶 mulberry leaf
白桑 white mulberry (Morus alba)
作茧 cocoon spinning
收茧 silk cocoons collecting
双宫茧 doupion cocoon
双宫丝 doupion silk
缫丝 silk reeling, filature
缫丝机 filature
缫丝厂 filature
热水缫丝法 hot-water reeling process
丝身 silk filament
蚕丝胶 sericin, silk gum
带胶丝身 bave
脱胶 degumming, boiling-off
脱胶丝身 brin
生丝 raw silk
丝绵 silk wadding
废丝 silk waste
落绵 silk noil
茧衣 cocoon stripping

(白，黄)长吐 long waste (white, yellow)
(黄)乱吐 short waste (yellow)
黄头带 yellow hard matte
绢丝 spun silk yarn
丝线 silk thread
䌷丝 noil yarn
桑蚕绵球 silk Peignee, silk tops
柞蚕 tussah, oak silkworm (Antherea pernyi)
栎树叶(柞树叶) oak leaf
辐照 irradiation
快中子 fast neutron
快中子辐照蚕卵 irradiation of silkworm eggs with fast neutrons
流动中子源载运车 mobile neutron source truck
柞蚕丝 tussah silk
柞蚕绵球 tussah silk spun laps, tussah silk spun Peignee
柞蚕落绵 tussah silk spun noil, tussah silk spun Bourette
大挽手(长度柞蚕废丝) tussah silk waste (long size)
二挽手(短度柞蚕废丝) tussah silk waste (short size)
柞绸 tussah pongee

## 养蜂业　Apiculture

养蜂场 apiary
副业养蜂 sideline beekeeping
蜂群 bee colony

蜜蜂 honey bee (Apis mellifera)
蜂房，蜂巢 beehive, bee-

comb, honey-comb

蜂箱　wooden beehive

十框蜂箱　ten-frame-hive

隔王板　queen-excluder

巢础　comb foundation

母蜂，蜂王　queen bee

雄蜂　drone bee

工蜂　worker bee

采蜜蜂　forager

蜂房内工蜂　house bee

饲幼虫工蜂　nurse bee

蜂王台　queen comb, queen's cell

产雄蜂王　drone layer

人工培育蜂王　grafting

除去蜂王　dequeening

蜜源植物　bee plant, honey plant

花蜜　nectar

蜜胃　honey stomach

(蜜蜂后腿上的)花粉篮　pollen basket

蜂舞　bee dances

婚飞　mating flight, nuptial flight

蜂粮　beebread

分封　swarming

人工分封　artificial swarming

割蜜　honey gathering, honey harvest

粒状蜂蜜　granulated honey, solidified honey, sugared honey

王浆，蜂乳　royal jelly, bee milk

蜂蜡　bee's wax

蜂蜜分离机　honey extractor, honey separator

蜂蜜分离装置　honey extracting equipment

蜂蜜过滤器　honey filter

倾析法　decantation system

沉积槽　sedimentation tank

防螫面罩　bee veil

蜂螫药膏　bee poison ointment

意大利蜂　Italian bee

卡尼拉蜜蜂　Carniolan bee

蜜蜂腐烂病　foulbrood

蜜导鸟　honey-guide

# 狩　猎　Game Hunting

狩猎　chasing, hunting

狩猎场　hunting-field, hunting-ground

狩猎法　game law

禁猎季节　closed game season

鸟兽禁猎区　sanctuary

猎人　huntsman, hunter

助猎手(惊兽手)　beater

狩猎术　huntsmanship

静猎　still hunt(ing)

围猎　enclosing of game

潜行猎　stalking

反向跟踪　back-tracking

追赶　chasing

装夹　set, trap

埋饵装夹　buried bait set

隧洞装夹　cubby set

陷阱，圈套，罗网　trap, snare

狩猎棚　shooting hut, ambush shed

猎枪　shot gun

乱射　pot shot

判准射　judged shot
杀射　fatal shot
放箭　loosing an arrow
猎兽犬　hound, hunting dog
猎鹿犬　deerhound
猎獾犬　basset
足迹味　foot-scent
猎物　game
小猎兽　ground game
棕熊(马熊)　brown bear (Uraus arctos)
黑熊(狗熊)　Asiatic black bear
熊胆　gall of bear
熊掌　bear's paw
獾　badger

果子狸(花面狸)　masked civet, gem-faced civet
猞猁(林狼)　lynx
獐　Chinese river-deer, Chinese water-deer
驯鹿　reindeer, caribou
小鹿　reeve's muntjac
虎　tiger
东北虎　Northeast tiger
华南虎　South China tiger
生皮　pelt
鸟枪　fowling piece
捕禽网　fowling net, clapnet
囮子鸟(媒鸟)　decoy bird
引鸟入网　decoying a bird into a net

## 农村手艺工人　Village Craftsman

生产小组　production group
锻工场　forge
锻工, 锻铁工人　wrought iron worker
铁匠的打铁助手　smith's striker
烧红的铁条　glowing bar
锤打铁条成一定形状　hammering the iron into shape
大锤　sledge
钢砧　steel anvil
造艇工人　boat builder
小帆船　small sailing craft
艇的骨架　skeleton of a boat
龙骨　keel
船首柱　stem
框架　frame
肋骨　ribs
板条　plank
鳞状叠板式　clinker system

平镶式　carvel system, flush system
电动手钻　electric-powered hand drill
卡钳　caliper
木工矩尺　carpenter's square
榫锯　tenon saw
横割锯　cross-cut saw
农村陶工　country potter, village potter
陶器作坊　pottery
采掘陶土　clay digging
陶坯制作工　thrower
陶工旋盘　potter's wheel
土团　lumps of clay
烧窑　firing
烧窑工人　kilnman
烧制瓦坯　pot baking
瓦盆　crock
(有嘴和把手)瓦壶　pitcher

高身大瓦埕　huge Ali Baba jar

烧炭工人　charcoal-burner

炭窑　charcoal-kiln

烧炭场　charcoal-kiln site

坑式烧炭法　charring in pits

堆积烧炭法　charring in heaps

箩筐编织工　basket-maker

箩筐类编织品　basketry, basketwork

柳条编织物　wickerwork

柳条　willow stick, osier twig, osier stick

竹条　bamboo cane

藤条　rattan

藤椅　cane chair

木片条篮子　chip basket

泡浸桶　soaking tub

刮刀　scraper

编织图案　weaving pattern

制桶工人　cooper

制桶工场　coopery, cooperage

打箍锤　hoop-driver, hoop-setter

桶板　stave

桶箍　hoop

绳索编造工　ropemaker

梳麻　hemp hackling

编索机　ropemaker's spinning machine

索心　rope core, rope heart

索的一股　strand

造车工人　cartwright, wheelwright

农用板车　farm wagon, farm cart

边板　side plank

辕杆　draught pole

弯轮胎机　tyre bender

镰刀锤　scythe hammer

打镰砧　scythe anvil

水磨坊　watermill

上射水车　overshot water-wheel, high-breast bucket wheel

中射水车　middleshot water-wheel, breast wheel

下射水车　undershot water-wheel, impact mill wheel

水车沟　millrace, raceway

引水渠　headrace

磨坊工人　miller

磨坊设计人　millwright

磨粉厂　flour mill

粉筛　flour sieve

石磨　millstone

上磨石　upper stone

下磨石　nether stone

# 渔 业 Fishery

## 一般用语 General Terms

海岸渔业 coastal fisheries
近海渔业 offshore fisheries
公海渔业 high seas fisheries
深海渔业 deep-sea fisheries
远洋渔业 distant fisheries
港湾河口渔业 estuary fisheries
内陆(淡水)渔业 inland (freshwater) fisheries
塘鱼养殖业 pond fisheries
养鱼业 fish farming
渔捞 fish harvesting
渔权 fishery rights
渔权范围 fisheries jurisdiction
渔权界线 fishery limit line
独占渔区 exclusive fishing zone
侵犯渔权 encroachment on fishery rights
渔业法 fisheries law
水产部 ministry of aquatic products
渔业资源保护 fisheries con-

servation
鱼类存储量 fishery stocks
滥渔 overfishing
捕鱼量 fish landings
每年捕鱼量 annual fish catch
一网网获量 haul
捕鱼定额 catch quota
网目规定 mesh-size regulations
一个航次捕获量 trip
鱼汛期 fishing season
规定渔季 legally open season
禁渔季节 closed season
禁渔区 fish sanctuary
渔港 fishing port, fish landing point
渔场 fishing ground
渔区 fishing area
渔村 fishing settlement, fishing village
渔民(整体) fisherfolk
渔民(个人) fisherman
渔船队 fishing fleet
陆上勤务人员 shoresman

## 渔 具 Fishing Gear

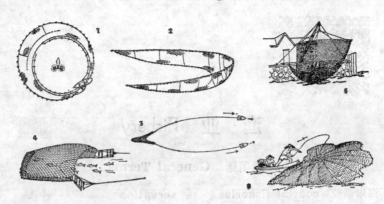

围网类  surrounding nets
围网  purse seine
双船环网①  two-boat ring net
伦巴拉网②  lampare
曳网类  seine nets
地曳网——无囊网  bearch seine without bag
地曳网——有囊网  bearch seine with bag
船曳网——有囊网  boat seine with bag
底曳网  bottom seine
双船底曳网,对曳网③  two-boat bottom seine, pair seine
拖网类  trawls
双支架桁拖网  double-rig beamtrawl
铅锤型桁拖网  beamtrawl of plumb staff type
网板拖网④  other trawl
双船拖网(对拖网)  pair trawl

底拖网  bottom trawl
中层拖网  midwater trawl, pelagic trawl
变水层拖网  semi-pelagic trawl
有翼拖网  wing trawl
V—D拖网  V-D trawl
高网口拖网  high opening trawl
船上操作采具器  boat-operated dredge
敷网⑤  liftnet
手提敷网  portable liftnet
船上操作敷网  boat-operated liftnet
岸边操作定点敷网  shoreoperated stationary liftnet
撒网⑥  castnet
有袋撒网  castnet with pockets
有闭合索撒网  castnet with closing lines

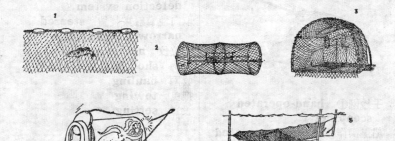

刺网① **gillnet**

底层定置刺网 **bottom-set gillnet**

底层定置缠络网 **bottom-set entangling net**

底层定置框刺网 **bottom-set frame net**

底层定置三层挂网 **bottom-set trammel**

混合式三层挂网刺网 **combined trammel-gillnet**

流网 **driftnet**

围刺网 **encircling gillnet, surrounding gillnet**

箱笼类 **pots**

鱼笼② **fish pot**

蟹虾笼③ **crab and lobster pot**

章鱼笼④ **octopus pot**

张网⑤ **fyke net**

无翼张网 **fyke net without wings**

有不等长翼张网 **fyke net with unequal wings**

有垣网张网 **fyke net with leader**

锚定长袋网 **anchored stownet**

旋围跳网 **encircling veranda net**

钓具 **fishing tackle**

手钓线 **handline**

活饵 **live-bait**

饵料袋 **bait pouch**

拟饵 **lure, artificial lure**

滚钓 **jig**

(有电动卷车)手钓线 **handline with electric reel**

(带花篮钓)手钓线 **handline with ripping hooks**

钓竿 **fishing pole**

延绳钓⑥ **longline**

底置悬浮延绳钓 **bottom-set floating longline**

漂动延绳钓 **drifting longline**

曳绳钓 **trolling**

手抄网① **hand-operated scoop net**

船上操作抄网 **boat-operated scoop net**

浮子网 **floatline, headline**

沉子网 **footrope, ground rope, leadline**

网板 **otter board, trawl board**

游纲 **pennant**

曳纲 **warp**

网衣 **netting, webbing**

泥索 **mudrope**

舷外突出撑杆 **outrigger**

光诱捕鱼(灯光捕鱼) **light fishing**

集鱼灯 **fishing lamp, jack light**

鱼泵 **fish pump**

光诱装置 **light attraction system**

鱼群搜索飞机 **spotter plane**

升级采蛤器 **escalator dredge**

拖网曳纲张度计 **trawl warp tensionmeter**

电子探鱼 **electronic fish detection**

换能器 **transducer**

回声横直面探鱼器 **CERES (Combined Echo Ranging Echo Sounding)**

渔用声纳站 **fisherman's asdic**

亨伯探鱼装置 **Humber fish detection system**

取向性窄射束装置 **steered narrow beam system**

网位仪 **net sounder**

放网 **shooting**

收网 **hauling**

拖曳 **towing**

设置 **setting**

鱼叉② **fishing spear**

标枪 **harpoon**

捕鲸炮③ **whale harpoon gun**

追猎索 **hunting line**

回收索 **retrieving line**

缩结系数 **hanging ratio, taper ratio**

混合钢索 **combination rope**

网衣缝合折缩比率 **take-up of meshes**

减目 **tapering**

缝边 **joining of net sections**

鱼栅 **stream net**

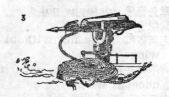

# 渔 船 Fishing Vessels

拖网船类　trawlers

舷拖网船　side trawler

升高艏楼甲板　raised fore-castle deck

前网板吊架　fore gallows frame

后网板吊架　aft gallows frame

拖网绞车　trawl winch

拖网索　trawl cable

鱼舱　fish hold

艇甲板　boat deck

艉(滑道)拖网船　stern (ramp) trawler

拖网加工船　factory trawler

艉滑道　stern chute (or ramp)

艉桥楼　stern bridge

后网板架滑车　aft gallows block

拖网桥楼　trawling bridge

(鱼)加工舱　(fish) processing room

鱼粉制造装置　fishmeal plant

鱼油槽　fish oil tank

冷冻机　freezer

冷冻机舱　freezer hold

吊货杆　cargo boom

吊网架　gantry

拖网捕虾船　shrimp trawler

双杆拖网法　double-rigged trawling method

对拖拖网船　pair trawlers

横桁拖网船　beam trawler

小型舷拖网船　dragger

围网船类　seiners

围网船　purse seiner

围网绞车　seine winch

收围网吊杆　pursing davit

围网甲板艇　seine skiff

混合渔船　combination vessel

双艇围网法　two-boat seining system

刺网船类　gill netters

漂网船　drifter

动力绞盘　powered capstan

动力起网滚筒　powered roller

导缆孔　fairlead

漂网拖网船　drifter-trawler

漂网捕鲑船　salmon drifter

钓船类　hook-and-liners

延绳钓船　longliner

延绳钓母船　longline mother ship

捕鱼艇　catcher boat

起延绳机　longline hauler

平底小渔艇　dory

起钓机　gurdy

竿钓艇　pole and line boat

诱饵钓艇　bait boat

诱饵　chum

羽毛拟饵　feathered lure

活动搁架　portable racks

曳绳钓艇　troller

捕鲸船　whale catcher, whaler

鲸鱼加工船　whale factory ship

鱼粉制造船　fishmeal factory ship

捕鱼艇母船　base ship

冷藏运输船　refrigerated transport

冷冻船　freezer ship

救援拖船　rescue tug

(拖网、加工、冷冻)联队捕鱼法 flotlla fishing
远洋渔船队 distant-water fishing fleet
科学研究船 scientific research vessel
教练船 training vessel
捕沙丁鱼艇 sardine launch
采蛤小艇 oyster canoe
划艇 rowboat
独木舟 dugout
鸬鹚捕鱼 cormorant fishing
金枪鱼捕捞船 tuna clipper
珊瑚采集船 coral boat

供应船 cog, cockboat
渔帆船 smack
采蛤单桅船 oyster sloop
渔船船长 skipper
捕鱼总指挥 chief fisherman
船级 class of ship
罐头工厂船 canning factory ship
渔业调查船 fisheries survey ship
出海 putting to sea
空手归航 broken voyage
网获很多 good catch, good haul

## 电力捕鱼 Electrical Fishing

带电围网 electrified seine
带电拖网 electrified trawl
隔鱼电网 electric fish fence
吸鱼电磁 fish magnet
脉冲电场 pulsed electric field
无网捕鱼 netless fishing
带电鱼泵 electrified fish pump
电延绳钓 electric longline
吸鱼电极 fish-attracting

electrode
电鱼叉 electric harpoon
电捕鱼器 electric fishcatcher
带电鱼钩 electrified hook
电幕 electric screen
电导 electric guide
电拖网捕虾装置 electrical shrimp trawling system
控制鱼的活动 controlling fish movements
电鱼至晕 stunning the fish

## 鱼的保藏 Preservation of Fish

雪藏鲜鱼 fish iced fresh
去了内脏的鱼 dressed fish, eviscerated fish, gutted fish
切鱼块 filleting a fish

切块作业线 filleting line
全鱼冷冻机 whole-fish freezer
冷藏鱼 iced fish, frozen fish
冷冻房 iced chamber, cold chamber

吹风冷冻间　air blast freezer
浸入冰冻法　immersion freezing
低温冰冻设备　low-temperature freezing facilities
冷藏舱　cold-storage hold
抗菌冰　antibiotic ice
超级冷冻　superchilling
海上加工　processing at sea

岸上加工　processing ashore
有效保存期　useful storage life
货架寿命　shelf-life
解冻装置　thawing plant
腌制场　salting yard
熏制场　curing yard, smoking yard

## 鱼类养殖　Fish Farming

海水养殖　marine fish farming
淡水养殖　freshwater fish farming
海水养殖场　marine farm
淡水养殖场　freshwater farm
选择性配种　selective breeding
选择种鱼　selection of brood stock fish
抽取鱼卵　stripping fish of eggs
抽取鱼精液　stripping fish of milt
人工授精　artificial fertilisation
盘内孵化受精卵　hatching fertilised eggs in trays
冷冻鱼精液　frozen milt
产卵力(生育力)　fecundity
基因组成　genetic make-up
促性腺激素　gonadotropin, gonadotropic hormone
炔雌醇　ethylestrenol
雌二醇　oestradiol
含类固醇饲料　steroid diet
给鱼做标志　fish marking
切鳍　finning
标签　tag

鱼的喂饲　fish feeding
自然喂饲　natural feeding
提高饲料转化率　improving food conversion ratio
海水笼养　marine cage farming
浮笼圈养　keeping stocks in floating cages
散放场养　free range farming, ranching
高蛋白颗粒饲料　high protein pellets
条件反射　conditioned response
配合饵料　synthetic fish food
补充喂饲　supplementary feeding
(海水)含盐量　salinity
(淡水)碳酸钙含量　calcium carbonate content
鱼的移殖　transplantation of fish
移殖鱼　transplanted fish
移殖河(原产河)　donor stream
移入河(接受河)　recipient stream
仿造天然环境　duplication of natural conditions
鱼苗死亡率　fry mortality

产卵回游 spawning migration, run

鱼梯 fish ladder, fishway

半咸水鱼池 brackish water fishpond

鱼池配套 fishpond system

幼鱼池 nursery pond

鱼围篱 fish corral

鱼种池 fry pond

养鱼池(成鱼池) rearing pond

捕鱼池 catching pond

进水渠 water-supplying canal

主水闸 main sluice gate

次水闸 secondary sluice gate

水口栅栏 screen

池底 pond floor

水口坝 bank, bund

池坝 ridge of a pond

食场 feeding pool

水域 water area, water space

水面面积 water surface area

鱼池的营养状况 nutrient status of a fishpond

浮游生物 plankton

浮游植物 plant plankton

浮游动物 zooplankton

藻类植物 algae

水中溶氧 dissolved oxygen in water

鱼塘施肥 pond fertilization

肥泥肥水 enriched pond soil and water

畜粪肥 animal manure

麸(糠) bran

田螺 pond snail

浮萍 duckweed

苏丹草 Sudan grass

苦草(鞭节草) vallisneria spiralis

黑藻(轮叶水草) hydrilla verticillata

施肥过度 overfertilization

分层养鱼 rearing fish at different depths

清除掠食鱼和野杂鱼 eradicating predatory and weed fish

干塘起捕 draining the pond to capture the fish

幼鱼 fingerling

未成年鱼 juvenile fish

成年鱼 adult fish

未产卵鱼 clean fish

经产卵鱼 foul fish

(未产的)鱼卵 roe

(产下的)鱼卵 spawn

热带鱼 tropical fish

吃草鱼 herbivorous fish

吃肉鱼 carnivorous fish

青草饲料 green fodder

补充鱼种 recruitment

年龄组成 age composition

年龄群 age group

鱼的行动习性 fish behaviour

溯游产卵鱼 anadromous fish

降海产卵鱼 catadromous fish

放鱼苗 seeding the fry

连续同种交配 breeding in and in

连续异种交配 breeding out and out

鱼池处理 fishpond treatment

## 养 蚝 Oyster Cultivation

养蚝场 oyster farm, oyster bank
蚝种 seed oyster
海底培养 bottom culture
离海底培养 off-bottom culture
蚝壳料 cultch, culch
木筏悬置蚝壳 shells suspended from rafts
养蚝筏 oyster raft
生长场 growing ground
肥育区 fattening area

采蚝 collecting oysters
蚝钳 oyster tongs
钳蚝工 oyster tonger
帆船捕捞 sail dredging
蚝卵,幼蚝 spat
蚝产卵 spatting
蚝幼体的附着 setting of oyster larvae
防止掠食动物 predator control
防淤 siltation prevention

## 珍珠养殖 Pearl Culture

珍珠贝 pearl shell
珍珠母 mother-of-pearl, nacre
银口珠母贝 silver-lip pearl oyster
采珠潜水员 pearl diver
采珠船 pearling lugger
采贝场 shell bed
珍珠养殖场 pearl culture farm
贝壳质 conchiolin
霰石晶体 aragonite crystal

皮细包 epithelial cell
套膜 mentle
珠核嵌入 nucleus insertion
宿主蚌 host oyster
移植技术 grafting technique
珠囊 pearl sack
贝壳质沉积 deposition of nacre, nacre deposition
皂石 soapstone
筏悬铁丝框 wire basket on floating raft
用完珠贝 spent shell

## 海洋鱼类 Marine Fishes

虎鲨 bullhead shark (Heterodontidae)
噬人鲨 man-eater shark, great white shark (Chach-

arodon carcharias)
须鲨 nurse shark (Orectolobidae)
沙锥齿鲨 nurse shark (Car-

charias arenarius)

鲸鲨　whale shark (Rhincodon typus)

吻沟双髻鲨(丁字鲨)① scalloped hammerhead (Sphyrina lewini)

角鲨　piked dogfish, spiny dogfish, spurdog (Squalus acanthias)

鱼翅(鲨鱼鳍)　shark's fin

锯鳐　sawfish (Pristidae)

中国团扇鳐② Chinese thornback (Platyshina sinensis)

犁头鳐　guitarfish (Rhinobatidae)

魟　stingray (Dasyatidae)

蝠鲼　devilfish, manta ray (Mobulidae)

膨鱼腮(蝠鲼鳃)　fills of devilfish, gills of manta ray

鸢鲼　eagle ray (Myliobatis tobijei)

电鳐　electric rey, torpedo (Torpedinidae)

银鲛　chimaera, ratfish (Chimaeridae)

黑线银鲛　silver shark (Chimaera phantasma)

鲟　sturgeon (Acipenseridae)

白鲟(象鱼)　paddlefish (Psephurus gladius)

遮目鱼(虱目鱼)　milkfish (Chanos chanos)

太平洋鲱(青条鱼)　Pacific herring (Clupea pallasii)

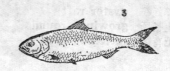

鳕(三来鱼)③　grenadier, rattail (Macrura reevesii)

鰳(曹白鱼)④　white herring (Ilisha elongata)

大西洋沙丁鱼　European pilchard (Sardinia pilchardus)

小沙丁鱼(青鳞鱼)　green pilchard, gilt sardine (Sardinella)

凤尾鱼　long-tailed anchovy (Coilia mystus)

鲑　salmon (Oncorhynchus)

大麻哈鱼　dog salmon, chum salmon, Pacific salmon (Oncorhynchus keta)

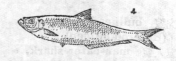

银鱼　salangid glassfish
　　(Salangidae)

蛇鲻(狗棍)　lizard fish
　　(Laurida)

龙头鱼(虾潺)　Bombay duck
　　(Harpodon nehereus)

鳗鲡(鳗,鳝)　common eel,
　　freshwater eel (Anguillidae)

白鳝　elever, glass eel

海鳗(狼牙鳝)　conger pike
　　(Muraenesox cinereus)

裸胸鳝　moray eel (Gymno-
　　thorax)

鲈(花鲈)　oriental spotted
　　bass, common sea bass
　　(Leteolebrax japonicus)

竹刀鱼(秋刀鱼)　saury (Colola-
　　bis saira)

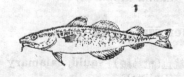

大头鳕①　Pacific cod (Gadus
　　Macrocephalus)

海龙　pipefish (Syngnathidae)

海马　sea horse (Hippocam-
　　pus)

鲻　mullet, grey mullet
　　(Mugil caphalus)

石斑鱼　grouper (Epinephelus)

胡椒鲷　thick lip (Plectorhyn-
　　chus pictus)

花尾胡椒鲷　thick lip (Plec-
　　torhynchus cinctus)

红笛鲷(红鱼)　red snapper
　　(Lutianus sanguineus)

千年笛鲷　emperor snapper
　　(Lutianus sebae)

圆鲹(池鱼)　scad (Decapterus)

石首鱼　croaker (Sciaenidae)

黄花鱼(大黄鱼)②　yellow
　　croaker (Pseudoscinena
　　crocca)

小黄鱼(黄花鱼)　small yellow
　　croaker (Pseudosciaena
　　polyactis)

单带绯鲤(红线鱼)　red goatfish
　　(Upeneus moluscensis)

金线鱼(红三)　golden thread
　　(Nemipterus virgatus)

宝刀鱼　wolf herring (Chino-
　　centrus dorab)

鳀　anchovy (Engrualidae)

乌鲂　sea bream (Sparidae)

莹斑蓝子鱼　rabbitfish (Siga-
　　nus oramin)

海鲶(赤鱼)　sea catfish (Arius)

非洲鲫　tilapia, bolti (Tilapia
　　mossambica)

玉筋鱼　sandeel, sandlance
　　(Ammodytidae)

鰕虎鱼　goby (Gobiidae)

带鱼③　cutlass fish, hair tail
　　(Trichiurus haumela)

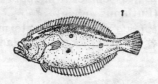

鲐　Japanese mackeral (Pneumato-phorus, aponicus)

马鲛　mackerel (Scombridae)

中华马鲛　Chinese mackerel (Scomberomorus sinensis)

大西洋马鲛　ero, king mackerel (Scomberomorus sinensis)

金枪鱼　tuna (Thunnidae)

鲳鱼(银鱼)　pomfret (Stromateoides argenteus)

沟鲹(黑鳍鲳)　thin crevalle (Atropus atropus)

牙鲆(左口鱼)①　summer flounder (Paralickthys olivaceus)

鲽　flounder (Pleuronectidae)

鳎　sole (Soleidae)

舌鳎　tonguefish, tongue sole (Cynoglossidae)

剥皮鱼(马面鲀)　filefish, leatherfish (Navodon modestus)

飞鱼　flying fish (Exocoetidae)

河豚　globefish, puffer (Fugu)

马鲅　threadfin (Polynemidae)

鲣鱼　skipjack tuna, oceanic bonito (Katsuwonus pelamis)

鲯鳅　dolphin fish (coryp haena hippurus)

## 其他海洋生物　Other Marine Life

鲍鱼(石决明)　abalone, earshell (Haliotis)

海参　sea slug, sea cucumber, beche-de-mer (Holothuroidea)

食用海参　trepang, beche-de-mer

章鱼　octopus (Octopus)

墨鱼(乌贼)②　cuttlefish (Sepia)

鱿鱼(枪乌贼)　squid, calamary (Loligo)

柔鱼　flying squid, sea arrow (Ommastrophidae)

海螺　conch

法螺　triton (Triton)

马蹄螺(公螺)　trochus (Trochus niloticus)

蝾螺　top shell (Turbo cornutus)

贻贝(淡菜)　mussel (Mytilus)

宝贝　money courie (Cypraea moneta)

扇贝　scallop (Pectinidae)

江瑶贝(干贝)　pinna, pen shell (Pinna)

文昌鱼 lancelet (Branchiostoma)

龙虾 spiny lobster (Panulirus)

锦绣龙虾 **Panulirus ornatus**

对虾 peneus (Penaeus)

小虾 shrimp

大虾① prawn

海蜇 jellyfish, sea blubber (Rhopilema esculenta)

海星 starfish (Asteroidea)

海绵 sponges (Spongia)

蟹 crab

梭子蟹(蝤蛑) swimming crab, portunid (Portunidae)

寄生蟹 hermit crab

高脚蟹 giant crab (Macrocheira Kaempfero)

招潮 fiddler crab, beckoning crab (Uca)

玳瑁 hawksbill sea turtle (Eretmochelys imricata)

棱皮龟(革龟) leatherback sea turtle (Dermochelys coriacea)

海龟 green turtle (Chelonia mydas)

海胆 sea chestnut, sea urchin (Echinoidea)

红珊瑚 red coral (Corallium nobile)

笙珊瑚② organ-pipe coral (Tubipora musica)

石芝 mushroom coral (Iungia)

抹香鲸③ sperm whale (Physeter catodon)

龙涎香 ambergris

长须鲸 razorback whale (Belaenoptera physalus)

海獭 sea otter (Enhydra lutris)

## 淡水鱼类 Freshwater Fishes

青鱼(黑鲩，螺丝青) snail carp (Mylopharyngodon piceus)

草鱼(鲩) grass carp (Clenopharyngodon idellus)

鲢(白鲢) silver carp (Hypophthalmichthys molitrix)

鳙(大鱼，花鲢) bighead carp (Aristichthys nobilis)

鲤 common carp (Cyprinus carpis)

鲫 crucian carp (Carassius carassius)

金鱼　goldfish (Carassius auratus)

鳊(北京鳊)　Beijing bream (Parabramis pekinensis)

鲮(土鲮鱼)　mud carp (Cirrhina molitorella)

鲶(鲇)　sheatfish (Parasilurus asotus)

黄鳝(泥鳝)　swamp eel, synbranch eel (Fluta alba)

乌鳢(生鱼)　snakehead mullet (Ophicephalus argus)

鳜(桂鱼)　Chinese perch (Siniperca chuatsi)

鳅　loach (Cobitidae)

鳑鲏　Japanese bitterling (Acheilognathus)

胡子鲶(塘虱)　catfish (Clarias fuscus)

鳅鮀(石虎鱼)　gudgeon (Gobio)

鳡(黄钻)　minnow (Elopichthys bambusa)

食蚊鱼(柳条鱼)　mosquito fish (Gambusia affinis)

胭脂鱼(火烧鳊)　Chinese sucker (Myxocyprinus asiaticus)

# 附　录 Appendix

# 常见动植物　Common Animals and Plants

## 灵长类　Primates

猩猩(褐猿)　(Pongo pygmaeus) orangutan

黑猩猩(黑猿)　(Pan troglodytes) chimpanzee

大猩猩(大猿)　(Gorilla gorilla) gorilla

长臂猿　(Hylobates) gibbon

狒狒　(Papio hamadryas) baboon

山都(豚尾狒狒)　(Papio comstud) chacma

山魈　(Mandrillus sphinx) mandrill

猕猴　(Macaca mulatta) rhesus monkey

长尾猴　(Cercopithecus) guenon

金丝猴　(Rhinopithecus roxellanae) golden monkey

卷尾猴(悬猴) (Cebus capuchinus) capuchin monkey

吼猴 (Mycetes) howler monkey

黑叶猴(乌猿) (Presbytis fransoisi) black leaf monkey

狐猴 (Lemur) lemur

指猴 (Chiromys madagascariensis) aye-aye

懒猴 (Nycticebus coucang) slow loris

眼镜猴 (Tarsius spectrum) tarsier

## 食肉兽类 Carnivores

狮 (Panthera leo) lion

虎 (Panthera tigris) tiger

金钱豹 (Panthera pardus) leopard

雪豹 (Panthera uncia) snow leopard

云豹 (Neofelis nebulosa) clouded leopard

猎豹 (Acinonyx venatica) cheetah

美洲狮 (Panthera concolor) cougar (puma)

美洲豹 (Panthera onca) jaguar

豹猫(狸猫) (Felis bengalensis) leopard cat

猞猁 (Felis lynx) lynx

家猫 (Felis domestica) cat

灵猫 (Viverra zibetha) civet

果子狸(花面狸) (Paguma larvata) masked palm civet

蛇獴 (Herpestes mungo) mongoose

鬣狗 (Hyaena hyaena) hyena

犬 (Canis familiaris) dog

狼 (Canis lupus) wolf

豺 (Cuon javanicus) dhole

狐(赤狐) (Vulpes vulpes) fox

白狐(北极狐) (Alopex lago-

pus) Arctic fox

貉(狗獾) (Nyctereutes procyonoides) racoon-dog

浣熊 (Procyon lotor) racoon

小熊猫 (Ailurus fulgens) panda

大熊猫 (Ailuropoda melanoleucus) giant panda

狗熊(黑熊) (Selenarctos thibetanus) Asiatic black bear

棕熊(马熊) (Ursus arctos) brown bear

白熊(北极熊) (Thalassarctos maritimus) polar bear

马来熊 (Helarctos malayanus) sun bear

紫貂(黑貂) (Martes zibellina) sable

水貂 (Mustela vison) mink

雪鼬(伶鼬, 银鼠) (Mustela nivalis) weasel

黄鼬(黄鼠狼) (Mustela sibirica) yellow weasel

白鼬(扫雪) (Mustela erminea) ermine

艾鼬(艾虎) (Mustela eversmanni) polecat

青鼬(蜜狗) (Charronia flavigula) yellow-throated marten

臭鼬 (Mephitis mephitis) skunk

獾(猪獾) (Meles meles) badger

沙獾 (Arctonyx collaris) sand badger

山獾(白猸) (Helictis moschata) ferret-badger

水獭 (Lutra lutra) otter

海獭 (Enhydra lutris) sea otter

海狗 (Callorhinus curilensis) kurilian fur seal

北海狮 (Eumetopias jubbata) sea-lion

海豹 (Phoca vitulina) harbour seal

海象(象海豹) (Mirounga) sea-elephant

海马 (Odobenus rosmarus) walrus

## 食草兽类 Herbivores

马 (Equus caballus) horse

驴 (Equus asinus) donkey

野驴(蒙驴) (Equus hemionus) Asiatic wild ass

骡 (Equus asinus X Equus caballus) mule

斑马 (Equus zebra) zebra

犀牛 (Rhinoceros) rhinoceros

貘 (Tapirus) tapir

野猪 (Sus scrofa) wild boar

猪 (Sus scrofa domestica) pig

河马 (Hippopotamus amphibius) hippopotamus

骆驼 (Camelus bactrianus) Bactrian camel

单峰驼 (Camelus dromedarius) dromedary

美洲原驼 (Lama guanicoe) guanaco (huanaco)

美洲驼 (Lama glama) llama

羊驼 (Lama alpacos) alpaca

鹿 (Cervus) deer

梅花鹿 (Cervus nippon) sika

马鹿(赤鹿) (Cervus elaphus) red deer

麝(香獐) (Moschus moschiferus) musk deer

毛冠鹿 (Elaphodus cephalophus) tufted deer

水鹿(黑鹿) Rusa unicolor sambar, waterbuck

驼鹿(犴) (Alces alces) elk

驯鹿 (Rangifer tarandus) reindeer

麅(狍子) (Capreolus capreolus) roe deer

长颈鹿 (Giraffa camelopardalis) giraffe

獾㹢狓 (Okapia johnstoni) okapi

水牛 (Bubalus bubalus) water buffalo

黄牛 (Bos taurus domestica) ox

瘤牛 (Bos indicus) zebu

牦牛 (Bos grunniens) yak

麝牛 (Ovibos moschatus)

musk ox

膨喉羚(羚羊) **(Gazella sub-gutturosa) goitred gazelle**

原羚 **(Procapra picticaudata) Tibetan gazelle**

藏羚 **(Pantholops hodgsoni) chiru**

青羊(斑羚) **(Naemorhedus goral) goral**

赛加羚羊(高鼻羚羊) **(Saiga tartarica) saiga**

羚牛 **(Budorcas taxicolor) takin**

岩羊(崖羊) **(Pseudois nayaur) bharal**

山羊 **(Capra hircus) goat**

绵羊 **(Ovis aries) sheep**

家兔 **(Oryctolagus cuniculus domestica) rabbit**

华南兔(山兔) **(Lepus sinensis) Chinese hare**

草兔(欧兔) **(Lepus europaeus) European hare**

鼠兔(啼兔) **(Ochotona) mouse hare**

印度象 **(Elephas maximus) Asiatic elephant**

非洲象 **(Elephas africanus) African elephant**

儒艮(人鱼) **(Dugong dugon) dugong (sea-cow)**

袋鼠 **(Macropus) kangaroo**

## 食虫兽类 Insectivores

树鼩 **(Tupaia belangeri) tree shrew (squirrel shrew)**

刺猬 **(Erinaceus europaeus) hedgehog**

鼩鼱 **(Sorex araneus) shrew mouse**

麝鼩 **(Crocidura suaveolens musk shrew**

鼹 **(Talpa) mole**

麝鼹 **(Scaptochirus moschatus) musk mole**

穿山甲 **(Manis pentadactyta) Chinese pangolin**

大食蚁兽 **(Myrmecophaga jubala) great anteater**

土豚(非洲食蚁兽) **(Orycteropus capensis) aard-vark**

## 鲸 类 Whales

蓝鲸 **(Balaenoptera musculus) blue whale**

长须鲸 **(Balaenoptera physalus) fin whale**

小鳁鲸(尖吻鲸) **(Balaenoptera acutorostrata) piked whale**

抹香鲸 **(Physeter catodon) sperm whale**

一角鲸 **(Monodon monoceros)** narwhal

虎鲸 **(Orcinus orca) killer whale**

海豚 **(Delphinus delphis) dolphin**

白鳍豚 **(Lipotes vexillifer) Chinese river dolphin**

江豚(江猪) **(Neomeris phocaenoides) finless black porpoise**

## 猛 禽　Birds of Prey

鹰　(Accipiter) hawk

苍鹰　(Accipiter gentilis) goshawk

雀鹰　(Accipiter nisus) sparrow hawk

鸢　(Milvus) kite

鵟　(Buteo buteo) buzzard

雕　(Aquila) eagle

金雕　(Aquila chrysaëtos) golden eagle

海雕　(Haliaectus) sea eagle

鹞　(Circus) harrier

鹗　(Pandion halio etus) osprey

隼　(Falco) falcon

游隼(鹘)　(Falco peregrinus) peregrine falcon

燕隼　(Falco subbuteo) hobby

小隼　(Microhierax melanoleucos) pigmy falcon

鸮(猫头鹰)　(Strigidae) owl

## 游 禽　Swimming Birds

鹅　(Anser domestica) goose

鸿雁　(Anser cygnoides) Chinese wild goose

豆雁　(Anser fabalis) bean goose

白额雁　(Anser albifrons) white-fronted goose

棉凫　(Nettapus coromandelianus) pygmy goose

天鹅(鹄)　(Cygnus cygnus) swan

家鸭　(Anas domestica) duck

绿头鸭(大麻鸭)　(Anas platyrhynchos) mallard

绿翅鸭(巴鸭)　(Anas crecca) teal

麝香鸭　(Cairina moschata) musk duck

绒鸭　(Somateria) eider duck

鹊鸭　(Bucephala clangula) goldeneye

秋沙鸭　(Mergus merganser) goosander (merganser)

鸳鸯　(Aix galericulata) mandarin duck

红头潜鸭　(Aythya ferina) pochard

潜鸟　(Gavia stellata) loon

䴙䴘　(Podiceps) grebe

鹈鹕(塘鹅)　(Pelecanus) pelican

鸬鹚　(Phalacrocorax carbo sinensis) Chinese cormorant

海鸬鹚　(Phalacrocorax pelagicus) pelagic cormorant

## 涉 禽　Wading Birds

苍鹭　(Ardea cinerea) grey heron

池鹭　(Ardeola bacchus) Chinese pond heron

白鹭 (Egretta garzetta) egret

鹳 (Ciconia) stork

鹮 (Threskiornithidae) ibis

白鹮 (Threskiornis aethiopica) sacred ibis

琵鹭 (Platalea) spoonbill

朱鹭(红鹳，火烈鸟) (Phoenicopteridae) flamingo

灰鹤 (Grus grus) grey crane

丹顶鹤 (Grus japonensis) white crane

蓑羽鹤 (Anthropoides virgo) demoiselle crane

秧鸡 (Rallus aquaticus) water rail

骨顶鸡（白骨顶） (Fulica atra) coot

红骨顶(黑水鸡) (Gallinula chloropus) gallinule

雉鸻 (Jacanidae) jacana

水雉 (Hydrophasianus chirurgus) pheasant-tailed jacana

蛎鹬 (Haematopus ostralegus osculans) eastern oystercatcher

金鸻(千鸟) (Charadrius pluvialis) golden plover

凤头麦鸡(绿田凫) (Vanellus vanellus) lapwing

鹬 (Tringa) sandpiper

丘鹬 (Scolopax rusticola) woodcock

燕鸻(土燕子) (Glareola maldivarum) pratincole

沙锥 (Capella) snipe

## 鸣 禽 Songbirds

百灵 (Alaudidae) lark

云雀 (Alauda arvensis) skylark

家燕 (Hirundo rustica) house swallow

黄鹂(黄莺) (Oriolus oriolus) golden oriole

乌鸦 (Corvus) crow

秃鼻乌鸦 (Corvus frugilegus) rook

寒鸦(慈乌) (Corvus monedula) jackdaw

渡鸦 (Corvus corax) raven

喜鹊(鹊) (Pica pica) magpie

松鸦 (Garrulus glandarius) jay

极乐鸟(凤鸟) (Paradisea apoda) bird of paradise

大山雀(白面山雀) (Parus major) great tit

䴓 (Sitta europaea) nuthatch

旋木雀 (Certhia familiaris) tree creeper

鸦雀 (Paradoxornithidae) parrotbill

画眉 (Garrulax canorus) babbler

红嘴相思鸟 (Leiothrix lutea) Beijing nightingale

白头鹎(白头翁) (Pycnonotus sinensis) Chinese bulbul

河乌 (Cinclus cinclus) dipper (water ouzel)

鹪鹩 (Troglodytes troglodytes) wren

鸫 (Turdus) thrush

乌鸫(百舌) (Turdus merula) blackbird

夜莺 (Luscinia megarhynchos) nightingale

蓝点颏(蓝喉歌鸲) (Luscinia suecica) bluethroat

红尾鸲 (Phoenicurus) redstart (firetail)

知更雀 (Erithacus rubecula) robin

柳莺 (Phylloscopus) willow warbler

苇莺 (Acrocephalus) reed warbler

戴菊莺 (Regulus regulus) goldcrest

鹟 (Muscicapa) flycatcher

鹡鸰 (Motacilla) wagtail

鹨 (Anthus) pipit

水鹨(冰鸡儿) (Anthus spinoletta) water pipit

太平鸟 (Bombycilla garrulus) waxwing

伯劳 (Lanius) shrike

椋鸟 (Sturnus) starling

八哥 (Acridotheres cristatellus) crested myna

鹩哥(秦吉了) (Gracula religiosa) hill myna

太阳鸟 (Aethopyga) sunbird

啄花鸟 (Dicaeum) flowerpecker

绣眼鸟 (Zosterops) silvereye

麻雀 (Passer) sparrow

织布鸟 (Ploceus) weaverbird

燕雀(花鸡) (Fringilla montifringilla) brambling

金丝雀 (Serinus canarius) canary

黄雀 (Carduelis spinus) siskin

朱雀 (Carpodacus) rose finch

锡嘴雀 (Coccothraustes coccothraustes) grosbeak

鹀 (Emberiza) bunting

黄胸鹀(禾花雀) (Emberiza aureola) yellow-breasted bunting (rice bird)

## 海 鸟 Seabirds

海鸥 (Larus) gull

银鸥 (Larus argentatus) herring gull

燕鸥 (Sterna) tern

海燕 (Hydrobates pelagicus) storm petrel

鹱 (Puffinus) shearwater

鹲(热带鸟) (Phaethon) tropic bird

鲣鸟 (Sula) booby

信天翁 (Diomedea) albatross

军舰鸟 (Fregatidae) frigate bird

## 其他禽鸟 Other Birds

鸵鸟 (Struthio camelus) ostrich

美洲鸵 (Rhea americana) rhea

鹤鸵(食火鸡) (Casuarius casuarius) cassowary

鸸鹋 (Dromaeus novaehollandiae) emu

无翼鸟 (Apteryx owenii) kiwi

䳍 (Rhynchotus rufescens) great tinamou

企鹅 (Spheniscus demersus) penguin

兀鹫 (Gyps) vulture

秃鹫(坐山雕) (Aegypius monachus) cinereous vulture

松鸡 (Tetrao) grouse

榛鸡 (Tetrastes bonasia) hazel hen

雷鸟 (Lagopus lagopus) ptarmigan

锦鸡 (Chrysolophus pictus) golden pheasant

环颈雉 (Phasianus colchicus torquatus) Chinese ring-necked pheasant

长尾雉(鷩雉) (Syrmaticus reevesii) long-tailed pheasant

白鹇 (Lophura nycthemera) silver pheasant

孔雀 (Pavo) peacock

鹧鸪 (Francolinus pintadeanus) partridge

石鸡 (Alectoris graeca) Greek partridge

鹌鹑 (Coturnix coturnix) quail

珠鸡 (Numida meleagris) guinea fowl

吐绶鸡(火鸡) (Meleagris gallopavo) turkey

三趾鹑(水鹌鹑) (Turnix tanki blanfordii) button quail

大鸨 (Otis tarda) great bustard

沙鸡 (Syrrhaptes paradoxus) sand grouse

原鸽 (Columba livia) rock dove

家鸽 (Columba livia domestica) pigeon

斑鸠 (Streptopelia orientalis) turtledove

鹦鹉 (Psittacula) parrot

虎皮鹦鹉 (Melopsittacus undulatus) budgerigar

杜鹃 (Cuculus) cuckoo

雨燕 (Apodidae) swift

金丝燕 (Collocalia vestita) collocalia

蜂鸟 (Trochilidae) hummingbird

翠鸟(钓鱼郎) (Alcedo atthis bengalensis) kingfisher

翡翠 (Halcyon) halcyon

蜂虎 (Meropidae) bee-eater

佛法僧 (Coracias) roller

戴胜 (Upupa epops) hoopoe

犀鸟 (Buceratidae) hornbill

啄木鸟 (Picidae) woodpecker

琴鸟 (Menura superba) lyrebird

## 啮齿动物　Rodents

松鼠(灰鼠) (Sciurus vulgaris) squirrel

树狗(巨松鼠) (Ratufa bicolor) giant squirrel

黄鼠(地松鼠) (Citellus dauri-
cus) ground squirrel

旱獭(土拔鼠) (Marmota
marmota) marmot

花鼠(五道眉) (Eutamias
sibiricus) Asiatic chipmunk

鼯鼠(大飞鼠) (Petaurista)
giant flying squirrel

河狸 (Castor fiber) beacer

大仓鼠 (Cricetulus triton)
ratlike hamster

田鼠 (Microtus arvalis) vole

麝鼠 (Ondatra zibethica)
musk rat

竹鼠 (Rhizomys sinensis)
root rat

黑家鼠(屋顶鼠) (Rattus rat-
tus) black rat

褐家鼠(沟鼠) (Rattus norve-
gicus) brown rat

小家鼠 (Mus musculus) mouse

巢鼠 (Micromys minutus)
harvest mouse

豚鼠(洋鼠，天竺鼠) (Cavia
cobaya) guinea pig

豪猪(箭猪) (Hystrix hodgsoni)
porcupine

## 两栖动物 Amphibians

泥螈(泥狗) (Necturus macula-
tus) mud puppy

小鲵(短尾鲵) (Hynobius
chinensis) Chinese land
salamander

大鲵(娃娃鱼) (Megalobatra-
chus davidianus) giant
salamander

虎螈 (Amblystoma tigrinum)
tiger salamander

瘰螈 (Trituroides chinensis)
Chinese newt

大蟾蜍 (Bufo bufo gargariz-)

ans) toad

中国雨蛙 (Hyla chinensis)
Chinese tree frog

虎纹蛙 (Rana tigrina) Indian
bullfrog

青蛙(黑斑蛙) (Rana nigroma-
culata) black-spotted frog

哈士蟆(中国林蛙) (Rana tem-
poraria chen-sinensis)
Chinese frog

牛蛙 (Rana catesbeiana)
American bullfrog

蝌蚪 tadpole

## 爬行动物 Reptiles

棱皮龟(革龟) (Dermochelys
coriacea) leatherback

玳瑁 (Eretmochelys imbrica-
ta) hawksbill turtle

海龟(绿蠵龟) (Chelonia
mydas) green turtle

蠵龟(赤蠵龟) (Caretta caretta
olivacea) loggerhead turtle

金龟(乌龟) (Geoclemys reeve-
sii) tortoise

陆龟 (Testudo elongata)
land turtle

象龟 (Testudo elephantopus) giant land turtle

鳖(甲鱼) (Amyda sinensis) Chinese freshwater turtle

鼍(扬子鳄) (Alligator sinensis) Chinese alligator

美洲鳄 (Alligator mississippiensis) alligator

非洲鳄 (Crocodylus porosus) crocodile

印度鳄 (Gavialis gangeticus) gavial

蟒蛇 (Python molurus) python

大眼镜蛇(眼镜王蛇) (Naja hannah) king-cobra

眼镜蛇 (Naja naja) cobra

金环蛇 (Bungarus fasciatus) gold-banded krait

银环蛇 (Bungarus multicinctus) silver-banded krait

灰鼠蛇(过树龙) (Ptyas korros) grey rat snake

游蛇 (Colubridae) colubrid snake

水游蛇 (Homalopsinae) colubrid water snake

海蛇 (Hydrophidae) sea snake

蝰蛇 (Viperidae) viper

极北蝰 (Vipera berus) common European viper

黑斑蝰 (Vipera russelli siamensis) daboia

蝮蛇 (Agkistrodon halys) pit viper

五步蛇(蕲蛇) (Agkistrodon acutus) moccasin

响尾蛇 (Crotalus) rattlesnake

避役 (Chamaeleon vulgaris) chameleon

壁虎(守宫) (Gekko japonicus) gecko

蛤蚧 (Gekko gecko) tokay

巨蜥 (Varanus salvator) kabaragoya

鳄蜥(雷公蜥) (Shinisaurus crocodilurus) Chinese montane lizard

石龙子 (Eumeces chinensis) Chinese skink

## 海洋鱼类 Marine Fishes

鲸鱼 (Cetacea) whale

鲸鲨 (Rhincodon typus) whale shark

吻沟双髻鲨 (Sphyrna lewini) scalloped hammerhead

鳐 (Rajidae) skate

犁头鳐 (Rhinobatos) guitarfish

鲟 (Acipenseridae) sturgeon

白鲟(象鱼) (Psephurus gladius) Chinese paddlefish

鳓鱼(曹白鱼) (Ilisha elongata) herring

鲱(青条鱼) (Clupea pallasi) Pacific herring

沙丁鱼 (Sardinops melanosticta) sardine

鲥鱼(三来) (Macrura reevesii) grenadier

遮目鱼 (Chanos chanos) milkfish

凤鲚(凤尾鱼) (Coilia mystus)

long-tail anchovy

大马哈鱼 (Oncorhynchus keta) pacific salmon

香鱼 (Plecoglossus altivelis) sweetfish

银鱼 (Salangidae) glassfish

龙头鱼 (Harpodon nehereus) Bombay duck

鳗丽(白鳝) (Anguillidae) common eel

海鳗 (Muraenidae) moray

飞鱼 (Exocoetidae) flying fish

鳕 (Godidae) cod

海龙 (Syngnathidae) pipefish

海马 (Hippocampus) sea horse

鲻 (Mugilidae) grey mullet

马鲅 (Polynemidae) threadfin

鲈 (Lateolabrax japonicus) oriental spotted bass

石斑鱼 (Epinephelus) grouper

红笛鲷(红鱼) (Lutianus erythropterus) red snapper

黄鱼(黄花) (Pseudosciaena) yellow croaker

鲅(马鲛) (Scomberomorus sinensis) Chinese mackerel

鲐鱼(青花鱼) (Pneumatophorus japonicus) Japanese mackerel

金枪鱼 (Thunnidae) tuna

带鱼 (Trichiuridae) cutlass fish, hair tail

鲳 (Stromateidae) pomfret

圆鲹(池鱼) (Decapterus) round scad

玉筋鱼 (Ammodytidae) sand-lance

牙鲆(左口鱼) (Paralichthys olivaceus) summer flounder

鳎 (Soleidae) sole

舌鳎(牛舌) (Cynoglossidae) tonguefish

河豚 (Fugu) globefish

狮子鱼(剥皮鱼) (Liparis tanakae) snailfish

## 淡水鱼类 Freshwater Fishes

鲤 (Cyprinus carpio) common carp

鲫 (Carassius) crucian carp

青鱼(黑鲩) (Mylopharyngodon piceus) black carp

草鱼(鲩) (Ctenopharyngodon idellus) grass carp

鲢 (Hypophthalmichthys molitrix) silver carp

鳙 (Aristichthys nobilis) fathead, bighead

鲮 (Cirrhina molitorella) mud carp

北京鳊 (Parabramis pekinensis) Beijing bream

鳡(黄钻) (Elopichthys bambusa) minnow

鳑鲏 (Rhodeus ocellatus) bitterling

鳅鲩(石虎鱼) (Gobio) gudgeon

鳜(桂鱼) (Siniperca chuatsi) Chinese perch

胭脂鱼(火烧鳊) (Myxocyprinus asiaticus) Chinese sucker

鳅 (Cobitidae) loach

黄鳝 (Fluta alba) symbranch eel

乌鳢(生鱼) (ophicephalus argus) snakehead mullet

胡子鲶(塘虱) (Clarias fuscus)

freshwater catfish

金鱼 (Carassins auratus) goldfish

非洲鲫 (Tilapia mossambica) bolti

## 软体动物　Molluscs

石鳖 (Chitonidae) chiton

鲍鱼 (Haliotis gigantea) abalone

宝贝 (Cypraea) cowrie

法螺 (Charonia) triton shell

蜗牛 (Eulota) snail

芋螺(鸡心螺) (Conus) cone shell

骨螺 (Murex) rock shell

竖琴螺(蜀江螺) (Harpa) harp shell

蝾螺 (Turbo) turban shell

蜘蛛螺 (Lambis) spider shell

荔枝螺 (Thais) periwinkle

蛾螺 (Buccinum) whelk

海兔 (Aplusia) sea hare

牡蛎(蚝) (Ostrea) oyster

贻贝(淡菜) (Mytilus) mussel

珍珠贝 (Pteria) pearl oyster

扇贝 (Pecten) scallop

蚶 (Arca) ark shell

蛤蜊 (Mactra) surf clam

蛏 (Sinonovacula) razor clam

砗磲 (Teidacna) giant clam

鹦鹉螺 (Nautilus) pearly nautilus

船蛸 (Argonauta) paper nautilus

章鱼 (Octopus) octopus

乌贼(墨鱼) (Sepia) cuttlefish

枪乌贼(鱿鱼) (Loligo) squid (calamary)

## 甲壳动物　Crustaceans

对虾 (Penaeus orientalis) prawn

龙虾 (Panulirus) lobster

大头虾 (Cambarus clarkii) crayfish

寄居虾(寄居蟹) (Pagurus) hermit crab

椰子蟹 (Birgus latro) coconut crab

梭子蟹(蝤蛑) (Portunus tri-tuberculatus) swimming crab

招潮 (Uca) fiddler crab (beckoning crab)

河蟹(螃蟹, 毛蟹) (Eriocheir sinensis) Chinese fresh-water crab

高脚蟹 (Macrocheira kaemp-feri) giant crab

虾蛄(螳螂虾) (Squilla orato-ria) mantis prawn

水蚤(金鱼虫) (Daphnia) water flea

## 棘皮动物 Echinoderms

海百合 (Metacrinus) sea lily
海星 (Asterias) starfish
海胆 (Echinoidea) sea-urchin

海参 (Holothurioidea) sea-cucumber

## 昆 虫 Insects

飞蝗 (Locusta) locust
蚱蜢 (Acrida chinensis) grasshopper
蟋蟀 (Gryllulus chinensis) cricket
蝼蛄(土狗子) (Gryllotalpa africana) mole cricket
螳螂 (Mantodea) mantis
薄翅螳螂 (Mantis religiosa) praying mantis
蜻蜓 (Odonata) dragonfly
蚱蝉(知了) (Cryptotympana atra) cicada
紫胶虫 (Laccifer lacca) lac insect
白腊虫 (Ericerus pela) wax insect
棉蚜 (Aphis gossypii) cotton aphis
椿象 (Hemiptera) plant bug
田鳖(桂花蝉) (Lethocerus indicus) lethocerus
臭虫 (Cimex) bed-bug
蛾 (Heterocera) moth
蝴蝶 (Rhopalocera) butterfly
棉铃虫 (Heliothis armigera) bollworm

桑蚕 (Bombyx mori) silk-worm
柞蚕 (Antheraea pernyi) Chinese tussah silkworm
甲虫 (Coleoptera) beetle
萤火虫 (Luciola terminalis) firefly
龙虱 (Cybister japonicus) cybister
日本金龟子 (Popillia japonica) Japanese beetle
蜜蜂 (Apis mellifera) honey-bee
熊蜂 (Bombus) bumblebee
胡蜂(黄蜂) (Vespa) wasp
蚂蚁 (Formicidae) ant
白蚁 (Isoptera) termite
蟑螂 (Blattaria) cockroach
蚊 (Anopheles) mosquito
虻 (Tabanus) gadfly
蝇 (Muscidae) fly
虱 (Anoplura) louse
蚤 (Siphonaptera) flea
蜉蝣 (Ephemerida) may-fly
衣鱼(蠹鱼) (Lepisma saccharina) silver-fish

## 其 他 Miscellaneous

蚂蟥 (Whitmania) leech
蚯蚓 (Pheretima tschiliensis)

earthworm
蜘蛛 (Araneida) spider

## 粮 谷 Cereals

小麦 **(Triticum aestivum) wheat**

大麦 **(Hordeum vulgare) barley**

裸大麦 **(Hordeum vulgare var. nuda) naked barley**

燕麦 **(Avena sativa) oats**

莜麦(裸燕麦) **(Avena nuda) naked oats**

黑麦 **(Secale cereale) rye**

稻 **(Oryza sativa) rice**

糯稻 **(Oryza sativa var. glutinosa) glutinous rice**

玉米 **(Zea mays) maize**

高粱 **(Sorghum vulgare) sorghum**

甜高粱(芦粟) **(Sorghum vulgare var. saccharatum) sorgo (sweet serghum)**

黍 **(Panicum miliaceum) millet**

粟(小米) **(Setaria itallica) foxtail millet**

龙爪稷(鸭脚粟) **(Eleusine coracana) Affrican millet**

穇(湖南稷子) **(Echinochloa crusagalli var. frumentacea) Japanese barnyard millet**

荞麦 **(Fagopyrum esculentum) buckwheat**

## 豆 类 Pulses

碗豆(麦豆) **(Pisum sativum) garden pea**

豇豆 **(Vigna sinensis) cowpea**

眉豆(饭豇豆) **(Vigna cylindrica) catjang**

长豇豆(长豆角) **(Vigna sesquipedalis) yardlong bean (asparagus bean)**

木豆 **(Cajanus cajan) pigeon pea**

大豆 **(Glycine max) soybean**

绿豆 **(Phaseolus radiatus) mung bean**

赤豆(小豆,红豆) **(Phaseolus angularis) adzuki bean**

菜豆(云豆,四季豆) **(Phaseolus vulgaris) kidney bean**

红花菜豆(龙爪豆) **(Phaseolus coccineus) scarlet runner (bean)**

雪豆(棉豆) **(Phaseolus lunatus) sieva bean**

蚕豆 **(Vicia faba) broad bean**

刀豆 **(Canavalia gladiata) sword bean**

矮刀豆(洋刀豆) **(Canavalia ensiformis) jack bean**

扁豆 **(Dolichos lablab) hyacinth bean**

兵豆(冰豆) **(Lens culinaris) lentil**

## 蔬 菜 Vegetables

卷心菜(椰菜) (Brassica oleracea var. capitata) cabbage

花椰菜 (Brassica oleracea var. botrytis) cauliflower

青菜(小白菜) (Brassica chinensis) *pakchoi*, Chinese cabbage

白菜(大白菜, 黄芽白) (Brassica pekinensis) *baicai*, Beijing cabbage

菜苔(菜心) (Brassica parachinensis) mock *pakchoi*

芥蓝 (Brassica alboglabra) cabbage mustard

芥菜 (Brassica juncea) leaf mustard

芜菁 (Brassica rapa) turnip

菠菜 (Spinacia oleracea) spinach

苋菜 (Amaranthus gangeticas) edible amaranth

马齿苋 (Portulaca oleracea) purslane

莼菜 (Brasenia schreberi) water shield

萝卜 (Raphanus sativus) radish

胡萝卜 (Daucus carota) carrot

荠菜 (Capsella bursa-pastoris) shepherd's purse

旱芹 (Apium graveolens) celery

枸杞 (Lycium chinensis) matrimony vine

辣椒 (Capsicum frutescens) red pepper

茄 (Solanum melongena) eggplant

马铃薯 (Solanum tuberosum) potato

番茄 (Lycopersicum esculentum) tomato

苦瓜 (Momordica charantia) balsam pear

丝瓜(水瓜) (Luffa cylindrica) sponge gourd, vegetable sponge

菜瓜(白瓜) (Cucumis melo var. conomon) white melon

黄瓜(青瓜) (Cucumis sativus) cucumber

冬瓜 (Benincasa hispida) wax gourd (white gourd)

节瓜 (Benincasa hispida var. chieh-qua) *jiegua*, hairy squash

葫芦瓜 (Lagenaria siceraris) bottle gourd

南瓜 (Cucurbita moschata) China squash

西葫芦(美洲南瓜) (Cucurbita pepo) pumpkin

茼蒿 (Cheysanthemum coronarium var. spatiosum) crown daisy

莴苣(生菜) (Lactua sativa) lettuce

慈姑 (Sagittaria sagittifolia) arrowhead

菱角 (Trapa spp.) water caltrop

荸荠(马蹄) (Eleocharis

dulcis) water chestnut
芋 (Colecasis esculenta) taro
番薯 (Ipomoea batatas) sweet potato
薯蓣(山药) (Dioscorea opposita) Chinese yam
参薯 (Dioscorea alata) white yam
豆薯(沙葛) (Pachyrhizus erosus) yam bean
葛 (Pueraria edulis) kudzu
水蔊菜(西洋菜) (Nasturtium officinale) watercress

茭白(茭笋) (Zizania caduciflora) wild rice shoots
龙须菜(芦笋,石刁柏) (Asparagus officinalis) garden asparagus
洋葱 (Allium cepa) onion
葱 (Allium fistulosum) Welsh onion (spring onion)
大蒜 (Allium sativum) garlic
韭葱(洋大蒜) (Allium tuberosum) leek
芫荽 (Coriandrum sativum) coriander

# 水　果　Fruits

苹果 (Malus pumila) apple
海棠果 (Malus pruniflora) crab apple
山楂 (Crataegus pinnatifida) haw
枇杷 (Eriobotrya japenica) loquat
雪梨 (Pyrus nivalis) snow pear
沙梨 (Pyrus pyrifolia) sand pear
桃 (Prunus persica) peach
梅 (Prunus nume) Japanese apricot
李 (Prunus salicina) plum
杏 (Prunus armeniaca) apricot
甜樱桃 (prunus avium) sweet cherry
榅桲 (Cydonia oblonga) quince
木瓜 (Chaenomeles sinensis) Chinese quince

贴梗海棠 (Chaenomeles lagenaria) flowering quince
红树莓(复盆子) (Rubus) raspberry
草莓 (Fragaria ananassa) strawberry
甜橙(广柑) (Citrus sinensis) sweet orange
柑 (Citrus reticulata) mandarin orange
柠檬 (Citrus limon) lemon
柚 (Citrus grandis) pomelo
葡萄柚 (Citrus paradisi) grapefruit
金桔 (Fortunella margarita) kumquat
黄皮 (Clausena lansium) wampee
荔枝 (Litchi chinensis) litchi
龙眼 (Euphoria longan) longan

韶子(红毛丹) (Nephelium lappaceum) rambutan

葡萄 (Vitis vinifora) grape

柿 (Diospyres kaki) persimmon

枣 (Zizyphus jujuba) jujube (Chinese date)

海枣(椰枣) (Phoenix dactylifera) date

猕猴桃 (Actinidia chinensis) Chinese gooseberry

石榴 (Punica granatum) pomegranate

番石榴 (Psidium guajava) guava

蒲桃 (Syzygium jambos) rose apple

番木瓜 (Carica papaya) papaya

五敛子(杨桃) (Averrhea carambola) carambola

榴莲 (Durio zibethinus) durian

凤梨(菠萝) (Ananas comosus) pineapple

木波罗 (Artocarpus heterophyllus) jack fruit

面包果 (Artocarpus communis) breadfruit

无花果 (Ficus carica) fig

芒果 (Mangifera indica) mango

山竹子(倒念子) (Garcinia mangostana) mangosteen

番荔枝 (Anona squamosa) custard apple

人心果 (Achras zapota) sapodilla

香蕉 (Musa sapientum) banana

粉蕉 (Musa nana) dwarf banana

橄榄 (Canarium album) Chinese white olive

西瓜 (Citrullus vulgaris) watermelon

香瓜(甜瓜) (Cucumis melo) musk melon

## 香 料 Spices

姜 (Zingiber officinale) ginger

姜黄 (Curcuma longa) turmeric

白豆蔻 (Amomum cardamomum) cardamon

肉豆蔻 (Myristica fragrans) nutmug

胡椒 (Piper nigrum) pepper

肉桂 (Cinnamomum cassia) Chinese cinnamon

丁香 (Syzygium aromatieum) clove

花椒 (Zanthoxylum bungeanum) prickly ash

八角茴香 (Illicum verum) star anise

茴香(小茴香) (Foeniculum vulgare) fennel

莳萝(土茴香) (Anethum graveolens) dill

香兰 (Vanilla fragrans) vanilla

薄荷 (Mentha arvensis)

field mint

留兰香　(Mentha spicita)
spearmint

胡椒薄荷　(Mentha piperita)

peppermint

众香果　(Pimenta dioica)
pimento (allspice)

## 油脂植物　Oil Plants

大豆　(Glycine max) soybean

花生　(Arachis hypogaea)
peanut

芝麻　(Sesamum indicum)
sesame

油菜　(Brassica campestris)
rape

油茶　(Camellia oleifera)
tea-oil tree

椰子　(Cocos nucifera)
coconut

油棕　(Elacis guineensis)
oll palm

油渣果(猪油果)　(Hodgsonia
macrocarpa)

油橄榄　(Olea europaca)
olive

胡桃(核桃)　(Juglans regia)
walnut

灰胡桃　(Juglans cinerea)
butternut

腰果树　(Anacardium

occidentale) cashew

毛棣(油种子树)　(Cornus wal-
teri) dogwood

油桐　(Aleurites fordii)
tung-oil tree

木油桐　(Aleurites montana)
mu-oil tree

石栗　(Aleurites moluccana)
candlenut

蓖麻　(Ricinus communis)
castor-oil plant

乌桕　(Sapium sebiferum)
Chinese tallow tree

白苏　(Perilla frutescens)
perilla

无患子(油患子)　(Sapindus
mukorossi) soapberry

鳄梨(油梨)　(Persea ame-
ricana) avocado (alligator
pear)

粗榧　(Cephalotaxus sinensis)
Chinese plum yew

## 纤维植物　Fibre Plants

树棉　(Gossypium arboreum)
tree cotton

草棉　(Gossypium herbaceum)
levant cotton

陆地棉　(Gossypium hirsutum)
upland cotton

海岛棉　(Gossypium harba-

dense) sea island cotton

苎麻　(Boehmeria nivea)
ramie, Chinese silk-plant

亚麻　(Linum usitatissimum)
flax

大麻　(Cannabis sativa) hemp

黄麻　(Corchorus capsularis)

jute

尚麻(青麻) (Abutilon theophrasti) Indian mallow (velvetleaf)

槿麻(红麻) (Hibiscus cannabinus) kenaf

蕉麻(马尼拉麻) (Musa textilis) abaca (Manila hemp)

剑麻(菠萝麻) (Agave sisalana) sisal

木棉 (Gossampinus malabarica) silk-cotton tree

吉贝(爪哇木棉) (Ceiba pentandra) kapok

## 药用植物 Medicinal Plants

麻黄 (Ephedra sinica) Chinese ephedra

柴胡 (Bupleurum chinense) Chinese thoroughwax

升麻 (Cimicifuga foetida) fetid bugbane

夏枯草 (Prunella vulgaris) self-heal

黄芩 (Scutellaria baicalensis) skullcap

黄连 (Coptis chinensis) Chinese goldthread

玄参 (Scrophularia buergerianna) figwort

藏红花 (Crocus sativus) saffron

紫草 (Lithospermum erythrorhizon) gromwell

金银花 (Lonicera japonica) honey suckle

连翘 (Forsythia suspensa) weeping golden bell

白头翁 (Pulsatilla chinensis) Chinese pasqueflower

穿心莲 (Andrographis paniculata) creat

了哥王 (Wikstroemia indica) wikstroemia

附子 (Aconitum carmichaelii) aconite (monkshood)

吴茱萸 (Evodia rutaecarpa) evodia

细辛 (Asarum sieboldii) wild ginger

高良姜(良姜) (Alpinia officinarum) lesser galingale

大黄(药用大黄) (Rheum officinale) rhubarb

巴豆 (Croton tiglium) croton

大戟 (Euphorbia pekinensis) Beijing euphorbia

藿香 (Agastache rugosus) wrinkled giant hyssop

广藿香 (Pogostemon cablin) patchouli

泽泻 (Alisma plantage-aquatica ssp. orientale) oriental water plantain

薏苡仁 (Coix lacry-jobi) Job's tears

木通 (Akebia quinata) akebi

威灵仙 (Clematis chinensis) Chinese clematis

前胡 (Peucedanum praeruptorum) hog fennel

贝母 (Fritillaria cirrhosa)

fritillary

桔梗 (Platycodon grandiflorus) balloon flower

仙鹤草 (Agrimonia pilosa) hairy-vein agrimony

三七 (Panax Pseudo-ginseng) false ginseng

川芎 (Ligusticum wallichii) lovage

白芷 (Angelica anomala) angelica

丹参 (Salvia miltiorrhiza) redroot sage

沙参 (Adenophora stricta) lady bell

益母草 (Leonurus) motherwort

人参 (panax ginseng) ginseng

党参 (Codonopsis pilosula) Asia bell

黄芪 (Astragalus mongholicus) Mongolian milkvetch

当归 (Angelica sinensis) Chinese angelica

黄精 (Polygonatum sibiricum) Siberian Solomon's seal

杜仲 (Eucommia ulmoides) cucommia

何首乌 (Polygonum multiflorum) tuber fleeceflower

巴戟天 (Morinda officinalis) Indian mulberry

菟丝子 (Cuscuta chinensis) Chinese dodder seed

天门冬 (Asparagus) wild asparagus

麦门冬 (Liriope spicata) lilyturf

芡实 (Euryale ferox) euryale fruit

诃子 (Terminalia chebula) chebule

远志 (Polygala tenuifolia) milkwort

钩藤 (Uncaria rhynchophylla) gambier plant

# 花 卉 Flowers

向日葵 (Helianthus annuus) sunflower

菊花 (Dendranthema morifolium) chrysanthemum

雏菊 (Bellis perennis) daisy

翠菊(蓝菊) (Callistephus chinensis) China aster

万寿菊 (Tagetes erecta) marigold

大丽菊 (Dahlia pinnata) dahlia

百日菊 (Zinnia elegans) zinnia

矢车菊 (Centaurea cyanus) cornflower

蜡菊 (Helichrysum bracteatum) strawflower

月季 (Rosa chinensis) China rose

玫瑰 (Rosa rugosa) rugosa rose

香水花 (Rosa odorata) tea rose

玉兰 (Magnolia denudata) yulan magnolia

含笑 (Michelia figo) banana

shrub

石竹(洛阳花) (Dianthus chinensis) China pink

香石竹 (Dianthus caryophyllus) carnation

荷(莲) (Nelumbo nucifera) lotus

西番莲 (Passiflora caerulea) passion flower

秋海棠 (Begonia evansiana) begonia

紫丁香 (Syringa oblata) lilac

茉莉 (Jasminum sambac) jasmine

木犀(桂花) (Osmanthus fragrans) sweet hibiscus

扶桑(朱槿，大红花) (Hibiscus rosa-sinensis) Chinese hibiscus

木芙蓉 (Hibiscus mutabilis) cottonrose

牡丹 (Paeonia suffruticosa) tree peony

芍药 (Paeonia lactiflora) Chinese peony

夹竹桃 (Nerium indicum) oleander

鸡蛋花 (Plumeria rubra) frangipani

紫罗兰 (Matthiola incana) stock

堇 (Viola) violet

绣球花 (Hydrangea macrophylla) hydrangea

百合 (Lilium) lily

郁金香 (Tulipa gesneriana) tulip

玉簪花 (Hosta plantaginea) fragrant plantain lily

晚香玉 (Polianthes tuberosa) tuberose

水仙 (Narcissus tazetta var. chinensis) Chinese sacred lily (Chinese polyanthus narcissus)

鸢尾 (Iris tectorum) iris

菖兰(剑兰) (Gladiolus gandavensis) gladiolus

兰花 (Cymbidium virescens) orchid

姜花 (Hedychium coronarium) ginger lily

鸡冠花 (Celosia cristata) cockscomb

凤仙花 (Impatiens balsamina) garden balsam

栀子(白蝉) (Gardenia jasminoides) gardenia

牵牛花 (Ipomoca nil) morning glory

美人蕉 (Canna indica) canna

蜡梅 (Chimonanthus praecox) wintersweet

杜鹃花 (Rhododendron simsii) rhododendron

吊钟花 (Enkianthus quinqueflorus) evergreen enkianthus

百岁兰 (Welwitschia mirabilis) tumboa

桃花 (Prunus persica) peach blossom

梅花 (Prunus mume) plum blossom

山茶花 (Camellia japonica) camellia

樱花 (Prunus yedoensis) Japanese cherry blossom

黄水仙 (Narcissus pseudonar-
cissus) daffodil

风信花(洋水仙) (Hyacinth
orientalis) hyacinth

仙客来 (Cyclamen) cyclamen

报春花 (Primula) primrose

一品红(圣诞树) (Euphorbia
pulcherrima) poinsettia

蒲包花 (Calceolaria) calcea-
laria

文冠果花 (Xanthocera sorbi-
folia) xanthocera

木棉花 (Gossampinus mala-
baria) kapok blossom

银柳 (Salix discolor) pussy
willow

紫藤 (Wisteria) wistaria

墨兰(春兰) (Cymbidium si-
nense) Chinese cymbidium

吊兰 (Chlorophytum capense)
pendulum orchid

紫菀 (Aster) aster

金鱼草 (Antirrhinum) snap-
dragon

铃兰 (Convallaria keikei)
lily of the valley

风铃草 (Campanula medium)
canterbury bell

金凤花(毛茛) (Ranuculus)
buttercup

罂粟花 (Papaver somniferum)
poppy

萱草(金针花) (Hemerocallis
fulva) day lily

万年青 (Rohdea japonica)
evergreen

金银花 (Lonicera) honey
suckle

三色堇 (Violet tricolor)
pansy

山指甲 (Ligustrum sinense)
Chinese privet

珍珠兰(米仔兰) (Aglais
odorata) aglais

凌霄花 (Campsis chinensis)
Chinese trumpet-creeper

天竺葵 (Pelargonium hor-
torum) geranium

蜀葵 (Althaea rosea) holly-
hock

番红花 (Iridaceae crocus)
crocus

盆栽金桔 (Fortunella marga-
rita) potted kumquat

四季桔 (Citrus microcarpa)
tangerine

肉质植物 succulent plant

仙人掌 (Cactaceae cactus)
cactus

仙人球 (Echinocatus grusonii)
barrel cactus, ferocactus

仙人柱(仙人鞭) (Cereus) ce-
reus, organ-pipe cactus

霸王鞭(三棱剑,剑花) (Zygoca-
tus truncatus) crab cactus

昙花 (Epiphyllum oxypeta-
lum) orchid cactus, leaf
cactus

## 常绿乔木　Evergreen Trees

铁树(苏铁) (Cycas revoluta)
sago cycas

油杉 (Keteleeria fortunei)

keteleeria

冷杉 (Abies) fir

铁杉 (Tsuga chinensis) Chinese hemlock

银杉　(Cathaya argyrophylla)

云杉　(Picea) spruce

雪松　(Cedrus) cedar

马尾松　(Pinus massoniana)
pony-tail pine

赤松　(Pinus densiflora)
Japanese red pine

油松　(Pinus tabulaeformis)
Chinese pine

红松　(Pinus koraiensis)
Korean pine

华山松　(Pinus armandil)
Huashan pine

白皮松　(Pinus bungeana)
lacebark pine

五钗松(日本五针松)　(Pinus
parviflora) Japanese white
pine

金松　(Sciadopitys verticillata) umbrella pine

杉(沙木)　(Cunninghamia lan-
ceolata) China fir

柳杉　(Cryptomeria fortunci)
Chinese cryptomeria

日本柳杉　(Cryptomeria japo-
nica) Japanese cedar

巨杉　(Sequoiadendron gigan-
teum) giant sequoia

南洋杉　(Araucaria) araucaria

侧柏(扁柏)　(Biota orientalis)
oriental arborvitae

柏木(垂柏)　(Cupressus fune-
bris) mourning cypress

干香柏　(Cupressus duclou-
xiana) Bhutan cypress

桧(圆柏)　(Sabina chinensis)
Chinese juniper

罗汉柏　(Thujopsis dolobrata)

hiba arborvitae

罗汉松　(Podocarpus macro-
phyllus)

紫杉　(Taxus) yew

红豆杉　(Taxus chinensis)
Chinese yew

香榧　(Torreya grandis) Chi-
nese torreya

木麻黄　(Casuarina equiseti-
folia) casuarina

榕　(Ficus microcarpa) littleleaf fig

垂叶榕　(Ficus benghalensis)
banyan

菩提树　(Ficus religiosa) pee-
pul (bo tree)

檀香　(Santalum album) white
sandalwood

樟　(Cinnamomum camphora)
camphor tree

楠　(Phoebe nanmu) nanmu

台湾相思树　(Acacia confusa)
Taiwan acacia

紫檀(青龙木)　(Pterocarpus
indicus) padauk

黄杨　(Buxus microphylla var.
sinica) Chinese littleleaf
box tree

沉香　(Aquilaria agallocha)
eaglewood

柠檬桉　(Eucalyptus citriodora)
lemon gum

蓝桉　(Eucalyptus globulus)
Tasmanian blue gum

大叶桉　(Eucalyptus robusta)
swamp mahogany

白千层　(Melaleuca leucaden-
dra) cajeput tree (paper-
bark)

乌木 (Diospyros ebenum) ebony

依兰香(依兰依兰) (Cananga odorata) ylang-ylang

## 落叶乔木 Deciduous Trees

银杏 (Gingko biloba) gingko (maidenhair tree)

落叶松 (Larix) larch

金钱松 (Pseudolarix amabilis) golden larch

水松 (Glyptostrobus pensilis) water pine

落羽杉 (Taxodium distichum) bald oypress

水杉 (Metasequoia glyptestroboides) dawn redwood

毛白杨 (Populus tomentosa) Chinese white poplar

银白杨 (Populus alba) white poplar

垂柳 (Salix babylonica) weeping willow

柽柳 (Tamarix chinensis) Chinese tamarisk

枫杨 (Pterocarya stenoptera) Chinese wingnut

山核桃 (Carya cathayensis) Chinese walnut

白桦 (Betula platyphylla) Asian white birch

桤木 (Alnus) alder

榛 (Corylus heterophylla) Siberian filbert

山毛榉 (Fagus) beech

栗 (Castanea mollissima) Chinese chestnut

栎 (Quercus) oak

榆 (Ulmus pumila) Siberian elm

榔榆 (Ulmus parviflora) Chinese elm

桑 (Morus alba) white mulberry

鹅掌楸 (Liriodendron) Chinese tulip tree

金缕梅 (Hamamelis mollis) Chinese witch hazel

苏合香 (Liquidambar orientalis) oriental sweet gum

法国梧桐 (Platanus orientalis) oriental plane tree

合欢 (Albizzia julibrissin) silk tree

凤凰木 (Delonix regia) flamboyant tree

皂荚 (Gleditsia sinensis) Chinese honey locust

紫荆 (Cercis chinensis) Chinese redbud

羊蹄甲 (Bauhinia variegata) mountain ebony (camel's foot)

槐 (Sophora japonica) Chinese scholar tree, Japanese pagoda tree

刺槐(洋槐) (Robinia pseudoacacia) locust tree

黄檀 (Dalbergia hupeana) rosewood

刺桐 (Erythrina indica) Indian coral tree

臭椿(樗) (Ailanthus altissima) tree-of-heaven

香椿　(Toona sinensis)
　　Chinese toon
楝树(苦楝)　(Melia azedarach)
　　Chinaberry
乌桕　(Sapium sebiferum)
　　Chinese sapium
丝棉木　(Euonymus bungeana) spindle tree
槭(枫)　(Acer) maple
七叶树　(Acsculus chinensis)
　　Chinese horse chestnut
椴　(Tilia) linden
梧桐　(Firmiana simplex)
　　Chinese parasol tree
珙桐　(Davidia involucrata)
　　dove tree
白蜡树(桦)　(Fraxinus chinensis) Chinese ash
水曲柳　(Fraxinus mandshurica) manchurian ash
梓　(Catalpa ovata) Chinese catalpa
楸　(Catalpa bungei)
　　Manchurian catalpa
柚木　(Tectona grandis) teak
栾(灯笼树)　(Koelreuteria paniculata) golden-rain tree
泡桐　(Paulownia) kiri

## 棕榈　Palms

棕榈　(Trachycarpus fortunei)
　　hemp palm
蒲葵　(Livistona chinensis)
　　Chinese fan palm
棕竹　(Rhapis humilis) bamboo palm (lady palm)
油棕　(Elaeis guineensis) oil palm
省藤　(Calamus platyacanthoides) rattan
麒麟血藤　(Calamus draco)
　　dragon's-blood palm
槟榔　(Areca cathecu) betel palm
桃榔　(Arenga pinnata) gomuti palm (sugar palm)
鱼尾葵　(Caryota ochlandra)
　　fishtail palm
椰子　(Cocos nucifera) coconut
海枣(椰枣)　(Phoenix dactylifera) date palm

## 藻类　Algae

葛仙米　(Nostoc commune)
　　star jelly
发菜　(Nostoc commune var. flagelliferme) flagelliform star jelly
海带　(Laminaria japonica)
　　tangle
羊栖菜　(Sargassum fusiforme)
　　fusiform sargassum
海蒿子　(Sargassum pallidum)
　　pale sargassum
紫菜　(Porphyra) red laver
石花菜　(Gelidium amansii)
　　gelidium

海萝 (Gloiopeltis) funori
麒麟菜 (Euchema) euchema
江蓠 (Gracilaria confervoides) gracilaria

仙菜 (Ceramium) rosetangle
海人草 (Digenea simplex) digenea

## 菌 类 Fungi

藻状菌 (Phycomycetes) algal fungus
毛霉 (Mucor) mucor
黑根霉 (Rhizopus nigricans) bread mould
虫霉 (Entomophthora) entomophthora
子囊菌 (Ascomycetes) sac fungus
赤霉菌 (Gibberella) gibberella
麦角菌 (Claviceps purpurea) ergot
冬虫夏草 (Cordyceps sinensis caterpillar fungus
担子菌 (Basidiomycetes) club fungus
银耳 (Tremella fuciformis) tremella
木耳(云耳) (Auricularia auricula) Jew's-ear
猪苓 (Polyporus umbellatus) agaric

灵芝 (Ganoderma lucidum) lucid ganoderma
茯苓 (Poria coccos) tuckahoe
牛肝菌 (Boletus) boletus
蜜环蕈 (Armillaria mellea) honey fungus
鸡㙡 (Collybia albuminosa) collybia (mushroom)
香菇(冬菇) (Lentinus edodes) lentinus (mushroom)
蚝菌 (Pleurotus ostreatus) oyster mushroom
蘑菇 (Agaricus campestris) champignon (meadow mushroom)
草菇 (Volvaria volvacea) volvaria (mushroom)
大马勃 (Calvatia gigantea) giant puffball
曲霉 (Aspergillus) aspergillus (green mould)
青霉 (Penicillium) penicillium (blue mould)

## 地 衣 Lichens

扁枝衣(树花) (Evernia) evernia
栎扁枝衣 (Evernia prunastri) oak moss lichen
松萝 (Usnea) usnea

石蕊 (Cladonia) cladonia
驯鹿苔(石蕊) (Cladonia rangiferina) reindeer lichen
石耳 (Gyrophora esculenta) edible manna lichen

## 藓 类 Mosses

泥炭藓　(Sphagnum) peat moss
水藓　(Fontinalis) brook moss
黑藓属　(Andreaea) slit moss
葫芦藓　(Funaria hygrome-
　trica) cord moss

灰藓　(Hypnum) carpet moss
大金发藓　(Polytrichum
　commune) pigeon-wheat
　moss (haircap moss)

## 蕨 类 Ferns

石松(过山龙)　(Lycopodium
　clavatum) lycopodium (club
　moss)
卷柏(还魂草)　(Selaginella
　tamariscina) selaginella
　(little club moss)
木贼　(Equisetum hiemale)
　scouring rush
瓶尔小草　(Ophioglossum
　vulgatum) adder's-tongue
　fern
海金沙　(Lygodium japonicum)
　climbing fern
蕨(乌糯)　(pteridium
　aquilinum var. latiusculum)
　bracken
狗脊　(Woodwardia japonica)
　chain fern

金毛狗脊(黄狗头)　(Cibotium
　barometz) scythian lamb
　(lamb plant)
桫椤　(Cyathea spinulosa) tree
　fern
贯众　(Cyrtomium fortunei)
　holly fern
鳞毛蕨　(Dryopteris) wood
　fern
水龙骨(岩蚕)　(Polypodium
　nipponicum) polypody
萍(田字草)　(Marsilea
　quadrifolia) clover fern
槐叶萍　(Salvinia natans)
　salvinia
满江红(红萍,绿萍)　(Azolla
　imbricata) mosquito fern

附　录：

# 简体字繁体字对照表

Appendix:

## Table of Simplified Chinese Characters
## Against Their Complex Forms

| | | | | |
|---|---|---|---|---|
| **2笔** | 习〔習〕 | 长〔長〕 | 邓〔鄧〕 | 号〔號〕 |
| | 马〔馬〕 | 仆〔僕〕 | 劝〔勸〕 | 电〔電〕 |
| 厂〔廠〕 | 乡〔鄉〕 | 币〔幣〕 | 双〔雙〕 | 只〔隻〕 |
| 卜〔蔔〕 | | 从〔從〕 | 书〔書〕 | 〔祇〕 |
| 儿〔兒〕 | **4笔** | 仑〔侖〕 | | 叽〔嘰〕 |
| 几〔幾〕 | | 仓〔倉〕 | **5笔** | 叹〔嘆〕 |
| 了〔瞭〕 | **【一】** | 风〔風〕 | | |
| | 丰〔豐〕 | 仅〔僅〕 | **【一】** | **【丿】** |
| **3笔** | 开〔開〕 | 凤〔鳳〕 | 击〔擊〕 | 们〔們〕 |
| 干〔乾〕 | 无〔無〕 | 乌〔烏〕 | 戈〔戔〕 | 仪〔儀〕 |
| 〔幹〕 | 韦〔韋〕 | **【丶】** | 扑〔撲〕 | 丛〔叢〕 |
| 亏〔虧〕 | 专〔專〕 | 闩〔閂〕 | 节〔節〕 | 尔〔爾〕 |
| 才〔纔〕 | 云〔雲〕 | 为〔爲〕 | 术〔術〕 | 乐〔樂〕 |
| 万〔萬〕 | 艺〔藝〕 | 斗〔鬥〕 | 龙〔龍〕 | 处〔處〕 |
| 与〔與〕 | 厅〔廳〕 | 忆〔憶〕 | 厉〔厲〕 | 冬〔鼕〕 |
| 千〔韆〕 | 历〔歷〕 | 订〔訂〕 | 灭〔滅〕 | 鸟〔鳥〕 |
| 亿〔億〕 | 〔曆〕 | 计〔計〕 | 东〔東〕 | 务〔務〕 |
| 个〔個〕 | 区〔區〕 | 讣〔訃〕 | 轧〔軋〕 | 刍〔芻〕 |
| 么〔麼〕 | 车〔車〕 | 认〔認〕 | **【丨】** | 饥〔饑〕 |
| 广〔廣〕 | **【丨】** | 讥〔譏〕 | 卢〔盧〕 | **【丶】** |
| 门〔門〕 | 冈〔岡〕 | **【乛】** | 业〔業〕 | 邝〔鄺〕 |
| 义〔義〕 | 贝〔貝〕 | 丑〔醜〕 | 旧〔舊〕 | 冯〔馮〕 |
| 卫〔衛〕 | 见〔見〕 | 队〔隊〕 | 帅〔帥〕 | 闪〔閃〕 |
| 飞〔飛〕 | **【丿】** | 办〔辦〕 | 归〔歸〕 | 兰〔蘭〕 |
| | 气〔氣〕 | | 叶〔葉〕 | 汇〔匯〕 |

| | | | | |
|---|---|---|---|---|
| 〔彙〕 | **6笔** | 划〔劃〕 | 传〔傳〕 | 冲〔衝〕 |
| 头〔頭〕 | | 迈〔邁〕 | 伛〔傴〕 | 妆〔妝〕 |
| 汉〔漢〕 | 【一】 | 毕〔畢〕 | 优〔優〕 | 庄〔莊〕 |
| 宁〔寧〕 | 玑〔璣〕 | 【丨】 | 伤〔傷〕 | 庆〔慶〕 |
| 讦〔訐〕 | 动〔動〕 | 贞〔貞〕 | 伥〔倀〕 | 刘〔劉〕 |
| 讧〔訌〕 | 执〔執〕 | 师〔師〕 | 价〔價〕 | 齐〔齊〕 |
| 讨〔討〕 | 巩〔鞏〕 | 当〔當〕 | 伦〔倫〕 | 产〔產〕 |
| 写〔寫〕 | 圹〔壙〕 | 〔噹〕 | 伧〔傖〕 | 闭〔閉〕 |
| 让〔讓〕 | 扩〔擴〕 | 尘〔塵〕 | 华〔華〕 | 问〔問〕 |
| 礼〔禮〕 | 扪〔捫〕 | 吁〔籲〕 | 伙〔夥〕 | 闯〔闖〕 |
| 讪〔訕〕 | 扫〔掃〕 | 吓〔嚇〕 | 伪〔偽〕 | 关〔關〕 |
| 讫〔訖〕 | 扬〔揚〕 | 虫〔蟲〕 | 向〔嚮〕 | 灯〔燈〕 |
| 训〔訓〕 | 场〔場〕 | 曲〔麯〕 | 后〔後〕 | 汤〔湯〕 |
| 议〔議〕 | 亚〔亞〕 | 团〔團〕 | 会〔會〕 | 忏〔懺〕 |
| 讯〔訊〕 | 芗〔薌〕 | 〔糰〕 | 杀〔殺〕 | 兴〔興〕 |
| 记〔記〕 | 朴〔樸〕 | 吗〔嗎〕 | 合〔閤〕 | 讲〔講〕 |
| 【乛】 | 机〔機〕 | 屿〔嶼〕 | 众〔眾〕 | 讳〔諱〕 |
| 辽〔遼〕 | 权〔權〕 | 岁〔歲〕 | 爷〔爺〕 | 讴〔謳〕 |
| 边〔邊〕 | 过〔過〕 | 回〔迴〕 | 伞〔傘〕 | 军〔軍〕 |
| 出〔齣〕 | 协〔協〕 | 岂〔豈〕 | 创〔創〕 | 讵〔詎〕 |
| 发〔發〕 | 压〔壓〕 | 则〔則〕 | 杂〔雜〕 | 讶〔訝〕 |
| 〔髮〕 | 厌〔厭〕 | 刚〔剛〕 | 负〔負〕 | 讷〔訥〕 |
| 圣〔聖〕 | 厍〔厙〕 | 网〔網〕 | 犷〔獷〕 | 许〔許〕 |
| 对〔對〕 | 页〔頁〕 | 钆〔釓〕 | 犸〔獁〕 | 讹〔訛〕 |
| 台〔臺〕 | 夸〔誇〕 | 钇〔釔〕 | 凫〔鳧〕 | 䜣〔訢〕 |
| 〔檯〕 | 夺〔奪〕 | 【丿】 | 邬〔鄔〕 | 论〔論〕 |
| 〔颱〕 | 达〔達〕 | 朱〔硃〕 | 饦〔飥〕 | 讻〔訩〕 |
| 纠〔糾〕 | 夹〔夾〕 | 迁〔遷〕 | 饧〔餳〕 | 讼〔訟〕 |
| 驭〔馭〕 | 轨〔軌〕 | 乔〔喬〕 | 【丶】 | 讽〔諷〕 |
| 丝〔絲〕 | 尧〔堯〕 | 伟〔偉〕 | 壮〔壯〕 | 农〔農〕 |

设〔設〕 纩〔纊〕 坞〔塢〕 衮〔窽〕 呜〔嗚〕

访〔訪〕 纪〔紀〕 坟〔墳〕 歼〔殲〕 别〔彆〕

诀〔訣〕 驰〔馳〕 护〔護〕 来〔來〕 财〔財〕

【コ】 纫〔紉〕 壳〔殼〕 欤〔歟〕 囵〔圇〕

寻〔尋〕 块〔塊〕 轩〔軒〕 觃〔覎〕

尽〔盡〕 **7 笔** 声〔聲〕 连〔連〕 帏〔幃〕

〔儘〕 报〔報〕 轫〔軔〕 岖〔嶇〕

导〔導〕 【一】 拟〔擬〕 【丨】 岗〔崗〕

孙〔孫〕 寿〔壽〕 㧑〔撝〕 卤〔鹵〕 岘〔峴〕

阵〔陣〕 麦〔麥〕 芜〔蕪〕 〔滷〕 帐〔帳〕

阳〔陽〕 玛〔瑪〕 苇〔葦〕 邺〔鄴〕 岚〔嵐〕

阶〔階〕 进〔進〕 芸〔蕓〕 坚〔堅〕 【丿】

阴〔陰〕 远〔遠〕 苈〔藶〕 时〔時〕 针〔針〕

妇〔婦〕 违〔違〕 苋〔莧〕 呒〔嘸〕 钉〔釘〕

妈〔媽〕 韧〔韌〕 苁〔蓯〕 县〔縣〕 钊〔剑〕

戏〔戲〕 刬〔剗〕 苍〔蒼〕 里〔裏〕 钋〔釙〕

观〔觀〕 运〔運〕 严〔嚴〕 呓〔囈〕 钉〔釘〕

欢〔歡〕 抚〔撫〕 芦〔蘆〕 呕〔嘔〕 乱〔亂〕

买〔買〕 坛〔壇〕 〔蠆〕 园〔園〕 体〔體〕

纤〔纖〕 〔罎〕 劳〔勞〕 呖〔嚦〕 佣〔傭〕

红〔紅〕 抟〔摶〕 克〔剋〕 旷〔曠〕 㑇〔像〕

纣〔紂〕 坏〔壞〕 苏〔蘇〕 围〔圍〕 彻〔徹〕

驮〔馱〕 抠〔摳〕 〔嚕〕 吨〔噸〕 余〔餘〕

纤〔縴〕 坜〔壢〕 极〔極〕 旸〔暘〕 金〔僉〕

〔纖〕 扰〔擾〕 杨〔楊〕 邮〔郵〕 谷〔穀〕

纥〔紇〕 坝〔壩〕 两〔兩〕 困〔睏〕 邻〔鄰〕

驯〔馴〕 贡〔貢〕 丽〔麗〕 员〔員〕 肠〔腸〕

纨〔紈〕 㧑〔搁〕 医〔醫〕 呗〔唄〕 龟〔龜〕

约〔約〕 折〔摺〕 励〔勵〕 听〔聽〕 犹〔猶〕

级〔級〕 抢〔搶〕 矶〔磯〕 呛〔嗆〕 狈〔狽〕

鸠〔鳩〕
条〔條〕
岛〔島〕
邹〔鄒〕
饨〔飩〕
饩〔餼〕
饪〔飪〕
饫〔飫〕
饬〔飭〕
饭〔飯〕
饮〔飲〕
系〔係〕
〔繫〕

**【丶】**

冻〔凍〕
状〔狀〕
亩〔畝〕
庑〔廡〕
库〔庫〕
疖〔癤〕
疗〔療〕
应〔應〕
这〔這〕
庐〔廬〕
闰〔閏〕
闱〔闈〕
闲〔閑〕
间〔間〕
闵〔閔〕
闷〔悶〕

灿〔燦〕
灶〔竈〕
炀〔煬〕
沣〔灃〕
沤〔漚〕
沥〔瀝〕
沦〔淪〕
沧〔滄〕
沨〔渢〕
沟〔溝〕
沩〔潙〕
沪〔滬〕
沈〔瀋〕
怃〔憮〕
怀〔懷〕
怄〔慪〕
忧〔憂〕
忾〔愾〕
怅〔悵〕
怆〔愴〕
穷〔窮〕
证〔證〕
诂〔詁〕
诃〔訶〕
启〔啓〕
评〔評〕
补〔補〕
诅〔詛〕
识〔識〕
诇〔詗〕

诈〔詐〕
诉〔訴〕
诊〔診〕
诋〔詆〕
诌〔謅〕
词〔詞〕
诎〔詘〕
诏〔詔〕
译〔譯〕
诒〔詒〕

**【乛】**

灵〔靈〕
层〔層〕
迟〔遲〕
张〔張〕
际〔際〕
陆〔陸〕
陇〔隴〕
陈〔陳〕
坠〔墜〕
陉〔陘〕
妪〔嫗〕
妩〔嫵〕
妫〔媯〕
刭〔剄〕
劲〔勁〕
鸡〔鷄〕
纬〔緯〕
纭〔紜〕
驱〔驅〕

纯〔純〕
纰〔紕〕
纱〔紗〕
纲〔綱〕
纳〔納〕
纴〔紝〕
驳〔駁〕
纵〔縱〕
纶〔綸〕
纷〔紛〕
纸〔紙〕
纹〔紋〕
纺〔紡〕
驴〔驢〕
纼〔紖〕
纽〔紐〕
纾〔紓〕

**8笔**

**【一】**

玮〔瑋〕
环〔環〕
责〔責〕
现〔現〕
表〔錶〕
珐〔琺〕
规〔規〕
匦〔匭〕
拢〔攏〕
拣〔揀〕

垆〔壚〕
担〔擔〕
顶〔頂〕
拥〔擁〕
势〔勢〕
拦〔攔〕
扛〔攏〕
拧〔擰〕
拨〔撥〕
择〔擇〕
茏〔蘢〕
苹〔蘋〕
茑〔蔦〕
范〔範〕
茔〔塋〕
茕〔煢〕
茎〔莖〕
枢〔樞〕
枥〔櫪〕
柜〔櫃〕
枫〔楓〕
枧〔梘〕
枨〔棖〕
板〔闆〕
枞〔樅〕
松〔鬆〕
枪〔槍〕
枫〔楓〕
构〔構〕
丧〔喪〕

画〔畫〕　国〔國〕　钒〔釩〕　肤〔膚〕　单〔單〕
枣〔棗〕　畅〔暢〕　钉〔釘〕　胨〔腖〕　炜〔煒〕
卖〔賣〕　咙〔嚨〕　钗〔釵〕　肿〔腫〕　炝〔熗〕
郁〔鬱〕　蚬〔蜆〕　钖〔鍚〕　胀〔脹〕　炉〔爐〕
矾〔礬〕　黾〔黽〕　钗〔釵〕　肮〔骯〕　浅〔淺〕
矿〔礦〕　鸣〔鳴〕　制〔製〕　胁〔脅〕　泷〔瀧〕
砀〔碭〕　咛〔嚀〕　迭〔疊〕　迩〔邇〕　泸〔瀘〕
码〔碼〕　咝〔噝〕　刮〔颳〕　鱼〔魚〕　泺〔濼〕
厕〔廁〕　罗〔羅〕　侠〔俠〕　狞〔獰〕　泞〔濘〕
奋〔奮〕　　〔囉〕　侥〔僥〕　备〔備〕　泻〔瀉〕
态〔態〕　崇〔崈〕　侦〔偵〕　枭〔梟〕　泼〔潑〕
瓯〔甌〕　峁〔嶩〕　侧〔側〕　饯〔餞〕　泽〔澤〕
欧〔歐〕　帜〔幟〕　凭〔憑〕　饰〔飾〕　泾〔涇〕
殴〔毆〕　岭〔嶺〕　侨〔僑〕　饱〔飽〕　怜〔憐〕
垄〔壟〕　剐〔剮〕　侩〔儈〕　饲〔飼〕　怄〔慪〕
郏〔郟〕　剀〔剴〕　货〔貨〕　饳〔飿〕　怿〔懌〕
轰〔轟〕　凯〔凱〕　侪〔儕〕　饴〔飴〕　峃〔嶨〕
项〔項〕　峥〔崢〕　侬〔儂〕　　　　　学〔學〕
转〔轉〕　败〔敗〕　质〔質〕　【丶】　宝〔寶〕
轭〔軛〕　账〔賬〕　征〔徵〕　变〔變〕　宠〔寵〕
斩〔斬〕　贩〔販〕　径〔徑〕　庞〔龐〕　审〔審〕
轮〔輪〕　贬〔貶〕　舍〔捨〕　庙〔廟〕　帘〔簾〕
软〔軟〕　图〔圖〕　剑〔劍〕　疟〔瘧〕　实〔實〕
鸢〔鳶〕　购〔購〕　郐〔鄶〕　疠〔癘〕　诓〔誆〕
【丨】　【丿】　怂〔慫〕　疡〔瘍〕　诔〔誄〕
齿〔齒〕　钍〔釷〕　籴〔糴〕　剂〔劑〕　试〔試〕
虏〔虜〕　钎〔釬〕　觅〔覓〕　废〔廢〕　诖〔詿〕
肾〔腎〕　钏〔釧〕　贪〔貪〕　闸〔閘〕　诗〔詩〕
贤〔賢〕　钐〔釤〕　贫〔貧〕　闹〔鬧〕　诘〔詰〕
昙〔曇〕　钓〔釣〕　戗〔戧〕　郑〔鄭〕　诙〔詼〕
　　　　　　　　　　　　　　卷〔捲〕

| | | | | |
|---|---|---|---|---|
| 诚〔誠〕 | 线〔綫〕 | **9 笔** | 茧〔繭〕 | 树〔樹〕 |
| 郓〔鄆〕 | 绀〔紺〕 | | 荞〔蕎〕 | 鸫〔鶇〕 |
| 衬〔襯〕 | 绁〔絏〕 | **【一】** | 荟〔薈〕 | 郦〔酈〕 |
| 祎〔禕〕 | 绂〔紱〕 | 贰〔貳〕 | 荠〔薺〕 | 咸〔鹹〕 |
| 视〔視〕 | 练〔練〕 | 帮〔幫〕 | 荡〔蕩〕 | 砖〔磚〕 |
| 诔〔誄〕 | 组〔組〕 | 珑〔瓏〕 | 垩〔堊〕 | 砗〔硨〕 |
| 话〔話〕 | 驵〔駔〕 | 顸〔頇〕 | 荣〔榮〕 | 砚〔硯〕 |
| 诞〔誕〕 | 绅〔紳〕 | 鞁〔靽〕 | 荤〔葷〕 | 砜〔碸〕 |
| 诟〔詬〕 | 绌〔紬〕 | 垭〔埡〕 | 荥〔滎〕 | 面〔麵〕 |
| 诠〔詮〕 | 细〔細〕 | 挜〔掗〕 | 荦〔犖〕 | 牵〔牽〕 |
| 诡〔詭〕 | 驶〔駛〕 | 挝〔撾〕 | 荧〔熒〕 | 鸥〔鷗〕 |
| 询〔詢〕 | 驸〔駙〕 | 项〔項〕 | 荨〔蕁〕 | 龚〔龔〕 |
| 诣〔詣〕 | 驷〔駟〕 | 挞〔撻〕 | 胡〔鬍〕 | 残〔殘〕 |
| 诤〔諍〕 | 驹〔駒〕 | 挟〔挾〕 | 荩〔藎〕 | 殇〔殤〕 |
| 该〔該〕 | 终〔終〕 | 挠〔撓〕 | 荪〔蓀〕 | 轱〔軲〕 |
| 详〔詳〕 | 织〔織〕 | 赵〔趙〕 | 荫〔蔭〕 | 轲〔軻〕 |
| 诧〔詫〕 | 驺〔騶〕 | 贲〔賁〕 | 荬〔蕒〕 | 轳〔轤〕 |
| 诨〔諢〕 | 绉〔縐〕 | 挡〔擋〕 | 荭〔葒〕 | 轴〔軸〕 |
| 诩〔詡〕 | 驻〔駐〕 | 垲〔塏〕 | 荮〔葤〕 | 轶〔軼〕 |
| **【ㄱ】** | 绊〔絆〕 | 挢〔撟〕 | 药〔藥〕 | 轷〔軤〕 |
| 肃〔肅〕 | 驼〔駝〕 | 垫〔墊〕 | 标〔標〕 | 轸〔軫〕 |
| 隶〔隸〕 | 绋〔紼〕 | 挤〔擠〕 | 栈〔棧〕 | 轹〔轢〕 |
| 录〔錄〕 | 绌〔絀〕 | 挥〔揮〕 | 栉〔櫛〕 | 轺〔軺〕 |
| 弥〔彌〕 | 绍〔紹〕 | 挦〔撏〕 | 栊〔櫳〕 | 轻〔輕〕 |
| 〔瀰〕 | 驿〔驛〕 | 荐〔薦〕 | 栋〔棟〕 | 鸦〔鴉〕 |
| 陕〔陝〕 | 绎〔繹〕 | 荚〔莢〕 | 栌〔櫨〕 | 虿〔蠆〕 |
| 驽〔駑〕 | 经〔經〕 | 贳〔貰〕 | 栎〔櫟〕 | **【丨】** |
| 驾〔駕〕 | 骀〔駘〕 | 荛〔蕘〕 | 栏〔欄〕 | 战〔戰〕 |
| 参〔參〕 | 绐〔紿〕 | 荜〔蓽〕 | 柠〔檸〕 | 觇〔覘〕 |
| 艰〔艱〕 | 贯〔貫〕 | 带〔帶〕 | 柽〔檉〕 | 点〔點〕 |

| | | | | |
|---|---|---|---|---|
| 临〔臨〕 | 峤〔嶠〕 | 钯〔鈀〕 | 狮〔獅〕 | 闽〔閩〕 |
| 览〔覽〕 | 贱〔賤〕 | 毡〔氈〕 | 独〔獨〕 | 闾〔閭〕 |
| 竖〔豎〕 | 贴〔貼〕 | 氢〔氫〕 | 狯〔獪〕 | 阃〔闃〕 |
| 尝〔嘗〕 | 贶〔貺〕 | 选〔選〕 | 狱〔獄〕 | 阀〔閥〕 |
| 眍〔瞘〕 | 贮〔貯〕 | 适〔適〕 | 狲〔猻〕 | 阁〔閣〕 |
| 眬〔矓〕 | 贻〔貽〕 | 种〔種〕 | 贸〔貿〕 | 阐〔闡〕 |
| 哑〔啞〕 | 【丿】 | 秋〔鞦〕 | 饵〔餌〕 | 阂〔閡〕 |
| 显〔顯〕 | 钘〔銒〕 | 复〔復〕 | 饶〔饒〕 | 养〔養〕 |
| 哒〔噠〕 | 钙〔鈣〕 | 〔複〕 | 蚀〔蝕〕 | 姜〔薑〕 |
| 哓〔嘵〕 | 钚〔鈈〕 | 〔覆〕 | 饷〔餉〕 | 类〔類〕 |
| 哗〔嘩〕 | 钛〔鈦〕 | 笃〔篤〕 | 饸〔餄〕 | 娄〔婁〕 |
| 贵〔貴〕 | 钗〔釵〕 | 俦〔儔〕 | 饹〔餎〕 | 总〔總〕 |
| 虾〔蝦〕 | 钝〔鈍〕 | 俩〔倆〕 | 饺〔餃〕 | 炼〔煉〕 |
| 蚁〔蟻〕 | 钞〔鈔〕 | 俪〔儷〕 | 饻〔餏〕 | 炽〔熾〕 |
| 蚂〔螞〕 | 钟〔鐘〕 | 贷〔貸〕 | 饼〔餅〕 | 烁〔爍〕 |
| 虽〔雖〕 | 〔鍾〕 | 顺〔順〕 | 【丶】 | 烂〔爛〕 |
| 骂〔罵〕 | 钡〔鋇〕 | 俭〔儉〕 | 峦〔巒〕 | 烃〔烴〕 |
| 哕〔噦〕 | 钢〔鋼〕 | 剑〔劍〕 | 弯〔彎〕 | 洼〔窪〕 |
| 剐〔剮〕 | 钠〔鈉〕 | 鸽〔鴿〕 | 孪〔孿〕 | 洁〔潔〕 |
| 郧〔鄖〕 | 钥〔鑰〕 | 须〔須〕 | 娈〔孌〕 | 洒〔灑〕 |
| 勋〔勛〕 | 钦〔欽〕 | 〔鬚〕 | 将〔將〕 | 浃〔浹〕 |
| 哗〔嘩〕 | 钧〔鈞〕 | 胧〔朧〕 | 奖〔獎〕 | 浇〔澆〕 |
| 响〔響〕 | 钤〔鈐〕 | 胨〔腖〕 | 疬〔癧〕 | 浈〔湞〕 |
| 哙〔噲〕 | 钨〔鎢〕 | 胪〔臚〕 | 疮〔瘡〕 | 浉〔溮〕 |
| 哝〔噥〕 | 钩〔鈎〕 | 胆〔膽〕 | 疯〔瘋〕 | 浊〔濁〕 |
| 哟〔喲〕 | 钪〔鈧〕 | 胜〔勝〕 | 亲〔親〕 | 测〔測〕 |
| 峡〔峽〕 | 钫〔鈁〕 | 胫〔脛〕 | 飒〔颯〕 | 浍〔澮〕 |
| 峣〔嶢〕 | 钬〔鈥〕 | 鸨〔鴇〕 | 闺〔閨〕 | 浏〔瀏〕 |
| 帧〔幀〕 | 钭〔鈄〕 | | 闻〔聞〕 | |
| 罚〔罰〕 | 钮〔鈕〕 | 狭〔狹〕 | 闼〔闥〕 | 济〔濟〕 |

| | | | | |
|---|---|---|---|---|
| 浐〔滻〕 | 诶〔誒〕 | 给〔給〕 | 莲〔蓮〕 | 轻〔輕〕 |
| 浑〔渾〕 | 【乛】 | 绚〔絢〕 | 莳〔蒔〕 | 轿〔轎〕 |
| 浒〔滸〕 | 垦〔墾〕 | 绛〔絳〕 | 莴〔萵〕 | 辂〔輅〕 |
| 浓〔濃〕 | 昼〔晝〕 | 络〔絡〕 | 获〔獲〕 | 较〔較〕 |
| 浔〔潯〕 | 费〔費〕 | 绝〔絕〕 | 〔穫〕 | 鸹〔鴰〕 |
| 浕〔濜〕 | 逊〔遜〕 | | 莸〔蕕〕 | 顿〔頓〕 |
| 恸〔慟〕 | 陨〔隕〕 | **10 笔** | 恶〔惡〕 | 趸〔躉〕 |
| 恹〔懨〕 | 险〔險〕 | 【一】 | 〔噁〕 | 毙〔斃〕 |
| 恺〔愷〕 | 贺〔賀〕 | 艳〔艷〕 | 劳〔勞〕 | 致〔緻〕 |
| 恻〔惻〕 | 怼〔懟〕 | 项〔項〕 | 莹〔瑩〕 | 【丨】 |
| 恼〔惱〕 | 垒〔壘〕 | 珲〔琿〕 | 莺〔鶯〕 | 龀〔齔〕 |
| 恽〔惲〕 | 娅〔婭〕 | 蚕〔蠶〕 | 鸪〔鴣〕 | 鸬〔鸕〕 |
| 举〔舉〕 | 娆〔嬈〕 | 顽〔頑〕 | 莼〔蓴〕 | 虑〔慮〕 |
| 觉〔覺〕 | 娇〔嬌〕 | 盏〔盞〕 | 桡〔橈〕 | 监〔監〕 |
| 宪〔憲〕 | 绑〔綁〕 | 捞〔撈〕 | 桢〔楨〕 | 紧〔緊〕 |
| 窃〔竊〕 | 绒〔絨〕 | 载〔載〕 | 档〔檔〕 | 党〔黨〕 |
| 诚〔誠〕 | 结〔結〕 | 赶〔趕〕 | 桤〔榿〕 | 唛〔嘜〕 |
| 诬〔誣〕 | 绔〔絝〕 | 盐〔鹽〕 | 桥〔橋〕 | 晒〔曬〕 |
| 语〔語〕 | 骁〔驍〕 | 埘〔塒〕 | 桦〔樺〕 | 晓〔曉〕 |
| 袄〔襖〕 | 绕〔繞〕 | 损〔損〕 | 桧〔檜〕 | 唢〔嗩〕 |
| 诮〔誚〕 | 经〔經〕 | 埙〔塤〕 | 桩〔樁〕 | 唠〔嘮〕 |
| 祢〔禰〕 | 骄〔驕〕 | 埚〔堝〕 | 样〔樣〕 | 鸭〔鴨〕 |
| 误〔誤〕 | 骅〔驊〕 | 捡〔撿〕 | 贾〔賈〕 | 唡〔啢〕 |
| 诰〔誥〕 | 绘〔繪〕 | 贽〔贄〕 | 逦〔邐〕 | 晔〔曄〕 |
| 诱〔誘〕 | 骆〔駱〕 | 挚〔摯〕 | 砺〔礪〕 | 晕〔暈〕 |
| 海〔海〕 | 骈〔駢〕 | 热〔熱〕 | 砾〔礫〕 | 鸮〔鴞〕 |
| 诳〔誑〕 | 绞〔絞〕 | 捣〔搗〕 | 础〔礎〕 | 唢〔嗊〕 |
| 鸩〔鴆〕 | 骇〔駭〕 | 壶〔壺〕 | 砻〔礱〕 | 唰〔喎〕 |
| 说〔說〕 | 统〔統〕 | 聂〔聶〕 | 顾〔顧〕 | 蚬〔蜆〕 |
| 诵〔誦〕 | 绗〔絎〕 | 莱〔萊〕 | 轼〔軾〕 | 鸯〔鴦〕 |

| | | | | |
|---|---|---|---|---|
| 崂〔嶗〕 | 铃〔鈴〕 | 颁〔頒〕 | 痉〔痙〕 | 涨〔漲〕 |
| 崃〔崍〕 | 铄〔鑠〕 | 颂〔頌〕 | 准〔準〕 | 烫〔燙〕 |
| 罢〔罷〕 | 铅〔鉛〕 | 脍〔膾〕 | 离〔離〕 | 涩〔澀〕 |
| 圆〔圓〕 | 铆〔鉚〕 | 脏〔臟〕 | 颃〔頏〕 | 悭〔慳〕 |
| 觊〔覬〕 | 铈〔鈰〕 | 〔髒〕 | 资〔資〕 | 悯〔憫〕 |
| 贼〔賊〕 | 铉〔鉉〕 | 脐〔臍〕 | 竞〔競〕 | 宽〔寬〕 |
| 贿〔賄〕 | 铊〔鉈〕 | 脑〔腦〕 | 阃〔閫〕 | 家〔傢〕 |
| 赂〔賂〕 | 铋〔鉍〕 | 胶〔膠〕 | 阄〔闖〕 | 宾〔賓〕 |
| 赃〔臟〕 | 铌〔鈮〕 | 脓〔膿〕 | 阄〔鬮〕 | 窍〔竅〕 |
| 赅〔賅〕 | 铍〔鈹〕 | 鸺〔鵂〕 | 阅〔閱〕 | 窝〔窩〕 |
| 赆〔贐〕 | 铍〔鑕〕 | 玺〔璽〕 | 阆〔閬〕 | 请〔請〕 |
| 【丿】 | 铎〔鐸〕 | 刏〔劋〕 | 郸〔鄲〕 | 诸〔諸〕 |
| 钰〔鈺〕 | 氩〔氬〕 | 鸲〔鴝〕 | 烦〔煩〕 | 诹〔諏〕 |
| 钱〔錢〕 | 牺〔犧〕 | 猃〔獫〕 | 烧〔燒〕 | 诺〔諾〕 |
| 钲〔鉦〕 | 敌〔敵〕 | 鸵〔鴕〕 | 烛〔燭〕 | 诼〔諑〕 |
| 钳〔鉗〕 | 积〔積〕 | 袅〔裊〕 | 烨〔燁〕 | 读〔讀〕 |
| 钴〔鈷〕 | 称〔稱〕 | 鸳〔鴛〕 | 烩〔燴〕 | 诽〔誹〕 |
| 钵〔鉢〕 | 笕〔筧〕 | 皱〔皺〕 | 烬〔燼〕 | 袜〔襪〕 |
| 钶〔鈳〕 | 笔〔筆〕 | 铧〔鏵〕 | 递〔遞〕 | 祯〔禎〕 |
| 钷〔鉕〕 | 债〔債〕 | 饿〔餓〕 | 涛〔濤〕 | 课〔課〕 |
| 钹〔鈸〕 | 借〔藉〕 | 馁〔餒〕 | 涝〔澇〕 | 诿〔諉〕 |
| 钻〔鑽〕 | 倾〔傾〕 | 【丶】 | 涞〔淶〕 | 谀〔諛〕 |
| 钼〔鉬〕 | 赁〔賃〕 | 栾〔欒〕 | 涟〔漣〕 | 谁〔誰〕 |
| 钽〔鉭〕 | 顾〔顧〕 | 挛〔攣〕 | 涢〔溳〕 | 谂〔諗〕 |
| 钾〔鉀〕 | 徕〔徠〕 | 恋〔戀〕 | 涡〔渦〕 | 调〔調〕 |
| 铀〔鈾〕 | 舰〔艦〕 | 桨〔槳〕 | 涂〔塗〕 | 谄〔諂〕 |
| 钿〔鈿〕 | 舱〔艙〕 | 浆〔漿〕 | 涤〔滌〕 | 谅〔諒〕 |
| 铁〔鐵〕 | 耸〔聳〕 | 症〔癥〕 | 润〔潤〕 | 谆〔諄〕 |
| 铂〔鉑〕 | 爱〔愛〕 | 痈〔癰〕 | 涧〔澗〕 | 谇〔誶〕 |
| | 鸽〔鴿〕 | 斋〔齋〕 | | 谈〔談〕 |

| | | | | |
|---|---|---|---|---|
| 谊〔誼〕 | 麸〔麩〕 | 硖〔硤〕 | 崭〔嶄〕 | 铫〔銚〕 |
| 讽〔諷〕 | 掳〔擄〕 | 硗〔磽〕 | 逻〔邏〕 | 铭〔銘〕 |
| 【乛】 | 掴〔摑〕 | 硙〔磑〕 | 帼〔幗〕 | 铬〔鉻〕 |
| 恳〔懇〕 | 鸷〔鷙〕 | 硚〔礄〕 | 赈〔賑〕 | 铮〔錚〕 |
| 剧〔劇〕 | 掷〔擲〕 | 鸸〔鴯〕 | 婴〔嬰〕 | 铯〔銫〕 |
| 娲〔媧〕 | 掸〔撣〕 | 聋〔聾〕 | 赊〔賒〕 | 铰〔鉸〕 |
| 娴〔嫻〕 | 壸〔壼〕 | 龚〔龔〕 | 【丿】 | 铱〔銥〕 |
| 难〔難〕 | 悫〔愨〕 | 袭〔襲〕 | 铏〔鉶〕 | 铲〔鏟〕 |
| 预〔預〕 | 据〔據〕 | 驾〔駕〕 | 铐〔銬〕 | 铳〔銃〕 |
| 绠〔綆〕 | 掺〔摻〕 | 殒〔殞〕 | 铑〔銠〕 | 铵〔銨〕 |
| 骊〔驪〕 | 掼〔摜〕 | 殓〔殮〕 | 铒〔鉺〕 | 银〔銀〕 |
| 绡〔綃〕 | 职〔職〕 | 赉〔賚〕 | 铓〔鋩〕 | 铷〔銣〕 |
| 骋〔騁〕 | 聍〔聹〕 | 辄〔輒〕 | 铕〔銪〕 | 矫〔矯〕 |
| 绢〔絹〕 | 萚〔蘀〕 | 辅〔輔〕 | 铗〔鋏〕 | 鸹〔鴰〕 |
| 绣〔綉〕 | 勚〔勩〕 | 辆〔輛〕 | 铙〔鐃〕 | 秽〔穢〕 |
| 验〔驗〕 | 萝〔蘿〕 | 堑〔塹〕 | 铛〔鐺〕 | 笺〔箋〕 |
| 绥〔綏〕 | 萤〔螢〕 | 【丨】 | 铝〔鋁〕 | 笼〔籠〕 |
| 绦〔縧〕 | 营〔營〕 | 颅〔顱〕 | 铜〔銅〕 | 笾〔籩〕 |
| 继〔繼〕 | 萦〔縈〕 | 喷〔噴〕 | 铟〔銦〕 | 偾〔僨〕 |
| 绨〔綈〕 | 萧〔蕭〕 | 悬〔懸〕 | 铠〔鎧〕 | 鸺〔鵂〕 |
| 骎〔駸〕 | 萨〔薩〕 | 啭〔囀〕 | 铡〔鍘〕 | 偿〔償〕 |
| 骏〔駿〕 | 梦〔夢〕 | 跃〔躍〕 | 铢〔銖〕 | 偻〔僂〕 |
| 鸶〔鷥〕 | 觋〔覡〕 | 啮〔嚙〕 | 铣〔銑〕 | 躯〔軀〕 |
| | 检〔檢〕 | 跄〔蹌〕 | 铥〔銩〕 | 皑〔皚〕 |
| **11笔** | 棂〔欞〕 | 蛎〔蠣〕 | 铤〔鋌〕 | 衅〔釁〕 |
| 【一】 | 啬〔嗇〕 | 蛊〔蠱〕 | 铧〔鏵〕 | 鸻〔鴴〕 |
| 焘〔燾〕 | 匮〔匱〕 | 蛏〔蟶〕 | 铨〔銓〕 | 衔〔銜〕 |
| 琎〔璡〕 | 酝〔醞〕 | 累〔纍〕 | 铩〔鎩〕 | 舻〔艫〕 |
| 琏〔璉〕 | 厣〔厴〕 | 啸〔嘯〕 | 铪〔鉿〕 | 盘〔盤〕 |
| 琐〔瑣〕 | 硕〔碩〕 | 帻〔幘〕 | 铰... | 鸼〔鵃〕 |

| | | | | |
|---|---|---|---|---|
| 龛〔龕〕 | 盖〔蓋〕 | 裆〔襠〕 | 续〔續〕 | 趋〔趨〕 |
| 鸽〔鴿〕 | 粝〔糲〕 | 祸〔禍〕 | 绮〔綺〕 | 揽〔攬〕 |
| 敛〔斂〕 | 断〔斷〕 | 谒〔謁〕 | 骑〔騎〕 | 颉〔頡〕 |
| 领〔領〕 | 兽〔獸〕 | 谓〔謂〕 | 绯〔緋〕 | 揿〔撳〕 |
| 脶〔腡〕 | 焖〔燜〕 | 谔〔諤〕 | 绰〔綽〕 | 搀〔攙〕 |
| 脸〔臉〕 | 渍〔漬〕 | 谕〔諭〕 | 骒〔騍〕 | 蛰〔蟄〕 |
| 象〔像〕 | 鸿〔鴻〕 | 谖〔諼〕 | 绲〔緄〕 | 絷〔縶〕 |
| 猎〔獵〕 | 渎〔瀆〕 | 谗〔讒〕 | 绳〔繩〕 | 搁〔擱〕 |
| 猡〔玀〕 | 渐〔漸〕 | 谘〔諮〕 | 骓〔騅〕 | 搂〔摟〕 |
| 猕〔獼〕 | 渑〔澠〕 | 谙〔諳〕 | 维〔維〕 | 搅〔攪〕 |
| 馃〔餜〕 | 渊〔淵〕 | 谚〔諺〕 | 绵〔綿〕 | 联〔聯〕 |
| 馄〔餛〕 | 渔〔漁〕 | 谛〔諦〕 | 绶〔綬〕 | 蒇〔蕆〕 |
| 馅〔餡〕 | 淀〔澱〕 | 谜〔謎〕 | 绷〔綳〕 | 蒉〔蕢〕 |
| 馆〔館〕 | 渗〔滲〕 | 谝〔諞〕 | 绸〔綢〕 | 蒋〔蔣〕 |
| 【丶】 | 惬〔愜〕 | 谞〔諝〕 | 绺〔綹〕 | 蒌〔蔞〕 |
| 鸾〔鸞〕 | 惭〔慚〕 | 【乛】 | 绻〔綣〕 | 韩〔韓〕 |
| 庼〔廎〕 | 惧〔懼〕 | 弹〔彈〕 | 综〔綜〕 | 椟〔櫝〕 |
| 痒〔癢〕 | 惊〔驚〕 | 堕〔墮〕 | 绽〔綻〕 | 椤〔欏〕 |
| 鸹〔鴰〕 | 惮〔憚〕 | 随〔隨〕 | 绾〔綰〕 | 赍〔賫〕 |
| 旋〔鏇〕 | 惨〔慘〕 | 枭〔燿〕 | 绿〔綠〕 | 椭〔橢〕 |
| 阃〔閫〕 | 惯〔慣〕 | 隐〔隱〕 | 骖〔驂〕 | 鹁〔鵓〕 |
| 阄〔鬮〕 | 祷〔禱〕 | 婳〔嫿〕 | 缀〔綴〕 | 鹂〔鸝〕 |
| 阅〔閱〕 | 谌〔諶〕 | 婵〔嬋〕 | 缁〔緇〕 | 觌〔覿〕 |
| 阆〔閬〕 | 谋〔謀〕 | 婶〔嬸〕 | | 硷〔鹼〕 |
| 阇〔闍〕 | 谍〔諜〕 | 颇〔頗〕 | **12笔** | 确〔確〕 |
| 阈〔閾〕 | 谎〔謊〕 | 颈〔頸〕 | | 詟〔讋〕 |
| 阉〔閹〕 | 谏〔諫〕 | 绩〔績〕 | 【一】 | 殚〔殫〕 |
| 阊〔閶〕 | 皲〔皸〕 | 绪〔緒〕 | 靓〔靚〕 | 颊〔頰〕 |
| 阋〔鬩〕 | 谐〔諧〕 | 绫〔綾〕 | 琼〔瓊〕 | 雳〔靂〕 |
| 羟〔羥〕 | 谑〔謔〕 | 骐〔騏〕 | 辇〔輦〕 | 辊〔輥〕 |
| | | | 鼋〔黿〕 | |

辋〔輞〕
椠〔槧〕
暂〔暫〕
辍〔輟〕
辐〔輻〕
翘〔翹〕

【丨】

辈〔輩〕
凿〔鑿〕
辉〔輝〕
赏〔賞〕
睐〔睞〕
睑〔瞼〕
喷〔噴〕
畴〔疇〕
践〔踐〕
遗〔遺〕
蛱〔蛺〕
蛲〔蟯〕
蛳〔螄〕
蛴〔蠐〕
鹃〔鵑〕
喽〔嘍〕
嵘〔嶸〕
嵚〔嶔〕
嵝〔嶁〕
赋〔賦〕
赌〔賭〕
赎〔贖〕

赐〔賜〕
赒〔賙〕
赔〔賠〕
赕〔賧〕

【丿】

铸〔鑄〕
锊〔鋝〕
铺〔鋪〕
铼〔錸〕
铽〔鋱〕
链〔鏈〕
铿〔鏗〕
销〔銷〕
锁〔鎖〕
锃〔鋥〕
锄〔鋤〕
锂〔鋰〕
锅〔鍋〕
锆〔鋯〕
锇〔鋨〕
锈〔銹〕
锉〔銼〕
锋〔鋒〕
锌〔鋅〕
锏〔鐧〕
锏〔鐗〕
锐〔銳〕
锑〔銻〕
锒〔鋃〕
锓〔鋟〕

铜〔銅〕
钢〔鋼〕
犊〔犢〕
鸽〔鴿〕
鹅〔鵝〕
颈〔頸〕
筑〔築〕
筚〔篳〕
筛〔篩〕
牍〔牘〕
傥〔儻〕
傧〔儐〕
储〔儲〕
傩〔儺〕
惩〔懲〕
御〔禦〕
颌〔頜〕
释〔釋〕
鸹〔鴰〕
腊〔臘〕
腘〔膕〕
鱿〔魷〕
鲁〔魯〕
鲂〔魴〕
颍〔潁〕
飓〔颶〕
觞〔觴〕
惫〔憊〕
馇〔餷〕
馈〔饋〕

馉〔餶〕
馊〔餿〕
馋〔饞〕

【丶】

亵〔褻〕
装〔裝〕
蛮〔蠻〕
脔〔臠〕
痨〔癆〕
痫〔癇〕
赓〔賡〕
颏〔頦〕
鹇〔鷳〕
阑〔闌〕
阒〔闃〕
阔〔闊〕
阕〔闋〕
粪〔糞〕
鹈〔鵜〕
窜〔竄〕
窝〔窩〕
誉〔譽〕
愤〔憤〕
愦〔憒〕
滞〔滯〕
湿〔濕〕
溃〔潰〕
溅〔濺〕
溇〔漊〕
湾〔灣〕

谟〔謨〕
裢〔褳〕
裣〔襝〕
裤〔褲〕
裥〔襇〕
禅〔禪〕
谠〔讜〕
谡〔謖〕
谢〔謝〕
谣〔謠〕
谤〔謗〕
谥〔謚〕
谦〔謙〕
谧〔謐〕

【乛】

属〔屬〕
屡〔屢〕
骘〔騭〕
毵〔毿〕
翚〔翬〕
骛〔騖〕
缂〔緙〕
缃〔緗〕
缄〔緘〕
缅〔緬〕
缆〔纜〕
缇〔緹〕
缈〔緲〕
缉〔緝〕

缊〔縕〕
缌〔緦〕
缎〔緞〕
缑〔緱〕
缓〔緩〕
缒〔縋〕
缔〔締〕
缕〔縷〕
骗〔騙〕
编〔編〕
缗〔緡〕
骚〔騷〕
缘〔緣〕
飨〔饗〕

**13 笔**

**【一】**

耢〔耮〕
鹋〔鶓〕
鹊〔鵲〕
辒〔轀〕
骜〔驁〕
摄〔攝〕
摅〔攄〕
摆〔擺〕
〔襬〕
赪〔赬〕
摈〔擯〕
毂〔轂〕
摊〔攤〕

鹊〔鵲〕
蓝〔藍〕
蒌〔蔞〕
鹋〔鶓〕
蓟〔薊〕
蒙〔矇〕
〔濛〕
〔懞〕
颐〔頤〕
献〔獻〕
蓣〔蕷〕
榄〔欖〕
榇〔櫬〕
榈〔櫚〕
楼〔樓〕
榉〔櫸〕
赖〔賴〕
碛〔磧〕
碍〔礙〕
碜〔磣〕
鹌〔鵪〕
尴〔尷〕
殒〔殞〕
雾〔霧〕
辏〔輳〕
辐〔輻〕
辑〔輯〕
输〔輸〕

**【丨】**

频〔頻〕

龃〔齟〕
龄〔齡〕
龅〔齙〕
龆〔齠〕
鉴〔鑒〕
韪〔韙〕
嗫〔囁〕
晓〔曉〕
踌〔躊〕
跻〔躋〕
跹〔躚〕
蜗〔蝸〕
嗳〔噯〕
赗〔賵〕

**【丿】**

锗〔鍺〕
错〔錯〕
锘〔鍩〕
锚〔錨〕
锛〔錛〕
锝〔鍀〕
锞〔錁〕
锟〔錕〕
锡〔錫〕
锢〔錮〕
锣〔鑼〕
锤〔錘〕
锥〔錐〕
锦〔錦〕
锧〔鑕〕

锨〔鍁〕
锫〔錇〕
锭〔錠〕
键〔鍵〕
锯〔鋸〕
锰〔錳〕
锱〔錙〕
辞〔辭〕
颓〔頹〕
穆〔穆〕
筹〔籌〕
签〔簽〕
〔籤〕
简〔簡〕
觎〔覦〕
颔〔頷〕
腻〔膩〕
鹏〔鵬〕
腾〔騰〕
鲅〔鮁〕
鲆〔鮃〕
鲇〔鮎〕
鲈〔鱸〕
鲊〔鮓〕
稣〔穌〕
鲋〔鮒〕
鲌〔鮊〕
鲍〔鮑〕
鲏〔鮍〕
鲐〔鮐〕

颖〔穎〕
鸽〔鴿〕
飓〔颶〕
飔〔颸〕
飕〔颼〕
触〔觸〕
雏〔雛〕
傅〔傅〕
馍〔饃〕
馏〔餾〕
馐〔饈〕

**【丶】**

酱〔醬〕
鹑〔鶉〕
瘅〔癉〕
瘆〔瘮〕
鹒〔鶊〕
阖〔闔〕
闻〔聞〕
阙〔闕〕
誊〔謄〕
粮〔糧〕
数〔數〕
滟〔灩〕
溁〔濚〕
漭〔漭〕
满〔滿〕
滤〔濾〕
滥〔濫〕
滗〔潷〕
滦〔灤〕
漓〔灕〕

| | | | | |
|---|---|---|---|---|
| 滨〔濱〕 | 缢〔縊〕 | 辕〔轅〕 | 锰〔錳〕 | 鲛〔鮫〕 |
| 滩〔灘〕 | 缣〔縑〕 | 辖〔轄〕 | 锻〔鍛〕 | 鲜〔鮮〕 |
| 溆〔漵〕 | 缤〔繽〕 | 辗〔輾〕 | 锼〔鎪〕 | 鲟〔鱘〕 |
| 慑〔懾〕 | 骗〔騙〕 | 【丨】 | 锾〔鍰〕 | 馑〔饉〕 |
| 誉〔譽〕 | | 龊〔齪〕 | 锵〔鏘〕 | 馒〔饅〕 |
| 鲎〔鱟〕 | **14笔** | 龈〔齦〕 | 锒〔鋃〕 | |
| 骞〔騫〕 | 【一】 | 鹍〔鵾〕 | 镀〔鍍〕 | 【、】 |
| 寝〔寢〕 | 瑷〔璦〕 | 颗〔顆〕 | 镁〔鎂〕 | 銮〔鑾〕 |
| 窥〔窺〕 | 赘〔贅〕 | 暖〔瞍〕 | 镂〔鏤〕 | 瘥〔瘥〕 |
| 窦〔竇〕 | 觏〔覯〕 | 暖〔曖〕 | 镃〔鎡〕 | 瘘〔瘻〕 |
| 谨〔謹〕 | 韬〔韜〕 | 鹖〔鶡〕 | 锁〔鑕〕 | 阚〔闞〕 |
| 谩〔謾〕 | 瑷〔靉〕 | 踌〔躊〕 | 锢〔錮〕 | 羞〔羞〕 |
| 谪〔謫〕 | 墙〔墻〕 | 踊〔踴〕 | 鸳〔鴛〕 | 眷〔養〕 |
| 谫〔譾〕 | 撄〔攖〕 | 蜡〔蠟〕 | 稳〔穩〕 | 椮〔椮〕 |
| 谬〔謬〕 | 蔷〔薔〕 | 蝈〔蟈〕 | 赟〔贇〕 | 鹝〔鷁〕 |
| 【乛】 | 嵘〔嶸〕 | 蝇〔蠅〕 | 箧〔篋〕 | 潇〔瀟〕 |
| 辟〔闢〕 | 薮〔藪〕 | 蝉〔蟬〕 | 箨〔籜〕 | 潋〔瀲〕 |
| 媛〔嬡〕 | 蔺〔藺〕 | 鹗〔鶚〕 | 箩〔籮〕 | 潍〔濰〕 |
| 嫔〔嬪〕 | 蔼〔藹〕 | 嘤〔嚶〕 | 箪〔簞〕 | 赛〔賽〕 |
| 缙〔縉〕 | 鹕〔鶘〕 | 黑〔羆〕 | 箓〔籙〕 | 窭〔窶〕 |
| 缜〔縝〕 | 槚〔檟〕 | 赗〔賵〕 | 箫〔簫〕 | 谭〔譚〕 |
| 缚〔縛〕 | 槛〔檻〕 | 罂〔罌〕 | 舆〔輿〕 | 潜〔譖〕 |
| 缛〔縟〕 | 槟〔檳〕 | 赚〔賺〕 | 膑〔臏〕 | 褥〔褥〕 |
| 辔〔轡〕 | 槠〔櫧〕 | 鹘〔鶻〕 | 鲑〔鮭〕 | 褛〔褸〕 |
| 缝〔縫〕 | 酽〔釅〕 | 【丿】 | 鲒〔鮚〕 | 谯〔譙〕 |
| 骝〔騮〕 | 酾〔釃〕 | 锲〔鍥〕 | 鲔〔鮪〕 | 谰〔讕〕 |
| 缩〔縮〕 | 酿〔釀〕 | 锴〔鍇〕 | 鲖〔鮦〕 | 谱〔譜〕 |
| 缡〔縭〕 | 霁〔霽〕 | 锶〔鍶〕 | 鲗〔鰂〕 | 谲〔譎〕 |
| 缠〔纏〕 | 愿〔願〕 | 锷〔鍔〕 | 鲙〔鱠〕 | 【乛】 |
| 缢〔繚〕 | 殡〔殯〕 | 锹〔鍬〕 | 鲚〔鱭〕 | 鹛〔鶥〕 |

嫱〔嬙〕　樱〔櫻〕　镐〔鎬〕　澜〔瀾〕　辚〔轔〕

鸷〔鷙〕　飘〔飄〕　镑〔鎊〕　额〔額〕　【丨】

缥〔縹〕　靥〔靨〕　镒〔鎰〕　谳〔讞〕　蹉〔蹉〕

骠〔驃〕　魇〔魘〕　镓〔鎵〕　褴〔襤〕　螨〔蟎〕

缦〔縵〕　餍〔饜〕　镔〔鑌〕　谴〔譴〕　鹦〔鸚〕

骡〔騾〕　霉〔黴〕　镉〔鎘〕　鹤〔鶴〕　赠〔贈〕

缧〔縲〕　辘〔轆〕　簀〔簀〕　谵〔譫〕　【丿】

缨〔纓〕　【丨】　篓〔簍〕　【乛】　镨〔鐠〕

聪〔聰〕　龉〔齬〕　鹛〔鶥〕　屦〔屨〕　镖〔鏢〕

缩〔縮〕　龊〔齪〕　鹢〔鷁〕　缬〔纈〕　镗〔鏜〕

缪〔繆〕　觑〔覷〕　鹗〔鶚〕　缭〔繚〕　镘〔鏝〕

缫〔繅〕　瞒〔瞞〕　鲠〔鯁〕　缯〔繒〕　镙〔鏍〕

**15笔**　题〔題〕　鲡〔鱺〕　　　镛〔鏞〕

【一】　颙〔顒〕　鲢〔鰱〕　**16笔**　镜〔鏡〕

耧〔耬〕　颐〔頤〕　鲣〔鰹〕　【一】　镝〔鏑〕

璎〔瓔〕　踯〔躑〕　鲥〔鰣〕　糯〔糯〕　镞〔鏃〕

叇〔靆〕　蝾〔蠑〕　鲤〔鯉〕　擞〔擻〕　氇〔氌〕

撵〔攆〕　蝼〔螻〕　鲦〔鰷〕　颞〔顳〕　赞〔贊〕

撷〔擷〕　噜〔嚕〕　鲧〔鯀〕　颟〔顢〕　穑〔穡〕

撺〔攛〕　嘱〔囑〕　鲩〔鯇〕　薮〔藪〕　篮〔籃〕

聩〔聵〕　颛〔顓〕　鲫〔鯽〕　颠〔顛〕　篱〔籬〕

聪〔聰〕　【丿】　徼〔徽〕　橹〔櫓〕　魉〔魎〕

觐〔覲〕　镊〔鑷〕　馔〔饌〕　橼〔櫞〕　鲭〔鯖〕

鞑〔韃〕　镇〔鎮〕　【丶】　鹥〔鷖〕　鲮〔鯪〕

鞒〔鞽〕　镉〔鎘〕　瘪〔癟〕　赝〔贋〕　鲰〔鯫〕

蕲〔蘄〕　锐〔鑥〕　瘫〔癱〕　飙〔飆〕　鲱〔鯡〕

赜〔賾〕　镋〔钂〕　齑〔齏〕　獭〔獺〕　鲲〔鯤〕

蕴〔蘊〕　镍〔鎳〕　颜〔顏〕　錾〔鏨〕　鲳〔鯧〕

樯〔檣〕　镏〔鎦〕　鹣〔鶼〕　辙〔轍〕　鲵〔鯢〕

| | | | | |
|---|---|---|---|---|
| 鲷〔鯛〕 | 瞩〔矚〕 | 鳊〔鯿〕 | 䲠〔鰆〕 | 鳔〔鰾〕 |
| 鲸〔鯨〕 | 蹒〔蹣〕 | 鳈〔鰁〕 | 鳍〔鰭〕 | 鳕〔鱈〕 |
| 鲻〔鯔〕 | 蹰〔躕〕 | 【丶】 | 鳎〔鰨〕 | 鳗〔鰻〕 |
| 獭〔獺〕 | 蟓〔蟓〕 | 鸳〔鴛〕 | 鳏〔鰥〕 | 鳙〔鱅〕 |
| 【丿】 | 嗫〔囁〕 | 辫〔辮〕 | 鳐〔鰩〕 | 鳛〔鰼〕 |
| 鹓〔鵷〕 | 羁〔羈〕 | 赢〔贏〕 | 鳒〔鰜〕 | 【丶】 |
| 瘿〔癭〕 | 赡〔贍〕 | 懑〔懣〕 | 【丶】 | 颤〔顫〕 |
| 斓〔斕〕 | 【丶】 | 【乛】 | 鹯〔鸇〕 | 癣〔癬〕 |
| 辩〔辯〕 | 镢〔鐝〕 | 鸺〔鵂〕 | 鹰〔鷹〕 | 谳〔讞〕 |
| 潍〔濰〕 | 镣〔鐐〕 | 骤〔驟〕 | 癫〔癲〕 | 【乛】 |
| 濒〔瀕〕 | 镤〔鏷〕 | | 羰〔羰〕 | 骥〔驥〕 |
| 懒〔懶〕 | 镥〔鑥〕 | **18 笔** | 谶〔讖〕 | 缵〔纘〕 |
| 黉〔黌〕 | 镦〔鐓〕 | 【一】 | 【乛】 | **20 笔** |
| 【乛】 | 锎〔鐦〕 | 鳌〔鰲〕 | 䴘〔鸊〕 | 【一】 |
| 鹥〔鷖〕 | 镨〔鐥〕 | 鞯〔韉〕 | | 瓒〔瓚〕 |
| 颏〔頦〕 | 错〔鐠〕 | 黡〔黶〕 | **19 笔** | 鬓〔鬢〕 |
| 缰〔繮〕 | 镩〔鑹〕 | 【丨】 | 【一】 | 颥〔顬〕 |
| 缱〔繾〕 | 锧〔鑕〕 | 黻〔黻〕 | 攒〔攢〕 | 【丨】 |
| 缲〔繰〕 | 镫〔鐙〕 | 颢〔顥〕 | 霭〔靄〕 | 鼍〔鼉〕 |
| 缳〔繯〕 | 簖〔籪〕 | 鹭〔鷺〕 | 【丨】 | 黩〔黷〕 |
| 缴〔繳〕 | 鹪〔鷦〕 | 嚣〔囂〕 | 鳖〔鱉〕 | 【丿】 |
| | 鳍〔鰭〕 | 髅〔髏〕 | 蹿〔躥〕 | 镳〔鑣〕 |
| **17 笔** | 鲽〔鰈〕 | 【丿】 | 巅〔巔〕 | 镴〔鑞〕 |
| | 鳁〔鰮〕 | 镬〔鑊〕 | 髋〔髖〕 | 臜〔臢〕 |
| 【一】 | 鳃〔鰓〕 | 镭〔鐳〕 | 髌〔髕〕 | 鳜〔鱖〕 |
| 藓〔蘚〕 | 鳄〔鱷〕 | 镮〔鐶〕 | 【丿】 | 鳝〔鱔〕 |
| 鹪〔鷦〕 | 鳅〔鰍〕 | 镯〔鐲〕 | 镲〔鑔〕 | 鳞〔鱗〕 |
| 【丨】 | 鳆〔鰒〕 | 镰〔鐮〕 | 簸〔簸〕 | 鳟〔鱒〕 |
| 黼〔黼〕 | 鳇〔鰉〕 | 镱〔鐿〕 | 鳘〔鰵〕 | 【乛】 |
| 龌〔齷〕 | | 雠〔讎〕 | 鳓〔鰳〕 | |